TES

1000 MILES

MINNESOTA

AKOTA

AKOTA

WISCONSIN

MICHIGAN

IOWA

SKA

ILLINOIS

INDIANA

OHIO

KANSAS

MISSOURI

KENTUCKY

OKLAHOMA

ARKANSAS

TENNESSEE

MISSISSIPPI

ALABAMA

GEORGIA

TEXAS

LOUISIANA

FLORIDA

VERMONT

MAINE

NEW HAMPSHIRE

MASSACHUSETTS

NEW YORK

RHODE ISLAND

CONNECTICUT

PENNSYLVANIA

NEW JERSEY

DISTRICT OF COLUMBIA

DELAWARE

MARYLAND

WEST VIRGINIA

VIRGINIA

NORTH CAROLINA

SOUTH CAROLINA

SUPERPOWER

SUPERPOWER

A Portrait of America in the 1970's

ROBERT HARGREAVES

ST. MARTIN'S PRESS, INC.   NEW YORK

Contents

Foreword

This book began, in a sense, as a byproduct of my assignment as correspondent in America for the British television news program *News at Ten,* an assignment that has taken me, during the past four and a half years, to almost every state in the Union, there to report on news events as varied as presidential politics and the Apollo moon missions, racial desegregation in the Deep South and the discovery of oil on the northern shore of Alaska, the Manson murder trial in Los Angeles and the unfolding drama of the Watergate affair. At first, these events would seem to have no common theme. How can an outsider from Europe's offshore island possibly hope to make sense of a country so vast, a people so diverse, a society so contradictory as that of the United States? One is inevitably overwhelmed by the sheer size and scope of the place. Only later did the realization come that all these events, and many others I have covered during my assignment here, are each, in their own particular ways, a part of the modern American experience. The book that has grown from them is an attempt to bring the themes together into a coherent whole.

The organization of the book is at once personal and arbitrary. I have tried, in the early chapters, to suggest something of the diversity of the United States, to get around the country geographically, to point up the contrasts between New York, say, and Los Angeles, between the ethos of the automobile town of Detroit and that of the oil state of Texas, between the life of the farmers of the Great Plains and that of the Chicano field workers who pick the crops in the Central Valley of California, and to deal only later with the great national institutions and the common social issues of the times. My approach to them all is that of a journalist: I am not an historian, or a philosopher, or any sort of ideologue—just a reporter. The portrait of the nation that emerges is therefore colored by the traditions of my own particular craft: It is America treated as news. Central to that tradition is an instinct for change, for movement, for drama, the search for a single significant event from which the reader is left to draw his own wider conclusions. The object is not to persuade, nor to convert, but to illuminate. In each of the chapters that follow, I have therefore tried to seek out the aspects of American life that are, in this broad sense, newsworthy, those that in some way illuminate the contemporary American dilemma. It has, in many ways, been an exhilarating experience. For a journalist from overseas, the United States is the best news beat in the world, a tour of duty here one of the most rewarding experiences of a lifetime.

In gathering the material on which this book is based, my debt to others has been immense. In trying to understand and explain their country, I have been guided, in most cases, by American journalists who have specialized for years in the particular fields I have covered, and I have drawn on their insights remorselessly and quoted from their writings extensively. Rather than clutter the text with too many footnotes, they are listed in detail at the end of the book in the bibliography. To each of them, my thanks. I would like here to express my particular gratitude to my employers, Independent Television News of London, both for the opportunity to gather all the material for this book and for the generous leave of absence during which I was able to complete much of the manuscript. I would like also to give a special word of thanks to David Haylock, Will Williams, and Janet Vaingat, the ITN newsfilm crew who have accompanied me on literally hundreds of news assignments throughout the United States. Their companionship and guidance have been more valuable than they know. For specific research, I am indebted to Nadia Wills, who helped to gather detailed information and background for several chapters, particularly those on health, lobbyists, and millionaires. For advice and countless hours of discussion on American affairs, I should like to thank Bill Watts, formerly of Dr. Kissinger's White House staff and now president of Potomac Associates, who also made available to me advance copies of many of Potomac's own publications. I also owe a great debt to Dr. Alan Pearce of the FCC and his wife, Kathy, both for their hospitality in providing me with a home in which to complete the manuscript and for their advice and assistance on several chapters. Leslie Pockell of St. Martin's Press, New York, has made more useful suggestions and comments than I can possibly enumerate; indeed, without his advice, the book would have taken a quite different form. I am grateful to Tom McCormack of St. Martin's Press and my London agent, Mark Hamilton, for their initial encouragement in persuading me to go ahead. Finally, only another author can understand the debt I owe to my wife, Olivia, whose help has been, in every sense, invaluable.

Washington, D.C., June 1973

Prologue

The State of a Nation

There once was a time, and it was not much more than a decade ago, when the people of the United States thought themselves at the threshold of a new Golden Age. The long night of the Cold War was beginning at last to recede, and the young President who had summoned them to the New Frontier and led them through the supreme perils of a nuclear missile crisis, was beckoning them now to reach, quite literally, for the moon. For Americans, and for most of mankind, it was a time of hope unparalleled in recent history. Their nation stood at the apogee of its power in the world. They were, they firmly believed, the keystone in the arch of freedom. In his last public speech, the President had referred again, in those haunting New England accents, to "this nation's place in history, to the fact that we do stand on the edge of a new era, filled with both crisis and opportunity, an era to be characterized by achievement and by challenge." Never was a nation more confident in its power, more certain of its destiny, than the United States during that last year in the life of John Kennedy.

It is hard, looking back upon the wreckage of the decade that has followed, to recall the spirit of those optimistic times. Proud in its strength, admired for its benevolence, envied for its wealth, America regarded itself more than ever as "the last best hope of mankind." The nation seemed to be intent on saving the world not only by its example, but by its own unaided exertions. "We shall pay any price, bear any burden, meet any hardship, support any friend, oppose any foe," Kennedy had declared in his inaugural address of two and a half years before, and there were few who had not been stirred by the rhetoric. Thereafter, every problem that arose, every crisis that developed, was accepted as a challenge to be overcome, an opportunity to be seized. Kennedy's handling of the Cuban missile crisis that had occurred in the autumn of 1962 was commonly regarded as a triumph of cool nerve and assured self-confidence. At home, the seemingly bottomless cornucopia of technology had brought the American people to a wealth undreamed-of by less fortunate lands. The future, as far as it could be foreseen, offered endless expectations of the same. The war in Vietnam was then no more than a shadow on a distant horizon—growing larger, it was true, but who in that era doubted that the application of American aid and American skills would not quickly resolve that conflict also? Even the grave problems of race were regarded, in 1963, as problems caused more by hope than by despair. The anticipation of black Americans, no less than those of whites, had been stirred by the optimistic spirit of the times as they, too, looked forward to the future and sang with all the fervor of expectation, "We shall overcome."

During those last months of his life, John Kennedy had seemed to tremble on the brink of greatness. Other Presidents in their first terms had achieved more, others had perhaps been more admired, others will be more highly regarded by history, but no other politician in memory had been loved by his fellow men as he had been loved. When he was shot that November morning in Dallas something died in the American spirit that has not yet been rekindled. At the distance of an entire decade, it is now possible to say that what died was hope. Grasping for destiny, America discovered Nemesis instead.

The brief Indian summer of the Kennedy Presidency is colored today by the same nostalgia as that once felt by Europeans when they looked back on that last summer of 1914 before the lights of civilization went out. An era of history had passed, and most people today realize that the ebullience of the Kennedy years has gone beyond recall. The aspirations of the New Frontier have been replaced by those of the Silent Majority. Three successive American Presidents have now, through one means or another, been destroyed. Following Edward Gibbon's remark about the Romans, the Americans of today must often reflect, with a just and melancholy recollection, on the instability of a happiness that depends on the character of a single man. The fatal moment was perhaps approaching, Gibbon wrote of the Age of the Antonines, when "some licentious youth, or some jealous tyrant, would abuse, to the destruction, that . . . power which they had exerted for the benefit of their people." American civilization has not yet come to that, but from Dallas to Watergate via the streets of Chicago and the paddyfields of South Vietnam, the institution of the Presidency has today sunk to its lowest point of regard since the United States first became a major figure on the world arena.

The nation as a whole has passed through what is certain to be remembered as its darkest decade since the Civil War of a century before. Across the entire land, there is hardly an institution that has not, at some time during that decade, passed through its own crisis of the spirit. Whether it is Wall Street or the army, New York City or big business, universities or the labor unions, the institutions of America have been afflicted by doubts about their role and uncertainties about their future that have left almost none of them unchanged. The worst traumas of the later 1960s are probably over, but the mood of introspection remains. The age of certainties has been overtaken by the era of doubt.

Not long before he died, former President Lyndon Johnson addressed himself to thoughts of a melancholy season. Each year with the coming of September, he said, we are reminded that the days are dwindling down to a precious few. "As it is with the calendar, so it sometimes seems to be with our country and its system. For there are those among us who would have us believe that America has come to its own September. That our own days are dwindling down to a precious few. That the green leaves of our best season are turning brown and will soon be falling to the ground. That before long we will feel the first chill winds of a long American winter—and that our nation's stand as mankind's 'last best hope' will be done." Johnson quickly dismissed such melancholy thoughts from his mind and reasserted his belief in the more traditional faith that his country was still guided by the light of the bright perceptions—America the beautiful, America the just, America the land of the free and the home of the brave—rather than what some have called the dark perceptions of America the unclean, America the unjust, America the unworthy. "We are not living in times of collapse," he affirmed. "The old is not coming down. Rather, the troubling and torment these days stems from the new trying to rise into place."

The new trying to rise into place: that, in a sense, is the theme of this book. For there is no doubt that the United States is today moving into a new period of its history. The old certainties of the past are gone forever; traditional attitudes, once regarded as wholly and typically American, are beginning to die. New perceptions, new values are rising to take their place. The chapters that follow are an attempt to identify and describe the main sources of that change, institution by institution across the country, an attempt to answer the question: What is happening to America today?

In portraying a country as vast as the United States, one is hampered by the fact that the subject will not sit still. Today more than ever, change and movement are the constant themes of American life, so that points which a bare decade ago seemed as constant as the Pole Star have vanished altogether from the American sky. Other movements, barely perceived in the early 1960s, seem to guide the nation's destinies today: an awareness of the limitations of their power, a new and wholly healthy concern with their environment, worries about the effects of pollution and unlimited economic growth, fear about the misuse of the tremendous powers of the Presidency, radical changes in the perceptions of the role of women and of the young. Some of the other phenomena that dominated perceptions about America during the last decade have come and gone like a comet passing through the heavens, notable among them the rebellion of the students and the black uprisings in the great cities. A nation does not of course change its character overnight, or even in the space of a single decade, and many of the old landmarks remain. But they have all, almost without exception, been altered in fundamental ways since the United States stood expectantly at the threshold of its new Golden Age.

That age has somehow slipped from America's grasp. Like Rome in an

earlier millennium, or Britain in our own, the nation today has turned its
attention inward, away from its earlier concern with the wider world. The
United States remains a superpower, a giant among nations, but the ideals of
the Pax Americana, the notion that decisions taken in Washington could
affect the destinies of half the globe, with Americans prepared to pay any
price, bear any burden, meet any hardship to support that role is no longer
credible in the 1970s. The internationalism of the older generation of Americans that led to that notion was, in the words of the historian Arthur Schlesinger, both spacious in design and noble in intent. "Its flaw," he writes, "is
that it overcommitted our country—it overcommitted our policy, our resources and our rhetoric. It was tinged with messianic pretensions. It estranged
our friends without intimidating our enemies. The time has surely come to
stop going abroad in search of monsters to destroy." In short, America has lost
its immunity to history. Like other, lesser nations, it too has discovered that
there are in fact limits to its enormous power. As a result, the nation is engaged
today in a slow, sometimes agonizing withdrawal from that earlier overcom-
mitment, a withdrawal that began with the trauma of Vietnam and will
doubtless continue to provide the main theme of American foreign policy
throughout the present decade.

At home, equally difficult reappraisals are also in progress. What is happening to America's domestic institutions today may in the long run prove to be
even more important than the role her leaders choose to play in the world
arena. For it is axiomatic that what happens in the United States today spreads
to the rest of the industrialized world tomorrow. Whether the American
experiment succeeds or fails is therefore of supreme and vital importance to
the whole of the rest of the world. A hundred years ago the British scientist
Thomas Huxley observed after a visit to the United States that "there is
something sublime in the future of America. But do not suppose that I am
pandering to what is commonly understood by national pride. I cannot say that
I am in the slightest degree impressed by your bigness, or your material
resources, as such. Size is not grandeur, and territory does not make a nation.
The great issue, about which hangs a true sublimity, and the terror of over-
hanging fate, is what are you going to do with all these things?"

A hundred years later, there is still something sublime in the future of
America and the great unanswered question remains: what are you going to
do with these things?

PART ONE

Environments

CHAPTER I

Cities

1. Suburban Flight, Urban Blight

"When the city loses its walls, the city ceases to be."

MAX WEBER

"Most cities by 1980 will be preponderantly black and brown and totally bankrupt."
Report of the Commission on the
Cities in the Seventies

Throughout its history, the shape of American society has been molded by the migratory habits of its people. From the day in 1607 when Captain John Smith set foot on the shores of Virginia to found the first English colony at Jamestown, the destiny of the continent has been in the hands of men and women who have been prepared to cut off all contact with their past, to pull up their roots and start life afresh in a new environment. They came for a variety of reasons, the early settlers: some willingly, some eagerly, some in search of adventure, some under force of compulsion or slavery, some simply to find an escape from a life in the Old World that had become too burdensome. However varied the motives that brought them here, they had one thing in common when they arrived: all were strangers in a new and alien land.

At first, it was a time for discovery, then for exploration, later for development. It is a strange thing, said Archibald MacLeish, to be an American:

> America is neither a land nor a people,
> A word's shape it is, a wind's sweep.

The theme continued for more than four centuries, until mobility had become the dominant characteristic of the American people. By the nineteenth century, the true pioneers had been joined by another, even greater tide of uprooted people—the flotsam of Europe, driven across the ocean by rural depopulation and industrial squalor in England, famine in Ireland, revolution and tyranny on the Continent—all attracted to America by the promise of religious and political freedom, social equality and economic opportunity, and changing the tenor of American civilization as they came.

The long voyages across the ocean, the treks across an unknown continent, are long since over, but even in our own century the dominant theme of mobility has continued, muted and less romantic, perhaps, than it was in the past, but no less profound in its implications for the future of American society. In the past thirty years alone the United States has seen three of the greatest migrations in its history, invisible migrations mostly, each overlapping and intermingling with the others and each having its effect on the other two. These three migrations of our era all began as a slow drift around the time of the Great Depression, gathering their fullest impetus in the twenty years that followed World War II and falling like breaking waves upon the shore in the decade of the 1960s. One wave has been the exodus of millions of blacks from the old rural South and into the slums of the northern cities. Another has been the slow but inexorable departure of farmers from their land, and the third and greatest has been the flight of the white middle classes out of the older cities and into the new suburbs beyond the city walls.

The effects of these three migrations have been felt across the country, in the rural areas of the South no less than the densely populated metropolises of the North, in the suburbs of Los Angeles and the small towns of the Great Plains. But nowhere has the impact been more painfully felt than in the older cities of the North and the East which, in the process of losing their middle classes, have become different in type and lifestyle from all other cities the world has ever known, populated increasingly by the poor and disadvantaged.

In the space of two generations, white America has become a largely suburban society. By the census of 1970, some 76 million people, more than a third of the total population, most of them white, most of them better off than average, had fled to the suburbs. At first, their flight from the city had been a way to exploit the new freedom of mobility brought by the automobile. It enabled them to find the space, the fresh air and quiet, and the residential amenities that were no longer available in the cities. But that first generation of suburbanites still went downtown to work, to shop, to go to church, to find good restaurants and theaters.

In the past decade, however, the suburbs have become much more than mere dormitories for the affluent. The people who live there have been followed in an ever-growing tide by the services and industries that belong by tradition to the city center. Offices and restaurants, churches and shopping plazas, cinemas and theaters are springing up today in and around the new suburbs. And they have changed the face of the country. The symbol of contemporary America is no longer the Statue of Liberty, holding her lamp to beckon the poor of Europe toward the promise of a new life; it is no longer the great white dome of the U.S. Capitol, which promised them democracy, nor even the production line of Henry Ford, which promised them affluence. It is instead the new suburban shopping mall, which promises them—domestic ease. They are no ordinary shops, these glittering plazas surrounded by acres of parking space that have arisen in the last ten years outside almost every self-respecting suburb. Like the banks in Samuel Butler's *Erewhon*, they are the temples of modern America. Already they have displaced the main street, the tavern, and the church as the focuses of social life. The bigger ones, with perhaps 150 or 200 shops under a single roof, come equipped with ornamental fountains and waterfalls twenty feet high, soothing piped-in music, and the gentle breeze of conditioned air; they have nurseries for the children, chapels for the weary, movie theaters for the bored, restaurants for the hungry. And they have utterly transformed the life of the affluent residents of suburbia.

The housewife who lives twenty miles outside Philadelphia or Detroit has no cause at all to travel any more to the downtown areas, while her husband goes only if he still works there—and increasingly, businesses and factories are also setting up in the suburbs away from the financial stranglehold of the inner city. Today, half of all employment in the fifteen largest metropolitan areas is generated outside the old city limits, while of the enormous number of workers who now live in the suburbs, only one out of every four still commutes from his suburban home to a job in the city. In Los Angeles and Pittsburgh, Boston and Detroit, fewer than 45 percent of all the jobs available in the metropolitan area are generated within the actual city limits. Across the country, work as well as housing is now to be found in the new suburban areas. Indeed, since the 1970s began, the suburbs have equaled, and perhaps even surpassed, the central cities as providers of jobs.

Through no fault of the new and poorer immigrants, the result for the inner cities has been a social and financial disaster. For when the rich move out and the poor stay behind, the tax base of the city is fatally weakened. In Boston, which has lost more than a fifth of its population in the past twenty years, fully one half of the city's real estate is now tied up in churches, schools, municipal offices, and other tax-exempt institutions, and the city today provides only one third of the jobs available in the metropolitan area. As a result, the downtown areas deteriorate, the welfare rolls get larger and larger, crime increases—and ever more city-dwellers are finally impelled to fly to the suburbs.

Much the same thing is happening in city after city across the country. Moon Landrieu, the mayor of New Orleans, has complained, "It is appalling to believe this country would let a city like New Orleans go down the pipe, but if you're going to save it, you'd better save it now, because two or three years from now may be too late. We are a city of 600,000. In the last decade we have lost 125,000 people—mostly white and affluent—moving out to the suburbs, and in their place, 90,000, mostly poor and black, moved in. We provide the transportation facilities, the parks, the zoo, the airport, the cultural facilities for a metropolitan area of 1.1 million. And we get nothing back from the suburbs. We don't even get a sales tax, because they have their own shopping centers. We don't have enough money even to put a coat of paint on our problems. We tax everything that moves, and everything that stands still, and if it moves, we tax it again."

Likewise in Baltimore, a city of more than 900,000 people, the roll of substantial taxpayers has been reduced to a mere 118,000. The more these remaining middle-class residents are hit by real-estate taxes, the more they move out—and the more Baltimore becomes, in the words of its mayor, "a repository for the poor." The same thing is happening elsewhere: in Philadelphia and Pittsburgh, Wilmington and Newark, Minneapolis and Atlanta. Only the brand-new cities of the South and the West seem so far to have escaped—burgeoning metropolises like Houston, Dallas, and Phoenix—and even there the suburbs are beginning to grow at an ominously faster pace than the inner city.

At first sight, it might appear that the solution to the problem of the cities lies in the stroke of a pen: to redefine their rigid boundaries so as to bring back the overflow suburbs where most of the affluent people now live. In Washington, D.C., to cite only one example, the city is still bounded by the old five-mile square laid down for the federal capital almost two hundred years ago. Yet those boundaries today bear no relationship whatever to the "real" size of the city. The result is that Washington must support its municipal services on a tax base of only 750,000 people, three quarters of them black, while over a million richer middle-class whites now live out of reach in the new suburbs of Virginia and Maryland, contributing little or nothing to the cost of running the city on which they ultimately depend. Much the same thing is true in New York, where the white-collar workers travel into the city each day in enormous numbers from their out-of-state suburbs in Connecticut and New Jersey (although New York does now impose taxes on its commuters).

The blunt truth is that the new dwellers of America's suburbia, secure at last in their middle-class fastnesses, want nothing more to do with the old cities they have abandoned. Most new suburban centers simply refuse to be incorporated into the central cities, and set up their own governments, schools, and other services instead, while suburban housing laws all too often forbid the building of publicly financed housing projects in order deliberately to shut out the poor. The arrogant insulation of the new suburbanites aptly parallels that of the old Puritans, who used to chant:

> We are the chosen few,
> And all the rest are damned;
> There's room enough in Hell for you—
> We can't have heaven crammed.

Minority groups are about as welcome in the suburbs as Dutch Elm disease. "The great irony of current history," says Richard Sennett, a sociologist at New York University, "may someday appear to be that this generation, seeking to avoid the disorder of city life, succeeded only in creating warring camps that had no way of communicating—other than through violence." Even those suburban dwellers who still find work in the old city centers commonly drive in to work each morning, use the city's services all day, and abandon it again at night, taking with them a large share of the income that belongs in equity to the city. The costs of supporting, educating, and policing the poor people who remain goes up every year; the tax money to pay for these services goes down. The old city centers become, in effect, colonies to be exploited by the suburban hinterlands that now support a larger population than the original cities that produced them.

The urban equation is complicated by the reluctance of the new suburbanites to decide what the modern inner city is *for*. In the classic cities of the past, the tendency was for the rich to live in mansions near the city center, the middle classes in a ring of inner suburbs, with the poor huddled on the outskirts. This was the standard pattern of history, followed from Athens and Rome to Paris, Vienna, London, and Madrid, and even by some of the older American cities like Philadelphia and New York. The postwar exodus to the suburbs has shattered that pattern in America. For two decades now, the middle classes have been leaving the cities at the rate of half a million every year, an exodus that has been accompanied and in many cases accelerated by the arrival of large numbers of disadvantaged blacks.

Already the District of Columbia is mostly black, and if the outgoing tide of whites keeps flowing at the present rate, it will be joined by 1980 by at least thirteen other major cities, including Chicago, Philadelphia, and Detroit. During the 1960s, Washington lost almost 40 percent of its white population, Newark lost 36 percent, Detroit 29 percent, Chicago 18 percent, Manhattan 15 percent. In this great reshuffling of population, a few of the traditional city-dwellers, of course, have chosen to remain behind: those who live in what are sometimes called "the gilded ghettoes," the very rich who can insulate themselves in old mansions or elegant new apartments; the elderly; single people, who can still find attractions in big-city life; a smattering of confirmed city-dwellers determined to stay on come what may. But for the rest, the older big cities today are inhabited mainly by the poorer blacks and browns, who find themselves unable to break out of the "white noose" that confines them within their ghettoes, and the remaining white ethnic groups who cannot wait for the day when they too can afford to leave for the suburbs. As a result, most American cities today are at once poorer, blacker, and smaller than they were ten years ago.

Although immigration from the South has dwindled recently, the population explosion within the new black ghettoes has more than made up for the decline in newcomers. Meanwhile, the white exodus continues, so that since 1950 nine of America's ten largest cities have lost a substantial part of their population, and of all cities with a population of more than three quarters of a million, only two—Los Angeles and Houston—have grown at all. The older ones have shown a constant decline in population since they reached their peak in 1950.

TABLE

		Population (1950)	Population (1970)
1.	New York, N.Y.	7,891,957	7,867,760
2.	Chicago, Ill.	3,620,962	3,366,957
3.	Philadelphia, Pa.	2,071,605	1,948,609
4.	Los Angeles, Cal.	1,970,358	2,816,061
5.	Detroit, Mich.	1,849,568	1,511,482
6.	Baltimore, Md.	949,708	905,759
7.	Cleveland, Ohio	914,808	750,903
8.	St. Louis, Mo.	856,796	622,236
9.	Washington, D.C.	802,178	756,510
10.	Boston, Mass.	801,444	641,071

(Source: U.S. Census Bureau)

In the intervening twenty years, Boston and St. Louis have dropped out of the top ten altogether, to be replaced by the rapidly growing Texas twins, Dallas and Houston. Houston, the fastest-growing city in the United States, increased its population from 596,163 in 1950 to 1,232,806 in 1970 to become America's sixth largest city. Los Angeles, which used to be the fastest-growing city, has actually suffered a decline in population since the 1970s began.

As long ago as the early 1920s, Henry Ford forecast that because of his new motor cars, "the cities are finished." Half a century later his forecast is coming close to fruition. "The city as we have known it, and the forms of economic and social organization which characterized it, are simply irrecoverable," wrote George Sternlieb, Professor of Urban and Regional Planning at Rutgers University. "The major problem of the core areas of our cities is simply their lack of economic value."

Lewis Mumford, the distinguished urbanologist, has compared the remaining city cores to the ruins of Pompeii. "This little town of some twenty-five thousand inhabitants," he wrote, "produced such an orderly and coherent and aesthetically animated life that even in its ruined state it gives a less ruinous impression than the central areas of most American cities of ten times that population." That may be an exaggerated view, a caricature of American cities today, although at its worst the modern city ghetto more than lives up to Mumford's description.

"My God! It looks like Dresden after World War Two," exclaimed Wes Uhlman, the mayor of Seattle, when he first cast eyes on the Brownsville section of Brooklyn in the summer of 1971.

Brownsville is not even the poorest section of New York City—that distinction belongs to the South Bronx—but it is perhaps the most awful example of the rot that afflicts an area after its middle classes have fled. Up until the war, Brownsville was largely a white working-class area of substantial homes —rather noisy, rather dirty, not at all rich, but a living community that was regarded with affection by its chiefly European inhabitants. Almost every block had its little family store; there were social clubs for the old folk, movie theaters for the young, restaurants for those who wanted them; the community, poor though it may have been, was *alive*.

Today, the whites have all but gone, the family stores are long since shuttered up, and Brownsville reeks—quite literally—of decay. Block after block teeters on the edge of physical collapse, and sometimes beyond it; corrugated iron sheets stand in place of glass in many of its windows; uncollected garbage stands up to eight feet high in its festering alleys; rats scurry through the rubble; little clusters of drug addicts lounge around, openly trading heroin on the street corners. Some tenements in Brownsville have even mounted "rat guards," where the tenants take turns staying awake all night to keep the rodents away from their sleeping children.

Brownsville has one of the highest infant-mortality rates, the worst disease rate, and some of the most appalling housing conditions anywhere in the nation. The illegitimacy rate here is more than 40 percent, and family after family is supported by an unemployed mother on welfare. The city slums have become matriarchies, and not only in Brownsville. Nationwide, the black urban family is in the process of disintegration, with a full third of them now headed by women. The unemployment rate for their teenage sons is almost as bad—up around 30 percent at the latest count for nonwhite youths between sixteen and nineteen years of age.

Brownsville is hardly typical of modern city life, but it may well be symptomatic, and there is hardly a big city across the country, from Baltimore to St. Louis to Phoenix, that does not possess, to a lesser or greater degree, its own example of urban squalor to put alongside Brownsville. The National Urban League, for example, recently documented the collapse of entire neighborhoods in six other cities outside New York: Chicago, Cleveland, St. Louis, Detroit, Atlanta, and Hoboken, New Jersey. "Entire neighborhoods housing hundreds of thousands of central city dwellers were on their way to a state similar to that caused by war—utter desolation," the Cities' Commission reported. In New York alone, estimates of the numbers of housing units that have been simply abandoned and left to rot run up to 100,000; in Baltimore, it is estimated that there are 7,000 vacant and decaying structures; in Philadelphia, 25,000. In Detroit, entire areas have been wrecked and vandalized in neighborhoods where the government holds title to some 8,500 homes that no one else wants. St. Louis has never had a major riot, "but block after block there looked as if the city had been bombed."

In Boston, there is a slum neighborhood that has an infant-mortality rate that compares unfavorably with the Congo, while Chicago's slum areas have 1,700 fewer doctors than they did a short decade ago. One third of all the slum families on welfare do not have enough beds for all members of the family; one in five has no private flush toilet; a full quarter of them do not have enough furniture for everyone in the family to sit down while eating.

Crime in these conditions is an ever-present problem, with ghetto families the commonest victims. One third of all robberies in America occur in cities with a population of more than one million. Even among the more affluent city-dwellers, the concern with crime leads to a self-protective withdrawal from their fellow men that can have appalling consequences, like the now-notorious incident which occurred in 1964 in Queens, a borough of New York City, when no fewer than thirty-eight people heard the screams of Kitty Genovese as she was being stabbed to death on a public sidewalk, and not one of them bothered to call the police.

"You forget about other people and focus on yourself," said a twenty-two-year-old Manhattan social worker after that incident. "You find yourself guarding every little piece of material you accumulate," said another New Yorker. "You find yourself afraid to go on a vacation that lasts longer than a week. You find yourself all keyed up about losing something. In the cities, I think it's going to boil down not to race riots, but to war between the haves and the have-nots. Survival of the fittest."

It is a depressing picture, and even the twelve hardened city mayors who toured Brownsville in the summer of 1971 were appalled at what they saw. Kevin White, the mayor of Boston, and himself no stranger to urban woes, declared afterwards, "This may be the first tangible sign of the collapse of our civilization." And New York's own mayor, John Lindsay, felt impelled to comment, "I have sometimes wondered if Brownsville had been discovered in Burma, whether our national government would not have responded far faster and with greater generosity than it has, so far, here at home."

Not long after the twelve mayors made their tour, the government of New York State seemed to fulfill Lindsay's prophecy when it announced it was making substantial cuts in its expenditures on the city slums. In Brownsville, the despairing inhabitants organized a protest march against the cuts that was to deteriorate into a fullscale riot—the first big-city riot of the 1970s.

Part of the demonstration was directed against the almost all-white make-up of the city's police and fire departments, which are manned 94 or 95 percent by whites, even though the city as a whole is now roughly one-third black and Puerto Rican. Considering that his own men had been stoned in the riot, a city fire official observed with considerable sympathy, "These are the people at the very bottom of our social scale. They know hunger and injustice. The American flag is to them a symbol. Can you imagine how they feel when fire engines manned by all-white crews race into their neighborhoods flying American flags? They throw things."

By recent standards, the riot in Brownsville was officially classified as a disorder of only "moderate" size: eighty-four fires, twenty-five stores looted, forty-six arrests, thirty-three injuries, no deaths. In the 1970s, a disturbance of that size is hardly even news, and the rest of the nation watched the fires for one night on television, then shrugged its shoulders and turned away, bored by the violence.

There is nothing new in America's neglect of its Brownsvilles: The country has always held its cities in low esteem. As far back as the War of Independence, the founding fathers feared that the cities would harbor the rabble of the nation, and urban life here has never had the same hold on the imagination as that displayed, for example, in Europe, where the prized attributes of civility, urbanity, and civilization itself are all derived from roots meaning "city."

Until the Industrial Revolution, the European city remained a kind of ideal state, the supreme instrument of civilization from Athens and Rome to Florence, Paris, and London. "The men who dwell in the city are my teachers," wrote Socrates, "and not the trees or the country."

The American heritage, with its stress on small towns, family farms, and the opening frontier, was very different. "Enthusiasm for the American city has not been typical or predominant in our intellectual history," say Morton and Lucia White in their thoughtful analysis *The Intellectual Versus the City.* "Fear has been the more common reaction. For a variety of reasons, our most celebrated thinkers have expressed different degrees of ambivalence and animosity towards the city, attitudes which may be partly responsible for a feeling on the part of today's city planner that he has no mythology or mystique on which he can rest or depend which he launches his campaigns in behalf of urban improvement. We have no persistent or pervasive tradition of romantic attachment to the city in our literature or in our philosophy, nothing like the Greek attachment to the *polis* or the French's writer's affection for Paris." From Emerson and Thoreau, Hawthorne and Poe, to Mark Twain, Walt Whitman and Frank Lloyd Wright the American intellectual tradition—literary, philosophical, even architectural—has sprung from largely antiurban roots. Where is New York's Dr. Johnson? Where is the Socrates of Chicago? In America, the list of great urban thinkers almost begins and ends with Ben Franklin in eighteenth-century Philadelphia. Even those patrician Bostonians Henry James and Henry Adams were more repelled than attracted by the quality of the American cities about which they wrote. And the landed gentlemen who drafted the U.S. Constitution never once mentioned the word *city,* although they took every opportunity to denigrate it in private. "I think our governments will remain virtuous for centuries," wrote Thomas Jefferson in 1787, ". . . and this will continue so long as there shall be vacant lands in any part of America. When [the people] get piled upon one another in large cities, as in Europe, they will become as corrupt as in Europe." From his rural mountaintop at Monticello, Jefferson dismissed all cities as "pestilential to the morals, the health and the liberties of man." The mobs of great cities, he wrote in his *Notes on Virginia*, "add just as much to the support of pure government as sores do to the strength of the human body."

It was largely because of this rural righteousness that so many of the state capitals were placed outside the main metropolises, as far away as possible from the pestilential influences Jefferson had warned them against. That is why today we find the capital of New York State in Albany, one hundred and fifty miles away from the noisy pressures of Manhattan; California's capital tucked away in Sacramento, isolated from the teeming masses of San Francisco and Los Angeles; the capital city of Illinois in Springfield, safely downstate from the modern Babylon that is Chicago.

In fact, of the fifteen largest American cities today, the only one to house the machinery of state government is Boston—and Boston, before the arrival of the Irish, was a unique city in America, governed by urban Brahmins who displayed a regard for their city that was almost European in its sense of community and culture. Elsewhere, the early Americans regarded—and their descendants still regard—their large cities with disdain.

The rise and subsequent fall of most of the great American cities is a phenomenon that has taken place within the span of a single century. Some cities, of course, were still growing even in the second half of the twentieth century—Los Angeles and Houston, for example—but by and large, the American cities had their heyday in the bare half-century between the end of the Civil War and the start of World War I. There was no doubt then what the big cities were for: they were staging areas for the great flood of immigrants from Europe: first the Irish, then the Germans, Italians, Poles, and Russian Jews. The tide reached its peak in the years immediately before World War I, when the outward migration from Europe ran at the rate of a million and a half every year, much of it to the United States.

The half century that followed the end of the American Civil War saw Chicago rise from a town of fewer than 30,000 souls to the nation's second largest city, with a population in 1910 that exceeded a million. St. Louis grew in the same period from a population of 78,000 into a city of nearly one million; New York City, the arrival-point of nearly all the European immigrants, had a population in 1850 of just over half a million, by far the country's biggest. Within the golden half-century it had grown to over 3.5 million, to become the first (and some say, the only) American city on a world scale.

While in the East, it was the immigrants who built the new cities, in the West, it was the railroads. From the day in 1869 when a golden nail driven into the railroad track in western Utah first linked the East Coast with the West, the growth of the cities west of the Alleghenies was assured. It has been said that while the eastern cities built railroads, in the West, railroads built the cities: Omaha, Kansas City, St. Louis, San Francisco, Salt Lake City, and Chicago all owe a large part of their rise to metropolitan stature to the arrival of the railroad.

The years that marked the great and uninterrupted growth of the cities were the years when the American dream was in full flower, immortalized by the famous lines on the pedestal of the Statue of Liberty in New York harbor, inscribed at the height of the migrations in 1903:

> Give me your tired, your poor,
> Your huddled masses, yearning to breathe free,
> The wretched refuse of your teeming shore,
> Send these, the homeless, tempest tossed, to me:
> I lift my lamp beside the golden door.

The promise held out in those lines by Emma Lazarus expressed the genuine idealism of that earlier America. But for the immigrants who sailed past the Statue of Liberty on their way to the processing sheds on Ellis Island, they contained more rhetoric than reality. Many were poor and illiterate and could not understand the English inscription anyway; others were halt and lame and old, arriving in an alien country that offered hope for only the young and strong. For them, a crueler reality awaited their arrival in the cities, a world that has been well described by Terry Coleman in his book *Going to America:*

> It was an old superstition, sometimes half believed by the simplest emigrants, that the streets of New York were paved with gold. When they got there, they learned three things: first, that the streets were not paved with gold; second, that the streets were not paved at all; and third, that they were expected to pave them.

The obstacles were particularly hard for the foreign-speaking immigrants, usually Catholics or Jews, who began filtering through the Ellis Island receiving sheds in the 1880s. Their alien appearance, emphasized by the foreign languages they spoke—Polish, Lithuanian, Czech, Hungarian, Russian, and Italian—seemed to pose a frightening new urban threat to the native-born, who sponsored the vehemently anti-Catholic and anti-Jewish movements that had already sprung up in many of the eastern states as an expression of the older America's distrust of the cities.

Although hostility between Catholic and Protestant endured until well into the twentieth century, it is nevertheless a remarkable testimony to the basic tolerance and resilience of American society that in the half century between 1860 and 1910 it was able to assimilate with as little enmity as it did the 17 million foreign-born immigrants who filled up the eastern cities. That is not to say the native-born Americans did not display hostility to the hordes of strangers who had arrived so suddenly in their midst. They did—and in many cases still do—mistrust the cities as repositories of alien influences; but they needed the new labor and, however grudgingly, they let the immigrants in without restriction, allowing them in time to become full-fledged American citizens. And gradually, as the newcomers were absorbed by burgeoning American industry and began to prosper, they—or at least their children—began to adapt to that process of Americanization known as "the melting pot."

Although the melting pot was never as pervasive as myth would have it, so that most immigrant groups have retained their strong ethnic and religious identities to this day, the impact of American culture on the new arrivals was profound, and the impact of American materialism perhaps even more so. The earlier "shanty Irish" thus became in time the "lace curtain" Irish, the Germans and the Poles went off to provide the manpower for the growing industries of Toledo, Chicago, and Pittsburgh, while many of the Jews stayed behind in the metropolises to staff the professions, providing a large share of the cities' doctors, lawyers, and schoolteachers.

The key to the nation's ability to absorb so many newcomers so quickly was the rapid industrialization that coincided with the arrival of the immigrants. For while in England and other developing countries in Europe the Industrial Revolution had been marked by great internal migrations away from the land and into the new factory towns and cities, in the United States a major part of the manpower needed by the new urban factories came direct from overseas. As a result, the process of industrialization took place perhaps faster and more smoothly than it might otherwise have done, the immigrants were absorbed with comparative ease, and the ironic side effect was to reinforce the traditional isolationism of rural America. The effect of the new immigrants was to cushion that older America from the shock of rapid industrialization that had so disrupted rural life in other nations, though the older Americans can hardly be said to have shown much gratitude and continued to display their small-town xenophobia and prejudice against the big cities until well into the present century.

Spurned and usually neglected by the state legislators in their remote rural capitals, the new immigrants in the big cities turned instead to self-help, led notably by the Irish, and city after city saw the rise of that unique American institution, the political machine. Always Democratic, often corrupt, and dominated by such legendary political chieftains as "Boss" Tweed and "Boss" Croker, the influence of the city machines that flourished until the arrival of the New Deal was paramount in bringing the immigrants into the mainstream of American political life.

If their influence was often corrupt, their organization was superb and undeniably more beneficial to the new arrivals and the health of the cities as a whole than the benign neglect they suffered at the hands of the old rural legislators. At least they paved the streets, provided the water supply, and arranged for the disposal of the city sewage.

In New York, the city machine known as Tammany Hall often established its hold on the immigrant the day he first set foot on American soil. Party organizers met him at the quayside and introduced him to the party there and then, found him a job and accommodation, and generally helped to put him on his feet in his new land. George Washington Plunkitt of Tammany Hall vividly explained what the machine was for, and how it functioned:

> What holds your grip on your district is to go right down among the poor families and help them in the different ways they need help. I've got a regular system for this. If there's a fire in Ninth, Tenth or Eleventh Avenue, for example, any hour of the day or night, I'm usually there with some of my election district captains as soon as the fire engines. If a family is burned out, I don't ask if they are Republicans or Democrats . . . I just get quarters for them, buy clothes for them if their clothes were burned up and fix them up until they get things running again. It's philanthropy, but it's politics, too—mighty good politics. Who can tell how many votes one of these fires brings me? The poor are the most grateful people in the world.

Most of the big city machines were undeniably corrupt, and the *sachems*, or leaders, who ran them were in politics not just as philanthropists, but to make money for themselves. Boss Tweed, who died in jail in 1873, is reputed to have plundered New York City of more than $200 million in the form of kickbacks from business contractors and bribes taken from the tax money of the poor. The graft continued well after his death, and right up to the 1930s the repeated attempts at reform all foundered on the massive political power the machine derived from the votes of the poor. The machine's demonstrable philanthropy always outweighed the denunciations, and it was only the interjection of national party politics into local affairs at the time of the New Deal that finally curbed the power of the Tammany Halls. Even today, the remaining vestiges of machine politics can be seen at work in Mayor Daley's Chicago, where his superbly efficient party organization still keeps its hold on the poor through techniques remarkably similar to those described seventy-five years ago by George Washington Plunkitt. But even in Chicago the departure of the old working classes for the suburbs has been making inroads on the efficiency of the party machine, and it is generally agreed that Mayor Daley offers the last living example of an old-fashioned city boss in action.

Back in 1888, Lord Bryce, the great British observer of the United States, wrote that the growth of the great cities was among the most significant and least fortunate changes that had taken place in the hundred years since independence. "The government of cities," he wrote, "is the one conspicuous failure of the United States." More than a lifetime has passed since Bryce wrote those words, and the cities have in the meantime changed beyond all recognition. Many would say they have changed only for the worse, and their problems today remain as grave as they have ever been.

What then does the future hold? After the race riots that erupted in many northern cities in 1967, the Kerner Commission reported that the causes of virtually all the riots lay in the conditions of life in the slums and ghettoes: racial discrimination in employment, education, and housing; the deterioration of physical facilities caused by the outward movement of middle-class whites; and the poverty that served to "destroy opportunity and hope and to enforce failure."

Four years later, the Commission on the Cities chaired by Senator Fred Harris and Mayor John Lindsay found that most of the changes since the riots had been for the worse. Housing, they found, "is still the national scandal it was then," schools were more tedious and more turbulent than ever, the rates of crime and unemployment and disease and heroin addiction were higher, welfare rolls were larger, and with few exceptions, the relations between minority communities and the police were just as hostile.

"In every city we visited," the commission reported, "the police and the people of the ghettoes—boys and young men, especially—regard each other with more or less fear and contempt." In Los Angeles, fifteen youths—five black, five Chicano, and five white—were induced to paste "Support the Black Panthers" bumper stickers on their cars. Within a month, they had each received at least one police summons, and the issuance of the tickets was accompanied by searches of cars and persons, verbal abuse, and an occasional gratuitous shove or blow. The contribution to safety or order, the Commission reported, was zero, but "the amount of resentment and hatred they provoked was substantial."

Elsewhere, the commission reported that "everywhere we went, the inner-city public schools were in disarray." In Detroit, where thirty of the school buildings in use in the ghetto area were dedicated during the administration of Ulysses S. Grant, members of the commission reported that at the time they visited the city "it was literally true that no one could tell on any day what schools would be open on the next one."

With the evidence of decay on all sides, the future for the neglected American inner city looks bleak indeed. Mayor Lindsay of New York, who has had more experience than most with America's urban maladies, believes it is finally time the federal government recognized that the largest metropolitan areas are indeed "national cities," and deserve a separate status in the political structure.

Lindsay is one of those rare Americans who says he actually *believes* in big cities. "The cities are not the problem," he has said. "They are the solution. They have always been the solution. And that's the reality we have lost sight of. The city is not the creator of social problems, and it doesn't spread them.

It solves them, for the city is the machine of social change. It is the city that transforms displaced rural populations and immigrant populations. When immigrants need education and jobs and housing they have always come to the city. When the economy failed in the rural South, its victims came north to the city. It is the city that gives human beings the education and skills and expectations that are the goals of the great urban working class and middle class."

But the cities that Lindsay believes in so fervently are today in dire straits. Somehow people assumed that they would work—financially, socially, educationally—by themselves, that they would automatically provide police protection and run the schools and build housing. "People *assumed* that it would happen," says Lindsay, "but it didn't—and no one paid any attention."

Indeed, under the Nixon Administration the problems of the central cities have become more invisible than ever. In his 1973 State of the Union message the President went so far as to claim that "the hour of crisis has passed" in American community life. In a speech the New York *Times* termed "a prolonged flight of fantasy," the President simply announced that his administration had caused the urban crisis to disappear. "The ship of state is back on an even keel," he said, "and we can put behind us the fear of capsizing." As evidence, the President cited the fact that civil disorders had declined, the air was getting cleaner, mass transit problems were being tackled, and the increase in the rate of crime was now dropping in "more than half of our nation's cities." He failed to mention, however, that violent crime in the cities had nevertheless increased by 30 percent in the previous four years. On closer inspection, his claim to have brought the crime wave under control simply meant that crime in the cities was worsening at a somewhat slower rate than it was during the 1960s. But at the same time, the population of the cities was falling, while the crime rate in the suburbs was increasing at a faster rate than ever. And nowhere in the President's speech was there any public recognition of the underlying financial and social problems that are the real cause of the chronic urban blight that so afflicts the modern American city.

Less than a year earlier, his Secretary of Housing and Urban Development, George Romney, had expressed a rather different view. "After long and careful study," Romney told a congressional committee, "it is my considered belief that the housing problem in our central cities results from all the social, economic and physical problems now afflicting our urban areas. And it is abundantly clear that the rotting of central cities is beginning to rot the surrounding suburbs. Despite all our efforts, despite the billions of dollars that have been expended, the decay of the core cities goes on. We continue to suffer continuing losses of human and economic resources." Romney had soon afterward gone to the White House with a plan to provide federal funds to solve city problems on an areawide basis. But the President rejected the plan. His own solution, reflecting his deep distrust of federal spending programs, was to turn over the problems of the cities to what he called "grassroots govern-ment." The code word for his plan was federal revenue-sharing: in other words, handing back to the states and cities a portion of the national tax income with which to tackle their local problems.

Unfortunately for the cities, the government decided to share out the available money on the basis of recent population growth, which meant the burgeoning white suburbs received a relatively large share of the cash, while the cities were again shortchanged, penalized for the very fact of being static, poor, and old. The formula seemed to overlook the very nature of the urban crisis: The areas that needed help the most were to receive the least. It was as though the nation were determined that its modern cities should live up to Thomas Jefferson's strictures as places that are "pestilential to the morals, the health and the liberties of man."

2. New York: The Big Apple

"Vulgar of manner, overfed,
Overdressed and underbred,
Heartless, Godless, hell's delight,
Rude by day and lewd by night."
RUFUS NEWTON on New York, 1906

It is not easy to write adequately of New York, at once the most magnificent and the most sordid of American cities. Visitors and inhabitants alike either love the city or hate it; and sometimes they love it and hate it both together. There are moments, says John Lindsay, especially in the spring and fall, when you would not want to live in any other place in the world. Yet it has moments in summer and winter when even its mayor feels he wants to leave it forever. The Manhattan skyline, still that pincushion in profile, is the most famous in the world, its slums among the most infamous. In the daytime, some of its streets are crowded with the most sophisticated shoppers to be found anywhere; at night, other streets are not safe to walk at all. For some, New York is synonymous with culture; for others, with crime. As Henry James wrote of London nearly ninety years ago, "It is not a pleasant place; it is not agreeable, or cheerful, or easy, or exempt from reproach. It is simply magnificent."

New York is magnificent too, and there is not an urban landscape anywhere in the world to match that glimpse of the glittering skyline at dusk as the visitor sweeps in across the Triborough Bridge, which leads into Manhattan from the airports—or, even better, sails in from the ocean under the graceful arch of the Verrazano-Narrows Bridge past the Statue of Liberty and on into the city's still-magnificent harbor, with the skyscrapers towering behind it like cliffs.

Its devotees deprecatingly call it the Big Apple, but for the visitor the first encounter with New York can be a bruising experience, too. In the summer of 1972, a middle-aged tourist from Kansas took one look at the teeming pornography shops that line both sides of Forty-second Street and declared to his wife, with pompous finality, "This is not America. This is a *jungle.*" Mrs. Kansas meanwhile had got herself involved in an altercation with a city cabdriver who had just shot a red light and almost run her down on a pedestrian crossing. But it was the cabbie, not the good woman from Kansas, who exploded in rage. "Lady!" he bellowed, groping for and finally finding the right New York expletive: "Lady, you're a *fink!*" Whereupon, Mr. and Mrs. Kansas, outraged to the core of their midwestern souls at this encounter with the metropolis, turned on their heels and fled. They were last seen disappearing back up Broadway, whence they had come, doubtless not stopping in their stride until they had caught the very next flight home to Topeka, where respectable folk are treated with a little more deference.

Manhattan is not as crowded as it was even seventy years ago, but it is still the most densely populated urban area in America, and it is true that the aggressive anonymity of its crowds often frightens strangers. There is without question a hostility abroad on the streets of New York that repels not only Mr. and Mrs. Kansas; you have to be tough here, just to survive. In a visitor's handbook to New York, the English writer James Cameron has said the New Yorkers' total oblivious unconcern with others is almost sublime. "No other city," he writes, "can relieve the visitor of so much money so quickly with so little enthusiasm. Paris clips the stranger with calculated insolence, London with casual gusto, Rome with a wink and Berlin with a leer. New York does it with absentminded indifference, tinged with contempt. The minimal civilities of a London bus queue are held to be effete in New York, if not subversive. In New York *Lebensraum* is so limited it must be gained by conquest, by the use of the elbow, the knee, breath, money, opportunism. There is a ceaseless struggle for a place to sit, eat, move, or stand in a queue." Recent experiments with rats have proved that when put in the same crowded environment as New Yorkers in the rush hour, the rats too began to display the same neuroses, the same antisocial aggressiveness that is encountered on any Manhattan street just after the offices have closed. Certainly, New York is not for the timid, although as Robert Manning, a Boston writer, has said, "It's not a bad place to visit—provided you've had all the appropriate innoculations and carry a return ticket hidden in your shoe."

Still, Manhattan, which to most outsiders *is* New York, remains the capital of the nation to everyone but the government. It dominates the culture of America, perhaps more than ever since the decline of Hollywood. Certainly it is still the only city in America where you could go out in the morning and buy a Cezanne—or just the same day's editions of the London newspapers. Its theaters, art galleries, and opera and concert halls are superb. It is the headquarters of all three television networks and the finest daily newspaper in the country. It has as many beaches within its city limits as Los Angeles and is within easy reach of some of the most beautiful countryside in the Northeast. It is America's undisputed financial center, and "head office" for thirty-one of the hundred biggest industrial enterprises, ten of the fifty biggest banks, six of the fifty biggest insurance companies and eight of the biggest transportation companies. They come here because this is where the power is. New York's senior senator, Jacob Javits, has said: "Notice how anyone who's running for President beats a path immediately to New York to raise a little dough. It's not just because there's money in New York—there's money in Dallas, too. It's because New York is an open market for ideas, and courageous enough to back new things. And this has been its role for a century or more."

Nevertheless, the economic base of New York is no longer quite as secure as it was even ten years ago. After rising steadily throughout the 1960s, employment in the city has begun to decline quite dramatically in recent years, and since 1970 New York has lost no fewer than 257,000 jobs—an ominous sign that all is not well in the Big Apple. The decline is due to what its director of labor statistics has called "weaknesses in all of New York City's major employment sectors," including those that had shown significant growth during the last half of the 1960s, particularly in service areas such as filling stations, dry-cleaning establishments, and clerical work. But some of the city's staple industries have been badly affected, too, particularly the garment trade, which has lost 54,000 jobs in the past decade, and the docks, where automation and the loss of many transatlantic passenger liners have led to a falling-off in employment.

The decline in the number of available jobs has been accompanied, and in part accelerated by a significant loss in the number of corporate headquarters in the city. In five years, twenty-two large firms pulled their headquarters out of New York altogether, including such giants as Shell Oil, which has moved to Houston; Eastern Airlines, lost to Miami; and Pepsico and General Telephone and Electric, which have both moved into new suburban headquarters outside the city. At one time the entire New York Stock Exchange even threatened to pull out and rebuild a new Wall Street across the Hudson River in New Jersey.

New Yorkers put a brave face on these losses. David Rockefeller, chairman of the board of the Chase Manhattan Bank, has said that the firms that have moved out will soon discover the suburbs are not as ideal as they first thought. Isolated in suburbia, company presidents will, he believes, come to miss the contact with their peers and the excitement of the cultural and intellectual life of the city. And even though there is now a surplus of office space in Manhattan, that has not halted an office-building boom that has transformed parts of Sixth Avenue and lower Manhattan in the past decade. Indeed, in 1974 the city will officially throw open the largest office building anywhere, the mountainous new World Trade Center, whose twin towers already dominate the skyline of lower Manhattan like gigantic human filing cabinets. A hundred feet taller than the Empire State Building, which held the crown for over forty years, the World Trade Center was for a while the tallest building in the world (or, more precisely, the tallest *two* buildings in the world) until it was overtaken by the new Sears Building in Chicago. Naturally, the Center has come in for a good deal of criticism from the environmentalists, although

New Yorkers on the whole are passionately attached to their skyscrapers. "I'm a New Yorker and I love big buildings," said Jerome Kretchmer, the city's former Environment Protection Administrator, when faced with grumbles about the almost arrogant mass of the new Center. However, the building is not yet fully in use, and the city has hardly begun to grapple with the problems that will be brought to lower Manhattan by the fifty thousand office workers who will spew out of the new building at the end of each working day. Maybe it will finish up, as some critics allege, as the last of the dinosaurs: the wrong building at the wrong place at the wrong time, another example of the decline of New York.

It is not the economic disorders of New York that most disturb those who love the city, however. "The truly terrible costs of New York are special and spiritual," writes Richard Whalen in his book *A City Destroying Itself*. "These accrue in endless human discomfort, inconvenience, harassment and fear which have become a part of the pervasive background, like the noise and the filth, but are much deadlier. For it is people who breathe life into an environment, who create and sustain a healthy city. If people are driven and their senses dulled, if they are alienated and dehumanized, the city is on the way to destroying itself."

Why? What has gone wrong with New York? Why do more and more of its people speak as though their city is doomed and on its way to becoming ungovernable? A modern Voltaire could continue almost endlessly about the miseries of life in New York today. More murders take place there now than ever before, well over thirty a week; in fact, New York has as many murders every ten days as all England suffers in a year, and mugging has become an ever-present problem—over 78,000 such crimes in 1972, which actually represents an *improvement* over previous years. That year, in a case chillingly reminiscent of the murder of Kitty Genovese eight years earlier, Dr. Wolfgang Friedmann, a distinguished professor of international law, was murdered in broad daylight, three blocks away from Columbia University, where he had just finished a day's teaching. As he lay bleeding to death on the sidewalk, passers-by ignored his cries for help, and for some time no one even thought of calling the police. "The jungle could not be more unfeeling towards its creatures," said the New York *Times* in a bitter editorial on the killing—a comment which led to a vehement reply from a local resident, who pointed out that the area was so noisy no one farther than ten feet away could possibly have heard a strangled cry for help. Later that same year there was a spate of armed holdups of teachers in their classrooms before the very eyes of their pupils. "Walk behind your desk and sit down," one holdup man had said. "There are a lot of children in your class. If you move, I'll blow your brains out."

Meanwhile, drug overdoses remain the largest single cause of death for New

Yorkers between the ages of fifteen and thirty-five. A total of 1,259 persons died of narcotics-related causes in the city in 1971, the worst year on record. There are many more statistics like that in New York for the most insatiable prophets of gloom. The city's air and its streets are the dirtiest in America, to the point where the *Times* has said it is hard to see New York as anything but an Augean stable, requiring a twentieth-century Hercules to run a river through it. Its subway trains run on 236 miles of the gloomiest, grimiest, most crime-infested railroad tracks anywhere. Every week, the city tows away 2,000 illegally parked cars from Manhattan alone, and its traffic jams can be so bad its traffic commissioner once remarked, "to get to the West Side, you have to be born there." New York's telephones break down more often than those of any other city. At least 400,000 of its housing units are condemned as substandard. Its school system verges on collapse, and in only 24 of the 158 intermediate and junior high schools are more than half the pupils able to read at the standard for their grade. Its overall crime rate has stabilized recently, although violence continues to increase.

Even in Greenwich Village, the legendary home of the city's bohemians and artists and traditionally the most liberal area in Manhattan, law and order has become a political issue. Yet back in the 1920s, Greenwich Village was the place of which the poet Floyd Dell was able to write:

> Here life went to a gentler pace,
> And dreams and dreamers found a place.

In the 1960s, Jane Jacobs, the well-known urban critic, held up Greenwich Village as the sort of community all New York should emulate. Even today, the West Village remains largely a quiet residential neighborhood, a stronghold of predominantly white upper-income professionals who voted more than 2 to 1 for Senator George McGovern in the Presidential election of 1972. Cheek by jowl with this largely affluent community, however, lies the very different East Village, whose dreams and dreamers have in recent years been transformed into a near-nightmare haunt of drug addicts, alcoholics, muggers, and sexual deviates. "It's a heavy scene here," a black artist told *Newsweek* magazine recently. "I've had it. I'm so tired of being scared." An elderly former resident remarked, "We had to lock ourselves in our apartment practically every night. In the morning, you would come down and find urine, feces, vomit and maybe a hypodermic needle in your hall. It was indescribable."

Poor schools, overcrowding, crime—these are some of the main reasons why so many middle-class whites are fleeing the downtown areas of all American cities for the suburbs. In New York, the same thing is happening, although the equation is complicated by the fact that there are several other "downtowns" here as well as the central one in Manhattan, which actually contains only 19 percent of the city's total population. The other boroughs, particularly

Queens and Brooklyn, have grown their own "inner cities" with problems not unlike those of Manhattan. With more than 2.5 million people, Brooklyn alone would rank as the nation's fourth largest city if it were independent of New York, and its downtown area suffers the same sort of blight that afflicts all urban areas, with two of the worst and largest ghettoes in the United States: Brownsville and Bedford-Stuyvesant. Queens has a more middle-class reputation, a more suburban air, and is in fact often the first way-station for middle-class and working-class whites on their way out of the central city. Its preoccupations tend to be the suburban ones of housing, high taxation, and transportation, rather than the typical big city problems of urban decay, and as a result Queens sometimes feels itself neglected by the city government across the river in Manhattan—a factor which played no small part in the precipitous decline in the popularity of John Lindsay in the borough. But short of fleeing the city altogether, the residents of Queens are trapped just as much as those of the other boroughs in the overall dilemma of New York. Citywide, 45 percent of the people who live there today are poor, one in every seven of them is on welfare, and the city's welfare bill has risen in the 1970s to a staggering total of $2 *billion* a year, of which the city's direct share is over half a billion. Paying this enormous bill is perhaps the biggest single factor in the decline of New York. And all the time, the balance tips further into the red as more and more whites leave for the suburbs and more and more—mostly poor—blacks and Puerto Ricans pour in, attracted often by the welfare benefits. A million whites have left New York in the past decade, to be replaced by half a million blacks and almost another half-million Puerto Ricans.

Nearly ninety years ago, Lord Bryce said of New York that it is "a European city, but of no particular country," and ever since New York has been the most racially mixed of any city in the world, a modern Babel that has more German-speakers than Cologne, more Jews than Jerusalem, more Irish than Cork, more Italians than Venice—and now, more Puerto Ricans than San Juan. Even today, over 3 million of the city's present population of 7.8 million were either themselves foreign born or had at least one foreign born parent.

Italians still make up by far the largest European contingent in the city, and in round figures the New Yorkers of foreign birth or parentage today include:

Italy:	682,000
"Other America":*	451,000
Russia:	394,000

*Latin America and the Caribbean, but not including Puerto Ricans, who are not classified as "foreign," since Puerto Rico is legally part of the United States.

Poland:	292,000
Ireland:	219,000
Germany:	146,000

Yet for all its diversity, New York is a place where the melting pot has failed to melt. There are Jewish neighborhoods that remain overwhelmingly Jewish in character, particularly in the Bronx; German is still spoken widely in Yorkville, Spanish in parts of Harlem. And each group of immigrants has established an ethnic hold on different parts of the city machinery, so that the flavor of the police force is still overwhelmingly Irish, garbage collection is under the control of the Italians, and schoolteachers are predominantly Jewish.

In the last decade, however, New York's racial mix has begun to change quite dramatically. According to the latest figures of the Census Bureau, the number of New Yorkers of European stock declined precipitously in the 1960s, while those from the Caribbean and South America more than doubled. The Spanish-language population of New York is more than a million and a quarter, many of them miserably poor emigrants from Puerto Rico, Cuba, and the Dominican Republic, while the black population, who are also in a sense immigrants to the city, has reached almost a million and three quarters. That makes over half the city either black, brown, or foreign-born.

Nowhere are the terrible spiritual costs of New York more apparent than in the noxious slums that house the two main minority groups: Harlem and Brownsville, Bedford-Stuyvesant and the South Bronx. At least 100,000 apartments and houses have been abandoned in the New York slums in the past eight years or so and simply left to fester and rot. In some of these areas four residents out of every ten are on welfare, and a third of the employable population has no work. Early in 1973 the New York *Times* ran a series of articles on the slums of South Bronx, which revealed a horror story of almost unbelievable proportions. "The South Bronx is a necropolis—a city of death," Dr. Harold Wise, a community leader, told the *Times*. "There's a total breakdown of services, looting is rampant, fires are everywhere." The *Times* wrote of packs of wild dogs roaming through the streets, of a drug-pusher murdered by a youth gang on a thirty-dollar contract from a rival pusher, of a youngster nearly stomped to death outside his school in an argument over a soda bottle. The area's 400,000 residents, who had long been afraid to go out at night, were now afraid to go out during the day into streets menaced by 20,000 drug addicts and 9,500 gang members. "This is the South Bronx today," wrote the *Times*'s reporter, Martin Tolchin; "violent, drugged, burned-out, graffitti-splattered and abandoned." And this close to the heart of the greatest city in America.

Many people saw in the South Bronx a social cancer which could end up destroying the city itself. Michael Gill, a banker who is engaged in many community programs, told the *Times:* "The reason my superiors at Bankers Trust support me is that they believe that if the South Bronx goes, the entire Bronx will collapse, and if the Bronx collapses, the city will collapse." Others have suggested quite seriously that the only solution is to raze the South Bronx like some latter-day Carthage, and then start to rebuild elsewhere. Robert Moses, who used to be known as New York's master builder, has said; "You must concede that the Bronx slum and others in Brooklyn and Manhattan are unrepairable. They are beyond rebuilding, tinkering and restoring. They must be leveled to the ground." The cost of this unlikely solution is estimated at around $10 billion for the external improvements alone. And even then, how much good would it do? The malaise that afflicts the New York slums is much more than mechanical: it goes right to the spiritual destruction of the people who live here. The Puerto Rican families, rural and foreign-speaking, fall apart when they get to the South Bronx. Unlike the earlier immigrants to New York, who were also forced to live in appalling slums but who could at least find jobs, many of the new Puerto Rican arrivals simply can't get work. They are unskilled and illiterate in a society that demands job training and a high level of literacy. Strong backs are no longer enough, although it is only strong backs that the new arrivals have to offer. Even the government, the employer of last resort, has failed the Puerto Ricans, according to Professor George Sternlieb. Nearly 14 percent of the heads of black households are employed by either the city, state, or federal governments. Only 4 percent of Puerto Rican heads of families are similarly employed. In every respect, the Puerto Ricans find themselves at the bottom of the pile, worse off by far even than the blacks who live in Harlem and Bedford-Stuyvesant.

"The time of happy platitudes is over," Professor Sternlieb says. "The old concept was that you take a group of people who were very poor and prejudiced against, and you add money and create a middle class. In small part, this was true. But what we're seeing is a tremendous division between those who are making it and those who are left behind."

When the first Dutch explorers sailed up the Hudson River in 1626 they purchased the island of Manhattan from the local Indians for twenty-four dollars in cash and trinkets. There is a New York wisecrack to the effect that the Dutch made a bad bargain: if they had taken their twenty-four dollars back to Amsterdam and invested it at compound rates of interest they would today be able to buy all of the real eastate on Manhattan six times over—and the city would still probably be a going concern.

That there is something wrong with the way their city is run, is the common complaint of all New Yorkers. Why, they ask, does it cost per head twice as much again to run the government of New York as it does to run Chicago? Why are the streets not kept in repair and adequately policed? Why are taxes so high and services so bad? Why are the schools not as good as they should be? And why does it all get worse and worse with no improvements ever in sight?

When they look for the answers they usually put the blame on the shoulders of the man who will have been their Mayor for a full eight years when his second term runs out in the New Year of 1974: John Vliet Lindsay. Lindsay has been blamed for just about everything and anything that has gone wrong in New York lately, from traffic jams to the crime wave, and the decline in his popularity has provided one of the most fascinating chapters in American politics in the past decade.

Lindsay, who recently passed his fiftieth birthday, came to power on a wave of enthusiasm unmatched since John Kennedy arrived at the White House in 1960. Like Kennedy, Lindsay was the epitome of the "media candidate": handsome and manly, energetic and articulate, with a burning determination to get things done. A fresh breeze seemed to blow through the city when he took over the mayor's elegant city home, Gracie Mansion, and he quickly developed a strong empathy with the poor and disadvantaged of the city. Often, the lean, six-foot-four frame of the mayor was to be seen striding purposefully through the ghettoes, cooling their tensions, receptive to their complaints, and above all *caring* about the way they lived.

Perhaps his finest achievement in office came during the periods of racial tension that swept America in the late 1960s, first during the long hot summer of 1967 in which dozens of other, lesser cities erupted in riots and looting, and then in the spring of 1968, just after the assassination of Martin Luther King, when it seemed that Harlem was about to explode, just as the ghetto in Washington had exploded. Most people now give Lindsay credit for saving the city that night from the sort of riot that had swept the Los Angeles district of Watts three years earlier.

Lindsay himself was at the theater when the news was brought to him that King had been shot. He left at once and drove into Harlem in the family station wagon. At 125th Street and Second Avenue, he stopped the car and got out, and for the rest of that long tense night walked with his entourage through the dark and turbulent streets.

"It was a dark night, hot for spring, and you could feel the anger," he wrote later. "I put my hand on the shoulder of each man as we passed, and expressed shared sorrow. There were no words spoken in exchange, only a nod of recognition. . . . Occasionally, I could hear my name shouted, and at other times I could hear men and women weeping or moaning. I was aware once in a while of groups of young men and boys running through the crowds down the street—and I heard sporadic sounds of breaking glass."

For hours the mayor kept on walking, touching shoulders, and going back from time to time to Gracie Mansion to check on progress in the rest of the city. New York held, the anger in the ghetto was kept within bounds, thanks largely to Lindsay's courage in going in person to the people. It was, without doubt, his finest hour as mayor.

There was, however, another side to Lindsay's tenure of office, and while he has always retained the affection and support of the blacks, he has at the same time lost—and lost massively—the support of the white voters in the city.

Lindsay, the first non-Democratic Mayor to be elected in New York since LaGuardia in 1934, had the misfortune to preside over the city during its years of decline. He came to office in the middle of a transit strike on New Year's Day in 1966 and ever since governed the city from crisis to crisis. The main complaint against him has been that many of those crises have been avoidable. In his handling of the inevitable disputes that arise with labor unions, the state legislature, and the city's financial Controllers, his technique often was one of crisis and confrontation, to the point where he has seemed more than once to bring the city to the verge of a nervous breakdown.

His relations with the municipal labor unions, for example, were marred by his rigidity and unwillingness to compromise. He really tried to live up to his image as "Mr. Clean," but his critics say this led him to become aloof, arrogant, and remote. Michael J. Quill, the late Transit Union president, publicly called him "a juvenile, a lightweight and a pipsqueak," and time and again during his tenure in office the city was crippled by strikes of municipal workers that at various times shut down schools, allowed tons of garbage to go uncollected, brought public transport to a standstill, and, on one famous occasion, stopped a large number of commuters from coming into the city when bridge mechanics blocked the rivers by leaving their drawbridges raised all day.

On each occasion, Lindsay was criticized for his clumsy handling of the labor leaders. He was seen as rigid and imperious in his negotiations, while his righteous refusal to act as a power broker prevented him from entering into the traditional process of wheeling and dealing that the labor leaders were used to. He appeared to be unable to recognize that the labor leaders had their own political problems to deal with, and it was only after the transit strike and, more significantly, the teachers' strike had reached catastrophic proportions that he finally entered into serious negotiations. During the teachers' strike he forfeited his own role as a mediator by denouncing the striking teachers as lawbreakers and unscrupulous enemies of the city. And during the garbage strike, he even urged Governor Rockefeller to call out the National Guard to break the strike rather than come to a settlement. Rockefeller refused, and that strike, like so many others, ended on terms that were worse for the city than if traditional negotiations had been entered into in the first place.

In an astute analysis of the mayor's difficulties with labour, Steven Weisman has observed that Lindsay's problems show that "for Americans weary of government overly attentive to selfish interest groups, a switch to government that ignores those interest groups can be a bold new shift to disaster."

Lindsay himself believes his own biggest contribution to the government of New York was his streamlining of the fifty or so city commissions he inherited into ten superagencies. New York's city government is notoriously ramshackle, inefficient, and riddled with out-of-date work practices, and Lindsay made a genuine effort at reform. When he walked into the mayor's office on his first day, he says, "I found a completely barren desk. Not a pencil, not a pad of paper was left. And the telephone communications between the mayor and the city departments consisted of a single two-button telephone. At a time when instant access was critical, there was no direct line between the mayor and police or fire and traffic."

By combining the old commissions into ten federal-style administrations, Lindsay attempted to streamline the rickety machinery of government. But according to his critics, the main result of the reforms has been to add one more layer to an already unwieldy administration, so that the city now employs over 413,000 workers, an increase of more than a quarter since Lindsay took office.

Whether the city is any more efficient now is a moot point. "Genghis Khan conquered Asia with an army only half the size of New York City's civil service," one of Lindsay's opponents has said. And in 1972, New York state auditors reported that what they termed "underutilization of employee time" was widespread in the city. Welfare employees, they reported, waste about two thirds of their time, while the productivity of water-meter readers was less than half that of workers doing similar jobs in private industry; this cost the city about $2 million a year more than it should have done. New Yorkers pay per capita half as much again for police protection as the average American and two thirds more for their garbage collection. One ancient work practice that still continues requires garbage collection crews to pick up a fixed weight of garbage each day. As soon as they meet their quotas, the crews can go home, with the result that some crews are said to soak their garbage with water to make it weigh more. Others are alleged to "leave a piece" after their truck is weighed in, so that what is left gets counted again at the next checkpoint. Partly as a result of these practices, it now costs more to collect a ton of New York garbage than it does to mine a ton of Kentucky coal.

Corruption has also been a perennial problem in New York. In the summer of 1972, the New York *Times* commissioned a special study on the city's construction industry and found that citywide payoffs to corrupt inspectors had reached the staggering rate of $25 million a year. "Hardly a skyscraper is built, scarcely a change is made in the world's most celebrated skyline, hardly a brownstone is renovated or a restaurant expanded without the illegal payoffs, ranging from five dollars to ten thousand dollars each," the *Times* reported. The payoffs were made to persuade inspectors and the police to overlook infringements of the building code such as dirty sidewalks, illegal parking by trucks, and storage of building materials in the street. Bribes were demanded by some inspectors simply to avoid delays in routine inspections, and in some cases payoffs were necessary just to avoid sabotage. "Keep the job moving," was the principle behind the bribes. "Avoid harassment. Time is money."

Even more serious charges of corruption were leveled by the crusading *Times* against the city's thirty-thousand-man police force, allegations which led Lindsay to undertake the most intensive investigation of corruption in New York City in the past forty years. When a commission under the chairmanship of Whitman Knapp, a Wall Street lawyer, published its findings in July 1972, it reported that corruption in the city's law-enforcement machinery was "widespread" and that the police were receiving millions of dollars a year in graft. Large numbers of policemen in virtually every unit assigned to arrest gamblers, the commission reported, received bribes ranging from $300 to $1,500 a month on a regular basis. Narcotics corruption was also commonplace, and although not as well organized as the corruption found in gambling, could bring in individual "scores" or bribes that were staggering in amount. The largest single payoff uncovered by the commission by a narcotics dealer was $80,000, yet the commission reported that "the size of this score was by no means unique."

The Knapp Commission found two main types of corrupt policemen in New York: "meat-eaters" and "grass-eaters." As the names suggest, the meat-eaters are those policemen who aggressively misuse their police power for personal gain. The grass-eaters simply accept the payoffs that the happenstance of police work throws their way. "Although the meat-eaters get the huge payoffs that make the headlines," the commission reported, "they represent a small percentage of corrupt policemen. The truth is, the vast majority of policemen on the take don't deal in huge amounts of graft."

And yet, they added, "grass-eaters are at the heart of the problem, since their great number tends to make corruption 'respectable.' . . . The rookie who comes into the department is faced with the situation where it is easier for him to become corrupt than to remain honest."

The Knapp Commission findings were vehemently criticized by spokesmen for the police, who charged that a few "rotten apples" had been used to besmirch the good name of the entire police department, but there was an uneasy feeling in New York that the hearings had uncovered a tale of corruption that was so widespread it was no longer possible to put it down to the wrongdoing of a few policemen on the take. In fact, as the commission pointed out, the mistaken belief that only a few "rotten apples" were involved had in the past proved to be one of the strongest bars to effective reform. There was, however, some evidence that the worst may already have passed, and the City's police commissioner, Patrick V. Murphy, was well under way with enlightened and fundamental internal reforms in the department. "I intend to leave this department with my whole skin and banners flying," Murphy had said when he announced the cleanup. "It will be either my hide or your hide on this corruption issue, and I don't intend to get nailed."

Scarcely had he spoken, however, when Mr. Murphy was forced to return at another press conference to announce "the worst instance of police corruption I have uncovered": the disappearance of hundreds of pounds of heroin and cocaine confiscated from the city's junkies and dealers and then apparently stolen from the office of the police department's property clerk. The dimensions of the loss emerged gradually: at first, it was thought that 57 pounds of heroin had been stolen from the police, with a street value estimated at $10 million. That heroin, originally seized in 1962 in the famous French Connection case, had in some cases been replaced on the property department shelves by worthless white powder. Next day, it was found that another 24 pounds of the French Connection heroin had been stolen, and ten days later it was discovered that a further eighty-eight pounds of heroin and 131 pounds of cocaine had also vanished from police custody. The dreadful conclusion could only be that this was an inside job, that someone in the police department was filtering the deadly narcotics back onto the streets. Even if it was confined to a few rotten apples, corruption within the police department was exacting a terrible toll on the city it was supposed to protect.

Corruption apart, Lindsay's main problem since the day he took office was that the city he inherited was broke and heavily in debt. New York City today spends nearly $10 billion a year—more than half the tax revenues of all of Great Britain—most of which goes on welfare, education, and health services. New York is bankrupt because its tax base is fixed, while the costs of maintaining the urban poor and the basic city services rise inexorably by about 15 percent each year. Lindsay himself believes the problem is compounded because the state government in Albany reserves to itself the more flexible forms of revenue raising, such as state income tax, leaving the city to raise its funds from such sources as sales and real-estate taxes, licenses, and a myriad of nuisance taxes that do more to enrage the populace than they do to solve the problem of the ever-mounting deficit.

Each year New Yorkers grumble that they pay over $3 billion into the state's kitty in Albany and get only half of it back. And each year, the argument over the city's budget between Lindsay and Governor Rockefeller has grown more and more bitter until they have almost reached the point of open fisticuffs.

About Eastertime each year, the mayor has made a pilgrimage to Albany to argue that New York should receive a fair share of taxes collected from the city and state. And each year the state legislature greets the supplicant with derision. "When I prepare for the Albany journey," Lindsay has written, "I think of Henry Hudson who began his own journey as captain of the stately *Half Moon* and ended it in a rowboat somewhere off the coast of Canada."

In recent years, Lindsay has come back from the annual charade in Albany to announce that because the state legislature had refused to give him the money he demanded, he would have to eliminate city government jobs. There was an emotional crisis in 1971, when the mayor announced he would have to fire up to sixty thousand city employees, close eight city hospitals, admit no further freshman classes to the City University, and close all the city-run kindergartens. To emphasize the point, he immediately curtailed the opening hours of the city libraries, museums, and cultural institutions, even though they were financed under the current year's budget.

In the end, the state legislature gave the city less than half what Lindsay had asked—and Lindsay's threats proved empty. The layoffs never materialized, the hospitals stayed open, and mysterious city funds with which to keep things going were unexpectedly "discovered" by the mayor's aides. Even within the city, critics charged the mayor with perpetrating a cruel hoax on the city employees. "The procedure . . . becomes unconscionable when it is translated into the fear it generates in the homes of the working people of this city," said the president of the City Council, Sanford D. Garelik.

For many of his critics, the mayor had cried wolf once too often; for Rockefeller the episode simply illustrated once again Lindsay's administrative rigidity and his inability to enter into meaningful negotiations without creating a wholly avoidable public confrontation.

The hostility between the two men began in private, but over the years it developed into one of the most roaringly open feuds in the history of modern American politics. Today Rockefeller no longer even tries to conceal his contempt for Lindsay's administration. He has said publicly that Lindsay was responsible for "declining city services due to inept and extravagant administration of the city government," and added for good measure that the city's fiscal problems had been "hindered by a growing loss of confidence in the mayor's administration of the city."

In his State of the State message delivered in January 1972, he launched into an even more caustic attack on the beleaguered mayor:

> Today, New York City has neither an effective city-wide, old-line political organization with all its faults, eager to respond to the individual's needs, nor does it have a true community or neighborhood elective government with the power to be either responsive to the people, or accountable to them in meeting their needs.
>
> While New York is still the cultural and financial capital of the country . . . for the people who live there it is presently a place where housing can't be found, streets are unsafe, corruption undermines public trust, garbage isn't picked up often enough, and, worst of all, no one can ever seem to get anything changed for the better because, as things now stand, there is no actual control over the functioning of city government despite the almost total centralization of power in City Hall.

It was a bitter message, and Lindsay could hardly be expected to take such a pounding without fighting back. Rockefeller's attack, he said, was "false and unworthy," and motivated by Rockefeller's national ambitions. "The governor reveals himself," huffed Lindsay, "as a tool of the White House in the politics of 1972. He has obviously decided to do everything possible to ingratiate himself with the President and his conservative supporters."

New Yorkers love a good fight, and here was one of the best: real heavy-weight stuff. Rockefeller was heard to remark as he bounced one day over the potholes that scar the streets of New York, "If I allowed the streets in Albany to get like this, I'd be impeached." Lindsay replied that New York could not afford better maintenance because it had been raped by the state government in Albany: "We've been raped, but we're being charged with prostitution."

"Poor fellow," said Rockefeller when Lindsay's remarks were reported back to him. "He's not responsible for what he's saying. He's emotionally upset. The poor man has been under a lot of pressure."

The feud reached its spectacular climax when the governor announced he was creating a special commission, at a cost of $250,000, to make a sweeping investigation of "the management, structure, organization and the fiscal gover-nance practices" of the Lindsay Administration. "We have a high—almost sublime—motivation," the Republican majority leader, Earl W. Brydges, told the State Senate when the commission was announced. "We're worried about a city—what was at least the greatest city in the world."

There were horse-laughs at Gracie Mansion when they read *that*. "They had to find some way to get rid of their venom," said one of the mayor's top aides. Sublimely motivated or not, the Lindsay Administration found the proposal disastrous, and promptly countered by forming a commission of their own to look into the state operations in the city, including the state-run subway system. And the bitter wisecracks continued: "I'm a little upset at how little they intend to pay for their investigation," Lindsay said. "They're spend-ing a million dollars on the Albany Mall and a measly quarter of a million dollars investigating the world's greatest city. We've been shortchanged again."

More and more New Yorkers say the only solution to this constant debilitat-ing feud with Albany is to break away and create the fifty-first state out of the New York metropolitan area, although Rockefeller has dismissed the notion as "childish." Lindsay himself believes the only real solution to the problem of the cities is federalization, to give them special powers to bypass the antique state governments and deal directly with the government in Washington in matters of trade, finance, and social welfare. But, as he sadly admitted to a visiting British reporter, "it is a solution you and I will never live to see." The flight of the middle class has transferred much of the old political power of the cities away into the suburbs, whose "Middle America" inhabitants choose to have as little as possible to do with the areas they have abandoned. Even a complete federal take-over of welfare payments, a step that would do more than anything else to relieve the awful burdens of the cities and states, is regarded as a political impossibility because of the opposition of the rural and suburban voting blocs. It is said such a reform could never get through Congress because it would mean half of all the payments would be made to only three states: California, Massachusetts, and New York.

So as Lindsay neared the end of his eight years in office what did the future seem to hold for New York? There may be some financial relief in prospect from increased state and federal assistance, but that may be a case of too little too late: New York's problems may simply have gone too far to be remedied by the mere infusion of money. And for the most part, the problems Lindsay hands over to his successor are much the same as those he inherited himself: crime, race relations, ghetto unemployment, housing, education, drug addiction, an eroding tax base and, above all, the flight of the middle class and its replacement by disadvantaged blacks and Puerto Ricans. Only the problems are all worse now than they were eight years ago, worse to the point where many of its citizens have come to believe New York is virtually ungovernable. Under its new mayor, New York will doubtless survive—cities do not just die silently in the night—but for too many of its citizens the price of living there is becoming intolerable.

And yet—and yet—there is, for all that, a magnificence about New York not possessed by any other city in America and not to be denied by even its most vehement detractors. Odd though it sometimes appears to the outsider, the people of New York remain passionately attached to their extraordinary environment. Yes, they will admit, much of the city is decaying, crime has become everyone's primary concern, fear has been the main theme of the 1973 election campaign—and yet, the passionate attachment remains. Heartless, godless, hell's delight—they wouldn't exchange it for any other urban environment in the United States.

3. Daley's Chicago

"I have seen the past—and it works."
                    New York official after visiting Chicago, 1971

"They have vilified me, they have crucified me, yes they have even criticized me."
                    MAYOR RICHARD J. DALEY, 1968

Chicago is commonly regarded as the most American of all cities, a place that still likes to think of itself, after Carl Sandburg, as "the city of broad shoulders," a masculine, handsome town, magnificently set on the shores of Lake Michigan, merchant, meat-processer, and financier to the heartland of the nation, a place Sarah Bernhardt described as "the pulse of America."

Like second cities everywhere, Chicago is at once provincial and proud of its provincialism, with a local patriotism that is more aggressive and more xenophobic than New York, the largest city. It is a less cosmopolitan town than its rival eight-hundred miles to the east, although one in every five white Chicagoans is foreign-born or of foreign parentage. But the ethnic mix is quite different here: Poles and Germans have been the leading white immigrants, with the once-dominant Irish down now in sixth place. Chicago is also one of the most rigidly segregated cities in America, with its black population, now up to well over a million, confined to ghettoes on the South and West sides.

The city's economy, once described by Theodore Dreiser as "a great orchestra in a tumult of noble harmony," is the most diversified in America, and still burgeoning. Chicago is at once a steel town with a greater output now even than Pittsburgh, the wholesale center of the entire Midwest, the largest railroad and air traffic center anywhere, and a manufacturing and financial city second only to New York. It boasts the highest building in the world (the Sears Building, 1,450 feet high), the busiest airport in the world (O'Hare, which handles more than half a million passengers every week), a city government that hasn't turned in a budget deficit in eighteen years, and a handsome central area that is clean, vibrant, and alive with people, even after dark.

Ten years ago, Frank Lloyd Wright said Chicago would eventually become the most beautiful city in the modern world. If you confine your gaze to the single square mile in the city center, it might be possible to say Wright's prophecy is coming true, although there is little beauty and much misery in the outlying ghettoes where the poor people live.

The skyscraper originated here, and central Chicago still possesses the most distinguished architecture in America, with the classic buildings of William Jenney and Mies van der Rohe interspersed now with several rising giants: the wedge-shaped Hancock Building, the Standard Oil Tower, and the Sears Building, all over a thousand feet tall. Its handsome Civic Center, confronted by a huge Picasso sculpture five stories high, stands in a spacious plaza lined with trees, and the top floors of its tall new buildings—unlike most of the skyscrapers of New York, which seem to die after dark—contain apartments as well as offices. Many people, mainly the affluent, still live in the city center, in the twin circular towers of Marina City or in one of the elegant apartment blocks overlooking Lake Michigan. Its commuters glide to work in clean, almost noiseless rapid-transit trains ingeniously built down the median strips of the new expressways that fan out from the city core, and the central area itself, which begins in the famous Loop* and ends on Lake Shore Drive, is even today that most remarkable of exceptions, a city center that actually works.

For many people, including those who live there, Chicago is one of the few cities left in America that is still fighting and has not simply given up on its struggle against crime, dirt, and decay. The resilience of the local economy has been one factor in that; another may be that Chicago's tax base has not been quite so badly eroded by the flight of the white middle classes as that in some other cities. "Downtown" is still an economically viable concept here.

Even so, some Chicagoans believe their city is just another New York at an earlier stage of decay. According to this view, the city's superb physical plant has been built at the expense of the poor and the black people, whose needs have been sorrily neglected in the past generation. For years whites have fiercely resisted integration with blacks, but now many white families are beginning to flee the city altogether for suburbs outside its boundaries. When blacks begin to rent houses in a Chicago community its whites leave almost overnight, and it has been forecast that by 1984 Chicago will have a black—and mostly poor—majority. If that forecast holds up, the price to be paid for Chicago's central elegance may yet be a terrible one, and the city may sooner or later suffer as a result from the worst explosion of racial and class hatred that any American city has yet seen.

Defenders of the city say No, Chicago got its priorities right, and as a result the city lives. Which is preferable, they ask: New York, which is run by a liberal and humane administration who will not—or cannot—resort to the cynical politics of the old power brokers, but whose city is crumbling before their very eyes, perhaps as a result; or Chicago, prosperous and efficient on the surface, but run by an antique political machine that can be despotic, ruthless,

*Named for the elevated railroad tracks that encircle the city's financial center.

and corrupt? Or is there some middle way that neither city has yet discovered? Answers do not come easily.

In Chicago, political power is a raw and sometimes brutal commodity known locally as "clout." And as everyone in Chicago will tell you, there is no one in their city with more clout than the man who, before his present term runs out, will have been their mayor for an unprecedented twenty years: the remarkable Richard Joseph Daley, otherwise known as "Hizzoner," son of an Irish steel worker, mayor of Chicago, and boss of the Cook County Democratic machine.

Daley himself is sensitive about calling his system of government a machine. "Organization, not machine," he once snapped at a press conference. "Get that? Organization, not machine." Whatever you call it, the machine (or organization) derives its immense local power from Daley's dual role as both mayor and chairman of the Cook County Democratic Committee.

He would hate to hear it, but Daley rules Chicago through an almost Soviet combination, in which the party and City Hall are almost indistinguishable, giving them the power of political patronage over some 35,000 city jobs. Through this elaborate system of patronage Daley controls all the jobs on the school board, the park board, the housing authority, large parts of the judiciary, and many important Illinois state offices as well. Most of them go to his handpicked and faithful party workhorses, and His Honor rules them all with what one writer has called a rod of flexible steel.

Sycophancy under such a system is naturally commonplace. In the Chicago Board of Aldermen, where thirty-eight of the fifty aldermen owe their positions directly to Daley, one of them, until his recent death, could be relied upon to jump to his feet at least once at every council meeting and cry, "God bless our mayor, the greatest mayor in America!" And no other mayor in the country could have packed the galleries of the Democratic National Convention, as Daley did in 1968, with city workers carrying signs saying, "We love our mayor." Every one of them depended for his livelihood on Daley; what he told them to do, they did.

Daley guards his power of patronage jealously and meets at least once each week with his patronage secretary to run through every application for every city job, right down to the lowliest streetsweeper's. As a result, nearly every family in Chicago has one member or another on the government payrolls and is thus beholden to the machine. Mike Royko, the Chicago *Daily News* columnist, has written of Daley's own neighborhood of Bridgeport: "In the East, some families register a newborn son at Harvard or Yale. In Bridgeport, they sign him on with the city water department."

Under this system, each ward is allotted some five hundred such jobs, and each recipient becomes, on admission, a part of the machine, expected to turn out and work on election day to get the Democratic ticket re-elected. In national elections, this has in the past cast Daley in the role of kingmaker in

Cook County, a role he has clearly relished. "Daley's the name of the ball game," said Bobby Kennedy in one widely quoted tribute to the power of Chicago's machine. And Lyndon Johnson, when he was in the White House, let it be known he was always at home to a call from the mayor of Chicago.

Adlai Stevenson III, the junior Senator from Illinois, has described Daley's machine as "a feudal system that rewards mediocrity, or worse, with jobs for the blind party faithful, special favors for businessmen and ineffectual civil servants." It may be mediocre at running, say, the park board, and feudal in its dealings with the poor blacks, but the machine has in the past been an undeniably efficient juggernaut when it comes time to get the votes out. In some black wards, which always used to vote overwhelmingly for the machine, the precinct captain has been known to march right into the voting booth to make sure his members voted properly. But usually a simple warning that they would lose their welfare check, their place on the public housing list, or their menial city job has sufficed to make sure they voted for the ticket.

And if promises fail, pressures can always be applied. When Ben Adamowski, a Republican, ran against Daley as he was coming up for his third term, the owner of a small Polish restaurant put up a big Adamowski sign.

Next day, Daley's precinct captain came around and, according to Mike Royko, their conversation went like this:

> "How come the sign, Harry?"
>
> "Ben's a friend of mine."
>
> "Ben's a nice guy, Harry, but that's a pretty big sign. I'd appreciate it if you'd take it down."
>
> "No, it's staying up."
>
> The next day the captain came back. "Look, I'm the precinct captain. Is there anything wrong, any problem, anything I can help you with?"
>
> "No."
>
> "Then why don't you take it down. You know how this looks in my job."
>
> But Harry would not budge. The sign stayed up.

On the third day, Royko says, the building inspectors came. The plumbing improvements alone cost Harry $1,200.

With tactics such as these, the Cook County machine has over the years turned in some phenomenal Democratic majorities, including Daley's own fifth-term victory in 1971 when he received more than 70 percent of the total vote and carried forty-eight of the city's fifty wards. The mayor was anxious to win a big victory that year because of the national criticism he had received three years before over his handling of the Democratic Party Convention. In the words of one of his aldermen, "We must win so big, so overwhelmingly, so abundantly, that never again will that array of so-called phony independents join up with the opposition or dare to challenge the big heart and mind and courage of our leader. We must win coming down the stretch like a thundering herd."

And so they did. In other years, however, the votes have not always come so abundantly, and there have been dark allegations that the Cook County machine has more than once stooped to outright vote-stealing, most famously in the national election of 1960 when there were charges that "Daley has stolen the White House." Just two more votes in each of Cook County's five-thousand-odd precincts would have given Nixon the national victory over John Kennedy, and when asked to make a recount, the machine replied that it would be glad to: at the rate of one precinct a day. Someone calculated that at that rate it would take twenty years to recount the votes, but by then Nixon had already conceded the election, and the issue was never pressed.

Apart from his control over the machine, which is absolute, Daley has built himself a unique alliance with both big business and organized labor. It is no accident that the city's business establishment, Republicans almost to a man and therefore on the face of it natural enemies of the Democratic Party machine, have come out so often in support of Daley and built such dazzling monuments in his city center: Daley wooed them there. And there is no denying that this has been good for the city. Commerce flourishes, business booms, taxes flow, and in exchange Daley has given the business community almost everything it has asked for, from favorable property tax rates, to speedy public transit for the office workers, to Daley's personal intervention as a peacemaker in labor disputes. "Daley realizes what makes an economy tick," says Robert S. Ingersoll, president of the Chicago Commercial Club.

The mayor's close links with big business, however, have never been allowed to interfere with his even closer ties with organized labor. Public strikes in Chicago are traditionally short and symbolic and, in contrast to Lindsay, Daley has been largely successful in avoiding prolonged and crippling public strikes ever since he came to office (although his record was marred in 1973 by a succession of bitter strikes in the city schools). Generally, when a strike starts, Daley lets it run on for a while, then steps in to demonstrate his ability as a mediator. In his five terms as mayor, he has personally settled over twenty major strikes, including one by the Chicago Symphony Orchestra. The one occasion on which he did not interfere with the progress of a strike was just before the Democratic Party Convention in 1968, when a walkout by electricians gave him a handy excuse for preventing the television networks from providing live outside coverage of the demonstrations that were threatening to mar the good name of his city.

After nearly twenty years in office, the story of Daley the man has become difficult to unravel from the story of Daley the mayor. He owes much of his strength as boss to his deep roots in the working-class community of Bridgeport, not far from the old Chicago stockyards, where he grew up in the company of many of the men who are now his associates. Bridgeport has not changed much since Daley was a boy, and the neighborhood retains its distinctly Irish, blue-collar atmosphere. The ethnic groups in Chicago, where forty languages once were spoken, have traditionally stuck to their own—the Irish on the South Side, the Germans on the North, the Italians and Poles on the West—and even today it is said to be unsafe for a black person to walk through Bridgeport after dark.

Daley still lives in Bridgeport in an unpretentious bungalow, indistinguishable on the outside from its modest neighbors and only a few blocks away from the house in which he was born over seventy years ago and the Catholic church where he once served as an altar boy. His wife, whom he calls "Sis," still bakes the family bread and does her own shopping at the local supermarket, where she pays her bills in cash.

A devout Catholic, Daley's first act when he leaves home each morning with his police escort is to attend mass at St. Peter's Church in downtown Chicago. His religion, strongly held, has been described as the pre-ecumenical sort that recognizes personal sin while ignoring social evils. Reporters who have seen it say the art in Daley's home is all religious, most of it bloody with crucifixions and crowns of thorns. The mayor's personal life is blameless, his honesty impeccable, his domestic ethics those of an old-fashioned—even puritanical —family man who does not like off-color stories and will not tolerate adulterous conduct on the part of his associates. He does not talk much in public about his personal beliefs, and most reports rely on a much-quoted statement he made during his first campaign for mayor back in 1955: "I will follow the training of my good Irish mother—and dad," he declared then. "If I am elected, I will embrace mercy, love, charity and walk humbly with my God."

The mayor is not given to philosophizing about his job, and it is inconceivable that he would ever write a book about his experiences, as John Lindsay has done. Daley's flights of rhetoric, which come most often when he is under attack, have a tendency to collapse into malapropisms, and over the years Chicago reporters have lovingly collected a whole anthology of their mayor's entanglements with the rules of English grammar, some of which are genuine treasures.

Back in 1960, he made a statement "for the enlightenment and edification and hallucination of the alderman from the fiftieth ward."

Five years later, he was to declare, "I resent the insinuendoes."

In perhaps the best example of all, he once told an audience, "Together we must rise to higher and higher platitudes."

In 1969, he said of a federal judge, "We have been boyhood friends all our lives," and while discussing the antiwar movement he announced, "I don't see any more serious division in our country than we had in the Civil War and at other times."

If it all seems good-humored and rather endearing, there is of course another, less pleasant, side to the character of Richard Daley: that of the vindictive bully who swore and yelled his way through the 1968 convention while his police clubbed down antiwar dissidents in the streets outside. The story hardly needs repeating here; it was told often enough at the time, from the mayor's orders to his police chief to shoot to kill arsonists and to maim or cripple looters in the race riots that preceded the convention, to the well-documented "police riot" that took place during the convention itself as Chicago's helmeted cops dealt out savage mass beatings to demonstrators and newsmen. For Chicago, it was an episode destined to become, as *Newsweek* magazine said at the time, "as indelible a part of its violent history as the Haymarket riot and the St. Valentine's Day Massacre."

Millions of television-viewers, both in America and around the world, were horrified at what they saw of Daley's Chicago. One scene from the scores of examples of unbridled police ferocity that took place that week still sticks vividly in the mind: that of a young blonde, kneeling before a phalanx of policemen, her head in her hands as the police pummeled her with their billy clubs and screaming: "Please God, help me. Please help me."

Inside the convention, the scene was almost as bad, as newsmen and delegates were beaten up on the floor of the hall itself. At one point the television cameras cut to a close-up of Mayor Daley, purple with rage, slashing his throat with his finger again and again as a signal for adjournment. Later, there was an episode even more ugly when Senator Abraham Ribicoff of Connecticut declared in the middle of his speech nominating George McGovern for the Presidency: "With George McGovern we wouldn't have Gestapo tactics on the streets of Chicago."

In the ensuing pandemonium, the television cameras again cut to a close-up of the enraged Mayor of Chicago, whose awesome temper appeared to be totally out of control as he bellowed obscenities and racial epithets at the slight figure of Ribicoff, who is Jewish. Fortunately for Daley there were no microphones near enough to pick up the sound of his outburst, though his sentiments were clear enough as his mouth gave shape to the expletive he is said never to have uttered in his life.

"How hard it is to accept the truth," said Ribicoff as he gazed down from the platform on the flailing arms of Chicago's Mayor. "How hard it is."

Altogether, Daley's performance inside and outside the hall was thought by many people to have lost the White House for the Democrats that year, although Daley amazingly came out of it with his local reputation untarnished and even enhanced in the eyes of his fellow Chicagoans, who rallied round to put most of the blame on the news media and the antiwar activists who were alleged to have provoked the riots.

But the turbulent events of that week took their personal toll on Daley, and Mike Royko has said in his biography of the mayor that for months after the convention he looked haggard and punch-drunk and could no longer go through a full day's work without showing signs of fatigue. At times, says

Royko, his head would nod sleepily at formal dinners, and he lost the thread of conversations.

Royko quotes a friend who stopped over to say hello to Daley in a private dining club. "I couldn't believe the shape he was in," the friend said. "His eyes were glassy and he seemed barely able to keep them open. We talked for a couple of minutes, but I couldn't understand what he was saying, that's how slurred his speech was. I thought he was drunk, but then I realized it was exhaustion. He seemed to be out on his feet."

For a while, his intimates were seriously concerned about his health, but gradually the mayor recovered his normal buoyancy and by the time he came up for re-election to his fifth term he seemed to be as physically fit and trim as he had ever been. The same could not be said, however, for the machine that had ruled Chicago for an uninterrupted span of forty years, and the events that have occurred since the debacle of 1968 have revealed serious flaking in the once-monolithic power of the party.

Like the Democratic Party everywhere in the North, the strength of the Chicago machine has rested since the days of the New Deal on a basic coalition of poor blacks and blue-collar whites. Nationally, the coalition put together by Roosevelt has shown signs of breaking up in the last four years, and the same thing may also be happening locally in Chicago, where Daley has never been able to establish the same hold over the new white suburbs as in the old ethnic neighborhoods in the city, while the blacks have become obvious potential allies for the independents and reformers.

The machine always took its black voters for granted, systematically shutting them out of white neighborhoods and depriving them of the services that the white areas enjoy. It remains a curious irony of Chicago politics that the enormous black vote remained for so many years the mainstay of the machine's electoral power. Come election day, and the machine, in spite of its faults, has until very recently been able to wheel out the black vote in droves. But no longer. After years of frustration, leaders of the blacks in the South Side ghetto have finally begun to break away from Daley's apparat, and an important catalyst in this process has been the alienation of the black community over the issue of law and order. There was a burst of outrage in the black community not long before the election of 1972 after two distinguished black dentists were roughed up by the police after minor traffic infringements. One of them, Dr. Daniel Clairborne, was booked for drunken driving and held for hours by the police, even though he was suffering from a serious stroke and in fact died a few days later. Leaders of the black community began to demand an end to what they called "flagrant police abuse of blacks." They were further annoyed when Daley ignored their invitation to meet with them to discuss police-community relations.

Daley's own attitude towards blacks is distinctly paternalistic. He has built them neighborhood swimming pools and row after row of high-rise apartment blocks (which have turned into instant slums), but he rarely enters the black ghettoes and has never undertaken the sort of walking tour through the black streets that made John Lindsay so popular in black neighborhoods in New York. Daley believes it is up to the blacks to pull themselves up by their own bootstraps, just as the Irish and later immigrants did.

Bootstraps, however, are in short supply in the black slums of Chicago, which remains the most segregated large city in the nation, with its black population—which is expected to become a majority in another dozen years —trapped by the new urban freeways and the iron "white noose" of the suburbs in their South Side and West Side ghettoes. More than 80 percent of Chicago's black youngsters go to schools that are 95 to 100 percent black. Poverty in the ghetto is endemic, with more than a third of its families living below the officially prescribed poverty line and an infant-mortality rate that is one of the worst in the country. "They're second-class citizens living in a second-class world, and they know it and hate it," wrote the Chicago *Daily News*.

Whites remain fiercely antagonistic to the blacks, and there are many in Chicago who remember with shame how Martin Luther King was stoned and spat upon when he led a march to demand open housing policies through white districts in the city during the early 1960s.

The police department's already-poor relationship with the black community took a spectacular turn for the worse at the end of 1969 after a raid on a West Side apartment belonging to members of the radical Black Panther Party, the repercussions from which have lasted until the present day. The raid by fourteen policemen, which had been ordered by Edward Hanrahan, Cook County's tough state's attorney and one of Daley's most closely trusted lieutenants, left two Panthers dead, three others seriously wounded, and more than eighty-two bullet holes in the walls and bedroom of their apartment. The surviving Panthers were enraged: their two dead members—Fred Hampton, the Chicago chairman, and Mark Clark—were said to have been sleeping when the police burst in, already firing. Not so, said Hanrahan, who planted a carefully rehearsed re-enactment of his version of the gun battle on a local CBS television station and supplied a photograph to the Chicago *Tribune* allegedly showing a wall riddled with bullets fired by the Panthers.

For a while, Hanrahan's story was accepted and the Panthers' disbelieved. Gradually, however, the true story came to light: the "bullet holes" in the *Tribune's* photograph were in fact nailheads, and visiting reporters taken by the Panthers through the apartment found clear evidence that most, if not all, of the eight-two bullets had been fired by the police. Fred Hampton had been shot dead in his bed.

A federal grand jury was summoned which supported the Panthers' version of the gun battle. Hanrahan, the jury found, had lied about the gun battle, and the police crime laboratory had lied about its ballistic tests. Hanrahan was accused of obstructing justice and interfering with the defense of the surviving Panthers, but was later acquitted, to courtroom cheers, after a noisy and turbulent thirteen-week trial in which the county special prosecutor, when he attempted to bring the indictments, had been shouted at, held in contempt, and fined fifty dollars an hour by the chief judge of the Criminal Court, who happened to be a neighbor, a former law partner, and a close friend of Mayor Daley.

For a while after the indictments had been handed up, Daley appeared to be willing to stand by his lieutenant at the polls as well as in the courtroom, but he promptly dumped him when he was persuaded that Hanrahan might hurt the entire Democratic Party ticket in the 1972 elections. Hanrahan, who had become a symbol of law and order for the white ethnic groups of Chicago, then did what no protege of the Mayor had ever done in seventeen years of Daley's rule: he challenged the machine.

Running as a maverick Democrat in the primary elections of 1972, Hanrahan waged a vigorous rightwing hardline law-and-order campaign, based on the slogan: "Would you want your law enforcement to be carried out by me, or by a nice fellow?" At first, no one gave him much of a chance. The son of the machine who had turned against his own was bound to be crushed by the juggernaut. Or so Chicago thought.

But Hanrahan's tough image was not displeasing to many white Chicagoans, and the fact that Daley had dumped him was seen by many as nothing less than a capitulation to a bunch of dangerous black radicals. Hanrahan, a surly man with an explosive temper, ran an inspired campaign, enlivened by touches of humor that impressed even the party loyalists. During the annual St. Patrick's Day parade he doffed his hat as he passed Mayor Daley to release a white dove, symbol of peace, and he stole the show at a luncheon for over a thousand of Daley's precinct workers gathered in support of his supposed replacement by engineering a supply of fortune cookies which, when opened, carried the message to every plate: "Hanrahan's the man." Even Daley was impressed. "In the fortune cookies," he was heard to exclaim as he left the luncheon. "It was in the fortune cookies. What do you think of that?"

Hanrahan, however, was not Daley's only problem in the 1972 primaries. Daniel Walker, his old enemy whose report on the convention disturbances had first coined the phrase "police riot," was running a liberal campaign against the machine for the Democratic nomination for the Illinois governorship. Beyond that, there was the problem of the national convention, in which the machine's power was being challenged by a liberal coalition determined to wrest away Daley's hitherto unchallenged position as chairman of the Illinois delegation and kingmaker to the national party.

The first blow fell in the spring of 1972, primary election night in Chicago and normally a festive occasion as ward bosses filed into Daley's office, one by one, to receive his grateful thanks for their work in achieving victory. This year, the mood was different. "It's like waiting outside the maternity room when someone is having a miscarriage," one ward boss was heard to mutter gloomily as he paced up and down a corridor waiting for the results to come in. Sure enough, the machine's fears were well-founded: the Cook County organization had lost its first primary since 1938. Not only had Hanrahan beaten the machine's candidate for state's attorney, but Walker had won too, and five other state legislators backed by the machine had been beaten by independent candidates.

The mayor accepted his defeat gamely. "Politics is no different than sports," he said. "You win 'em and you lose 'em." But for the machine it was clearly a shattering experience, which several writers saw as the beginning of the end for Richard Daley.

The worst was yet to come. After his own re-election a year earlier, Daley had been asked at a press conference if the main Democratic presidential hopefuls—Muskie, Humphrey, Kennedy, and the outsider, George McGovern—had telephoned with their congratulations? "All of them did," Daley had replied with a satisfied smile. A year later, the smile had vanished, and it was beginning to look doubtful if Daley would even be in attendance at the 1972 convention, still less be in a position to play his accustomed role as kingmaker. The machine was being challenged by a vigorous reform group running under the new rules for picking delegates to the party convention, and their fight with the machine got all the way to the convention floor, where the McGovern-dominated assembly finally snatched away Daley's own seat as a delegate, together with those of fifty-eight other members of his team. The liberals had finally exacted vengeance for what Daley did to them in 1968.

Soon afterwards, articles began appearing in the press with headlines that would have been heretical only two years before: "Is Daley Done?" "Debacle for Daley," and "The Mangled Machine." All of them suggested that his dominance of Chicago politics might finally be coming to an end—forecasts that proved only too well founded on election night in November. Hanrahan, by this time back in the fold (dropping him had been "just a mistake," Daley said), was crushed by his Republican opponent as black voters rebelled against the machine at last, splitting their tickets by the thousand to keep Hanrahan out of office. Walker had won, too, and an ashen-faced Daley told the press he had just experienced "a very unique and extraordinary day," the worst setback for the machine in almost forty years.

Perhaps the worst sign of the machine's deterioration was the victory of a Republican, Bernard Carey, as Cook County state's attorney, an office that has always been regarded as crucial to the maintenance of Daley's power— the one sure office that could keep a lid on the party's scandals. But now they had lost it, and when they realized that Carey had won, jubilant Republicans danced outside his election headquarters, shouting over and over again: "They're all going to jail! They're all going to jail!" Daley professed not to be worried: "An honest man has nothing to fear from the state's attorney or any other attorney," he said on election night. But while the mayor himself has always been personally untainted by corruption, scandal has come perilously close to some others in his administration. Now, with both the U.S. attorney's and the state's attorney's offices in the hands of his opponents, the machine's dirty laundry has started to come to the wash. Already the former Governor of Illinois, Otto Kerner, hand-picked by Daley, has been convicted of taking graft from racetrack interests, and the Cook County clerk found guilty of accepting bribes from a voting machine manufacturer. Other indictments had meanwhile been served on several members of the county assessor's office, including a former alderman, members of the police department for alleged ties to organized crime, and seventy-five of the machine's election judges and precinct workers for alleged vote fraud in the spring primary.

After years of sneering at New York's misfortunes, it's beginning to look, as Mike Royko commented, "as though Chicagah ain't so great, either." But there was something puzzling about the stories of Chicago's recent disasters, Royko found:

> When the same things were happening in New York they were always Lindsay's schools, and Lindsay's crowded subways. They were Lindsay's crooked cops, and Lindsay's unsafe streets. He was Lindsay's crooked aide, and it was Lindsay's higher taxes, and it was Lindsay's city that didn't work. But in Chicago, those aren't Daley's schools that are shut down, although he appoints that bumbling school board. It isn't Daley's C.T.A. [Chicago Transit Authority] that is on the verge of collapse, although he appoints the majority to the bumbling C.T.A. board. They aren't Daley's crooked cops, although he picks the commissioner and has a big say in many of the other top jobs. Those aren't Daley's pals showing up at the Kerner trial, although he put all of them in positions of power and influence. It isn't Daley's Loop when it is unsafe; it is his only when he leads a parade down State Street. Those aren't Daley's expressways on which traffic is almost moving backwards. They are his only when he lets the fat contracts and cuts the ribbons.
>
> That must be how you get the reputation for being the one man who can make a city work. When it turns out that the city doesn't work after all, you let someone else take all the credit.

Clearly, they are beginning to sharpen their knives in Chicago after all those years of acquiescence in machine politics. And while Royko's thrusts were sometimes a little unfair (Chicago's transport system, for example, is still more efficient than most, in spite of its faults), they are at the same time symptomatic of a growing desire for reform.

Daley's own term of office runs on until 1975, by which time His Honor will have reached the age of seventy-three. He has dropped no hints that he might then like to retire, and it is entirely possible that he might choose to fight back as he has done so often in the past and run for yet another four-year term. But whatever his decision, the legend about the invincibility of his machine has been shattered for ever. Daley looks more and more like the very last of America's big city bosses.

4. L.A.: A Thousand Suburbs in Search of a City

"We know we are mad and so can survive. The other cities . . . refuse the knowledge of their own insanity and so will self-destroy."
                    —RAY BRADBURY, *"Los Angeles is the Best Place in America,"* 1972

"But there's no there there."
                                        —GERTRUDE STEIN *on Los Angeles*

"Eureka!" proclaims the state motto of California: "I have found it." The sentiment expressed in that single exuberant and youthful cry captures perfectly the Californian idea that theirs is the land of El Dorado, the Golden West, a country that beckons man to follow the most alluring of all human prospects: the chance to start again. From the day that gold was first found in the hills of Sacramento a century and a quarter ago successive generations of Americans have followed the same tenacious dream. The continent tipped, said Ambrose Bierce, and everything that was not tied down rolled westward.

They rolled, in a never-ending tide, through four successive generations, a curious mixture of ambitious men and failures, hopeful men and losers—the nation's drifters, most of them drawn there by the promise of some personal metamorphosis. So many of them came that California grew "like a gourd in the night" into the largest state in the Union, with a population that by the mid-1960s had reached twenty million people. If El Dorado means affluence, most of them found that, too: California today produces a combined wealth greater than all the independent nations of the world save six* and enjoys a per capita income higher than that of any nation anywhere, including that of the United States. "I do not mean to say that everybody in Southern California is rich," said Charles Dudley Warner back in the 1880s—"but everybody expects to be rich tomorrow."

Its wealth, its Mediterranean climate, and its physical isolation from the rest of the country have given Southern California the air of a land apart, a separate and distinct civilization, so that even today the westbound traveler comes upon

---

*The United States, the Soviet Union, Japan, West Germany, France, and Britain. California's GNP is now calculated at more than $100 billion and its per capita income in excess of $4,500.

the state with surprise. It takes five hours to fly in a modern jetliner from the cities of the Eastern Seaboard across the continent to the Pacific Coast, and at first the feeling is that one is leaving the great centers of civilization behind. The densely populated areas of the East stop abruptly with the Appalachians; beyond them comes a thousand miles of farmland, flat rectangular fields laid out as regularly as a chessboard. Centers of population grow sparser as the land gradually changes color from green to a burnt ocher and then gives way to the snowcapped granite of the Rocky Mountains. West of the Rockies is emptiness: the arid deserts of Utah and Nevada, barely scratched by the marks of man, a land so dry that from forty thousand feet it is sometimes possible to pick out the trails left behind by the wagon wheels of the pioneers a hundred years ago or more. Eventually, the desert yields to more mountains, the Sierra Nevada; and still, the land below is desolate, wild, and empty. At last, quite suddenly, beyond the last range of mountains, there comes into sight one of the most breathtaking prospects of the modern world: the city of Los Angeles seen from the air, a seemingly endless megalopolis stretching from horizon to horizon, its back to the mountains, its face to the ocean, its serpentine freeways—already its most prominent feature—surging with cars like corpuscles making their way through the bloodstream.

To some, Los Angeles appears as the graveyard of western man; to others, as the ultimate city of our age. It is, at any rate, the last outburst of a civilization that has been pressing westward every since Europeans first arrived in North America four hundred years ago. Ten million people live in Southern California today, seven million of them spread out across greater Los Angeles, which is in area the largest major metropolis of the western world and in population the second largest in America, having overtaken greater Chicago in the mid-1960s. As large cities go, it is also one of the youngest. At the end of World War II Los Angeles had precisely one freeway and a population less than half of that it supports today. The physical transformation that has taken place in the past generation has been prodigious. Anyone who has spent his whole life in this kaleidoscopic environment must feel, in Richard G. Lillard's words, "as if the whole history of civilization were passing him by in quick review."

The reputation of Los Angeles as the first big city to build itself around the automobile is too well known to be labored; the city has over three hundred miles of freeway within its boundaries today, roads and parking lots cover 55 percent of the available land area, there are two automobiles here for every three people, and the average Angeleno spends an hour and thirty-six minutes in his car every day. In a sense the freeways *are* Los Angeles, certainly the dominant symbol of its mobile, technologically dominated civilization. In other, older cities the introduction of modern highways, cleaving their way like brutal juggernauts through residential areas and parkland alike, has all too frequently come as an environmental disaster, but in Los Angeles there is an undeniable majesty to its sweeping eight-lane and ten-lane freeways, bringing unity to an area that would otherwise possess none. They are the axes around which the city has developed, and without them L.A. would disintegrate into a thousand isolated suburbs. The visitor to this city looks in vain for the "central" shopping district, the "good" residential quarter, the "main" industrial area, or the business district clustered around the central railroad station. In Los Angeles such old-fashioned city amenities simply do not exist, and do not need to exist. (In the past few years there has been something of a building boom in the old central area, and Los Angeles now has skyscrapers in its brand-new "downtown" business sector, but it is an area that is more lifeless after dark even than the decaying centers of most eastern cities.)

Because of its huge lateral spread, Los Angeles is a term that means different things to different people. The City of Los Angeles proper is a bizarre organism, shaped rather like the two halves of an amoeba, connected by a long, half-mile-wide corridor, and riddled with autonomous enclaves such as Beverly Hills and Santa Monica. The population of the political city is now almost three million, but when most people talk of Los Angeles they normally include the rest of Los Angeles County, bringing the total population up to some seven million. Lately, it has also become common to include the sprawling suburbs of Long Beach and Orange County to make a Greater Los Angeles conurbation of some four thousand square miles with a population of more than nine million.

The fragmented nature of its boundaries goes some way toward explaining the curiously elusive character of the city's administration. There is almost no such thing as a centralized political establishment in Los Angeles, no power structure to compare with that of New York's, and certainly nothing remotely comparable to Daley's machine in Chicago. Los Angeles's mayor, Thomas Bradley, a former black policeman, holds none of the patronage of most other big-city executives, with such services as health, schools, transportation, and welfare coming under control of the county or special-purpose districts. But when Bradley came to office in the middle of 1973 after a surprisingly decisive victory over the incumbent Sam Yorty, who had been mayor for twelve years, it was widely regarded as a turning point in the history of Los Angeles politics. No other city in America had elected a black mayor with the help of so many white votes, and in the years to come Bradley could become an important national leader in black electoral politics, a man to watch. His victory in Los Angeles proved that, with the right backing, a black candidate *can* attract white votes, even in the face of open appeals to racial prejudice and fears of black radicalism. That this should come in the city where the racial violence of the 1960s first erupted, in the Watts riots of 1965, has been the most hopeful sign for many years that the divisions and the discord that marked the decade of the 1960s are beginning at last to subside. Los Angeles may once again have provided the first signpost to the future.

It can be argued that Los Angeles really came of age not with the automobile but with the arrival of the transcontinental jetliners that were first introduced at the end of the 1950s. Suddenly, southern California became accessible; the isolation of living there had to some extent been ameliorated. (For even the so-called midwestern city of Chicago is as far away from Los Angeles as London is from Cairo.) But although it has been physically isolated from the rest of the United States for most of its history, Los Angeles has remained at the same time quintessentially American, an outgrowth almost of the ethic of the Midwest, from which so many of its people have come. While San Francisco, its elegant neighbor four hundred miles to the north, has always been a cosmopolitan city, with most of its early population arriving by sea— and then largely from other *urban* areas—Los Angeles has been built by people who came on the overland route, midwesterners mostly, who brought with them the provincialism and the materialistic outlook of smalltown life on the Great Plains. So that whatever "Middle America" is, Los Angeles is the same, only more so. Farnsworth Crowder put it well when he wrote that "what America is, California is, with accents, in italics. National currents of thought, passions, aspirations, and protest, elsewhere kept rather decently in subterranean channels, have a way of boiling up in the Pacific sun to mix in a chemistry of queer odors and unexpected crystallizations: but it is all richly, pungently American and not to be disowned, out of embarrassment and annoyance, by the rest of the nation which is in fact its parental flesh and blood, its roots and its mentor." Here, he says, "American institutions sharpen into focus so startling as to give the effect, sometimes, of caricature. Here the socio-economic class conflict is vividly posed in burning silhouettes against the walls of the factory and the hinterland. Here American scholarship and research are at their best; American culture and quasi-religions are at their shallow and shabby worst; here are America's indignant soap-boxers and pamphleteers, bigots surrendered to some over-simplified ideal, its scared reactionaries and its grim stand-patters; its baronial aristocracy, its patient poor, its sober, good natured, self-centered middle class; its promoters, racketeers, opportunists, and politicians; its fagged-out oldsters and its brash, raw youth."

But more than that, Los Angeles is above all things a crucible of change. Like the state of California as a whole, it has raced through the normal evolutionary process of urban growth in the span of a single lifetime. At the beginning of this century its main occupation, incredibly enough, was agriculture, and even that had been made possible only by a characteristic recourse to technology, needed in this case to bring in an artificial water supply—for thanks to its dry Mediterranean climate, Los Angeles is technically a desert.

Then, in rapid succession, came the discovery of oil; the arrival of the movies and the growth of Hollywood; the industrial development of World War II, particularly in aviation and shipbuilding; the upsurge of homegrown industry just after the war; and finally, the growth of the so-called knowhow industries that transformed Los Angeles once again into the postindustrial society it is today. When Richard Nixon, the region's most famous living son, was born on the outskirts of Los Angeles in the tiny rural community of Yorba Linda, its economy was based entirely on the growth of oranges and lemons. Today, Yorba Linda's orange groves have all but gone, swallowed up like so much else by the inexorable growth of the city. Another famous Angeleno is Adolph Zukor, one of the founding fathers of the movie industry; in 1973 Adolph Zukor celebrated his one hundredth birthday, but the Hollywood he knew as the center of the movie industry is moribund, having arrived, grown, flourished, withered, and declined all within a period of some sixty years.

Hollywood's mushroomlike growth followed by a gradual decline is all too typical of the life of Los Angeles as a whole. Some people fear that much the same thing is now happening in the aerospace industry, which established roots here not long before World War II and grew to gigantic proportions just afterward. Lockheed, Douglas, Hughes Aircraft, Northrup, North American Rockwell, and the Rand Corporation all have their headquarters in the Los Angeles area, and it is estimated that between ten thousand and twelve thousand other firms in southern California serve the industry in one way or another. So the slump in aerospace jobs that came at the start of the 1970s hit the metropolitan area with especial severity, the unemployment rate rising at one point to almost 8 percent. The slump stopped the growth of Los Angeles in its tracks, and for the first time in its history the population of the area has actually begun to decline (much to the surprise of most Angelenos, who had expected their city to go on growing for ever).

The city has never experienced an unemployment slump on this scale before —even during the Depression years, over 400,000 people moved into Los Angeles to find work, more than *ten times* as many as moved into San Francisco—and it will be interesting to see whether its traditional resilience will carry it forward into yet another new field of endeavor. Once before, just after World War II, Los Angeles showed that it was able to defy the normal laws of economic growth. At that time, Hollywood was just entering its period of decline, the oil industry was preoccupied with filling local needs, while the production of warships and warplanes stopped abruptly with the end of hostilities. For most other cities, the result would have been depression and unemployment. But as Jane Jacobs has explained in her *Economy of Cities*, Los Angeles found a new affluence in the challenge by starting up hundreds of brand new grassroots industries. The city's physical isolation from the rest of the country was an important factor in this new growth: Isolation taught the city to be self-sufficient, to produce for itself what it would otherwise have to import from thousands of miles away. As it was, one eighth of all the new businesses started in the United States during the latter half of the 1940s were started in Los Angeles. They multiplied swiftly, says Jacobs, mostly by the breakaway method, pouring forth furnaces, sliding doors, mechanical saws, bathing suits, underwear, china, furniture, cameras, hand tools, hospital equipment, scientific instruments, engineering services, and hundreds of other products.

The economy secured, Los Angeles continued to grow, and until the start of the 1970s, the people poured in. Government contracts were a recent and increasingly important source of employment, particularly in the new and esoteric fields of space exploration, missile engineering, and research into atomic energy. Technologists especially seemed to find the area congenial, and by the mid-1960s new people were still arriving in California at the steady rate of 300,000 a year. So great was their need for new houses and land that the undeveloped areas of Los Angeles were being urbanized at the rate of 260 acres every day.

The quick rise and fall of its staple industries and the comparative newness of so many of its people have combined to give Los Angeles its characteristic air of impermanence. There is a rootlessness here, as apparent in its architecture as in its people, whether it is in the cardboard-carton appearance of the suburban homes packed into the San Fernando Valley or the lavish but somehow alien chateaux still to be found in Hollywood. Something in the intense Van Gogh–like nature of the southern Californian landscape, in the almost artificial quality of the sunlight—and even of its smog—gives its man-made structures an incongruous look, as if they had been dropped down from the sky. It is not just that so many of the buildings in Los Angeles look so flimsy: they also look unreal, like a Hollywood film set. All over the city, the hodgepodge of architectural styles leaves the impression that even the houses have not yet adapted themselves to the peculiar environment of southern California. Carey McWilliams believes that as much as anything else, it is the lack of a functional relationship between the homes of Los Angeles and the land on which they rest that creates this illusion of unreality. The character of the architecture, while reflecting the restless character of the occupants and their recent arrival in the region, also contributes to their rootlessness and their feeling of unreality about the land in which they live. "How can they feel at home in such a house in such a land?" he asks. "It may be built of stone and steel, but it is as unreal as though it were built of papier-maché."

How to explain the restlessness of the Angelenos? Three out of every four people here move home every year, always in search of a better plot, a bigger swimming pool, a grander patio. And even when they have found it, it is not long before they are feeling the urge to move on again, to escape from the smog, to get nearer to the office—or farther away, as the taste dictates. Partly, this restlessness has to do with the tremendous lateral growth of Los Angeles in the past two decades: A quiet suburban home on the edge of the city very soon gets swallowed up and surrounded by the expanding acres of brick and concrete, creating its own pressures to move on ever outwards. Partly, too, it has to do with the nuclear structure of the typical Los Angeles family, or at least those that are white and newly arrived. All across suburban America the characteristic white middle-class family has become fragmented, so that it is becoming uncommon to find parents, children, grandparents, uncles, aunts, and cousins all living in the same neighborhood, or even in the same state, and rare indeed to find them living in the same household in the pattern of some other cultures. As in all other things, what America is, so is Los Angeles —only more so. The nuclear family is the Los Angeles norm, a unit made up only of parents and their younger children. Singles live alone, in apartments, or with their friends; old people often become lonely and tragic castoffs, condemned to spend their declining years with the geriatric set in a colony of other old people, or even worse, to spend them alone in some isolated apartment block. No wonder such social diseases as suicide and alcoholism are more prevalent here than elsewhere.

But while much of the frustration and loneliness that afflicts American society can be put down to the rise of the suburban nucleus as the normal family unit, some sociologists see strengths in the pattern as well as weaknesses. Talcott Parsons of Harvard University (quoted by Christopher Rand in *Los Angeles, The Ultimate City*) claims that a great deal of America's industrial efficiency is due to the structure of family life, since it gives flexibility to the labor force by allowing people to move freely from place to place and from class to class, encouraging its adventurous young folk to fare forth and make their own way in the world. It is at least arguable that the brash and easy mobility of Los Angeles is a healthier social phenomenon than the decay that afflicts some older industrial societies where the people insist on clinging to the familiar land even after the old staples of employment have gone, as has happened in some of the mountain regions of West Virginia and Tennessee, for example, or in the mining regions of South Wales.

The loneliness of Los Angeles is perhaps the price that has to be paid for the efficiency and the affluence that people seek here. But in terms of the quality of life it is a price that can lead to some unhappy side effects, not only in the destruction of the traditional family unit but also in terms of a wider cultural loneliness. What de Tocqueville said of America before California ever entered the Union, applies with redoubled force to Los Angeles today— that "not only does democracy make every man forget his ancestors, but it hides his descendants and separates his contemporaries from him; it throws him back forever upon himself alone and threatens in the end to confine him entirely within the solitude of his own heart."

The effects of this solitude are to be found throughout Los Angeles, mani- festing themselves in all sorts of odd and sometimes amusing ways. It is to be found in the quest for sex and companionship in the classified section of the Los Angeles *Free Press;* it is obvious in the popularity of radio, especially of those "conversational" programs where listeners telephone in to chat about trivialities with the announcer; it is to be found also in the enormous ratings of those programs produced specifically for the lonely commuters on the freeways. One senses, too, a yearning for human communication coming from all those isolated drivers who, as a sort of substitute for conversation, cry out to each other in the cryptolanguage of the bumper sticker, "HAVE A NICE DAY" or "HONK IF YOU LOVE JESUS." As Christopher Rand has said, "a citizen of New York, by walking a few midtown blocks, can rub shoulders with rich and poor and experience a thousand interesting sights, sounds and smells. But a moving Angeleno is insulated from these things by his wall of metal and glass (nor is there much good sidewalk life to be found anyway, on the freeways and main boulevards)."

Rand also notes an interesting corollary to the loneliness of the southern Californian, and that is the tendency in this environment for the traditional American puritanism to invert itself, for dutifulness to change to hedonism, an attribute that is just about mandatory in L.A. The hedonism of the Angeleno is apparent, like the loneliness, in many ways: the sun cult of California, the adulation of youth, the active purposelessness of the beach life, and the extraordinary preoccupation with the human body. "I have seen the future," declared one newly returned visitor from Los Angeles, "and it plays." And, one might almost add, it has its face lifted, its muscles toned, its nose plastically reshaped, and its hair dressed more often than any other city in America in its efforts to keep young, to go on playing. But there is something in the air that seems to go to the head of those who write about Los Angeles. For example, Tim Tyler, an adopted Angeleno, wrote recently in *Time* about California's girls:

> In bathing suits these are not just any girls. California Girls. There is a difference. Maybe it's the orange juice. Or the incessant sunshine. Or the surfing and and the skiing. But there's something transporting about a California Girl; the legs are longer, the eyes clearer, the skin more exuberant. Maybe an out-of-towner can become a California Girl if she comes here early—say at about age three. After that, it's too late. She can be beautiful. And healthy. And sexy. But she can never quite be that combination of maximum looks and minimum restraint, that tranquil body and restive psyche that is the California Girl!

This is, of course, almost total nonsense. There are just as many girls in California with acne and skinny legs as anywhere else in the nation. But the passage is interesting for the image it portrays of what California girls are *perceived* to be. Exuberance is in the eye of the beholder, not in the orange juice. Yet so strong is the cult of the Californian body that it becomes almost an act of impoliteness not to praise in extravagant terms the beauty of its girls and the tanned and healthy virility of its menfolk. It is rather like omitting to comment on the quality of the sunshine or the beauty of the mountains —failing to make an expected and harmless civility.

Most of it *is* harmless of course, even if strangers do tend to find it odd, although many amateur psychologists were quick to blame the rootless hedonism of Los Angeles for the demonic murders committed by Charles Manson and his band of female dropouts, who terrorized the more affluent parts of Los Angeles towards the end of the 1960s. Some people perceived in the murders a bizarre and troubling extension of the malaise that afflicts southern California as a whole, and it is certainly true that the region has an almost hypnotic attraction for the nation's dropouts and misfits. The canyons and the desert regions on the fringes of the city have become the haven of dozens of hippie communes, most of them of course of the gentle and nonviolent sort, but in any case outcasts from the hedonistic materialism of the southern Californian culture. Alexis de Tocqueville once remarked, "it is said the deserts of Thebaid were peopled by the persecutions of the Emperors and the massacres of the Circus; I should say rather that it was by the luxuries of Rome and the Epicurean philosophy of Greece." It may be that the same strange influences are now at work in modern Los Angeles.

Since this decade began the gilt on the California dream has begun to fade: the state as a whole and Los Angeles in particular have lost some of their earlier attractions, not only for would-be immigrants from the East and Midwest but also for many Angelenos themselves. As recently as 1967, 73 percent of its residents told the California Poll that the state was "one of the best places" in America in which to live. By 1971, many of them had changed their minds: Twenty-nine percent now said they would like to move elsewhere, while of the newcomers, those who had arrived in the previous eight years, almost half said they wanted to leave again. They give many reasons, including high taxes, overcrowding, and poor job opportunities, but the factor that influences them most is smog. "The Los Angeles basin has been unlivable for the past ten years," declares Clare Dederich, an official of the Sierra Club. That may be an exaggerated view, but it is one that is shared by many Angelenos, who in a bare quarter century have seen their once-blue skies turn into a metallic green because of air pollution. "The great things that brought people to California were climate and jobs," says one resident, "and now they've both gone to hell."

It is no ordinary smog that afflicts Los Angeles; the variety found here has a chemical consistency and an irritation level unlike any other—the result of what were supposed to be the city's two great boons, cars and sunshine. Mingled together, the effect is poisonous. Fumes from the cars, notably unburned hydrocarbons and nitrous oxides, get trapped in the still air of the L.A. basin. As the sun comes up, a process of photosynthesis takes place, turning the fumes into a choking haze that irritates the eyes and attacks the lungs. It is a phenomenon that begins afresh each working day. At dawn the air is usually reasonably clear and the San Bernardino Mountains can still be seen on the rim of the basin. Then, as the morning rush hour starts—and it starts early in Los Angeles, around seven—the smog begins to build up, yellow at first, then green, finishing up on the really bad days in summer as a huge brown mushroom hanging over the entire city and pushing its poisonous fingers up through the canyons and over the mountains into the desert beyond. Already it has killed more than a thousand acres of lovely ponderosa pines in the hills and has begun to attack also the citrus trees and vegetables in the rich agricultural land outside the city. In the summer months the smog sometimes gets so bad the elementary school playgrounds are closed and the children forbidden to take exercise for fear of what the smog might do to their lungs. The California Medical Association has warned of "a state of chronic and increasing emergency." For two thirds of the year the smog now exceeds the oxidant limits fixed by both state and federal authorities, and occasionally it has exceeded those limits by more than fifty times.

What then is to be done? It was not until the late 1950s that the blame for the smog was put where it really belongs—on the exhaust fumes of the cars, which are largely invisible when they enter the air. Before that it had been assumed the smog arose from industrial pollution, and the state launched a vigorous attack on these static sources of fumes. But to no avail. The smog continued to grow worse throughout the 1960s, and even the recent introduction of mandatory pollution-control devices on the automobiles seems to have made little difference to the quality of the air. The federal government has lately tried to take a hand, and in 1970 Congress passed a new Clean Air Act laying down stringent air-quality standards to be imposed by a deadline in 1977. Unfortunately, there appears to be no way in which southern California can comply with the new law without paralyzing its economic and social life. The Environmental Protection Agency, which has the task of enforcing the new law, has drawn up formal plans that to most Angelenos seem almost laughably drastic: imposition of gasoline rationing with the object of reducing auto travel in the Los Angeles basin by 80 percent. In a city so totally dependent on the motor car and without any sort of alternative system of public transport the imposition of gasoline rationing would be almost as crippling as an air raid. In Los Angeles, of all places, the proposals can't work, won't work—and perhaps were never even meant to work. The agency's then administrator, William Ruckelshaus, was apologetic in submitting his proposals, admitting himself that they would probably never be put into effect, but confessing he knew of no other certain way by which the Los Angeles area could comply with the law inside the legal deadline. "This is the crunch," one EPA official declared. "People have to come to grips with the question of what price they want to pay for what benefits."

The point of course was a political one: the EPA's drastic solution to the problem was an indirect way of putting pressure on Congress to weaken its new air standards. As a tactic, it was shrewd and will probably work, for there is almost no one in California prepared to accept gasoline rationing as a solution to the smog problem, and the effect is almost bound to be a weakening in the federal standards. Nevertheless, the Angelenos are caught in a difficult dilemma. Already, for more than two hundred days every year, their skies are clouded with pollutants in excess of the air-quality standards held to be essential for public health. There is no real amelioration in sight, in spite of all the present controls. "The chances of Los Angeles or any neighboring county meeting the federal oxidant standard even by 1977 are zero," says the director of the local air-pollution control program flatly. He adds that they will never be met "unless we depopulate Los Angeles County."

Just below the surface of the golden image projected by the white residents of the city lie the *barrios* and the ghettoes of another Los Angeles, barely considered by analysts of the Californian way of life: the areas where the city's minority groups live. The black population of Los Angeles, which arrived here even more recently than many of its whites, now ranks in size with that of New York, Chicago, and Detroit; its Mexican community, a million strong, is second only to that of Mexico City itself; its Japanese population is the largest on the continent, surpassed in the United States only by that of Hawaii. All three communities have escaped the experience of the Californian melting pot and together make up about one quarter of the total population of the metropolitan area.

But even so, and in spite of their high numbers, the three minority communities remain to a remarkable degree unintegrated into the technological life of Los Angeles and, indeed, with each other. The hundred thousand or more Japanese are perhaps the closest to acceptance in this society, and are beginning to spread out through the greater city—although they have in the past suffered their share of racial discrimination. They were packed off, after Pearl Harbor, into detention camps without appeal and with only forty-eight hours' notice, often having to abandon their businesses, fishing boats, and small farms, for which they commonly received only token compensation. They came back after the war, however, and in more recent years have been enjoying a certain prestige, largely because of the immense amount of trade that grew up in the 1960s between California and Japan.

The outlook for the other two minority groups remains bleaker, and it is hard to decide whether it is the Mexicans or the blacks who find themselves at the bottom of the Los Angeles heap. Both suffer from appalling unemployment problems. Although the blacks have a marginally lower per capita income, the Mexicans are handicapped more by poor educational facilities (in part because of the language barrier) and inadequate health care (due to a combination of factors, including the more rural, peasantlike life many of them lead and the fact that many of them are not yet American citizens, which makes it harder for them to obtain welfare benefits).

The 700,000 blacks who live in Greater Los Angeles are more urbanized than the Mexicans and find it harder to break out of their ghetto. Indeed, Los Angeles is today one of the most heavily segregated cities in the United States, with fewer blacks living in the suburbs than any other metropolis except Chicago and Cleveland. The black heartland is Watts, with a population that is over 90 percent black and a name that will be remembered as the scene of the first and worst of the big-city riots of the mid-1960s.

At first sight, Watts seems an unlikely place for a riot—and even an unlikely place for a ghetto. The streets are broad and lined with palm trees, the houses are substantial and separate, there are none of the rotting tenements here that mar Harlem and other northern slums. "A New Yorker walking through Watts, weighing the so-called 'slums,' would go out of his mind with envy," says Ray Bradbury in an article boosting the assets of Los Angeles. Yet this is the area that exploded in rage and violence during the 1965 riots, which left thirty-four killed, over a thousand injured, and a one-square-mile area looted and burned out. Even today, there is a mood of almost palpable hatred and racial antagonism in Watts. The reasons are to be found not far below the apparently tranquil surface, and are largely connected with the technological nature of Los Angeles society. Most available jobs here call for a high level of literacy, which the blacks, many lacking even rudimentary education due to their southern rural background, often do not possess. In a sprawling and motorized city, moreover, the industrial jobs that are available to blacks are to be found many miles away from the ghetto. Bus services are notoriously inefficient, and the majority of the black families in Watts cannot afford a car, so they find it difficult, if not impossible, to get to work. The commission that looked into the 1965 riots found, for instance, that the nearest employment agency was an hour and a half away from the ghetto via three different bus lines, while the nearest public hospital was two hours away by bus. Police harassment and substandard schools were another direct cause of the riots ("Now we're on top and they're on the bottom," said the L.A. police chief after the riots had been put down—an attitude hardly calculated to earn the trust of those "on the bottom"). There has been some noticeable improvement in Watts since then, particularly in the field of self-help, with several black-run industries moving into the area, although unemployment remains an intractable problem. The juvenile unemployment rate in the black area has for years been up as high as 25 to 30 percent; even for adults the rate is still at 12 to 15 percent, half again as high as the rate for the city as a whole. The impression remains that blacks are neither needed nor welcomed in Los Angeles.

In the Mexican ghetto of East Los Angeles, known as the barrio, conditions are scarcely any better, but because of their comparative passivity the Mexican-Americans have in the past received less national attention than the blacks. Yet less than half of them finish high school, and the unemployment rate is three times as high as that of the whites in Los Angeles. As a result, attitudes are beginning to change. There is an anger abroad in the barrio today scarcely less than that to be found in Watts, and a new pride in their ethnic identity. They have started calling themselves by the tougher name *Chicano* and have in the 1970s struck a new pose of militancy. "We have a new nationalism now," one of their leaders has said. "There is no more *Tio Taco*, which is our version of Uncle Tom. We may be a few years behind the blacks in our militancy, but we are getting there very fast. . . . We are demanding better housing and jobs now. We will fight and picket and sit in until we get them. And we will have our confrontations with the police, too, and they will be worse than those of the blacks because there are two million of us here" (i.e. throughout California, with about one million living in Greater Los Angeles). In 1970, there was indeed a serious Chicano riot in the city, during the course of which Ruben Salazar, a respected Mexican-American columnist for the Los Angeles *Times,* was killed by a police tear-gas canister fired into a crowded bar.

For all their anger, the Chicanos are still in a sense the least alien of all the ethnic groups who live in Los Angeles, not excepting the whites. They are, after all, not far from home; the landscape and the climate are familiar, an extension, indeed, of that to be found in Mexico itself, only a hundred and fifty miles or so to the south. Psychologically, therefore, escape is at hand, and this has the paradoxical effect of reinforcing the separateness of the Mexican community here. There is just not the same pressure to assimilate, to learn the English language, to "make it" in the melting pot, when the home country is so near. "The Mexican-American has not cut the umbilical cord from Mexico," one academic study reports. "Why are they not found at concerts and lectures? It is not just that they are not asked, or do not feel welcome: they are watching the bullfights on TV. The culture is constantly being reinforced from Mexico; and they are constantly bombarded by Spanish language newspapers, radio, etc.; this, plus the fact of being physically identifiable, keeps them from moving more into the broader community."

Nor does Mexico family life encourage an exodus from the barrio into the wider world of opportunity. Chicanos still live to a great extent in linear families in the old rural tradition, often with grandparents, parents, and grownup children all living under the same roof. While this gives a warmth and a unity to their relationships unknown to the white nuclear families here, it also, as we have seen, discourages efficiency and flexibility in the labor force.

So the different communities of Los Angeles seem destined to pursue their own separate cultures, hardly communicating with one another, sometimes hardly showing themselves aware of one another's existence. This can be seen as no loss to L.A., says Christopher Rand, "since East Los Angeles—with its little houses and rich front-porch life, its lovingly watered flowers, and its shop-windows full of Anglo-forgotten things like sewing trays—is a relief to visit after the so different and monotonous main city. But many Anglos don't feel that way about it. They look on the poorer and culturally different Mexicans as inferior, and often as sinister if they are dark. They are made nervous by them, or, more commonly, ignore them. L.A. may be a dual city, but there is great mutual indifference between its halves."

CHAPTER II

The Land

1. Corn Belt

"Our farmers round, well pleased with constant gain,
Like other farmers, flourish and complain."

GEORGE CRABBE (1754–1832)

Every autumn, when the corn harvest is gathered in across the fertile lands of the Great Plains, the American horn of plenty appears literally to overflow. In Iowa, mounds of grain are often piled five feet high along the streets for lack of storage space, waiting to be converted into produce for the consumer. This is the heart of the midwestern corn belt, an area of deep black earth stretching across five states, unimpeded by trees or rocks, where the pioneers found they could plough in a straight line all day long and which today produces 70 percent of all the maize (corn)* grown in the world. Corn is the staple of American agriculture, worth more than twice as much as wheat, the second largest crop.

In the early years of the American Republic, when the new land was being won with eighty acres and a mule, Thomas Jefferson laid down the principle that the physical production of goods, not the merchandising of them, was the basic source of wealth and therefore the most meritorious occupation. Agriculture, according to the Jeffersonian creed, was not only a business, but a way of life; the new republic must encourage its people to move out onto its abundant land, for those nations prospered most which had the greatest part of their population working on farms they themselves owned. For over a century, the American farmer, like Cincinnatus, was looked up to as the ideal citizen: hardworking, self-supporting, politically independent, and socially stable. In the farm-working communities of the Great Plains the ideal still persists, although the reality perished more than a generation ago with the introduction of subsidies and the consequent reliance on government intervention and support for their livelihoods.

*In all the old Anglo-Saxon and Norse tongues, corn, or *korn*, was used to describe any kind of grain or seed, a meaning it still retains in England. But when the first settlers arrived in America, it was natural that they should call the strange crops grown by the natives "Indian corn." Over the years, this has been universally abbreviated in American usage simply to "corn."

Today, the main problem of the American farm is overabundance: the land produces far more food and fiber than the people can consume. Thus, in the fall of 1971, the mounds of corn in the streets of Iowa were higher than they had ever been. That year's harvest of 5.5 billion bushels was by far the biggest ever, more than 18 percent above the previous record of 1967 and 28 percent greater than the 1970 harvest, much of which had been destroyed by blight. Yet even as they gathered in the most bountiful harvest in their history, the farmers of the corn belt spoke grimly of impending disaster—disaster brought about by their own overproduction.

That year their corn stood in the streets because they were unable to sell all they had produced. "I feel like I'm beating my head against a brick wall," said one small farmer in Illinois. "I work harder and make less." The over-abundant harvest had pushed down prices to their lowest level in eleven years, down to less than a dollar a bushel on the open market, compared with $1.62 just before the bumper harvest. To sell their crops at that price would on the face of it leave many farmers on a precarious knife-edge between profit and loss that for the smaller ones could have deadly consequences. "Farmers are the only ones in the country who get stuck for being too efficient," said Marty Myers, an Agriculture Department official. "Another year like this and you'll see lots more farm sales."

Myers's forecast was not intended to be taken too seriously, however. It was a blatant example of special pleading on behalf of farmers who "flourish and complain," since in nationwide terms it is not the farmer who is penalized for his efficiency: it is, as usual, the consumer. After the bumper crops of 1971, food products cost about the same as they always had; there was no spectacular decline in the selling price of grain. Instead, the consumer, as taxpayer, was called upon to pay even greater subsidies to the farmers, with the most efficient receiving the greatest subsidies.

The public actually gets caught twice by the economic consequences of the overabundant soil—once as taxpayers and once as consumers—for surplus farm produce in America is deliberately kept off the market by two devices: government payments for keeping land fallow, and purchase of excess supplies at support price levels. This system of subsidies had its birth in the early days of Roosevelt's New Deal, before which surplus farm produce actually did find its way onto the market, thereby driving down farm prices to disastrous levels. American farmers still look back on the years of the Great Depression with the clutch of fear, and the demands of the farm lobby today echo the distress they suffered forty years ago. In those days, the farmers who went bankrupt were the most efficient; the venturesome ones who had invested their capital in such progressive areas as power machinery, chemical fertilizers and selective breeding techniques. The effects of the Depression shook their faith in the free-market system and undermined their confidence in their own basic creed, which since the pioneers had been based on independence and self-reliance.

What saved them from the slump was government intervention, imposed in direct conflict with their own deeply held ethic.

The great nineteenth-century observer of America, Alexis deTocqueville, believed that agriculture was an occupation suited only to the wealthy, who already had great superfluity, or to the poor, who only wanted to live. The American middle class, he observed, quickly developed a distaste for agriculture, since it enriched them only slowly and with great toil, so that they tended to turn instead to risky but lucrative jobs in the city. A century and a half of American farm experience seemed to belie that hypothesis, and only a generation ago the neat white farmhouses of the corn belt stood as seemingly permanent symbols of prosperous middle-class agriculture. In the 1970s, however, deTocqueville's analysis is beginning to fit the American farm scene once again, and it is possible to forecast that by the end of this decade, those who are left to cultivate the land will either be very rich—or very poor. All across the corn belt, farmhouses are today falling empty or being rented by city workers who commute to factory jobs in Des Moines or Omaha.

American farmers are going out of business at the rate of 2,000 every week. Since 1945, 3 million of them have left their farms, and the pace is not expected to slacken until around 1980 when, according to the Secretary of Agriculture, the figure will stabilize at around 1.75 million, or a million fewer farms than there are today. By the time it has ended, the drift from the land will have encompassed in less than forty years one of the greatest social upheavals in American history, comparable in its impact to the migrations from Europe at the turn of the century or the postwar movement of blacks from the cotton-growing states of the South to the slums of the northern cities. For farmers, the postwar revolution in agriculture has doomed a cherished way of life. The rural America of the future is beginning to look more and more like a scattered colony of factory farms. "It's simply that small acreages won't work any more," says Richard Ellis, an Iowa corn farmer. "They're economically dead." Or, as Earl Butz, the Secretary of Agriculture, has put it: "There are a lot of people who think there is something inherently good about a nation with a lot of small land owners out there. That's not true if they don't have enough land to make a decent living." So the Jeffersonian creed is now officially dead.

Of the 2,831,000 farms in the United States in 1973, over 1,000,000 gross less than five thousand dollars a year. With the operator and his family living in abject poverty and possessing woefully inadequate resources, this group of poor farmers, scattered across the United States, makes up more than a third of the total farm population, yet is responsible for only around 6 percent of the total farm product. These are the ones who suffer most in the years of surplus, and the ones who are in most danger of being driven from the land by the broad technological revolution that is in the process of transforming farming into agribusiness.

At the other extreme stand the gigantic corporate farms which many fear are in the process of becoming the dominant force in American agriculture, and whose rise in the past decade has introduced to the land the morality and ruthlessness of big business. So far, there are not many of them: only 22,000 at the latest count, fewer than one out of every hundred. But these farms now control more than 8 percent of the total farm acreage and do almost 15 percent of the total farm business.

Between these two extremes are squeezed the great majority of America's family farmers—about a million and a half of them, many of whom now find themselves in a state of transition, neither large enough to compete efficiently with the corporate farms, nor small enough not to bother. The median net income of these million and a half family farms in 1970 was only $7,980, which compares poorly with the wages earned by an unskilled industrial worker and very poorly indeed with the average white-collar worker, whose city-based earnings in 1970 were almost twice as high. With only a few hundred acres of land, plenty of debts, and little capital, more and more of the smaller family farmers were finding themselves forced to merge their land into multi-million-dollar cooperatives, able to compete in price and efficiency with the big business corporations. Often the only other choices were to fall back into the ranks of poverty and inefficiency, or to get off the land altogether. It is this final alternative that farmers who have been brought up to treasure their individual way of life worry about the most, but whichever course he chooses, the prosperous small farmer is today in real danger of disappearing forever from the American landscape.

The farmers themselves tend to blame their dilemma on the invasion of the land by agribusiness: the huge corporations that in the past decade have started growing and harvesting their own crops. Senator Gaylord Nelson of Wisconsin, who represents many dairy farmers, declares: "Corporate farming threatens an ultimate shift in power in rural America, a shift in control of the production of food and fiber away from the independent farmers, a shift of control of small town economies away from their citizens." And it is estimated that for every six farmers who leave the land, one smalltown businessman is also forced to pack up and leave.

Attracted by the generous tax concessions, farming, like oil, has become a favorite tax haven for the excess capital generated by wealthy corporations. The ITT conglomerate, for example, produces not only international Telex equipment but also such unlikely byproducts as Smithfield hams, while farmers as improbable as Boeing Aircraft, the Greyhound Bus Line, and the John Hancock Insurance Company have started hauling manure and planting potatoes.

The corporate farms are also big farms. The Tenneco Oil Corporation, one of the biggest, owns or leases 135,000 of the most productive acres in California as well as contracting to buy the crops from dozens of other farms in the area. Tenneco's stated goal is the total integration of its production and marketing operations "from seedling to supermarket." The giant corporation not only tills the soil; it also makes its own tractors, the fuel oil to run them, and the pesticides to control its crops. Irrigation of the land has been automated and is now controlled by a computer, as is the company's marketing procedure. Where possible, crops are harvested by machine—not always with improved results for the consumer. The quality of most American tomatoes has declined in recent years because only hard tomatoes with thick skins can be successfully picked by machines. Strawberries, table grapes, and many vegetables are being similarly toughened up in the interests of efficient harvesting.

Across America, every farmworker now has an average forty-six-horsepower machine at his elbow. Giant four-wheel drive tractors averaging more than two hundred horsepower have become commonplace on the corporate farms, many of them fitted with air-conditioned cabs and stereo tape-decks. With them farmers can plough eight fourteen-inch furrows at a steady four and a half miles an hour, thirty-six to forty acres a day. In their drive to use all this machinery efficiently, the big farms are moving toward what they call "vertical integration" of their operations, whereby the farm operator, by cutting out the middleman, is able to control all the stages his produce goes through. This is the trend that causes most anxiety to foes of corporate farming. Already the poultry industry has been almost totally integrated and the trend is spreading to potatoes, cattle feed, citrus fruits, and other crops. Throughout America, big supermarket chains now buy their lettuce direct from the fields, where their huge purchases naturally set the market price.

Until about twenty years ago family farmers used to pick up useful extra money from the small flocks of chickens that were to be found in almost every farmyard. Today, fewer than twenty huge corporations are in control of the country's poultry industry, and the barnyard rooster has virtually disappeared. The once independent farmer who actually raises the chickens is reduced to a sharecropper's role of feeding company feed to company chickens which he houses in a shed built with a company loan. When his birds are mature, the company takes them away for slaughter and packaging to be shipped off, still under company control, to the supermarkets. Ralph Nader's organization has called this process "poultry peonage," and has bitterly criticized the power the big companies hold over the poultry-raising farmer, who has lost every shred of his once-cherished independence. The producers reply that their methods have drastically reduced the cost of chicken, which is one of the few foods that has gone down in price since the end of the World War II. As a result, Americans now eat about twice as much chicken as they did twenty years ago, and many more farmers have been given work raising them. The farmer is paid around fifty dollars for every thousand chickens he rears, but the broiler companies frequently make arbitrary cuts in the growing fees, sometimes by as much as a half. Chicken-raisers in northern Alabama recently refused to sign new contracts and began picketing the offices of the broiler company to protest against a proposed cut in their fees. But the companies simply refused to negotiate, and most of the strikers were quickly forced back to work at the reduced rates. Those who refused to sign the contract had the mortgages foreclosed on their chicken houses, which were of course financed by the broiler companies. One grower said of the failure of the strike, "Us growers are the only slaves left in this country."

In the fruit, vegetable, and poultry industries the arrival of agribusiness has undeniably driven thousands of small farmers from the land. In the citrus areas of California and Florida, where the old colonial traditions of vast land-holdings still persist, agribusiness is today the rule rather than the exception. But in the traditional farming areas, especially in the Midwest where wheat and corn are grown, the threat of agribusiness has been considerably exaggerated. The vast majority of farms in these areas—in fact, over 90 percent of them—are still owned by the family that operates them. It is true that the number of farms in these areas is falling just as fast as anywhere else in the country, but the farmers who are being driven off the land are being taken over not by agribusiness but by other family farmers, who have expanded their holdings to the size of small factories.

It is technology, not big business, that drives the small farmer from his land; the enormous machines that have now been introduced to the land make it possible for one farmer in the corn belt to work a thousand acres or more almost entirely singlehanded. And in spite of populist claims to the contrary, big farms are undeniably more efficient than smaller ones, at least in the strictly business sense. An Iowa State University study has shown that on the state's smaller farms it costs eighty-five dollars an acre to raise a crop of corn and only fifty-six dollars an acre on the biggest farms. And as costs fall, productivity increases. Twenty years ago, farmers spent 15 billion hours of labor to produce their crops. Today, they use only 6.5 billion labor hours and produce more crops. The average American chicken today produces 212 eggs a year, compared with only 115 eggs in 1950, and the average cow produces twice as much milk as she did thirty-five years ago. The introduction of hybrid corn has doubled the yield per acre and many farms are now able to afford to have their soils custom-built, spoon-fed with the right nutrients to increase yields even further.

But still the myth persists that these changes have been brought about by the stealthy wiles of big business, which is often represented as forcing the true sons of the soil off the land and into the sinful city. The simmering conflict between the traditional family farmer and the new giants flared up into open warfare at the end of 1971, when President Nixon nominated as his new

Secretary of Agriculture Dr. Earl Butz, a longtime advocate of agribusiness and a large shareholder in some of the biggest companies. The heat generated by the appointment surprised everyone, particularly Butz. "I feel like the man who walked into the post office, saw his picture on the wall, and said he didn't know he was wanted," Butz had declared when he first appeared before his confirmation hearing in the Senate.

For the farmers, Butz had at first seemed to represent the worst possible appointment: a man who actually *believed* in agribusiness and went around the country preaching that present farm trends were not just inevitable but also represented "progress."

Butz, a fluent defender of big business on the farm, started his career as an agricultural economist and later became an Assistant Secretary of Agriculture under Ezra Taft Benson, an Eisenhower appointee whose memory is still detested in the farm belt as an enemy who tried to beat down prices. In the Kennedy years, Butz returned to Purdue University, the West Point of agribusiness, where he ran the department of agriculture while at the same time serving on the board of four big corporations: Ralston Purina, Stokely–Van Camp, International Minerals and Chemicals, and J. I. Case. In defending himself at the Senate confirmation hearing, Butz admitted that he owned two thousand shares in Ralston Purina and IMC and a thousand in Stokely–Van Camp, worth altogether about $109,000. His four directorships brought in a further $26,800 in addition to his $35,000 university salary. He told the committee he did not regard his holdings as representing any conflict of interest and offered to place his agribusiness stock into a "blind trust." The committee was not impressed and only confirmed his appointment on condition that he sell his stock within ninety days.

Much of the opposition to his appointment was admittedly partisan and at least partly inspired by the presidential ambitions of the clutch of Democratic senators who were angling for the votes of the farm belt. Senator Hubert Humphrey, for example, made much of falling farm prices and the farm program of the Republicans without ever mentioning the agribusiness ties of the President's nominee. It was left to *New Republic* magazine to point out that Humphrey himself receives much financial support from big agricultural corporations and their executives. Democratic strategists also admitted that they did not really want to block Butz's nomination, since they hoped to make him a campaign liability in 1972.

Their hopes in this direction, however, were sadly dashed, for in spite of the opposition that had at first greeted his nomination, Butz rapidly became a sort of folk hero to much of rural America. "Butz is beautiful!" one Iowa hog-raiser exclaimed just before the election. "He doesn't think it is bad for farmers to get higher livestock prices than we were getting twenty years ago." "Butz has probably done more good for farmers than any Secretary of Agriculture I can remember," said another.

Butz had achieved this remarkable transformation by ensuring the election-year prosperity of the farmers, whose total income in 1972 rose to the highest level ever. Partly through the biggest government subsidies in history, partly through Butz's efforts to sell surplus wheat to the Russians, and partly by taking the side of the farmer against the consumer, who was paying more for his food than ever in spite of the overabundant harvest, Butz had ensured for the President a completely clean sweep of the farm states in the national election. It was, said *Time* magazine, "a bounty that ended the mutiny."

Nevertheless, Butz has hardly begun to tackle the longer-range problems that face America's farming community, central among them the controversy that is now beginning to erupt over the subsidy payments. In the election year of 1972, the year after the great corn harvest, farm payments were the most expensive on record, costing the American taxpayer over $4 billion. Half of that went to the farmers of the corn belt, who were paid some $2.5 billion *not* to grow corn in 1972. The Department of Agriculture's feed-grain program had called on the corn-belt farmers to leave idle at least 38 million acres —twice the acreage left fallow in the previous year—in return for price support and payments, and across the country the government allowed some 60 million acres—equivalent to almost one half of the agricultural land in the country of Denmark—to be taken out of production.

But the fact is that the farm subsidies go mainly to the big farmers and so help to drive the small farmer off the land altogether. Nationally, one third of all farm subsidies today go to fewer than one twentieth of the nation's farmers, although there is now a $55,000 ceiling on individual subsidy payments for any single crop of wheat, cotton, or feed grain. Before that provision had been voted into law in 1970, there had been no upper limit on the size of individual subsidies, so that in 1969 five agribusiness operators were able to qualify for subsidies of over a million dollars apiece. One of them, the J. G. Boswell Land Company, which farms 96,000 acres in the San Joaquin Valley in California, picked up a colossal $4.4 million that year—more than all the farmers of Pennsylvania put together. Many congressman-farmers were themselves benefiting from their own subsidy programs, including George Mahon, chairman of the House Appropriations Committee, and Senator James O. Eastland, whose Mississippi cotton plantation was subsidized that year to the tune of $146,000. The loophole was stopped by the vigorous advocacy of a Republican congressman from Massachusetts, Silvio Conte. "It is high time," he declared, "that congressmen and senators who have their faces in the public trough stop collecting subsidies or do not vote on these bills." Nevertheless it was not long before many big farmers found a neat and simple way around the new ceiling. They simply divided their farms in half, putting one of them in the name of a close relative, and so were able to collect the maximum subsidy not on one crop, but on two.

The subsidy system had worked fairly well until the late 1950s, when America first began to produce the huge surpluses of grain, mostly wheat and corn, which now appear to have become a permanent feature of American agriculture. Many agricultural economists believe the subsidy system is as a result out of date and should be abandoned; even Earl Butz has said that the greatest challenge he faces in the next three or four years is "to get government out of agriculture." He is uncomfortable, he says, with the billions of dollars a year now handed out to farmers "for doing—or not doing—anything." And with their election landslide safely behind them, Butz and the President set out to do exactly as he had promised. Early in 1973, the President proposed to eliminate direct payment to farmers altogether, arguing that they had become "drastically outdated." At the same time, he proposed large reductions in the amount of land allowed to lie fallow in future. "Our goal is very simple," the President said. "The farmer wants, has earned, and deserves more freedom to make his own decisions. The nation wants and needs expanded supplies of reasonably priced goods and commodities."

Acting out of his own deep faith in free enterprise and a free-market system, the President was proposing nothing short of a Republican counter-revolution down on the farm, a restoration of the old Jeffersonian principles that forty years of Democratic Party intervention seemed to have eradicated. It was a bold move, which Nixon had been pushed toward by two new factors that have recently entered the farm subsidy equation: an alarming increase in food prices in the supermarkets, especially of meat, which had been brought about in part by the feed-grain shortages caused by the subsidy system; and a series of crop failures elsewhere in the world, which had led to the huge, although perhaps temporary, purchases of American grain by the Russians, but which had also had the effect of further driving up domestic food-prices.

The President's new farm policy was thus shrewdly timed. Who could object to proposals which would help to bring down the price of food? But that, alas, was not the only consideration. The President's good intentions notwithstanding, political realities meant a bitter fight with the Congress over his proposals. The ideal of farming as a way of life is too deeply implanted in the soil of both the South and the Midwest for the politicians in Congress who set the subsidies to risk supporting the dangerous notion that America today might simply have too many farmers, for there is no doubt that the fierce competitive pressures of a completely free market would drive even more of the smaller and less efficient farmers off the land. In the Senate particularly, those farmers still have a powerful constituency—Iowa and North Dakota, for example, have voices as strong there as New York or California—and it was inevitable that Nixon's proposals should be met with explosive hostility.

The storm was not long in breaking. Senator Herman E. Talmadge of Georgia, chairman of the Senate's Agriculture and Forestry Committee, at once expressed his opposition to the new proposals: "Congress is not about to repeal minimum wages," he said. "Congress is not about to repeal a citizen's right for collective bargaining. Congress is not about to break up large businesses. Without some aid in the way of price supports, virtually every small farmer in America would be ploughed under. I do not believe Georgians sent me to the United States Senate to help liquidate the small farmers of our nation."

Talmadge predicted that the President's new subsidy proposals would never be enacted, and it certainly appeared that the entrenched farm interests in Congress would fight them to the bitter end—even though for twenty years now American farmers have been producing far more food and fiber than the United States can possibly consume here or profitably sell overseas. It is ironic, in an era when it has become fashionable to forge gloomy prognoses of the future on the basis of the "population explosion," that the 200 million people who live in the United States are not sufficient to consume the available fruits of the land. Another 50 million people or so would solve the surplus farm problem overnight.

2. La Causa

"Respect for another's rights is the meaning of peace."
> Quotation from Benito Juarez, displayed in
> the United Farmworkers' headquarters,
> Keene, California.

The great Central Valley of California, four hundred miles long, forty miles across, and bounded on both sides by mountain ranges, was at the turn of the century little more than a barren desert. Today, thanks to an elaborate and highly efficient system of irrigation, it contains the most profitable agricultural land in America. Here, with the possible exception of the valley of the Nile, is the most fertile land on earth; its flat, monotonous fields blown by the hot dry winds between the mountains producing specialty crops as diverse as nectarines and walnuts, melons and olives, figs and many varieties of grape. The Central Valley's two almost equal halves—Sacramento in the North and San Joaquin in the South—make California the richest agricultural state in the union, ahead even of Iowa, with a cash income from its crops worth over $4 billion a year.

Valley society is, by the standards of the rest of California, static and hierarchical. The upper class, all white, consists of landowners and growers, including several well-known corporations. A step down the hierarchy there is a substantial middle-class, also white, made up mainly of the merchants and shopkeepers who cater to the needs of the growers. And below them both there is a scarcely considered yet far more numerous third class of fieldworkers, most of them migrants, nearly all Spanish-speaking Chicanos and Filipinos, the last of a long line of exploited minorities who have worked the land in the Central Valley.

The native Indians were the first fieldworkers here, held in virtual slavery by the Franciscan padres who opened up the California missions towards the end of the eighteenth century. There was no irrigation then, and the Franciscans worked only on the fringes of the valley, but years later, after California entered the Union, large numbers of Chinese were brought in, first to work as coolies on the Central Pacific Railroad, and then, a generation later, to harvest the abundant crops on the now well-irrigated land. Mass immigration from China was stopped during World War I, and the Chinese who remained gradually drifted away from the valley land into their urban concentrations in San Francisco, but the gap was quickly filled by the first unofficial wave of Mexican "wetbacks",* followed in the 1920s by the Filipinos. In the 1930s came the Okies and the Arkies, poor farmers from Oklahoma and Arkansas who had been driven off their own land by the farm slump and whose tragedy has been immortalized by John Steinbeck in *The Grapes of Wrath*. Their plight was a temporary one, however, and most of them stayed on the land only long enough to see out the Depression; when they moved on, either to join the armed forces or to work in the wartime factories of Los Angeles, they were succeeded by a new wave of temporary immigrants, brought in from their native Mexico under an official U.S. government *bracero*† program.

The bracero program came as a boon to the big and increasingly mechanized California farmers, who found they could get through about eleven months of the year with a skeleton labor force, but then at harvest time would need to employ a massive army of stoop-laborers to pick the crops. For more than twenty years, the braceros filled this role perfectly. Hundreds of thousands of workers were imported from Mexico each year at harvest time to live in temporary encampments, and then conveniently re-exported in the off-seasons, carrying with them dollar savings which at one time made up a third of Mexico's foreign-exchange income. On the surface the program profited everyone; it was good for Mexico, good for the braceros, and certainly good for the California farmers themselves, for whom it provided a cheap and docile labor force without the inconvenience of having to look after them in the off-seasons. Elsewhere, however, the program was widely detested: The resident Americanized Chicanos saw the temporary migrants as scabs brought in to keep down their own wages, while it was also argued that the system perpetuated an alien style of life in the Central Valley, based on a relationship between the landlords and an essentially landless rural proletariat. The concept was un-American, and largely as a result of the pressures brought to bear by the labor movement the bracero program was scrapped in 1964.

Since then, whether for good or evil, the field work in California has been carried out chiefly by resident Mexican-American Chicanos. In the entire United States there are now 4 million Americans of Mexican origin, making up one of the country's biggest ethnic minorities, of whom more than 250,000 are field workers in California. Their lot has improved considerably since the braceros were sent home—and certainly since Steinbeck wrote *The Grapes of Wrath*—but the life and the work remain among the most unpleasant and grueling in America. In the San Joaquin fields where the expensive cash-crops

*So called because many of them, farther south in Texas, arrived in the United States by swimming across the Rio Grande.
†*Bracero*, from the Spanish *brazo*, "arm," simply means a manual day-laborer.

grow, the temperature in summer often rises to well above one hundred degrees, shade is nonexistent, and field workers are notoriously subject to back and muscle ailments. Although by the old standards—and even by comparison with peasant farmers in Europe—the Chicano fieldworkers are now quite well off financially, the majority of them still live in filthy, unsanitary camps as they move from crop to crop across the Valley. Health care is a perennial problem, and schooling for their children is difficult because of the nomadic nature of their lives. And while for years the Chicanos were thought of as a lazy, placid peasant people who had found in the United States a higher standard of living than that they had left behind in their native Mexico, during the past decade a revolution has taken place in their ranks that has brought to national attention the harsh and sometimes squalid conditions of their existence.

The new Chicano movement, known as *La Causa,* is led by the remarkable and charismatic Cesar Chavez, a man regarded by some as a saint, by others as a political fanatic. Chavez's famous strike against the table-grape growers of San Joaquin, which ended in victory only in 1970, made him an international figure. Today, broken in health by the fasts he undertook during *La Huelga*—the strike—Chavez is revered by his people as the leader who brought them dignity.

Born in Yuma, Arizona, in 1927, of Spanish and Indian blood, Chavez's early life was a cut above that of most of his fellow Chicanos. He is a native-born American citizen whose parents owned their own eighty-acre farm in the Gila Valley of southern Arizona, where he lived until he was ten. In the Great Depression, the farm failed, and the family was forced to pack everything they owned into a decrepit old station wagon and head west to the fields of California. Chavez spent the impressionable teenage years moving with his family from crop to crop as migrant laborers, working each harvest in turn: first the asparagus in the southern Imperial Valley; then up the San Joaquin Valley for the potatoes, beans, plums, and apricots; finally on northward to the Napa Valley near San Francisco for the grape harvest. When the first winter came, the entire family lived in an eight-by-ten-foot tent on a diet of beans, tortillas, and an occasional potato. Finally, after war broke out, the family settled in Delano, a small, dusty market town in the center of the San Joaquin Valley, where until recently Chavez lived in a tiny two-bedroom house with his wife and eight children.

Here Chavez received the first taste of the racial discrimination practiced against Mexican-Americans in California. At a Delano movie-theater with his fiancée, he refused to sit on the righthand side of the theater with the Mexicans and sat instead on the left, which was reserved for Anglos. "The assistant manager came," Chavez recalls, "the girl who sold the popcorn came, and the girl with the tickets came. Then the manager came. They tried to pull me up, and I said, 'No, you have to break my arms before I get up.' " Chavez was sixteen years old.

His formal schooling had been irregular, and he dropped out altogether in the ninth grade to become a *pachuco*, a street tough, affecting a zoot suit, a broad flat hat, and a ducktail haircut in an aggressive display of his separateness from the locally predominant Anglos. To all outward appearances, he was a typical Chicano, a fieldworker with not much of a future and with none of the special charisma that surrounds him today. He began to involve himself in union affairs only in the 1950s, when he discovered his flair for leadership and public speaking.

"It really started for me," he says, "when I was working on an apricot farm." Chavez had got together one night with some of the Chicano hoodlums of San Jose to break up a meeting called by a white social worker called Fred Ross, who ran the Community Service Organizations, which had been set up to improve the lot of the Mexican-Americans in the cities. "We were going to have a little reception for him to teach the gringo a little bit of how we felt," Chavez says. "There were about thirty of us in the house, young guys mostly. I was supposed to give them the signal—change my cigarette from my right hand to my left, and then we were going to give him a lot of hell. But he started talking and the more he talked, the more wide-eyed I became and the less inclined I was to give the signal. A couple of guys who were pretty drunk at the time still wanted to give the gringo the business, but we got rid of them. This fellow was making a lot of sense, and I wanted to hear what he had to say."

Before long, Chavez had been completely won over and was soon working for Ross fulltime. He served a long apprenticeship, and it was from Ross that he obtained most of his education. Eventually, in 1958, Chavez broke away to found his own National Farm Workers' Association, the NFWA, which has been the basis of his power ever since. He began cautiously with the task of organization, investing his life savings of $1,200 in the union and crisscrossing the San Joaquin in a battered 1953 Mercury station wagon, soliciting support and working on the NFWA's insurance plans and credit union. It seemed a hopeless task: the shifting, transient fieldworkers were indifferent to unionism, and after two years the NFWA had only a thousand members, fewer than a third of one percent of the California fieldworkers.

Then in 1965, three years after his union had been founded, a local strike broke out among the Filipino workers in the grape fields near Delano. The growers refused to negotiate, cut off the water, gas, and electricity in the company-owned houses, and waited for the strikers to capitulate. Chavez saw his opportunity and quickly took over the strike as his own, offering the Filipinos the unconditional support of the NFWA. No one gave him much hope of success, but Chavez had timed his first big strike well. The growers of table grapes are especially vulnerable to strikes, since the value of their product is largely dependent upon appearance, which means the grapes have to be skillfully picked by hand at exactly the right moment. Against a determined strike at harvest time, the growers therefore begin at a disadvantage.

On the other hand, strikes of this sort had happened often in the past and had never been pursued with much determination. The workers had always returned to the fields after a few days when their meager savings had run out. Besides, they lived in company houses while working the fields and could always be evicted if they caused too much trouble. So at first the growers affected lack of concern.

But under Chavez the striking Chicanos began to use tactics never before employed by agricultural workers. When their savings ran out, the union set up a field kitchen for the strikers and began soliciting donations from other unions: forty pounds of hamburger a week from one union, a hundred dozen eggs from another, a hundred loaves of day-old bread from Los Angeles. When the growers began to bring in nonunion labor, the Chicanos picketed them with a vehemence never seen before in the Central Valley. Once, nonunion Filipinos were persuaded to go away and work in unstruck olive fields, sixty miles away, and Chavez actually provided them with the buses they needed to get there. Two weeks after the strike began there were fewer than five hundred workers in the vineyards, where there should have been five thousand. The grapes began to rot on the vines; the growers to show their first signs of concern. They tried shipping nonunion grapes out of the Valley at night, but union pickets trailed them to the dockside at San Francisco, where they persuaded the longshoremen not to load them. The consignment rotted on the quayside; and when the winter rains came, the strike still held. Chavez had won the first round.

The strike was to last for five full years, during which Chavez and his devoted band of followers refused all offers of compromise. "Either the union will be destroyed," he said, "or they will sign a contract. There is no other alternative." In 1967, Chavez organized the national boycott of California table grapes that spread the news of *La Huelga* across the country. He led a dramatic march of strikers from Delano to Sacramento, the state capital, where they called for a special session of the state legislature to give the farm workers the same rights that other workers had. In 1968, after a violent clash with local—white—police, Chavez, a devout Roman Catholic, began a twenty-five-day fast "as an act of penance, recalling the workers to the nonviolent roots of their movement." When the fast ended, Senator Robert Kennedy, then in California seeking the Democratic presidential nomination, knelt beside him in the open air to receive the Catholic communion. In August 1970, Chavez won his biggest victory when the twenty-six major grape-owners in the area finally capitulated and signed a contract with the union, now known as UFWOC, the United Farm Workers' Organizing Committee. As a result, Chavez's Chicano fieldworkers won the second highest agricultural wages in the world, a basic $2.05 an hour, plus $.25 a box during harvest time—piece rates which can more than double the basic wage. Only in Hawaii are field rates higher than that.

Chavez won his victory through singlemindedness and an organizing zeal akin to fanaticism. "I feel complimented when you call me a fanatic," he says. "We're an action movement, and the only ones who make things change are fanatics. If you're not a fanatic around here, you can't cut it." Chavez's acknowledged fanaticism is something that has always worried his opponents as well as some of his non-Chicano sympathizers. Today, as he runs his union affairs often from his bedside, trying now to spread his influence across the country to Florida, where the field workers are mostly Cubans and blacks, he still speaks of *La Causa* as though it were a religious crusade rather than a labor movement. Much more than any ordinary union leader, he has cast himself as the spiritual leader of his people, closely following the teachings of two famous papal encyclicals: *Rerum novarum*, published by Pope Leo XIII in 1891, which contends that the rich of the world have enslaved the poor, and *Quadragesimo anno*, in which Pope Pius XI criticized the effects of the economic slump of the 1930s. As a Catholic, Chavez bitterly opposes the introduction of birth control among his people, which he argues would diminish the numerical power of the poor. It is this mystic side of him that so exasperates the growers, who see the issues in simple terms of management and labor, while Chavez preaches to them about the rights and dignity of his people.

Chavez freely admits that he seeks not only a fair wage but a social revolution to bring to his people the rights enjoyed by other men. "We want the existing social order to dissolve," he writes. "We want a new social order. We are poor, we are humble, and our only choice is to strike in those ranches where we are not treated with the respect we deserve as working men, where our rights as free and sovereign men are not recognized. We do not want the paternalism of the rancher; we do not want the contractor; we do not want charity as the price of our dignity. We want to be equal with all working men in the nation; we want a just wage, better working conditions, a decent future for our children. To those who oppose us, be they ranchers, police, politicians or speculators, we say that we are going to continue fighting until we die, or we win. WE SHALL OVERCOME."

While he behaves in many ways like a mystic, on the practical level his control over the United Farm Workers is absolute, his rule authoritarian. At the rambling union headquarters known as La Paz, once down in the valley among the workers but now housed in a picturesque former sanitarium in the foothills of the Tehachapi Mountains, field assignments are handed out to workers not by the employers or their contractors but by the union, on a strict seniority basis. Chavez has ruled that any worker who does not report for a job assigned to him by the union goes automatically to the bottom of the list. In slack times, that can mean no job at all. The Chicano workers seem to accept the system placidly enough, although since his victory in 1970 Chavez has been running what amounts to a closed shop, and anyone who falls out of line not only loses his standing with the union but all chance of field employment anywhere. In the early days of La Huelga the Chicanos complained that they were not given the same rights as other workers who came under the National Labor Relations Board: a minimum wage, unemployment insurance, and the right to collective bargaining. Today it is Chavez who opposes placing farm workers under the Board, since that would make his closed shop illegal under the Taft-Hartley Act.

The union has also been handicapped in its fight for justice by the poor administration of the new union-run hiring halls, a factor which has led to a certain loss of support from the less ideologically committed field workers. Families of workers, for instance, were often split up against their wishes and assigned to separate jobs sometimes many miles apart. Others found there was no effective machinery for the adjustment of their legitimate grievances, that the new union administrators could be just as high-handed and insensitive in their allocation of jobs as the old labor contractor had been. As one of the growers, not completely unsympathetic to Chavez, put it: "There is a great misconception in the public mind about Cesar Chavez. There's no question that he's an honest, dedicated leader. In 1969 and 1970, many people equated him with Martin Luther King, Bobby Kennedy and Mahatma Gandhi all rolled into one, and he won a great victory. But unfortunately he's turned out to be the world's worst administrator. He did not know how to run a routine trade union. It should have been very dull, humdrum business, but instead Chavez brought in people exuding hate and malice. They wanted to shout and fight and tell people off rather than doing their job."

Furthermore, the UFW has no printed bylaws, there are no elections of officers and members must accept the rule of Chavez whether they like it or not. In negotiating with the agricultural producers, for example, Chavez insists that all new contracts contain a clause stating that any worker who fails to pay his union dues, initiation fees, and assessments is to be immediately dismissed by the employer. Chavez reserves the right to raise or lower these fees at will, without any vote from the workers. Another clause states that the growers must immediately discharge any worker whom the union advises is not in "good standing." Neither Chavez nor anyone else at the UFW will put into writing a statement of what the union regards as "good standing," so that in practice the union exercises a final veto over which workers shall be given a job. The union claims these clauses are necessary because of the bad faith shown in the past by many growers, who have exploited any loophole to bring in outside labor and so dilute the bargaining strength of the union. Discipline, Chavez argues, is essential if the union is to survive. Nevertheless, such clauses exasperate even the moderates among the growers, who are powerless to resist, since when they hesitate over a particular clause, or ask for clarification, Chavez tells them, "If you don't sign, we will strike you and force you to sign an even tougher agreement."

Should this be seen as an abuse of power, or simply as a proper regard for the rights of a hitherto deprived and exploited people? The truth, as usual, is hard to disentangle. The vineyard owners, many of whom are themselves of humble central European origin and hard to cast as villains, have become bitter since their unconditional surrender to the union. They claim that the tactics lately employed by Chavez amount to coercion, that without his closed shop most migrant workers would be happy to work outside the union or as members of the Teamsters, the other agricultural union in the Central Valley. The growers say the workers they employed were in any case as highly paid as any agricultural laborers in America, even without the UFW contract. They also point out that while Chavez is himself a passionate believer in nonviolence who includes in his personal pantheon of heroes such figures as Gandhi, Nehru, and Martin Luther King, his followers are not always so scrupulous. They tell of foremen beaten up, tires slashed, packing sheds set afire by UFW pickets. Union officials reply with stories of pickets sprayed with sulphur and even of a growers' plot to assassinate their leader.

While in the California vineyards Chavez was at first victorious, in other areas the growers have in recent years begun to strike back. The weapon they have used against him is the International Brotherhood of Teamsters, the biggest union in the country and long reputed to be one of its most corrupt. For years, the Teamsters had claimed exclusive rights over the California fieldworkers, and Chavez's early struggles were directed almost as much against the white-dominated union as they were against the growers. Chavez felt the Teamsters under Jimmy Hoffa, later sent to jail for corruption, had shown little concern for the exploited Chicanos in the fields and had in fact been one of the instruments used to deny them their just rights.

At first, it seemed Chavez had effectively driven the Teamsters out of the vineyards, and for about three years after he won his famous victory, a fragile truce prevailed between the two unions. But in the spring of 1973, when the UFW's contracts came up for renewal, the growers began to exploit the undoubted weaknesses in Chavez's organization. Many of them, rather than sign a new contract with the UFW, hastened instead into agreements with the Teamsters—although no effort was made to find out whether the workers who actually harvested the crops would have preferred to be represented by Chavez. While in industry such inter-union disputes are settled by a secret ballot of the workers, the law which provides for that does not apply to agriculture, and the field workers of California have never once been asked which union they prefer. Moreover, the new contracts with the Teamsters also violated an informal peace agreement worked out between the two unions, whereby Chavez was given undisputed jurisdiction over the field workers, the Teamsters over workers in the packing sheds, transport and processing operations.

The result of this renewed assault by the Teamsters—who are widely believed to be acting in collusion with the growers—has been a resumption of the bitter inter-union struggle for power in the grape fields of California, with the United Farm Workers fighting once more for its very survival. There can be little doubt that the vast majority of the growers want to see Chavez driven out of the vineyards once and for all, and to that end they have joined up with the Teamsters in a concerted effort to destroy his tiny union. Chavez has the backing, both moral and financial, of the mighty AFL-CIO, but by the summer of 1973, as the cry of *La Huelga* was heard once more across the fields of the Central Valley, the plight of the UFW in California was as grave as it has ever been.

Another problem that faces Chavez as he moves toward a countrywide base for his power is the difficulty in getting his message across to farm workers who are not Mexican-American, and he has yet to demonstrate that he can win support from the blacks who make up the majority of field workers in many states, including the important Florida citrus groves. Even in California, there is evidence that the blacks and other minorities have difficulty in relating to the Chicano leadership of the UFW and to the Roman Catholic overtones of Chavez's struggles.

In the long run, however, the biggest threat of all to the success of Chavez's revolution might lie in the accelerating move towards mechanized harvesting, once held back by the abundant supply of bracero labor but now being introduced at a rapid pace in the San Joaquin Valley, at least partly in retaliation against Chavez's revolutionary tactics. The UFW now includes in its contracts a clause requiring growers to contribute two cents an hour for each worker into an economic development fund to retrain those displaced by automation. While this is a step forward, it does nothing to solve the age-old dilemma of the worker who is forced out of an unpleasant and demeaning occupation into something even more unpleasant. In good times, the problem solves itself and the workers displaced by automation move on to better jobs and higher pay in the cities. But in hard times, when city jobs are scarce, as they have been in California since the seventies began, mechanization can drive people into unemployment or into even less desirable jobs than those in the fields. Chavez has not yet faced up to the possibility that the numerical power of the poor may not be as absolute as it seemed when La Huelga began back in 1965. By the end of the seventies, mechanized harvesting, together with the introduction of new tough-skinned crops, seem likely to drive many Chicanos from the land altogether. It seems certain, as the migrant farmworkers' movement expands, that Chavez will be forced to allow some dilution of his personal leadership and perhaps also some diversification in union representation as La Causa draws in the membership of blacks and other minorities who owe no special allegiance to the charismatic man from La Paz.

CHAPTER III

The South

New Days for Dixie

"We in the South have a better opportunity than any area of America to solve the American dilemma, to become a model for race relations. We in the South have an opportunity to take hold of the energy of industrialization and urbanization and show how it can be shaped into a graceful, humane and liveable environment—and one that too can be a model for the nation and indeed the world."
—GOVERNOR LINWOOD HOLTON OF VIRGINIA, 1972

The American Deep South is more a state of mind than a place on the map, a product of history rather than geography, the region where the common generalizations about the United States break down. While America as a whole has been nurtured on success, the Southern heritage has included defeat and military occupation. While America as a whole is affluent, through most of their history many of its Southern states have been familiar with grinding poverty. While other Americans are among the most mobile and rootless people on earth, Southern society has until very recently been static, its people retaining a deep and abiding relationship to the small towns and rural areas in which they grew up. While other regions have assimilated wave after wave of newcomers in the past hundred years, the South has almost totally eluded the common American experience of immigration and the melting pot, as the home of the two hugest and (except for the Indians) oldest minority groups of all: the descendants of original white Anglo-Saxon settlers and their contemporaries, the black slaves. That alone is enough to make it the most American region of all in a quite literal sense, with well over 80 percent of its people native-born Americans of old American stock.

The people of the South, both black and white, live closer to the earth than they do in the rest of the United States; their passions are more primeval, more tribal; violence is more commonplace here than in other states. Religion flourishes among its people still—religion of a fundamental, Bible-reading, hymn-singing sort—and they have retained an old-fashioned, even Gothic sense of sin. "If God were permissive," says the signboard at the approach to one town in North Carolina, "He would have given Moses the Ten Suggestions." In the South that is meant not as an existentialist joke, but as a fundamental fact of life, seriously suggested and seriously accepted.

Physically, it is not easy to tell just where the South begins and where it ends. The Southern historian, James G. Randall, was close to the truth when he wrote that "Poets have done better in expressing the oneness of the South than historians in expressing it." The region has no natural geographic boundaries, so that while Illinois is regarded as a midwestern state, its region known as "Egypt" is as southern in its social structure as Memphis or New Orleans. Texas is not nowadays looked upon as a part of the Deep South, although it formed a part of the old Confederacy that seceded during the Civil War, and it has towns like Galveston and San Antonio that have an undeniably Southern flavor. Florida, on the other hand, is without question a Southern state, although Miami, its largest city, is not southern in its outlook at all, but almost like a part of New York City set down in the tropics: atypical, immigrant, alien, isolated.

Loosely speaking, the modern South covers a fifth of the entire country, embracing the foothills of the Appalachians and the endlessly flat Everglades of Florida, the pine forests of Georgia and the cotton fields of Alabama and Arkansas. It stretches from the Atlantic beaches of Virginia and North Carolina down through the steamy bayous of Louisiana, where the Gulf of Mexico is stained far out to sea by the alluvial deposits carried down by the mightiest and most southern of all American rivers, the Mississippi, which pours out of its delta a volume of water thirty times greater than that carried by the Thames.

In the 1970s, however, the oneness of the Deep South is no longer quite so monolithic as it once was. This, the first American frontier—opened up in the first decades of the new republic by Anglo-Saxon settlers of predominantly Presbyterian Ulster and lowland Scottish stock who pushed down from the original colonies in Virginia and North Carolina—is today in the process of becoming the last frontier, finally beginning to catch up with the rest of the country, economically, socially, educationally, even politically. The two dominant southern themes of race and poverty have both begun to soften, while the great exodus from the South—of blacks to the northern cities, of whites to the more prosperous and challenging air of California and the northern suburbs—has been almost halted in the past decade. For the first time since the end of the Civil War more people are now moving into the southern states than they are into other parts of the country. The outward flow that reached its peak in the decade between 1940 and 1950, when over 3.5 million Southerners emigrated elsewhere, was finally reversed in the census of 1970. At the beginning of World War II, seven of every ten blacks lived in the South, two thirds of them in rural areas. Today, less than half the black population has remained in the South, and 55 percent now lives in the cities.

The wellspring of the change that is overtaking the new South is economic. Six of the ten states with the largest recent growth in manufacturing were states of the old Confederacy. Successful industrialization has brought phenomenal growth to cities like Atlanta, Memphis, and New Orleans, which have grown into genuine regional metropolises, pushed along by the South's entrenched power in Congress, which has brought in government contracts, military bases, space-age facilities, and agricultural subsidies, and has helped to buffer the region from the effects of the Nixon recession of the early seventies.

There are other harbingers of the new day, so long promised, so long delayed, that is now coming for the South, most notably the desegregation of its schools and the new political power of the blacks. The transformation of the southern-school-systems since this decade began has been little short of revolutionary. As recently as 1967, only 4.3 percent of the South's black children were in school systems that had been desegregated; within two years the proportion reached 27.2 percent, and by the fall of 1970 was up to 90.5 percent. In individual schools progress was somewhat slower, of course, mainly due to segregated housing patterns, but even so, the number of black children attending all-black schools in the South has dropped in three years from 68 percent to only 14 percent. Statistically, at least, the schools of the Old South are now more racially integrated than those of the North and West.

Political changes are taking place, too. There are now over one thousand elected black officials in the South, and even in Mississippi, traditionally the most vehemently segregationist state of all, there are now towns that have elected black mayors, sheriffs, or councilmen—not as many as there should be, perhaps, but a start has been made. The 3 million black voters who live in the Old Confederacy have at last become a power to be reckoned with, not least by the new generation of white politicians who have been forced to take account of the blacks' aspirations and their growing political strength.

Since this decade began, several states in the South have replaced the old white demagogues who used to sit in the governors' mansions with men of a decidedly more liberal mold: Linwood Holton of Virginia ("let our goal in Virginia be an aristocracy of ability, regardless of race, color, or creed") John West of South Carolina, Reubin Askew of Florida, Dale Bumpers of Arkansas, James Earl Carter of Georgia. In his inaugural address to the people of Georgia in 1971, Carter had spoken at last the words not uttered by a white southern politician in over ninety years: "I say to you quite frankly that the time for racial discrimination is over. Our people have already made this major and difficult decision. No poor, rural, weak, or black person should ever have to bear the additional burden of being deprived of the opportunity of an education, a job, or simple justice."

On the surface, that may seem a small and insignificant sign of progress, an easy promise for a white politician to make, but to see what a transformation has been wrought in the South in the past ten years, it is only necessary to turn back through the pages of John Gunther's description of life in the South written in 1947, in which he described the predicament of a black professor at the University of Atlanta at that time. The professor worked in conjunction with a number of whites, Gunther wrote. But meeting him on the street after hours, they were not likely to recognize or greet him. In a hotel, he traveled in the freight elevator, and under no circumstances could he eat in anything but a segregated restaurant or lunchroom. Too proud to go to a Jim Crow theater, he could hardly ever see a first-run movie or go to a concert. When he traveled by train, by was packed like an animal into a villainously decrepit wooden car. If he visited a friend in a suburb, he found that the water, electricity, and gas stopped where the segregated quarter began. He was not allowed to try on a hat or a pair of gloves in a white store. Not conceivably would a true southern white shake hands with him, and at a bus terminal he would have to use the "colored" toilet and drink from a separate water fountain. He was expected to give way to whites on the sidewalk, and he almost never saw the picture of a fellow black in the newspaper, except that of a criminal. His children attended a segregated school, and when they grew up, no state university in the entire South would receive them.

Those were the years in which blacks who traveled on the buses in Mississippi were not only compelled to sit in the back, they were often divided from the white passengers in the front by a heavy curtain—a state of affairs that lasted until well into the 1960s, when segregation finally began to break down, first under the inspired leadership of Dr. Martin Luther King, later under pressure from the Kennedy and Johnson administrations, the Civil Rights Act of 1964, and the various rulings of the Supreme Court on school desegregation, many of which only began to have a practical effect in the South after the start of the 1970s.

While in the words of the old Negro spiritual there is undoubtedly a new day a-coming in the South, the ingrained prejudices of four generations do not disappear overnight. All along, progress has been punctuated by violence— Little Rock, Selma, the assassination of Dr. King—and by the implacable, romantic, unyielding resistance of whites, who have had every significant change forced upon them from outside. That there is still discrimination practiced against the blacks in the South is undeniable. They are even today far poorer on the whole than their white neighbors, they still live in a segregated part of town and find it harder to get jobs. Thousands of them, especially in the remote rural areas, live in conditions of appalling poverty. Yet it is also undeniable that the most evil manifestations of the segregation chronicled by John Gunther only twenty-five years ago have become a relic of the past as outmoded as the statues of the Confederate soldier that are still found in the center of every southern community.

Race and poverty; poverty and race. These two themes have been intertwined in the history of the South since its earliest days. Like most of the other problems of the South, both had their modern genesis in the traumas of the Civil War and its aftermath, Reconstruction, when for eight or nine years the states that had gone into rebellion were ruled by martial law. "The war," wrote James Truslow Adams, "left the South prostrate; Reconstruction left it maddened."

The South lost a quarter of its white male population in the war; with Reconstruction many of those who remained were classified as rebels and deprived of the vote. The region was divided into five military districts ruled by an unholy coalition made up of the northern army, the newly freed black slaves, Yankee carpetbaggers (so called because of their suitcases, made of carpet bagging, in which they carried their possessions) and southern white collaborators who became known as scallawags. Black voters outnumbered whites in five of the Confederate states in these years, and with the help of the carpetbaggers and the scallawags they were also able to dominate the majority of the other states in the name of the Republican Party. "Fifteen years have passed over the South," one traveler observed gloomily of this period, "and she still sits crushed, wrecked, busy displaying and bemoaning her wounds."

The Reconstruction experiment finally collapsed in the compromise of 1877, when President Rutherford B. Hayes, in exchange for the South's electoral votes, agreed to pull out the remaining northern troops and leave the newly enfranchised blacks to the mercies of the embittered whites, who moved at once to establish one-party rule under the Democrats, based on the doctrine of White Supremacy. But it was not mere dominance that the whites imposed on the South in the years after Reconstruction. It was "the absolute elimination of the Negro from every social activity that involved one iota of equality with the white man." In most states, he was deprived even of his vote, that heritage most highly treasured by Americans. The expedient often used was the brutally simple one of subjecting him to a registration test of such bewildering complexity that even the white registrars who administered it could not have passed.

"Well, Rastus," goes the bitter old black joke,' "tell me what it means when it says that no state shall grant letters of marque or reprisal?"

"Why, suh," replies the black. "It means this ol' nigger ain't gonna get no vote in Sunflower County!"

As late as 1960, only 6 percent of the blacks in Mississippi eligible for the vote were actually registered; a single decade later 60 percent of them were, and hundreds of thousands of them turned out in 1971 to vote for Charles Evers, the first black candidate for governor of that backward state since the days of Reconstruction. The fact that Evers lost was perhaps less significant than the fact that he was allowed to campaign unmolested, without violence, on the steps of almost every courthouse in the state—the courthouse that for a hundred years had been the symbol of white supremacy.

Two years earlier, Evers (whose brother Medgar, a fieldworker for the National Association for the Advancement of Colored People, had been murdered in Jackson in 1963 by a white sniper) had become Mississippi's first black mayor in the tiny town of Fayette, where 75 percent of the inhabitants are black, with an average income of less than a thousand dollars a year. "We're going to show the whites—the whites who have done so much to hurt us—that it's easy to do good," he had declared just before his inauguration. "We're going to say to all the blacks: Don't get mad, get smart. Don't shoot your brother, and don't bomb him. Just vote him out of office. Because the right will prevail. All the mean folks in the country will someday be gone. And then the country will belong to the good folks.

"Our schools will be open to everybody," Evers had declared. "Maybe what we do in Mississippi will help our black brothers and our white brothers all over the country. I'm only here to say: Let's help ourselves. Let's not cast anybody off and let's not hate anybody. I'm not even going to hate that old chief of police, whom I'm going to fire on July the eighth."

It had taken twenty years of civil rights legislation, black voter-registration drives, court decisions, executive orders—and not infrequently the use of federal force—to enable men like Charles Evers to run for public office in the South. "Self-enlightenment was not the take-off point," one black leader has said. "The most potent factor has been the national policies that *forced* the South to change its way of doing business."

Many areas in the South were forced into the biggest turning point in a lifetime one cold and sunny January day in 1970. On that day the barriers of segregation finally came down in the first of some thirty school districts in Mississippi—and they came down peacefully. Ever since the Supreme Court had ruled in 1954 that schools in the South should be desegregated "with all deliberate speed," school boards in Mississippi and other states throughout the South, all of them controlled by whites, had dragged their heels on desegregation. They interpreted "all deliberate speed" to mean the slowest speed the whites could get away with, so that as late as 1964 there was not a single black child at an integrated school in Mississippi. But in 1969, the Supreme Court had passed a further ruling which in effect prohibited the old dual school-system and made "all deliberate speed" no longer permissible. The school barriers were ordered down throughout the South. And desegregation came to the small towns of Mississippi not slowly, but all at once. *"Mississippi!"*one local newspaper editor had exclaimed when the effects of the ruling became apparent. "The one damn place where Yankees and everyone else says this can't work, and it's becoming the battlefront. It's part of the screwy system of this nation that the one state least equipped, financially and emotionally, to deal with all the implications of it is finally having to do it first."

His fears were to prove largely unfounded. As the day approached, Fannie Lou Hamer, the black Mississippi leader, addressed a group of children who for the first time in their lives were to attend school together with white children. "You not just *frightened*," she told them, her strong local accent doubly stressed by the presence of reporters and television cameras. "You scared to death, ain't you? You scared to death. But just remember, they ain't gonna be savin' *you*. You gonna be savin' *them*."

The day came and passed without a single incident. The children, both black and white, *were* scared; but over the next few days, as school after school in the deeply rural area opened its doors to mixed classes, it was clear that there was going to be no violence. Unlike some of the earlier test-cases of the 1960s, the whites had come to accept the changes as inevitable—grudgingly perhaps, unwillingly certainly—but nevertheless, inevitable. Diehards had threatened to withdraw their children from the school system altogether, but that threat proved worse than the reality. In the event only 12 percent of the white parents put their children into private segregated academies—far fewer than the earlier pessimistic forecasts.

Most whites showed that they preferred to accept integration rather than see the public school system destroyed. In coming to this decision—a radical one for the South—they were helped by several factors. Economically, integration was difficult to resist: many of the white families in these rural areas were themselves too poor to afford private schooling for three or four children. There were no suburbs to flee to as the whites in the north had fled. In most of the Mississippi schools the ratio of blacks to white was fairly even, so that their children were not overwhelmed by blacks, as they had been in some of the bigger northern cities, where the school enrolment was often 80 or 90 percent black. But above all, in the small towns of Mississippi the school boards were not compelled to resort to widespread and long-distance busing to achieve the decreed racial balance—the busing that had caused such severe political problems in other parts of the country, even in other parts of the South.

For the whites, therefore, it can be argued that the acceptance of school desegregation will gradually lead to a more widely tolerant attitude towards their black neighbors—not in this generation perhaps, but maybe in the next, in the attitude of the white children who are for the first time attending the same schools as blacks. "Never again will we experience the horror and fear that anticipates desegregation," says one leader of the moderate whites. "And most of us will never again completely ignore the black sections of town. For the first time, it dawned on us that there were no sidewalks there. For the first time in their lives, whites were working with blacks for a common cause."

For the blacks, however, the gains since that 1970 day have been uneven. Less than two years after the schools in Mississippi and other southern states had been desegregated, there was a gloomier mood than ever among the region's black leaders, a mood of disillusionment, a feeling that under President Nixon the gains of the 1960s had been brought to an end, a feeling that in any case integration was really not solving the black educational problems.

That mood was perhaps more acute in the new big cities of the South than it was in the rural areas, for the cities of the South have now begun to spawn white suburbs on the pattern of older cities in the North, leaving behind an urban core populated more and more by blacks and a school system that is becoming segregated again, not by law, but by the more intractable problem brought about by de facto patterns of segregated housing. Atlanta, for example, has changed from a school system that was only one-third black in 1950 to one that is more than half black today, largely because whites have left for suburbs that are outside the boundaries of the city.

Even in the rural areas, where most schools are now integrated, many *classes* in those schools are not. And for black teachers integration has brought many difficult problems, not least the discrimination they still suffer at the hands of their white colleagues and parents of their white children. Time and again in those first few weeks after integration, white parents would complain that they had for the first time met their child's new black teacher and asked her (it was usually her) what subjects she taught. "Ah teaches English," came the alleged reply. One heard the same story in town after town—an expression more of white prejudice than of black teaching standards. Many black teachers also found they had been demoted at their new integrated schools. This problem was particularly acute for black principals who were nearly always demoted to *assistant* principal in the new school—or in some cases fired from their posts altogether.

There was disillusionment also at President Nixon's opposition to desegregation, a feeling that the gains of the 1960s had been brought deliberately to an end under the political pressures of angry white parents in the cities, who were vehemently opposing the new busing guidelines. At the very moment when in Mississippi the old barriers had been broken down, there was a feeling that the nation as a whole had faltered in its progress toward equal schooling just as it had faltered in the period after Reconstruction. "The force of reformist zeal expends itself and the disenchantment sets in," says C. Vann Woodward, the distinguished Yale historian. "The leaders of the resistance are emboldened; the Negroes feel deserted. After a period of promise, they go from disillusionment to a sense of unfulfillment and withdrawal."

Nevertheless, in spite of the growing disenchantment, progress had been made in the South. At least 40 percent and perhaps as many as 45 percent of the three million black schoolchildren in the South today attend schools with white majorities—and almost certainly there is now a bigger percentage of children attending desegregated schools in the South than there is in the schools of the urban North and West. It has been a remarkable transformation, achieved peaceably and accepted at last by the segregationist whites who a decade earlier had forced the federal government to bring in troops to escort the first few black students into school and college and where less than ten years before George Wallace had declared at his oath-taking ceremony on the steps of the Alabama state capitol in Montgomery, "In the name of the greatest people that have ever trod this earth, I draw the line in the dust and toss the gauntlet before the feet of tyranny. And I say, segregation now! Segregation tomorrow! Segregation forever!" George Wallace still campaigned through the South in the early 1970s making speeches against what he called "this asinine policy of busin' little chil'ren," but by this time even Wallace had stopped talking openly about segregation—and that in itself was a considerable advance.

After race, the other enduring problem of the South is poverty—poverty of a nature not encountered in most other parts of the United States, poverty that persists in the more rural areas in spite of the vast economic changes that are sweeping the newly industrialized areas of the South. Even today, one quarter of the total population of Mississippi, more than 400,000 persons, are eating federally paid-for food, and there are counties in South Carolina that have even refused to let in the federally aided food program on the grounds that by covering up the problem of hunger, the state would prove more attractive to new industry. Across America there are still twenty-six million people—the majority of them in the South—who live at or below the federally defined poverty level and who therefore cannot afford to purchase an adequate diet.

For the blacks who live in the old cotton-growing areas of the South, where much of the poverty is concentrated, there is nothing new in hunger and hardship. But the plight they are in today contrasts sadly with the progress that is being made in other parts of the region, a plight that has been accentuated by the decline of cotton as the South's staple industry, coupled with the almost complete mechanization of the cotton farms that remain. In Mississippi alone, the cotton acreage has been more than halved in the past twenty years, while 90 percent of the crop is now gathered by machines, which can pick as much cotton in an hour as a man with a mule used to be able to pick in a week. Tens of thousands of former cotton hands have left the land altogether; some of these who are left have found better jobs than they had before, driving the tractors, operating the new machinery, guaranteed a daily minimum wage. Others less fortunate, however, have been forced into a life as sharecroppers, relatively poorer now than they have ever been.

They live in rural shanties, often made of no more than corrugated iron and tarpaper, looking picturesque enough when viewed from the distance of the main road, perhaps surrounded by hanging fronds of Spanish moss and set against the majestic backdrop of the Mississippi River. Inside, however, conditions can be as squalid and unsanitary as in any hovel on the poverty-stricken island of Haiti. It is common to find listless children with swollen bellies, protruding navels, and all the other signs of pellagra or other forms of malnutrition. In the entire state of Mississippi, the infant mortality rate remains the highest in the country, ominously higher today than it was even in 1940, with around 55 deaths for every 1,000 live births. In Tunica County, which borders the Mississippi River in the far north of the state, the infant mortality rate was recently up to 64.5 per 1,000 live births, some three times the national average, the majority of the infant deaths coming from such preventable conditions as pneumonia and diarrhea. Out of the County's total population of some 17,000, almost 80 percent of it black, the median income was not much more than $1,250 a year. Of the 11,000 people below the official poverty level, only 1,500 were receiving public assistance and only 6,000 had been permitted to take part in the government's food-stamp program, largely because the others simply cannot afford to take part. Tunica County and others like it have sent thousands of their people fleeing in desperation to the North —-where their poverty is at least visible—yet thousands of others remain, many of them showing clinical signs of malnutrition.

There are pockets of poverty like Tunica County all across the South, where the black sharecroppers, the poorest of the poor, have no money whatsoever. No one in these areas buys anything or sells anything, and what trade there is, is conducted by a primitive form of barter. "They work or they don't work," Robert Sherrill has written. "But when they do work it is for past debts or to establish future credit. No money changes hands. They wear cast off clothes, they eat charity food. They buy nothing."

Statistically, there are between forty and sixty thousand incomeless families in the Delta region of Mississippi alone. Because they are able-bodied, the men are not qualified for welfare payments. And because they have no money, they cannot afford to join the Food Stamp Program, under which poor families are supposed to pay around two dollars a month a head for stamps they can exchange for food. But when the poor cannot afford to buy the food stamps in the first place, they do not qualify for the subsidies and are forced instead to rely on charity handouts from the Commodities Distribution program— food which is declared surplus by the Department of Agriculture, most of it cornmeal, flour, and dried milk. It is not meant to provide the staple food for these people, merely to supplement their diet, but thousands upon thousands of people in the South subsist almost entirely upon this hardly adequate supply.

As recently as 1967, a working party for the Senate Subcommittee on Manpower and Employment visited poor people in rural Mississippi and came away shocked at what they had found: people by the thousands "living outside of every legal, medical and social advance our nation has made in this century." They found homes where children were lucky to eat one meal a day— children who never drank milk nor ate any fruit, green vegetables, or meat. "They live," said the report, "on starches—grits, bread, Kool-Aid. . . . We saw children fed communally—that is by neighbors who give scraps of food to children whose own parents have nothing to give them." Not only were these children receiving no food from the government; they were also getting no medical attention whatsoever. "They are living under such primitive conditions," the report went on, "that we found it hard to believe we were examining American children of the twentieth century."

It is a melancholy story, and while there has been some small improvement in the five or six years since the report was compiled, conditions today remain for the most part just as the committee reported them. As late as 1972, it was found that of the 30 million people in America who qualify for food stamps, only 11.8 million actually receive them. Some live in areas where food stamps are not furnished, others drop out of the program voluntarily, the remainder —that is, perhaps 4 or 5 million people—are program "pushouts," people who for one reason or another cannot effectively control their meager cash flow to meet the program's inflexible demands, outside the American mainstream, victims of an ethic which decrees that there must be something inherently wrong with people who have no money. The ironic effect is that the country takes care of its poor—but withholds its care from the poorest of all.

PART TWO

Work

CHAPTER IV

Money

1. Trillion-Dollar Economy

"Business is what makes the mare go."

LYNDON B. JOHNSON

Of all the assumptions made about the United States throughout the past generation, none seemed safer than faith in the enduring strength of the American economy. It was economic dominance, indeed, that enabled her to assume the burdens of world leadership in the postwar era; and if America is regarded as a superpower, it is not just because of the might of her nuclear arsenal or the sense of national destiny expressed by her leaders, but because of the enormous strength of her industry. It was a wealth that underpinned everything else.

And it was a wealth that led in the 1960s to an overweening sense of pride. Along among the nations of the world, past or present, the United States had assumed she was so wealthy she could afford both guns *and* butter. McGeorge Bundy, President Johnson's national security adviser, had said so quite explicitly back in 1964, and Johnson had tried to achieve it in the years that followed by fighting the war in Vietnam without raising taxes to pay for it. For a while, it seemed he might get away with this defiance of the laws of economic logic, but by the time he left office in January 1969 it was already apparent he had failed. The American economy was in trouble. It was not that America hadn't the money to pay for the war in Vietnam; even at its worst, it never directly accounted for more than 3.5 percent of the gross national product. But by dissembling about the true costs of the military involvement and attempting to pay for it out of deficit spending, Johnson and McNamara had unleashed forces that would sooner or later—but inevitably—bring America to the reckoning. Pride could do no more.

Just over two years after he left office, Johnson's pigeons came home to roost; and they came home all at once. By the summer of 1971, the economy was in an acute state of crisis. With the war gradually winding down, industry had sunk into the longest and worst recession since the Eisenhower years. At home, 5.5 million Americans were out of work, business growth was at a standstill, yet inflation—the inflation caused by Johnson's taxfree war—was the worst anyone could remember. Abroad, the situation looked even graver.

The balance-of-payments deficit that year alone dropped down in the red to a colossal $30.5 billion, three times the official value of all the gold in Fort Knox. Even the balance of trade, the difference between what the United States buys and sells overseas, was going steeply into deficit for the first time since World War II. Together, these alarming trends had undermined the stability of the dollar, which had once been the very symbol of American prosperity, but which was now being humbled daily on the exchange markets of Western Europe and Japan.

The economic crisis had come to a head in the middle of August that year, when President Nixon was compelled to impose the first wage-and-price freeze the United States had ever known. That same Sunday night, the value of the dollar was unpegged from its exchange rate in gold, and next morning when a tourist in Paris tried to pay his hotel bill in dollars his offer was spurned by the French desk clerk. "Those aren't worth anything any more," he was told in a statement of Gallic arrogance that reverberated back home on the wires of the Associated Press, to be related in shocked tones by the television newscasters. For many Americans the experience was as humiliating as it was novel.

Now and again, however, even in 1971, the aggressive optimism that was once regarded as the chief characteristic of the American people still shone through. The most aggressive optimist of them all, John Connally, then Secretary of the Treasury, expressed the more traditional view with his usual trenchancy at a press conference called to defend the President's freeze. "You're assuming the bottom's going to fall out of the dollar," he told one persistent questioner. "Well, let me remind you that in terms of the free world gross national product, the United States produces forty-eight percent of it. Let me remind you that this is the strongest economy on the face of the earth. And let me remind you that every country in the world pegs the value of its currency to the dollar."

Unfortunately, Secretary Connally was not only out of date with his figures and a touch cavalier with his facts;* he was also to prove wrong in his confidence in the strength of the dollar. There have been not one but two devaluations of the dollar since he spoke, and that, as even *Time* magazine ruefully admitted, is something that once upon a very recent time could have happened only to a banana republic.

Nevertheless, most people would agree that the thrust of Connally's argument was true: the United States economy is and will remain far and away the strongest on the face of the earth. So why then has the world lost confidence in the once-mighty dollar?

The easy answer is that ever since the early 1950s the United States has

---

*In 1971, the American share of the world's GNP had actually fallen to 30.2 percent, or about 40 percent of that of what Secretary Connally quaintly called "the free world."

been living beyond her means in the world, spending overseas billions of dollars more than she has been earning, not only in trade imports, but on troop costs in Europe, the war in Vietnam, foreign and military aid, and dollar investments in overseas factories. As long as the U.S. economy remained proportionately so much stronger than all the others, and as long as she maintained the role of the world's reserve banker with a stable currency against which all the others were measured, the imbalance in overseas payments was a burden which could be borne fairly lightly. America could spare the dollars; and the dollars, as the unit of international trade—what the French used to call the "imperial" currency—were always welcomed overseas. But when other countries, particularly Germany and Japan, began to build up enormous trade surpluses, as they did throughout the 1960s, the days of the dollar's hegemony were numbered. As the other currencies as a result grew stronger, the dollar, undermined by Johnson's inflation, grew weaker. The crisis came when vast quantities of liquid capital—held sometimes by foreign countries, sometimes by international speculators, sometimes by American companies operating overseas—began to be converted away from dollars and into the new and even stronger currencies of Germany and Japan. And with inflation and a trade recession running simultaneously at home and apparently nothing being done about the hugely mounting balance of payments deficits, all the dollars that were loose in the world, the vagabond greenbacks, suddenly looked less valuable than they used to. A great rush began to convert them into yen, marks, Swiss francs—anything that looked as though it might hold its value. The more dollars were unloaded, of course, the less valuable they became. A basic principle of economics was at work: the principle that says a glut of any product brings down its price. It is true of bacon, and it now proved to be true of dollars.

Ironically, when it came, the devaluation of the dollar was received relatively calmly by most Americans. President Nixon was praised by the business community for courageously facing up to the new realities, and hardly anyone, except perhaps Secretary Connally, believed that devaluation marked a loss of national virility. Attitudes had changed beyond measure since those days in the 1960s when American governments thought they could afford guns *and* butter *and* a never-ending balance of payments deficit: power, even the vast economic power of the United States, had its limits after all.

In the end, the main effects of devaluation were felt not at home but abroad. That is because the American economy is self-supporting to a greater degree than most others. So, while for such countries as Britain, Canada, and Sweden exports traditionally amount to about 20 percent of the national income, and for the Netherlands, Norway, and New Zealand they amount to nearly 40 percent, exports make up only about 5 percent of the national income of the United States. So the humbling of the dollar is likely to have a more profound impact on the rest of the world than on home industry.

On the face of it, indeed, the two devaluations of the dollar ought to have restored quite quickly the deficit in the American balance of trade. They at once made imports into the United States more expensive, so in theory Americans would buy less of them; and they made American goods cheaper for the rest of the world, so that in theory they should have bought more of them. But by 1973, it was clear that was not happening, and for several reasons, all connected with the mysterious complications of international trade.

First, America had found herself in a sudden and unexpected energy crisis, so that today she is buying more foreign oil than ever before, and because of devaluation having to pay more for it. Secondly, devaluation was followed by a consumer boom at home, and America has found to its alarm that domestic industry has lost its competitive edge in such basic consumer goods as television sets, cars, and textiles, which choosy American consumers still continued to buy from foreign producers in spite of the new high prices.

The third factor in the equation arises from the curious nature of much of America's exports, which tend to come from extreme ends of the economic spectrum. A surprisingly high proportion of them are either basic raw materials —agricultural produce mostly, such as soybeans, wheat, rice, and cotton—or highly technological items like jumbo jets, computers, and machine tools. Demand for American food produce, on the one hand, depends not so much on its competitive price edge as on the basic world shortages—on crop failures in Russsia, China, India—while demand for jumbo jets and computers are what the economists call *price-inelastic*, since not many airlines in the world are likely to buy an extra 747 jumbo jet just because its price has been shaved by devaluation.

For all these reasons, the United States continued to run a balance of trade deficit even after devaluation. And for these reasons, too, demands for protectionist legislation, designed to shut out foreign goods by high tariffs, have grown strident in the 1970s. The old days of laissez-faire are over. Nevertheless, the retreat from hegemony, which will continue throughout the 1970s, is not likely to mean a complete withdrawal into prewar isolation, but rather an acceptance of the more modest role of *primus inter pares*. As Roy Jenkins, the British M.P., said in his lecture at Yale University at the end of 1971, the dollar *could* be managed with the most brutal disregard for international consequences. the United States *could* move far in a fully protectionist direction. The damage to the rest of the world and the repercussive effects on America in these wholly imaginary circumstances would not be very great. "But this is not remotely the position today," Jenkins said. "America is not becoming post-imperial Spain. Her every move will still have a greater effect on the prosperity and trading health of the whole world than those of any other three countries put together."

Devaluation and inflation notwithstanding, the fact is that the American economy in the 1970s remains and is likely to remain for the rest of this century far and away the richest and most productive in the entire world. In spite of the aura of gloom that now surrounded it, the American economy passed another landmark in 1971, a year which would be remembered not only for devaluation and the freeze but also as the year of the trillion-dollar economy, the first year in which the gross national product of the United States broke through to one *trillion* dollars—$1,000,000,000,000, a third of the world's total, and a figure which is moreover expected to double not long after the end of this decade. The trillion-dollar breakthrough had been marked, amid the anguished breast-beating that seems to accompany any American success these days, in a small ceremony at the White House early in January. There were grumbles that the ceremony was a few weeks premature, and that what President Nixon was celebrating was not growth, but inflation. To many outsiders, it seemed that these critics, like so many Americans, had become so preoccupied with their immediate problems they no longer fully comprehended how materially rich their country still was in comparison with the rest of the world.

In every sense, America is still a country where more people die of too much food than of too little; her problems are the problems of plenty, not the problems of want with which less fortunate nations and less fortunate eras have traditionally been compelled to grapple. In their present mood of pessimism and introspection too many Americans seem unaware of that crucial fact; to paraphrase Evelyn Waugh, many of the older countries of the world count it as a good day when one thing goes right, while the Americans, who have grown used to easy success, count it as a bad day when one thing goes wrong. When things go wrong as they have in the past decade, Americans lose their self-confidence and look toward the imminent collapse of the Republic.

In this new mood of pessimism, the arrival of the trillion-dollar economy was greeted more as the harbinger of Armageddon than as the simple proof of prosperity. Studies were produced to show that economic growth could not go on for ever, and that the present trends would lead inevitably to collapse. Economic growth had become not a blessing, but a curse, which submerged the individual to the needs of the corporate state. Wealth today was doom tomorrow. A British economist, after a cursory look at America in the 1970s, wrote in the New York *Times* that growth could—and perhaps should—have stopped after World War I. "There was enough technology to make life quite pleasant,'" wrote Ezra J. Mishan. "Cities weren't overgrown. People weren't too avaricious. You hadn't really ruined the environment as you have now, and built up entrenched industries so that you can't go back."

This elitist argument has become very fashionable lately, but in the end it is overwhelmed by the statistics of the American economy. There can be no going back now, and nostalgia for the days before the automobile (and, incidentally, for the days of the robber barons) wilts away before the sheer size and diversity of the modern American economy. In land area, the United

States stands only fourth among the nations, and fourth also in population, but in terms of industrial output she has stood throughout the postwar era head, shoulders, and torso above anyone else, richer until very recently than Western Europe, Japan, and the Soviet Union combined. The United States today produces one quarter of the world's oil and consumes about a third of it. Her steel mills produce nearly a third of the western world's total, and her aircraft manufacturers have built 85 percent of the ten thousand commercial airliners now in service. Her people buy 10 million new automobiles every year (70 percent of them, in 1973, equipped with air conditioning), and they own nearly half of all the cars running anywhere. Her biggest private company, AT&T, known to friends and enemies alike as "Ma Bell," is richer than Sweden, and her largest manufacturer, General Motors, has an annual income greater than the government of France. A list of the forty richest organizations in the world includes thirty-two sovereign states—and eight private American corporations.* General Motors falls in size between the Netherlands and the Argentine, the Ford Motor Company just behind Czechoslovakia, and Exxon just ahead of the Union of South Africa.

*Based on a table in which the gross national product of the leading nations was compared with the net sales of the largest corporations.

2. The Big Board

"Downtown, there are two emotions: fear and greed. The rest is bullshit."
New York broker, quoted in Harpers Magazine, *May 1971*

The heart of the American capitalist system lies just across the street from the steps of the federal Subtreasury Building at the toe of Manhattan where George Washington took his oath of office as first President of the United States. Here, where the narrow canyons of Wall Street and Broad Street converge, stands the home of Mammon, otherwise known as the New York Stock Exchange. The Exchange, whose pompous and heavily pillared façade proclaims to all who pass the confidence and permanence of the awesome world of high finance, has a venerable history, older even than its classic-revival architecture. It began in 1792, not long after George Washington was first sworn in, when twenty-four merchants of the neighborhood met under a local buttonwood tree and there signed an agreement to organize a central market-place where they would buy and sell securities.

Today, on entering the Exchange through its massive porticos, reminders of this venerable past confront the visitor at every step. The effect is almost one of overkill: The plush red carpeting of the boardrooms, the high-vaulted gilt ceilings, the enormous oil paintings of humorless, tight-lipped men combine to create an atmosphere of pseudo-Victorian solemnity and stability. The outsider is awed, as the architect meant him to be. Later, as he looks down on the arena-like floor of the Exchange where the trading is carried out, watching the brokers scurry busily between the eighteen horseshoe-shaped trading posts, most of them too preoccupied with the affairs of the moment to worry about the ghosts of the bulls and the bears and the panics that are said to hover there, the effect is altered somewhat. Here, it is like looking down on a gigantic but rather old-fashioned gambling casino, an institution the Exchange resembles in more ways than one.

Up in the public gallery, quiet-spoken guides reel off statistics meant to be as awesome as the architecture of the building. On a busy day, they tell you, the ticker will cough out about one third of a mile of tape; only yesterday, 20 million shares were traded on the Big Board; over $30 billion in new corporate capital is raised here every year; 32 million Americans—one in every six men, women and children in the nation—are now said to invest directly in the stock market; half a million miles of telephone and teletype wires link the Big Board to the brokerage houses, enough to spin out to the moon and back.

They make it sound like the very model of efficiency and sound management. But Wall Street, alas, is very far from that, and what the statistics and the architecture conceal is the specter of crisis and even panic that has haunted the Exchange since the bear market of 1969–1970. The bear market is over now, but the damage done in eighteen short months may force Wall Street into a transformation more profound than that which followed the great crash of 1929. Today, it is no exaggeration to say the Big Board itself is in peril, and many observers doubt that it can survive in its present form beyond the 1970s. Internally, the Exchange is rent by bitter disputes among its member brokers as they face the breakup of the monopoly they have enjoyed since 1792. The bear market showed that the capital structure of many of the brokerage houses was built on sand; the Exchange now admits that in its efforts to avert financial disaster and the collapse of the Street's paperwork system it was compelled to intervene in the affairs of no fewer than 196 of its member firms, including some of the most distinguished names on Wall Street. At the height of the crisis, in the autumn of 1970, it seemed the very cornerstone of the edifice was about to crumble. The Exchange announced that its special trust fund of $25 million had been exhausted in the attempt to rescue the customers of failed brokers and so maintain its proud boast that since the 1930s no customer has lost money through the failure of a member firm. Later, even the addition of a further $30 million that the Exchange had put aside for a new building was not enough to plug the drain and stop the panic, and by the time it was over the Exchange had spent $57 million to bail out the customers of firms that had gone under. Even now, it is estimated that brokerage houses owe their customers over a billion dollars' worth of securities that they failed to deliver because of the breakdown in the Street's paperwork system.

Many brokers, surveying those months with a shudder, believe the effect on the Street itself was worse than anything they had experienced in the 1930s. Altogether, 139 brokerage houses failed and went "belly up" or were forced into shotgun mergers. The vice president of the Exchange, Lee Arning, put together so many forced mergers he became known on the Street for a while as "Marryin' Sam." Robert W. Haack, who was then president of the Exchange, declared that at one time 30 percent of the Exchange's 646 member firms could have been put out of business. "The problem of insolvency," he said, "was more critical than the world will ever know."

How did it happen? The scene of the 1970 panic was set during the easy get-rich-quick bull market of the previous eight years, the longest bull market in Wall Street history, when the greed of many brokers overcame their prudence. They encouraged the public to join in the pied-piper's dance after wealth with promises, as painted by one of the stock-market schools, that appealed to pure avarice:

Trading in stocks is an ideal business when you know how to operate scientifically. Hours 10 to 3. Stay away when you like. Take long weekends. And frequent vacations. Travel abroad for months. Surely those frequent trips to Zurich would be tax-deductible. Go and come when you please. No overheads. No partners. No employees. No *boss.* You are in business for yourself. Bank account increases steadily after you know how.

The public fell for it, hook, line and sinker. From beginning to end of the bull market the number of people directly owning stocks soared up from fewer than 12 million to nearly 32 million. And naturally, it was not usually the gullible public who grew rich, but the brokers, with their handsome fixed-rate commissions and the trading knowledge of the insider. "Where are the *customers'* yachts?" goes the old Wall Street saw; but the customers never seemed to notice that their chief role in the market was to make their brokers wealthy.

The dramatic upsurge in public investment in the stock market during the 1960s was matched by the increased participation of the great institutional investors, the life insurance companies, the big pension funds, the trust companies, and the banks that began to switch the money they had to invest from the traditional, slow-growing fixed-income securities into industrial stocks that they bought on the floor of the New York Stock Exchange. The brokers naturally welcomed them: with millions to invest, they brought in enormous commissions, particularly when they began to buy and sell on a shortterm basis.

Many investors had discovered a new cult during those dazzling years. They found that by concentrating on the so-called go-go funds they could sometimes double their money in as little as six months. The technique, which after 1965 became fashionable even with the staid institutional investors, was to swing quickly in and out of glamour issues that were judged to have "growth potential." These were the go-go funds, many of them conglomerates, which in a rising market yielded easy profits for the insiders and fat commissions for the brokers. Growth was the cry, "performance" the criterion of whether a stock was worth trading. As the cult grew and stocks changed hands with greater and greater frequency the cult became a stampede and the volume of trading on the floor of the Exchange grew to the point where the brokerage houses lost control of their own prosperity. Commissions flowed in, paperwork accumulated, and for eight years the market went nowhere but up, up, up. Trading volume rose from an average 3 million stocks a day in 1960 to 7 million in 1966, 8 million in 1967, and an impossible 13 million by 1968. "There was a bit of collective insanity in those days," said Howard Stein, head of the large Dreyfus Fund and one of the Exchange's leading critics. "The market lost its reason, and almost lost its future."

For a while, the market's inherent weaknesses were concealed in the glut of easy money; the bonanza seemed as though it would go on for ever, and as profits rose, so did the brokers' expectations. Those were the years Wall

Streeters leased the third house in the South of France, the yacht in Florida, the grouse moor in Scotland, and the expensive showroom in Manhattan crammed with electronic gadgets to lure in more and more investors. There were brokers who ran a Cadillac, a Rolls-Royce, *and* a Mercedes. But like the grasshopper in the fable, the brokers had failed to prepare for the winter. As many of them had taken out virtually all the profits from their companies in the good years, they were unprepared to meet the losses when the bad year came. That it was the only bad year they have experienced in a decade is a measure of the shortsightedness, the incompetence, and the sheer greed that dominated Wall Street throughout the 1960s. Modernization, attention to their own capital structure, and the vital reorganization of the brokerage houses' back offices that was needed to keep up with the growth in paperwork, was often sadly neglected, with the predictable result that when the crisis struck, they too broke down.

Several observers have remarked on the hypocrisy of Wall Street in those years, in particular the insistence of the brokerage firms on the virtues of sound management in the companies they recommended to investors. Analysts arrived at a firm demanding to see their accounting department, their systems analysis, their research, their staff. "Their word affects the prospects for its stock like a review in the New York *Times* affects the box office of a Broadway play," wrote Lewis H. Lapham, a well-known Wall Street commentator. "Yet the management of their own firms was so inadequate many were later suspended from trading."

The comments of the Exchange's own president, Robert Haack, were even more damning: "You had an industry that was under-manned operationally," Mr. Haack declared in a 1971 press release. "It was geared to production and sales, and not to the servicing thereof. It was faced with volume that it could not accommodate. There was no facility for handling it on a backlog basis. The next thing you knew, the industry had created a Frankenstein."

The breakdown came first in the neglected back offices of the brokerage houses. They were buried under an avalanche of paper they could not begin to cope with. When stocks change hands, speedy and accurate record-keeping is the only way the change in ownershp can be traced. Every step of the transaction must be recorded: the customer's order to buy or sell, the execution of his order on the floor of the Exchange, the payment of cash, and the delivery of his bonds. Under the rules for most Stock Exchange transactions, the seller's broker is allowed five days to deliver the stock certificates to the buyer's broker. If he is late, he must enter a "fail to deliver" item on his records.

Wall Street has made almost no attempt to mechanize this process, which was—and largely still is—carried out manually by an army of clerks working in almost Victorian conditions in the brokerage houses' back offices, known colloquially as "the cage." Wages in the back office are low, conditions squalid, the workers neither very ambitious nor well educated. Supervision is generally lax, and staff turnover can rise as high as 60 percent in a single year. Until 1968, the only time the back-office workers came into prominence was during Wall Street's famous tickertape parades, during which they showered tons of paper from their skyscraper windows onto the heads of visiting astronauts and baseball teams. There are rumors, always hotly denied, that when the New York Mets baseball team drove through Wall Street after winning the World Series, they were bombarded not only with the traditional tickertape and toilet paper but also with several tons of vital investment records and stock certificates—the back offices' revenge for the years of neglect and carelessness.

When the Wall Street cage collapsed at the end of 1968, record-keeping broke down over a wide front, and the Street simply lost control of the securities and certificates that were vital to its business. Some may easily have been torn up and thrown out of the windows onto the heads of visiting dignitaries, others fell behind the radiators or into trash bins, and many were stolen, but more often they simply piled up on the desks of the back-office clerks into mountains of paper so huge it became physically impossible to handle them with the staff available. Christopher Elias, editor of the Exchange's official magazine until he was fired for writing a book about the Wall Street collapse, said the extent of the chaos was hard for an outsider to imagine:

Physically, the scene of many back offices raised the image of a public toilet in which paper towels had been tossed everywhere. . . . Among the people working in the offices, the capacity for error, carelessness, and theft was limitless. Stock certificates were left for weeks piled haphazardly on any level surface—on filing cabinets, behind which the certificates occasionally fell, or on tables, from which they were often brushed into waste baskets. Stocks sent to investors were mailed to wrong addresses or not mailed at all. An investor who bought 100 shares might receive 1,000—or 100 shares of a different stock, a bond, or just an empty envelope. A man in Pennsylvania wrote the Exchange that the monthly statement his broker was sending him credited him with owning a million dollars worth of bonds, and he couldn't get the statement corrected.

The problem grew and grew throughout 1968, until in December New York Stock Exchange members failed to deliver a staggering $4 billion worth of stocks that had been traded on the Big Board that month. Even the mighty Merrill Lynch, the biggest and most efficient brokerage house on Wall Street, lost track of over $375 million of its customers' money. "It all boils down to this," a Merrill Lynch spokesman explained. "It's gotten to the point where we just can't get our hands on the securities we buy and sell." At one leading firm that later went into liquidation, auditors turned up approximately *thirty-one thousand* bookkeeping errors in the 1968 audit

The problem had become so enormous the Exchange itself was forced, somewhat reluctantly, to intervene, although it usually found itself helpless to remedy a situation which had run almost totally out of control. With three of its biggest firms headed for disaster, the Exchange felt the severity of the paperwork problem was so great an orderly liquidation would prove impossible if the firms were suspended. In order to avoid a collapse of investor confidence in the stock market, therefore, the three big firms in trouble were allowed to continue trading, their problems hidden from the general public. "Suspension could have emptied these firms of clerical staff at a time of intense competition among brokerage firms for skilled operations employees," said the Exchange's official report on the collapse. In other words, brokerage houses had started to raid one another's back offices for extra staff in the now-desperate scramble to get their records straight. The overall effect, of course, was simply to compound the problem, and firms that lost experienced backroom staff were left even more firmly embedded in the mire.

In the wake of the collapse of the cage came the thefts. Brokerage houses had undertaken a crash recruiting and training program to raise the back-office staff needed to process the accumulated snowdrifts of paper. It turned out later that many of their new recruits came from Mafia-controlled employment agencies, with the result that the back offices were infiltrated by criminal elements at the very moment they were least able to keep track of the flow of securities through their firms. Too late, the alarm bells began to ring at the Exchange. Thefts increased so sharply among member firms that insurance companies were beginning to turn down requests for policies to cover the brokers against these losses—for naturally, the brokers were liable for the loss of securities and bonds they held for their customers. If they could no longer get insurance against theft, it meant they had to go back to the floor of the Exchange and buy replacement stocks out of their own money. One well-known company, W. E. Hutton, was granted insurance only on condition it accept a $50,000 deduction on each and every claim. Another firm was forced to agree to a 92.7 percent deduction, while some insurance companies began turning down this sort of business altogether.

But the thefts continued. Robert M. Morgenthau, the U.S. attorney in New York, described securities thefts as "a modern day alternative to bank robbery, which requires no gun, no get-away car, no bravado, but which can generate an illegal wealth of which Dillinger would have not even dreamed." The extent of the stealing that goes on in Wall Street is hard for the layman to imagine. A back-office clerk walked out of the F. I. DuPont company one day with one million dollars' worth of IBM stock wrapped in a newspaper. The press reported it as one of the biggest single thefts of all time, but Attorney General John Mitchell told a Senate hearing in 1971 that Justice Department records indicated that "upwards of $400 million worth of stolen securities [were] not recovered for the years 1969 and 1970." That represents an *average* of $800,000 worth of thefts for every working day of the year.

At first, the problem of securities thefts was kept secret. They would probably have been kept secret indefinitely had not Wall Street been hit by yet another wave of disaster, which revealed its weaknesses to the entire world. This came in the form of the bear market of 1969–1970, which brought the golden days of the sixties to an abrupt end. Ironically enough, the Street at first welcomed the turndown in prices that first became noticeable in the spring of 1969. The Big Board had hit 968 points in January of that year, its highest point of the decade, and at first the slide downwards was a gentle one, accompanied by a welcome slackening in the hectic pace of trading. Brokerage firms felt that they had been granted a breathing space in which to catch up with their back-office problems. But as 1969 progressed, it became clear that the turndown was more than just a temporary one, and the market kept going down for almost a year and a half, touching bottom in May 1970, when the Dow-Jones average fell to 631 points. Even more serious for the brokers was the accompanying decline in trading volume, which dropped during the same period from an average 13 million shares a day down to 7 or 8 million. The simultaneous decline in sales volume and the drop in prices dealt many brokers a one-two blow they were unable to withstand. The weaker ones began to collapse.

The Exchange at first pooh-poohed the idea that the difficulties its member firms were experiencing were in any way critical. As late as April 1970, Haack testified before Congress that the Exchange would be able to handle its own problems and live up to its boast that in more than thirty years "no customer of an NYSE member organization has sustained a loss of securities or funds as a result of a liquidation of an NYSE firm." The Exchange, he said, administered its rules in "a conscientious and vigorous way" and no crisis was foreseen. Yet within two months the collapse of member firms had forced the Exchange to hand out its entire emergency trust fund to customers facing a direct and immediate loss of securities and funds. At the same time, another firm— Hayden, Stone, one of the biggest—had been given an emergency loan of $5 million to shore it up against collapse. With 100,000 customer accounts, the eighty-eight-year-old firm carried one of the most prestigious names on Wall Street. To all outward appearances, it had been one of the most successful and go-ahead in the business. It had pioneered many of the slick marketing and stock-selection techniques of the previous decade. At the end of 1968, the firm's unsuspecting copywriter was given a sales booklet to write. He ended it with the words, "We are proud of our past, but the best is yet to come." At that very moment insiders were quietly withdrawing their investments from the firm. "I left to do something else," said one Hayden, Stone insider who took his money out. "I could see that unless something was done to halt our losses, the firm was in deep, deep trouble." The Exchange can do nothing to prevent such withdrawals, which are perfectly legal, although they clearly have the effect of pulling out the rug just at the moment the troubled firm needs it most. The crisis at Hayden, Stone was documented by a former officer in *Fortune* magazine in December 1970:

> There was only one executive who, at a relatively early date, sensed the real peril of the situation. That was the Treasurer, Walter Isaacson, and in the middle of 1969 he would spread out his charts at every directors' meeting and make, with variations, the same speech: "Look, fellows, revenues are going down like this and costs are going up like this and we have to cut back now or be in real trouble." Nobody wanted to believe him. Finally, Isaacson got to be such a nuisance that Hayden, Stone did what any red-blooded management would do: it fired him.

Hayden, Stone's back offices had been the scene of some of the worst shambles on Wall Street, and for more than a year before it collapsed the company had been accepting far more orders than it could handle. It had also failed to maintain the required ratio of capital to match its debts and was placed under restriction by the Exchange in 1969, several months before the bear market finally brought the roof down. The firm found itself in financial difficulties virtually overnight when high-flying stocks in which it held a portion of its capital stalled and began to nosedive. One of them was the Four Seasons Nursing Centers of America, a firm in which Hayden, Stone held $4 million worth of collateral stock. When Four Seasons went bankrupt, Hayden, Stone's paper capital was wiped out and so, in effect, was the brokerage house. A 1967 profit of over $7 million was converted into a loss of nearly $11 million by 1969. A year later, the firm was dismembered.

The brokers by this time were in full retreat. No less than 35 percent of the Street's total work force had been laid off and horror stories began to appear in the press of stock salesmen who had sold their yachts and taken to selling pretzels in the street. A former San Francisco broker who in 1968 had thought he was well on the way to his first million dollars had been forced to sell his twenty-two-room mansion, his art collection, and his library of rare books. "I've gone from a black Rolls Royce to a yellow Datsun," he told the newspapers. "But at least I'm still driving." Another broker boasted that he slept each night that year like a baby: "I wake up every three hours and cry."

As the crisis grew, firms began a major bloodletting campaign in an attempt to cut overhead. One brokerage house claimed it was saving $6,000 a month by discouraging employees from duplicating their personal correspondence and their children's homework on the office Xerox machine. Executive dining rooms were closed down; business slumped at Delmonico's, one of the Street's favorite eating houses. The number of sales branches was cut back drastically, especially overseas, although this attempt at economy sometimes backfired. When the Francis I. duPont company got into trouble and tried to save money by closing down its office in Kuwait, its key personnel were seized by the local sheik and held hostage until the firm settled its outstanding accounts.

By now, the extent of the crisis had begun to dawn on a hitherto unsuspecting public, and the press began to cry alarm. "An investor who buys stocks through a reputable brokerage house would have reason to think that he really owns the shares," wrote *Time* magazine. But now that turned out in many cases not to be true: the public discovered that brokers commonly used their customers' margin stock as collateral for their own bank loans. Thus, if the brokers failed, the bank took possession of the customers' money. That is one of the problems the Exchange's emergency fund had been set up to prevent, but as the Exchange's own coffers were now empty, it was unable to help any further, and when a Philadelphia-based firm, Robinson & Company, filed for bankruptcy, many of the shares owned by the firm's eight thousand customers became the property of the banks. Robinson & Company had resigned its Exchange seat three months earlier when its troubles first began. Because it was now technically no longer a member, the Exchange refused to pay off the bankers and get the customers' stock back. The Exchange still clung to its claim that no customer of a member firm had been let down, but to many observers the excuse was beginning to wear rather thin.

As 1970 wore on, the crisis deepened. Other firms went into liquidation, and one of Wall Street's giants, Goodbody & Company, was forced into a merger with Merrill Lynch. One of the first really big brokers to fail, McDonnell & Company, had ironically been one of the few firms in Wall Street that had tried to bring its back-office system up to date. In 1968 it had installed a new computer to do the job, but the experiment had turned out to be a disaster. McDonnell's, whose president for a while was the former Postmaster General Lawrence O'Brien, later chairman of the Democratic Party's national committee, was another firm that had been beguiled by the prospects of expansion. It had dreamed the corporate dream of becoming "another Merrill Lynch" with millions of cutomers served by branches throughout the world, and had spent lavishly towards that goal. Some $400,000 had gone on a Manhattan salesroom, equipped with chairs costing $300 each for the secretaries, but the most extravagent gesture of all turned out to be its installation of a new IBM 360 computer. A firm unqualified in Wall Street paperwork had been engaged to program the new computer, which was finally plugged in three months late, in November 1968. Three days later, it broke down. "It just didn't work," a former McDonnell vicepresident told Christopher Elias. "It aborted. Trade got lost. There were no confirmations. It was as simple as that." The firm had unwisely removed an old backup system before the new computer had been fully tested, with the result that McDonnell's entire back office then went out of control. Two more days and the firm would have been compelled to stop all public business there and then. As it was, a third of its statements to customers had at least one error in them that it was impossible to correct. The computer system was quickly scrapped, and a new one installed in a last hope of saving the firm. But there was no way to undo the damage that had been done. "We're putting garbage into the system; we are getting garbage out," one executive complained. The firm began a desperate retrenchment: It disposed of twenty-three of its twenty-six branches, resigned one of its three seats on the Exchange, and lost or fired most of its office staff. The end was not long delayed and in April 1970 McDonnell & Company was liquidated, the first of the really big brokers to go under.

The man whose unhappy task it was to preside over the chaos of 1969 and 1970, the dapper, handsome Robert W. Haack, was the full-time paid president of the Exchange until he lost his job in the middle of 1972. Haack was the most visible spokesman for the securities industry at this time: "I slept very well between two fifteen A.M. and two thirty A.M.," he says wryly of his role.

Years ago, President Franklin D. Roosevelt used to describe Haack's post as "the second toughest job in the world" (presumably after his own), yet to many of his colleagues Haack appeared more of a quiet, unimaginative manager than an innovative reformer. To several observers he appeared to be awed by the mighty Board of Governors, and press reports often pointed out unkindly that he had in fact been the board's third choice for the post, having been chosen for the $125,000-a-year job only after two other prospective appointees had dropped out.

The surprise therefore was great when in November 1970 Haack stood up in public before the Economic Club of New York, stuck out his strong Dutch jaw, and delivered one of the most explosive and courageous attacks on the very system over which he had presided for nearly three years.

"The day of the casually managed brokerage firm is over," he declared. "And perhaps that is just as well. Many of the hundred-odd firms which have vanished from the roster of the New York Stock Exchange membership offer testimony in absentia to the folly and consequences of careless or disingenuous management."

To many members, this attack by a man they regarded as a hireling was little short of treason. They sat back in astonishment as Haack went on first to question their sanctified system of fixed commission rates and then to suggest a restructuring of their own Board of Governors so that the Exchange could get rid of what he called the "private club" atmosphere. Fear of competition, said Haack, prevented the professional staff of the Exchange from dealing with the current crisis as effectively as they should. Throw open the doors, he urged, let in the chilly but invigorating winds of competition. Fixed commissions may have made brokers rich, but at the same time they had lost business for the Exchange as a whole. Already the institutional investors were taking their business away from the floor of the New York Stock Exchange into the unregulated so-called third market.* Members were clinging to a system of antiquated and unequal rules that prevented these urgently needed reforms. Furthermore, he went on, to bypass these rules many members indulged in "intrigues and machinations" and "mazes of blatant gimmickry" that he believed were tending to undermine "the entire moral fabric" of the industry.

Once they got over the initial shock, members of the Exchange greeted Haack's speech with cries of outrage. "He makes me sick," exclaimed one senior and hitherto distinguished member. "We do not require the moralisms of a paid hireling," sniffed another. The chairman of the Board of Governors, Bernard J. "Bunny" Lasker, declared that "the policy of the New York Stock Exchange is made by the board of Governors, not by the president." There were rumors that Haack would be asked to resign, but he saw the crisis through, although he did in fact announce later that he would not seek an extension of his contract when it ran out in July 1972.

Haack himself was not surprised by the vehemence of the reaction to his speech. "They'd only come to my funeral if they could cut out my heart and sell it for an eighth," he is reported to have said of his Wall Street critics. The speech was, he feels, "a calculated risk," intended to trigger reform, and he would make it all over again if he had the opportunity. "What I've been trying to say for the last couple of years is that I'm fearful many people in the Exchange community fail to realize that the stock exchange is in a competitive fight for its life," he says. His main worry is that since the 1970 panic the Exchange has been losing business at a steadily rising rate to the outside "third market." "The dominance of the New York Stock Exchange is being undermined," he believes. "And my position is that our anticompetitive stances are fragmenting this market and are a boon to other markets." As evidence for this belief, he points out that the NYSE's share of the market is now at an all-time low: around 80 percent, the last 10 percent of which has fallen away since 1967.

When their initial surprise at Haack's outspoken speech had worn off, some of the more thoughtful members of the Exchange came around to agree with him. Donald Regan, chairman of Merrill Lynch, the most powerful brokerage house of all, believes it is inevitable that the present Exchange system will collapse. "The Exchange hasn't emerged from the technology of the nineteenth century," he believes. "It's an anachronism." In his view, the Exchange will be replaced by a fully automated market linking the entire country by electronic means, a system sometimes known on the Street by the acronym

*Members of the Big Board are compelled, under the rules, to conduct all their business on the floor of the Exchange. Nonmembers, however, have in recent years taken to trading stocks listed by the Big Board among themselves. This is the trading operation known as the Third Market, whose "over-the counter" trading in listed securities has done much to sap the strength and profits of the member firms.

OBC: "One Big Computer." That this would probably force many NYSE brokers out of business gives Regan no pause at all. "So what if they go bust?" he says. "What God-given right do they have to stay in business?" In his view, many of the floor interests at the Exchange are like the firemen on the railroads: obsolete.

The crisis at Hayden, Stone and some of the other brokerage houses had pointed up the flimsy capital structure on which many Wall Street firms had built their businesses. From this experience it was clear that capital reserves, which were supposed to protect the customer against loss, were of little value when they were themselves used to speculate on the market—and were in any case largely made up of money or securities that could be withdrawn on only ninety days' notice. Consequently, when the market slumped, the principals with inside knowledge pulled out their investments, leaving the customers and the Big Board's trust fund to sort out the mess. Senator Edward Brooke commented on this practice at a Senate committee hearing:

> I think we have a simple rule involved here. It involves the fundamental difference between mine and thine. If I hold your money in safekeeping for you and use that money for my own personal uses, I think it is quite clear that I have been guilty of embezzlement and that I would be chargeable for the use of the money. There should be no difference because the securities industry is involved.

Another problem that had been brought to light was the increasing fragmentation of the market referred to by Haack. Fragmentation was accompanied by a loss of liquidity that seriously disrupted the basic function of the marketplace: the provision of a stable and ready flow of capital with which to finance American industry. The arrival of the institutional investors had overwhelmed the specialist traders who were supposed to maintain an orderly market by intervening on the floor to prevent abrupt price changes. But when the institutionals began their big block trading, the specialists were simply unable to muster enough cash to absorb it, with resultant disturbance of the trading process. Then the institutions began to bypass the Exchange altogether and were reported to be trading big blocks of shares between themselves in private—a form of under-the-counter selling that further disrupted the market and, even worse, created a wholly artificial picture of what was really happening to the stocks they exchanged. On the Big Board itself, the institutions had traded only one third of all the shares sold a decade earlier; by 1971, they accounted for almost 60 percent of the total and were becoming impatient with the Exchange's persistent refusals to admit them to membership. So when the market finally began to climb back again from the slump, radical reform of the entire market procedure had become an urgent priority.

The traditionalists at the Exchange had been alienated forever, but as the market recovered, the views of the progressives gradually came into the ascendancy. The Exchange's first fulltime president, William McChesney Martin, Jr., a man of legendary uprightness, was recalled to make a study of the Exchange's operating methods. His twenty-page report, presented in August 1971, called for sweeping changes on the Big Board: integration of all stock exchanges in the country into one computer-fed system, elimination of the paper stock certificate (to be replaced by information stored on magnetic tape), and widespread reorganization of the Exchange itself so as to give the public a bigger voice in its affairs.

Gradually, Wall Street was also becoming increasingly subject to direct rule from Washington. Congress had already passed a bill establishing a public corporation to insure investors against loss in case of broker failures. A year later, when a new boom appeared to be fueling the stock market, the government's own regulatory body, the Securities and Exchange Commission, endorsed the Wall Street reform movement. The SEC's then chairman, William J. Casey, submitted a set of proposals to Congress that, if enacted, would severely curtail the Big Board's sovereignty over its own affairs. He also proposed to allow the institutional investors to participate in the market, a move that has since begun and which in the years to come seems certain to strip the NYSE brokerage houses of many of their lucrative institutional commissions. Other reforms proposed by the SEC would eventually establish a central computer-fed marketplace for the buying and selling of stocks and introduce a measure of competition in the commission rates charged by brokers.

By 1973 real reforms were being cautiously introduced to the conservative world of high finance. The SEC opened up the Exchange for the first time to outsiders, ordering it to admit the institutional investors—although only on condition that they conduct 80 percent of their business directly with the public. The reform was so cautious, indeed, that there were many observers who believed the institutions allowed to do only 20 percent of their business on their own account would be unable, or unwilling, to meet the new requirements. But at least it was a start—the first time the government had intervened to tell the exchanges whom they can and cannot admit, and under what conditions.

The Big Board also has a new chairman now, James J. Needham, a flamboyant accountant still in his mid-forties, who has worked hard to restore the flagging morale of the industry. Some people say he is presiding over a dying institution, that before long the Big Board will be replaced by a central market system, with the broker sitting behind a desk looking at the screen of a cathode-ray tube on which will be displayed the bids and offers for any particular stock all across the country. Fundamental reform of this dimension, however, is still years away from practical application, and before it comes Needham is determined to re-establish the primacy of the Big Board in any new automated and streamlined Federal Stock Exchange. Besides, he still believes in the virtues of the stock market. "It is no exaggeration to say that our sophisticated network for distributing securities is the eighth wonder of the world," he wrote in a 1972 article not long after he had been appointed to his $200,000-a-year post. "It is the envy of every capitalist country that seeks to encourage rapid economic growth and the efficient allocation of resources. To risk dismantling this system . . . is to risk dismantling the American economy."

Since then, however, Needham has begun to institute several reforms of his own, including support for the complete abolition of the fixed-rate commissions through which the brokers are paid. For Wall Street as a whole, the reforms can hardly come too soon. The market during the 1970s has acquired what the analysts call "bad breath": The average American investor, the traditional small capitalist whom the Big Board did so much to boost in the 1960s, has begun to abandon the market altogether, largely as a result of the losses he suffered in the 1969–1970 bear market. "I'll tell you why the public isn't in the market," said one fund manager in a 1972 interview. "It's gotten wise. It's been eaten alive in the last several years by inflation and by the money it lost in stocks."

By the summer of 1973 Wall Street had slipped once more insensibly into crisis. Three years earlier, crisis had been brought about by too much business; now it was the result of too little. By May of that year more than half the Exchange's member firms were operating in the red and up to eight thousand employees had been dismissed. A total of sixty-eight firms had been put on the Exchange's "early warning list" and it was widely expected that several of them would be forced into insolvency before the year was out. A new sense of panic was beginning to grip Wall Street, and the heady days of the 1960s seemed to have passed, perhaps forever.

But Wall Street finds it hard to cast off its bad habits, and whenever stocks bounce back, as they did in 1972, so does the Wall Street silly season. That not much had changed on Wall Street, after all, was forcibly brought to public attention when a nineteen-year-old student of accounting threw the market into an uproar with his own foray into consumerism. He was Abraham Treff, an evening student at St. Joseph's College, Philadelphia, who took upon himself to "investigate" the market. Treff had watched an interview with Ralph Nader on his local television station and decided that he too could expose some of the more questionable practices of big business. "I said I'd investigate the stock market," he recalls. "My friends said I didn't know what I was talking about. 'What'll you find out about the stock market?' they asked."

Treff succeeded beyond his wildest expectations. He simply picked up the telephone and told brokers in New York, Pennsylvania, and Texas that he wanted to buy. Within five weeks he had accumulated over $200,000 in stocks without ever once meeting a broker face to face and without putting up a single penny of his own money. When the SEC finally caught up with him, he was summoned to Manhattan to give a report on his activities. "I was trying to show that the brokerage firms weren't going by the rules," he told them. Possible charges against the youth for federal fraud offenses were quietly dropped when the reasons for his Wall Street foray became clear. But in a wider sense, the Treff affair illustrated the fact that not much had changed in the Wall Street sales offices in spite of the hammering they took at the start of the decade; they are as hungry as ever for business, even when it means flouting their own firmly established rules for credit and trading. Clearly, there is nothing like a bull market to help Wall Street forget.

3. Super-Rich

"In a plague, corner the market in coffins; in an earthquake, invest in concrete; in a war, sell guns or oil; in a depression, sell short."
KENNETH LAMOTT, THE MONEYMAKERS, 1969

From its beginnings, American society has been distinguished by the pursuit and honor of wealth. Even before the great fortunes of the Rockefellers and others were amassed in the Industrial Revolution, Alexis deTocqueville observed of the United States that "to clear, cultivate, and transform the huge uninhabited continent which is their domain, the Americans need the everyday support of an energetic passion; and that passion can only be the love of wealth." So, according to deTocqueville, Americans attached no stigma to the love of money and even regarded as "noble and estimable ambition that which our mediaeval ancestors would have called base cupidity." From that day to this, Americans have pursued money, individually and collectively, to the point where their society has become far and away the richest the world has ever known.

In the 1970s, the median income of American families for the first time exceeded $10,000 a year, the highest anywhere. But in the midst of this affluence, there are pockets of sometimes appalling poverty, with some 7 percent of the population earning less than $2,500 a year. In fact, sociologists sometimes argue that at least seven Americans out of every ten are in fact poor, in the sense that although they enjoy the highest material standard of living in the world, the loss of a job or a catastrophic illness would quickly leave them destitute. They own a car, a mortgaged house, furniture, clothes, and a television set; they perhaps hold a life insurance policy and a few stocks and bonds; but they play no significant part in the ownership of corporate America, other than as the minions of the really wealthy. The top one-tenth of one percent of the population—only 200,000 people—is said to be in effective control of the nation's economy.

The uneven distribution of wealth has led to an enduring myth, profoundly cherished by reforming sociologists, that the American plutocracy is a distinct and separate class, dominated by a hierarchy of some sixty families who act in concert to dictate policy to the government of the United States. Thus

Ferdinand Lundberg in his prewar study of wealth claimed that these sixty families, buttressed by no more than ninety families of lesser wealth, dominated modern America. They were, he wrote, "the living center of the modern industrial oligarchy," forming a *de facto* government, absolutist and plutocratic in its lineaments, which he asserted, "is actually the government of the United States—informal, invisible, shadowy. It is the government of money in a dollar democracy."

The myth, however, is hollow. The American plutocracy today does not act as a homogeneous mass. It consists just as much of creators of wealth as it does of inheritors; it has been largely succeeded in influence by a new generation of industrial bureaucrats who today wield the real levers of power in America; nor are its favors lavished exclusively, as the myth would have it, on rightwing candidates for office who would shield their privilege and their money from the encroachments of the egalitarians on the left. In the landslide election of 1972, several of the country's richest men donated huge sums of money to the campaign of George McGovern, a liberal Democrat whom no one would accuse of rightwing bias. In short, the political affiliations of the very rich are much like those of other Americans, supporting ideologies that run all the way from the crackpot right to the liberal left. Even in the politically active and stupendously rich Rockefeller family, the new generation of heirs has shown signs of turning away from the traditional Rockefeller Republicanism, and one member of the family, John D. Rockefeller IV, ran in 1972 for the governorship of West Virginia as a Democrat. (He lost—which destroys another old myth that the very rich can buy their way to political office in America wherever and whenever they choose.)

The proportion of the national wealth held by the top one percent of the population in America, moreover, has been dropping steadily since the 1920s. In 1922, the top one percent controlled 32 percent of all wealth; by 1953 the figure had dropped to 25 percent; and today it is estimated to be little more than 20 percent—a smaller proportion than that in most other western countries.

Indeed, so far has this process gone that (with a little aid from inflation) to be a dollar millionaire in the egalitarian seventies is to be regarded as no more than a member of a solid and remarkably substantial middle class. The editors of *Fortune* magazine, who keep an eye on these things, declared wistfully after their last headcount of the richest men and women in America that "the U.S. has become so affluent . . . there no longer is any great prestige in being a mere millionaire." To speak of "mere" millionaires may sound a little eccentric, even in America, but *Fortune* declared flatly that the very word has acquired an almost quaint sound today: "to have a net worth of one million dollars is to be, much of the time, indistinguishable from members of the omnipresent middle class." Or, as John Jacob Astor tartly put it many years ago: "A man who has a million dollars is as well off as if he were rich."

There are in fact so many "mere" millionaires in America today that they can no longer be counted with any precision, although it is estimated that somewhere around the start of this decade their total for the first time exceeded 100,000—enough millionaires to fill a city the size of Charleston, South Carolina, twice over—or enough millionaires to make up one third of the entire population of the state of Wyoming.

American millionaires are a diverse lot, to be found in almost every city and of almost every class: they include men and women, young and old, new rich and established rich. Although only some thirty-five of them are black, it has been estimated that twenty—and possibly as many as thirty—of the one hundred members of the U.S. Senate are millionaires, while perhaps most surprising of all is the fact that at least half of America's millionaires are *new* rich, having made their money by their own exertions in their own lifetime, often in the span of a single decade. As a class, millionaires are also growing at a more rapid rate than any other segment of American society. Back in 1953 there were 27,000 Americans with a gross estate worth more than a million dollars; by 1965, the figure had grown to about 90,000 and today it is over 100,000, a growth only partly explained by the rise in inflation that has occurred in the past twenty years. Herman P. Miller of the U.S. Census Bureau found after a recent count that their numbers were growing so rapidly "it suggests that the new millions are largely earned and not simply passed down through inheritance—that is, they come from the creation of goods and services we can all enjoy. A large proportion of today's new millionaires derive their wealth from scientific inventions, home construction, new products and other things that enrich our lives in many ways."

While the ownership of a million dollars may to ordinary mortals represent wealth beyond reach, it is no longer the touchstone of what *Fortune* magazine and others define as "great wealth." When *Fortune* last compiled its list of the richest men and women in America, it drew the line of superwealth at $100 million and after four months of research announced there were 153 individuals in the United States whose net worth, including wealth held by spouses, minor children, trusts, and foundations, made them centimillionaires. The size of the great fortunes held by these members of the super-rich passes almost beyond the bounds of comprehension, especially when compared to the earnings of the ordinary mass of mankind, even in the affluent society of the United States. The average American worker, who today earns more than ten thousand dollars every year—and spends most of it—would have to have been working at the same rate of pay since the Stone Age, *ten thousand years ago,* before he had earned a hundred million dollars: and even then, there would still be 153 Americans richer than he was.

Wealth on this scale is not of course unique to the United States: Dr. Marcus Wallenberg, the Swedish banker; Sir John Ellerman, the British shipping magnate; Aristotle Onassis and Stavros Niarchos, the Greek tanker kings; and the family of Friedrich Flick, the German steel manufacturer, are all at least as rich as the richest Americans. But no other country in the world boasts so many multimillionaires as America, and in no other country are the ranks of the Super Rich so open to newcomers. Indeed, it can be argued that the American plutocracy survives in part because, like the British aristocracy, it has always welcomed ambitious newcomers. Unlike the nobility of prerevolutionary France, who lived a life of privileged insulation from hoi polloi, or the landowners of some South American countries, who keep national wealth firmly within the control of a few rich families, the gates of the American super-rich have never been closed to outsiders. In fact, of the 153 centimillionaires today, only half inherited their fortunes; the rest were largely self-made men, and fully one third of the total had been men of modest means and obscure reputation only one decade earlier, having made the bulk of their wealth in a single ten-year span.

They do, however share certain characteristics. While there are plenty of women and a sprinkling of blacks in the ranks of the common-or-garden millionaires, the super-rich are white to a man. (The thirty-five known black millionaires fall well below the $100 million threshold of great wealth, and most of them have made their money by catering exclusively to black customers—as bankers, insurance agents, or publishers. Few of them indeed have yet made it in the white world of wealth.) It has been estimated that the new self-made super-rich are statistically the sons of lower-middle-class white parents from city environments in either the Northeast, the Southwest, or the Midwest. Only one was born on the Pacific Coast and none at all in the South outside of Texas.

If there is any distinction to be made in the diverse ranks of the very wealthy, it is between the old rich and the new rich. As a class, the old rich, who inherited their wealth, tend nowadays toward philanthropy, good works, and fame, and (apart from the huge sums they spend on works of art) seem to have abandoned the spectacular and ostentatious consumption of bygone generations of inheritors. The new rich, on the other hand, tend to work singlemindedly and often anonymously at making themselves ever richer: Dr. Edwin Land, Daniel Ludwig, and Howard Ahmanson are hardly household words in the United States, yet they each have made fortunes of more than $300 million in the past twenty years or so.

The two richest Americans of all, both worth more than one billion dollars, are a curious mixture of old and new wealth. They are J. Paul Getty and Howard Hughes, both of whom now live out of the country. Both men inherited substantial fortunes from their fathers but worked with the singlemindedness that is normally a sign of the nouveau riche to transform their inherited millions into billions. Both men are today so rich it is impossible to make any precise estimate of their wealth. The editors of *Fortune*, after careful and detailed analysis of their holdings, finally threw up their hands in despair and called it a tie, with both men estimated to own anywhere between $1 and $1.5 billion.

Counting Getty and Hughes as self-made men, the wealthiest of the New Rich today are:

		Age (1973)	Estimated Worth	Main source of Wealth
1.	J. Paul Getty (England)	80	$1 billion to $1.5 billion	Oil
2.	Howard Hughes (England)	67		Aircraft, oil drills, real estate.
3.	H. L. Hunt (Dallas)	84	$500 million to $1 billion	Oil
4.	Dr. Edwin H. Land (Cambridge, Massachusetts)	63		Polaroid cameras
5.	Daniel K. Ludwig (New York City)	75		Shipping
6.	N. Bunker Hunt (Dallas; son of H. L. Hunt)	47		Oil
7.	John D. MacArthur (Chicago)	76		Insurance and real estate
8.	William L. McKnight (St. Paul, Minnesota)	85	$300 million to $500 million	Minnesota Mining & Manufacturing
9.	Howard F. Ahmanson (Los Angeles)	76		Savings and Loan Asstn.
10.	Charles Allen Jr. (New York)	70		Investment banker

Perhaps the most interesting of the new centimillionaires is Dr. Edwin H. Land, a gentle scientific genius who founded a fortune of more than half a billion dollars through his invention of the Polaroid camera. Propelled by more than a simple love of riches, Land has devoted the last seven years of his life to research and development of the ultimate Polaroid camera, which is expected to revolutionize the art of photography during the last half of this decade. Land, who is revered by his staff, often spends eighteen hours a day in his laboratory, where he acts as chief scientific researcher as well as president, chairman, and principal stockholder in the company. He has been working on his idea since he was eighteen, when as a student at Harvard University he dropped out of college altogether to work fulltime on his inventions. His first thought was to use the polaroid filters he had devised in the headlights of all new automobiles, which he was convinced would reduce glare and thereby make night driving much safer. Detroit, however, turned him down, partly because they found his filters were vulnerable to heat. Land turned instead to polarized sunglasses, which became an instant success, and during the war went on to produce millions of glarefree goggles for the armed services.

He got the idea for the first Polaroid camera during a walk with his three-year-old daughter Jennifer in 1943, after she had asked him how long it would be before she could see some photographs he had just snapped. The idea of using his polarizing techniques to develop and print films inside the camera came to him in a flash, and he told *Time* magazine in a rare interview that by the time he and Jennifer had returned from their walk he had solved all the problems "except the ones that it has taken from 1943 to 1972 to solve."

After the war, the Polaroid Corporation became one of the fastest-growing companies of modern times, and it has been estimated that anyone who had the foresight to invest a thousand dollars in the company when it was founded would today be worth almost $4 million. (Although the road to riches has not been without its potholes: in the Wall Street slump at the end of the 1960s, Land and his wife watched the value of their Polaroid holdings drop by $42 million in a single day). Like many of the other very rich men, Land is intensely shy, although he remains the most attractive and likable of the new generation of centimillionaires.

As a class, however, the New Rich do not make up an especially attractive gallery of personalities: the majority of them, like rich men throughout history, have been propelled to wealth by motives that are often pathological and sometimes pathetic. In his study *The Moneymakers*, Kenneth Lamott concluded that "the energy of the very rich man chasing after still another million is healthy in the sense that the rosy cheeks of the tubercular, the high spirits of the maniac, the ambivalent beauty of the homosexual are healthy." Others attempt to explain their singleminded pursuit of wealth in Freudian terms, on the theory that the adult impulse to collect large sums of money arises from unusual anal pleasure during infancy; to put it more simply: money equals feces.

At least three of the new centimillionaires are said to be misanthropes, one of them left his wife with the comment that "behind ever great man was a woman—who hindered him every step of the way." The associates of another report that he has the manners of a wart hog, while a number of the richest Americans have virtually cut themselves off from contact with the outside world, including of course the richest and best-known recluse of them all, Howard Hughes.

Hughes became world-famous in the early 1970s thanks to the forged biography written by Clifford Irving, but the most fascinating thing about the man who may be the richest individual in the world is not the story of Irving's hoax or even the puzzle of why Hughes has withdrawn so totally from human society, but rather the mystery of how he has managed to hold on to his amazing fortune in the face of some of the most disastrous business misjudgments of the century: misjudgments that under anyone else would have constituted a death-wish. He ran the RKO Corporation to the point of bankruptcy, he was forced to sell Trans World Airlines by its creditors and was later sued for $140 million because of his alleged mismanagement, he built the biggest white elephant in the history of aviation, his Las Vegas gambling empire has been a disastrous failure—and yet somehow Hughes has emerged from the succession of wreckages with his fortune not only intact but greatly enhanced. It makes the most extraordinary story of success through failure in the history of American capitalism.

Hughes began as a golden boy, the archetype of the successful, open American adventurer. When he was nineteen, he inherited a bare half-million dollars from his father, a dominating man known as "Big Howard," who had been the inventor of a revolutionary oil drill and founder of the Hughes Tool Company, which was to become the cornerstone upon which the later empire was haphazardly built. The young Hughes became a Hollywood moviemaker and later a famous aviator who once held the transcontinental speed record and was given a tickertape parade in New York. Already displaying a tendency to ricochet from one undertaking to another, Hughes returned to Hollywood to make more movies, including his best-known work, *The Outlaw*, during the filming of which he is said to have taken time out to design the mechanically perfect brassiere that made the breasts of Jane Russell famous throughout the world.

Between the bouts of moviemaking, the restless tinkerer returned to aviation and the scene of perhaps his most spectacular failure of all: the Hercules troop carrier, otherwise known as the "Spruce Goose," a plane made entirely of plywood that is even today the biggest aircraft ever built. Unfortunately, the Spruce Goose, which was designed to carry seven hundred troops and their equipment, did not prove to be particularly airworthy. The plane was promised first for 1943, then for 1944, but it had still not been completed by the end of the war. Finally, during Senate hearings on the scandal that had cost the American taxpayer some $60 million, Hughes bravely took the huge plane into the air before a skeptical audience of dignitaries at Long Beach, California. It flew for about one mile—and has never been in the air since. Hughes is reported to have spent about $50 million of his own money on the Spruce Goose, but today it is still there in the Long Beach sheds, a moldering and forgotten anachronism that would have brought certain ruin to many a less fortunate millionaire.

Somehow the Hughes Aircraft company survived the catastrophe and moved on into the manufacture of sophisticated electronics equipment for the U.S. Air Force. The Korean War came along and probably saved the company, bringing in enormous profits, but by 1953 Hughes Aircraft was on the point of collapse because of quarrels among its senior managers, whom Hughes was never able effectively to control. It is said that when Harold Talbott, then Secretary of the Air Force, visited the company's Culver City plant and learned how badly it had been managed, he raged at Hughes, "You have made a hell of a mess of a great property, and by God, as long as I'm Secretary of the Air Force, you're not going to get another dollar to do business."

Incredibly, as the wheel turned, Hughes Aircraft recovered its balance and made its peace with the Air Force and also with NASA, the great new patron of technology of the 1960s, so that soon profitable contracts were coming in once again: the Syncom communications satellite, the Surveryor spacecraft, and the Early Bird satellite, three highly successful ventures that brought Hughes Aircraft from the brink of disaster to further glittering success. However, Hughes is said to have missed his chance to turn his aircraft company into the General Motors of the new technology, since by this time there were other competitors in a field he had previously dominated.

Finally came the Las Vegas venture, in which Hughes is reported to have lost at least $50 million, and possibly a great deal more, much of it through fraud, theft, waste, and incompetent management. By the time it began, in 1966, Hughes had withdrawn into his eccentric and even paranoiac seclusion, hanging blankets over his windows to keep out germs, compelling the typists who prepared his papers to wear rubber gloves for the same reason, cutting himself off even from his closest advisors, who received their orders in writing and were reported not to have seen their employer in years, even though he sat just down the street in a penthouse on top of the Desert Inn.

Hughes poured some $300 million into his Nevada gambling and mining operations over the next four years—a truly incredible sum of money. The scale of the disaster that overtook his venture began to come to light only in 1972, months after Hughes had fled the Desert Inn in dead of night—first to the Bahamas, then to Nicaragua, to Canada, back to Nicaragua, and finally, after his hideaway had been destroyed in the Managua earthquake, to London, where he was last heard of living in seclusion on the top floor of a West End hotel.

After he left Las Vegas, an investigation was begun by some twenty Internal Revenue officials, two Justice Department organized-crime strike forces, and a private intelligence service retained by the Hughes organization. Their investigations will take years to complete, but they have already revealed that Hughes was cheated on a scale that beggars the imagination. A probe into the

Hughes Las Vegas empire undertaken by the *Wall Street Journal* disclosed a massive loss of cash, much of it through fraud and theft:

> When Howard Hughes stepped off a private railroad car in 1966 and began buying Nevada, he was hailed as the savior of the gambling industry and the man who would drive the underworld sharks out of town. It is now clear, however, that if anyone was taken for a ride, it is Howard Hughes himself.

According to the *Journal*, Hughes's casino revenues had been heavily skimmed by his own employees. "The Indians were stealing hell out of the place," said one Justice Department official. "Dealers were walking away from the tables with their pockets lined with chips. At some hotel restaurants, more food was going out of the back door than was coming in the front. Thieves were running off with God knows how many plants and trees and selling them all over town." At the same time, Hughes's own officials were living like lords; some of the seven hotel and casino properties he owned had been bought at grossly inflated prices—and even then proceeded to lose some $16 million during the recession years of 1970 and 1971. Elsewhere in Nevada, the *Journal* went on, the billionaire was roundly fleeced by a group of promoters who cajoled him into paying nearly $20 million for claims on dubiously productive gold and silver mines that could have been bought for a fraction of that cost. It was as though Hughes had never heard Mark Twain's definition of a mine: "a hole in the ground with a liar on top."

Even today, it is not known where Hughes's money went. But, said the *Journal*, "along the way it passed through a strange world inhabited by salty old prospectors, professional swindlers, Latin American generals, a mysterious international money courier rumored to have many aliases, a former governor, a would-be Senator and Richard Nixon's brother Donald."

It is not easy to tell what the wayward billionaire will turn to next. There was much astonishment on Wall Street in the autumn of 1972 when a prospectus arrived at the offices of the Securities and Exchange Commission, putting up for public sale the very cornerstone of the empire, the Hughes Tool Company, which Hughes once vowed he would never part with. The sale seemed to follow the standard pattern. His former financial adviser, Noah Dietrich, speculated that Hughes was in dire need of cash with which to meet a $140 million judgment awarded to TWA and to shore up his crumbling gambling investments and one of his airlines, Hughes Air West, which had been hard hit by the recession of the early seventies. But once again, Hughes may win a further fortune from apparent disaster, having timed his sale at the moment the Hughes Tool shares had risen to one of their highest points in history. And a few weeks after the company had been offered for sale, the Supreme Court overturned the TWA judgment, leaving Hughes apparently richer than ever.

There is nevertheless a sense of tragedy and a desperate loneliness about this modern Midas who sees all he touches turned instantly into gold. Is it shrewdness, or is it simply luck, that has led him time after time to pluck a new fortune from the very jaws of catastrophe? Perhaps there is no pattern, no rational explanation of Hughes's extraordinary career; perhaps once a fortune has grown large enough it will go on multiplying itself for ever and ever, defying even the laws of prudence and business judgment and common sense. But to what ultimate purpose? The billionaire has no heir, and it is likely that his great fortune will be fragmented and dissipated after his death. Yet still, long after most men of his wealth would have retired, Hughes keeps up his peripatetic wanderings, buying an airline here, a gold mine there, keeping up to the end one of the strangest and saddest success stories of modern times.

The old rich of America are a staider and more stable group than the new billionaires, although the men who founded some of the great fortunes of the past displayed in their time just as singleminded a pursuit of wealth as any of their modern successors. There is a story, perhaps apocryphal, that Cornelius Vanderbilt, the Howard Hughes of his day, once wrote to a group of his colleagues who had tried to gain control of one of his companies the following letter:

> Gentlemen:
> You have undertaken to cheat me. I will not sue you, for law takes too long. I will ruin you.
>
> Sincerely yours,
Cornelius Vanderbilt

Vanderbilt was one of the first great nineteenth-century American billionaires, a group whose members later came to be called robber barons, as remarkable a collection of unscrupulous cheats and swindlers that the world has seen since the rise of the Borgias three hundred years earlier. Even today, a roll call of their names inspires a sense of awe entirely absent from contemplation of the new super-rich: John D. Rockefeller, J. Pierpont Morgan, Cornelius Vanderbilt, John Jacob Astor, Jay Gould, Edward Henry Harriman, Andrew Carnegie, and of course many others. The story of their rise to wealth has become an American legend, not least because of the ruthless means by which they accumulated their fortunes. "Law?" exclaimed Commodore Vanderbilt, "what do I need with law? Hain't I got the power?" And so it went, down through the entire list: Rockefeller built his Standard Oil monopoly by systematically crushing his competitors; Jay Gould established his fortune by watering the stock of the Erie Railroad; J. P. Morgan made an unscrupulous effort to corner the money market; Harriman employed gangs of toughs armed with dynamite to establish the rights of way for his railroad. They were all, in President Theodore Roosevelt's memorable phrase, "malefactors of great wealth."

While every great fortune that rolled out of the nineteenth century may well have been rooted in fraud, the robber barons were also in large part responsible for the creation of the modern industrial society in the United States. In the period that ran roughly from the end of the Civil War to the start of the World War I, they accomplished a vast job of construction, building the railroads, the refineries, the steel works, the industries, the banks that were the foundation of the modern capitalist system.

The Civil War of the 1860s was the crucible in which modern American capitalism was forged. It dislodged forever the political power of the great plantation owners, most of whom were Southerners, and replaced them with a new breed of northern industrialists, who were to become the dominant force in American society for the next forty years. Later they were joined by an entirely new type of technological entrepreneur, a twentieth-century phenomenon that brought enormous riches to men like Henry Ford, who virtually invented the production line; Andrew Mellon, who founded one of the greatest fortunes of all on the smelting of aluminum; the du Pont dynasty, who made chemicals and provided 40 percent of the explosives used by the Allies in World War I. Later still came the stock-market and real-estate speculators who coolly plucked fortunes from the Great Crash, prominent among them Joseph P. Kennedy of Boston.

Today, their heirs sit collectively on fortunes of considerably greater size than those accumulated by the new rich, although a combination of estate taxes and the division of large fortunes among a multitude of heirs has actually reduced inheritance as a source of great wealth over the past generation or so. The name of Vanderbilt or Astor, for example, is today nowhere to be found on the list of the super-rich, although at the turn of the century they were regarded as the two most spectacularly rich families of all. Other old rich families, however, remain: the Rockefellers, with five centimillionaires still in the family; the Mellons of Pittsburgh, who also have five; and the du Ponts with three.

Considered as family groupings, the four key American dynasties of wealth today are:

1. *Mellon*
   Pittsburgh: Alcoa, Gulf Oil, real estate, banks.
   Total family fortune: $1.9 billion–$3.6 billion.
2. *du Pont*
   Wilmington, Delaware: E. I. du Pont de Nemours, General Motors.
   Total family fortune: $1.5 billion–$2.0 billion.
3. *Rockefeller*
   New York: Standard Oil, Chase Manhattan Bank, Rockefeller Brothers' Fund.

Total family fortune: $1.2 billion–$1.7 billion.
4. *Ford*
   Detroit: Ford Motor.
   Total family fortune: $600 million–$800 million.

Spectacularly absent from the list of America's richest families today are the Astors, once regarded as the very richest family of all. The original John Jacob Astor had set out from the German village of Waldorf as early as 1783, nearly drowning on the way when the ship in which he sailed ran into the winter ice packs on Chesapeake Bay. When the captain ordered the passengers to prepare to abandon ship, Astor, with the prudence that befitted a future millionaire, appeared on deck in his best suit.

As his biographer, Cleveland Amory, tells it, the captain then bellowed at him, "What are you dressed up for?"

In his thick German accent, which he was never to lose, Astor replied: "If ve are saved, I haf my Sunday suit on. If ve are drowned, it von't make no difference vot kind of clothes I haf on."*

Astor and the rest of the passengers were saved, and he went on to found a remarkable dynasty, but it is one which today has fallen upon sad times. Six generations of inheritance taxes, a multiplicity of heirs, some lurid divorce settlements and reckless spending show that in America great fortunes can be lost as well as won. The last of the very rich Astors was Vincent, who died in 1959 without an heir, leaving the bulk of his fortune to charity. His much-married stepbrother, John Jacob Astor VI, who was himself once worth over $70 million, appealed for Vincent's money in court, confessing he was down to his last $5 million, poor fellow. The court turned him down, doubtless remembering his ancestor's remark that a man who has a million dollars "is as well off as if he were rich."

Sixty years earlier, not long before John Jacob Astor VI was born, the Astors had been involved in bitter social rivalry with the Vanderbilts, a rivalry which came to a dazzling climax in the Gilded Age of the 1890s. Led by their womenfolk, the rival families built themselves splendid mansions on Manhattan's Fifth Avenue and million-dollar "cottages" on the ocean front at Newport, bought themselves huge and lavish yachts, threw fancy-dress balls costing hundreds of thousands of dollars each, bought diamonds for their dogs and works of art for their drawing rooms, and between them spent literally hundreds of millions of dollars in a span of perhaps thirty years, an orgy of spending that has no parallel in American history.

At the turn of the century, the Vanderbilts' collective fortune was worth some $400 million, that of the Astors' almost as much; today, both fortunes

---

*The incident provided a curious prologue to the disaster which overtook John Jacob Astor IV, who drowned when the *Titanic* went down in 1912.

have been greatly diminished by successive generations of spendthrifts. "In-herited wealth is a great handicap to happiness," William K. Vanderbilt had observed sadly back in 1905. "It is as certain death to ambition as cocaine is to morality."

Is this then to be the fate of the great inherited fortunes of today? Will future generations of Rockefellers, Mellons, Fords, and du Ponts go the way of the Astors and the Vanderbilts?

It hardly seems likely. For one thing, the reckless goings-on of the Gilded Age have now passed wholly out of fashion; since the death of William Randolph Hearst (who is justly remembered as the last and the best of the big spenders, having poured $20 million into his incredible mountaintop palace at San Simeon and another $50 million to equip it with the plunder of Europe, including Cardinal Richelieu's bed) the very rich today are far more discreet about their wealth than they were in the past. Lavish yachts, enor-mous cars, medieval castles, ostentatious banquets are today not the status symbols they once were. Given the normal propensity of money to multiply itself, it would take extravagance on a truly staggering scale to dissipate a fortune of more than $100 million.

There is no sign that any of the great modern dynasties, or their immediate heirs, have any such destructive inclinations today, and the four cardinal families have all taken care to wrap up much of their wealth in trust funds and foundations, which relieve them of much of the burden of inheritance taxes. Indeed, the big tax-exempt private foundation may well be the chief symbol of American capitalism in the last half of the twentieth century, a curious phenomenon through which the rich are at once enabled to preserve their great wealth and institutionalize their philanthropy. Altogether, there are some 25,000 private foundations in America, 33 of them with assets of $100 million or more each. The biggest of all are institutions of enormous power and influence, comparable in their impact to a great private university or to the medieval church—the Ford Foundation with assets of nearly $3 billion, the Rockefeller Foundation ($757 million), the Andrew W. Mellon Founda-tion ($697 million), and the Lilly Endowment ($778 million).

Often the foundations are little more than tax havens for the rich, a means through which they can keep their fortunes intact and under family control. Sometimes they are used to provide safe and comfortable incomes for favorite protégés: John Connally, for instance, is the recipient of $750,000 in fees from the Richardson Foundation, set up by a Texas oil family, while former mem-bers of Robert Kennedy's staff were well taken care of by the Ford Foundation. The du Pont philanthropies are almost exclusively devoted to preserving the family's own baronial manors and estates in the Delaware chateau country, with fellowship programs in such subjects as ornamental horticulture. ("The need for skilled horticulturalists has never been greater," declared one du Pont official). Yet others, notably the Ford, Rockefeller, and Carnegie foundations, have over the years embarked upon immensely ambitious and undeniably beneficial programs, and have on the way attracted some of the best minds in the country to work for them.

But, as Peter Steinfels has said, America has never quite made up its mind about foundations: "Nothing which has given us yellow fever vaccine, better schools, the National Gallery of Art, Gunnar Myrdal's *An American Dilemma*, kidney machines, the Green Revolution, and *Sesame Street* could be all bad. And yet we continue to suspect that organized philanthropy, like hypocrisy, is the compliment that vice pays to virtue. We question the large foundations' motives; we worry about their power—and we take their money."

In any case, the foundations have become the means whereby the rich American dynasties have been able to ensure their own survival; although as the generations pass, it might be supposed that the inevitable multiplicity of heirs is bound to dilute the size of individual inheritances. In financial terms, however, the very rich do tend to hang together as true dynasties. While the du Pont fortune is now divided among some 250 principal heirs, some of whom have never yet met, they are still able to act as a remarkably cohesive group when it comes to preserving the family's wealth. The cousinhood of the du Ponts gives a single unified thrust to the family enterprise through its network of holding companies and trust funds, all under family management, and the same is true of the Rockefellers, the Fords, and to a lesser extent the Mellons. Members of the current generation of all these families have shown they have the character, the talent, and the ambition to use their money, rather than spend it, and most of them would probably despise the Vanderbilt observation that inherited wealth is the cocaine of ambition.

The Rockefellers, brothers and sons, are as ambitious in their various fields as any member of the nouveaux riches: Nelson, four-term governor of New York State; David, the enormously powerful chairman of the board of the Chase Manhattan Bank, who is often described as the most influential capitalist in the world, and in the next generation, John D. (Jay) Rockefeller IV, who confidently expects one day to become President of the United States in spite of his 1972 setback at the polls of West Virginia. *Noblesse oblige*.

Professor Lundberg points out that not the least of the assets of the Rockefellers is intelligence: "although actually the intelligence at their disposal—the pooled family intelligence derived from long experience with a mercurial world plus that of their large professional advisory and research staffs—greatly exceeds their personal intelligence. Like the ruler of a great state, they have more relevant information at their ready disposal than they can carry with them in their own heads. As far as the contemporary world is concerned, they are thoroughly *informed*. They can, in fact, out-think most contemporaries."

The future of the Mellon family is more problematical. Three of the four most able members of the family have died during the past decade, leaving a power vacuum at the center of the vast family holdings that members of the new generation of Mellons, many of whom are still only in their twenties or early thirties, have shown little inclination to fill. Indeed, so shy are they of publicity that a few years ago the family hired a public-relations firm to keep the Mellon name out of the newspapers, although they are by any standards one of the richest and potentially most influential families in the United States.

The last surviving member of the older generation is Paul Mellon, now in his mid-sixties, and he too has shown more interest in giving away his millions than in wielding the power that could have been his for the asking. "I do not think that I would be a great success as a banker or industrialist," he admitted on one occasion. "Commerce and banking hold no particular interest for me."

Art and horses are the twin passions of Paul Mellon's life. The guardian angel of the Washington National Gallery, Mellon has been known to carry a Degas under his arm at airport terminals, much like anyone else might carry a newspaper; he once imported an entire pack of hounds and a huntmaster from England, and there is a story that when a classmate of his stepdaughter came to lunch one day, she looked up at a Van Gogh on the wall and asked: "Oh, who paints in the family?" "No one here," the daughter replied with the insouciance of the very rich. "Dad buys them in the store."

Paul Mellon is a contented man: "at least part of the purpose of life is enjoyment," he once told a graduating class of schoolchildren. He is the only son of the founder of the Mellon fortune, Andrew W. Mellon, a man of dour Ulster stock who accumulated vast wealth without his contemporaries ever becoming aware of it. He owned a bank and became a moneylender to industry, never building himself but slowly acquiring an interest in each plant he financed until he had come to control a large segment of American industry, most noticeably the corporation that later became the Aluminium Company of America, better known as Alcoa. The old New York *Herald-Tribune* reported that "almost every American pursuing his everyday life was constantly contributing something to the upbuilding of that fortune and that power, for the Mellon group in the industrial realm reached out in myraid lines —to gas, coal, aluminium, coke, petroleum and all its byproducts, heat and power, iron and steel, glass and brick, transport by land, sea and air, finance, real estate, and a thousand derivatives of machine-age fundamentals."

Andrew Mellon became the richest individual in the country, although hardly anyone had heard of him, and when a colleague proposed him to President-elect Harding as Secretary of the Treasury, Harding, just as unaware of his accomplishments as everyone else, asked, "Who's he?" Mellon resigned his directorships in sixty companies and went on to become the dominating political figure of his age, serving under three successive Presidents—Harding, Coolidge, and Hoover—which led the late Senator Robert La Follette to remark, "Andrew W. Mellon today is the real President of the United States.

Calvin Coolidge is merely the man who occupies the White House." Mellon was at first given much of the credit for the spectacular boom of the late 1920s, but later had the misfortune to preside over the Treasury in the year of the Great Crash, and was later much abused for his contribution to that disaster. Hoover packed him off to Britain as U.S. ambassador, but he was recalled after Roosevelt's victory in 1932 to find himself accused in court of defrauding the government of $3 million in unpaid income taxes. By the time he was finally cleared of the charge in 1937, Mellon was dead.

After his death the country learned to its surprise it had become the beneficiary of the largest single gift it has ever received: the $50 million Mellon art collection, with another $16 million thrown in to build a gallery in which to house it. Throughout his life, Mellon had been collecting masterpieces around the world—Rembrandts, Titians, Goyas, El Grecos, Holbeins, French Impressionists—including some twenty-one priceless paintings he had secretly acquired from the Soviet Government in 1931 when they were selling off some of the treasures from the Hermitage in order to bridge a critical shortage of foreign exchange. The Mellon art collection became the nucleus of the American National Gallery, an institution which today ranks among the half-dozen finest galleries of art in the world. The National Gallery was opened in 1941 (Mellon refused to let it carry his own name) and has since received further abundantly generous donations from the family, including $20 million jointly presented by Paul and his sister, Ailsa Mellon Bruce, to add a new wing in 1967, and an early Cézanne for which Paul Mellon in 1970 was said to have paid almost $2 million dollars—the highest figure ever paid for a French painting.

Paul Mellon is a philanthropist who takes his duties seriously. "Giving away large sums of money is a soul-searching problem," he once remarked. "You can cause as much damage with it as you may do good."

While they are thus far from dying out, and indeed remain as wealthy as ever, the American super-rich today, both the inheritors and the self-made, are no longer the immensely powerful social and political forces they once were. They are, in a sense, survivors of a world that has passed, along with the railroad, which became the symbol of so much of their earlier power. Individual entrepreneurs on the model of Henry Ford and John D. Rockefeller are no longer at the cutting edge of industrial progress, however crude and unscrupulous that progress might have been, while the great business enterprises of today no longer come under the control of a single all-powerful individual but are more typically publicly owned corporations, run by vast bureaucracies, such as Boeing Aircraft, General Motors, ITT, and IBM. Traces of the legendary pattern remain, but today the typical head of a giant corporation acquired his position through a steady climb to power in a rigid white-collar hierarchy.

Fifty years ago, the super-rich were the essential movers and shakers of the

American system of capitalism. Today they are the irrelevant, if interesting survivors of an earlier epoch. Howard Hughes and J. Paul Getty, the Mellons and the du Ponts, can all be safely left in luxurious seclusion, symbols of another age.

CHAPTER V

Industry

1. The Bigness of Business

"The business of America is business"
—Speech given by CALVIN COOLIDGE *before the Society of American*
Newspaper Editors, January 17, 1925

It is not only Texans who stand in awe of bigness. Americans generally tend to be thrilled by sheer size, to think that a thousand square miles is more wonderful than one square mile, and that a million square miles is almost the same as heaven. E. M. Forster was not thinking of American business when he wrote that the awe of bigness was the vice of vulgar minds, but the comparison is apt. The pursuit of bigness has become the vice of American industry. In the 1970s, only two hundred corporations own two thirds of the manufacturing assets of the United States. A generation earlier, that share was spread among a thousand corporations, and at the turn of the century among nearly two thousand. In one quarter of the nation's manufacturing industries today, the four largest companies hold 50 percent or more of the available market. The domestic market in automobile manufacture, for example, is dominated by three strong companies—GM, Ford, and Chrysler—and one weaker one, American Motors. The only other competition comes from overseas. In the steel industry, the bulk of the nation's production comes from no more than half a dozen companies. In commercial aviation, the only competitors are two powerful giants—Boeing and McDonnell Douglas—with one less powerful giant—Lockheed—struggling to break back into the market. The result in every case has been a decline in real competition between these supposedly competing firms, and in many cases there has been active collusion to keep prices artificially high. In the midst of the recession in 1970, at a time when American automobile manufacturers were faced with a large drop in sales and ever fiercer competition from abroad, the Ford Motor Company actually announced it would *raise* the price of its basic model to "match" the price charged by General Motors. And at the height of the slump in domestic air travel in the early 1970s, the airlines jointly increased the cost of their tickets, when according to all the classic laws of economics they should have been reducing them.

Respectable academics sometimes argue that the trend toward giantism is not only inevitable but beneficial, on the general theory "the bigger the better," in which by "better" they presumably mean more efficient. The phenomenon is by no means confined to the United States; one of the principal driving forces towards European economic unity within the Common Market has been the desire to create Continental-scale industries on the American pattern. Indeed, several of the giant European corporations like Royal Dutch Shell, Unilever, and the Volkswagenwerke lag not at all behind their American counterparts either in the scale of their operations or in the diversity of their activities. Giant companies are permanent modern phenomena, straddling the economies of the industralized world like so many Gullivers in Lilliput. They are here to stay, and the modern world will have to learn to live with them.

The phenomenon is there for all to see. We all know, there are private corporations bigger than sovereign states and we all expect the 1970s to go on producing more and more of these multi-national, multi-industry Leviathans—yet there have been very few convincing explanations as to why the successful modern corporation has grown to be so colossal. Antony Jay would have us believe in his witty analysis of *Corporation Man* that the drive toward bigness is the result of a basic subconscious urge on the part of top management; that the modern corporation is nothing more than an extension of the ancient tribal hunting-band in which man's primitive instinct as a hunter is a more powerful factor than reason and logic. In this analysis, corporations expand for the same reasons the Roman Empire expanded. Perhaps, like the Roman Empire, they also contain the seeds of their own destruction and will eventually collapse under succeeding waves of barbarian invasions, in which Sonys and Volkswagens will presumably take the place of the Vandals and the Visigoths.

A more prosaic view has been expounded by Professor John Kenneth Galbraith, who believes that the need for large scale planning is the basic reason for giantism. He argues that for planning—the control of supply, control of demand, provision of capital, minimization of risk—there is no clear limit to the desirable size. "It could be," he says in *The New Industrial State*, "that the bigger the better." In another passage he speaks of a "benign providence" that has made the modern industry of a few large firms "an excellent instrument for inducing technical change." Professor Galbraith argues that the concentration of economic power must be accepted; modern technology makes it inevitable.

During the 1960s, this concentration of the nation's manufacturing and financial assets into fewer and fewer hands appeared to be a process both irresistible and irreversible. Some companies grew by the simple process of producing more and more of the products they knew best, but toward the end of the decade many others grew into giants as the result of what Senator Philip Hart has called "company-eating contests," a process whereby the biggest corporations systematically bought control of their less wealthy—but often more efficient—competitors in a move toward bigness for its own sake.

The humorist Art Buchwald once looked forward to a time when every corporation west of the Mississippi had been merged into the single corporation Samson Securities and every corporation east of the Mississippi had been merged into the Delilah Company. Eventually, of course, Samson and Delilah decide to merge and negotiate with the President to buy up the United States.

Buchwald's column was more than just a joke. In 1969 alone, some 4,550 firms disappeared by merger. It has been estimated that if the trend continued, 300 giant corporations would dominate the economy of the world by 1980. Concern was expressed by humorists, economists, sociologists, and politicians alike. John Mitchell, who was then U.S. Attorney General, expressed his alarm in a 1969 speech before the Georgia Bar Association in which he warned that the dangers of this superconcentration of power to the country's economic, political, and social structure could hardly be overestimated. It eliminated existing and future competition. It created nationwide marketing, managerial, and financing structures whose enormous physical and psychological resources barred smaller firms from participating in a competitive market. "This leaves us," he declared, "with the unacceptable probability that the nation's manufacturing and financial assets will continue to be concentrated in the hands of fewer and fewer people—the very evil that the Sherman Act, the Clayton Act, the Robinson-Patman Act and the Celler-Kefauver Amendment were designed to combat."

The wave of mergers that prompted Mitchell's alarm stopped abruptly during the Wall Street slump of 1969–1970, although some of its effects are likely to be lasting. Nor were the dangers he warned against all that new. The trend has been apparent at least since the 1950s, when the late Senator Estes Kefauver declared, "Through monopolistic mergers the people are losing power to direct their economic welfare. When they lose the power to direct their economic welfare they also lose the means to direct their economic future." Back in those days Senator Kefauver was talking of the dangers of monopolistic mergers within a single industry in the classic way that General Motors swallowed up, one by one, so many of the famous independent automobile producers: Buick, Pontiac, Oldsmobile, Cadillac. Since he spoke, a new and even wider danger has emerged, a danger disguised by the inelegant title of "conglomerate."

Conglomerates have been defined as companies which are not what the public supposes them to be. The *Wall Street Journal* once explained how they worked with effective simplicity: An executive who checks out of his room at the Sheraton Hotel, steps into his Avis Rent-a-Car, drives to his broker's to check on his Hamilton Mutual Fund shares, mails a quarterly premium for his American Mutual life insurance policy, checks on financing some capital equipment through the Kellogg Corporation, fires off a cable to Britain, then motors to Camp Kilmer, New Jersey, for a session with the purchasing agent at the federal Job Corps there. "It's just a routine morning dealing with a variety of matters," said the *Journal*. "But so far the man's business has been entirely with divisions or operations of the inappropriately named International Telephone and Telegraph Corp."

ITT is perhaps the classic conglomerate, a hungry leviathan that has so far bought its way into such unrelated businesses as insurance, electrical equipment, chemicals, world communications, engineering, and transport. It was once also on the point of swallowing up the American Broadcasting Corporation, until the Justice Department decreed that marriage would have been a little *too* bigamous. ITT itself shuns the word conglomerate and prefers to call itself "a unified-management, multiproduct corporation." Whatever the title, ITT has become in less than a decade a huge amalgam of some 331 directly or indirectly owned companies in over 65 countries with over 400,000 employees and sales that by 1972 exceeded $8.5 billion.

ITT's director, president, and chief executive officer is Harold Geneen, a benign, bespectacled former Englishman who in the space of fifteen years has proved himself to be one of the most brilliant business managers of the era. He holds his vast empire together by enormous attention to detail. He demands monthly reports from all his divisions and, it seems, he reads them all himself. To make sure he gets the details he wants, down to such minor details as a lost order, he has a staff that tours the world, dropping in on the subsidiaries to check up on things. And, *Forbes* magazine reports, "line people know that if Geneen finds out anything negative about a man's operation, no matter how petty, from anyone else but the man himself, he explodes; so the reports are highly detailed."

ITT's drive to expand, to join the "company-eating contest," came as the result of a deliberate and rational decision taken back in 1963 "formally to start a goal program for acquisition." Since then, ITT's drive has been very basic: Geneen once admitted he had only two criteria for buying up another company—"The company should be growing faster than ITT. And it should have plenty of room to grow as the industry it is in grows." Not efficiency of production, not the public interest, not the welfare of its employees, not even ITT's devotion to the industries it so assiduously devours, but simple profit is the sole *raison d'être* of the conglomerate. For ITT the results have been spectacular. At the end of 1970, Geneen reported the company had completed a continuous record of *forty-six consecutive quarters* in which sales, net income, and earnings per share had each increased over the corresponding period of the prior year. And while ITT is the biggest and best-known conglomerate, it is by no means the only company in the United States that is "inappropriately named."

Litton Industries, once a small firm manufacturing microwave tubes, gained a reputation as the fastest-growing company in American history, absorbing fifty companies in twelve years and branching into such unrelated fields as typewriters, nuclear submarines, calculating machines, and frozen food.

General Motors is well-known as America's largest producer of automobiles. It is not so well known as one of the largest single producers of domestic washing machines and color television sets.

The Radio Corporation of America—RCA—owns the National Broadcasting Company and makes television sets. But it also owns Hertz Rent-a-Car and Random House, the publishers.

Gulf and Western Industries, which began by manufacturing automobile bumpers, branched out during the 1960s to purchase companies that made cigars, fertilizers, zinc, and electric organs, and also bought several huge farms and the Paramount Pictures Corporation.

Westinghouse Electric bottles Seven-Up and owns five TV stations; the W. R. Grace shipping company brews Miller's High Life beer; Boeing has moved into farming; and the list of conglomerates grows.

By the late 1960s, it seemed entirely possible that the whole of American industry would be swallowed up by the conglomerates. But somehow it didn't happen. The great wave of mergers collapsed as rapidly as it had begun in the aftermath of the Wall Street slump and the Nixon recession of the early 1970s. Heavily burdened by debt, many of the newer conglomerates came close to bankruptcy and only saved themselves through desperate "remnant sales," retrenchment, and loans from local bankers. Many of them, in one phrase, had tried to build a house from the roof down; and it was surprising that so few of them actually collapsed. "It was a time of intense insanity in which greed and fear were the ruling emotions," said one Manhattan banker. "We have not yet paid the full price for what happened."

The fact is, most conglomerates were made on Wall Street, the result of financial razzle-dazzle and corporate sleight-of-hand, making their profits during the boom years by financial manipulation rather than by actually producing goods of genuine economic value. Contrary to the popular mythology of the late sixties, it proved in the end they could not, by brilliant management, produce more than the sum of their parts. As the Celler Commission reported, "A good manager's intuitions, like those of a good card player, come from his long experience with the special rules, technology and markets of a particular industry. Only in extraordinary individuals—so few as to be practically negligible—do we find the ability to absorb a new game intellectually and then compete successfully with experienced players." If anything, according to the Celler findings, conglomerates frequently have an injurious effect on efficiency, productivity, and corporate values. Even conglomerates found they could not get something for nothing. In industry, there is no such thing as a free lunch.

American industry is still digesting the lessons learned from the great merger frenzy. For one thing, the Federal Trade Commission now requires advance notice of all acquisitions of companies with sales above $10 million by companies with sales of $250 million, which has put a stop to some of the stealthier attempts at take-over, like the rush by Gulf and Western that in 1969 nearly succeeded in buying Pan American World Airways. The Justice Department has also invoked the antitrust laws to prevent several conglomerate mergers, while the investing public itself has become much more wary of the promises of instant wealth held out by the manipulated profits brought by some of the trickier mergers.

But most of the new big corporations of course are here to stay, and some of their values have stuck, among them the interesting and unexpected effect they have had on basic company loyalties. Until the mid-sixties, the average American executive stayed with the same company all his life, climbing slowly up a rigid white-collar hierarchy, working hard and diligently until, when he was sixty years old, and if he was lucky, he became the company president. As the prisoner learned to love his chains, so did the American executive learn to love the corporation that enveloped him. Back in the late fifties and the sixties, their plight was exhaustively surveyed under such suggestive titles as *Organization Man, Man in the Gray Flannel Suit, Corporation Man, Life in the Crystal Palace,* and many others. There was one chilling story from those years of a list headed "PYM" carried around by the president of General Electric. It turned out that "PYM" stood for "Promising Young Men." That was twenty years ago, but even then the company was so large the president had no personal contact with his key executives; he had to carry their names around on a written list. The effect that such a list was bound to produce on the PYMs themselves, on their efforts to keep their names on the list, and above all on their efforts to conform, keep in line, and not become un-PYM, staggers the imagination.

The problem was expressed at its most trenchant by T. K. Quinn, once also a top executive at General Electric, who wrote a fierce attack called *Giant Business: Threat to Democracy.* It was Quinn's contention that economic concentration was producing a new and dependent generation that had already lost the drive and individualism Americans of an earlier epoch treasured so highly:

> Every one of the thousands of absorbed and merged corporations represents a lost opportunity for the young men of tomorrow to find more important places, where a man could assume responsibility and develop his ability and serve the community in the spirit of independence. Where will the leaders of the future come from? Surely not from the bureaucratically-minded subordinates of the third and fourth generations in giant corporations who line up and move from speciality jobs automatically to the next level as death or resignation overtakes their predecessors.

They are not creative towers of strength; they are more like the trusting, clinging vines which hug these towers for their weak existence.

Twenty years later, events have shown that in one respect at least Quinn was wrong. The middle ranks of industry may well be choked with weak and clinging vines, even in the 1970s, and some of them doubtless carry their habits of bureacracy and caution with them to the very top. Yet since this decade began there has been a dramatic shift in the tradition that demanded an executive should stay with the same company all his working life. There is suddenly room at the top, and the instruments of this change, often enough, have been the big conglomerates, whose speciality, after all, was management. Indeed, *Newsweek* magazine reports that job-hoppers from General Electric and Litton Industries have become so common they have been given the nickname "Lidos" and "Gedos." Executive turnover from the level of vice-president up was almost nonexistent until the mid-sixties, but since 1968 corporate nomads have occupied about 5 percent of the top industrial jobs. That hardly represents a mass migration, but it does indicate a new trend, one that is expected by many businessmen to increase in significance as this decade goes by. Increasingly, the more modern executives now tend to identify not with a single company but with the profession of management. And more than anything else, the inducement for them to move over is the chance to run their own show.

In any case, whether home-grown or imported from a rival company, the heads of modern American industry are today overwhelmingly professional managers rather than capitalist entrepreneurs in the traditional sense. There are those who still believe these executives are merely the nominees and puppets of individual rich men who wield power in the bygone manner of J. P. Morgan or the original John D. Rockefeller. But as Professor Galbraith has pointed out, most of the power implicit in the running of the big modern firms has passed to the "technostructure," men of a quite uniform and identifiable social type. They are, with very few exceptions, white, Protestant (preferably Episcopalian or Presbyterian), American-born, and college-educated. Few of them are country boys who have made good in the city. Even fewer are immigrants, poor or rich. Not many are Catholics or Jews, and almost none of them is black. In his study of *The Power Elite*, C. Wright Mills has shown that when he made his analysis, 71 percent of the country's leading business executives were the sons of businessmen or professional men and only 12 percent were the sons of workers or of lower blue-collar employees.

Romantic writers used to describe these top business executives as "captains of industry" whose momentous decisions could affect the stability of sovereign states and the prosperity of entire continents, and whose names were known and recognized in every household in the land. Today, the romance is gone. American business executives, even at the very top, are notable chiefly for their anonymity. Henry Ford II is probably the only head of a large American corporation whose name would be instantly recognized by the average newspaper reader anywhere in the world. The rest of them remain anonymous. Like ordinary mortals, they have to produce evidence of their identity when they cash a cheque or pay a hotel bill. Yet they probably hold in their hands more collective power than any other group of men outside the walls of the Moscow Kremlin.

Every year, *Fortune* magazine produces a list of the top corporations of the United States, measured in terms of annual sales. In 1972, the top twenty companies—the elite of the elite, every one of them household names producing goods used every day by almost every American—were listed as follows:

		Sales (1972) $000	Employees
1.	General Motors (Detroit)	30,435,231	759,543
2.	Exxon (New York)	20,309,753	141,000
3.	Ford Motor (Dearborn, Mich.)	20,194,400	442,607
4.	General Electric (New York)	10,239,500	369,000
5.	Chrysler (Detroit)	9,759,129	244,844
6.	IBM (Armonk, N.Y.)	9,532,593	262,152
7.	Mobil Oil (New York)	9,166,332	75,400
8.	Texaco (New York)	8,692,991	76,496
9.	ITT (New York)	8,556,826	428,000
10.	Western Electric (New York)	6,551,183	205,665
11.	Gulf Oil (Pittsburgh)	6,243,000	57,500
12.	Standard Oil of California (San Francisco)	5,829,487	41,497
13.	U.S. Steel (New York)	5,401,773	176,486
14.	Westinghouse Electric (Pittsburgh)	5,086,621	183,768
15.	Standard Oil of Indiana (Chicago)	4,503,372	46,627
16.	E. I. Du Pont de Nemours (Wilmington, Del.)	4,365,900	111,052
17.	Shell Oil (Houston)	4,075,898	32,871
18.	Goodyear Tire (Akron, Ohio)	4,071,523	145,201
19.	RCA (New York)	3,838,180	122,000
20.	Procter & Gamble (Cincinnati)	3,514,438	45,000

2. GM: Troubled Giant

*"For years I thought that what was good for the country was good for General
Motors, and vice versa."*
— CHARLES E. WILSON, *chairman, General Motors, 1958*

It is on the size and strength of her gigantic private corporations that the
United States ultimately depends for her power in the world. They ARE the
United States, Professor Ferdinand Lundberg has said. Take them away, and
what would be left?

The name of the chairman of the largest industrial corporation of all is
Richard C. Gerstenberg. Outside Detroit, it is reasonable to assume few
people have heard of him. In that respect Dick Gerstenberg is the classic
modern American executive: hard-working, conservative, eminently respectable, little-known, and exceedingly powerful.

Like all his recent predecessors, Gerstenberg is a General Motors man
through and through. Now in his early sixties, he joined the company after
his graduation from the University of Michigan in 1931 and has never worked
for anyone else. He got the top job at the end of 1971 after four years as the
heir apparent, the company's chief financial expert, whose specialist talents
were picked as the ones thought necessary to tackle the problems of cost and
profits that confront the corporation in the 1970s.

A rather dry, serious man who wears horn-rimmed glasses, Gerstenberg
looks exactly like the accountant he is. Once, when he was being questioned
about GM's products by a Senate committee, he told them, "You are talking
to old Gerstenberg, the bookkeeper. I am not an engineer." A colleague
describes him as "a broadgauge guy who will do the industry some good" in
the age of eroding profit margins that lie ahead. As chairman, he draws a salary
of $250,000 a year, plus bonuses and stock options that could increase his
income in a good year to around $800,000. He dresses in a rather less austere
style than his colleagues, occasionally sporting a broadknot tie and a polkadot-
ted pocket handkerchief—an affectation that passes in Detroit for the height
of sartorial daring.

Gerstenberg grew up in the upstate New York town of Mohawk, where his
father, a German immigrant, was an inspector for the Remington typewriter

company. He recalls that his father once told him, "I wish there was some way you could get a good education so you could get a big job with a big company and take things easy." Young Dick Gerstenberg found a way to get his good education at the University of Michigan in Ann Arbor, but he graduated in the year of the Great Depression, when jobs with big companies were hard to come by. "I think I came to Detroit at least once every week looking for a job, but there were no jobs available anywhere," he says. "So I shoveled sand all during that summer in a little foundry back of Ann Arbor, in the town of Milan."

Finally, his perseverance paid off and the young college graduate one day landed a job as timekeeper for GM's Frigidaire Division at Dayton, Ohio. For his first two and a half years at GM, his function was to pick up the employees' timeclock cards every day and check that their working hours were properly calculated. At the end of the two and a half years he was moved to the Fisher Body Division in Detroit, whence his rise has been solid, sound, and unspectacular. Today, as one of Detroit's chief corporate diplomats, he is a passionate believer in the American system and the profit motive, which on his appointment as chairman he described as "the key to all progress."

Gerstenberg's background as a smalltown boy who has made his own way in the world resembles that of most of his colleagues, although his special expertise differs greatly from that of his immediate predecessor, James M. Roche. Roche was a brilliant administrator and a public-relations man who spent much of his time as chairman defending with great dignity the good gray ways of General Motors to an increasingly skeptical public. Gerstenberg is an "inside" man, recognized as the leading financial expert in the entire automobile industry, equipped with a keen, tough mind that will be stretched to the full in trying to hold down the crisis of costs that now afflicts all four automobile makers.

General Motors has a flair for choosing its top men with great shrewdness, and each of the seven men who have held the chairmanship has been endowed with the special qualities needed to lead the company at the particular time he took over. In the 1920s, when General Motors was still very much number two to Henry Ford, the company was directed by a genius called Alfred P. Sloan, who set up GM's formidable organization plan on the principle of centralized control and finance and decentralized production operations. Sloan realised that Ford's concentration on only one car, the Model T, was out of date in an era of rising expectations, and he formulated a new policy for GM: "a car for every purse, every person, and every purpose." Sloan sensed that Americans wanted something more than mere wheels. "Mr. Ford," he later recalled, "failed to realize that it was necessary for new cars to do more than meet the need for basic transportation. Middle-income buyers created the demand for progress in new cars, for comfort, convenience, power, and style. This was the actual trend of American life, and those who adapted to it prospered."

No one adapted to it or prospered from it with more success than General Motors. When Sloan retired in 1956 it was GM, with more than half the market, that dominated Detroit. Today, Ford, Chrysler, and American Motors are, in a sense, mere satellites of the gigantic GM. When General Motors sets a new style, or a new price, the other three manufacturers have little choice but to follow suit. General Motors, by tradition, is the company that understands the consumer—a company that once even employed seven psychologists to study the sounds and smells of its new cars to discover the hidden desires of its potential buyers. Chevrolet's general manager, introducing a new model, was then able to claim with pride, "We've got the finest door slam this year we've ever had—a big car sound." The company understands that the public does not buy its cars on any kind of a rational basis.

Gerstenberg, like the rest of the men who run General Motors, embodies all the old-fashioned American virtues. Most of them are kind, grandfatherly figures, conforming Christians, dedicated to the good, abundant middlewestern way of life. They rise early, often at five or six o'clock, and glide down the freeway in vast Cadillacs from their pleasant suburban homes to the fortress-like GM Building in Detroit, where they work in their locked and isolated fourteenth-floor executive suites for as many as ten or fourteen hours a day. They have little time for outside pursuits. Gerstenberg says he once started to read *Wheels*, Arthur Hailey's bestselling novel about the automobile industry, but gave it up after a hundred pages. "I thought there'd be some interest in the story," he says, "but there wasn't." Many of the GM executives lead the same inbred, monklike existence. Their critics often say they are cut off from contemporary currents of thought. In a sense they *are* curiously out-of-date figures, stuck in the mode of thought of the late 1950s, when the lifestyle they projected seemed to represent the very essence of America. The turbulent 1960s somehow passed them by; they still run GM on the old principles of Alfred Sloan when in the 1970s the old principles no longer suffice.

Nearly all the top executives have been with the company thirty years or more, and an impressive number of them are graduates of GM's own school, the GM Institute. They were picked for promotion early under a system in which each of the corporation's 760,000 employees is regularly and carefully screened for signs of managerial ability. Every six months, those who show the greatest potential are listed in a confidential "black book" and methodically shifted from one job to another to test their caliber. The survivors eventually make it to the "Greenbrier Group," a select party of executives who are invited to GM's Staff College at Greenbrier, West Virginia, to reflect on the company's performance. The method of promotion is very like that of the army, an organization GM resembles in several other ways, with an accent on uniformity, official titles, a rigid chain of command, and a rather brusque military approach to its problems.

The founder of the Greenbrier system, Alfred Sloan, declared that General

Motors was "not the appropriate organization for purely intuitive executives, but it provides a favorable environment for capable and rational men"—a doctrine that his successors have raised almost to the status of a religion. They have created, says William Serrin of the Detroit *Free Press*, "a wonderfully fascinating institution, almost incomprehensibly large, exceedingly powerful, rich, secretive, inbred, smug, full of politics and personalities, as worthy of study as the Kremlin, Peking, or the Catholic Church, all of which, in ways, it resembles."

In its own terms, the empire created by Alfred Sloan has been startlingly successful, the most successful and widely imitated corporation of its type ever known. Its annual sales now exceed $30 billion, a sum approaching in value the total annual exports of Britain and the Netherlands put together. It produces over 7,750,000 vehicles every year and employs an overall work force of nearly 800,000 people. And yet, for all its material success, the giant is sorely troubled; the capable and rational men who now stand in Sloan's place have, in the past six years, presided over the most severe buffeting their company has ever known. In the 1970s, GM appears to be under siege from all sides.

Consumer groups, led by Ralph Nader, began the assault in the mid-1960s with charges that GM's Corvair was a deathtrap on wheels—a campaign that has left deep scars on GM's corporate image. Later, the environmentalists, disenchanted with the automobile, joined the attack, claiming that GM's products were suffocating the cities with pollution, a condition they claimed GM could prevent if only it tried hard enough. Antiwar demonstrators joined in the attack with a march on the company's headquarters in which they carried banners reading: GM GETS RICH, GI's DIE. It was an unfair charge, as GM receives only 3 percent of its revenues from defense contracts, but because of its colossal overall size, GM seemed to offer a convenient and vulnerable target to social critics, who think they see in big business all the symptoms of an ailing society. GM's president, Edward N. Cole, once declared, "We're under the gun from the critics because of what we are. The biggest is the most vulnerable. It's easier to get headlines by attacking GM."

On top of all this, the corporation appeared to be faltering even by its own standards of success. In the 1970s, for the first time since the war, its share of the domestic market fell to a bare 50 percent, and its profit margins have been dwindling since 1965. In 1970 it made one of its rare misjudgments of the market, which allowed foreign competitors—chiefly Volkswagen and Toyota—to seize an unprecedented 16 percent share of domestic automobile sales. That was largely GM's own fault, as the company traditionally disdains small cars because the profit margins are so narrow. A GM executive once told the New York *Times*, "if the public wants to lower its standard of living by driving a cheap, crowded car, we'll make it." General Motors clearly thought it could go on for ever persuading American consumers that their rising expectations would lead them to buy perpetually bigger and bigger cars with lots of chrome, steel, and profitable options. But in the 1970s the worm turned, and many consumers, especially in the high-density markets of New York and California, seemed happier with their European and Japanese imports. There were even suggestions that they ran better, and no one could deny that they were cleaner and, for city driving, more convenient. GM had missed the trend, and as a result one sixth of all American motorists now drive around in imported automobiles.

There were other "traditional" problems with which to grapple in the early 1970s. The automobile industry was imperiled by a grave "crisis of cost," led by hugely inflated union demands which were forcing American manufacturers to price themselves out of world markets. The workers' demands were only settled after a costly and damaging strike, and then only after a private meeting between Roche and Leonard Woodcock, head of the United Auto Workers, a man who has described GM as "a gold-plated sweatshop." After a twenty-minute talk with Woodcock, Roche gave in completely and directed the company to accept the UAW demands on the basis of an average fifty-one-cent-an-hour increase, the start of a five-hundred-dollars-a-month pension plan, and an unlimited cost-of-living escalation clause—a settlement that, it has been argued, added fuel to the runaway inflation of the early 1970s and was one of the main factors that led President Nixon to impose his wage-and-price freeze. In the end it was the consumer who was, as usual, forced to pay. GM could only give its workers a larger piece of the pie if it took it away from its customers in the form of thinner steel, inadequate bumpers, and slightly less car for their dollar.

The attitude of its workers is also in urgent need of improvement: some managers believe it is one of the most crucial problems facing the automobile industry today. GM's absenteeism rate, which was only 2 percent in 1960, had climbed to 6 percent by 1970 and in some plants rises as high as 15 percent. Never buy a car that came off the production line on a Monday or a Friday, goes the old Detroit saw: those are the days on which absenteeism is highest and the production lines staffed with standin workers who make many errors. The Cadillac plant has now begun an experiment in which the old assembly-line has been abandoned so that each worker can build at least one complete part in an attempt to make him feel he is doing a good job and get satisfaction from his work. The program has had some success in reducing absenteeism, but it is hard to visualize how it can be applied to the industry as a whole. The dreadful monotony of the assembly line has been frequently chronicled, but has to be seen and experienced before it can be truly understood. On the assembly line, cars move past each work station at the rate of fifty to sixty-five cars an hour; that is about one car every minute on which the worker must perform his appointed task. The line never stops: day in, day out, he repeats the same, seemingly pointless task, week after week, year after year throughout his working life. Boredom is inevitable, the high wages providing the only compensation for the never-ending mental agony of the work. The absenteeism and shoddy workmanship that results presents General Motors and the other American automobile makers with one of the greatest challenges of the decade—one which they have so far scarcely begun to tackle.

At the end of 1971 another blow fell upon the beleaguered prestige of the company: GM was forced to recall nearly 6.7 million of its Chevrolet automobiles and trucks to correct what federal authorities and other critics called a major safety defect affecting the vehicles' rubber engine-mounts. As expected, General Motors denied the safety allegations and said it had announced the recall simply to avoid "misunderstandings." Nevertheless, the recall was far and away the largest, most damaging, and most expensive in automobile history, costing the company an estimated $33 million, not to mention the untold damage to its reputation.

Meanwhile, the attacks by outsiders continued with unabated strength. Richard Ottinger, a former New York congressman, described GM's big brass as "the leading Neanderthals of the business world," and accused Roche of "leading the corporation down a path that will certainly spell its own destruction and endanger the very system he claims to be championing." Pressure began to build up from black groups for more jobs, and there were more general charges from consumer groups that GM was failing in its social responsibilities.

Perhaps because of the ingrown structure of its management, GM was felt to respond inadequately to these outside pressures. Its executive board has become, in the eyes of its detractors, a self-serving, self-justifying, and self-perpetuating industrial oligarchy, answerable ultimately only to itself. Its board of directors is chosen not by its 1.3 million stockholders but by a system of cronyism candidly described by the former chairman himself: "Different members of the board," Roche said, "get together and agree on the proposed candidates submitted to the entire board for their approval."

Dissatisfaction with these ingrained habits boiled over at the company's annual general meetings in both 1970 and 1971. The 1970 AGM in Detroit's Cobo Hall was perhaps a turning point in American business history. A group of lawyers backed by Nader and calling their movement Campaign GM had bought a dozen shares in the corporation and put up a series of consumer-oriented resolutions to be voted on at the annual meeting. One resolution would have created a "Shareholders' Committee for Corporate Responsibility" to watch over GM's action on pollution control. Another would have added three "public representatives" to the corporation's twenty-three-man board to speak for consumers and minority groups.

Up on the fourteenth floor, the executive reacted to these proposals with undisguised horror. At first, they brusquely refused to put the activists' resolutions to a vote. Nader's lawyers promptly appealed to the Securities and

Exchange Commission, who, to the company's chagrin, overruled the board's decision. When the meeting was finally convened, feelings on both sides were running high. For six and a half hours, Roche fielded hostile questions from the activist stockholders in a meeting that sometimes looked more like a noisy production of *Hair* than the sober meeting of conservative stockholders the executive had been used to handling.

Assigned fifteen minutes' speaking time each, the activists paraded to the microphone all day long to deliver a steady and unfriendly stream of complaints against the company. Some of the proposals made that day were just plain silly. Stewart Mott, son of GM's then oldest director and largest single shareholder, Charles P. Mott, pleaded with GM to join in efforts to control population growth. Albert P. Appleby, a Los Angeles businessman, wanted to enlist the corporation in an effort to end the war in Vietnam. Later speakers were more to the point. A young Washington lawyer, Geoffrey Cowan, asked the directors if they ever discussed pollution and whether they employed an expert on the subject. "I think the shareholders are entitled to know what goes on at board meetings," he exclaimed, to the obvious astonishment of the assembled board members.

A black law student from UCLA, Barbara J. Williams, demanded to know why no black person had ever been named to the board. "No black has been nominated and no black has been elected," Roche replied. "Our directors are elected by our stockholders."

Miss Williams asked, "How are they nominated?"

"They are nominated at the annual shareholders' meeting, just as they were today."

Staring directly at Roche, Miss Williams declared, "Mr. Roche, you have not answered my question. Why are there no blacks on the GM board of directors? Why no women?"

Under this cross-examination, Roche replied again, "Because none was elected."

It was not the answer his critics wanted to hear, and another Washington lawyer, Harry Huge, took up the cross-examination. "Mr. Roche," he declared, "*you* nominate the board of directors because eleven members of the board are your officers and former officers of the board of General Motors." Roche would not accept this definition of his powers, saying he merely "can make recommendations." Huge answered with another question: "Have you ever made a recommendation that wasn't acted upon favorably?" Roche said he had, but under further questioning admitted that the board had never gone so far as to reject any of his recommendations for election to a directorship.

Afterwards, Roche spoke of his critics with respect. "They were very precise," he told a *Business Week* reporter. "It was obvious they did a lot of homework. I'm sure there's going to be continued interest."

Other directors were not so sanguine. John T. Connor, a GM Board member, was shocked at the suggestion that ordinary stockholders were entitled to know what went on in the boardroom. "This was a new departure," he said. "Up until this time, stockholders have always appreciated and observed the sanctity of the boardroom. I think it is essential for a board to have free and frank discussions. I was quite upset at the nature of the questions and the tone of the questions . . . as if the board was a public body whose deliberations were a matter of public record."

The GM management had gone to extraordinary lengths to prepare itself for the encounter. Before the meeting, every shareholder had been sent a twenty-one-page booklet defending the company's record on safety and pollution. Roche himself wrote to the heads of foundations, bank trust departments, and university endowments—all large GM stockholders—urging them to vote down the proposals. Lesser officials were instructed to follow up his letter with phone calls.

It was an unequal contest that the management was bound to win. As expected, the two proposals introduced by Campaign GM were soundly defeated, winning less than 3 percent of the vote. Their defeat was a reflection of the entrenched power of the management, which, when pressed, can usually marshal the proxy votes of the vast silent majority of shareholders.

Nevertheless, GM was shaken by the experience. Its hometown newspaper, the Detroit *Free Press*, thought that while the company had won the battle of the votes, the Nader lawyers had won "an enormous psychological and publicity victory." The *Free Press* added, "The idea that a corporation needs some free-standing souls around to prod it in the public interest is not as apocalyptic as it sounds."

GM is not a company that likes to admit it is wrong. When it recalled its defective Chevrolets it refused to answer any questions on the issue, and rather than blame the recall on its own defective engineering, GM preferred to describe it as "the result of misinformation and misunderstanding" that the company was anxious to eliminate. Back in 1966, its spokesman had protested vigorously against a proposed California law establishing stringent standards for auto exhausts. It would be technically impossible for GM to comply, the spokesman said. But once legislation had been passed, it turned out not to be impossible after all. The resultant credibility gap has left the public with the impression that GM has to be pushed into nearly every improvement it makes. And so it proved with Campaign GM. After publicly denouncing its critics, the company quietly began to institute some of the very reforms called for by the Campaign GM organizers. Within a year, GM had appointed its first black board-member, and an authority on pollution control was appointed vice president in charge of environmental activities. A public policy committee was set up, composed of five distinguished businessmen and educators, including James R. Killian, chairman of the prestigious Massachusetts Institute of Technology. GM deposited $5 million in 35 black-owned banks as part of a federal program to encourage black capitalism and put a further $2 million into low-cost housing developments sponsored by civil rights groups in towns where it has factories.

Having quietly instituted its own reforms, the company characteristically mounted a counterattack on its critics. A new hard line was adopted in speeches by both Roche and Edward N. Cole, the company president—"as if they were serving notice that they can be pushed only so far," said *Time* magazine—and since Gerstenberg took over he has worked hard to counter what he regards as the woeful ignorance of the American public about the free enterprise system and what it means to their future prosperity. In 1973, he had been distressed to discover that the average American, according to one opinion poll, believed that company profits in the United States were nearly seven times higher than they actually were—ignorance that he found quite deplorable. "Great issues swirl around him," he wrote of his "average" fellow-countryman. "His judgment is critical, yet he has little or no economic knowledge or experience. Because he thinks profits are seven times higher than they are, because he is unaware of the direct linkage between profits and jobs and a prosperous society, he is often willing to accept regulation or legislation that would limit profits. He is a ready target for the propaganda of those who would break up what they call 'big business,' and subject the entire business community to progressively tighter governmental control and regulation. In my opinion, lack of understanding underlies much of the apathy which the public is showing towards efforts to eliminate or cripple the free enterprise system. . . . We cannot afford to let this continue. We cannot because the harsh lesson of history is that freedom lost in one sphere of human activity—in private enterprise, for example—inevitably leads to the loss of freedom in another. By our actions we must demonstrate that free enterprise is the most effective instrument that man ever devised for both economic and social progress."

GM's devotion to the principles of freedom is touching, and it would be churlish to question its sincerity. But not everyone would agree with the underlying implication that GM's loss of freedom to pollute the air or to produce unsafe vehicles represented any threat at all to the individual freedom of Americans. Indeed, many critics would argue that the reverse was true. But Gerstenberg seemed to be giving notice that *all* governmental control and regulation was unacceptable—that while GM was prepared to bend with the wind, to give the appearance of change, on fundamentals it had not changed at all. It seems astonishing that in the 1970s the head of America's largest corporation could criticize the public's willingness to accept regulation or legislation "that would limit profits." In Detroit, the spirit of free enterprise flows pure and deep indeed.

Gerstenberg's new approach was encouraging to those GM subordinates who had thought all along the company was taking too soft a line with its critics. There are still men at GM today who have never forgotten or forgiven the company's biggest humiliation, when as new chairman, Roche had gone to Washington to apologize for the company's behavior to Ralph Nader. To the old guard, 22 March 1966 was the day the dam broke. Roche remembers it as the bitterest day of his life.

The affair had begun at the end of the previous year, when GM's intelligence system had learned that Nader, then an unknown thirty-two-year-old lawyer, had written a critical book about the company—his famous attack on the dangerous design defects in the Corvair, entitled *Unsafe at Any Speed.*

Before the book was published, Aloysius F. Power, the head of GM's legal department, ordered an investigation into Nader's background. The company paid $6,700 to hire Vincent Gillen, a former FBI agent turned private detective, to "investigate" Nader. Power said later it was a normal action to find out whether Nader was connected with lawyers who were pushing safety claims against General Motors. But Gillen went further. In a letter to his agents telling them what they were supposed to accomplish, he wrote that "our job is to check Nader's life and current activities, to determine what makes him tick, such as his real interest in safety, his supporters, if any, his politics, his marital status, his friends, his women, boys, etc., drinking, dope, jobs, in fact all facets of his life." Gillen's agents went about their task with clumsy and hamfisted relish. Nader's unlisted telephone would ring in the middle of the night, and ominous-sounding voices would ask such questions as "Why don't you go back to Connecticut, buddy-boy?" Mysterious private eyes were seen tailing him in such widely separated points as Des Moines, Philadelphia, and Washington. A pretty blonde tried to lure him into her apartment while he was shopping for cookies in a Washington supermarket. Friends and associates were quizzed about his political affiliations, his alleged anti-Semitism, and why he had never married.

Inevitably, the story leaked out. Equally inevitably, GM denied it. Then, on the night of 8 March, as yet another denial was being drafted, a GM official telephoned Roche, who was staying late in his office to handle the matter, and told him, "There is something you must know." The corporation, he said, did have detectives investigating Nader.

Appalled, Roche sought his colleagues' advice. How was GM to respond? Some of the top men reportedly wanted to deny what General Motors had done; others wanted to camouflage it. The legal department wanted to counterattack: to admit what they had done but to claim this was what any redblooded corporation would have done in similar circumstances.

Roche listened carefully. The next night, a new statement was released, pointedly timed just before midnight so as to miss both the main editions of the morning newspapers and the main television and radio news programs. Dictated by Roche himself, the statement said GM had conducted "a routine investigation through a reputable law firm to determine whether Ralph Nader was acting on behalf of litigants or their attorneys in the Corvair-design cases pending against General Motors." Such investigations, the statement added, were "a well-known and accepted practice in the legal profession."

If Roche hoped the matter would rest there, he was to be rudely disappointed. Nader denounced his statement as "misleading," and both Nader and Roche were invited to testify at a public hearing of Senator Abraham Ribicoff's subcommittee on traffic safety. GM was caught in a trap, largely of its own making. After further agonizing thought, Roche decided there was only one honorable course of action: "We must go to Washington and apologize."

Many of his colleagues were shocked. General Motors never apologizes, they said. We must not apologize.

"Goddammit," Roche told him. "What the hell do you want me to do? This is the only thing that can be done."

Two weeks later the huge marble caucus room of the old Senate Office Building in Washington was jammed with reporters, cameramen, and public citizens as Roche arrived for the hearing. The scene, said *Newsweek* magazine, "had all the fascination of a public whipping." But first, there were more revelations. It turned out that Gillen's gumshoes had started looking into Senator Ribicoff's private life, hoping to turn up some sort of connection with Nader. Then Gillen told Senator Robert Kennedy they had looked into Nader's background so carefully "in fairness to Ralph."

"What the hell's this fairness to Ralph?" Kennedy shouted. "You have to keep running around the country proving he's not anti-Semitic or not queer? Ralph's doing all right."

Then came Roche's turn. Stuttering slightly, he said in a quiet baritone, "I deplore the kind of harassment to which Mr. Nader has apparently been subjected. I am just as shocked and outraged as the members of this subcommittee. I am not here to excuse, condone, or justify in any way our investigating Mr. Nader. To the extent that General Motors bears responsibility, I want to apologize here and now."

It was a courageous and dignified statement delivered in a manner that did much to redeem General Motors's reputation in the company's darkest hour. Even Nader conceded that the gentlemanly, grandfatherly Roche had been the perfect figure to make the apology. But it was also a moment of public humiliation that General Motors has never forgotten, and it set the tone for the rest of Roche's chairmanship, during which the automobile industry went onto the defensive for the first time in its sixty-year history. It has remained on the defensive ever since. In the years that have followed, General Motors has paid dearly for its abuse of power in attacking Ralph Nader. The price in bad publicity has been incalculable. A year afterwards, Congress pushed through the Highway Safety Act, which for the first time put strict regulations on the auto industry. "We all decided then, when we heard about Vince Gillen and GM," one senator recalled, "the hell with them." The Corvair, Nader's particular target, which he had attacked as "uniquely unsafe," was discontinued in May 1969. Nader himself was projected overnight into a hero figure, America's Crusader Consumer. He eventually settled out of court with the company for $425,000, which his lawyers said was the largest amount ever paid as damages for invasion of privacy.

Even then, GM was reluctant to concede it had been in the wrong. Its lawyers were instructed to say they had agreed on the settlement only "to avoid the very substantial additional expense and demands upon time of corporation personnel" that would be incurred if the case dragged on. "My heart bleeds for them," replied Nader. He said *he* had agreed to settle only because he was convinced that GM would otherwise continue to delay the suit until "all the culpable officials would have retired." Nader took the money and invested the residue in a fund he has set up to monitor in perpetuity General Motors's activities in the safety, pollution, and consumer-relations areas. Nader said dryly it would be General Motors's contribution to the consumer movement: "They're going to be financing their own ombudsman."

Many people see in all this the end of America's love affair with the automobile, though naturally the men at General Motors do not agree. In the very last interview he gave before he retired, Roche was asked the self-same question: Did he still think America was in love with the automobile? "Very definitely I do," he replied. "I think the average American today would give up about anything before he gives up his automobile."

Cynics immediately answered that they might *have* to. But even the sternest critics of General Motors would have to concur that the automobile retains its central place in American life. In the 1970s it may be shorn of its once-fantastic trimmings, the idyllic love affair may have turned with the years into a quarrelsome marriage, the air of Los Angeles may be thick with its fumes, and its freeway system may have paved over an area as large as the whole of New England—but the automobile remains, and the industry that produces it is still central to the success or failure of the domestic economy. As the men who sit astride fully half that industry, Dick Gerstenberg and his colleagues up on the fourteenth floor still wield an impressive amount of power.

3. The Oil Game

"Texas could exist without the United States, but the United States cannot, except at very great hazard, exist without Texas."
—SAM HOUSTON, *Texas patriot, 1793–1863.*

Eleven hundred miles to the southwest of the gray industrial town of Detroit lies the sprawling state of Texas, a land the more reserved northerners look upon with decidedly mixed emotions. Texans are everything the staider industrialists of the North are not: brash, boastful, uninhibited, and given to exaggerated local patriotism. Outsiders, especially those from the North and East, tend to regard these traits with disdain. A northern visitor once declared that Texas had more cattle and less milk, more rivers and less water, and more landscape and less to look at, than any other state in the Union. Today, Texas still has its cattle barons, and its local patriotism is, if anything, shriller than ever, but it also has something most of the northern and eastern states do not: oil.

Of the 254 counties in Texas, 195 produce oil. Everywhere, one is confronted with a paraphernalia of the industry. On the new U.S. Highway 45, which runs south from Houston to the Bay of Galveston, the flat, marshy landscape is dominated by drilling rigs and refineries, petrochemical plants, and gleaming storage tanks. Everywhere in Texas, perhaps the most familiar sight of all is the prehistoric nodding head of the device known locally as the pumping jack. Over it all lingers the characteristic, faintly nauseating smell of crude oil. Texas, which produces a third of America's oil, now has over 200,000 wells, or one well for just about every filling station in the country. Oil has been discovered in every conceivable location; the pumping jacks nod away, twenty-four hours a day, on farmland and bayous, graveyards and suburban gardens. There even used to be one in the middle of the Houston municipal dump.

Each year the oil and natural gas produced in Texas sells for well over $5 billion. That is equivalent to $45 worth of oil for each inhabitant of the state. Oil has brought so much wealth to Texas that the local author J. Frank Dobie has remarked that the proceeds from cattle now look like tips. Of the country's ten largest businesses, four are oil companies. Measured in terms of its share capital, the industry is by far America's biggest, worth at current stock-exchange prices more than the steel, automobile, and chemical industries put together. And with oil has come that other Texas phenomenon, the oil millionaire. In other states, a millionaire is a man who owns a million dollars. In Texas, a man is not counted as a real millionaire until he *earns* a million dollars every year. And some of them still earn more than that in a month. Harold Lafayette Hunt, the richest Texan of them all, now estimates his income at roughly a million dollars a week.

Better known as a crackpot philosopher of the extreme right, Hunt's background is obscure. He dropped out of school in the fifth grade in his home town of Vandalia, Illinois, and according to Texas legend then went to work as a cowhand in Canada and as a lumberjack in Arizona. He had a fling at cotton growing in Arkansas back in the 1920s and only became a rich man after he went into oil in the East Texas fields just after the Depression. Legend has it that he won his first oil well in a game of poker at a place called El Dorado, though he claims he bought it fair and square. By the end of World War II, Hunt owned more oil reserves than all the Axis nations put together.

Now in his eighties, Hunt is a Texas eccentric, devoted to the causes of the extreme right, which he propagates through a privately sponsored radio program called Life Line, which is said to reach some five million people a day over several hundred radio stations. Hunt's politics can be judged from the Life Line slogan: "The battle for Freedom is a battle between Communism and the Profit Motive system." In 1963, just before President Kennedy's assassination in Dallas, Life Line put out a series of venomous programs on the tyranny of the Kennedy administration and its supposed affinity for communism. It was probably Hunt as much as anyone who led Kennedy to remark on that fateful visit, "We're now entering nut country."

In spite of his aversion to the liberalism of the Kennedys, Hunt is rumored to have invested several hundred thousand dollars in the political campaigns of President Lyndon Johnson, who was a well-known supporter of the oil industry's special tax status. After LBJ's retirement in 1968, however, Hunt came out in support of George Wallace, whom he is also said to have provided with considerable financial support. Wallace's campaign assistants have denied this, saying all he ever gave them was four cartons of his books.

One of Hunt's books is a novel called *Alpaca*, a love story in which his hero and heroine set to work perfecting a new system of government in which the biggest taxpayers are given the most votes. "It's like a corporation," the author explains. "The greatest stockholders have the greatest votes." Asked by a reporter whether he expected to make money out of his book, Hunt snapped, "Certainly. Everything I do, I do for profit."

Hunt's lifestyle is as eccentric as his politics. He lives in a replica of George Washington's home at Mount Vernon, although naturally, since this is Texas, Hunt's version is on a considerably larger scale than the original. Mean in his personal habits, Hunt trims his own hair and usually eats his lunch from a brown paper bag containing dried prunes, low-calorie cheese, and a slice of bread baked from Deaf Smith County wheat. He neither smokes nor drinks, but is an ardent gambler, who once kept two men on his payroll whose sole function was to keep a Western Union line open on which to place the millionaire's bets on horse races and baseball games.

Many observers have commented on the close affinity between gambling and "the oil game," as it is almost universally known by its practitioners. In the early nineteenth century, long before oil had been discovered in Texas, de Tocqueville observed that "the whole life of an American is passed like a game of chance." In the twentieth century, the Texas oil men maintain this tradition. "It's just like running a dice-table—one that's honest, open, and above board," Ted Weiner, a Fort Worth oil millionaire, has said of his profession. And H. L. Hunt, when asked for his formula for making money in oil, replied, "You have to be lucky."

The great Texas oil gamble began in 1901 when oil was struck at a place in East Texas called Spindletop, an event that marked the end of John D. Rockefeller's monopoly of the American oil industry. Before Spindletop, Rockefeller's Standard Oil Company directly controlled 83 percent of all oil produced in the United States, though of course that was in the days when petroleum was used chiefly for lighting and lubrication. In its way, the gusher at Spindletop marked the beginning of the modern age. Oil had become a source of cheap power just at the moment the internal combustion engine was poised to transform first the United States and then the rest of the world with the revolutionary concept of personal mobility.

For thirty years the area around Spindletop was the only important oil-producing region in Texas. The great modern oil boom began only in 1930, as a result of a discovery by a gentle and impoverished old-age pensioner known to everyone as "Dad" Joiner, King of the Wildcatters. In Texas terminology, a wildcatter is an oilman who drills speculatively for oil, usually with makeshift equipment and a secondhand rig—a technique known as "po'-boying." After striking several "dusters," or dry holes, Dad Joiner struck it rich on a farm in Rusk County owned by a widow called Daisy Bradford, after whom he named his wells. Daisy Bradford No. 3 was the one that came in a gusher—the largest single pool of oil ever discovered in the continental United States, spreading over an area of some 240 square miles.

Dad Joiner's strike effectively ended the Depression in East Texas, although for a while it threatened to ruin the industry in the process. The Daisy Bradford well was producing oil in such abundance that the price dropped from $1.30 a barrel to as low as 5 cents. A quota system was introduced in an effort to bring order into the industry, but the producers ignored it and began running "hot oil." There were fights and bloodshed on the oilfields, and the Texas National Guard had to be called in before order was restored. State and federal laws were enacted enabling the state to set the amount of oil each operator would be allowed to produce. Today, once a month, usually on a Friday, the Texas Railroad Commission meets in the Commodore Perry Hotel in Austin, the state capital, to decide, as it has done since the 1930s, how much oil the state's wells can produce during the next month.

Like most wildcatters, Dad Joiner died broke at the age of eighty-seven in his modest house in Mockingbird Lane in Dallas. But several of the shrewder men who followed him made their fortunes from his discovery. Two of the richest, Sid Richardson and Clint Murchison, as engaging a pair of multimillionaires as the state has produced, got their start back in the depression days when Murchison pulled Richardson out of a poker game in Wichita Falls to investigate rumors of a wildcat strike near the Oklahoma border. They found the area fenced off and guarded, but got near enough literally to smell oil, and next morning borrowed $50,000 to buy the leases. A day later, they sold them again for $200,000 and so established the basis of two of the greatest fortunes in the United States.

Texas tales of the partners' deeds abound. In 1958, they teamed up to help a friend gain control of the New York Central Railroad. Murchison made the arrangement over the long-distance telephone for what he thought was an investment of $5 million each. Through a misunderstanding, it turned out to be twice that, and when Richardson found out, he simply called his partner back to inquire, "Say, Clint, what was the name of that railroad?"

That is the way oilmen do business. When they meet in the Petroleum Club in Houston or Dallas, their deals are clinched in an informal, almost nonchalant manner. Their personal honesty is unimpeachable, and a handshake is usually regarded as sufficiently binding evidence for a deal worth millions of dollars. "You know, those eastern fellows just don't know the way we do business down here," one of Murchison's former partners has said. "They want to fool around exchanging lots of papers. They can't believe it when they sit down around here and see how we frame a deal over the phone in fifteen minutes that it would take their lawyers months to handle. After those Eastern fellows been around for a while, though, they begin to go along in the small denominations. But when they get into the big denominations, then they start going slow again. They never really seem to catch on to the basic idea, which is that it's the *ratios* that count. Just the *ratios*. Them noughts at the end don't mean nothin'."

The offhand manner in which Clint Murchison used to conduct the annual stockholders' meeting of the Delhi-Taylor Oil Corporation would scandalize the prim executives of General Motors—not to mention GM's consumer-oriented critics. A typical Murchison AGM has been recorded by John Bainbridge in *The Super Americans*. "If you'll all come to order," Murchison began, "I'll run through my annual reading lesson. First, let's have a motion to waive the reading of the minutes of the last meeting. Does anyone so waive?" Somebody did, and Murchison launched into a casual review of the events of the past year: "Canadian Delhi is so conservative we kicked it out of Delhi. . . . Gas can't go anywhere but up." Then came questions from the stockholders. "Clint," asked one, "how can you make the stockholders' meeting in Calgary and the Kentucky Derby, too?" "Afraid I can't, Roy," Murchison replied. "I'll have to pass up the stockholders' meeting." Finally Murchison announced, "I make a motion you make a motion we adjourn." The stockholders obliged and retired to Murchison's house for a garden party.

It is all very folksy and engaging, and the romantic stories of how poor men can singlehandedly make a fortune from oil have an irresistible appeal, even in the drab and egalitarian 1970s. There is another side to the story, however, and of the thousands of hopeful roughnecks who have tried their hand at the oil game, only a tiny proportion have made it to the top. These days, the roughnecks who make fortunes out of oil are also more likely to be rich men before they start. Investing in oil wells has become a popular gamble with the very rich and the very famous, who find in oil a convenient way of cutting down their taxes while making a sizable extra fortune. One industrialist, worth $85 million, told the *Wall Street Journal*, "When a fellow is in my income bracket, he automatically goes into oil. This is a legal way to escape confiscation of earnings." Bob Hope and Bing Crosby also found oil a useful way of cutting down taxes on their Hollywood salaries, and the two entertainers each bought a 16 percent share in an oil lease in Scurry County. After one dry hole, they hit twenty-eight oil producing wells in a row, which made them both millionaires. Other Hollywood stars joined the oil rush: Gene Autry had six wells near Wichita Falls, and Jimmy Stewart went into association with a Fort Worth operator and also owns some wells in Utah.

With or without Hollywood backing, the roughnecks are very probably representatives of a dying breed. They are known in the industry as "independents," of whom there are getting on for seven thousand in Texas alone. Their role is to produce and discover oil for the "majors," the famous large oil corporations without whom they could not exist. It has been estimated that the independents find 85 percent of the oil in Texas and own 15 percent of it. The majors find 15 percent and own 85 percent. Rich though they are, the independents are dwarfed by the leading majors, the big eight of which are Exxon, Mobil, Shell, British Petroleum, Texaco, Gulf, and the Standard Oil companies of California and Indiana.

Exxon, until 1972 known as Standard Oil of New Jersey, is the dominant force among the majors. Everything about the company is immense: Its assets of $20 billion are twice the size of the U.S. government's gold reserves, and its shareholders outnumber the population of Hawaii. Its tanker fleet of about 150 vessels, including 19 new supertankers, is comparable in tonnage to the British Royal Navy. The company is estimated to sell one out of every seven gallons of fuel marketed in the western world.

Unlike the domestic independents, the majors tend to favor overseas investment and the importation of foreign oil, which until very recently has been much cheaper. The independents, however, through the power of their Washington oil lobby, have been able to curtail foreign imports by means of a quota system specifically designed to protect their interests and keep the cost of American gasoline artificially high (although the cost of gasoline in America is still very much cheaper than elsewhere in the western world: an average 37 cents a gallon in 1972, compared to 77 cents in West Germany, 81 cents in France, and 99 cents in Italy).

Since the 1970s began, however, the United States has, to its surprise, became a major oil importer. The fact is that the country now consumes so much energy the domestic fields can no longer keep up with the demand. In 1972, for the first time in twenty-four years, the Texas Railroad Commission announced that the Texas wells would in future be allowed to pump oil at full capacity. "We feel this to be an historic occasion," said Byron Tunnell, chairman of the commission. "Damned historic, and a sad one. Texas oil fields have been like a reliable old warrior that could rise to the task, when needed. That old warrior can't rise any more." Or, as former Commerce Secretary Peter Peterson put it, "Popeye is running out of cheap spinach."

As a result, oil imports have more than doubled since 1965–67. Serious studies have been produced to show that as early as 1975 the United States will be compelled to import $14 billion worth of oil each year, more than a third of the total consumption, most of it from the Arab countries of the Middle East. Indeed, the soaring importation of Arab oil has perhaps been the most important single factor in the recent U.S. balance of trade deficits, and the enormous quantities of dollars held by the Arab countries played no small part in the double devaluation of the dollar in 1971 and 1973.

For all that, the United States itself is nowhere near running out of oil. The huge new fields in Alaska are themselves enough to increase proved U.S. reserves by two thirds. A study by the Interior Department has estimated that American fuel minerals—petroleum, natural gas, coal, oil shale, uranium, and thorium—are enough to last 190 more years at the rate of consumption in 1970. The study added, "the potential resources of fuel minerals that are on the verge of use but await technological advance will last 16,500 years at the rate of energy use in 1970." Meanwhile, 55 percent of the discoverable oil and 66 percent of the discoverable natural gas in the United States are still in the ground, waiting to be found. Why, then, the sudden alarm over the energy crisis that erupted in 1972? One reason is that the American drillers have almost exhausted their best sites, where oil was both available in abundant quantities and easy to bring to the surface. Increasingly, reserves are now found in deeper wells, where oil has to be forced to the surface by complicated and expensive pumps, or in inaccessible and difficult sites, such as the new offshore wells in the Gulf of Mexico and California, or the even more inhospitable region on the Arctic coast of Alaska. Foreign oil is not only more plentiful these days, it is also cheaper to drill, so that in the Arab countries oil costs on average only twenty cents a barrel to bring to the surface, against nearly two dollars for U.S. oil. The American producers, moreover, have been simply unable to keep up with the increasing domestic demand. The energy needs of an advanced technological civilization are prodigious so that human labor now accounts for less than one percent of the work performed in the United States; artificial energy for the rest of it. The country consumes about one third of the world's total output of fuels, or about eight times as much energy per capita as the rest of the world, and more than three quarters of it comes in the form of liquid petroleum or natural gas.*

For all these reasons, the old oil import quota has now been all but rescinded. For fourteen years, the quota had limited crude oil imports to 21 percent of domestic production—one of the oil industry's special privileges that so outraged its critics, who saw the quota as an open subsidy for rich and powerful Texans. It has been estimated that the quota system, which worked in tandem with the state laws controlling local production, was worth between $5.2 and $7 billion a year to the oilmen. The quota was instituted by President Eisenhower in 1959 as a "national security measure" that was supposed to free the United States from its dependence on foreign-drilled oil and encourage exploration for more domestic reserves. While Ike's quota certainly had the desired effect of encouraging exploration, the argument that this increased the national security rested at best on doubtful logic. As Senator Edward Kennedy observed, the industry's attitude seemed to imply that "our reserves will be conserved if we use them first."

Other examples of the special tax privileges granted to the oilmen, however, remain, chief among them the oil depletion allowance, a deduction based on the argument that oil is capital and by taking it out of the ground, the oilmen are reducing the value of their property. The depletion allowance is an article of faith in the industry. As the former president of Standard Oil of New Jersey, M. J. Rathbone, remarked, "The allowance was granted on the basis that when a prospector found an oilfield and produced the oilfield he was in effect going out of business."

Since Congress forced through the 1969 Tax Reform Act, the depletion allowance has allowed owners of oil wells to deduct from their taxable income 22 percent of the value that each well yields. For forty-five years before that the oilmen had been granted a depletion allowance of 27.5 percent: thus, for each $1 million worth of oil he sold, the oilman was allowed to deduct $275,000 on his tax return. Although this has now been reduced to $220,000, the tax allowance may, and very often does, exceed the cost of producing the

*In 1971, liquid petroleum supplied 44.2 percent of the U.S. energy needs, natural gas 32.9 percent, coal 18.2 percent, hydropower 4.1 percent, and nuclear power 0.6 percent, according to the Department of the Interior.

oil in the first place. The effect is to provide a very handsome subsidy to an already rich industry, which its critics claim costs other taxpayers some $1.3 billion every year. The depletion allowance is the main reason some 155 millionaires, mostly oil men, were able to pay no tax whatsoever for several years in the 1960s. It is also the reason that Atlantic-Richfield, one of the wealthier oil companies, avoided paying any federal taxes in 1964–1967, while at the same time accumulating a federal tax credit of $629,000. The company's profits in those years amounted to a total of $465 million. Little wonder murmurings of revolt began to rise from the ranks of the middle-class taxpayers who had no such loopholes to resort to.

"Did you pay an average tax rate of 25 percent of your income last year?" Representative Bertram Podell asked in Congress. "Shed a tear, ungrateful wretch, for persecuted Shell Oil Company, which paid 13.1 percent of $342 million in 1967 in the form of federal taxes. Weep for the Union Oil Co., which paid 6.3 percent tax. Or how could we forget the terrible fate that overtook Getty Oil Company in 1967? . . . Shall we expand the food stamp program to include starving oil-company executives and their ragged families huddled in pitiful groups on the Riviera and in the Caribbean? How can they keep polluting our beaches, killing our wildlife, keeping out cheap foreign oil, and taking that 27.5 percent depletion allowance on a pitiful diet of filet mignon, paté de foie gras, and ten-year-old whisky?"

The story of how the depletion allowance passed into law and how it was maintained unchanged for forty-five years provides a classic study of what Senator Pastore has called "the raw political power" of big business to influence the legislative process. Ever since the Depression years, President after President has criticized the allowance; none has been strong enough to remove it. As long ago as 1933, President Roosevelt described it as "a pure subsidy to a certain class of taxpayers." His successor, President Truman, declared in 1950, "I know of no loophole so inequitable." Ike was a friend of the oilmen and did not even try to cut their allowance, but Senator Robert Taft, known as "Mr. Republican," said the allowance was "to a large extent a gift." John Kennedy announced in his 1960 campaign that if elected he intended to take a close look at depletion, but thanks largely to his Vice President, Lyndon Johnson, another open friend of the oil lobby, he never did. Johnson said of the Democratic Party's tax platform that year, "the platform pertains only to loopholes, and I see none in oil." And H. L. Hunt, although violently opposed to Kennedy, approved of the fellow Texan who succeeded him. "Johnson is the kind of President who can lead Congress around by the nose," he declared. "I wouldn't mind seeing *him* there for three terms." Under LBJ the issue lay dormant for four years, only to be raised again in the 1968 campaign, when candidate Richard M. Nixon declared of the depletion allowance, "As President, I will maintain it."

The oilmen obtained their extraordinary armhold on successive Presidents and their Congresses chiefly through the considerable amounts of largesse they are able to distribute at campaign time. No one knows exactly how much money oil pours into politics, although oil producers are known to be traditionally generous donors to the election campaigns of Richard Nixon. The Mellon family (Gulf Oil) reportedly gave $215,000 to his 1968 campaign, Sun Oil another $84,000, and oil interests are reported to have donated several millions to Nixon's 1972 campaign. In exchange, the representatives of the industry were granted easy access to the Nixon White House, where one of the President's senior aides, a millionaire called Peter Flanigan, had as one of his many assignments the job of listening sympathetically to the oilmen—and presumably of making sure their political contributions continued to flow. Soon after the President took office, Flanigan arranged a private meeting between Nixon and Michael L. Haider, the retired chairman of Standard Oil of New Jersey. Haider, known in the trade as "Iron Mike," came out of the meeting saying, "I am feeling more optimistic about the handling of the petroleum industry's problems in Washington." He felt the President had "a good grasp of the problems" surrounding the industry's import controls and expressed his confidence that the outcome of the negotiations then in progress would be favorable.

Although most of the Texas oilmen describe themselves politically as Democrats, they distribute their money on a strictly nonpartisan basis for services rendered. Johnson, a fellow Texan, they could support; he, after all, supported them. But Hubert Humphrey, his successor and an avowed opponent of the depletion allowance, was not acceptable, so in 1968 the oilmen's money went elsewhere. The Democrats were desperate for money that year, and several top aides were dispatched to the Houston Petroleum Club to plead the party's case and to ask for the traditional campaign contribution from the oil millionaires. The oilmen at once asked what their candidate intended to do about depletion. "We told them the Vice President would not promise them a thing," Jeno Paulucci, a Humphrey supporter, told the Los Angeles *Times*. "We told them he would not be a political prostitute. The oil men wouldn't give us a dime."

There are even cruder examples of the oilmen's arm-twisting techniques to maintain the depletion allowance. When Frank Moss, then a county attorney, was running for his Senate seat in Utah, he one day received a telephone call from a Democratic Party functionary in Washington. According to the late Senator Paul Douglas,* the conversation went like this:

"Judge, how would you like ten thousand dollars?"

"Would I like ten thousand dollars? Why, it could make the difference between victory and defeat." Moss said he could finance two television programs and probably three on radio, which would make a big difference in a large state like Utah. "Have you got the ten thousand dollars?" he asked.

"Well, I'm sorry to say there's a catch to all this," the functionary replied.

---

*Quoted in *Atlantic Monthly*, September 1969.

"You can have the ten thousand dollars provided you will agree to maintain the twenty-seven and one-half percent allowance on oil."

There was a long silence. Finally, Moss said, "Well, I don't know. We've struck oil in this state. It may be all right. But I don't *know* about it. If the only way to get the ten thousand dollars is to be for something I'm not sure about, I'll just have to say I won't accept it."

Curses were heard at the other end of the line. "Oh, my God," exclaimed the party man, "We've got an honest man, and we're sending him down to defeat."

The story actually had a happy ending for Moss, as the party told the story to a wealthy liberal supporter who immediately sat down and wrote out a check for ten thousand dollars—with no strings attached.

Even without Moss's support, the influence of the oil lobby on Capitol Hill, although less absolute than it was ten or twenty years ago, is still pervasive. Its hard core includes as a matter of course the two Senators from Texas, John Tower and Lloyd M. Bentsen—one a Republican, the other a conservative Democrat—as well as eight other aging and conservative Senators from the South and Midwest. On the fringes of the lobby even the archliberals Fulbright and McCarthy (before he retired from the Senate) relied to some extent on oil for their backing and could usually be relied upon in turn to support the oil interests when it came time to vote. According to the New York *Times*, Gene McCarthy raised $40,000 in one afternoon at the Houston Petroleum Club during his 1968 presidential campaign—even though his party's eventual candidate got nothing.

Today, the acknowledged leader of the oil lobby in the Senate is Russell Long of Louisiana, the now-aging son of a famous demagogue father, and chairman of the prestigious Finance Committee, where the depletion allowance is set. Long, who fought tooth and nail to prevent any reduction in the 27.5 percent depletion allowance, says coyly that his own income from oil wells "exceeds" what he makes in the Senate. "Most of my income is from oil," he admits. "I don't regard it as any conflict of interest. My state produces more oil and gas per acre than any other state in the Union. If I didn't represent the oil and gas industry, I wouldn't represent the people of Lousiana." It has been estimated that in the years between 1964 and 1970 Long received $1,196,915 from his oil and gas leases—$330,000 of which was exempt from taxes. Long also holds seven private leases whose royalty reports are not available for public scrutiny. The mutual support that Long receives from oil and oil receives from Long is clearly substantial, yet the protective shield he holds around the industry is no longer as secure as it once was, and his attempts to defend depletion and the import quotas sometimes carry a faint air of desperation. He has been known to defend the import quota, which used to shut out Canadian oil, by invoking the possibility of war between the U.S. and its northern neighbor. The oil lobby has never sounded so apologetic and so defensive as it does under Long's leadership in the 1970s. "Frankly," says Michel L. Halbouty, a Houston oil producer, "all of us took it for granted that our little red house would never be blown down by those howling wolves. The people would automatically support depletion if they knew what our industry meant to them." The trouble is, said the chairman of the America Petroleum Institute, Jake Harmon, "most people in the United States think we are a bunch of overbearing braggarts with a tax gimmick. Unless we change that unfair image, we're going to lose our depletion allowance and generally go down the drain."

Such statements are a far cry from the aggressive tone adopted by the oilmen in the heady days of the late 1950s when the two party leaders in the Senate, Lyndon Johnson for the Democrats and Everettt Dirksen for the Republicans, were between them able to ensure that no antidepletion man ever made his way onto the Finance Committee, where the decisions were taken. For years, LBJ stood with his fellow Texan, House Speaker Sam Rayburn, like Horatio on the bridge defending depletion against all comers, using his tremendous influence first as Senate Majority Leader, then as Vice President, and finally as President to keep the opponents of the depletion allowance at bay. His role in preserving the oilmen's privileges can hardly be exaggerated: "Almost any oilman knows that without 'Lyndon and Mr. Sam' there might be no depletion provision today," says the Houston *Post*.

Johnson's technique was to use his seniority to prevent Senators opposed to the depletion allowance from obtaining membership on the Finance Committee. In the lower house it was Sam Rayburn's role as Speaker to keep all measures affecting the allowance confined within the House Ways and Means Committee, where tax bills originate. "Let it out of committee," he once remarked, "and they'd cut it down to fifteen, ten, five percent—maybe take it away altogether. Do you think you could convince a Detroit factory worker that the depletion allowance is a good thing? Once it got to the floor, it would be cut to ribbons." Naturally, under Rayburn, the question never did get to the floor of the House of Representatives, although there were one or two close calls in the Senate.

Today, with Johnson, Rayburn, and Dirksen all dead, the oil lobby is itself somewhat depleted. When the Tax Reform Act of 1969 finally cut the allowance from the mystical figure of 27.5 percent to a still healthy 22 percent, Senator Thomas McIntyre of New Hampshire, a longtime opponent of depletion, declared that Congress had once and for all rejected its role as the bastion of the oil industry. "We have finally made a crack in oil's protective shield," he declared—even though at 22 percent the oilmen still find themselves better padded against taxation than any other branch of industry.

Three and a half thousand miles away from the oilfields of Texas, in the ramshackle and windswept city of Juneau, capital of Alaska, the Senate of

America's biggest state was called to order one day in 1970 for an opening prayer by the State chaplain. "We thank Thee, O Lord," he intoned, "for the oil Thou hast given us for a natural resource." The chaplain's thanksgiving was another way of saying the poorest state had hit paydirt. Only two years earlier, oil had been struck at Prudhoe Bay on Alaska's Arctic coast, and now it was known the field was the richest on the continent, with reserves estimated at a minimum of fifty million barrels, but probably as much as ten or fifteen billion barrels—enough, if it could be produced, to mark both the end of Texas's domination of the American oil industry and Alaska's emergence from its backward and undeveloped state.

The oil rush had hit Alaska like an epidemic. Atlantic Richfield, the company that until then had been paying no federal taxes, was the first to strike oil in January 1968. The news spread, and other companies joined the hunt, braving weather fifty-five degrees below zero to establish the whereabouts of the oil. The competition was fierce and maintaining secrecy was an important ingredient of success. Some companies hired helicopters to spy on their competitors' drilling rigs. From the size of a pile of pipe, for example, they could work out the depth to which their rivals planned to drill. The competitors' crews in turn switched on hot-water hoses to throw up screens of steam to shield their secrets. Drilling results were reported to head office either by private courier or by coded radio message. A joke went the Arctic rounds: "Are you in oil?" "No, I'm incognito."

By the time the drilling leases were auctioned in Anchorage in September 1969, the secrecy surrounding the rival bids had become bizarre. The state had ruled that bids for its drilling leases must be submitted in sealed envelopes no later than the morning of the sale. The oilmen went to extraordinary lengths to prevent their rivals from learning the size of their bids. One company staying at the Anchorage Westward Hotel reserved the rooms on either side of their own and the rooms above and below to protect themselves against bugging. Another executive turned up with his bid wrapped in aluminum foil in case his competitors had discovered a way of taking X-ray photographs. A consortium headed by Continental Oil hired a private train to shuttle back and forth between Calgary and Edmonton for four days while executives worked out their bids in total secrecy. On the morning of the auction they flew into Anchorage in a company jet to take part in an event Governor Keith Miller of Alaska described as "our rendezvous with destiny." Sitting in a huge concrete auditorium with a map of the north shore pinned up behind them, state officials raffled off in a few hours leases to drill oil worth more than $850 million, a sum that represented more than a hundred times the price the United States paid for the territory in 1867 and the equivalent of $3,000 for every one of the men, women, and children who live there today. Alaska seemed to be awash with money it hardly knew what to do with. The state had received down payments of $180 million in cash, with the balance due ten days later. Officials had calculated that to pay the checks into a bank through the normal channels would cost them $180,000 in lost interest, so they chartered a jet to fly the money to the Bank of America in San Francisco, where it began earning interest next morning.

For a while it seemed as if another Klondike era was about to begin. The national press carried ecstatic articles about the Alaskan "oil fever" and the exploitation of America's last frontier. The air of romanticism was further heightened when the Humble Oil Corporation refitted one of its oil tankers as an icebreaker and sent it off to smash its way through the legendary Northwest Passage.

Although the S S *Manhattan* did make it through to Prudhoe Bay, the voyage was not a success. She arrived in port with a hole in the side of her hull big enough to drive a truck through. The passage the *Manhattan* eventually took was also far to the south of the one originally planned, and even though the pioneer voyage had taken place in September when the Arctic icefloes were at their furthest ebb, the giant tanker was twice stuck in impassable icefloes and had to be rather ignominiously rescued by an accompanying Canadian naval vessel. The fanfare that had accompanied the $40 million voyage obscured these uncomfortable facts for a while, but no further voyages of exploration took place. It looks today as though the plan to ship oil through the Northwest Passage has been quietly dropped, although the General Dynamics Corporation is reported to be working on a scheme to carry the oil *underneath* the twenty-foot icepack in giant tanker submarines.

The oilmen turned instead to their original idea of building a pipeline to carry the oil eight hundred miles across the Arctic tundra to the warmwater port of Valdez, on the southern shore of the state. This project, which they christened TAPS, for Trans-Arctic Pipeline System, placed Alaska's two most precious commodities—oil and the Arctic wilderness—in direct conflict, and when news of the pipeline project was released the environmentalists successfully campaigned to stop it. "I hear them talk, and I hear trees falling in the forest," said one woman conservationist with more poignancy than accuracy (for most of its length, the planned TAPS would run across the bare tundra and not through forests). Still, the environmentalists had a point. The original explorations had been carried out with a reckless disregard for the environment, and the damage left behind by the geophysical survey crews who roamed the Arctic in search of oil can still be seen four or five years later. One bulldozer operator carved his company's initials on the tundra in letters a hundred feet long, and wherever their tracked vehicles went they left a trail of destruction and garbage that seems in the Arctic as durable as the Egyptian pyramids. In summer, tracked vehicles destroy the delicate mat of vegetation that covers the tundra; the ruts they cause later erode into ditches of water several feet deep, so that the damage can never be repaired. The survey crews frequently set up their winter camps on frozen lakes, leaving behind oil drums and heaps of garbage that polluted the water as soon as the ice melted the following spring. Seismic explosions stripped more vegetation from the tundra. Every point they touched, the crews despoiled with the junk of their civilization, which in the Arctic is almost impossible to dispose of. Criticism of these practices was in those days met with outright hostility: "Two years ago this was the frozen hostile North," one oilman irritably declared. "Now all of a sudden, it's the goddam delicate tundra."

The oilmen are more sensitive to the environment today, thanks to the work of the conservationists. Their drilling operations at Prudhoe Bay are in many ways claimed to be models of careful industrial practice. But the damage they had done earlier was not easily forgotten, and when their pipeline project was unveiled it ran into a barrage of criticism. The most colorful objection, and therefore the most publicized, was based on the argument that an overland pipeline would create an impassable barrier right across the path of the annual cariboux migrations. The oilmen replied that in that case they could build their pipe underground, but that proposal raised even greater objections. Oil is pumped while it is quite hot (at about 150 degrees Fahrenheit). At this temperature the pipeline would melt the permafrost, causing the pipe to sink and fracture, with the prospect of spilling oil all over the tundra. Since most of the pipeline route lies across federal land, the Interior Department in Washington intervened and ordered work on the project halted until the oilmen came up with satisfactory answers to these politically dangerous questions.

Fierce debate followed in the Alaska Senate. State Senator Robert Blodgett, the representative from Nome, made a bitter attack on what he called "those damn conservationists in Washington." Over the border in Canada, he declared, not altogether truthfully, "you don't find conservationists messing about with economic development. I'm sick of hearing people in the U.S. who've made garbage cans of their own state. All these do-gooders and bug hunters and bird watchers can mind their own damn business." In spite of Blodgett's angry rhetoric, work on the pipeline project ground to a halt. In 1970, a federal court sided with the environmentalists and ordered the oilmen to produce proof that their pipeline would not cause severe ecological damage. For three years after that the on-again-off-again drama of the pipeline dragged its way through the courts, until President Nixon was forced to asked Congress to pass special legislation to allow construction work to begin. It is expected to take at least until 1974 for work to start, pending the arrival in Washington of an acceptably safe design. Meanwhile, as estimates of the cost grew from the original $900 million to more than $3 billion, hundreds of miles of stockpiled pipe lay rusting in Alaska, and the state complained it faced "unprecedented economic disaster" unless work started soon. The Alaskan oil rush seemed, temporarily at least, to be over before it had ever really begun. "The state," said Newsweek magazine, "has had all the sensations of boom except the smell of real oil and the feel of real money."

4. Company Town

"Will the last person out of Seattle please turn off the light."
—Breadline joke, Boeing factory, 1971

Just before Christmas 1971, a Japanese freighter docked at the quayside in the port of Seattle with an unusual cargo. The ship carried food parcels, donated by the prosperous Japanese for the aerospace workers of Washington State whom the Tokyo press had reported were out of work—and hungry.

The food parcels were admittedly something of a stunt on the part of the status-conscious Japanese, although with one in every eight of its workers out of a job, the need for food in the Seattle area was a real one. Incredible though it may seem in the 1970s, isolated pockets of people *were* going hungry in the pleasantly suburban, once-prosperous city on the far northwestern Pacific seaboard, which was now being described by its own mayor as the "Appalachia of the West."

Seattle had become a classic one-industry town, dependent for its livelihood on the fortunes of a single firm: the Boeing Aircraft Company. For the best part of thirty years Boeing had provided most of the jobs and most of the wealth that had created a boom town out of Seattle. Since the end of the war, its population had increased by more than a third, its per capita income had almost exactly doubled, two families in every three lived in their own detached homes, and with plenty of space still to expand it provided one of the most agreeable city environments in the United States.

Among its population of highly skilled, well-educated scientists and engineers there had been glamour as well as affluence in working for the aerospace industry. In a society dedicated to material success, they had been the winners, the vanguard of America's technological revolution. Boeing had recruited them from as far away as western Europe, and over the years had used their talents to build the Saturn V rocket that carried the first men to the surface of the moon, the bulk of America's strategic bomber fleet, most of its intercontinental ballistic missiles, and the great family of commercial jetliners that had revolutionized the traveling habits of the entire world. By the end of the 1960s, Boeing's jets were outselling its nearest rivals by a ratio of nearly ten to one and were in service with almost every single major airline around the world.

Each year, more and more billions of dollars were poured into the industry to fuel the technological advances that seemed as though they would go on for ever. When the boom reached its peak in 1968, aerospace sales in America were running at the rate of $30 billion a year and providing work for over 1.25 million people, including some of the most highly skilled, best-trained workers in industry. Boeing alone employed 101,500 in the Seattle area, and to most of them their futures seemed completely assured.

It was true that the company had not landed a new defense contract for the previous seven years, and orders were finally tailing off for its family of commercial jets. But as the acknowledged leader of its industry, Boeing had ambitious new plans for the 1970s that promised even greater prosperity. A new commercial jet, the 747 jumbo, then at an advanced stage of planning, was expected to repeat the success of the 707 jets that had been introduced a decade earlier. Beyond that, there was a contract to build the prototype of America's first supersonic passenger aircraft, the SST, which one enthusiastic researcher forecast would be the country's leading export item from 1975 to 1990.

Up in the third-floor boardroom, the company's top executives were not quite so sanguine. They realized the 747 project was a gamble—but it was one they felt fully justified in taking. Boeing was an aggressive company that had fought its way to the top by taking exactly similar hardheaded commercial gambles in the past. The company was proud of its tradition of longterm planning, often for projects as far as ten or fifteen years into the future. Its analyses had nearly always proved to be shrewd, well-timed, and enormously profitable. Under their chairman, William M. Allen, the board concluded they had no alternative to developing the new jumbo jets if they were to keep their commercial lead.

Ironically, the decision to build the jumbos came from Boeing's failure to win a Defense Department contract for the C-5A cargo plane. Lockheed and General Electric had won the competition to build that ill-fated aircraft and its engines, leaving the two losers, Boeing and Pratt & Whitney, looking for a market for their rejected designs.

The result was the 747. Technically, the development of the aircraft was a near-miracle of good planning and brilliant organization. Boeing spent nearly a quarter of a million dollars just to clear an eight-hundred-acre site north of Seattle on which to build an entirely new factory for the 747 production line —the biggest single building in the world. Within three years of the acceptance of the original design, the first 747's had been certified for commercial flight.

At first, the public reaction was ecstatic. "There was an almost frantic move by the airlines to buy this plane," said the general manager of Boeing's commercial aircraft division, Tex Boullioun. "We just invited the presidents of the airlines out and the minute any one of those guys walked into the mockup they realized they couldn't let their competition get ahead on this. They all wanted the best position they could afford."

The scramble to buy was so intense that before the first aircraft had ever flown, Boeing had sold 183 of the jumbos at a cost of around $23 million apiece. The airline executives were just as enthusiastic as Boeing in ushering in what they liked to call the new air age, while their publicity men had a field day with the new aircraft's statistics. Visitors to the 747 plant at Everett were told that the fuselage of the new aircraft was twice as long as Orville Wright's first flight; its tail stood higher off the ground when parked than the Wright brothers' planes ever flew; its cabin, which could hold up to five hundred passengers, was compared to an ocean liner; and there were jokes about "when does this place get to England?" It was pointed out that the tractors that would be used to haul the jumbos around at the airports would themselves cost more than the old DC-3 airliners. A jubilant Pan American executive, in a forecast he must have later regretted, declared that the jumbos would transform the competitive position of his airline, coming just at the right moment to prevent his company from going into the red.

The Nixon recession that ushered in the 1970s brought an abrupt end to Boeing's dreams. The company had been cruelly unlucky in the timing of its jumbos, which began to roll off the production line at the very moment domestic air travel went into its worst slump in history. Simply put, the airlines found they could no longer afford the large fleets of 747's they had ordered. Purchases declined, and as work dried up, Boeing's profits fell in the space of a single year by 88 percent. By 1970, it had sold only half the number of 747's it had projected, and even as it braced itself for the commercial storms that lay ahead, every possible adverse contingency hit the company, one after the other. In a single eighteen-month period, 747 sales dried up into a trickle, defense spending was pared by $4 billion, several potential defense contracts went to other firms and Congress canceled the SST project on which Boeing had built its hopes for the future. In the middle of the crisis, its president and chief executive, Thornton A. Wilson, was stricken with a heart attack. No amount of forward planning could have warded off the disaster that was now imminent.

William Allen, who had managed the company for twenty-five years, was brought back from the verge of retirement to take over again as chief executive. At once he began a desperate program of retrenchment. In the following months, Boeing's workforce fell from its peak of over 100,000 to fewer than 38,000, and the company town that had for so long enjoyed a Boeing boom learned what it was like to suffer a Boeing bust.

It is estimated in Seattle that every Boeing employee creates one other job in the local area, so when the Boeing layoffs began there were no jobs to spare anywhere. The recession that had hit the airlines also struck even harder at the northwest's only other major industry, timber, while the third largest employer, agriculture, was crippled by a prolonged dock strike. At its worst, in May 1971, unemployment in the Seattle-Everett area rose to a devastating 15 percent. The town had been overtaken by the worst economic disaster since the slump of the 1930s.

At first, the townspeople responded to their plight with a grim gallows humor. "Will the last person out of Seattle please turn off the light," went one current joke. "Want to work for a small company?" asked another. "Wait a few months."

But for many in Seattle, the slump brought real tragedy. The people without jobs were for the most part a type of unemployed never seen before in America: well-educated, formerly prosperous professional people, whose plight was made infinitely worse by the trappings of affluence they had gathered during the good years—principally, their houses and their cars. As they tried desperately to hold on to suburban houses they could not afford with a car in the garage they could not run, many of these new poor actually began to starve. Because they still owned property, they were technically ineligible for welfare benefits, and thousands of them were left without any income whatever.

Even if they did want to sell, they found their houses and cars had become unsalable assets in Seattle. A Senate Committee reported on the problem much later:

> The irony of the assets of the New Poor is that they have only bargain-sale value in the open market and therefore could only be sold at staggering losses. The primary problem is that people can't afford food stamps because it requires cash and they won't or can't sell their house or car or other vital family asset.

The fact that people were actually going hungry in Seattle dawned only slowly on the rest of the nation. But local people, only too aware of the distress in their midst, rallied round nobly to help their hungry fellow citizens. A community program called Neighbors in Need was set up by several church groups to distribute free food through a network of thirty-four food banks scattered throughout the area. In its first year, Neighbors in Need gave away an estimated $1.5 million worth of free food to the needy unemployed. Bakeries were persuaded to give away their day-old bread, an airline donated surplus cases of cocktail nuts, farmers gave imperfect but edible produce. A special appeal by the Seattle *Times* brought in $200,000 for the program, mostly from local sources, and the people of Kobe in Japan, Seattle's sister town, made their symbolic gift of food.

It was perhaps the arrival of food parcels from Japan that first brought Seattle's plight to the center of national attention. Until that time, the U.S. Department of Agriculture had declined to participate in the food-bank program, even though surplus farm produce was going to waste all across the nation. Senator Warren G. Magnuson of Washington State made effective propaganda of the Japanese shipment in an emotional speech delivered on the floor of the Senate. "I stand in total humiliation," he told his fellow Senators. "The hungry people of Seattle, Washington, are being kept from starvation by mercy shipments of food from Japan while the U.S. government . . . refuses to open its warehouses to these starving women, children, and unemployed men." USDA's decision, he said, was "the most hard-hearted disregard of human suffering I have ever witnessed."

It is not for nothing that Magnuson is sometimes known to his colleagues as "the Senator from Boeing." Within fifteen minutes of his searing attack, an Agriculture Department official telephoned the governor of Washington State, Daniel J. Evans, to tell him a government food-relief program would be established immediately. Three weeks later, the first USDA store was opened in Seattle, and while the financial hardships continued, the crisis of suburban hunger seemed to be finally at an end.

"There is still a lot of tragedy around," said the mayor of Seattle. "The only hope we have lies in our people. They are rugged and resourceful, and eventually we will perhaps come out all the stronger for this." His optimism was shared by many of the unemployed. Having enjoyed a privileged position in society, many aerospace workers retained a surprisingly strong faith that good times would return again; that they only had to sit out the slump and, sooner or later, the Boeing boom would come back. "These aerospace people are well-trained," said a Washington State social worker. "They have a lot of confidence in themselves. They are confident they can make it, and many of them just aren't leaving."

For nearly a year, almost no one moved out of Seattle. The slump in aerospace was countrywide, so there were no jobs to go to anyway in other cities, but still they hung on with great tenacity. Eventually, about a third of Boeing's unemployed scientists and engineers did find other work, even if it was only a parttime job at the local filling station. One man with four degrees earned a parttime income peddling correspondence courses. Even those on the breadline stayed on in the hope that Boeing would eventually win new contracts and take them back.

But gradually, the realization began to dawn that the slump was likely to last longer than any of them had anticipated. By the summer of 1972, Boeing had fallen from its proud place as the state's largest employer into third place, with a payroll that was stabilizing around 45,000 workers. "Many people held out a long time," said a state official. "But now they are confronting the hard reality that they will have to transfer."

One of the biggest ironies was Boeing's discovery that, when it had to, it could produce its 747's with far fewer workers than it had previously thought possible. Also, the great demands for labor arise mainly during the research and prototype-testing phases, and with the cancelation of the SST, Boeing was left with no prototypes, no big new aircraft coming along, and therefore no work in prospect for the specialists who draw the plans, make the tools, and test the countless parts that go into a new aircraft. It looks today as though the 747, now in routine production, may be the company's last big new development for many years to come.

The employment boom of the late 1960s had also led to what the management euphemistically called "skill dilution." In other words, rapid sales had been acquired at the cost of productive inefficiency, and the company made it clear it intended never again to fall into the trap of over-rapid expansion. Boeing's president, T. A. Wilson, by then recovered from his heart attack, summarized the company's new problems in a 1972 address to the local chamber of commerce. "We will not soon forget," he said, "the traumatic experience we have been through in the past few years and neither will you in the community, I expect. We don't like to turn down available business, but thinking of the future, we would not want to expand again in one location as fast as we did prior to 1968. Adding people at that rate is not necessarily good for the community—or for the company."

By this time, Boeing was busy with plans for diversification. Never again did the company intend to get caught with all its eggs in one basket, and Wilson appointed a board-level committee to study the possibility for new projects. "Our objective," he said, "is to have thirty-three percent of Boeing's total business in nontraditional areas by 1980." As a result, the company is already involved in building a mass-transit system in West Virginia, a desalination project in the Virgin Islands, and an experimental agricultural community in northern Oregon. "Even for the Boeing Company," said a senior vice president, "it's never too late to start hauling manure, irrigating land, and planting potatoes."

Those brave words epitomize the peculiarly American notion that technological solutions can be found for almost any problem, that skills and manpower—and above all, expertise—have only to be applied at the right places in the right quantities for the problems to disappear. It is a trait that comes from deep within the American psyche. While older nations often claim to find it naive, it has for generations been the source of the self-confidence they so envy in the American people. It remains to be seen whether Seattle's aerospace workers can successfully transform themselves into farmers, or even whether the complicated problems of the 1970s and 1980s are amenable to the simplistic technological solutions of the past. But there can be no doubt that the energy is there—and so is the will to succeed.

5. The Air War

"For my part, I travel not to go anywhere, but to go. I travel for travel's sake. The great affair is to move."
— ROBERT LOUIS STEVENSON, *Travels with a Donkey, 1879*

More than any people on earth, Americans are a nation of travelers. Like Stevenson on his donkey, their great affair is to move. By car, by train, but above all, by air, they are a people in motion, crisscrossing their great country from the Atlantic to California, from the Great Lakes to the Gulf of Mexico. On any normal weekday, half a million of them take to the air with one of the main domestic airlines for business trips or family reunions, annual vacations or just an evening out in another town. In 1972, the airlines carried a total of 175 million passengers across the sprawling continent on journeys that account for 60 percent of all the air travel anywhere in the world.

Geography is the reason that Americans travel by air. In the 1970s, there is no other practical way for a businessman to make the three-thousand-mile journey from New York across to California, or for a holidaymaker to take the thirteen-hundred-mile escape-route from the bitter snows of Chicago to the winter sunshine of Miami.

It is no exaggeration to say the country has been transformed by the jetliners of Boeing and McDonnell Douglas that were introduced in the late 1950s. In the following decade, domestic and international airlines boomed as never before, as they catered to the peripatetic cravings of this nation of travelers.

In the ten years from 1959, when the first longrange 707 jet went into service with Pan American World Airways, Boeing and McDonnell Douglas between them sold over 2,000 of their jets to the airlines of America. United, the biggest airline of all, now has a fleet of over 380 jets, which together fly over a million miles every day of the year.

In the mid-1970s, the ten biggest airlines, measured in terms of their operating revenues, were:

		Employees
1.	United Air Lines (Chicago)	52,312
2.	Trans World Airlines (New York)	58,606
3.	American Airlines (New York)	35,469
4.	Pan American World Airways (New York)	36,181
5.	Eastern Air Lines (Miami)	30,900
6.	Delta Air Lines (Atlanta)	20,800
7.	Northwest Airlines (St. Paul)	10,114
8.	Braniff Airways (Dallas)	9,466
9.	Continental Air Lines (Los Angeles)	8,349
10.	Western Airlines (Los Angeles)	9,039

Traditionally, air travel has always been something of a switchback business, lurching from champagne to cinders and back again in an exaggerated parody of the national business cycle. Good times bring untold riches to the airlines; bad times grind them to the point of bankruptcy. Since President Nixon came to office, the American airlines have ridden the switchback more fiercely than ever before, dropping from the heights of the biggest boom in their history down to the depths of their worst slump ever and then back again, with a recovery so sudden it startled even the sober accountants who manage the airlines' finances.

As recently as 1970, the twelve major domestic airlines lost $200 million. Several of them had been brought to the verge of bankruptcy, including some of the most familiar carriers of all: TWA, Pan American, and United. Trans World that year lost nearly $100 million,* the largest loss any airline has ever suffered in a single twelve-month period; United lost $46 million, the biggest loss in its forty-six-year history; Pan Am lost $48 million.

What tipped them so dramatically into the red was a sharp slump in air travel, brought on by the Nixon recession, coupled with their own spending spree on new aircraft that left them with a huge excess seating capacity at the very moment they least needed it.

When they are hit by a travel slump, there is very little the individual airlines can do to increase their competitive position; that is one of the reasons for their melodramatic drop in profits. The cost of almost everything in air transportation is decided elsewhere: fares are regulated by the Civil Aeronautics Board, a body that also allocates the routes; landing fees are further controlled; and the cost of fuel and new aircraft is the same for everyone. In the middle of a slump, the best a hard-pressed airline can do is fire as many of its staff as it dares and join in the competition to provide the service frills that attract passengers away from other airlines—tastier cocktail nuts, sexier stewardesses, and more exotic meals. Real competition is in fact illegal: the CAB will not allow them to cut fares (or increase them), or except in very rare

---

*Pushed down in the books to $64 million by pulling in tax credits and some hotel sales.

cases to cut their flights on unprofitable routes, or even to give their passengers a few more inches of leg room. The result, inevitably, is empty aircraft in the skies and red ink in the ledger.

When the recession became apparent in the summer of 1969, the better-managed airlines began an immediate economy drive and waited hopefully for the passengers to return. United Airlines, for example, ordered the pilots on its fleet of DC-8 jets to cut their cruising speed by fifteen miles an hour. Company experts had worked out that this would save the airline seven million dollars a year in fuel bills. The savings in the first year actually came to nine million dollars, and it is doubtful if one passenger in ten thousand knew the reason why it was taking them a few extra minutes to reach their destination.

Similar economies were made at TWA under its aggressively competitive chairman, Charles Tillinghast, who fired nearly 12 percent of his staff. Five thousand people lost their jobs with TWA, from the top of the company to the bottom. Cargo flights were cut by about one fifth, and as many jets as could be spared were sold off or leased out to charter lines. As a result, by the skin of its teeth, TWA survived. Its record loss of 1970 was turned around within twelve months into a small profit. A dramatic upturn in passenger traffic in the final quarter of 1971 came just in time to save the airline from probable bankruptcy. "The traffic turnaround came up from one day to the next," said a TWA official. "It's probably what saved us."

Pan Am, however, has been less fortunate. While most of the other airlines are now recovering from the losses they incurred during the recession, Pan Am is not. The company's problems are more intractable than those of the other carriers. In the first place, it has no domestic routes and must rely entirely on overseas business for its revenue. That was a policy imposed on the company by its founder, Juan T. Trippe, who lobbied hard to make Pan Am the country's "chosen instrument" in international aviation. Trippe worked effectively on his contacts at the State Department to win for Pan Am a near-monopoly position in many overseas markets, in exchange for which the airline flew many low-density development routes that were deemed to serve the State Department's foreign policy objectives. Gradually, however, Pan Am's monopoly was eroded, first by the foreign airlines that were granted reciprocal service rights, then by the invasion of some of its most profitable routes by other American airlines. Pan Am suffered badly, for example, when National Airlines was granted the lucrative franchise for daily flights on the Miami-to-London run, while other airlines nibbled away at the edges of the Pan Am empire in the Caribbean and the South Pacific.

Pan Am was also unlucky in timing the introduction of the new 747 jumbo jets. Its thirty-three jumbos, far more than any other airline possesses, cost the company over $750 million, which it raised mostly in longterm loans. On top of this it paid $90 million for a new maintenance-and-service installation at Kennedy Airport in New York, and another $50 million-odd on its new passenger terminal there, the first to be built specially to handle the 747 traffic.

Ten years earlier, Pan Am had gambled heavily on the introduction of the first jet aircraft, and had seen that gamble pay off royally. This time, it was not so lucky. The argument in favor of the 747's had been based on increased productivity: the jumbos were designed to operate at a cost per passenger of about one third below that of the conventional jets—provided they were able to fill a comparable number of seats. Projections based on the growing traffic of the 1960s had been optimistic; according to all the best calculations, the yield per passenger mile, the standard by which airlines measure their revenue, should have shown a sensational improvement. But Pan Am's calculations were erroneous. In 1971, the carrier's fleet of jumbos were flying on average with only 45.7 percent of their seats filled. The 707's they replaced had never flown less than half full.

At the same time, operating costs for the jumbos increased sharply, due largely to inflation, while on the most profitable routes across the North Atlantic, the charter airlines were taking a greater and greater share of the business. But perhaps the biggest blow came during merger talks with TWA, which was then believed to be in far worse trouble than Pan Am. The Pan Am directors learned with shock that even while it was suffering the worst year in airline history, TWA was being run more efficiently. Over the North Atlantic routes, where the operations of the two lines could be most fairly compared, TWA's costs were several percentage points better than those of Pan Am. Had it been able to run its fleet as efficiently as its rival, its losses would have been converted into a substantial profit.

The chairman of Pan Am during the crisis was Najeeb E. Halaby, a former Air Force general of Syrian extraction, known to his colleagues as "Jeeb." Halaby took over as chief executive just as the recession began in 1969, having been handpicked for the succession four years earlier by Juan Trippe. The two men had first met when Halaby was head of the Federal Aviation Agency, a post he was given by President Kennedy. From the first, Jeeb Halaby was Pan Am's heir apparent, although, having had no previous airline experience, he was regarded by many of his colleagues as an interloper and given inadequate training to run the company. For four years after he joined Pan Am, Halaby's job had nothing to do with running the airline business. He held instead a post he later called "senior vice president—miscellaneous," running the business-jet division, military rest-and-recreation flights from Vietnam, and some of the company's international hotel operations.

When he took over the company, first as president and chief executive, then as chairman, Halaby quickly gained a reputation for boardroom ruthlessness. Within two years of his accession, no fewer than thirty-six of the company's top managers had been fired, retired, or forced to resign, and Halaby sought to replace them with his own—outside—appointees. Unfortunately, according to an old associate quoted in *Newsweek* magazine, "His guys weren't winners either." Pan Am, said the associate, remained "full of bickering, jealousy, and animus . . . Halaby was never able to handle it."

Halaby had attempted to restore company morale by hiring a team of industrial psychologists, who promptly spent $100,000 on a "management laboratory." High-ranking executives were summoned by the psychologists to attend sensitivity-training sessions, and *Fortune* chronicled the story of one senior vice president, James Weesner, who was ordered to take his top staff a hundred miles to attend a "management and organizational development laboratory" at Montauk Point on the eastern tip of Long Island. After a couple of days, Weesner said, the psychologists in charge gave up in frustration. "They said we were the most hopeless group they had seen," he recalled, "and that we might as well go home." The senior executives resented it when Halaby consulted the psychologists on matters of sensitive company policy, and the shrinks were finally discredited after one of them turned up at the company's annual meeting of shareholders wearing a knitted one-piece jumpsuit. For the conventional executives from New York, that was just too much to take, and thereafter the psychologists' influence waned noticeably.

Another source of friction inside the company was Halaby's attempt to divide executive responsibility among a team of four vice presidents who were supposed to work in tandem, but who in fact fell out among themselves and became known in the firm as "the Alexandria Quartet."

Halaby can hardly be blamed for all of Pan Am's problems. The decision to buy the fleet of jumbos was made personally by his predecessor, and the slump in business was shared by all the airlines. He was also unable to do much to alleviate the longterm problems that arose from the company's lack of any domestic routes. He did his best to cut operating costs, and in good times would probably have been able to negotiate a successful merger with one of the domestic carriers and so develop a more viable network of air routes. But with cumulative losses that were climbing near to a hundred million dollars, Pan Am could not offer much of a dowry.

Because of the intricacies of airline accounting, Pan Am could go on running up losses for several more years before it actually ran out of money, but when the other airlines climbed back into profitability and Pan Am did not, the board finally ran out of patience.

In the first two months of 1972—long after most other airlines were showing a healthy profit again—Pan Am's losses were worse than ever: $12 million in January, another $11 million in February. The board looked around for a scapegoat and found one in Halaby. In April 1972, he was fired.

He did not leave quietly, as the board had probably hoped. "I did the best I could in the time available to me," he said in his resignation statement. "I truly believe it will be a miracle if the new team does any better. Pan Am is in deep, deep trouble."

Many in the airline industry agreed. It was widely believed in the industry that Washington would sooner or later have to be called in to mount a major rescue operation for its chief overseas carrier. No airline could absorb indefinitely the sort of losses that Pan Am had piled up in the early years of the Nixon Administration.

CHAPTER VI

Labor

1. Blue-Collar Blues

"Above all, the average worker wants a job in which he does not have to think."
—HENRY FORD, *1922*

"Do you know what I do? I fix seven bolts. Seven bolts! Day in and day out, the same seven bolts. What do I think about? Raquel Welch!"
—GM striker, Tarrytown, New York, 1970

To the college-educated, a man who earns his living by physical toil is nowa-days often referred to as a "hardhat"—a pejorative term, which in current American usage has taken on the overtones of a sneer, a term denoting not just a worker, but a political reactionary, a racist, a bigot, and an ignoramus. This use of a nickname clearly intended to demean is a measure of the abrupt decline in status suffered by the average working-class American during the chaotic decade from which he has just emerged.

The decline in the worker's status has been sudden, for barely a single decade ago he was still regarded as a fully paid-up member of the affluent society, secure in his role and firm in his belief in the traditional working-class virtues of hard work, unspoken patriotism, and a steady and orderly mode of life. In those days, he also carried a more dignified title, and liked to call himself a "blue-collar" worker, a term that at least *implied* full equality of status with his better-educated, better-paid fellows who wore white collars and worked in an office. Yet today, overwhelmed by social and technological changes that have transformed both his workplace and his neighborhood, he has become a resentful and bewildered "hardhat."

Many hypotheses have been offered to explain the crisis of morale that affects the American working community today. It is often claimed—fre-quently by the workers themselves—that the blue-collar malaise is the result of a double bind: an economic squeeze on one side, caused by inflation and rising prices which are not matched by the workers' increased paychecks, and on the other a social squeeze, in which the working man sees his valued position in society threatened by minority groups, especially blacks, whose wage gains have exceeded those of white workers in recent years. These are the fears that lead to the accusations of bigotry and racism and the political exploitation of such artificial hardhat issues as school busing and law and order. President Nixon began it in the election campaigns of 1968 and 1970 with his appeals to the "Silent Majority" and what he called "The Forgotten Americans." The movement received further impetus with the appeal to baser prejudices launched by Governor George Wallace in his two presidential campaigns. The workers themselves often echo these emotions: Eugene Schafer, a New York ironworker who ran as Democratic candidate for the state assembly from Brooklyn, delcared in a 1970 election address, "I think I'm a forgotten American because my community is falling apart. The streets are caving in, the sanitation's lousy, the sewer system stinks, industry's gone out of the community, welfare's on the rise."

Politicians and many workers themselves have helped to implant these impressions of the blue-collar stereotype; a man mad at government for burdening him with an unfair tax load, pushed around by "pointy-head" bureaucrats in Washington, and hurting financially because of inflation. In fact, most of the assumptions that underlie blue-collar discontent are based if not on untruths, at least on gross oversimplifications. The discontent is real enough, but it is based mostly on the workers' *perception* of what is wrong, and many of them think they are much worse off than they really are. A recent symposium,* for example, found that financially, in spite of the inflationary squeeze that undoubtedly existed, blue-collar workers had achieved the same relative increase in earnings as other workers during the past decade. Nor were they paying disproportionately for such items as welfare contributions and other public-assistance programs that were thought to account for the strong antiblack feelings often found in working-class neighborhoods. In reality, the study found, "tax as a proportion of income . . . has probably not changed very much; and the magnitude of the change—one tenth of one per cent—suggests that this change could not have caused a significant rise in blue-collar alienation."

Yet the paradox remains. Manual workers are, without doubt, increasingly disillusioned and disenchanted with their role in American society. The reasons are perhaps deeper and more profound than is commonly realized, the result of a basic transformation of the old work ethic and a marked change in the attitude of society, which has tended in recent years to downgrade the traditional dignity and honor of manual work. "You make fun of the plumber and the carpenter and the working man," says Nat Goldfinger, a trade-union research director. "Today, all the emphasis is on the Ph. D. degree, upon the mathematician, the scientist, the engineer, and so forth. The hardhat . . . is viewed almost as the enemy within."

His point is reinforced by the Assistant Secretary of Labor, Jerome Rosow,

*Blue Collar Workers: A Symposium on Middle America, edited by Sar A. Levitan, McGraw-Hill, New York, 1971.

who believes that "all blue-collar workers, skilled or not, have been denigrated so badly, so harshly, that their jobs have become a last resort, instead of decent, respected careers. Fathers hesitate—and even apologize—for their occupation, instead of holding it up as an aspiration for their own sons." Rosow's impressions were repeated, almost word for word, in a controversial government-sponsored study* in which a research team reported, "Our interviews with blue-collar workers revealed an almost overwhelming sense of inferiority. The worker cannot talk proudly to his children about his job, and many workers feel that they must apologize for their status." Significant numbers of workers were dissatisfied with their working lives, the study found, suggesting that increasing prosperity and better education were important factors in this, as well as a yearning for "interesting work." In fact, among all the workers surveyed, "good pay" was ranked only fifth in importance in weighing the value of their jobs; individual responsibility, job interest, and the chance to use personal skills were all rated higher.

The HEW study group also found an interesting corollary between job dissatisfaction and alienated behavior from society as a whole—an indication that the blue-collar malaise may be psychological, even spiritual, in its origins, rather than merely economic. It seems no accident that workers employed in degrading production-line jobs are the most likely to support extremist candidates for public office, those like George Wallace, whose exploitation of the workers' frustrations with big business, big government, court-ordered busing, and high taxes carried him in 1972 to primary election victory in states such as Michigan, once a reliable bulwark of the New Deal Democrats and their successors. There is real evidence, the HEW report said, that political and social attitudes are related to work expectation and experience. Where aspirations relating to work were not realized, it was common to find a degree of bitterness and alienation among workers that was reflected in a reduced sense of political efficacy. "These alienated workers," the report continued, "tend to participate less in elections, and when they do vote, tend to cast their ballots for extremist or 'protest' candidates. These dissatisfied workers are far more likely than satisfied workers to believe that the lot of the average person has been getting worse. They are more authoritarian in their views. They tend to prefer strong leaders to democratically developed law."

Not all American workers find themselves in this bind, of course. White-collar workers now make up almost half the total work force and another 16 percent work on farms and in service industries. In fact, of the 83 million Americans holding fulltime or parttime jobs, only about 19 million are engaged in manufacturing industries, with perhaps one million of them working on assembly lines, where the crisis has been concentrated. So it is easy to

---

* *Work in America*, published in December 1972 by the Upjohn Institute for Employment Research under a grant from the Department of Health, Education, and Welfare.

exaggerate the extent of the alienation, and a Gallup poll conducted in 1973 did not altogether bear out the sweeping pessimism of the HEW study. Gallup found 77 percent of the workers he interviewed were satisfied with their work, which is still a very tidy majority, even though this represents a decline of about 10 percent since the same question was asked in 1960. However, Gallup did find young workers under thirty were substantially more dissatisfied with their jobs than older workers, adding that the results indicated "a greater degree of discontent today than we have found for a number of years—particularly among young persons. I think it is safe to say that young workers dissatisfied with their jobs pose a growing threat to United States industrial output."

The same findings are repeated in study after study, all suggesting the same thing: there is a growing generation gap within the working community and, among younger workers at any rate, a loss of pride in their position and their workmanship that represents a basic change in the old attitudes towards the work ethic. Hard Work is no longer its own reward.

In a perceptive series of articles on the labor movement prepared for the Washington *Post*, the most striking conclusions concerned the changing attitudes of young workers towards their jobs. "The young worker's complaint is simple," wrote the *Post*'s reporters. "He says he hates his job, particularly the monotonous factory job. At times, he hates it so much that he deliberately will throw a monkey wrench into the machinery, or turn to drugs to escape the boredom." To a remarkable degree, they found young workers shared common attitudes with the far more publicized—and favored—young college students. "Call it what you will," they concluded, "counter-culture, drug culture, anti-establishment feeling or youth rebellion—the same forces are motivating both groups."

It is this new attitude toward work that lies behind the workers' dropping morale as well as the associated absenteeism, the industrial sabotage, and the problems of quality control that plague much of American industry today. In the automobile industry both Ford and General Motors have on occasion had to close down entire plants because not enough employees had turned up for work. When this happened at one plant in Baltimore, the plant manager sent out letters to the workers addressed "Dear fellow employee and family" and asked for their "best efforts in being at work every day on time." But the workers are not often impressed by such pleas. William Serrin tells the story of one welder who was asked why had had taken an unauthorized day off, why he was willing to get by on four days of pay a week instead of five. "The welder stopped," Serrin said, "raised his welding gun, tipped back his visor, and said, 'Because I can't get by on three.' "

A massive example of this contemporary malaise came to light early in 1972 during a threatened strike over working conditions at GM's much-vaunted new factory at Lordstown, Ohio, where the company's new Vega cars are produced. The plant had been built in Ohio farmland, away from the sup- posedly malign city influence of Detroit, and opened only two years earlier as a model factory, constructed around entirely new principles of automation and intensive worker motivation which the management believed the employees would take to "very strongly."

In its efforts to increase productivity, GM had both simplified and inten- sified the work expected from the men on the assembly lines. Instead of the usual sixty cars an hour, the Vega assembly line moves at an incredible one hundred cars an hour, a speedup made possible by brilliant new engineering practices, including robot welders known as Unimates and greatly simplified assembly methods. As a result, the workers on the line face no fewer than eight hundred Vegas in every eight-hour shift—or one car every thirty-six seconds. Some workers, conjuring up latter-day visions of Charlie Chaplin in *Modern Times*, complained that they actually had to run along the assembly line to keep up with their jobs. "B-z-z-t! It runs past you," said one worker describing his assembly-line job. "You know, b-z-z-t! Well, how much concentrated thought does it take to do that? It makes you feel unwanted, it makes you feel part of the machinery."

So at Lordstown, whose employees incidentally are among the highest-paid industrial workers in the world, the men rebelled. The GM management began to complain of "tardiness, loitering, failure to follow instructions, and abuse of employee facilities." In some periods, absenteeism rose as high as 16 percent, and there were complaints that workers had attacked the paint, bodies, upholstery, and controls of cars. A reward of five-thousand dollars was offered for information about a fire in the electrical controls of the assembly line itself.

Nor was the problem confined to GM. At a nearby Chrysler plant in Detroit, a recent study found that in some departments nearly 65 percent of the workforce were using drugs of one form or another, often heroin. The company tried to cover it up; they did not want the public to get hold of the idea that their cars were being built by junkies. But the problem had become so acute, the employees themselves had felt compelled to start their own drug-abuse control program.

Management claims this sort of discontent has no connection with the speedup and the increasingly monotonous nature of assembly-line work. Jo- seph E. Godfrey, the head of GM's Assembly Division, which runs the Lordstown plant, echoed Henry Ford when he declared in an interview with *Automotive News* that the factory experienced its biggest problems when the so-called "monotony" of the work was disturbed. "The workers complain about monotony," he said, "but years spent in the factories leads me to believe that they like to do their jobs automatically. If you interject new things, you spoil the rhythm of the job, and work gets fouled up."

Other observers, especially the workers themselves, disagree with Mr. Godfrey's assessment. "Sure, we read how the working man today has no pride in his work," said an auto union leader. "And it's true. But what you don't read is how the company has broken down the work into smaller and smaller units, so that no man can feel pride in what he's doing. If they'd just let us build a car occasionally. Just one."

That plea for the restoration of the working man's pride in his job is echoed throughout industry. Robert Georgine, secretary-treasurer of the building trades department of the AFL-CIO, told the Washington *Post*, "When I go on the job today, I get sick at what I see. Pride in workmanship is almost nil. It is a fact that today, for many reasons, the young fellow coming in now is not as productive as his counterpart before. Productivity is our biggest problem."

Whatever the reason, whether they are exploited by management or pampered by it, whether they are too powerful or not powerful enough, alienated by the nature of the work or just plain bored, the young American workers of the seventies have lost their fathers' rock-firm belief in the work ethic. They have begun to demand more, and offer less. Since 1967, industrial productivity has risen only 4 percent; at the same time, unit labor costs have gone up by over 16 percent. Partly as a result, many industries run grave risks of losing their markets to foreigners through their inability to compete. Even GM's automated Vega had to be sold for $211 more than the imported Volkswagens that it was supposed to replace—the result, according to GM, of higher US labor costs. Similar examples have arisen in the steel industry, chemicals, radio, television and typewriter manufacture, and many others. In the 1970s, Americans buy almost all their tape recorders and still cameras from foreign suppliers, together with 70 percent of their radios, 49 percent of their sewing machines, 40 percent of their glassware, 35 percent of their shoes, and around 16 percent of their motor cars. Not all of this can be put down to the workers, of course, but there is a real danger in the 1970s that American industry is losing its competitive edge. It is perhaps unfair to blame the workman, but many consumers and many managements do, while the workers themselves tend to put the blame on cheap foreign labor—both of which are perhaps simplistic analyses. It is true that for years American wages have been the highest in the world, but this has been more than compensated for by high productivity. The real blame lies elsewhere: the restrictive trade policies of Japan, for instance, which have systematically shut out American goods, and even more important, the combination of domestic inflation and rigid exchange rates that, until devaluation, allowed foreign competitors to sell their goods in the United States at unrealistically low prices, establishing in those years a foothold in the American consumer market that is proving difficult to dislodge.

All this marks, perhaps, the end of the American blue-collar dream, which flowered briefly in the period from the end of the Great Depression until sometime in the middle of the 1960s. The American worker then lived in a world in which his rising expectations were matched by actual achievement, with a standard of living that was far and away the highest of any working community in the world, double that of his nearest rivals in Western Europe. He had his own house, his own car, his expensive hobbies, he was the envy of workers everywhere else, and the cornucopia of technology seemed to offer him endless expectations of the same. But somewhere in the 1960s, the dream soured; the technology which had helped to make his standard of living so high became enshrined as an end in itself, instead of just the means to a better way of life. He discovered that the same technology that had given him affluence at the same time took away from him qualities which in the end may prove to be even more precious than wealth. The real roots of the hardhat's discontent lie in the loss of respect for himself as a craftsman, loss of pride in a dead-end job, and above all, loss of that social status which is important to any member of the community.

It is too early yet to say where this disenchantment will lead him and his country. Some observers profess to see America withdrawing under the pressures into a protective shell of economic isolationism. There have certainly been plenty of cries for protection fom the entrenched leaders of the American unions. Once, when asked how he proposed to keep competitively priced foreign goods from coming into the United States, George Meany replied simply, "Lock them out, the same as they lock us out." Mr. Meany and many other labor leaders believe that if industry were forced to compete at home with foreign products, the result would be a low-wage economy, with a low standard of living for the American people. "It's just that simple," he says. "We would have to reduce our wages to the wages of the Japanese or the Formosans or the people in Hong Kong, or something like that."

To other nations, such words come as a shock. .To most of them it is inconceivable that the United States could withdraw behind such an archaic barrier of subsidized production and national mercantilism, the most likely outcome of which would be a world trade recession on the scale of the 1930s. Yet protectionism is now the official policy of the American labor movement, and the experience of the seventies has so far served to harden rather than soften the isolationist line taken by many of the labor leaders. Should those views ever be translated into real political action, the whole world would be made to pay for the disillusionment of the American hardhat.

2. Old Leaders, New Problems

"A lot of my colleagues are products of an era and an environment that is no longer in existence."

—JERRY WURF, *president, American Federation of State, County & Municipal Employees*

The outstanding characteristic of American trade unionism, and the one that distinguishes it from trade-union movements just about everywhere else in the world, is its devotion to the principles of capitalism. Members of American unions stand by no firm political ideology, as do, for example, the workers of Britain, Australia, and West Germany. Still less do they flirt with communism, as do some unions in France, Italy, and Japan. Here in America, they buy the system and are bothered not at all by the political side-issues that occupy trade union movements elsewhere; such goals as the pursuit of socialism, the nationalization of industry, or the organization of a political "Labor" party on the British model. In the eyes of some, the sole political slogan of the American union movement is "more"—more wages, more power, more old-fashioned "pull," more influence on the legislative process. As a result, the American union movement is unique—at once stronger and yet in some important respects weaker than its counterparts in the rest of the world.

The unions themselves have traditionally shunned the quest for party power. "I don't think we're ready and I don't think we're qualified to run the government" is the view of George Meany, President of the American Federation of Labor—Congress of Industrial Organizations. "I don't think any special-interest group is qualified to run the government. I don't think General Motors should run the government, and I don't think the AFL-CIO should run the government."

All of which is not to say that the American union movement does not possess immense political power. Quite clearly, it does possess that power, although it chooses to use it for simpler and perhaps narrower ends than union movements elsewhere. "George Meany is not running a labor movement," says Herbert Hill of the NAACP. "George Meany and his colleagues are now businessmen engaged in the business of unions."

Labor owes this business tradition to the man who virtually founded the union movement in America, a London-born cigarmaker called Samuel Gompers, a man of legendary conservatism. In a period when free-enterprise America was bitterly hostile to labor organizations, Gompers evolved the peculiarly capitalistic principles on which the movement is still based. As president of the American Federation of Labor from its formation in 1886 until his death in 1924, he was the man who made unionism respectable in America. Gompers' deep distrust of intellectual reformers and socialists, traits fully inherited by his modern successors, helped to concentrate the labor movement's sights on purely economic goals and away from the dangers of radical politics and "irresponsible" strikes.

Gompers died in harness in 1924, his goals only partly accomplished. Since then the AFL has been led by only two other men: William Green, who held office from 1924 until his death at the age of eighty-two, and George Meany, who was Green's chief assistant for twelve years before succeeding him in 1952. From his wood-paneled office in the center of Washington, with a window that looks *down* on the White House, Meany has ruled the labor roost now for a full twenty years and reaches his eightieth birthday in 1974. There are some who believe this irascible, cigar-chewing labor leader may be the most powerful man in America today. Like Gompers, his spiritual grandfather, Meany too is a man of legendary conservatism, a leader whose views on many issues have been well to the right of every President since the war. On the domestic front, he speaks with sulphurous fury about "long-haired kookies," and in foreign affairs, which he looks after for the AFL-CIO almost as a personal hobby, he stood steadfastly in support of the war in Vietnam and even came out against President Nixon's visit to China, which he described with a characteristic snort as "the number one stunt by the number one stunt man of our time."

His relations with Nixon have been stormy, although by withholding support from George McGovern in the presidential election campaign of 1972, Meany was responsible as much as anyone for the President's re-election landslide that year. But while he has given the President support on such issues as the Vietnam War, the supersonic transport, and the Lockheed loan, he has withheld it on Nixon's supposedly antilabor Supreme Court nominations and the early Pay Board. As one of the central building-blocks on which the New Deal coalition had been built, the labor movement had been taken for granted by the Democrats, but since 1972 Meany has struck a decidedly neutral pose. "My opinion," he once said, "is that the Republican Party stinks, and the Democratic Party is almost as bad. . . . If we are in the pockets of the Democrats, we are not that important." George Meany has made it quite clear he does not sit in anyone's pocket, though his support has been carefully wooed by every President since Kennedy. President Johnson, with his passion for statistics, recalled that he personally conferred with Meany forty-nine times during his tenure of the White House, and another eighty-two times on the telephone.

Meany, an Irish-American, left high school at sixteen to become an apprentice plumber in his home neighborhood in the Bronx, but from the start he seems to have had his eye on a union career, following in the footsteps of his father, who was president of a Bronx plumbers' local.

In 1922, Meany became a union business agent. By 1934 he was president of the New York State Federation of Labor. His success as a lobbyist in Albany brought him to the attention of national labor leaders, and in 1939 he came to Washington as the AFL's secretary-treasurer, taking over as president in 1952. In union affairs, his prime achievement in his early years as president was the merger of the AFL with the Congress of Industrial Organizations, the other main union body in America, then headed by Walter Reuther. The alliance they forged was, in the scornful words of John L. Lewis, "a rope of sand," but it is one that, like its leader, has stood the test of time, even though the two biggest unions of all have since left the fold: the United Auto Workers quitting to preserve their social idealism, the Teamsters expelled because of corruption.

Meany is sensitive to charges that he has become too old and too out-of-touch with contemporary currents of American life. Yet the organization he heads is said to have the oldest leadership of any body in the western world outside the Vatican Curia. By 1973, the average age of the thirty-five men who make up the executive council of the AFL-CIO had reached sixty-five years, and most of the senior ones were well over seventy, products of an era in American life that has long since passed away. The common forces that shaped them, including the bitter antiunion antagonisms of the 1920s and the slump of the 1930s, are today not even memories to the majority of the young workers they lead.

The power of these old men is immense, although it is by no means as deeply entrenched as is commonly supposed, and rests on a comparatively narrow—and dwindling—constituency. Of the more than eighty million Americans currently listed in the labor force, fewer than twenty million are union members; that is, only one in every four, or more precisely 27.4 percent of the total. Union membership is still expanding, but not nearly so fast as the work force and the percentage belonging to the unions has been declining ever since it reached its peak in 1955.

Meany himself worries not a whit about the declining proportion of workers who join the unions. When asked by *U.S. News & World Report* why union membership was not growing as fast as the country's labor force, he replied bluntly, "I don't know. I don't care." He argues that American unions have never had a large proportion of the work force and numbers make no difference anyway. "It's the organized vote that counts," he says. "The organized fellow is the fellow who counts—not just in legislation; anyplace. . . . Why should I worry about organizing groups of people who do not appear to want to be organized?"

The ten biggest unions today, measured in terms of their membership, are:

		Membership	*President*	*Age*
1.	Teamsters	2,020,000	Frank E. Fitzsimmons	65
2.	United Auto Workers	1,350,000	Leonard Woodcock	61
3.	Steelworkers	1,200,000	I. W. Abel	63
4.	Electrical Workers	977,295	Joseph D. Keenan	74
5.	Machinists	900,000	Floyd E. Smith	59
6.	Carpenters	808,000	M. A. Hutcheson	74
7.	Laborers	650,000	Peter J. Fosco	78
8.	Retail Clerks	650,000	A. Suffridge	62
9.	Meat Cutters	550,000	Joseph Belsky	n.a.
10.	State, County & Municipal Employees	525,000	Jerry Wurf	52

Among them, these unions wield a power far beyond their actual numerical strength. They do this by a combination of great wealth and superb organization. Their total assets can only be guessed at; they run into billions of dollars. Some unions own their own banks; all have big pension funds and enormous investments in real estate, hotels, and life-insurance companies. They are also known to collect between $75 and $100 million in membership dues every month. The amount of money they spend on politics can also only be estimated, although they are forbidden by law to use union dues to finance federal election campaigns. They spend their wealth instead on organization and things like voter registration. In some states the local AFL-CIO office can produce within seconds a computerized list of workers and their wives, families, party affiliation, age, and latest home address, which can of course then be used by the labor-backed candidate to canvass a whole district. The AFL-CIO's Committee on Political Education reckons to spend about $1 million a year on voter registration drives, and it is estimated that COPE spent between $5 million and $7 million in the unsuccessful bid to get Hubert Humphrey elected in 1968.

The Presidential election of 1968 aroused labor to the greatest political exertions of its history to keep Richard Nixon out of the White House, an effort vividly described by Theodore H. White in *The Making of the President 1968*:

"The ultimate registration, by labor's efforts, of 4.6 million voters; the printing and distribution of 55 million pamphlets and leaflets out of Washington and 60 million more from local unions; telephone banks in 638 localities, using 8,055 telephones, manned by 24,611 union men and women and their families; some 72,225 house-to-house canvassers; and, on election day, 94,457 volunteers serving as car poolers, materials-distributors, baby-sitters, poll-watchers, telephoners."

Quite apart from its effort to help elect presidents and legislators who are sympathetic to labor, the unions also wield tremendous influence on Capitol Hill, where they run one of the biggest, smoothest and most influential lobbies in Washington, as well as one of the most visible.

As a result of all these activities, American unions have, in the Meany thesis, delivered more to the American worker than any labor movement that ever existed. Yet the workers they represent, in spite of their vociferous complaints, are not the downtrodden or the neglected, but in a sense an élite. The average union member today earns at least three to five dollars an hour, a sum far above that of the unorganized, often unskilled, nonunion worker. Broadly speaking, the unions represent the "haves" in the American working community. The really poor working man, who as often as not is also unskilled, black and frequently out of work, is not a member of a trade union. Indeed, in some unions, particularly in the construction trades, a black worker performing other than an unskilled job is about as rare as a woman stockbroker on the floor of the New York Stock Exchange.

It is this élitism that leads to the charges that Meany is just a businessman engaged in the business of unionism, blind to restrictive work practices and insensitive to the needs of really deprived minority groups. To many social critics, the AFL-CIO under Meany has become one of the most reactionary forces in America, a narrow and protectionist special-interest group, superbly equipped to look after its own in economic terms but inadequate to deal with the wider social problems. It is for these reasons, among others, that the United Auto Workers broke with Meany in 1967. "In our judgment, the AFL-CIO had become stultified," said Irving Bluestone of the UAW. "It was no longer a cause. It was a kind of business."

Meany does not allow this sort of criticism to bother him much. He is a tough man, shaped in an old school, and he seems quite content to hammer away on the old Gompers theme of "more"—meaning more pie for his members. It is no accident that Meany, a plumber, heads a federation whose central core of power has traditionally rested in the construction industries. At the federation's conventions in Miami, it is George Meany and his cronies from the seventeen building trade unions who always occupy the most prestigious row of hotel suites. And critics say it is also no accident that the construction unions are among the most restrictive in the country. All seventeen of them tightly resist entry from outsiders and run what is virtually a closed shop in most of their trades. Featherbedding is universal, interunion violence is commonplace, and the unions monopolize most of the hiring halls, running many of the functions normally reserved for management. They decide on the number of workers required for any particular job, even though many of them are what are known as "nail keg" jobs, in which the worker is just assigned to sit on a metaphorical nail keg and watch the work. Wage rates for the insiders are inflated, blacks almost entirely excluded from these so-called craft unions, other workers virtually shut out. "The carpenters for instance take the attitude that Jesus Christ was a carpenter and that they were here first, so the rest of you guys stand in line," a sheet-metal worker told the Washington *Post.*

And George Morris, a General Motors vice president, told the *Post,* "We have building-trade-union members rubbing shoulders with our own auto-worker-union skilled mechanics who perform the same jobs. The building trade people are not above saying, 'Hey, buddy, if you were a member of the electrical workers' union instead of the auto workers, you'd have this kind of check.' They jab them and irritate them, so that our electrician goes down to his UAW local and says, 'Goddamn. How come that guy gets eight-fifty an hour and I get five-eighty?' So we have a hell of a lot of pressure inside the union from the skilled trades groups, and the UAW has to reflect that when they sit down and bargain with us."

Meany of course rejects these charges as he settles down to his role as labor's angry, demanding elder statesman, and his on-again-off-again feud with President Nixon has run almost from the day Nixon took office. There had been bad blood between the two leaders for many months before the final explosion, which occurred at the 1971 AFL-CIO convention in Miami, a meeting to which the President had somewhat rashly invited himself. The feud seems to have begun because Meany felt the President had not treated him "straight." At a Labor Day dinner at the White House in 1970, Meany had replied to an overeffusive Nixon toast with some blunt words, reviewing his personal acquaintance with every President since Franklin Roosevelt. He concluded with what was intended to be a friendly, if clumsy, compliment: "No matter how political they might have been," he said, "and let me tell you, Franklin Roosevelt, he was just as tricky as anyone who bore the name of 'Tricky Dick' could possibly be; and let me tell you, Lyndon Johnson, he was no slouch at politics—when they get into this house, I have found they have one thing in common: they want to be the best President they possibly can for the American people." He finished his oration, with a nod towards Nixon: "And this applies to this man here. I may be bouncing on your head tomorrow morning, but this goes [tonight]."

They were private words, spoken at an intimate inside dinner, but the White House committed the tactical error of making a verbatim transcript of Meany's toast and circulating it widely throughout the country. Meany was furious. He felt that he had been betrayed by the President and that issuing the transcript of his speech was an unpardonable attempt to demean him. "What the hell do these yokels know?" he bellowed of the White House staff. "They give a dinner and they think it's a tremendous honor. We've got a stake in society. We're not selling out for a lousy steak at a dinner!" The relationship, already bad, quickly got worse. There was another row about the President's original wage-and-price freeze, about which Meany only heard an hour before it was announced, when a White House functionary phoned to say, "You ought to watch the President's speech on TV."

The climax came at the labor movement's annual meeting in Miami, to which Nixon had originally been invited to appear by the labor leaders. But they heard nothing until the day before, when a White House aide called to say the President would like to appear next day. "Put on your best bib and tucker," Meany told the members—then adjourned to discuss the manner in which they should receive the President. They were in the middle of their quarrel over Nixon's income policy at the time, and his request for an invitation to their convention had put them into a neat quandary. Enthusiastic applause would obviously not be suitable, but on the other hand, they realized that to receive the President with hostility would be bad for labor's public image. They resolved, instead, to be cool but polite. When the moment came, alas, their effort to keep either cool or polite was not exactly an unqualified success.

In the first place, Meany had ordered the band not to strike up "Hail to the Chief," the President's customary entry fanfare, although it had greeted Meany himself with a stirring rendering of "My Wild Irish Rose." Meany then introduced Nixon in a cursory manner the Miami *Herald* later described as "loutish," and in a speech highly critical of the President's economic policies told the delegates in his rough Bronx accents, "If the President of the United States doesn't want our membership on the pay board, he knows what he can do!"

Nixon chose to meet the challenge head on. Trembling slightly and with a nervous and shaky voice, the President took the rostrum and declared, more to the watching millions on television that to the labor delegates in the hall, "Mr. Meany is correct. I know exactly what I can do, and I am going to do it. It is my obligation as President to make this program of stopping the rise in the cost of living succeed, and to the extent that my powers allow it, I shall do exactly that."

The President thereupon plunged into the body of the hall and began shaking hands, campaign style, with all in sight. From his seat on the platform, George Meany leaned over to his neighbor and whispered, sotto voce, "Disgusting, isn't it?" Unfortunately, his microphone was still open, and his comments were carried via television to the watching world. Finally, when the President had left the hall, Meany stepped to the podium, pounded his gavel, and announced, "We will now proceed with Act II." It brought down the house.

The feud was now running at full tide. Meany launched into a series of attacks on the inequities of the President's pay freeze in which he successively criticized the pay board as "a stacked deck," the leader of its business representatives as "a pipsqueak," and Nixon's whole policy as "a complete miserable failure."

So it came as no surprise when a few months later Meany led the unions out of the President's pay board altogether. "George Meany has walked off the job," said the President. "I cannot permit any leader representing a special interest, no matter how powerful, to torpedo and sink a program which is needed to protect the public interest."

For his part, Meany was convinced the public would come around to his realization that price controls had been a failure. "The program is a sham," he declared. "The pay board has been a device to undermine and destroy collective bargaining. . . . The wage-earner is expected to fight inflation by surrendering his job or cutting his standard of living and digging deeper to make up the tax deficit left by giveaways to big business. But we in labor do not intend to close our eyes and pretend it isn't happening."

The result was widely expected to be organized labor's biggest effort to defeat an incumbent President. But it never happened. Meany completely reversed his stance toward both the President and the Pay Board and virtually assured Nixon's re-election when he refused to endorse McGovern's candidacy, the first time since the AFL-CIO was formed that it has not officially supported the Democratic nominee. As a result, Richard Nixon, who got only 14 percent of the labor vote in 1968, is estimated to have collected more than half of it in 1972. Meany's decision—which, as a measure of his enormous power within the movement, was his alone—grew in part out of his contempt for McGovern, whom he described during the campaign as "an apologist for the Communist world" and whom he regarded as an amiable nonentity who had allowed his party to be taken over by all the groups Meany detests the most: antiwar activists, New Left socialists, radical women, militant blacks, and all the rest.

Whether, after Meany has gone, these assorted radicals can find a home in the same party as the labor movement is one of the most fascinating conundrums of American politics. It may be that Meany has finally shattered the coalition that has for so long provided the Democratic Party with a permanent national majority. The defection of union members in such large numbers in 1972 was based on a number of factors, which may or may not turn out to be lasting: class opposition to the so-called college-educated elitists, antiblack and antiwelfare emotions, economic opposition to the Democrats' proposals to cut the defense spending on which so many union jobs depend, and several other issues which also may in the end turn out to be ephemeral. That so many of its members should find a home with the Republicans is a measure of the way the labor movement, or at least a large segment of it, has now become a part of the American establishment, with a vested interest in preserving the status quo. Nevertheless, its courtship by Richard Nixon is one of those dangerous romances that threatens to go onto the rocks at any moment. There have been very few political parties, if any, that have succeeded for long in reconciling the interests of those natural antagonists, big business and big labor. There is evidence, too, that Meany himself regarded the romance as a strictly business affair, a marriage of convenience. "Just watch George," one of his intimates was quoted as saying not long after the election. "He'll milk this thing for everything he can get out of it."

Meany has always prided himself on his achievement in "keeping the boys together," but while he personally pushed through the decision to keep the AFL-CIO politically neutral, the strains have begun to show in the labor federation since the 1972 election. Thirty-two of the federation's 116 member unions broke away during the campaign itself and supported George McGovern anyway; many others are forecasting that Meany's decision will not only weaken COPE, the Committee on Political Education, which is the federation's chief political arm; it will also split the entire labor movement even more badly than it split the Democrats—although as long as Meany remains in charge the cracks have not been allowed to show. And what happens to the movement after Meany goes? He is, after all, an old man who has held the federation together for the past twenty years more through the force of his personality than through any underlying institutional philosophy. Already, the two biggest unions of all fall outside the influence of the federation, and with no obvious successor in view and no real political philosophy to hold it together, the institutional influence of the AFL-CIO could suffer a precipitous decline before the end of this decade.

3. Two Leaders

"Business unionism, with its invitation to complacency and corruption, need not be the sole shape that the labor movement must assume."
—WALTER REUTHER, *president, UAW, 1946–1970*

Outside the federal hierarchy of the AFL-CIO, the most powerful union leader in America today is the soft-spoken and intellectual head of the United Auto Workers, Leonard Woodcock. Woodcock, who succeeded to the job in 1970 after the death of the legendary Walter Reuther, also holds what is probably the toughest union job in the country: a delicate balancing act, intended on the one hand to achieve the highest economic rewards for his members, and on the other to preserve the socially responsible and progressive traditions established by his distinguished predecessor.

Reuther, by any standards the most influential trade unionist of his generation, has been a hard man to follow. Woodcock had spent his entire union life working in the shadow of the great man and was thrust into the top job at the moment many observers believed his career had come to an end. The problems that faced him were immense. The union was in the midst of a severe economic crisis, caused in part by a drop in membership and the hugely inflated costs of an educational center for union members and their families that had been Reuther's "dream project."* Then there had been a strike of secretaries and maintenance personnel at the UAW's own headquarters, Solidarity House, in Detroit, when Woodcock and his colleagues were forced to run the gantlet of union pickets calling "scab" and "fink" as they entered their own building. And finally, he was forced to lead the union into its biggest and costliest strike for a generation, against the gigantic General Motors.

Woodcock emerged from his fiery initiation with greatly enhanced prestige. The GM strike was settled on terms that amounted to total victory for the union. Woodcock won an immediate fifty-one-cent-an-hour increase for his members, an enlightened cost-of-living escalator clause, and a revolutionary "thirty and out" clause which permitted union members to retire on full

*Reuther had been killed in a private plane crash while on an inspection tour of the project at Black Lake in northern Michigan.

pension after thirty years. At fifty-nine, Woodcock had finally won his spurs, and the GM settlement ensured his virtually automatic re-election to the presidency when his original term ran out in 1972.

Now in his early sixties, Woodcock is described by some of his colleagues as a cold and calculating man. Born in Providence, Rhode Island, and brought up in Britain until his teens, Woodcock had originally wanted to be an accountant. But like many others of his generation, he left school at the time of the Depression and had to take whatever work he could find, becoming a machine assembler with Borg-Warner. A lonely man, still troubled by ill health after two bouts with tuberculosis, he has impressed his colleagues by his unique combination of sensitivity and toughness. "We're always very orderly in Detroit," he said at the height of the conflict with GM. "We may have the longest strike in our history, but it will be an *orderly* strike." William Serrin of the Detroit *Free Press,* who has watched his rise closely, says "there are those in Detroit labor circles who will say, privately, that he surpasses Reuther in several areas: intellect, ability to analyze problems, and ability to speak quickly and concisely." What he lacks is Reuther's color and the evangelical streak through which he almost singlehandedly transformed the nature of collective bargaining in America.

During his twenty-four years as president, Reuther had involved the UAW in many causes far beyond the aims of traditional business unionism. "In many ways, Walter remained our conscience," declared an AFL-CIO official at the time the UAW withdrew from the federation. And at the time of his death, he was deeply involved in such wide-ranging causes as equal rights for black workers, the fight for cleaner air and water, national health insurance, and mass-produced low-income housing. Under his impetus, the UAW became the most democratic union in America, and by the time he died well over 20 percent of the UAW membership was black. In an obituary statement, the National Urban League declared, "He fought with a rare and noble passion for true equality for even the least among us. . . . Walter Reuther represented the best in the trade union movement, the best in the civil rights movement, the best in America." A UAW official paid a more practical tribute: "Walter succeeded in keeping the union together for two reasons," he said. "He was a skillful negotiator who delivered at the bargaining table, and there was no question of his honesty. Nobody suspected he was on the take or had anything but the welfare of his members at heart."

His funeral was attended by the establishment of Detroit as well as civil rights leaders from across the country. Henry Ford II was there to offer his final tribute, and so were the chairmen of General Motors and Chrysler. It therefore comes as a surprise to recall that a bare twenty-five years earlier this same man of "rare and noble passion" had been reviled and hated like no other union leader in the country. George Romney, then at American Motors, had called him "the most dangerous radical in America," and a prewar trip to the

Soviet Union had led to repeated charges that he was a Communist, though in fact he had always been a socialist in the old German tradition and a passionate defender of the democratic process. In 1933, he had been fired by Ford for union activity. Four years later he was viciously beaten up by company thugs, hired by the violently antiunion Henry Ford in an attempt to keep unionism out of his plants. But in 1941, Ford was finally forced to capitulate, and unionism was established at last in his bastion of twentieth-century capitalism. Wages in auto manufacture rose from the five dollars a day paid by Henry Ford during the Depression to the five dollars an hour paid at the time of Reuther's death. Today, the auto workers are the highest paid industrial workers anywhere, and the union inherited by Woodcock faces problems very different from those of the union taken over by Reuther in 1946.

Where Reuther's problems were largely external, Woodcock's are mainly centered on the union itself. Worker morale is as big a headache for Woodcock as it is for the automakers; over 40 percent of his membership today is under thirty, and the more extreme demands of the younger workers are directed just as frequently against the union bureaucracy as they are against management. Meanwhile, in spite of the UAW's relatively large proportion of black members, racial tension has also been building up in many union districts. Much of the white membership, a goodly proportion of whom are also migrants from the South, tend toward reactionary rightwing politics; several local UAW presidents are open supporters of George Wallace, and there has been quite severe violence between black and white UAW members in several of the factories around Detroit. Militant blacks, centered on the Chrysler plant, caused much of the trouble by promising to free blacks from "the racist, tyrannical, and unrepresentative UAW"—a charge that, however unfair, promises to bring more trouble—and a white backlash—in its wake.

Under Woodcock there are now signs that the UAW is beginning to tilt away from the radical social stance it adopted under Reuther towards a more conventional position. UAW watchers at the 1972 union convention in Atlantic City reported two significant signs of increasing conservatism: the rejection of Paul Schrade, a liberal activist, from his position as the union's director on the West Coast, and a decision to hold the next UAW convention in 1974 at Miami Beach.

The decision to move the convention away from Atlantic City was opposed by the liberals for reasons of nostalgia. Miami had always been the favorite meeting place for George Meany's AFL-CIO, and Meany's poker-playing train journeys to the annual convention had become famous in the labor movement. Reuther, however, had always opposed holding his conventions in that sybaritic town for fear it would symbolize that the union was getting fat and soft and moving away from the cause of social justice. So the decision of the new leaders to put the plebeian glories of Atlantic City behind them may mark a real, as well as a symbolic, turning point for the UAW.

Schrade's eviction from office may have a deeper significance. He was the union's West Coast regional director, had been wounded when Senator Robert Kennedy was assassinated in 1968, and had become well-known for his stand against the Vietnam War and his involvement with the blacks in the Watts area of Los Angeles and with Cesar Chavez's farm workers. He was defeated in Atlantic City by a candidate who declared, "I feel very strongly that our union has to get back to the people in the shop"—in other words, cut back on all this idealistic social work and community action among the poor and the disadvantaged. The union claimed Mr. Shrade lost his job because he did not pay enough attention to union affairs, and not because of his liberalism, but his rejection seemed to symbolize a movement away from the ideals of Walter Reuther that had for more than a generation motivated America's second largest and most socially committed labor union.

In any event, the UAW today has become, in the view of many of its critics, out-of-date and old-fashioned, "a right-of-center union with a left-of-center reputation." As Schrade himself has said, "The United Auto Workers has been going through a quiet process of transformation the extent of which has not yet become apparent to its million and a half members." In this analysis, the union is as much to blame as the big automobile companies for the drudgery of the production line and the alienation of the young workers. The "civilized relationship" with management that Woodcock likes to boast about has had the effect of bureaucratizing the union, of bringing it closer in outlook to management than to its own rank and file, with the result that at bargaining time both sides tend to let slide the fundamental issues that the UAW stresses so strongly in its public relations statements—things like pollution control, job enrichment, changing the production-line system—and settles instead for the one gut issue of more money. Ted Jacobs of the Nader organization has pointed out that "the company and union respond to bureaucratic demands and political exigencies which are often determined by the nature of the relationship that parties have evolved. General Motors is not and will not respond to the problems of the 1970s *sua sponte*. It will respond when challenged, pushed, and prodded. It is here that institutions such as the UAW can fulfill their once promising vision of not so much 'More' as 'Better.' "

Sadly, the UAW in the 1970s seems to have laid aside Walter Reuther's stricture that business unionism need not be the sole shape that the union movement in America must assume. The cycle has returned to the answer given by old Samuel Gompers, who when asked in 1898 what labor wanted, replied simply, "More."

4. Coal-Black Shame

"If I do run, Ralph, they'll try to kill me."
— *"Jock" Yablonski to Ralph Nader, 1969*

Along the hilly coalfields of Appalachia, which run in a northeasterly direction from Kentucky through West Virginia and on into the western corners of Maryland and Pennsylvania, no section of the working community feels so abandoned, so full of despair as the men who mine America's coal. Numerically, they are only a quarter as strong as they were at the end of the war—down from a total of 400,000 to some 95,000 today. But their decline in numbers tells only part of the story, for those who remain, far from being the élite, highly mechanized workforce that had been promised by the introduction of automation, have been among the most neglected and exploited workers in the country, still haunted, even into the 1970s, by the triple specters of death, disease, and decay that have been part of the miners' lot for generations.

Throughout the industry, the pervading notion that men are cheaper than coal still persists, with the result that the American coal mines are among the most dangerous in the world. Since records have been kept, 120,000 American miners have died underground, an average of 100 a month for a century—a death rate per unit of work that has over the years been three times higher than the Russian, four times higher than the British, and six times higher than the German. During the last war, according to one authority, German coal mines, operated by slave labor and under constant aerial bombardment, had a better safety record than the mines of Appalachia. The death rate has finally been falling since the introduction of much-heralded safety legislation, passed at the end of 1969 as a result of seventeen massive underground explosions that killed seventy-eight men in Farmington, West Virginia, but men still continue to die down in the mines—over six hundred of them since the new legislation was passed. "To be honest," a Bureau of Mines official has said, "the act is not being fully enforced, and probably won't be for some time. We have a serious manpower problem. . . ."

Chronic lung disease, however, may be an even worse killer of American miners than accidents. At a conservative estimate, 100,000 retired and active miners are today suffering from the gasping breathlessness of pneumoconiosis, or black lung disease, which is caused by prolonged inhalation of the fine coal dust thrown up by the new electric mining machines. Black lung is thought to be a graver threat to the health of the miners than the old silicosis, which is caused by rock dust, yet astonishingly few miners receive compensation when they contract the disease. Of the coal-mining states of Appalachia, only Pennsylvania had paid any compensation claims for black lung, and even there the benefits are paid by the state's taxpayers and not by the industry. Some coal operators have taken the position that the disease does not exist, hiring doctors to testify that the suffocating miners were probably smoking too many cigarettes. One company doctor testified in West Virginia's statehouse that physicians who were crusading for changes in the compensation laws were "alarmists" who did nothing but harm to the coalminer when they told him to quit the only work he knew just because he was a little breathless.

Perhaps the biggest tragedy of all for the miners of Appalachia during the past decade is the way they were abandoned and neglected by their own union, the United Mine Workers of America, a body shrunken to a corrupt and self-serving parody of the once-mighty organization headed by John L. Lewis. For forty years and more, Lewis had been the miners' champion, leading his men in the manner of an Old Testament prophet, promising them in his fiery Welsh rhetoric, "I shall speak your name not in the feeble whisper of a spokesman for mendicants asking for alms, but in the thunderous roar of the captain of a mighty host demanding the justice to which free men are entitled." His relations with the mine-owners were frequently violent. He was a man, said Huey Long, "who fights moving locomotives in the early morning just to warm up." But toward the end, Lewis had realized that the only way to save the industry from the ruinous competition of oil and gas was to agree to largescale automation in order to hold down the cost of coal and make it a competitive source of fuel for the country's growing number of power-generating plants. At the cost of some 300,000 coal miners' jobs, he did save it, assuming the burgeoning postwar economy would take care of the displaced men and his own union would protect those who remained. In exchange for his agreement on automation, the owners imposed a royalty of forty cents on every ton of coal produced, with which to finance a welfare and retirement fund that gave UMW miners the best pensions in industry and the only industrywide scheme of free medical care.

The fight for the welfare fund had been bitter. "If we must grind up human flesh and bones in an industrial machine—in the industrial machine that we call modern America," Lewis had thundered, "then, before God, I assert that those who consume coal, and you and I who benefit from that service, because we live in comfort, owe protection to those men first, and we owe security to their families after, if they die. I say it! I voice it! I proclaim it! And I care not who in heaven or hell opposes it!" Not long thereafter, the owners made their greatest bargaining concession ever, and when Lewis retired in 1960, peace reigned on the coal fields for the first time in his long life; coal was once again prosperous, and the miners were being paid wages that matched the best in industry.

But Lewis had made two major miscalculations. He had not foreseen—who could have foreseen?—that instead of humanizing the miners' work, the new electric machines that are now used to cut the coal would create vast clouds of dust that assault the miners' lungs more cruelly even than the accidents and economic abuses of the past. And his own autocratic personality had been so vast, he had failed to provide the union with effective leadership to take over when he retired.

His handpicked successor was a former miner from Montana called W. A. "Tony" Boyle, an obscure figure who had worked most of his life in the shadow of the great man. "It was," said Lewis before he died, "the worst mistake I ever made." Lewis lived until he was eighty-nine, long enough to watch through the mists of old age the degradation of the union he loved, to the point where he was reported to have said in private of his successors, "Let them sink in their own slime."

Boyle had carefully modeled his image after his master's, running the union as a personal fiefdom, just as Lewis had done. But where Lewis had used violence to combat worse violence, Boyle used violence to silence and intimidate his opponents within the union. Where Lewis had initiated the collaboration with the owners to save the industry, Boyle used collaboration to make sweetheart ties with the owners that fattened the bank balances of the UMW but did nothing for the men who mined the coal. Where Lewis used the coal royalties to provide adequate pensions for his men, Boyle used the pension fund for his own ends, denying old age or disability pensions to many miners on flimsy technicalities. And where Lewis had taken over central trusteeship of many UMW districts to preserve the unity and integrity of the movement, Boyle used the trusteeships to keep all the main district offices of the union under his own control.

The union attempted to build up as big a cult of personality around Boyle as it had around Lewis, engaging in ludicrous attempts to make a legend out of the natty, diminutive man who had inherited the mantle of the master. The union spent $117,000 on framed photographs of its president and his politburo, which hung in every union office and hall. When Boyle appeared before a union convention soon after his first election, he was given an hour-long, foot-stomping ovation, led by hired cheerleaders and kept going by five bands brought in at a cost of thousands of dollars. And at big union gatherings, choirs were hired to sing (to the tune of "The Foggy Foggy Dew") a workers' ballad that must be unsurpassed for industrial bathos even in the Soviet Union:

> When Tony was a young man, he went underground;
>> He worked at the miner's trade.
> And many, many times the bosses passed the word,
>> He's a dangerous renegade.

All this buffoonery concealed for a while the United Mine Workers' disdain for its own members, but slowly, after two major tragedies, the true state of the union began to emerge. The first came after the explosions in 1968 at the supposedly "safe" mine in Farmington that had been allowed to ignore citations for literally hundreds of safety violations, often with the connivance of the UMW. The dramatic pithead vigil that lasted from Thanksgiving until Christmas was interrupted from time to time by a parade of VIPs, among them UMW President Boyle, who came to laud the company that owned the mine as "one of the better companies as far as cooperation and safety is concerned." If this "safe" mine blew up, he said, "you can imagine what the rest are like." Then he added, philosophically, "as long as we mine coal, there is always this inherent danger of explosion."

Reformists outside the industry challenged Boyle's statement. Ralph Nader and Congressman Ken Hechler of West Virginia suggested the union itself bore a large part of the responsibility for the industry's poor safety standards. It had up to that time failed to support a single piece of mine-safety legislation and had constantly compromised and "snuggled up" to management on safety issues until the position of the union had become markedly less reformist even than the owners'. Nader and Hechler were rewarded for their comments by a front-page editorial in the UMW *Journal* labeling them "finks" and "Johnny-come-lately experts." "We're not going to destroy the coal industry to satisfy the fanatic ravings of the self-appointed and ill-informed saviors of the coal miners," said President Boyle. Later he avowed that the UMW would not abridge the rights of mine operators in running the mines. "We follow the judgment of the coal operators, right or wrong," he declared.

The Farmington disaster, however, had revealed to the world the extent to which the union under Boyle had married itself by "sweetheart" contracts to the industry by which the UMW allows favored companies to pay its members less than the agreed rate for the job in exchange for "favors" paid to union headquarters. A blind eye toward safety requirements was widely believed to be an implicit part of many such "sweetheart" contracts.

As the union's complicity became clear, a tentative reform movement began to grow up in the UMW itself, led by Joseph (Jock) Yablonski, a craggy-browed Pennsylvanian who had served the union for thirty-six years and had been closely identified with the old-guard leadership. Yablonski broke loose in May 1969 with the encouragement of Ralph Nader, abandoning his $30,000-a-year sinecure and declaring that he intended to run against Boyle for the union presidency later that year. "I participated in and tolerated the deteriorating performance of this leadership," he said. "But with an increasingly troubled conscience. I will no longer be beholden to the past."

The campaign was marked by appalling bribery, intimidation, and corruption and was constantly marred by violence. The Boyle faction attempted to stop Yablonski's nomination by such tactics as offering open bribes to members as they turned up to vote at local branches. At one meeting, Yablonski's supporters arrived at the appointed hour of 7:00 P.M. to find the clock on the wall set forward and Boyle's nomination already pushed through. Other Yablonski nominating meetings were declared invalid by rump sessions held after most members had left. At one rally during the campaign proper, Yablonski was knocked unconscious and nearly paralyzed by a karate blow to the neck delivered by one of Boyle's hired thugs. But Yablonski kept going, and as he did, the true state of the United Mine Workers came under closer and closer scrutiny. "This union is a private government—like the Mafia," said Joseph L. Rauh, Jr., Yablonski's campaign adviser. "It operates above the law." Just how far above the law it operated became clear as the campaign progressed.

In spite of the Landrum-Griffin Act, which stipulates that rank-and-file union members have the right to choose their own representatives, the officers in twenty of the twenty-five UMW districts were appointed directly by Boyle under trusteeships inherited from Lewis. Not one of the working miners of West Virginia was allowed a say in the election of his own union officials, and many of the West Virginia branches were made up entirely of retired miners, beholden to union headquarters for their pensions. "We haven't got the heart to revoke the charters," the union declared when asked for an explanation of this anomaly. In reality, of course, the bogus branches were to be used to supply large blocs of pro-Boyle votes in the union election. (The UMW membership is made up of 95,000 working miners, 20,000 unemployed, and 85,000 retired, all of whom pay dues and vote in union elections.)

Financial scandals also came to light. Salaries of $40,000 a year were being paid to second-echelon functionaries. Boyle's daughter, Antoinette, a union lawyer in Billings, Montana, was reported to have been paid $43,809 in salary and expenses for duties that were never made clear. It was learned that since 1964, Boyle himself had drawn more than $30,000 in director's fees from the National Bank of Washington, which was itself 75 percent owned by the UMW. What was worse, the union had kept $67 million in a *checking* account at the bank, thereby foregoing interest on the miners' hard-earned contributions, but earning good profits for the bank. It was disclosed that top officers of the union had transferred $850,000 from the union's treasury to a special "agency fund" to finance their own retirement on full salary. And finally, as the day of the election approached, Boyle, as trustee and chief executive of the pension fund, declared a 33 percent increase in union pensions in an attempt—successful—to ensure the support of the retired miners, even though he was warned that this would lead to the eventual insolvency of the fund.

Yablonski's supporters appealed to the Labor Department to intervene. President Nixon's then Secretary of Labor, George Shultz, refused. "The department should not investigate and publicize the activities of one faction in an election in order to assist the campaign of the other," he declared. He said the Department would observe the longstanding rule to wait on the sidelines until the balloting was over. There was a widespread feeling at this time, doubtless shared by the lawyers of the Labor Department, that Yablonski was little if any better than the man he sought to replace. "He's just one of the boys in the kitchen trying to move into the living room," was the attitude of George Meany. Yablonski was certainly no saint, and had been in and around violence all his life; in his youth he had served an eight-month prison term for theft, and he was described by *Time* as "a rasp-voiced man with bushy eyebrows and a kind of wild glint in his eye." He did not, said *Time*, establish an air of calm and reasonableness: "He was a man haunted by many demons."

Nevertheless, Yablonski's commitment to reform was genuine enough, and his campaign had attracted the attention and support of Walter Reuther, Ralph Nader, and John D. Rockefeller IV. But when the votes were counted on 9 December, the union announced Boyle was the victor by a margin of 35,000 votes, having won a full 93 percent of the pension votes. Yablonski refused to concede the election, charging there had been widespread bribery and fraud, and retired to his lonely farmhouse near Clarksville, Pennsylvania, where he was bothered by a strange car that was often seen parked near to the entrance road to the farm. "Ed," he had said to one of his campaign workers, Ed Monborne, "I think they're after me."

A few days before polling, Yablonski's agent had again appealed to Shultz for intervention by the Labor Department. "The failure to take strong measures to ensure a fair election may well bring in its train ugly violence," he said. The statement was to prove more prophetic than he knew. On New Year's Eve, a band of assassins broke into the Yablonskis' farmhouse and killed the three occupants in their beds. First, Yablonski's twenty-five-year-old daughter, Charlotte, was shot through the head as she slept. They fired at least five bullets into Yablonski as he tried to grab for the shotgun he kept by his bedside, then shot his wife, Margaret, through the bedcovers which she pulled over her head in terror. Their bodies were found five days later.

When he heard of the murders, Tony Boyle scoffed at the idea that the union was in any way involved, and offered a reward of $50,000 for information leading to the capture of the criminals. But gradually, a different story came to light. The three murderers were tracked down and caught, confessing to the FBI that they had been paid to kill the Yablonskis by officials of the UMW. It was alleged the $15,000 death kitty came from a special "Research and Information Fund" set up by the union, of which only $4,500 had found its way down to the actual killers. Silous Huddleston, a local union president from La Follette, Tennessee, confessed in 1972 his own complicity in the killings, also implicating Albert Pass, a member of the UMW executive board, and William J. Prater, a union field representative, both of whom have since gone on trial for murder; in 1973 Boyle himself was indicted.

Meanwhile, Tony Boyle was sentenced in 1972 to five years in jail* for illegally contributing nearly $50,000 of the union's money to political campaigns, much of it going toward Hubert Humphrey's 1968 bid for the Presidency. (Humphrey had attended the UMW conference that year, declaring effusively, "Mr. President—Tony Boyle—the one and only Tony Boyle—it is good to be with you. . . . I am mighty glad to rub shoulders with this fellow Tony Boyle. He has been giving me counsel and advice for a long time.") Earlier, a federal judge had added to Boyle's troubles by setting aside his 1969 victory over Jock Yablonski on the grounds that the evidence of illegalities was "too strong to resist." Boyle was forced to run for office again, this time under the watchful eye of a thousand federal agents, whose presence on the coal fields insured the fairest union election in history. When the results came through at the end of the year, Boyle was out, defeated by a quiet-spoken former miner named Arnold Miller, a grizzled man with silver-gray hair and deep facial scars from machine-gun wounds he received in the Normandy landings in World War II.

Miller acted promptly to erase as much as he could of the Boyle era's image, although with a large number of Boyle's former supporters still on the UMW board he has had a stiff fight. He immediately cut his own salary from $50,000 to $35,000, pledged that he would raise miners' pensions to $200 a month, and swiftly dismissed scores of pro-Boyle officials at the union's Washington headquarters. Tony Boyle's black Cadillac, equipped with a back-seat bar, was auctioned off to the highest bidder, and Boyle's own pension cut back to $16,000 from the $50,000—the equivalent of his fulltime salary—that had been hastily voted by the old board in the last days of its life.

Setting his own house in order, however, was not Miller's only concern after he had taken over. One big issue that seems bound to increase in importance as the years go by is the problem of strip mining, reaching the coal by literally stripping away the earth that conceals it, a practice that has left ghastly environmental scars in parts of the Appalachians (and increasingly in the western deserts, where much new coal is now being uncovered). For the miners, strip mining brings new problems, for while it is on the whole far safer and far healthier than deep coal mining, it is also more automated, with consequent threats to the miners' jobs. The new mines are also often operated by nonunion labor, and what is more, the miners have become perhaps too dependent on the royalties from stripmined coal to pay for their welfare fund. If the conservationists have their way, such coal will become an even less important source of American energy in the years ahead, with untold consequences for the retired miners, who have already seen their welfare fund dwindle alarmingly during the Boyle regime.

Miller's first concern, however, has been to look to the problems of safety

---

*The sentence was suspended, pending appeal.

and disease that have so afflicted his members in past years. Himself a victim of black lung disease, which compelled him to retire prematurely from the mines in 1970 at the age of forty-seven, Miller has undertaken to press for adequate compensation for the black lung victims. It will be a long and uphill struggle, and he knows it, but it is a reform that could do more for the neglected miners of Appalachia than any that has occurred in his lifetime.

PART THREE

The Constitution

CHAPTER VII
The Presidency

1. Puritan in the White House: The First Term

"Nixon's the One"
—Campaign Slogan, 1968

When Richard Nixon arrived at the White House in the New Year of 1969, pledged to bring his divided countrymen together again, there were many among them who thought him uniquely unsuited to the task. After four of the most tormented years in their history, Americans were in almost desperate need of a leader who could calm their passions, restore their sense of national unity, and bind up the wounds of an unpopular and unwinnable war. Beset by problems, though not yet devoid of hope, they yearned for the soothing and avuncular charms of another Eisenhower. Through the accidents of assassination and the vicissitudes of one of the most bizarre election years in memory, they got instead—Richard Nixon. Here was a man who, in a public career that spanned virtually the entire postwar era, had stirred their passions like no other politician of his generation. Feelings about him, both favorable and unfavorable, ran strong and deep. And the shadow of his reputation had preceded him into the White House.

In the overheated atmosphere of the late sixties, it was impossible for anyone to be neutral on the subject of this man they had just elected President. Among his own constituency, those who were later to be labeled the Silent Majority, Nixon inspired, if not love, at least a fierce admiration, particularly when he struck his tough, simplistic pose on those social issues that worried them the most: crime, riots, student dissent, and what has come to be loosely called "permissiveness."

Among his opponents, Nixon provoked even more visceral emotions. Indeed, it is hard to think of another politician who stirred in the breasts of the liberal middle class a more cordial dislike: There were traits in his character, episodes in his background, that aroused in them an emotional and almost irrational hostility. His irritating habit of rising again and again from the political dead merely served to heighten their distaste. Three times at least they had watched his career collapse in ruins, twice in the past decade they had written *finis* to his presidential ambitions, yet he had somehow confounded them all and come back from his humiliations, apparently indestructible, to rise to the pinnacle, there to survey the wreckage of the liberal hopes of an entire decade: two Kennedys dead, Johnson discredited, the Democratic Party divided, dispirited, defeated. Of that generation of political leaders who had fought the battles of the sixties, Nixon alone survived. For good or evil, he was now likely to remain President for the next eight years. The prospect, to those who disliked him, was deeply disturbing.

Although he had hardly been out of the news since that day in 1948 when as an ambitious and rising young congressman he had challenged and triumphed over a largely mythical Communist conspiracy within the government, there was a curiously unknown quantity about the nation's thirty-seventh President in those early days of his tenure. He was an opportunist—even his allies conceded that—so where exactly did he stand on the great issues of the day? On what principles would his Presidency be anchored? What exactly did he intend to do with the office now that he had finally won it? His election campaign, which had been largely defensive and negative, offered few if any clues to these questions that so puzzled his countrymen. True, he had hinted that if elected he would end the war in Vietnam, but he had never talked in specifics and it soon became clear that this was an election promise that would not be carried out quickly. He had talked, in stereotypes, about ending crime on the streets, about stamping down on permissiveness, about tackling the problem of the "welfare loafers" who were costing the taxpayers so much money, but these hardly amounted to a political program. So was there, in fact, anything more to him than a political opportunist who had seen and seized the chance to win power?

More than any other President of this century, Nixon was—and has remained—an enigma, one of the most difficult personalities to understand and to explain that has ever occupied the White House. Yet, by a curious paradox, he is also a man who has been trying to tell America about himself since the moment he first arrived on the national scene, who has revealed more about the inner workings of his mind and soul almost than is decent. He is, he freely admits, an introvert in an extrovert profession. But his is an introspection that he somehow needs constantly to put on public view, with Nixon himself the most critical member of the audience. Whenever he meets a crisis, he has a need to step outside himself and examine his own performance. "Did you feel you have learned anything new about basic strengths in your personality," he asks himself in the introduction to his autobiography, "or did you discover any personal weaknesses about which you were previously unaware? Have you found that you had an extra strength which you had not anticipated when you were confronted with a crisis? Could you recall your feelings when the crisis had passed? Was there a sense of relief from tension or anxiety?" The recurrent theme in his life is this desire to prove himself in difficult situations, to demonstrate his toughness to the entire world, a trait at least one psychiatrist sees as "the mark of an insecurely held self." For such a personality, to win is everything. "When I am attacked," he has said, "my instinct is to strike back."

In another revealing passage in his autobiography (which, typically, he called *Six Crises*), Nixon has described his own feelings as the time of trial approaches:

> When a man has been through even a minor crisis, he learns not to worry when his muscles tense up, his breathing comes faster, his nerves tingle, his stomach churns, his temper becomes short, his nights are sleepless. He recognizes such symptoms as the natural and healthy signs that his system is keyed up for battle. Far from worrying when this happens, he should worry when it does not. Because he knows from experience that once the battle is joined, all these symptoms will disappear—unless he insists on thinking primarily of himself rather than the problem he must confront.

Not that Nixon actually *enjoys* his churning stomach, his sleepless nights. "Crisis can indeed be agony," he says. "But it is an exquisite agony which a man might not want to experience again—yet would not for the world have missed." The self-portrait that emerges from his descriptions of himself as a man in crisis is that of a tense and single-minded Puritan, possessing determination of almost heroic proportions, yet at the same time showing himself emotionally incapable of compromise. Once his course has been set, he *must* win. If the North Vietnamese raise difficulties in the peace talks—bomb them; if the Congress challenges his programs—crush them; if the press brings up awkward issues—vilify them. From somewhere deep within his psyche, comes the recurrent refrain: Nixon is not a man to trifle with. He demands and sometimes he pleads for the *respect* of his fellows. Not that it is mere popularity that Nixon seeks, nor the simple acclaim of the crowds that satisfies some lesser politicians. Indeed, during his first term he sometimes seemed to go out of his way to pick out the tough option, the one that, however unpopular, would win him the respect that was his due as President. And sometimes he left the impression that he had determined upon a particular course of action just because it *was* the tough option, a trait that was especially noticeable in his early decisions over Vietnam. But in his public statements justifying the American invasion of Cambodia, the mining of Haiphong harbor, and the bombing of Hanoi, he revealed more about his motivations than he perhaps intended. Thus, if the United States were to allow a Communist takeover, "the office of the President will lose respect, and I am not going to let that happen." In invading Cambodia, "we will not be humiliated," it is "our will and character" that are being tested: "I would rather be a one-term President than be a two-term President at the cost of seeing America become a second rate power and see this nation accept the first defeat in its proud 190-year history." In this intense concern with the effect of the crisis upon himself and his own career, Nixon comes very near to that other lifelong characteristic, self-pity. Americans that night were interested in the effect the Cambodian invasion would have on them and on the country. They could hardly have cared less about its personal impact on the President.

The forces that led this grim and relentless Puritan to drive himself onward until he reached the top were formed during the hardships of his early child-hood in southern California. The Nixon family had settled in the Quaker community of Yorba Linda, in those days a rural and isolated village set amid the orange groves, today a declining oasis long ago engulfed in the character-less urban sprawl of greater Los Angeles. The contrast between Nixon's boy-hood home and that of the man who beat him for the Presidency in 1960 could hardly be more striking. John Kennedy grew up a millionaire in the security and salt air of the famous family compound at Hyannisport, mixing from his earliest days with the famous and the mighty. Three thousand miles away in the balmier airs of southern California, Nixon was to experience a very differ-ent boyhood, haunted by family poverty and illness, dreaming the dream as he lay awake at night listening to the rumbling of the Santa Fe freight trains that one day the railroad would carry him away to the wider world of challenge and opportunity.

His father, Frank, who had with his own hands built the house in which the young Nixons grew up, had in his youth been a characteristic American rolling stone, glassworker, potato-farmer, telephone linesman, and motorman on the electric trolleycars in a small town in Ohio. In that last job, standing in the open vestibules of the trolleycars during the bitter midwestern winters, Frank Nixon had contracted frostbite in both his feet. California in those days of this century was perhaps the logical destination for such a man, and it was there, for the sake of his health, that he finally settled down to make his home. In 1908 he met and married a devout and gentle Quaker called Hannah Milhous, descended like himself from archetypal Americans of old Protestant Scots-Irish stock. Ancestors on both sides of the family had come over to the New World in the first half of the eighteenth century, humble hardworking pioneers who had soon pushed out to help develop the old frontier. One of Nixon's ancestors had fought in the War of Independence with George Washington, another lies buried on the battlefield at Gettysburg, and in Indiana the Milhous family was long remembered for the underground escape route they helped to organize for runaway southern slaves. For generations, the family had been farmers, with a scattering of preachers and teachers, hardy folk, close to the soil, the sort that is sometimes known as the salt of the earth.

The Nixon household in California grew up also in this tradition. The family was stable and united, devoted to those same pioneer virtues of self-reliance, piety, and hard work. What they lacked was luck. For all his energy and the driving ambition he was to pass on to his son, Frank Nixon was a failure. He was forced to give up a lemon orchard he had planted in Yorba Linda and move back into town, where he opened a general store and a filling station. But even then the family remained poor and plagued by the specter of ill-health: Nixon's father suffered badly from ulcers, which seems to have affected his temper, and two of the Nixon brothers died in childhood. Then for two years Nixon's mother had to take the eldest son, Harold, away from home to the desert air of Arizona in the hopes of finding a cure for his tuberculosis. She resolutely refused to accept any financial help and paid for the treatment he received at the nursing home by her own hard work as a general maid, cook, and furnacehand. Eventually, Harold and Mrs. Nixon returned from Arizona, but the ravages of tuberculosis had gone too far, and not long afterwards he died. Harold's end came suddenly: Early one morning Richard had driven him into town to buy a birthday present for their mother —an electric mixer—and when they got back, Richard left for school. When he got there, a message was waiting for him: "Come home. Your brother has died." Mrs. Nixon was stoical in her grief. "It is difficult to understand the ways of the Lord," she said. "But the best happens for every person."

To this day, Nixon still speaks with a fierce and justifiable pride of his mother's "courage and determination not to break down, whatever the physical and emotional strain." This experience, perhaps the most traumatic of his boyhood, also left him with a deep conviction, one that he has never abandoned, that triumph over adversity comes to those who are prepared to help themselves, that the acceptance of hardship and suffering is the price of independence. This is the voice of authentic Puritanism. "The average American," he was to say more than forty years later, "is just like a child in the family. You give him some responsibility and he is going to amount to something. If, on the other hand, you make him completely dependent and pamper him and cater to him too much, you are going to make him soft, spoiled and eventually a very weak individual." And he has spoken often, in criticizing what he calls "welfare loafers," of the time his mother scrubbed floors, emptied bedpans, and wore her hands raw to pay for her eldest son's medical bills.

The fierce pride of his parents' independence and the loyalty to the memory of their struggle imbued in him from his earliest days an unquestioning belief in the verities of the Puritan ethic in which he grew up. It is an ethic, deeply held by many Anglo-Saxons, which dictates that life is a battle to be fought rather than enjoyed, that success is a mark of virtue, that "making it" or "getting on" is the principal purpose of existence and that doubt and self-questioning are in some ways a measure of weakness. So strong was that belief in Richard Nixon that in 1968 when he was nominated for the second time to the Presidency he was able to declare, with the utmost sincerity, "I believe in the American Dream because I have seen it come true in my own life." In his entire career, Nixon never appears once to have doubted the validity of his American Dream: He accepts the maxims of his youth as wholly true and has acted always within the accepted rules. He is, in short, totally conventional. But unlike most conventional people, his strengths, which are substantial, arise perhaps not from too much inner security as from too little. There is an inescapable feeling that his toughness is a façade, erected to persuade the world—and perhaps to persuade himself—that he is a cooler and calmer and more controlled person than he really is. It leads also to what may be his most interesting characteristic of all: his willingness to place huge stakes on a single dramatic gamble. The mining of Haiphong harbor on the eve of his visit to Moscow, the huge risks he took in bombing Hanoi in order to reach a speedier peace settlement—these are not aberrations, but part of a pattern that has been discernible throughout his career. In order to win, to show the world that he can "make it," Nixon has taught himself to be a risktaker of colossal nerve and calculation. Again and again, he has gambled heavily on the outcome of his crises: The Hiss case, the Checkers speech, his presidential campaigns, the tough line in Vietnam all carry the stamp not only of a man who means to win but also of one who is prepared to stake his entire future, if necessary, on the outcome. "I cannot understand anyone," he once remarked, "who is not prepared to risk failure."

Taken together, Nixon's qualities of iron determination, sheer diligence, striving to win, and willingness to take courageous gambles, make an altogether out-of-the-ordinary and formidable combination. Those traits in his character were of course acquired long before he began his public career, and most of the anecdotes about the youthful Nixon illustrate the same familiar themes. Back in his college days at Whittier, for example, it was a matter of class pride to come up with a wooden privy to burn on the annual college bonfire. Student leaders before him had occasionally produced a twoholer, which had won for them considerable prestige. But that was not enough for Nixon. In his senior year, he typically came up with a fourholer, a record that stands at Whittier to this day—a triumph which must have cost him considerable singleminded effort. Later, as a junior navy officer in the Pacific during World War II, Nixon taught himself to play poker—with equally predictable results. He studied the cards for days, carefully working out his game plan, trying out all the options, preparing himself mentally for the test, and going on from there to become a gambler of legendary nerve, so that he returned home from the war with a nest egg of some ten thousand dollars, made up entirely of his poker winnings. "Show him the rules," Garry Wills has written, "and he will play your game, no matter what, and beat you at it. Because with him it is not a game."

These are not exactly likable qualities in any man. While all his biographers relate the anecdote about his pokerplaying, not one of them has ever suggested that Nixon took to the game for *fun*. Even pokerplaying he approached with a Puritan sense of purpose—he needed the money—and when the game had served its purpose, he dropped it entirely and apparently has never played since.

It would be absurd to pretend that Nixon is the first singleminded opportunist ever to sit in the White House—Franklin Roosevelt is another who immediately springs to mind—and mere dislike of his personal qualities only partially explains the especial abhorrence with which so many of his opponents regard him. He is, they will admit, more than ordinarily able, he is courageous, he is an exemplary husband and father; he is, in a sense, a living embodiment of the American Dream, the poor boy who has risen from humble beginnings to the highest position in the nation. During his first term, he was acclaimed as a strong President whose policies, especially in foreign affairs, won wide approval. And yet the impassioned dislike persisted, typified by that ancient and indestructible nickname "Tricky Dick" and the outrageously unfair campaign slogan, "Would you buy a used car from this man?"

Nixon's reputation for divisiveness has a long history, going back to his campaigns against domestic communism in his early days as a congressman from southern California. But it was perhaps with the Hiss case, the first of his *Six Crises,* that he became the chief bête noire of the liberals. The Hiss affair brought him immense national attention and led directly to his selection as Eisenhower's running mate. But, as Nixon himself acknowledges, "it also left a residue of hate and hostility toward me—not only among the Communists but also among substantial segments of the press and the intellectual community—a hostility which remains even today . . ."

It is difficult, a quarter-century later, to recall the intense emotions that this celebrated case aroused in Americans of all persuasions. The facts of the case are plain: Alger Hiss, a senior official at the State Department and a product of the Eastern establishment, had in his youth been a Communist; he had lied before the Senate about his communism; he had lied when he denied that he had ever known his accuser, Whittaker Chambers; and Nixon had caught him out in his lies. Typically, Nixon had taken a huge personal gamble when he persisted in pursuing his hunch that Hiss was perjuring himself when almost everyone else in Washington had convinced themselves that a terrible mistake had been made. President Truman himself had intervened to call the investigation "a red herring" and Nixon's own mother had pleaded with him to abandon the inquiry. But Nixon doggedly persevered. "I warn you," one Washington reporter had told him, "you'd better be right, or you're a dead duck."

Again, Nixon had done his homework more thoroughly than his opponents. His judgment was vindicated; the issue won him immense public support. Hiss went to jail and Nixon, having clearly done his duty, went on to become Eisenhower's Vice President. And there, in ordinary times, the case might have rested. But times, in the summer of 1948, were far from ordinary. For a poison had entered the nation's bloodstream—the poison of an hysterical anti-Communism that saw Reds under every bed and the Hiss case as proof positive that there was a deadly conspiracy aimed at the very heart of the government. And none believed in the conspiracy theory more fervently than

Richard Nixon. The threat of domestic Communism, he declared in a speech in the House of Representatives, "permits the enemy to guide and shape our policy; it disarms and dooms our diplomacy to defeat in advance; before they go into conferences traitors in the high councils of our own government make sure that the deck is stacked on the Soviet side of the diplomatic table."

The charge was patently absurd. Hiss, it was true, had been a Communist. It was also true that buried in the ranks of the government bureaucracy there might have been a scattering of others like him. But to go from this to the charge that they represented, as Nixon claimed, "a real and present danger to the security of the nation," was to pursue a delusion. And to move from there to the equally absurd proposition that the conspiracy had been fostered by the Democrats was, to put it delicately, a wild exaggeration. Yet it was a progression Nixon was soon to make. Before long, he was showing no scruples in tarring *anyone* who opposed him with the conspiratorial brush. Thus, the Democrats became, in one lurid phrase, "Dean Acheson's college of cowardly Communist containment." And when during the 1952 campaign Nixon was falsely accused of financial impropriety, he counterattacked with a further outburst on the influence of the Communists:

> You folks know the work I did investigating the Communists in the United States. Ever since I have done that work the Communists and left-wingers have been fighting me with every possible smear. When I received the nomination for the vice-presidency I was warned that if I continued to attack the Communists in this government, they would continue to smear me. They started it yesterday. They tried to say that I had taken sixteen thousand dollars for my personal use.

Here was the first use of a political technique that will always be associated with the name of Richard Nixon. When you are attacked, strike back, take the offensive, but above all, *shift the ground*. The financial charges against Nixon were unfair and, as he later demonstrated in the famous Checkers speech, wholly unfounded. But simply to deny them was not enough; they had come about, according to Nixon, solely because of his attacks on "the Communists in this government." Thus the ground had been shifted, with great astuteness, away from the charges against Nixon and back onto the allegations that the Democrats were somehow tied up with the Communists. Twenty years later, as tenant of the White House, Nixon was still using the same technique, and always with the same devastating effectiveness. The classic example came perhaps with the Senate's rejection of G. Harrold Carswell as Nixon's nominee to the Supreme Court. Carswell, in the judgment of the Senate, was simply not high enough caliber for the job, so they rejected him. But Nixon, emotionally incapable of accepting his defeat, once again shifted the ground. Carswell was a southerner; Nixon sought southern sympathy; it was therefore not Carswell's quite obvious lack of qualifications which led to his rejection, but the accident of his birth. Behold, therefore, Nixon's conclusion: "The next nominee must come from outside the South." In the following year's elections, he obtained considerable further mileage out of his allegations that the Senate had prevented him from appointing a southerner, any southerner, to the Supreme Court—which was of course not really the issue at all. Never mind—it gave Nixon the opportunity for attack, to seize a wider victory from the jaws of this defeat. After creating his diversionary giants, he is then able to destroy them with all the absurdity, though little of the grace, of Don Quixote tilting after his windmills. Only in Nixon's case, he *knows* his giants are really windmills. After all, he put them there.

In office, by deliberate intent, Nixon made himself a figure of almost monarchical aloofness. Indeed, there can hardly have been a national leader since Moses who arrived at his great decisions in such lonely isolation as the current President of the United States. Not for him the open court of Kennedy's Camelot or the drumming up of a consensus that typified Lyndon Johnson's approach to an impending decision. Nixon retreats, sometimes quite literally, to the mountaintop, his tablets of yellow legal paper in hand, to wrestle with his own soul in the privacy of one of his three retreats: Key Biscayne, San Clemente, or his favorite, Camp David in the hills of Maryland. "I find that up here on top of a mountain it is easier for me to get on top of the job," he has remarked of Camp David. Nothing more aptly illustrates the monarchical tendencies of the modern Presidency than Nixon's belief in the essential loneliness of his burden.

It was perhaps inevitable under the American system of government that the White House should have drawn to itself all the trappings of a court. The President lived in a sort of splendid isolation from reality, his every bodily whim catered to by a staff of loyal courtiers, his inner sanctum—the Oval Office—carefully screened from all unwelcome visitors by his keeper of the gate, who more than once physically prevented distinguished visitors from entering to see the President. Even adversaries have found it inadvisable to be anything other than respectful when they are ushered into the Presidential suite. George Reedy, once Lyndon Johnson's press secretary, has written:

> The aura of reverence that surrounds the President when he is in the Mansion is so universal that the slightest hint of criticism automatically labels a man as a colossal lout. The wise Senator, therefore, enters cautiously, dressed in his Sunday best and with a respectful, almost pious look on his face. He waits to speak until the President has spoken to him and his responses are couched in the same careful language employed by cabinet members. He emerges in the same manner and if, for any reason, he must express a dissent, it is most deferential, almost apologetic. There have been exceptions, of course, but they often end disastrously for the Senator."

The two key courtiers in Nixon's first-term White House were his chief of staff, H. R. Haldeman, and his domestic-affairs aide, John Ehrlichman, who were sometimes referred to by Dr. Henry Kissinger as the "Praetorian Guard" and by others, in reference to their German ancestry, as "The Berlin Wall." Both were essentially functionaries, Haldeman in particular acting as the keeper of the gates, a seemingly secondary role, but one which under a President such as Nixon grew into a position of formidable power. And as in any other royal court, in a battle of wills between the palace guard and the nominally more powerful barons out in the country, the palace guard always won. They had the ear of the King. Thus, it was Haldeman who decided who got to see the President—and who did not. It was Haldeman, too, who selected which memoranda the President should receive and it was Haldeman who protected a very private President from the bruising encounters with the outside world.

Even before the tragedy of the Watergate scandal swept them from office, there were many who believed the Teutonic structure of their staff had further served to isolate the President, to cut him off from the hard realities of opposition. Richard Whalen, a conservative Republican who resigned from Nixon's staff during the 1968 campaign, did so partly because of what he regarded as the malign influence of the President's closest aides. "Nixon's own insecurity caused him to need the protection of men willing to do whatever he wished," Whalen wrote. "In return they wielded unmeasured influence. By controlling the environment in which he moved, every person, paper and choice presented to him, they exercised power beyond argument or appeal. If I remained, I would no longer work for Nixon but for these men whom I did not respect. Yet they were only incidental foes. The true conflict was between my desire to serve Nixon and his inability to accept service on terms that were not humiliating to the servant."

Haldeman created the impression of an Oval Office that was not just isolated, but almost besieged. One morning, after Arthur Burns, then a senior and distinguished White House Counselor, had been in to see the President, he remembered on his way out of the office something he had forgotten to mention to the President and turned to re-enter. Haldeman physically blocked the door, declaring bluntly, "Your appointment is over." Burns explained why he needed to return, but Haldeman was adamant. Submit a memorandum, he said, and it would be placed in the President's reading folder. Burns, speechless, simply walked away.

If there was something of the bully in Haldeman—and some others on the President's staff—he had on occasion been known to meet his match. When John Connally was Secretary of the Treasury he quickly made it plain that no one was going to block *him* from the Oval Office. Haldeman tried it only once: A memorandum from the imperious Texan was returned, undelivered, with a note asking him why he wished to raise this particular subject with the President. The outburst of rage that this prompted down the road at the Treasury is remembered there to this day. Connally demanded, and received, a written apology for this intolerable interference with his personal access to the President. Unfortunately, there were not many of Connally's temperament and status around in the Nixon Administration, and for most of them, until Watergate the order remained, "Go see the staff."

Just as the crises of Nixon's early life seemed to come in sixes, so too, with a not entirely spurious symmetry, can the great decisions of his first term in office be put at six. During those first four years, his times of greatest trial included three crucial decisions concerning the war in Vietnam: the commitment of American troops to the invasion of Cambodia in the spring of 1970, the mining of the harbors and ports of North Vietnam on the eve of his departure for Moscow, and the unleashing of the B-52s over Hanoi in the Christmas season of 1972. At home, there was the Supreme Court crisis, which led to a major defeat. Then there was the spectacular announcement of his visit to Peking (which may well have been more spectacular than the visit itself) and, finally, the sudden devaluation of the dollar. The events could hardly be more disparate, but in each and every case, Nixon's approach was the same. First, the retreat into himself, "the period of soul-searching and doubt to determine whether to fight the battle or fly from it." And, doubtless at these times too, the churning stomach and the sleepless nights as he keyed himself up for the battle ahead—although later his aides denied that he ever displayed emotions so human: they might, after all, be construed as weakness. The lonely decision having been arrived at, there came the dramatic announcement to a startled world. And afterwards, the monarchical retreat into a further isolation that brooked no interference either from Congress, from the press or, least of all, from the people. "It is often said," Nixon remarked after he had renewed the bombing of Vietnam in 1972, "that when a President makes a hard decision, the so-called opinion leaders of the country can be counted upon to stand beside him, regardless of party." When the President acts, he seems to be saying here, he *must* be supported in whatever he has decided to do. Dissent was somehow seen as an assault on the presidential authority, even as disloyalty to the country. That in itself is a sweeping enough claim from the head of a democratically elected government, but Nixon went on to state that the country's "opinion leaders" were bound by duty to support the bombing:

Who are the opinion leaders? They are supposed to be leaders of the media, the great editors and publishers and television commentators and the rest. They are supposed to be the presidents of our universities, and the professors and the rest, those who have the educational background to understand the importance of great decisions and the necessity to stand by the President of the United States when he makes a terribly difficult, potentially unpopular decision. They are supposed to be some of our top businessmen who also have this kind of background.

Let me tell you that when that decision was made, there was precious little
support from any of the so-called opinion leaders of this country who I have just
described.

The conclusions that the President drew from this unpalatable fact are
almost absolutist in their implications. Here was the most explicit statement
yet that the President really did look upon his office as some kind of monarchy.
Dissent equals disloyalty—and as for the people, like the loyal soldiers of Henry V,
"we know enough if we know we are the King's subjects."

The sense of the President's intolerance of criticism was never more apparent than during the aftermath to his invasion of Cambodia in the spring of
1970. The college campuses, which had been peaceful, even serene, ever since
the President came to office, exploded in protest. Nixon's initial reaction was
one of ill-concealed contempt. Characteristically striking back at his critics, he
let fly an almost incoherent outburst to a group of office workers outside the
Pentagon:

You see these bums. You know—blowing up the campuses. Listen, the boys that
are on the college campuses today are the luckiest people in the world, going to the
greatest universities, and here they are burning books, storming around about this
issue. You name it—get rid of the war and there will be another one. Then out there,
we have kids who are just doing their duty. They stand tall and they are
proud . . .

Three days later, National Guardsmen trying to quell a student riot at Kent
State University in Ohio opened fire without warning, leaving four students
dead and ten wounded, and presenting Nixon with the most difficult crisis
since he arrived in office. But still, the administration kept up its hardline
attitude. The President himself coldly dismissed the Kent State shootings as
the inevitable consequence of "the resort to violence," while Vice President
Agnew, then at his raucous worst, spoke harsh words about "the new politics
of violence and confrontation."

It was a pity that at this crisis in their fortunes the President and his
spokesmen paid so little heed to the theme of unity and conciliation he had
expressed so eloquently at his inauguration—words that contrasted sadly with
his attitude now that the crisis had arrived. "We are caught in war, wanting
peace," he had said then. "We are torn by division, wanting unity. We cannot
learn from one another until we stop shouting at one another—until we speak
quietly enough so that our words can be heard as well as our voices." Unfortunately, the voice that had been heard most loudly around the land in the weeks
before the Kent State tragedy was not that of the President at his inauguration,
nor even that of the students in their outrage, but that of Vice President
Agnew on a polysyllabic rampage against what he was unwise enough to call

"the criminal left" and "the kid extortionists." What hope was there of conciliation with an administration whose chief spokesman, only two weeks before Kent State, had likened the nation's colleges to "circus tents or psychiatric centers for overprivileged, underdisciplined, irresponsible children of the well-to-do blasé permissivists"? In the face of this divisive and unyielding attitude, the gulf between the administration and the students, already broad, widened into a chasm. There were reports that up to half a million students were planning to march on Washington in protest against Cambodia and the killings at Kent State. The administration gave the impression that they could hardly care less.

Although the student protests had fallen upon hard hearts at the White House, their agony did not pass unheeded elsewhere in the administration. By one of those curious ironies of the times, their cause—when it looked the most hopeless—was unexpectedly taken up by a member of the President's own Cabinet. Walter Hickel, a shrill and abrasive Alaska land-developer who had gone on to become Nixon's Secretary of the Interior, was an unlikely rebel. This self-made millionaire had seemed on his appointment to be an archetypal Republican businessman, who had at first stirred much concern with his outspoken criticisms of the environmental movement. What was the point, he had asked at his maiden press conference, of "conservation for conservation's sake"?—"A tree looking at a tree really doesn't do anything." But over the following months Hickel had become a convert. And like most apostates he took to his new faith with an impassioned zeal and touching sincerity. Now, at this critical point in the fortunes of the government, Wally Hickel took up the cause of the students.

Hickel had watched the Cambodian invasion and the subsequent student revolt with a mounting sense of alarm. American youth had been needlessly polarized, and the President, in his isolation, did not seem to be aware of it. "I have to get my thoughts through to the President to help him," Hickel declared. He then set about the task, half comic, half tragic, of making contact with the man in the Oval Office. He tried to reach him on the telephone, but thanks to the Berlin Wall, he failed. Next, he tried to set up an appointment. Again, he failed. "It's going to be very difficult to see the President," a White House aide told him. Hickel exploded. "What the hell do I have to do?" he burst out. "Call a press conference? Is that the only way I can reach the President?"

So this member of the Nixon Cabinet, who had seen his chief privately only twice since his inauguration a year and a half before, sat down to write him a letter. Unfortunately someone on his staff leaked a copy of it to the press, and Bob Haldeman learned through the Associated Press wire that it was on its way. The letter, naïvely direct, was not calculated to sooth any ruffled feelings at the White House, but it expressed with some passion the despair of Hickel's new constituency, the young. It began:

Dear Mr. President,

I believe this administration finds itself, today, embracing a philosophy which appears to lack appropriate concern for the great mass of Americans—our young people.

Addressed either politically or philosophically, I believe we are in error if we set out consciously to alienate those who could be our friends.

Today, our young people, or at least a vast segment of them, believe they have no opportunity to communicate with Government, regardless of Administration, other than through violent confrontation . . ."

Hickel went on to argue that during the Great Depression American youth had also lost its ability to communicate with a Republican administration, and as a result had gone on to become the predominant leaders of the next two decades as Democrats. What was happening today, he thought, was not unrelated to what happened in the 1930s, only now, "being unable to communicate with either party, they are apparently heading down the road to anarchy." Youth in its protest must be heard, he argued, going on to take a swipe at the divisive speeches of Vice President Agnew. Initially, Hickel said, Agnew's speeches had answered a deepseated mood; "however, a continued attack on the young—not on their attitudes so much as their motives, can serve little purpose other than to further cement those attitudes to a solidity impossible to penetrate with reason." Hickel ended his unorthodox letter with a personal plea to the President that he consider meeting, "on an individual and conversational basis," with members of his Cabinet—a remark that could only be construed as a direct criticism of the President's isolation and of Haldeman and Ehrlichman's Berlin Wall.

According to strict protocol, Hickel should of course have submitted his resignation with such a critical letter. But Hickel was a cussed man as well as a rather naïve one, and it was clear he was not going to make things easy for a White House beside itself with fury about the publication of his letter. The administration also had sound political reasons for not firing him out of hand. They are said to have feared that if they did so he might go back to Alaska to run in the impending election for his old job as governor as an anti-Nixon independent. They accordingly decided to placate him until the election had passed—and fire him afterwards. But their anger at Hickel's temerity in criticizing the President, in stabbing him in the back, as they saw it, at the most critical moment in his administration, was not assuaged. At first, Hickel was ostracized. He received a call the following weekend asking him not to attend the regular White House prayer service, and he was "disinvited" from another trip to the White House to brief reporters on what he considered to be his crowning achievement: the creation of a marine sanctuary off the California coast, which had been terribly scarred by an oil spill.

But the appearance of unity had to be preserved, and it was not long before

Hickel got his desired face to face meeting with the President. It was, by all accounts, an embarrassing encounter, with the President exceedingly ill-at-ease in the presence of his adversary. After forty-five minutes of desultory conversation, Hickel finally blurted out, "Mr. President, do you want me to leave the administration?"

The President thereupon jumped from his chair, "very hurried and agitated," according to Hickel's account. "That's one option we hadn't considered," he said. Having to fire someone is a task Nixon loathes and will go to almost any lengths to avoid. He hates the sight of blood on the floor, and normally leaves the distasteful task of slaughter to his staff. But Hickel had forced his hand, caught him off guard, embarrassed him. So the President instantly called in John Ehrlichman to spare him any further agony. "John," he said, "I want you to handle this. Wally asked whether he should leave. That's one option we hadn't considered." And like the White Rabbit hurrying off with his eye on his watch, the President left the room.

For a while, the cracks were papered over. Ehrlichman privately told newsmen there was now "no problem" between the President and his Interior Secretary. It had all been a terrible misunderstanding, Ehrlichman implied: Hickel had in fact seen the President scores of times since the inauguration and what he probably meant in his letter was that he had not had the chance to meet with him alone on matters of broader interest than just departmental matters. "But that's not the way we run the White House," Ehrlichman explained. "There's always a staff member present when Cabinet people come in unless it's just a personal visit. The President is an awfully busy man. He doesn't have the time just to put his feet up on his desk and say, 'How are you, Wally? What's on your mind these days?' "

By this time, the White House had become thoroughly alarmed at the storm that had blown up over the Cambodia invasion and its domestic aftermath. The country was in a ferment more profound than any since those awful days of 1968. The earlier hard line against dissent had backfired; several members of the White House staff had resigned in protest over the invasion; and it was clear Richard Nixon was riding his worst crisis since he came to office. The mood of the administration was, in the words of one insider, "close to panic."

On the night of May 8th, barely a week after he had taken his big gamble and sent American troops to "clean out" the Communist sanctuaries in Cambodia, President Nixon appeared before a press conference and pledged their early return. Of the student protestors, who were even then gathering in their tens of thousands outside the White House, Nixon declared: "I agree with everything they are trying to accomplish." And for Vice-President Agnew he had this advice: "When the action is hot, keep the rhetoric cool." On all three issues the President had made a complete *volte face:* perhaps the biggest of his career up to that time.

That night, he was unable to sleep. He had gone to bed only at 2:30, but was up again before five. Summoning his valet and his Secret Service guards he decided it was time to meet the people. He drove down to the Lincoln Memorial, less than a mile away, to seek out some of the students who were gathering in Washington for the following day's protest marches. Never at ease in making casual conversation—"I cannot become a buddy-buddy boy" he had said once—the President chatted with them for about an hour, recalling his own days as a student, urging them to keep their demonstration peaceful, and telling them: "Remember, I feel just as deeply as you do about this." He urged them to get to know China, Prague and Warsaw, and when one student called out, "We are not interested in what Prague or Warsaw look like, we are interested in what kind of life we build in the United States," Nixon replied, "The purpose of my discussing Prague and other places was not to discuss the city but its people. We are going to be living in all parts of the world and it is vitally important that you know and appreciate and understand people everywhere. Ending the war and cleaning the streets and the air and the water are not going to solve spiritual hunger, which all of us have." It is interesting, in recounting his memories of that encounter, that what the President remembers is not what the students said to him, but what he said to *them.* As for the students, what they remembered—or said they remembered—most was the President's awkwardness at making easy conversation. "The surfing's great down there," he said to one group of students from California. "Do you enjoy it?" It was hardly a relevant remark to a group of students from a state whose entire system of higher education was at that time paralyzed and who had traveled the breadth of the continent to express their antiwar sentiments. But at least, Nixon had tried.

Eventually, of course, the troops that had gone into Cambodia came out again, a great victory was claimed, the campuses quietened down, and the administration resumed its criticism of dissent in time for the midterm elections. The attempt at conciliation had been a strictly shortterm operation.

Some months later, the Hickel episode, too, was to have a curious epilogue. The Interior Secretary, by this time grown even more reckless in his comments, had decided to brazen out his disagreements with the administration, even though he had been told the time was now ripe for a quiet resignation. Far from resigning, the Secretary instead went on national television. "If I go away," he said in an interview, "I'm going away with an arrow in my heart, not a bullet in my back."

The only man who could ask him to quit, he indicated, would be the President himself. So once again, Nixon was forced into a disagreeable encounter with a man who had become an outright encumbrance. But even then he found it next to impossible actually to deliver the blow. Hickel walked into the Oval Office and sat down on a chair close to the President's desk. Nixon stared uncomfortably out the window for a time, then began making inconsequential conversation about the new lighting that had been installed around the White House. He seemed quite unable to steel himself to the task before him. Finally, it was Hickel who was compelled to take the initiative. "Mr. President," he said, "get to the point." The President launched into another discussion about the work Hickel had done at Interior and during the campaign, then, unable to escape any longer, declared abruptly, "Wally, you're a strong man, so I'd like you to be strong when I tell you what I'm going to tell you. I believe that's the way you'd want it." At last, it came out: the President wanted him to go. Hickel was fired.

The story is revealing for the insights it gives into the private Nixon, a side of the man even his closest associates seldom see. Far from being the ruthless gut-fighter of popular mythology, the President in private displays an acute sensitivity to the feelings of others, an unwillingness to inflict injury that amounts almost to squeamishness. If there is dirty work to be done, bad news to be broken, let it be done out of sight, behind the arras. The contrast with his predecessor, who actively relished putting people down, is both striking and refreshing. While the public Nixon comes across as a man who is needlessly insulting to his opponents, referring to dissenting students as "bums" and welfare recipients as "loafers," face-to-face one gets a glimpse of a warmth and sensitivity he has never been able to project to the wider world. In private, he is, it seems, unfailingly courteous—a man who is polite even to movies. His daughter Tricia told one interviewer, "My father is very patient and very loyal to a movie. He's the last one to walk out if one is bad. The rest of us keep saying let's go, come on, this is lousy, but he says no, let's wait a bit and maybe it will get better. He is a perpetual optimist about everything, including people."

Yet, somehow, the appealing side of Nixon, so apparent to his family and close friends, vanishes like a wisp in the wind once he ventures again onto the public stage. On Nixon's sixtieth birthday, early in 1973, James Reston, one of Washington's most respected and sober columnists, felt obliged to write of the President, "He has used his power . . . not to unite, but to divide." As Nixon began his second term, talking still about bringing the people together, his behavior had been precisely the opposite, Reston said—more war without presidential consultation or explanation; more confrontation between executive and legislative branches; more vindictive reaction to dissent. "It is almost as if the President coming up on sixty was determined not to heal old sores, but to settle old scores."

The President at that time had just ordered the most severe bombing of the war in Vietnam without any personal explanation of its purpose. When congressional leaders were summoned to a breakfast briefing on the President's domestic programs, he had turned his back and walked out on them without allowing any questions. When the Washington *Post* criticized the Republicans for bugging the Democratic headquarters at the Watergate, it suddenly found its society reporter barred from covering social events in the White House. And when peace finally did come to Vietnam, Nixon in his moment of triumph could not resist a petty dig at the reporters who had gathered to cover his announcement that this represented "peace with honor." "To write down that phrase," he told them, "will probably stick in your throats."

This, then, is the elusive and enigmatic man who guided the United States during one of the more troubled periods in her recent history onward—to what? One can capture, through anecdotes, a feeling for the shades of his character, and through his own writings and actions, a sense of the inner drive of his ambitions. But what of his ideology? What of his accomplishments? What of his essential political convictions? If these were questions that puzzled his countrymen when he first came to the Presidency, the answers were no less tentative, no less shadowy when, four years later, he won re-election by one of the biggest landslides in American history. Not that Nixon had been a weak President; on the contrary, the accomplishments of his first term, especially in foreign affairs, had been substantial and solid; and if for nothing else, he is likely to be remembered by history for his daring initiatives in dismantling the antiquated apparatus of the Cold War and establishing in its place the foundations for what may well turn out to be "a full generation of peace." But it is not so much Nixon's accomplishments that are so puzzling, as his motives. Evidence that he adhered to a political philosophy of any permanence was as hard to come by after half a decade in office as it was during all those years in the wilderness. Indeed, he seemed to be picking up his political positions as he went along, to be modeling himself, self-consciously, on a succession of heroes with whom for the moment he could identify. So at first, he was Charles de Gaulle, the man who united his country after a divisive colonial war. Then he was Woodrow Wilson, the peacemaker acting on the world stage. And by the end of his first term, Nixon was comparing himself to Benjamin Disraeli, the Victorian imperialist, whose biography by Robert Blake he had been reading recently and in whose life he professed to detect several startling similarities to his own (although skipping, one supposes, those passages in which the author discusses Disraeli's reputation as "an insincere charlatan, a dreamer, an opportunist adventurer, a sphinx without a riddle—like Louis Napoleon.")

At first sight, the personal comparison between the intense and joyless Puritan in the White House and the languid Sephardic Jew who became Queen Victoria's favorite Prime Minister is so improbable it verges on the ludicrous. Disraeli in his youth had been a dandy, a romantic, a novelist of no little distinction, a sexual adventurer, a social climber, and a noted wit. Even as prime minister he was an exotic figure, his hair flowing down to his shoulders, his fingers festooned with diamonds, his cheeks heavily coated with rouge. One cannot imagine the crewcut Haldeman ever allowing *him* into the

Oval Office. Yet here was the prudish, respectable Nixon adopting this believer in the principles of aristocracy as a fellow spirit and larding his speeches
with Disraeli's better-known bons mots. In appropriating Disraeli's language,
however, one was always left with the uncomfortable feeling that Nixon had
somehow not quite grasped the full point of his hero's sallies, that something,
somewhere, had got lost in the transition. For example, Disraeli had once
remarked sardonically that the Liberal Cabinet, sitting side by side on the
front bench of the House of Commons, reminded him of one of those marine
landscapes not very unusual on the coasts of South America. "You behold,"
he said, "a range of exhausted volcanoes." Tickled by the phrase, although not
quite understanding the imagery, Nixon promptly applied the metaphor not
to the opposition but, with an earnestness that would have amused Disraeli,
to his *own* Cabinet. Then Disraeli, not without a touch of malice, had written
in his novel *Coningsby* the following snippet of dialogue: " 'A sound Conservative government,' said Taper musingly: 'I understand: Tory men and Whig
measures.' " Again, Nixon seized upon the phrase and made it his own. "Tory
men and liberal principles," the President declared, "those are the ones who
have enlarged democracy." Which is not *quite* the principle Dizzy had in
mind. The phrase was meant sarcastically; he was, after all, trying to satirize
the unimaginative Conservative politicians of his day for *betraying* their Tory
principles by embracing the policy of the Whigs. Indeed, in *Coningsby* Disraeli displays an utter contempt for the emerging middle classes of England
—the Nixons of his day. The aristocracy was to him a race apart and meant
to rule, while the masses needed to learn the qualities of "loyalty and religious
reverence." But that was a nuance that seems to have escaped both Nixon and
the acolytes who had pressed Blake's *Disraeli* upon him. Yet if they had only
read a little further into *Coningsby* they would have found one or two even
less flattering epigrams on the nature of the mid-nineteenth century conservatism they seem to have taken as their model: "an unhappy cross-breed, the
mule of politics that engenders nothing"; a political philosophy that "discards
Prescription, shrinks from Principle, disavows Progress"; a party that having
rejected all respect for antiquity "offers no redress for the present and makes
no preparations for the future." Is *this* the conservatism Nixon had in mind
for America? One assumes not, although it is hard to be sure.

Even Disraeli's famous claim that he had brought home "peace with honor"
from the Congress of Berlin was appropriated by the President, who used the
same phrase to describe his own ceasefire settlement in Vietnam. Unfortunately, he seems not to have realized that it had been borrowed once before
—by Neville Chamberlain, who returned from his journey of appeasement to
Munich waving a scrap of paper bearing Hitler's signature and claiming that
this, too, brought "peace with honor." If, to use the President's own words,
the phrase now stuck in the throats of those who recorded it, that was perhaps
because· of the less-than-happy consequences that had followed closely upon

Chamberlain's unfortunate journey and his even more unfortunate use of a phrase that has for ever afterward been associated with a very special kind of dishonor. Of all this, however, the President appeared to be blithely unaware.

In comparing Nixon's performance with that of Disraeli in office, students of the President find themselves on more solid ground. Here, it is true, there are some startling similarities between the two men. Both were capable, in office, of dazzling flexibility: Disraeli, having brought down his own prime minister on the issue of protectionism, abruptly became a supporter of free trade; Nixon changed almost overnight from a traditional Republican budget-balancer to a self-avowed Keynesian. Both men undertook major reform of the government bureaucracy; both based their foreign policy on an unsentimental balance of power; both reached across the despised liberal middle classes to find support among the workers—Disraeli with his Tory laborers, Nixon with his Forgotten Americans. And both subscribed to a distrust of Liberal reform. "In a progressive country," Disraeli wrote, "change is constant: and the great question is not whether you should resist change, but whether that change should be carried out in deference to the manners, the customs, the laws and the traditions of a people, or whether it should be carried out in deference to abstract principles and arbitrary and general doctrines." In other words, no ideology—a theme that found its precise echo in Nixon's definition of his approach to government as that of "strong adherence to the basic values that the nation believes in, and to conserving those values, and not being destructive of them, but combined with reform, reform that will work, not reform that destroys."

If Nixon does have a personal political philosophy on the subject of domestic politics, it can be summed up as mistrust of the government bureaucracy, an attitude he seems to have acquired as a temporary civil servant just after the war when the pragmatist in him had been horrified at the waste of both money and manpower and appalled at the lack of efficiency in the lower branches of the government machine. "I honestly believe that government in Washington is too big and too expensive," he remarked just after his re-election. The country, he believed, had enough on its plate in the way of spending programs, social programs, throwing dollars at problems. What America needed basically was sound, pragmatic administrative reform. And that is what he set out to achieve and had hoped to be remembered for. "What people don't understand," said one of his speechwriters, "is that the old man is *serious* about holding down spending and taxes. Why, he even talks about 'the damned government'!"

Beyond this passion for administrative efficiency, however, Nixon never displayed much interest in domestic affairs and gave the impression that on the home front at least he was running an improvised Presidency. His real passion has always been for foreign affairs, as he himself admitted not long before the 1968 election. "I've always thought this country could run itself domestically, without a President," he observed then. "All you need is a competent Cabinet to run the country at home. You need a President for foreign policy." And, true to his word, it was to foreign affairs that Nixon has devoted most of his attention and displayed the greatest flexibility of principle. His conversions were sometimes dazzling. For he had come to office with the reputation—and more than the reputation, the actuality—of being a fervent anti-Communist. "Nixon's hatred for Communism," wrote one of his biographers during his first year in the White House, "is the one real and genuine passion of his otherwise sterile political personality." Yet here he was, only two years later, the harshest anti-Communist of his day, clinking glasses with Chou En-lai in Peking and speaking of peace to the Russian people on Moscow television. It was, given all Nixon had said about the Communist powers in the past, an astonishing sight. Disraeli would have been proud of him. More than that, it demonstrated beyond any doubt that Nixon had come to the Presidency really without any ideology. In a nation of pragmatists, he was the pragmatist supreme—a brilliant political improviser who knew precisely how to calculate the direction of the prevailing winds and how to set his own sails to catch them.

The argument here does not necessarily imply criticism. It is simply that Nixon knew better than his recent opponents how to calculate the middle course. Ask him to choose any number between one and ten, someone once remarked—and he will invariably pick five. "My position is of the center," he observed after his landslide victory in 1972, and he believes, rightly, that he won so handsomely then because his opponent failed to understand that the battle in national politics is always for the middle ground. And in seeking out the constantly changing center, it is obviously helpful to be unencumbered by ideological baggage.

It is of course an approach to politics that requires a certain amount of cynical calculation. When the urban crisis exploded in riots in the spring and summer of 1968, for example, Nixon chose not to confront the issue because his campaign staff were unable to establish a consensus. No one around him had any idea of what his true feelings were on the issue, and it was felt safer to say nothing rather than take up a position that might lose votes. For more or less the same reasons Nixon was even reluctant to attend the funeral of Dr. Martin Luther King, although he finally agreed to go after one of his advisers pointed out that "if he stays home there won't be any moral difference between him and Wallace." But throughout the later campaign Nixon worried that he might have made the wrong calculation, rebuking those who had urged him to go and calling the decision "a serious mistake that might have cost us the South."

Some would call this approach to politics opportunist, and so, in a sense, it is. But it is an opportunism that allows for a flexibility that is perhaps essential in guiding the destinies of great nations. Nor is Nixon the first

President whose deeds in office do not always coincide with his rhetoric on public platforms. In the election campaign of 1932, Franklin Roosevelt—of all people—made a speech in Pittsburgh in which he promised to cut spending and balance the national budget. When, during the torrent of spending that marked his first hundred days in office, he was reminded of his promise by the Republicans, he handed the problem over to one of his advisers. Back came the reply: "Mr. President, there is only one way to explain this speech. Deny you ever made it."

In practice, Roosevelt's opportunism served the country well. And so too, in matters of policy, did Nixon's. It enabled him, for example, to reverse completely his earlier unsuccessful economic policies. It enabled him to seize the opportunity to reach an accommodation with the Communist powers. It enabled him to come to terms with his former enemies in the labor movement after their support had been spurned by the Democrats. It enabled him, further, to play cool political poker with the proposals of his opponents, which again and again he plucked from their platform and presented as his own. As Disraeli once remarked of Sir Robert Peel, "He caught the Whigs bathing and walked away with their clothes." When he returned to the White House in triumph after one of the biggest landslide victories of the century, that quotation from his own hero looked as though it would serve well enough as an interim epitaph for the uncompleted Presidency of Richard Nixon. But the opportunism which enabled him to take over the programs of his opponents had been directed also to a more sinister purpose. Unknown to most of the electorate, there was a time bomb ticking away beneath the Nixon Presidency as he began his second term in January 1973. When it exploded, barely three months later, Nixon was engulfed by the biggest and most dangerous scandal ever to afflict a President in office. The label on that time bomb was Watergate.

2. Watergate: The Unmaking of the President, 1973

"Watch what we do, not what we say."
—JOHN MITCHELL, *on taking office as U.S. Attorney General, 1969.*

The fuse on the Watergate time bomb had been lit, almost casually, during meetings of Nixon's campaign strategists early in 1972, at a time when the fortunes of the President seemed to be at a low ebb. The historic visit to China had not yet taken place, the war in Vietnam looked as far away from settlement as ever, and, surprising though it now seems, the consensus among most political observers at the time was that on election day Nixon would be a vulnerable candidate. Senator Edmund Muskie was still the Democrats' front runner, with his reputation then at its peak, and it was the opinion of the Nixon men that he would be the toughest candidate for them to beat. Larry O'Brien, who had just taken over as the Democrats' National Chairman, was meanwhile making effective political capital out of the administration's involvement in the ITT scandal, and the discomfited President's men were casting around for a means to discredit him. Specific dirty tricks were perhaps not yet in their mind, but in the almost paranoid atmosphere that prevailed in the Nixon White House, it was now considered time to start plotting the downfall of their opponents—only to the bland and self-righteous ideologues who surrounded the President, the Democrats were not merely political opponents to be defeated in fair and open fight: they were, in the later words of one of them, political enemies to be "screwed."

To that end, they had pulled out of the White House a flamboyant former FBI agent called G. Gordon Liddy and re-assigned him to the Committee to Re-elect the President, an organization formed in the previous year which later came justly to be known as CREEP. As a lawyer, Liddy was given the title of Counsel to the Committee, and among his tasks was the preparation of a plan for gathering intelligence on the Democrats. The campaign was still in its early days, the Committee had not yet thought out its full election strategy and Liddy was at first given little guidance in preparing his schemes. But as a willing self-starter, the Committee's new counsel set about his task with a zeal akin to fanaticism.

He had a mysterious career behind him, this man who was to play a central role in the affair that began to unfold. He had been in and out of right-wing politics in upper New York State, had served as assistant District Attorney in Dutchess County, where he had once gained notoriety by firing off a revolver in the courtroom, and had run for Congress as a law-and-order Conservative in the elections of 1968 on the slogan, "God help us if the thin blue line of protection crumbles." After the election, he had been recommended for a job in Washington with the new Nixon administration, and in 1969 joined the Treasury Department as special assistant for organized crime, where he was later instrumental in organizing Operation Intercept, a scheme for combating illegal narcotics traffic. Liddy's brusque manner and clipped moustache gave him a somehow military bearing, but behind it was concealed an awesome temper and a wilful disposition, and his new colleagues in Washington soon found him to be an awkward man to deal with.

Given to violent and headstrong enthusiasms, Liddy quickly gained a reputation as one who often balked at orders and constantly tried to set policy. His stormy career at the Treasury lasted less than two years, ending with his dismissal, according to his superiors there, for attempting to subvert their official policy on the control of handweapons known as "Saturday night specials." An ardent gun fancier, Liddy had given an unauthorized speech in favor of the National Rifle Association's gun lobby, who opposed the Treasury restrictions on Saturday night specials, and he had also, it was claimed, entered into his own private and wholly irregular negotiations on the matter with officials at the White House and the Justice Department. So Liddy was dismissed. "We couldn't control him," a Treasury official said later.

But Liddy's habit of going over the heads of his own superiors had not gone unnoticed at the White House, where his activities in the war against drug smuggling had caught the eye of powerful friends, notably Egil (Bud) Krogh, the top aide to John D. Ehrlichman. Consequently, on the same day that he was fired from the Treasury, Liddy's more powerful new friends in the White House stepped in to his rescue. It was now July, 1971, and the White House was in a state of agitated alarm over the publication of government secrets in the aftermath of the Pentagon Papers affair. Liddy was just the sort of man they were looking for to help them plug the leakage of information that had so infuriated the President, and he was at once taken on board to join the White House intelligence unit that later became known as "the plumbers." There he worked closely with Krogh and another undercover agent called E. Howard Hunt, taking part in a variety of secret and sometimes illegal missions —among them an ill-fated attempt at burglary on the Los Angeles offices of the psychiatrist who had been treating Daniel Ellsberg, the source of the Pentagon Papers revelations which had just been published in the *New York Times*. All these activities, however, were carefully concealed from the public and came to light only in the aftermath of the Watergate affair.

Liddy's job with the plumbers lasted about five months, but that was enough to establish his reputation as an intelligence gatherer of uncommon dedication and zeal, and he had on one occasion won praise from the President himself for the quality of a legal paper he had prepared. So when the Nixon men began to put together the staff for their Committee to Re-elect the President, Liddy was once again the right man in the right place. His new duties, vaguely defined, were to co-ordinate what were called "demonstration intelligence" and "security operations" for the Re-election Committee. After a brief interview with John Mitchell, then still U.S. Attorney General but soon to become Nixon's campaign director, Liddy was hired and given his title as "counsel" to the Committee. Precisely what instructions he was given when he took over his new job has never been clearly established, and Liddy himself has steadfastly refused to talk about his role in the affair that followed. But it is known that he discussed "a broad-range intelligence plan" with John Dean III, the President's Counsel at the White House, and that when he joined the Committee staff on December 13th, he at once began to put together a plan of political spying, burglarizing, bugging and kidnapping that had no parallel in American political history. Liddy appears to have set out on his new task with his characteristic headstrong relish, and, according to later testimony, was apt to dash into his superior's offices crying, "Listen: I've got this great idea—" Whether they did listen isn't clear, but before long he was ready to unfold his grandiose plan.

Subsequently, on January 27th, Liddy became the central figure at a fateful meeting in John Mitchell's office at the Justice Department. Present with Liddy and the Attorney General were John Dean and Jeb Stuart Magruder, another bland young Nixon aide who had not long before left his White House post as special assistant to the President to set up the Re-election Committee. Liddy had taken immense care to prepare himself for this vital meeting and had brought with him a series of professionally prepared charts, in color, for which he claimed to have spent some $7,000. Thus from the very outset it was clear this was no free-wheeling discussion session, but a carefully prepared and formal presentation of an elaborate and expensive plan of political espionage, with the calculated aim of subverting the democratic process.

As the others at the meeting have since recounted it, Liddy began by displaying his charts on an easel, each headed by a mysterious code name: Gemstone, Target, Ruby I, Ruby II and two others. Liddy, ever the professional intelligence-gatherer, went through the charts with a pointer, explaining his plans in detail to the other three men, who reportedly watched him in total and shocked silence. One of the projects dealt with wiretapping, electronic surveillance and illicit photography of the Democratic candidates, including the interception of ground-to-air communications with the candidates' campaign planes. Another dealt with the problem of radical demonstrators who were expected to give trouble at the Republican Party's Convention, at that time planned to take place in San Diego. Liddy's mind-boggling proposal was that the leaders of the radicals should be kidnapped by teams of undercover agents and spirited away across the border into Mexico, where they would be detained, out of harm's way, until the Convention was over. Another plan was for call girls—high-class girls, he said, the best in the business—to be hired during the Democratic Party Convention in Miami Beach; the girls would then lure important Deomocrats onto a hired yacht, there to be photographed and taperecorded in compromising situations. Finally, Liddy came to his last chart, on which he outlined the cost of his outrageous schemes: one million dollars, all told. When he finished his presentation, the other three men were, according to their later testimony, appalled. John Dean called the scheme "Mission Impossible," Mitchell sucked pensively on his pipe and told Liddy dryly that this was not quite what they had in mind—the proposals were both unrealistic and far and away too expensive. Liddy was told in effect to go back to the drawing board. According to Dean's later testimony, he thought the plan had died there and then, and as Liddy dejectedly took down his charts from the easel and prepared to leave the room, Dean recalls that Mitchell had said the plan is "certainly out of the question." The plan was so far out, Dean was to say later, "that there was no hope in my mind that anyone was going to approve a plan like this. So I just assumed it was going to die a natural death." John Mitchell later said gruffly he wished he had not only thrown Liddy out of his office—he wished he had thrown him out of the window.

But Liddy's proposals were in fact far from dead; instead of being thrown out of the office (he was, after all, proposing criminal acts in the presence of the U.S. Attorney General) he was simply told to go away and do better next time, to produce "a more realistic plan." At the same time, Magruder says he prepared a report on Liddy's proposals and sent them over to the White House in a memo addressed to Gordon Strachan, whose job it was to brief the top men there on the activities of the men from CREEP. It thus seems likely that at least some of Nixon's top aides received their first report on what was afoot in this report from Jeb Magruder.

Liddy left the meeting in distress. He had confidently assumed that everyone there would accept his plan at face value, and he was upset that it had been so decisively rejected. But he managed to hide his disappointment from his junior colleagues back at the Committee, and in fact indicated to Jim McCord, the Committee's Security Officer, that the plan had been approved. In any event, he set to work again to produce a revised plan in time for another presentation the following week. Once again, a meeting was set up in the office of the Attorney General, and once again, Liddy, Magruder and Dean trooped in to discuss the revised proposals.

This time, Liddy had followed Mitchell's instructions and produced a much scaled-down plan. The scheme to abduct the demonstrators had been dropped altogether and the staffing proposals had also been cut back drastically. All the same, Liddy's second plan, for an estimated cost of some $450,000, called for an elaborate scheme of illegal bugging and wiretapping of Democratic National Committee headquarters, electronic surveillance of the Fontainebleau Hotel, which was to be the Party's Convention headquarters at Miami Beach, and a bizarre scheme to raid the Las Vegas offices of a former associate of the millionaire recluse Howard Hughes.

One again, however, Liddy's proposals were turned down. But once again, they were not rejected out of hand. Long and careful discussion had taken place on a proposal to eavesdrop on Larry O'Brien, the Democratic Party chairman. "Mr. O'Brien had been a very effective spokesman against our position on the ITT case," Magruder remembered, "and I think there was a general concern that if he was allowed to continue as Democratic National Chairman, because he was most certainly their most professional operator, that he could be very difficult in the coming campaign. So we had hoped that information might discredit him." The arrogance contained in the assumption that the men from CREEP were the ones to decide who could and who could not be "allowed" to remain as Democratic National Chairman is positively breathtaking; but for the moment the main outcome of this second meeting with Mitchell was that Liddy's proposals were once again turned down. And for the second time, a report on the meeting was sent up to the White House, this one direct from John Dean to the President's chief aide, H. R. Haldeman. According to Dean's later recollection, he told Haldeman that Liddy's schemes were "incredible, unnecessary and unwise," and that the Re-election Committee had no need of bugging, mugging, prostitutes and kidnappers.

Dean's memory may well by that time have acquired a self-protective coloration, but it demonstrates once again that at least the outlines of the Liddy plan were probably well known in the very highest echelons of the White House and that, incredibly, nothing was done there to stop it. It was now clear that at the meetings of these four men—three of them lawyers, one of them the highest law officer in the United States—was coming close to criminal conspiracy. Given the way the White House was run during Nixon's first term, one must assume that a single word from any one of the men of authority who now knew about the scheme would have been enough to kill Liddy's harebrained schemes stone dead. But the word was never given.

This time, as it happens, Gordon Liddy did not hide his disappointment that his plans had not been approved. He was again bitterly disappointed at his rebuff and seems to have had several violent arguments with Jeb Magruder, even threatening on one occasion to kill him. Magruder did not take the threat seriously, but he was becoming worried about Liddy's habit of openly carrying around a gun. Considering him an unstable character, he told the White House he wanted to fire him. Exactly what happened next is a matter of some dispute, but the outcome was that Liddy stayed, although in a slightly different capacity. He had by now struck up a renewed working acquaintance with E.

Howard Hunt, his old associate in the burglary of Ellsberg's psychiatrist's office of the previous year and had brought Hunt over from the White House to work with him on "Gemstone" and the other plans.

Hunt had worked twenty years for the CIA, had taken part in the abortive Bay of Pigs invasion in 1961 and had written a string of some 47 thrillers under a variety of pen names, each drawing on his inside knowledge of the agency's operations. Hunt and Liddy were birds of a feather, and Liddy seems to have confided to Hunt his disappointment that all his espionage plans were being turned down. At any rate, Hunt passed the message on to Charles Colson, another high White House aide, and a few nights later Jeb Magruder got a telephone call from Colson, who asked him, in Magruder's words, "to get off the stick and get the budget approved for Mr. Liddy's plans, that we needed information, particularly on Mr. O'Brien." Magruder claims Colson never mentioned wiretapping or espionage, but he assumed Colson knew at least the outline of Liddy's plans. Thus, imperceptibly, the conspiracy was broadening. By now, at a conservative estimate, at least six of the President's top aides had inside knowledge of what was afoot.

To Magruder, Colson's message was clear enough. The White House wanted information on O'Brien, and Magruder felt he had been instructed to revive Liddy's proposals. Accordingly, at the end of March, two months after Liddy had seen his first schemes rejected, a third meeting was set up with John Mitchell, who was at this time vacationing near the President's retreat at Key Biscayne. There, a long strategy session was held with Magruder, Mitchell, and the Attorney General's confidante, Fred la Rue, during which they discussed a series of some thirty decision papers concerned with the campaign, most of them dealing with direct mail and advertising. The last item on the agenda was the Liddy proposal, by now further scaled down to a cost of some $250,000. For a while, the entire project hung once more in the balance. "I can honestly say that no one was particularly overwhelmed with the project," Magruder testified later. "But I think we felt that the information could be useful." Mitchell then reportedly circled three of Liddy's proposals: first, for a bugging operation on the Democratic National Committee offices at the Watergate, and then, if funds were still available, for entry into the Presidential contenders' offices, and later into the Convention headquarters at Miami Beach. "Okay," Mitchell is said to have remarked, "Let's give him a quarter of a million dollars and see what he can come up with."

Mitchell has since vehemently denied he ever made this remark attributed to him by Magruder, but whether or not the conversation occurred, Liddy was informed that his scaled-down plan had at last been approved. The die was now cast for the political crimes that came to be known as Watergate. Liddy went to the CRP's treasurer, Hugh Sloan, and asked for an initial $83,000 to get the operation moving. Sloan was not told what they money was for, and, worried by the request, approached Maurice Stans, the former Commerce

Secretary, who was now Nixon's chief fundraiser. Stans went in turn to Mitchell; Mitchell came on to Magruder to ask why Liddy needed so much money. Magruder says he explained that it was "front-end money" needed to buy the necessary bugging equipment and the other early costs of getting Liddy's operations together. Mitchell professed himself satisfied with this explanation, and so approval for the scheme was finally given.

Finding the money needed to front these covert operations was actually the least of the Committee's problems at this time. The men from CREEP were in fact awash with money—and the corrupting effect of the millions of dollars they had collected for the President's re-election effort was at least partly responsible for the senseless crimes that followed. Maurice Stans turned out to be the most successful—and ruthless—fundraiser in electoral history, bringing in an estimated $55 million to the coffers at CREEP, which was thereby enabled to run the most lavishly-financed Presidential campaign America has ever known.

The use of Stans as the President's chief bagman was itself a questionable ploy. As former Secretary of Commerce, he was now turning for political cash to those corporations whose profits were once directly influenced by his own Department—and were likely to be so influenced again if, as was then expected, he returned to his Commerce Department post after Nixon's re-election. The methods he now used to raise funds for CREEP amounted to little less than outright extortion. At one time, a list was drawn up by the Committee's finance officers of corporations and individuals "who had problems with the Government" and a financial quota set for their expected contributions. "Can the guy who gave the President $20,000 pick up the phone and call the White House if he gets into trouble with the feds?" asked a Houston oil man rhetorically. "You bet. Does he realize this when he gives? You bet."

Corporations dependent on the Government for their business were another obviously vulnerable target. Thus, American Airlines, one of the largest in the nation, was induced to make an illegal contribution of some $55,000 out of company funds at a time when the airline had a merger pending with Western Airlines. "A large part of the money raised from the business community for political purposes is given for fear of what would happen if it were not given," commented George A. Spater, American's chairman, after the incident came to light.

Then there was the sale of ambassadorships, a practice of dubious morality which has had a long history in the United States, but one which was now cynically raised to the level of almost open auction. Contributions from some would-be ambassadors were regarded as no more than their first bid: if they really wanted the post, the committee would come back to them and ask for more, and there was an understanding that if, as expected, the President was re-elected, the campaign bids would afterwards have to be raised. In this manner, Mrs. Ruth Farkas, a lady of ready wealth but no other obvious qualifications, was bilked of $300,000 to purchase the post of U.S. Ambassador to Luxembourg—$200,000 of which she had prudently made payable *after* the election.

Practices of this nature had been used before in Presidential politics—but never before had they been used so openly, or the funds solicited so blatantly. What was more, much of this money was solicited in *cash* in order to make it more difficult to trace; and, presumably, easier to use for illicit activities as the need arose. Equally cynical was the manner in which the funds were drummed up secretly before the deadline, in April, for a new federal law which required the full disclosure of the sources of all large campaign contributions. Thus, when cash was needed for the Watergate operation, there was no need to report whence it had come. And just to make sure the source would not be traced, much of the money subsequently used for the Watergate break in was first "laundered" by a process in which it passed from the original contributor through a bank in Mexico and back into the hands of G. Gordon Liddy and his cohorts.

Part of the reason for this secrecy over funds was to be found in the curious nature of the Committee to Re-elect the President, a political oddity that was again the product of the particular arrogance that afflicted the Nixon entourage during its first term in office. Disillusioned after his unsuccessful intervention on behalf of Republican Party candidates in the mid-term elections of 1970, Nixon had turned his back on the GOP and set up his own private apparatus at CREEP in an attempt to win a purely personal victory at the polls in November. For the first time, a Presidential candidate was thus cut off almost entirely from contact with his own party: another decision, born of arrogance, for which the Nixon men were later to pay dearly. Not only did the men from CREEP ignore entirely the state parties for most of the subsequent campaign, they were themselves strictly amateurs in the world of professional politics. None of them had ever run for political office, all of their loyalties were concentrated around one man—Richard Nixon—and none of them had a wider constituency in the country as a whole. Their sin was pride, the almost passionless crimes they now planned motivated by a perverted sense of loyalty to the President. To this day, there is evidence that many of them still do not accept the idea that what they did was wrong—that the acts they committed were worse by far than the simple corruption or personal greed that had marked earlier Presidential scandals. For as Mr. Justice Brandeis observed back in 1938: "The greatest dangers to liberty lurk in insidious encroachment by men of zeal, well-meaning but without understanding." His phrase describes precisely the character of the men with whom Richard Nixon had chosen to surround himself.

This was a crime of the managerial classes, the Babbitts of the 1970s, men with closed minds and pragmatic hearts. And these were the men who now set the scene for a series of political crimes unique in American history. Yet, as it later turned out, Liddy's raids on the Watergate were but a small part of the whole chilling picture. For in conjunction with his now comparatively modest espionage operations, the men around Nixon were also busy with a variety of other stratagems designed to do down their opponents and, if possible, to destroy the Democratic Party as a Presidential campaign force. In other words, they set out to rig the results of the Presidential election and to steal from the citizens of America their most precious heritage—the right to choose their own Government in a free and open election. This was not politics, at least not politics as it has been traditionally understood in America; this was warfare. For as Stewart Alsop has perceptively pointed out, the techniques used against their opponents by the men from CREEP were exactly those used by the allied secret services in waging covert and unconventional war against the Germans. But to transfer the subversive techniques used in the efforts to bring down Nazism to the political process inside America was, as Alsop said, "a genuinely terrifying innovation." Yet this is now exactly what the men from CREEP had set out to accomplish. At its peak, three networks of covert agents were set up, each with the specific task of espionage or sabotage. Their campaign followed almost exactly the fourfold patterns of the wartime Secret Service operations—Secret Intelligence, Secret Operations, Morale Operations, and Black Propaganda.

Marcus Raskin and Robert Borosage, both of the Institute for Policy Studies, see this operation as an almost inevitable outcome of the license granted to the President and the bureaucracies in conducting national security affairs. "Men have been trained to murder, bribe, lie and sabotage in the national interest," they write. "High executive officials have learned to order lawless activity without compunction, to lie without shame. They have invented a system of para-law, ersatz law that is based on command and higher authority as a way to rationalize criminal activity in the name of the state or the leader. The Watergate only demonstrates the obvious: such training not only warps the conduct of foreign affairs but our own democracy. If *raison d'etat* can justify bribery and subversion to influence the outcome of elections in Chile, Guatemala or South Vietnam, then it is hardly mysterious that a program of sabotage and wiretapping was similarly justified to re-elect President Nixon."

As in any wartime operation, one of the tasks the Nixon men had set themselves was to discredit their opponents with any useful "black propaganda" that came to hand. For example, at a time when it still seemed possible that Senator Edward Kennedy might be the Democratic nominee, E. Howard Hunt was sent over from his office in the White House to read through old State Department cables to see if he could find any evidence there that would blacken the reputation of President John Kennedy, and in particular he was asked to discover if there was any truth in the persistent rumours that Kennedy had acquiesced in the murder of South Vietnam's President Ngo Dinh Diem.

Hunt came back from his mission with some not very incriminating cables and showed them to Charles Colson, his White House superior, who, according to Hunt's sworn testimony, then declared: "Well, this isn't good enough. Do you think you could improve on them?" Whereupon Hunt set to with the White House Xerox machine, a razor blade and a typewriter and, using his novelist's imagination, concocted a cable of his own, purporting to connect Kennedy with the Diem assassination. Hunt and Colson then tried to interest *Life* magazine in publishing their "discovery", but after showing initial interest, the *Life* reporter became suspicious and nothing came of that venture.

Meanwhile, as the Democrats' front runner, Senator Muskie now became the prime target for the covert operation. A Nixon supporter was infiltrated into the Muskie campaign organization, where he intercepted several confidential documents which were used to embarrass the candidate. Later, as Muskie's campaign got under way, his organization began to experience a series of inexplicable incidents—all apparently organized by the men from CREEP and the White House. A campaign flight bound for Portland, Oregon, was mysteriously rerouted to Salem, throwing a whole day's campaign effort into disarray. At one fundraising dinner for Muskie, someone sent round hundreds of dollars worth of liquor and food, including 200 hot pizzas —all unordered, and all sent COD. A dozen African diplomats were invited to the dinner and chauffeur-driven limousines provided to drive them there, while two magicians—one flown in from the Virgin Islands—suddenly materialized to entertain them. During the New Hampshire primary campaign, voters in that conservative and largely white northern state would receive telephone calls in the middle of the night from an organization claiming to be the "Harlem for Muskie Committee", urging them to vote for Muskie because of his record in supporting black people. Finally, came the most successful dirty trick of all—the famous forged letter alleging that Muskie had sneered at New Hampshire's "Canucks", one of the allegations that caused the candidate to break down and weep in the snow—an event which is thought by many to have seriously affected his performance at the polls a few days later.

With that success behind them, the men from CREEP may fairly be said to have at least influenced the eventual result of the 1972 election campaign, and they now took the decision that the candidate whom Nixon could most easily beat in the November elections would be George McGovern. They accordingly set out to do what they could to help assure his nomination.

These, then, were the black propaganda operations, designed to throw the Democratic party into disarray and, it now seems, carried out with chilling efficiency. Meanwhile, morale operations were also in progress. The White House was flooded with cables supporting the President's policies in Vietnam —most of them forged in an attempt to persuade the electorate that the President's policies were more popular than they really were. Campaign funds already gathered were on one occasion diverted, in cash, to the proceeds for a fundraising dinner for Vice-President Agnew in an attempt to make it appear the organizers had taken in $50,000 more than they actually did.

The minds that dreamed up all these plans were also turned to other purposes, not specifically connected with the forthcoming election, but designed nonetheless to intimidate anyone who had too openly criticized the Nixon regime. According to one story, the White House had seriously considered blowing up the Brookings Institute, a well-regarded Washington think-tank; the idea was that after the explosion one of the Washington "plumbers" could dash into the building in the confusion and make off with some papers the White House wanted to acquire. The mind reels at such tactics, and in fact that plan was never carried out. On a more practical level, one White House memo penned by John Dean spoke of using the federal bureaucracy to "deal" with people known to be active in their opposition. "Stated a bit more bluntly," he elegantly added—"how we can use the available federal machinery to screw our political opponents." To this end, the FBI was called out to make a full field investigation of Daniel Schorr, a news reporter with CBS, who had aroused the wrath of the Nixon entourage for his investigative reporting on the Washington bureaucracy. Chet Huntley, the former NBC newscaster, was given difficulties at the Department of the Interior in getting underway with his resort plans in Montana, apparently on the basis of a single hostile comment he had made about the President. But perhaps the most notorious of these activities was the plan to use the federal tax system to harass known opponents of the administration. Attempts were made—not altogether successfully—to crack down on the multitude of tax-exempt foundations that were, in the White House view, "feeding left-wing causes", to infiltrate the bureaucracy of the Internal Revenue Service with Nixon supporters and to stimulate tax audits and other legal difficulties for people who were critical of the President. One such audit was made against a comparatively lowly reporter who had once written a hostile article about Nixon's friend Bebe Rebozo. Yet another memo written inside the White House represented a flagrant attempt to put political pressure on the IRS commissioner, John Walters. The memo said, in part:

> Walters must be made to know that discreet political actions and investigations on behalf of the administration are a firm requirement and responsibility on his part.

The mentality thus displayed is sinister in its implications. Here were intelligent men, entrusted with running the most powerful office in the world, revealing themselves as ready, for the pettiest of motives, to subvert the practices of democracy, to cast aside with hardly a thought the minimum standards of decency without which power comes very close to tyranny. The philosophy of ruthless pragmatism which seemed to guide these men was, in a very real sense, subversive. They were, as Connecticut Senator Lowell Weicker later remarked, the men who almost stole America.

Watergate and its associated crimes were not attempts by a single man of evil intent; it was rather a matter of crime by group. None of the participants was evil in the traditional sense, hardly any of them really considered they were doing wrong; they were, to all outward appearances, utterly normal Americans, young men on the rise mostly, loyal, smooth and bland, and quite unburdened with ideas. "I am guilty," one of them was to say later, "of a deep sense of loyalty to the President of the United States." And that was precisely the flaw in their characters; their unquestioning loyalty to Richard Nixon, to the "team", was so strong it overrode all other considerations. Loyalty, indeed, was the main reason most of them had been chosen for their jobs in the first place. As Chief of Staff for the most isolated President of the century, H.R. Haldeman had surrounded himself with young men beholden to him for their careers, men without any political ties of their own, who did not dare to question his instructions. And for four years they ran the country as though they were running an election campaign.

Haldeman himself was the classic administrator, the office manager, an insider whose previous experience of practical politics had been as a Nixon advance man, versed to the point of perfectionism in the public relations techniques of packaging his candidate in the manner in which he had once sold Black Flag insecticide for the J. Walter Thompson advertising agency. Long before Watergate, Richard J. Whalen, a conservative Republican who had worked with Haldeman in the 1968 campaign, wrote in his book *Catch the Falling Flag* that "the once prestigious title of 'Special Assistant to the President' was bestowed wholesale on ex-advance men who had proved their fitness to govern by releasing the balloons at precisely the moment the candidate's arms shot skyward in a V. They were sober, industrious, efficient, and almost completely unaware of a wider world and a larger politics than they had known." Even during the 1968 campaign, Whalen had concluded that "we were under the heel of men basically unsure of themselves, second-raters playing over their heads and fiercely resentful of anyone who dared approach them at eye-level. Nixon's own insecurity caused him to need the protection of men willing to do whatever he wished."

Although neither Haldeman nor any of his henchmen had any previous experience of national politics when they assumed power with Richard Nixon in the New Year of 1969, they had set about, with a zeal that was part arrogance, part naiveté, to draw into their own hands the greatest concentration of executive power the United States had ever seen. Before their downfall they had effectively stripped the Cabinet of all members with any independent standing, replaced them with pliable and obedient men and brought virtually all the executive power within the confines of the White House. John Ehrlichman, the other half of the "Berlin Wall", once sent a letter to a member of the Cabinet which, as Hugh Sidey has recounted it, went something like this:

"The President has asked me to tell you how displeased he is with what you have done about——" The Cabinet member was petrified lest the letter should get out. "Can you imagine what would have happened under Ike or Johnson if such a letter had been received?" an official said. "Their Cabinet members would have taken the White House apart."

Yet for all their immense power, "The German Mafia" had not a shred of idealism in their souls. "We believe in what works," was their pragmatic catchphrase. And in the court-like atmosphere they had created in the Nixon White House, the exercise of individual judgment and morality was not a quality to be prized—but rather a weakness to be despised. The supreme virtue was to be "on the team", and anyone who dared to question the group's decisions was cast out of the team like some latter-day pariah. Thus, when asked why he had gone along with crimes he knew were being committed, Bart Porter, yet another young CREEP executive, was able earnestly to reply: "In all honesty, probably because of the fear of group pressure that would ensue, of not being a team player."

The silence in the face of conspiracy, the acquiescence in crime that follow from this attitude are the qualities that made Watergate possible, qualities long embodied in the American ideal of "belonging," of being part of a group that is larger than the individual. Such ideals have been around for quite a while, and were well described back in the 1950s by William H. Whyte in his bestselling book *The Organization Man*. The organization man, Whyte wrote, was caught in a modern trap. "Every decision he faces on the problem of the individual versus authority is something of a dilemma. It is not a case of whether he should fight against black tyranny or blaze a new trail against patent stupidity. That would be easy—intellectually at least. The real issue is far more subtle. For it is not the evils of organization life that puzzle him, *but its very beneficence.* He is imprisoned in brotherhood. Because his area of maneuver seems so small and because the trappings so mundane, his fight lacks the heroic cast."

Twenty-five years later, Whyte's perceptive analysis found its precise echo in the anguish of Hugh Sloan, the young treasurer of the CREEP finance committee, and one of the few men on the Nixon team who had the strength of character to refuse to go along with crime by the group. "There was no independent sense of morality there," Sloan was to say of his years at the White House. "I mean if you worked for someone, he was God and whatever the orders were, you did it—and there were damned few who were able to make or willing to make independent judgments. It was all so narrow, so closed. Nobody listened to anybody who wasn't in a superior position. They were guys who had committed themselves economically to politics—you know, in a way in which it was not only what they were doing at the moment but what they were going to be doing all their lives, and because of that there emerged some kind of separate morality about things."

Yet even Hugh Sloan, who honorably resigned when he realized what was being done with all the loose cash he handed out, was imbued with a sense of loyalty to the group. "I want you to know," he said, "that I feel I did not leave the team. As far as I am concerned, the team left me."

Sloan at least had the good sense to get out while he honestly could. But the other members of the team blindly went along with whatever was asked of them, assuming that just by being members of the wider body, by simply following "official" orders, they were absolved from all personal responsibility and all taint of wrong-doing. They were, for the most part, pitiful figures, caught up in a senseless human tragedy that would destroy their careers, send some of them to jail and prevent others from ever again practicing their chosen profession. Much later, when Senator Sam Ervin sought to explain their motives, he reached into Shakespeare for the lament of Cardinal Wolsey in *Henry VIII*: "Had I but served my God with half the zeal I served my King, he would not in mine age have left me naked to mine enemies."

Meanwhile, the plot that was to lead all of these men to their downfall was gathering momentum. Liddy, who was putting together, on his reduced budget, the ragged group of agents who were to conduct the Watergate break-in, had already picked Hunt to supervise the overall operation, and for his team of "hit men" it was natural that Hunt should rely on his old cronies from the CIA. His first contact was with Bernard Barker, a Miami real estate operator who had been his second-in-command during the Bay of Pigs landings of eleven years previously, and to whom he had turned once before, to help with the burglary at the offices of Daniel Ellsberg's psychiatrist.

Of all the participants in the Watergate crimes, Barker is the one who perhaps deserves the most compassion. His motives for joining the operation, although muddled and obviously misguided, were in a strange sense honorable. An American citizen who had lived for much of his life in Cuba, Barker had retained both an intense loyalty to Hunt and an equally intense hatred of the Cuban regime of Fidel Castro. This man who saw politics in such simple terms of black and white looked upon Hunt as a symbol of Cuba's freedom, and he still referred to his former commander under his CIA code name of Eduardo.

Hunt had apparently persuaded Barker that the mission for which he was now recruited was a "national security" operation, designed to produce proof that the Castro regime was helping to finance the Democrats' election campaign, particularly that of George McGovern. Later, when asked by the Senate investigating committee how he could possibly have become involved in such an operation, Barker replied simply: "Eduardo represents to the Cuban people their liberation. I cannot deny my services in the way that it was proposed to me on a matter of national security, knowing that with my training I had the personnel available for this type of operation. . . . We had hopes that Mr. Hunt's position in the White House would be a decisive factor at a later date for obtaining help in the liberation of Cuba."

Barker, in short, was simply a misguided fanatic, easily persuaded to become the tool of other, more subtle minds. And he had the additional advantage of bringing with him into the operation a group of similarly-minded men, some of them Cuban exiles, who could be likewise trusted to conduct the operation with discipline and discretion. For Barker and his men, this was to be another CIA-type mission, based on the philosophy: "If you are caught by the enemy, every effort will be made to retrieve you, all of your expenses will be taken care of, and your family will be provided for." According to their code, the mission, once explained, was never again discussed, either with each other or with Hunt. All Barker was told by Hunt was: "Get your men into training going up and down stairs." Barker unquestioningly obeyed.

The final member of the Watergate "hit team" was to be James McCord, CREEP's security officer and another former veteran of the CIA with a shadowy background. As a specialist in wiretapping, McCord's job was to install the actual eavesdropping equipment in the Democrats' headquarters.

To his neighbors in suburban Maryland, McCord was a respected pillar of the community, a practicing Methodist who spent half a day each week working for his church, and as the father of a retarded child, was chairman of a local group devoted to helping other handicapped children. "They are just a lovely family, and wonderful neighbors," one of the housewives from the area was quoted as saying after he had been arrested. Like the others, McCord now went along with the Watergate plans out of a misguided sense of loyalty, because, he believed, the break-in had been "directed" by the U.S. Attorney General. To men of an authoritarian cast of mind, as McCord seems to have been, orders from above are to be loyally obeyed—not questioned.

After an initial abortive attempt to plant eavesdropping bugs in the offices of Senator McGovern—thwarted because there was always someone in the office working late—McCord now received his instructions for the bugging operation at the Watergate. On Memorial Day weekend at the end of May the break-in was successfully accomplished and two bugs planted, one of them on O'Brien's phone, a second on the phone of Spencer Oliver, another Democratic Party executive. At the same time, photographs were taken of a number of documents taken from the office safe. The operation was financed with cash taken from Maurice Stans' safe, which had been carefully "laundered" through the bank in Mexico.

This was the point at which things began to go wrong. Liddy, with a foolhardy bravado—which he later blamed on the lack of proper funding—had gone along himself on one of the earlier missions to McGovern's headquarters, and to help accomplish their breakin had drawn his pistol and shot out the office light bulbs. When Magruder and Strachan heard of this, not long after the initial break-in at the Watergate, they were furious with Liddy and deeply concerned lest his participation in the nighttime missions should be traced back to the Re-election Committee. So Liddy was already in disgrace when the first fruits of his Watergate venture began to come through. And they too, according to most accounts, were deeply disappointing. As John Ehrlichman declared later: "They learned a great deal more about Mr. Oliver than anyone really wanted to know." What was worse, the attempt to monitor O'Brien's phone was a mechanical failure.

Disappointing though they were, Magruder has since testified that he took the results of the break-in to a meeting with John Mitchell (which Mitchell has since strongly denied) and showed them to the Attorney General, together with the photographs of the stolen documents, the thieves' fingers in rubber gloves showing around the edges. But again, the photographs were found to contain little of substance. Although Mitchell disputes this account, Magruder says the Attorney General then called Liddy up to his office and gave him a severe tongue-lashing. He is alleged to have told Liddy the job was not satisfactory, the mission had been valueless and not worth the money that had been paid for it.

Much chastened by the humiliating failure of his expensive mission, which came on top of all his other troubles, Liddy now took the most fateful decision of all—to go back to the Watergate, to break in again, and put right the defective equipment. Although Hunt was by now having his doubts about the operation, Liddy is reported to have told him: "We can't call it off. We are doing this on Mr. Mitchell's orders. We must go ahead."

Whether Liddy was using Mitchell's name to conceal his own frustrations at having failed in his initial mission, or whether he was truthfully reporting Mitchell's instructions has not been satisfactorily resolved. In any event, Liddy took it upon himself to organize a second break-in, scheduled for shortly after midnight on June 17th, and he spent the day before the operation personally forging documents purporting to entitle "the bearer" to enter the DNC premises. The denouement was now at hand.

Shortly after midnight on June 17th, Frank Wills, a young security guard, was making his round of the Watergate office complex when he noticed that masking tape had been placed over the latches on two of the office doors so that they would not lock when closed. Thinking the tapes had been placed there by maintenance men and later forgotten, he removed them and continued on his rounds. Ten minutes later, when he passed the same two doors again, he found the tape had mysteriously reappeared—and more tape had been placed over other locks on the floor.

Wills went immediately to the lobby of the Watergate and called the Metropolitan police, who at once sent round an unmarked squad car. Inside the Democratic National Committee offices, police found Barker and his team, well-dressed, wearing rubber surgical gloves. The hit team had been caught red-handed, and from them police confiscated break-in equipment, cameras, forty rolls of unexposed film, three pen-sized tear gas guns, a walkie-talkie radio, bugging equipment, and thousands of dollars in cash, most of it in hundred-dollar bills with the serial numbers in sequence. In a small diary carried by one of the men appeared the notation: "Howard Hunt, W.H.", and after it, the White House telephone number. The hit team had been astonishingly careless, and from those small clues was pieced together the ingredients for the most explosive political scandal in American history. Sooner or later, full disclosure of the whole unsavory story was now inevitable.

Within days, the links with both the White House and the Committee to Re-elect the President had been publicly established, thanks largely to some persistent police beat reporting by the metropolitan desk of the *Washington Post.* By the end of the month, John Mitchell had resigned as the President's campaign director in mysterious circumstances, and not long after that it became publicly known that a campaign contribution for $25,000 which had been handed to Maurice Stans had found its way into Barker's bank account in Miami. By August, it was known that a "secret" horde of cash, $350,000, mostly in $100 bills, had been kept during the campaign in Stans' safe in the Re-election Committee offices. Throughout the rest of the election campaign, right up until polling day in November, the newspapers, led by the *Washington Post,* kept up a steady drip-drip-drip of revelations, each more damning than the last, each more firmly implicating the men around Nixon not only in the Watergate affair but also in a massive campaign of political spying and sabotage. And yet, for fully ten months, the public seemed not to care.

Perhaps the most mysterious aspect of the whole Watergate affair is its almost inexplicable lack of impact during the subsequent election campaign, and indeed well into the President's second term as well. Public opinion during a period of some ten months remained utterly dormant, apparently accepting at face value the repeated denials of wrongdoing that flowed from the White House. In spite of Nixon's personal lack of popularity, the institution of the presidency seemed to have become so hallowed that the American people wanted desperately to believe the best. The ironic conclusion must be that if the President had at any time before his second inauguration had the knowledge and the will to admit the wrong and order an immediate housecleaning, the matter would have been quickly forgotten—or at least forgiven by a tolerant electorate.

But as it happened, the American people were never asked the easier question which could have been put to them at any time in the months that followed the break-in—that is, were they prepared to condone the bugging of one party's headquarters by spies from another? With hindsight, it can be said with near certainty that the majority of them would not have looked unkindly upon such an admission, if it had been made promptly and frankly and been accompanied by some minimum sign of contrition. Indeed, the evidence suggests that they might well have been eager to do so. But thanks to the arrogant belief of the men around the President that they had no need to confess their wrong-doing, the easy question was never put. Instead, when it came, the question was the infinitely more difficult one of whether public opinion was prepared to condone the greater crime of obstructing the course of justice in order to hide that initial wrongdoing. And this time, the answer was no. The *New Yorker* put it well when it wrote, in a commentary on the Watergate coverup, that in a democracy certain forms of truth do more than compel our minds' assent; they compel us to act. Truth and justice have shaped and determined the fundamental structures of American institutions, said the magazine. "In a democracy, we are free to do many things, but we are not free to ignore the truth. It holds the system itself, and our individual liberty, hostage. In the end, it is by virtue of this power that our nation consents to march to the tune of a piece of paper—the Constitution."

It is a part of the genius of the American system that in the end, when the truth came out, no power on earth, not even the immense power of the presidency, was strong enough to conceal it; and that once the truth was out, the system was compelled into action. But at the same time, it is worth recalling that it was not public opinion which forced the truth out into the open. It was the law.

Right through the summer of 1972 and well into the following winter, the senior echelons of the White House, the President's Re-election Committee, the Justice Department and several other branches of the federal bureaucracy all labored to conceal the administration's involvement in the associated crimes of Watergate. Attempts were made to intimidate the press, muzzle the courts, suppress the evidence. The members of the hit team were induced, by outright bribery, to plead guilty and thus prevent their cross-examination in open court, an event which might have produced evidence implicating officials more senior in the hierarchy. President Nixon's personal attorney was instrumental in raising hundreds of thousands of dollars to buy this vital silence and promises were made that if the defendants kept quiet they would be granted executive clemency after a short spell in jail. Meanwhile, incriminating documents were burned and shredded by the bucketful and attempts were made by both Haldeman and Ehrlichman to bully the FBI into not pressing its investigations. At one point, a plot was discussed to pass off the burglary as a CIA operation—and thus cover it up in the interests of "national security." The strategy of the Nixon men during this entire period was to hold the line at Liddy, to maintain by every means in their power the implausible story that the Watergate plot had begun and ended with the unauthorized excesses of this flamboyant ex-FBI agent.

By the President's second inauguration, as John Dean has testified, the Watergate cover-up had become a way of life, for him and for many other senior officials around Washington. And right until the spring of 1973, it seemed they might still get away with it. Public opinion continued to be dormant, and it was doubtless the fervent prayer of the now enormous number of senior officials who were involved that once the seven convicted burglars were safely in jail, the issue would quietly die away. But that was not to be. On the very eve of his sentencing, Jim McCord broke his silence and brought the whole tottering edifice crumbling into ruins.

He was induced to do so largely because of the pressures placed upon him by an upright federal judge, John Sirica, a conservative 69-year-old jurist who had been demonstrably angered at the rampant perjury that had been committed in his courtroom during the trial of the seven defendants and by the pusillanimous case brought by the federal prosecutors and the continued refusal of the defendants to implicate their superiors. Sirica, who was known in Washington as "Maximum John" because of the severity of the sentences he frequently handed down, had for some time been putting pressure on McCord through his probation officer, and on the day of his sentencing, McCord publicly broke the nine-month silence maintained by the defendants —in spite of the fact that this tough former CIA agent was in fear of retaliation, even death, should he now disclose the truth. Most of the defendants were under the impression that they would be sent to jail for a year, or maybe two, but they were visibly shaken when Sirica handed down his sentence on Liddy: up to twenty years in prison, as an example, with a fine of $40,000 thrown in on top. As the others followed, one by one, Sirica sentenced them each to "provisional" terms of 35 to 40 years, with the strong hint that the sentences would be reconsidered if they broke their silence.

McCord had by this time already agreed to talk, and in a letter to Judge Sirica he admitted that political pressure had been applied to the defendants to plead guilty and remain silent, that others were involved in the Watergate affair who had not yet been identified and that perjury had occurred during the trial itself. McCord had been under intense pressure from the White House for several months on end, and had once been summoned, by a mysterious caller, to a phone box near his home, where he received the following message:

Plead guilty. One year is a long time. You will get executive clemency. Your family will be taken care of and when you get out you will be rehabilitated and a job will be found. Don't take immunity when called before the Grand Jury. . . .

In retrospect, it seemed McCord's composure had begun to crack during the early part of the trial when he heard Jeb Magruder perjure himself. And when he saw a picture of the smiling Magruder in the newspapers, the feeling began to grow that he and the other defendants were being set up as the "fall guys" in the operation, the scapegoats, and that the role of the big shots— he mentioned Mitchell, Dean and Magruder—was to be covered up. He believed they were lying to save their own skins and that, he said, was not his idea of American justice, the trial was a sham, and he was prepared to make his unhappiness known. On one occasion, he says, he was offered $100,000 in cash to keep his silence, and on another he was summoned to a rendezvous with a former White House aide, Jack Caulfield, who was allegedly helping in the coverup. There, in a car park overlooking the Potomac River, he was told: "The President's ability to govern is at stake. Another Teapot Dome scandal is possible, and the government may fall. Everyone is on track but you. You are not following the game plan. . . ."

But by now it was too late. McCord was suffering from a deep sense of injustice, determined that the role of the higher-ups should be disclosed. This one man in possession of the truth had within his hands the power to bring the government of the United States to a shuddering halt.

The whole coverup operation now began to fall apart, and some of the others who were implicated, notably Dean and Magruder, began a desperate scramble to save their own skins. When he got wind that he had been implicated, Magruder went to see the prosecutors and told them the whole story. A day later, he is reported to have bumped into Bart Porter in Lafayette Square, just across from the White House. "It's all over," he declared emotionally. "A lot of people are going to jail—Mitchell, La Rue, Mardian, myself, Dean, Colson, Strachan and maybe Haldeman. Silbert [the prosecutor] may indict *you*."

The elaborate coverup operation had finally collapsed. All through April and well into May the revelations came pouring out, wrecking reputations, humbling the mighty, driving shoals of high Nixon officials out of office and threatening at any moment to engulf the President himself. For weeks on end, the country lived in a state of acute crisis, perhaps the gravest crisis any American administration had experienced in living memory. And at its center was Richard Nixon.

Only a few short months before, the President had been returned to office in one of the more memorable landslides in electoral history, finally freed, as he must have thought, from all those insecurities that had plagued him throughout his political career, respected at last, confident of his abilities, and now even demonstrably popular with the electorate. How sweet the cup of triumph must have seemed as he took his oath of office at his second inauguration in January! And with what cruel swiftness it was immediately afterwards dashed from his lips!

Within weeks of his inauguration, Nixon's administration lay in ruins, with Haldeman and Ehrlichman both forced from their offices, Mitchell and Stans under indictment for perjury and conspiracy, lesser fry squabbling publicly among themselves as they strove desperately to avoid being sent to jail, and Nixon himself caught out in earlier untruths about Watergate which his press secretary was now obliged to characterize, in the language of George Orwell's Newspeak, as "inoperative."

As the country looked on in a sort of fascinated horror, the issue now was the credibility of Richard Nixon. At stake was his survival as President. And the questions his countrymen pondered went straight to Nixon's personal involvement in the whole sordid affair: Did he know, in advance, about the Watergate operation? Did he authorize it? Did he know about or participate in the coverup? If firm evidence was produced which would answer any one of these questions in the affirmative, Nixon was surely doomed.

On April 30th, the President took his case to the people. Appearing on national television, a bust of Abraham Lincoln prominently displayed behind him, Richard Nixon was now face to face with the biggest crisis of his career. And, perhaps for the first time in his life, he failed to rise to the occasion. Looking haggard and nervous, the President addressed himself to generalities when the occasion demanded specifics, leaving the impression that he regarded Watergate as a minor diversion, one which he said had already claimed "far too much of my time and my attention." Leave me alone, he seemed to be saying, "I must now turn my full attention—and I shall do so—once again to the larger duties of this office. . . . There is vital work to be done. . . . work that cannot wait, work that I must do." This master manager of the personal crisis, the man who had once written that the most difficult part of any crisis is the moment when one must either face up to it or fly from it, chose now to fly. He failed to deal openly with any of the major issues that had been raised, accepting "responsibility" for Watergate, but spending much of his speech protesting his own innocence and putting the burden of guilt on his subordinates, people, he said, "whose zeal exceeded their judgment" at a time when he himself had been too busy to pay attention to the day-to-day details of his campaign. Towards the end, he fell back on self-pity, that lifelong characteristic, speaking of "my terrible personal ordeal" in ordering the bombing of Hanoi, and a maudlin form of patriotism that caused him to conclude, in pious tones: "God bless America. And God bless each and every one of you."

It was, quite probably, the worst major speech he had ever made, and one which left the firm impression in the minds of the majority of Americans, confirmed in a subsequent Gallup poll, that Nixon knew much more about the affair than he was prepared to admit. For the first time in his life, Nixon's techniques of crisis management had let him down. Always before, he had been at his best in moments of extreme stress; his spiritual home had seemed to be in the last ditch, whence, at the very moment of defeat, he had sprung back like a cornered tiger to scatter his enemies, real or imagined, with a devastating counterattack. So as they settled down before their television sets on that Monday night, experienced Nixon watchers had expected to see something like a second Checkers speech, another Pumpkin Papers surprise, a skilful master stroke that would have diverted attention elsewhere, as had happened so often in the past. They received instead a series of lame excuses that stretched the credulity of even the most loyal of his viewers.

Garry Wills, the author of *Nixon Agonistes*, has suggested that Nixon floundered in his attempts to use television to recruit public sympathy because he was deprived of a kickable foe. He had been betrayed, he seemed to be saying—but he could not kick out at his betrayers, since they held his political fate in their hands. "He had to praise them while dismissing them," Wills wrote—"as if he had told us, back in 1952, that his funds were in good order, but, to appease his critics and get on with the nation's business, he had sent Checkers off to be chloroformed." Nor could he easily set up a straw man to attack, as he had also done so often in the past. The Communists would no longer serve, since Nixon himself had just engineered the detente with the two big Communist powers. He could hardly turn on the press, since the Washington *Post* had just been so resoundingly vindicated in its earlier Watergate exposures. He could no longer deride the government as soft on crime—since he was the government. There could be no more talk of "crooks in the White House", no angry speech about restoring law and order, no promises that, if elected, he would appoint a new Attorney General. He did, at a later date, make a somewhat feeble counter attack on "people who steal the government's secrets and publish them in the newspapers," but since Daniel Ellsberg's trial had by then been dismissed because of the gross misbehavior of the government, even that weapon was now blunted in his grasp.

There were times, in the nightmare days that followed, when it seemed the President would be swept at any moment from office, and it is known that on at least one occasion as he wrestled with his dilemma, he seriously discussed, in the intimacy of his own family, the possibility of his resignation. The world will probably never know what private agonies of mind and conscience Richard Nixon went through as the public drama unfolded. In his rare public appearances, he often looked haggard and woebegone and already years older than he had done at his inauguration three and a half months before. He spoke, from time to time, of "this deplorable incident" and when he appeared before a crowd in Florida he seemed to be moving around in a daze, guided along by Secret Service agents carrying walkie-talkies. "Turn him right there, and have him walk into the faculty," a reporter overheard one agent say. The President turned. "Have him wave." The President waved.

Under a parliamentary system of government, an administration caught in the embrace of such a widespread scandal would by this time certainly have fallen, but thanks to the inflexibility of the American structure, with its separation of powers and its fixed term of office, the only available machinery for dealing with the crisis it now faced was the cumbersome and destructive one of impeachment by the Congress. And this was the prospect before which the members of Congress recoiled. To most of them, the idea of impeaching an incumbent President, especially at the outset of a new term, was almost sacrilegious. Even George McGovern now rallied round to save the administration of Richard Nixon. "He is the elected leader of the nation," McGovern said, "and he is struggling to restore his leadership. We must help him for the sake of the office he holds." Melvin Laird, the former Secretary of Defense who was now called back to the rescue of the crippled Nixon White House, went still further. When asked whether he thought the President was involved in the Watergate coverup, he replied: "I don't want to know. I'm confident that the President didn't have any knowledge of this, but I don't want to put the presidency in a position where it's on trial. A trial of the presidency would be very dangerous, a bad mistake."

It was ironic that the same truth which had forced the system into action when dealing with the lesser fry, forced it now into paralysis when dealing with the President. This system which, in Senator Sam Ervin's words, had the strength and the resilience to endure the ferocity of the various investigations that were then under way, was not, it seems, considered strong enough to face the consequences of those investigations. What was at issue, of course, was not the survival of Richard Nixon, or even of the Republican Party, but the preservation of the presidential system of government. Yet this pervasive belief that the institution of the presidency was not resilient enough to survive the downfall of a single occupant demonstrated an appalling lack of faith in their institutions on the part of Americans who ought to have known better. Laird in particular seemed to be arguing that what the country needed now was to live in a world of silence and pretense and, like the three wise monkeys, "see no evil, hear no evil, speak no evil." In the last analysis, his argument implied that Americans must close their eyes to what was happening to the presidency for the sake of preserving the presidency. But would an office preserved on those terms be an office worth preserving? On those terms, indeed, could it be preserved at all as an office of honor and leadership?

An argument which failed to make the distinction between the institution of the presidency and the man who happened temporarily to occupy the office was based, in any case, on faulty logic; it was not the presidency which was on trial, it was the administration of Richard Nixon. It was true, however that, in a wider sense, the system was in conflict with itself. A rift had arisen between the two bedrock principles of government in the United States: that which holds that theirs is a government of laws, not men, and that no man is above the law; and the other which provides for the separation of powers in order to leave the President free to do his job without interference from the other branches of government. The members of Congress who had to consider the possibility of impeachment were thus placed in a terrible dilemma.

Without a doubt, impeachment would be a messy and divisive business, which if Nixon chose to fight it, could tear the country apart more tragically than had the Vietnam war, with untold consequences for the future. There were many who sincerely believed that impeachment in any but the most clearcut of circumstances would do infinitely more harm than good. There were others, more cynical, who opposed impeaching Nixon because it would lead to the presidency of Spiro Agnew. And that was an outcome which neither Republicans, who feared for the future of their Party, nor Democrats, who feared the fight against an incumbent Agnew in 1976, were particularly anxious to bring about.

On the other hand, the prospect of living for nearly four more years under an enfeebled President, no longer in control of his office, was equally appalling to contemplate. And by this time, Nixon's presidency had, to all intents and purposes, been destroyed, everything he did or said overshadowed by a growing impression of presidential guilt. For whether or not concrete evidence could be produced to implicate Nixon directly in the crimes that had been committed, Watergate was still the equivalent of murder in the Cathedral, the President's Thomas à Becket, and like Henry II he must be held accountable to history for the actions of his subordinates.

There were some who argued that this assumption was unjust, that every man, even the President, should be assumed innocent until proven guilty. This is an argument which equates, falsely, the fitness to hold high office with the protection of a private individual's rights before the courts. However, on the face of it, this is an assumption that the U.S. Constitution demands; before a President can be forcibly removed from office by impeachment, the Congress would need evidence sufficient to convict him for crimes in a court of law. There is no machinery, under the American system, for removing a President from office on the grounds that he has lost the confidence of the country, or even on the grounds that he has lost his ability to govern. On this particular point, a constitutional flaw was revealed. And it was due to this flaw that the country was thrown into such an anguished crisis of conscience over the Watergate affair. A President was clearly losing his ability to govern, while the country was left with no easy means of getting rid of him.

In its immediate consequences, Watergate therefore became a national trauma much greater than the sum of its parts. All through 1973 the crisis continued, getting worse rather than better, as the allegations crept nearer to the door of the Oval Office. The focus had switched now to the appearance of the perpetrators, one by one, before the Senate investigating committee headed by Senator Sam Ervin of North Carolina, the effect of which was to bring before the American public, in chilling detail, the full horrors of the affair, while at the same time further paralyzing the presidency of Richard Nixon.

The consequences of all of this, for the system, for the country, even for the world, can hardly fail to be profound. Watergate, with hindsight, will probably come to be regarded as historic a moment in the development of American political institutions as the arrival of the New Deal a generation and a half earlier, one of those cataclysmic upheavals that occur in all societies from time to time, destined to alter in fundamental ways the underlying relationship between the people and their government. To some, that is no bad thing. In the years since the New Deal, the presidency had imperceptibly acquired almost monarchical powers; and as Watergate had demonstrated, those powers had become too easy to abuse.

Daniel Webster once observed that "whatever government is not a government of laws is a despotism, let it be called what it may." Under Nixon, the presidency had come to be an office of such power that his men felt free to substitute their own will for the law, to spy on their fellow citizens, to subvert their most hallowed institutions, to usurp many of the constitutional powers of the Congress, to unleash what was in effect a secret police force on the citizenry, and then conspire to rig a presidential election in order to keep themselves in power. It was perhaps not yet tyranny, but it certainly represented a creeping drift towards arbitrary and lawless rule by the most authoritarian President in memory, a dress rehearsal, almost, of the means through which tyranny might be established in America. From this point of view, at least, Watergate was a crisis that came just in time.

3. Ins and Outs

"I know nothing grander, better exercise, better digestion, more positive proof of the past, the triumphant result of faith in human kind, than a well-contested American national election."

— WALT WHITMAN, *"Democratic Vistas"*

"There's nothing wrong with this country that a good election can't cure."

— RICHARD NIXON, *1968*

It is one of the clichés of American politics, generally although by no means always true, that the Republicans do not win national elections—the Democrats lose them. In a nation where registered Democrats outnumber their Republican rivals by a ratio of almost 2 to 1, how else can one explain the presidency of Richard Nixon, the first partisan Republican to win the White House since the days of Herbert Hoover (leaving aside the Eisenhower interregnum, for as a Republican candidate Ike was made in heaven and owed his elections to his personal popularity rather than his nominal party allegiance; He would have won just as handily as a Democrat)? The answer must be that he won because of a massive Democratic default, climbing to power in 1968 on the wreckage of the Democrats' convention in Chicago and consolidating his hold in 1972 against perhaps the weakest and most divisive candidate the Democrats have nominated for high office in a generation. So, while on the surface it would appear that Nixon's 1972 achievement in carrying every state except Massachusetts and the District of Columbia represented a massive mandate for the Republicans, a closer scrutiny of the results would indicate that the public was voting not so much for Nixon as against Senator McGovern. In the first place, Nixon's victory cut huge swathes in the nominal party registration figures for 1972: nearly 62 million Democrats against only 35 million Republicans, with slightly over 5 million independents. Second, his triumph was a purely personal one. In every other landslide in American history (Harding in 1920, Roosevelt in 1936, Johnson in 1964), the presidential candidate carried his party with him into overwhelming control of Congress, while Nixon was left facing a Congress still firmly under the control of the opposition party. Indeed, the Republicans have not held control of either House of Congress for close to twenty years.

Political scientists, journalists, and party professionals on both sides are still picking over the electoral entrails in the hopes of discovering the "real" significance of America's last remarkable election result. The Republicans, naturally enough, would like to think it signifies a turning point in political history as decisive as that heralded by Roosevelt's first victory in 1932, in which he created the modern Democratic Party coalition, or that of Lincoln, which first brought the new Republican Party to power in 1860, or that of William McKinley in 1896, which put the then agrarian and populist Democrats into the wilderness for a generation. These Republicans, led by the President himself, would like to believe they have laid the foundations of a new coalition in which the South, the suburbs, and what they call the "Sunbelt" have been permanently added to the traditional ranks of Republican voters and which, they fondly hope, will keep their party in power for years to come.

Their Democratic opponents, with an equally natural sense of self-preservation, disagree with this thesis. Their defeat in 1968, they argue, was due to an unfortunate alienation of the liberals over the Vietnam War, which is now over, while their even more disastrous defeat four years later can be put down to the selection of an inept and ideologically unacceptable candidate—temporary aberrations both. Come 1976, they claim with engaging plausibility, and the old coalition will be back together again, although with some admitted defections in the South. The party, having learned its lesson and perhaps purged its soul through the temporary flirtation with McGovernism, will swing once more to the center and win back all those "natural" Democrats in the unions and the so-called ethnic working classes who voted so heavily for Nixon in 1972 but could never expect to find a permanent and comfortable home in the party of big business and WASP respectability.

Other analysts, outside the party mainstream, have argued that the election of 1972 simply proved that the old two-party system seems to be collapsing. Nationally, the Democratic coalition sprang a slow leak at the end of World War II and has now outlived its usefulness, its political objectives worn so thin that today "they are little more than platitudes." These theorists, ignoring perhaps the enduring strength of the two main parties, look forward to the not-so-distant day when three or even four separate parties will compete for tenure of the White House, the Wallace movement or its successor splitting away to the right, the ideological "liberals" to the left, with the rump of the Democrats and Republicans struggling for what is left of the middle ground. Still others profess to believe that the political parties have become irrelevant to the choice of a presidential candidate and will somehow just wither away, leaving candidates to run as individuals outside the party organization, just as the Founding Fathers intended they should. The Constitution, after all, says nothing about the role of political parties, which were at that time regarded as dangerously factious innovations. Indeed, George Washington had warned in his farewell address against "the dangers of party in the state," although his words have been cheerfully ignored throughout this century and the last.

It is of course undeniable that a decade of unpopular war and unprecedented domestic turmoil have alienated large segments of the electorate from the modern party mainstream. In Nixon's impressive landslide a bare 55 percent of the electorate bothered to go to the polls, and of those who did turn out, an astonishing number split their tickets, voting for a Republican President in one column and Democratic Members of Congress in the other. Clearly, traditional party allegiances do not mean today what they once did. Studies have shown that in the seven elections since the end of World War II only 22 percent of the electorate who are old enough have voted consistently for a presidential candidate of the same party. The rest, almost four fifths of them, have switched their votes back and forth from Democrat to Republican (or in 1968 to Wallace) with scarcely a twinge of disloyalty.

Dramatic swings of voters from one national election to another have thus become a commonplace of American politics in the past decade. A 60 percent landslide for Johnson in 1964 was transformed only eight years later into a 60 percent landslide the other way. At least in presidential elections the American electorate has proved itself to be remarkably nonpartisan, showing no sign of giving either party a lasting majority. In spite of all the talk of "emerging majorities" and "new coalitions," that state of affairs seems likely to continue at least until the end of the present decade and perhaps beyond. It would be simply foolhardy to predict which party has the edge to win the next presidential election in 1976, although less so to predict that the next President will rise to power in the manner of his predecessors through the normal machinery of national party politics. The decay of the two-party system has not yet gone so far that it can be bypassed altogether. For all their limitations and shortcomings, for all the alienation of minority groups on both the left and right wings of the political spectrum, the traditional parties will both be around for the foreseeable future. They are, in short, indispensable to the proper functioning of American democracy.

In every national election since 1952, a political scientist called Samuel Lubell has toured the country asking voters a standard question: "What do you see as the big difference between the parties, in what the Democrats and the Republicans stand for?" In recent years, he has been startled to discover that as many as half of the persons interviewed replied, "There is no difference."

Their answer will come as a relief to outside visitors who regularly ask the same question when they come to America, and just as regularly go away puzzled by the answers. How is it possible to define the ideology of a party that shelters beneath its ample umbrella such disparate viewpoints as those held by Senators Edward Kennedy and James O. Eastland, George Wallace and Shirley Chisholm, Richard Daley and Bella Abzug? One can only stand in awe of the forces—in Clinton Rossiter's words, "memory, habit, inertia, and vested interest, especially an interest in defeating the Republicans"—that keep such people in the same party. The gaps within the parties, particularly the Democrats, seem in such a light much greater than that between the parties. The fiercest ideological battles in American politics nearly always take place inside one or the other of the two parties, and only the electoral battles outside them—a matter that has confounded foreign observers for generations. What are the principles of the two great parties, asked Lord Bryce back in the 1880s, what are their distinctive tenets, their tendencies?

> This is what a European is always asking of intelligent Republicans and intelligent Democrats. He always asks because he never gets an answer. The replies leave him in deeper perplexity. After some months the truth begins to dawn upon him. . . . Neither party has any principles, any distinctive tenets. Both have traditions. Both claim to have tendencies. Both have certainly war cries, organizations, interests enlisted in their support. But those interests are in the main the interests of getting or keeping the patronage of government. Tenets and policies, points of political doctrine and points of political practice, have all but vanished. They have not been thrown away but they have been stripped away by Time and the progress of events, fulfilling some policies, blotting out others. All has been lost, except office or the hope of it.

Times have changed since Bryce wrote that somewhat cynical appraisal, but they have not changed that much. Party politics in America boils down sooner or later to the intensely practical issue of getting elected. Alexander Hamilton once forecast that the time would come "when every vital question of state will be merged into the question, 'who will be the next President?' " That time is now, just as much as it was in 1880 or even in 1800. As the Republicans who marched under the banner of Barry Goldwater in 1964 and the Democrats who strode off into the ideological wilderness with George McGovern in 1972 both discovered to their cost, the only party that stands a chance of winning is that which best succeeds in making its appeal as universal as the dictates of a diverse electorate will allow. The battle, that is to say, is for the middle ground, and even in the polarized society of the 1970s those parties which ignore that truism do so at their peril.

Except for a few months every four years there really is of course no such thing as a national American party. The various component parts assemble as a unified force only at their great nominating conventions in the summer, then hold together as best they can until the presidential election is over in November. If they lose, the party then fragments for another four years, without any cohesive "central office" to keep up party discipline, sometimes without even a titular head, a "leader of the opposition," who can speak to the nation with the authority of the entire party against the policies of the incumbent President. Who speaks for the Democrats today? Certainly not George McGovern, the man the party turned to as their leader in 1972. Nor their next presidential candidate either, for he has not yet been chosen. The party, as a national force, is in effect leaderless and will remain so until the next nominating convention in 1976. This is perhaps the great failure of American politics, the great void at the center of political life. Without leadership there can be no organized opposition, and without an organized opposition the inherent power of the presidency, which many Americans already believe is too great, becomes greater still.

As George McGovern bitterly observed after his 1972 defeat, "The loyal opposition is neither loyal to a specific set of principles nor effective in its opposition. The Democratic Party is in peril of becoming a party of incumbency out of power, much like the Whigs in the nineteenth century—a party with no principles, no programs, living only from day to day, caring only for the prerogatives of office, doing nothing, and worse, not caring that nothing is done." Under the American system of government, however, the party out of power has always found itself cast in this role that Senator McGovern finds so reprehensible, the Democrats today no less than the Republicans in the Roosevelt-Truman or Kennedy-Johnson eras, when they too lived from day to day, a party "with no principles and no programs, caring only for the prerogatives of office."

It is sometimes expected that Congress should move in to fill this vacuum of opposition. Indeed, under President Nixon the electorate seems quite deliberately to have put the Democrats in charge of Congress in order to balance the powers of the Republican who sits in the White House, to pit one institution against another, Congress versus the Presidency, with Congress cast in the novel but almost medieval role of barons balancing the powers of a feudal monarch. But the monarch speaks with a unified voice, while the Democratic barons in Congress, who have no single recognized leader, speak with all the tongues of Babel. "I belong to no organized party," Will Rogers once remarked. "I am a Democrat."

Where then does the party go from here? Is it enough simply to sit out the lean years of opposition and hope that come next election day the party will have somehow pulled itself back together again, as it has done so often in the past? Will a move toward the center suffice to bring back into the fold all the defectors of 1972? Is there indeed an identifiable center still to be found in American politics today?

As they ponder the answers to these and other equally difficult political conundrums, many of its adherents believe the Democratic Party is today in greater danger of falling apart than at any time in a century. The huge and amazing coalition put together by Franklin Roosevelt under the economic stresses of the Great Depression of forty years ago seems to have lost the vital cement of loyalty and self-interest in the past two elections. Worse still, the great electoral "building blocks" which Roosevelt used to put the coalition together are themselves beginning to fragment, are not really "blocks" any longer. While they always overlapped to some degree, and were never quite as homogeneous as some social scientists liked to pretend, the old political classifications of Labor, Jews, the South, the cities or Catholics, provide a wholly inadequate basis on which to do one's political arithmetic in the 1970s. The power of the big-city machines, perhaps the most vital component of the old coalition, has been on the wane for years now, largely because of the drift of so many of its adherents away from the urban centers and into the more conservative and less easily organized suburbs. The South, once even more solid for the Democrats, became politically schizophrenic some time during the past decade, going for Wallace in 1968 and Nixon in 1972, while even on the local level, Republican senators, congressmen, and governors have established a small but perhaps strategic toehold in the states of the once-monolithic Confederacy. Meanwhile, other elements of the old coalition, such as organized labor, urban Catholics and Jews, and even the intellectual community, have been growing increasingly conservative in their social attitudes in recent years and can no longer be taken for granted by the Democrats.

As if this process of natural attrition did not give them problems enough, the Democrats' presidential candidate in 1972 won the party's nomination by deliberately spurning the old interest groups, by carrying his own ideological faction to victory over a divided opposition, by trying to win the election on a platform of ideological purity rather than a broad appeal to all the parts of the coalition. As the world now knows, McGovern's campaign collapsed in the biggest disaster the Democrats have experienced since the 1920s. By insisting on the sanctity of their own ideological platform, the pacifists, the feminists, the consumer advocates, and other radical groups with whom McGovern came to be identified simply drove away the more conservative voters and thereby ensured the electoral defeat of the party as a whole. The base on which they built their platform was just not broad enough and across the country commanded the loyalty of fewer than 40 percent of those who bothered to vote. "The McGovernites' intellect, idealism and unity of purpose were fatally flawed by their habits of overlooking the needs of working people, of slighting their value and folkways and of excluding them from the new Democratic coalition," wrote Richard Krickus in the aftermath of the defeat, while a Polish-American precinct worker in Philadelphia declared of McGovern's campaign staff, "They won't listen to anybody who tells them that the issues they talk about don't mean much to people who live in working-class neighborhoods like the one I come from."

Apart from the defects in its overall appeal, the campaign was also an organizational catastrophe. As a factional candidate, McGovern was probably doomed anyway, but the campaign was barely underway before he had irrevocably sealed his fate by changing his mind in public first about his proposals to redistribute national income by giving away a thousand dollars to every citizen and then, even more disastrously, about dropping his runningmate, Senator Thomas Eagleton, after the now-notorious disclosures about the vice-presidential candidate's mental health. The tragedy turned into farce as McGovern shopped around in public trying to find a replacement for Eagleton, running through a half-dozen refusals before he settled on Sargent Shriver. There were other blunders, too, so that as early as August, McGovern was giving the impression, as a staff member put it, of "a guy who'd have a hard time running Peoria."

As bitter in defeat as he had been inept in victory, McGovern promptly described the November landslide as a national rejection of "morality and decency." Doubting whether his party could be brought together again, or even "should be brought together again," he went on to characterize as "wreckers" those labor leaders whose support is vital if the party is ever to be rebuilt, vowing to keep them from ever coming back into a dominant role.

Today, it seems doubtful if he will be able to live up to his promise. For in spite of the bitterness of their candidate in defeat, things were not quite as bad as they seemed for the Democrats when they woke up on the morning after the election. It was quickly apparent that McGovern's loss was to a large extent a personal one, and he disappeared from view as even a titular leader more rapidly than any other beaten candidate in memory. Besides, the party somehow managed to survive the tidal wave that engulfed their candidate, retaining impressive majorities in the Senate, the House of Representatives, and statehouses across the country. Things could have been much worse. Furthermore, in the last surviving Kennedy brother, the party even had an heir apparent, the man to whom the popular wisdom had already conceded in advance the next nomination, the one man who, the party fervently hopes, can pull its warring factions together in time for the challenge of 1976.

Politically, Edward Kennedy stands just about as far to the left as George McGovern ever did, a vigorous critic of the Vietnam War with impeccable liberal credentials on domestic matters such as health care and civil rights. Yet such is the loyalty of the party regulars to this remarkable family dynasty that he commands the support not only of McGovern's radical supporters on the left but of most other segments of the old coalition too: labor and the cities, blacks and Chicanos, the old guard and the new youth votes, and above all the Roman Catholic workers of the Eastern Seaboard who voted so heavily for Nixon in 1972 (although it is hard to see how he could ever carry the South). As a candidate and perhaps as a man he remains flawed by the tragedy at Chappaquiddick, an incident that will never be entirely forgotten as long as Kennedy stays in politics. By 1976, however, Chappaquiddick will have become a distant memory to most Democratic voters, many of whom have displayed a willingness, even an eagerness, to forget and forgive.

There are also questions, it is true, about Kennedy's underlying seriousness, doubts about his youth (he will be only forty-four when the next election comes around), and perhaps also fears for his physical safety. But as the Democrats dust themselves down after the disaster of 1972, circumstances seem to have presented Kennedy with an opportunity for healing past wounds unique in American politics. It is hard to recall another time when a single candidate stood out as such an obvious frontrunner so far in advance of the election: not Roosevelt in 1928, not John Kennedy in 1956, certainly not Harry Truman or Lyndon Johnson, Adlai Stevenson or George McGovern. Kennedy is certainly not yet regarded as the leader of his party, not yet the recognized head of the opposition, but if he wants the nomination, if he can keep himself out of trouble, if he decides his obligation to the memory of his two dead brothers demands it, it is hard to see anyone else beating him. Those are, of course, big "ifs," and no one with even the most superficial memories of the improbable ups and downs of the past ten years can yet speak of certainties. One has only to run through the doleful political rollcall of the recent past to realize there are no longer any certainties in national politics: Who could have foreseen Dallas, the Vietnam imbroglio, the LBJ withdrawal, the assassination in Los Angeles, the political resurrection of Richard Nixon that led to the final improbable result of the 1968 election? Or who would have dared to set the equally melodramatic scenario for the election four years later, beginning with the tragedy at Chappaquiddick, which effectively removed Senator Kennedy from the scene in the first act? "Even Edgar Allen Poe, drunk or sober, wouldn't have dared to begin one of his dramatic tales with such a startling event," wrote James Reston in the New York *Times.* The only thread that connects the events that followed is once again that of implausible melodrama: the shooting of George Wallace, which removed him as an effective candidate on the very day when he seemed to be poised to capture the balance of power between the two main parties, the sight of Senator Muskie weeping in the New Hampshire snow, the dropping of Senator Eagleton after the revelations about his mental health. Even the subplot in that election seemed to have been lifted straight from the pages of a thirdrate political thriller, most notably in the case of the Watergate Seven, in which Republican spies, burglary tools in hand, were arrested inside their rivals' headquarters, an event closely followed by the resignation of John Mitchell as the President's campaign manager after his talkative wife, Martha, had threatened to spill the beans and had been forcibly subdued and drugged by her own security agents. Wild and unlikely accidents have thus played almost as important a part in the making of recent Presidents as more mundane considerations such as party tactics, the great issues of war and peace, or the philosophy of the rival candidates.

In the light of the almost irrational sequence of events in the recent past, there would seem to be great dangers for the Democrats in their apparently universal assumption that in 1976, in the words of one party pro, "Kennedy will be the nominee or will name the nominee." Events may yet conspire to shatter that assumption, but today there can be little doubt that the junior senator from Massachusetts is in the process of emerging as the party's natural leader, the inheritor of the mantle of his two fallen brothers. As a candidate, he would be, like Ike, made in heaven, surrounded by an aura of glamour and (dare one use the word today?) a sense of charisma possessed by none of his contemporaries. So much of his appeal lies in the magic of his name, however, that it is next to impossible to determine what sort of President he would make. Would he, in office, unite or divide? Is he really qualified for the job intellectually? Does he possess the moral stamina to withstand the pressures of the Presidency? Or is he, as the jibes of jealous colleagues sometimes have it, a cardboard figure, carried by his devoted and able staff? When he first ran for the Senate seat vacated by his brother, John Kennedy his opponent declared, "His academic career is mediocre. His professional career is virtually nonexistent. His candidacy is both preposterous and insulting." Kennedy has of course been through the fire since then, but the doubts remain. They arise not just from the taint of Chappaquiddick or from the even more ancient memories of his cheating at Harvard, but from a more generalized concern about his personal and political ability to fill what is perhaps the most awesome office in the world. Opponents in Congress, for example, ruminate on the sloppiness with which he ran the office of his party's Senate whip—and subsequently lost it to the conservative Senator Robert Byrd from West Virginia—or to his ill-considered intervention in the Ulster crisis, when his call for the immediate withdrawal of British troops and the "repatriation" of Protestant Ulstermen won him a unique double rebuke from both the British and Irish Prime Ministers. While these incidents reflect what are perhaps serious flaws in his judgment, they are more than balanced in the eyes of his supporters by his more positive achievements in the Senate. He was largely instrumental in winning the vote for the eighteen-year-olds, and has made himself the Senate's leading expert on the problems of health care, on which he has introduced an impressive mass of legislation. It is Kennedy more than any other single person who has been responsible for opening the eyes of the country to some of the more flagrant abuses and failings of the present lack of national health insurance. On civil rights, open housing, gun control, and the care of the elderly, his liberal credentials have been equally impeccable.

In any event, whatever his flaws, whatever his virtues, Edward Kennedy stands today so far above any of his colleagues in electoral popularity that the nomination of his party would seem to be his for the asking. There is also irony in the fact that by removing him from serious contention in 1972, even the tragedy at Chappaquiddick may in the end work to his political advantage. For Kennedy realized before many of his rivals that no Democrat stood much change of winning against the incumbent Richard Nixon. "I think it's going to be difficult to beat the President under any circumstances," he declared in an interview a whole year before the election. "It would be extremely difficult to beat him if, for instance, he ends the war. If the SALT talks succeed. If the trip to Peking is effective. If the cities are quiet. If the economy recovers and unemployment goes down . . ." Kennedy's assessment was a shrewd one, his "ifs" all worked out in favor of the President, whose position was probably unassailable by the time the country went to the polls a year later. By allowing another standardbearer to lead the party to a defeat that was anyhow inevitable, Kennedy's own position has been immeasurably strengthened. As a result, the Democrats can now look forward to selecting a viable leader with broad popular support, undamaged by the 1972 defeat and possessing a cohesive political philosophy around which most of the elements of the old coalition can rally once again. While the penalties of another failure would be enormously damaging, perhaps even lethal, for the moment at least there appears to be a signpost leading the Democrats out of the wilderness in which they have been unaccustomedly wandering since the collapse of the old consensus at the end of the 1960s. Their prospects could be much, much worse.

What then of their opponents? Where does the Republican Party go from here? What is the future of the Grand Old Party after the scandals that have now engulfed the Republican in the White House? "For forty years," one senator has said, "we carried the image of being the party of the Great Depression. Now are we going to spend another forty as the party of Watergate?" Only one thing is certain: the party will be without the presence of Richard Nixon for the first time in over twenty years. By 1976, the Republicans as well as the Democrats will be forced to turn to new leadership, although the Republicans have no natural heir-apparent, and speculation as to who the party might choose is even less productive than it is for the Democrats. Nixon himself was once said to favor John Connally, his former Secretary of the Treasury and a man he enormously admires. But Connally was still a Democrat (albeit a "Democrat for Nixon") in the last election, and he would have powerful opposition to overcome among the party faithful, who do not much care for turncoats, however charismatic. Then there is Spiro Agnew, who would certainly like the job but might have a hard time winning a national election, especially now that he has his own personal scandal to live down; Charles Percy, the liberal senator from Illinois, who has yet to show his hand and is in any case detested by the Nixon regulars; Nelson Rockefeller, whose political ambitions still burn brightly, even though he will be 68 years old before the office next falls vacant; or maybe one of the dark horses, like Senator Howard Baker, who acquired a national reputation overnight during the Senate Watergate hearings in the summer of 1973.

Much more relevant than the perennial Washington chitchat about personalities, however, is the intriguing question whether *any* Republican candidate can win the presidency in the aftermath of Watergate. Nixon would like to have gone down in history as one of the handful of Presidents who transformed the fortunes of their parties, leaving them in a position of dominance, and he has worked hard towards that goal. Whether he had succeeded in forming the permanent conservative coalition he talks about was already a dubious proposition, with or without Watergate, and it could be that his administration will be remembered as just another passing Republican interlude, much like Eisenhower's, or Wilson's during the long period of Republican ascendancy that collapsed under the weight of the Depression.

Among what James Reston calls the "writers of advanced political nonsense" there are those who see the two great American parties as the sun and the moon, a tidy theory in which of course the moon can only shine after the sun has set. From the beginning of this century until the Depression, according to this theory, the sun represented the Republican Party, the moon the Democrats. After Roosevelt came to power, the roles were reversed and the Democrats became the sun, allowing the moon to shine only when they were in temporary eclipse. Now, after another period of transition, the argument goes that the two parties are once again in the process of changing roles—a theory that has the additional advantage of being unprovable until at least a generation after the event.

At any rate, the theory has Nixon as the agent for transforming the Republicans into the party of the sun, or in other words the part of the ascendancy. In office, his battle plan for achieving this objective has been twinpronged—the famous "Southern strategy" providing one main thrust, a "suburban strategy" the other—the aim of course being to split the Democratic opposition. In practice, however, the plan has turned out to be more of a political tightrope act than the forging of a new and permanent coalition, an act of political opportunism that worked well enough against a divided opposition, but one that holds out more peril than promise for the future.

The dangers to the party that would result from basing their appeal on a conservative-cum-Southern strategy were in fact spotted as long ago as 1950 by Governor Thomas Dewey when he rejected the advice of "impractical theorists" who were then seeking "to drive all moderates and liberals out of the Republican Party and then have the remainder join forces with the conservative groups in the South. Then they would have everything neatly arranged, indeed," the governor said. "The Democratic Party would be the liberal-to-radical party. The Republican Party would be the conservative-to-reactionary party.

"The results would be neatly arranged, too. The Republicans would lose every election and the Democrats would win every election."

Such a strategy was tried out in the midterm election of 1970, and found wanting, just as Dewey had forecast. In spite of the President's personal efforts, the Republicans failed completely in their hopes of winning control of either the Senate or the House of Representatives. A softened version of the strategy was tried in the congressional elections of 1972 and again found wanting. The Republicans, for all their efforts, and in spite of the President's own personal landslide, were as far away as ever from winning a majority in either chamber. In national elections, the party has found it cannot make a pitch to narrow regional or class interests while at the same time holding out a wider vision for the country as a whole. Haunted, moreover, by Barry Goldwater's defeat, neither can they afford to tilt too blatantly towards the right and the South without at the same time alienating other voters in the more moderate East and West.

So while it is probably true that many white voters in the South, having used Wallace as a temporary way-station, will move over permanently to the Republicans, the battleground in the country as a whole will remain, as it always must in a responsive and representative democracy, in the famous and much scorned middle ground. The trick—and it is not as easy as it sounds, as Ed Muskie found to his cost—is to identify the middle ground. Richard M. Scammon and Ben J. Wattenberg made the point succinctly in their analysis of *The Real Majority:*

"The winning coalition in America is the one that holds the center ground in the attitudinal battlefield. In the years until the election of 1968, the battlefield had been mostly an economic battlefield, and the Democrats held the ideological allegiance of the machinist and his wife from the suburbs of Dayton, and tens of millions of other middle-income, middle-educated, middle-aged voters who wanted a high minimum wage, Social Security, Medicare, union protection, and so on. That seems to be changing. For the seventies, the battlefield shows signs of splitting into two battlefields: the old economic one and the new social one that deals with crime, drugs, racial pressure and disruption. To the extent that this transformation occurs, then the party and the candidate that best occupy the center ground of the two battlefields will win the presidency."

In other words, the two parties must quite consciously grow closer together rather than further apart. "Cynics may ask," say the two authors, "what is the sense of parties that must always move toward the other-party position to gain political strength. They may be answered by noting that this is the procedure that guarantees the responsiveness of the American system." And that in itself remains the best argument in favor of a healthy two-party system: It guarantees as can no other, that government does remain responsive to the needs and aspirations, the fears and foibles of the great majority of its citizens. So long as the two parties remain broad enough in their general appeal there is no important minority, be they women or workers, blacks or conservatives, the elderly or big business, who should not find a home in one or the other of the great coalitions. As Judge Charles Wyzanski put it to an audience at Lake Forest College, Illinois, "Anyone who really studies democracy will find out that democracy is pluralistic in character. It is those already in power who scorn the pressure groups. But it is pressure groups—whether it be voter leagues formed by women, labor unions formed by workers, black organizations formed by colored people—that in the end count and enter into the total social fabric. Democracy is a struggle based not only on high ideals; it is power against power."

Disillusionment comes when a substantial segment of society finds its legitimate interests ignored or bypassed, when people can find no home in either party and feel compelled to act in a state of permanent opposition outside the two-party system. Balancing their often-conflicting aspirations is of course the whole art of politics, a difficult art at the best of times, but one that becomes next to impossible in times of turmoil, as in 1968 when the two-party system came as close as it has ever done to breaking down. Disillusionment came then because two substantial but very disparate segments of society—the frustrated voters who supported George Wallace on one flank, and the opponents of the war in Vietnam on the other—found themselves shut out from their "natural" party. That year some ten million voters broke away from the system with Wallace to form a third party on the right, while countless others on the left vented their frustrations in ultimately futile, even nihilistic, demonstrations on the streets.

All but a hard core of antiwar extremists returned to the system in 1972, however, even succeeding in capturing temporary control of the Democratic Party. Indeed, it may well prove to be the one lasting achievement of George McGovern that he brought back to the fold those radical Democrats who four years earlier looked as though they might well break away and form a fourth party of the left under the leadership of Eugene McCarthy. With the American involvement at last over, Vietnam will cease to be the tragically divisive issue that has dominated the politics of the past decade. But while the involvement may be over, the lessons for the parties remain. Vietnam was, in a sense, perhaps the greatest failure of responsive party politics in this century, the result of isolating foreign policy from partisan debate. Both parties had in fact abdicated their responsibilities for foreign policy in the aftermath of the last war, long before Vietnam became such a burning issue, but the so-called nonpolitical aspects of foreign policy, agreed to by both Republicans and Democrats, had the result, as John Kenneth Galbraith has pointed out, of removing foreign policy from the influence of men who had any personal stake in the future of the Democratic Party, the President apart. Thus, when John Kennedy arrived in the White House, instead of Adlai Stevenson, W. Averell Harriman or J. W. Fulbright, with their Democratic party associations, the new President gave the key foreign policy jobs to such nonpolitical Establishment men as Dean Rusk, Robert McNamara, Roswell Gilpatric, and the Bundy brothers, McGeorge and William. "If only one of them had ever run for sheriff," Lyndon Johnson once sighed. And, as David Broder has put it:

It is these men, with their marvelous self-confidence and their well-developed contempt for politicians and public opinion, who wrote the clever scenarios and the cynical memoranda that comprise the history of Vietnam policy under three administrations contained in the Pentagon Papers. It is they who stand ready to advise a President how he can dupe the Congress and the public and maneuver the nation into war without disclosing his intentions.

For ten long years, the greatest single issue facing the American people remained, politically speaking, beyond their reach. It has been the most massive and ultimately tragic breakdown of the responsiveness of the two-party system in a lifetime.

CHAPTER VIII

Congress

The Pendulum Swings

"To get along, go along."
—LYNDON JOHNSON, *then Senate Majority Leader, 1958*

The framers of the American Constitution gave the paramount place in their logical, eighteenth-century scheme of things not to the President, but to Congress, a body they fully expected would become "the first branch of government." It was a daring innovation, based on impeccable theory. The House of Representatives and the Senate "in Congress assembled" were to frame the federal laws, scrupulously independent and separate from the President, whose chief duty under the Constitution was to administer, not determine, those laws. The ink was hardly dry on that venerable document, however, when the theory began to break down. From the earliest days of the Republic, Congress was never able to operate in the logical, watertight compartment assigned to it by the Founding Fathers.

Today, nearly two centuries later, it is clear that the President, not Congress, has become the first branch of government and the principal initiator of all important legislation. Indeed, so far has that process gone that no fewer than 80 percent of the major laws enacted in the past twenty years have started out in the executive branch, while Congress, in the words of one of its senior members, "has become a third or fourth-class power, a separate and thoroughly unequal branch of our national government."

In the 1970s, that has become the fashionable view. Congress is nowadays widely dismissed as "a constitutional relic." Thus, Ralph Nader opened his study of Congress in 1972 with the opinion that it had become "the great American default," while the Washington *Post* in a recent article on the balance of power began with the rhetorical question: "Is Congress dead?"

For Americans, who are deeply attached to their written Constitution, such conclusions are perhaps inescapable. On any strict interpretation of the words actually contained in that document, Congress today does not fill the role assigned to it. It is not the prime initiator of legislation. It is not the first branch of government. It has lost the sole power to declare war. Even its power of control over the federal pursestrings is no longer absolute.

For all that, the U.S. Congress remains one of the most powerful legislative bodies in the world, far from the mere rubber stamp that many of its recent critics have called it. While it has lost or surrendered a large part of its positive power to initiate new laws, it has nevertheless retained virtually intact its negative powers to check and balance the powers of the Presidency; a role that, it can be argued, is the true test of legislative effectiveness in any democracy. Since President Nixon came to office, Congress has rejected his plans to build a supersonic aircraft, subjected his defense budgets to unprecedented scrutiny, thrown out two of his nominees to the Supreme Court and forced him to drop another as head of the FBI, extended the provisions of Social Security, and pushed through an extension of the franchise to include eighteen-year-old voters. It has also played a central role in exposing the seamy abuses of the Watergate scandal. In terms of power, that is no mean record. True, it at the same time failed to impose an effective curb on the President's power to wage an undeclared war, but that was due as much to its own inability to reach a consensus as to any inherent lack of power. It has also seen the President seize control over federal spending which by right belongs to the House of Representatives. But as Nixon entered his second term, it already seemed that the congressional worm was about to turn. Members of both houses of Congress, perhaps a majority, felt the Presidential usurpation of their powers had gone far enough, that it was time to flex muscles grown flabby with disuse. As a result, the final years of the Nixon Presidency were ready for an epic struggle for power between the two principal branches of government. It would be a mistake to assume that the outcome of that battle is a foregone conclusion.

When John Kennedy left his seat in the Senate to seek the Presidency, he said he wanted to go to the White House because "that is where the real power is." But once he reached the executive mansion, he discovered that the powers of Congress were greater than he had earlier supposed:

> The Congress looks more powerful sitting here than it did when I was in Congress. But that is because when you are in Congress you are one of a hundred in the Senate or 435 in the House, so that power is so divided. But from here I look at a Congress, and I look at the collective power of the Congress, particularly the bloc action, and it is a substantial power.

Here, then, is the paradox. Critics of Congress who look for it to fulfill the exact role assigned to it in the Constitution conclude that Congress is a failure. Presidents, who are forced to look at Congress with a less theoretical eye, conclude on the other hand that it retains "substantial power." Both views are, in their way, correct, but they are also irreconcilable. To reach any valid assessment of the true constitutional power of the modern Congress, therefore, it is necessary to go beyond what is written about those powers in the Constitution.

What the Founding Fathers specifically intended when they created the

Constitution is, in the last analysis, irrelevant. The doctrine of separated powers they embraced was in the first place based on a major misconception, a doctrine that had been articulated for them in the theories of the French philosopher Montesquieu, who wrote in 1748 that "when the legislative and executive powers are united in the same person or the same body of magistrates, there can be no liberty." Montesquieu had based his theory on his studies of the British constitution, where he had concluded that the Crown represented the executive branch of government, Parliament the legislature. Their powers were separate; therefore in Britain there was liberty. But Montesquieu had failed to take into account that some years before he had articulated his doctrine, the British Parliament had finally established its supremacy over the Crown by forcing the king to accept a Prime Minister chosen by—or at least acceptable to—the House of Commons. The executive and legislative powers of government in Britain were thus firmly in the hands of Parliament, at least in domestic affairs, so that by the time Montesquieu had published his theories in *The Spirit of the Laws*, its main thesis was out of date.

The American Founding Fathers, who had just concluded their own struggle with the British Crown, nonetheless accepted Montesquieu's doctrine with gratitude, fallacies and all. As Senator Joseph Clark has pointed out, he offered them a sophisticated rationale for conclusions they probably held already; in the American context, the doctrine made sense. But as a result, the form of government they created turned out to be quite different from that of the mother country that Montesquieu had taken as his model. To all intents and purposes, they had created in America an elective monarchy without a king, balanced by a Parliament without a prime minister. While that may not have been their intention, it turned out to be a stroke of genius which for close on two hundred years has served well the cause of American democracy. However, it has meant that the true constitutional balance between President and Congress is not to be found in the dead letters of an eighteenth-century document, but in the living interpretation of each succeeding generation of politicians who occupy the twin palaces of American government: the White House and the U.S. Capitol. Consequently, the American Constitution today is based in practice not on a separation of powers, but in the words of Richard Neustadt, "separated institutions sharing powers."

When power is shared, of course, the exact balance between the two branches of government will vary from President to President, from Congress to Congress. Under Johnson and later under Nixon the executive branch had become so dominant that Congress began to fear for its very survival as a real constitutional force, yet only ten years ago the worry about Congress was exactly the opposite one: how to make a conservative body more responsive to the will of a liberal President. This is in fact the pattern of history. In the United States the pendulum of power has always shown a tendency to swing quite dramatically back and forth from Capitol Hill to the White House. There is some reason to suppose that if the members of Congress can steel themselves for the task the pendulum will swing in their direction once again, in a sort of delayed reaction to the usurpation of their powers in the past decade.

This always-fascinating tug of war has seen the power of Congress rise and fall again and again, with strong Presidents like Lincoln and Franklin Roosevelt able to override the Congress on most issues and weaker ones like Grant and Harding prisoners of the congressional will. In the 1890s, under President McKinley, Congress had become so strong it was able to force the country into a wholly unjustifiable war with Spain against the President's wishes—quite the reverse of the manner in which the United States later went to war in Vietnam.

Crisis has come when strongminded Presidents have faced equally strong minds in the Congress. Before America's entry into World War I, when Woodrow Wilson sought to arm merchant vessels against the threat of unrestricted submarine warfare, the move was at first blocked by twelve senators who seized upon the Senate's rule allowing unlimited debate to filibuster against the arming and so prevent the issue from coming to a vote. Although seventy-five other Senators declared they were in favor of the President's measure "if a vote could be had," the filibuster by the twelve isolationists continued until Congress had adjourned, and the measure thus expired. (As a result of this extraordinary affair, the Senate changed its rules to allow for a motion of cloture to cut off debate if two thirds of its members so decide. But filibusters still continue.) Angered by this "little group of willful men representing no opinion but their own," Wilson armed the vessels anyway by executive order, a precedent that has been followed more than once in our own times. When war came, Wilson's authority had grown so strong one senator was moved to lament as he was herded to vote for one presidential initiative after another, "The lash, forever and eternally the lash, is laid across the legislative back. More and more we cringe."

Wilson's triumph did not long survive the war. Once again the pendulum swung, and before Wilson left office congressional supremacy had been firmly re-established after a major battle of wills on the great issues of foreign policy. Wilson was compelled to stand by helplessly as the Senate, emboldened by its constitutional powers to approve foreign treaties, rejected his attempts to bring the United States into the League of Nations. It is worth remembering today that it was Congress and not the President that turned the United States upon the isolationist course it was to pursue for close on two decades. Indeed, Wilson died believing the balance of power had swung permanently to the Senate, remarking bitterly before he did, "Senators have no use for their brains, except as knots to keep their bodies from unraveling."

It took the crisis of the Depression and the initiatives of Franklin Roosevelt to seize back for the White House the presidential powers that had been allowed to lie fallow under Harding, Coolidge, and Hoover. From the first, Roosevelt left Congress in no doubt that he fully intended to be master. "While the Constitution wisely declared a separation," he announced at the height of the crisis, "common purpose declares a union." On his very first day in office he closed the banks by executive order, declaring that he sought from the Congress "broad executive power to wage war against the emergency as great as the power that would be given to me if we were in fact invaded by a foreign foe." The famous Hundred Days that followed had a shattering effect on the powers of the Congress, as Senator Joseph Clark has recounted:

> Congress was overwhelmed. Its leaders became Parliamentary lieutenants, participating with Cabinet members in the drafting of legislation and then marching it to a vote. Committee action was but a momentary pause. Senators and Congressmen voted for bills they had never read and of whose contents they had only the foggiest notion. An emergency banking bill was debated for forty minutes; eleven of the President's most important bills were passed with an average of three and two-thirds hours' debate.

Under Roosevelt, the constitutional balance of power had tilted once more towards the White House, and there it has remained to this day. It is true there has not been a President since then who has not had some part of his legislative program checked or curtailed by the Congress, but never again has the major policy initiative come from anywhere except the White House. Under the American system of government, that is perhaps as it should be. Congress after all has not always been on the side of the angels in its battles with the White House, and one need only recall the excesses of Joe McCarthy, the isolationism of the prewar era, and the filibustering against civil-rights legislation to realize that the power of Congress as well as the power of the Presidency can at times be abused. Those who call for the strengthening of Congress today might well bear in mind the words of the *Christian Science Monitor* in an editorial on Senate reform in the spring of 1970. Fine, said the newspaper, it was clearly the intention of the Founding Fathers that both the Presidency and Congress should have their say. Then it went on to add:

> But hold on a moment. Which Senate are we speaking of? Are we talking of the Senate which has over and over again balked at constructive foreign initiatives, crippled foreign efforts, ignored foreign opportunities? Are we talking of the Senate which blocked American entry into the League of Nations, held back full support for the World Court, is presently cutting back further and further on foreign aid, which has no hesitation over passing resolutions mixing in the affairs of other countries for political rather than diplomatic reasons?
> Of course, this is not the Senate which today's "strengthen-the-Senate" advocates have in mind. They visualize an upper chamber full of wisdom and goodwill, a bulwark of reason and foresight in a reckless world. . . .
> But, alas, in the world of politics, we must expect the bad with the good, the

unwise with the far-seeing, the heedless with the prudent. A Senate which has asserted an iron hand over the President on South-east Asia might also be inclined to assert an equally hard fist where other very different issues are concerned.

Congress, unlike the Presidency, is an extremely parochial body. There is a saying on Capitol Hill that most members tend to think what is good for Podunk must be good for the country, whereas the President must act on the opposite assumption that what is good for the country is probably also good for Podunk. Power in Congress is too diffuse, too regional, too negative for its members to exercise effectively anything but a check on the presidential power. Again, that is perhaps as it should be. As Dean Acheson once remarked, "The central question is not whether Congress should be stronger than the President, or vice versa, but how the Congress and the President can both be strengthened to do the pressing work that falls to each to do and to both to do together."

For the average American citizen who takes the mandatory tour of Capitol Hill on his visit to Washington, Congress must seem a puzzling institution. Under the great white cast-iron dome that dominates the Washington skyline, the statue of Freedom on its pinnacle facing resolutely *away* from the White House, nothing much ever appears to be happening. The tourist, who has been brought up to look upon his national institutions with reverence, will keep a proper silence as he files through corridor after corridor crammed not with the living members of Congress he might have expected to find there but with rows of overblown marble statuary commemorating members long since dead and mostly forgotten. Arriving in the rotunda beneath the dome, he will look around with awe at the allegorical scenes that encircle that magnificent chamber, each depicting an heroic moment in American history. "If your neck troubles you," the guide intones, "remember that the artist had to lie flat on his back on a scaffold 180 feet above the floor to execute this masterpiece." Surmounting it all is Brumidi's fresco depicting George Washington's ascent into heaven attended by Liberty, Victory, and Fame, and accompanied by thirteen voluptuous women representing the original American colonies, a work that actually killed its artist, who slipped one day from the scaffolding and died of shock soon afterwards.

Having been suitably uplifted by this glimpse of his heritage, the tourist will eventually make his way into the northernmost wing of the building where, if he is lucky and he has made the right arrangements, he will find the Senate in open session. Looking down from the visitors' gallery, he may perhaps spy a familiar face down on the floor as a handful of senators—sometimes scarcely even a handful—pay almost no attention to another of their members who is droning on interminably about such subjects as the importance of water conservation in California. He will be diverted, however, by the impressive surroundings. The Senate chamber is a handsome place, hung with gold silk damask, with a semicircular arrangement of desks in four rows, one small mahogany desk for each Senator, set perhaps three feet apart, so that when in session the members of this august body look like nothing so much as a senior class of undergraduates sitting for their final examinations, an effect that is only heightened by the small glass bottle that stands on each desk and said once to have been filled with sand to blot ink. The language they use here is courtly, the wit ponderous. "If you think a colleague is stupid," Senator Alben Barkley once remarked, "refer to him as 'the able, learned, and distinguished Senator.' If you know he is stupid, refer to him as 'the *very* able, learned, and distinguished Senator.' " In debate, the senators never refer to each other by name but as "the distinguished senator from Virginia," or wherever it may be, although in times of stress they have been known to refer to each other simply as states, like "Texas" and "New York," as though they were medieval peers in a history by Shakespeare.

But debates on the floor are of almost no importance in the Senate nowadays, except to lubricate the vanity of the senators and fill the pages of the Congressional Record. "You've got to work things out in the cloakroom," Lyndon Johnson once remarked, "and when you've got them worked out, you can debate a little before you vote." Indeed, one of the main functions of Senate debate is quite literally to kill time, to filibuster so that it becomes impossible to move on to the next item of business, to talk an unpopular bill to death, a technique used most notoriously to prevent the passage of civil-rights legislation by recalcitrant southern senators, who have used this ingenious machinery, in Joe Chamberlain's phrase, "to save themselves from the natural consequences of being outnumbered." When it is in this mood, the Senate, as one of its members has sadly observed, represents the South's revenge on the North for having lost the Civil War. In 1957, Strom Thurmond held the Senate floor for a record of twenty-four hours and eighteen minutes in his attempt to stop the civil-rights bill of that year. And although debate can be stopped these days by a motion of cloture supported by two thirds of the members "present and voting," this has succeeded only eight times since the rule was adopted in 1917. Forty-five other attempts to stop filibustering have failed.

Filibustering apart, the days of great debates taking place on the Senate floor are long since past. Today, the only words a senator utters that are likely to be remembered are those he speaks to the television cameras set up in the halls outside his committee rooms. The bleak truth is that most speeches on the floor are made to a virtually empty chamber and almost none of them is reported in the daily press.

Perhaps even more surprising than the absence of debate in the Senate is the complete breakdown of any sort of party discipline. Members are nominally Democrats or Republicans, but this appears to influence not one whit

the way in which they cast their vote, a state of affairs which occasions great
astonishment among visiting British M.P's, for whom the withdrawal of the
party whip would be tantamount to a public execution. But here in the Senate,
and to some degree in the House, liberal Republicans will cheerfully and
consistently vote with the Democrats against the wishes of a Republican
President, while Southern Democrats vote just as happily with conservative
Republicans. The party leadership lacks any positive power to influence the
votes of its members one way or the other, and the days have long since
vanished when a vote in the party caucus bound all its members to vote the
same way on the floor. Today, even regional allegiances do not have the power
they once possessed to influence a senator's vote. William Fulbright and John
McClellan, for example, are both Democrats, both voted into office by the
same electorate in the same southern state of Arkansas, yet in twenty key votes
in the first Nixon Administration they voted the same way only seven times.
It stands as a remarkable tribute to the individuality of the senators, but it is
also in the long run a source of weakness for the Senate as an institution when
power has grown so diffuse.

Over in the other wing of the Capitol Building, where the House of
Representatives sits, things seem busier, more worldly. There are, after all, four
times as many congressmen as senators, although they can be just as ponderous
in their public utterances as members of the Senate, which they always refer
to as "the other place," and *never* as the Upper House. It was not for nothing
that the House was once described as the greatest organized inferiority complex in the world. Contrary to general belief, say the cynics, the major occupation of the House is not legislating but trying to make itself appear important
and significant. That, alas, it will never be, for power in the House is not
concentrated but scattered, party discipline is virtually nonexistent, and debate here, while subject to a time limit, is even less meaningful than it is in
the Senate.

Those who have the power—"petty barons" Woodrow Wilson once called
them—use it quite cynically and shamelessly for their own ends. Thus in May
1970, when the House was considering amendments to cut off military aid to
Cambodia, the hawks, who controlled the powerful Armed Services Committee, and who therefore controlled the time for debate, used up most of it
themselves. At the end of the day, the doves, who were in favor of the
amendment, were granted precisely forty-five seconds apiece in which to make
their speeches. The hawks then added insult to injury by walking out of the
chamber as the minispeeches began. Don Riegle, a young congressman from
Michigan, recalled what happened when his turn came to use his forty-five
seconds:

> I grabbed the microphone at the Republican committee table and started to
> unload. "What a sham!" I cried, speaking directly to the people in the gallery. "I
> ask you, have you ever seen a worse sight in your life?"

I was dimly aware that Doc Hall from Missouri had jumped to his feet and was angrily shouting, "Point of order! Point of order!" And I could hear the acting Speaker pounding the gavel on his desk. But I ignored them. "For eight years," I continued, "we have fought an undeclared war. What can be more important than fully debating this issue? And where are those members who minutes ago voted to cut off debate? They're down in the House gym playing paddle ball!"

The bedlam in the chamber made it impossible for me to go on. The gallery spectators were applauding furiously and so were anti-war members. Doc Hall was still shouting, "Point of order!" and Dan Rostenkowski from Illinois was sitting in the Speaker's chair, still flailing away with the gavel with all his might. My time had expired so I left the mike.

Riegle discovered afterwards that by addressing the people in the gallery he had violated the rules of the House. He had also deeply wounded many of his colleagues by referring to Cambodia and the House gym in the same speech. "You know darn well we need a House gym," one member told him reproachfully. "Members just don't get enough exercise!" Somewhat chastened by this charade of a debate, Riegle concluded that junior membership in the House did not provide the powerful public platform he had expected. "The right idea expressed by the President at the right time and in the right way may be worth all the votes that I could cast in this House in the next forty years," he observed mournfully. That did not prevent him, however, from seeking and winning another term in office at the next election, which for the House takes place every two years, although by 1973 he had changed his party allegiance from Republican to Democratic.

The fact is that the debates that take place on the floor of either chamber are today as irrelevant as the senators' archaic glass bottles of sand. They are form without substance. For it is not during debate that the real work of Congress is done, but behind the doors of the various committee rooms, which dominate Capitol Hill, in the words of a member, "like a string of forts." Woodrow Wilson, in his classic study of the workings of power on Capitol Hill, declared that "the House sits not for serious discussion, but to sanction the conclusions of its committees as rapidly as possible." That is as true today as it was then. Wilson went on to add, "Congress in session is Congress on public exhibition, while Congress in its committee rooms is Congress at work."

The committee system is at once the great strength and the great weakness of the modern Congress. It is strong because that is where the real power of Congress lies: If a bill passes unanimously out of committee there is almost nothing an individual senator or congressman can do to alter it. If the bill fails in committee, it is as good as dead in Congress as a whole. For this reason, the chairmen of the main committees in both the House and the Senate are men of enormous power and influence, with control over millions of dollars of the federal budget. It is said of former congressman Carl Vinson that when asked to resign as chairman of the House Armed Services Committee to become Secretary of Defense, he replied, "I would rather run the Pentagon from here." When Wilbur Mills, the enormously powerful chairman of the House Ways and Means Committee, considered running for the Presidency early in 1972, a colleague asked him, "Wilbur, why do you want to run for President and give up your grip on the country?" These men are the autocrats of the Hill, the real leaders of the Congress. As Morris Udall has observed, "The committee member who has served twenty years is not just five percent more powerful than the member who has served nineteen years. If he is the chairman he is one thousand percent more powerful."

The great weakness of the committee system, however, is the manner in which its members—and in particular its chairmen—have traditionally been chosen. Each party's Committee on Committees, which makes the assignments, takes great care to screen out nonconformists whose views might cause trouble. In the past no one ever made his way onto the Senate Finance Committee or to the House Ways and Means Committee, until he had passed a kind of loyalty test on the question of oil-depletion allowances. And when one freshman congressman was being interviewed for membership on the House Interstate and Foreign Commerce Committee, he was first asked, "What's your position on tobacco?" "I don't smoke," the congressman replied, perhaps facetiously. Needless to add, he did not get the desired appointment. In the Senate, a new member will normally get a minimum of two committee appointments, one of them on a committee of real substance, so that it is not too difficult for him to make his mark from his earliest days. But even in the upper chamber, committee allocations can be made or broken by the established leadership. It is said that when Ed Muskie first arrived in the Senate back in 1959, he rubbed Lyndon Johnson, then majority leader, the wrong way. Instead of being assigned to the committees of his choice, he finished up instead on Public Works. In the House, the original committee assignments a member receives can make or break his political career, although in the 1970s some of the more aggressive new members, particularly those from New York City, have begun with some success to challenge this establishment system. When Congressman Herman Badillo first arrived in the House from his district in the Bronx—perhaps one of the most urban areas in the country—he found himself assigned to the House Agriculture Committee. "There isn't any crop in my district except marijuana," he complained and actually succeeded in getting his assignment changed. So did another New York freshman, Shirley Chisholm, who was heard to remark that she had been assigned to Agriculture because the House leadership had read the book *A Tree Grows in Brooklyn.* However, another New York congresswoman, Bella Abzug, a vociferous opponent of the war in Vietnam, failed in her persistent attempts to get an appointment to the Armed Services Committee, one of the most powerful and conservative committees in the House.

Once appointed to a committee, however, the member is usually there for life—provided, of course, that he can keep his congressional seat. The best appointments go by tradition to the most senior members. Thus the dominant members of any committee are not necessarily the ablest, or the most experienced, or the most representative members, but those who have managed to get themselves elected to office the most often. They progress through the hierarchy by the simple accumulation of seniority; the chairman of each committee, in both the House and the Senate, is in practice the member of the majority party who has survived on the committee the longest. Reform is now on the way, but for years length of service has been the sole qualification for his office—a system of appointment used by no other legislative body in the world.

One consequence of this system is that the most influential committees are rarely representative of Congress as a whole. In the House especially, those members who accumulate the most seniority are those who manage to get themselves re-elected again and again to "safe" seats. And, almost by definition, the safest seats these days are to be found in rural areas, in the virtually one-party South, and in stable suburbs. The big-city machines, which in the past have produced such senior members as Emanuel Celler and John Rooney of New York and John McCormack of Boston, have lost much influence lately, due in part to the flight of so many of their constitutents to the suburbs. Big cities today tend to be politically volatile, with a bigger-than-average turnover of members, who therefore find it difficult to accumulate the necessary seniority within the committees. The committees in their turn therefore tend to be dominated by members who are older, more rural, more cautious, and more conservative than the House as a whole. As a result, congressional power gravitates towards minority, not majority, rule.

There also seems to be a tendency for conservatives to understand better than the liberals where the real levers of power in Congress are to be found. Those from the South in particular show a natural instinct for political maneuver and a fascination with the minutiae of parliamentary procedure and thus tend to gravitate towards the less glamorous but often more influential "backroom" committees like Appropriations, Ways and Means, and Finance. There is a saying in Congress that the conservatives will allow the liberals to say "what" if the conservatives can say "how much"—and today, the committees that deal with money in both houses are all dominated by conservative southerners and members from other rural areas. Elizabeth Drew, a perceptive and sympathetic observer of Congress in action, has quoted one senator as saying, "the liberals are always ten years late in figuring out where the real power is." She goes on to say that for years "the liberals scrambled for seats on committees dealing with issues that seemed more glamorous, such as foreign policy, or of more concern to their constituents, such as education and labor and housing. When they began to understand the substantive consequences of committee allocations, and some liberals attained sufficient seniority to seek seats on tax and revenue committees, many were reluctant to do so. They were loath to surrender the seniority they had attained within their own committees, to move to committees where the work is a complex and sometimes heavy going, where they would be outnumbered and outmaneuvered by the conservatives, and where there might be less opportunity for publicity. Many a liberal prefers a press release to power."

Reform, combined with the normal attrition of illness, old age, and defeat at the polls, has caused some crumbling in the seniority system in both houses in the 1970s, although even today Congress can still be fairly defined as a Union army led by Confederate generals. In the Senate, only one important committee chairmanship in in the hands of an easterner, while the three most populous states of all—California, New York, and Illinois—have not held an important standing committee chairmanship in years. The South holds no fewer than nine, including all the major ones. The great bloc of southern Democrats still represents the Senate establishment, and nowhere in their ranks are to be found the internationally famous senators who have considered themselves powerful and capable enough of running for the Presidency: Humphrey, Muskie, McGovern, Goldwater, and Kennedy, who do not possess an important standing-committee chairmanship between them.

The rural southerners who hold the reins of power in the Senate today are:

Committee	Chairman	Age in 1973
Agriculture	Herman Talmadge (Georgia)	60
Appropriations	John L. McClellan (Arkansas)	76
Armed Services	John Stennis (Mississippi)	72
Banking, Housing, & Urban Affairs	John Sparkman (Alabama)	74
Finance	Russell Long (Louisiana)	55
Foreign Relations	William Fulbright (Arkansas)	68
Government Operations	John L. McClellan (Arkansas)	77
Judiciary	James Eastland (Mississippi)	69
Rules & Administration	B. Everett Jordan (N. Carolina)	77

Perhaps the most unrepresentative chairman of them all is James Oliver Eastland of Mississippi, who has been chairman of the Judiciary Committee since 1956 and president pro tempore of the Senate since the summer of 1972, a largely ceremonial post in which he presides over the Senate in the absence of the Vice President, but which also puts him third in line for the Presidency of the United States behind Agnew and the Speaker of the House of Representatives.

In appearance Eastland is cut in the classic mold of southern Senators: florid and rotund, a supreme master of parliamentary procedure who tends to chew impassively on an unlighted cigar and who has described himself as "a living symbol of conservative leadership in the Senate." The owner of a vast cotton plantation in Sunflower County, one of the most backward corners of a backward state, Eastland has in the past used his position as chairman of the Senate Judiciary Committee to almost singlehandedly bottle up civil-rights legislation. Back in the days when Earl Warren was Chief Justice, he suggested that the entire Supreme Court should be impeached for what he termed its "pro-Communist decisions." Under both Johnson and Nixon, Eastland has been closer to the Republicans than he has to members of his own Democratic Party in the Senate. As a member of the Agriculture Committee, he has been bitterly criticized for collecting subsidies on his cotton crop that he has himself helped to set, apparently unaware—or uncaring—that this might represent a conflict of interest. In 1971, according to the New York *Times*, Eastland collected some $38,000 in subsidies on his cotton plantation, but Ralph Nader's organization says the figure for Eastland and his wife in that year was no less than $159,000.

When President Johnson nominated Abe Fortas to succeed Earl Warren as Chief Justice of the Supreme Court, Eastland told him the appointment would "tear the country apart"—apparently on the grounds that Fortas was an ardent advocate of civil rights for black Americans. Eastland particularly objected to a speech in which Fortas—a Jew—had compared the struggles of the blacks for equality with those of the Jews and said that the Jews must therefore help the blacks in their fight for civil rights. Interpretating Fortas's statement as "a conspiratorial call for Jews and Negroes to take over America," Eastland was instrumental in blocking Fortas's appointment, having received assurances from Richard Nixon that a Chief Justice more to his liking would be appointed when the Republicans took over the White House, which is exactly what happened after the presidential election of 1968. Today, Eastland still holds his chairmanship, by virtue of his seniority, in spite of a brief and unsuccessful attempt by Hubert Humphrey and Fred Harris to strip him of his office in the spring of 1972.

Change, however, is now on the way. There is a school of thought that believes the seniority system will itself bring about the reforms most desired by the liberal critics. According to this argument, most recently propounded by David Broder of the Washington *Post*, the conservative southern Democrats who have dominated the Senate for the past forty years are in fact the last of the line, and as they gradually die or retire from office they will be replaced by the group of mostly northern liberals who were elected when President Kennedy came to office at the start of the 1960s. Given the hazards of life in general and politics in particular, says Broder, some and perhaps most of the oldtime southerners will be gone by the end of the present presidential term in 1977. Behind them is a new generation of Democratic senators quite unlike their own: representatives of the populous states of the East, the Midwest, and the West. "These men," Broder adds, "tend to be energetic, programmatic, progressive, urban minded—and on the move." Before Richard Nixon leaves office it can therefore be expected that such liberal senators as McGovern and Proxmire, Muskie and Church, McIntyre and Ribicoff, will have begun to replace the thin and aging remnant of the southern old guard. "In both politics and personality," Broder believes, "the old place won't be the same."

In the House of Representatives, the elections of 1972 brought about the biggest changes in years, and the erosion of the power of the old guard has already begun. The 1972 elections saw the electoral downfall of several of the old diehards, notably including John McMillan, the autocratic chairman of the House committee that in effect rules the city of Washington (and who once described the black residents of the federal city as "interlopers"); Wayne Aspinall, chairman of the Interior Committee, defeated in the election by the ecologists; and William Colmer, an eighty-two-year-old Mississippian, chairman of the mighty Rules Committee, whose approval was needed to get a bill onto the floor for a vote, and who has now been replaced by Ray Madden, a relatively liberal representative from the industrial city of Gary, Indiana. In all, the 1972 elections saw the end through defeat or retirement of six Democratic committee chairmen and nine Republicans who were in line for chairmanships if the Republicans ever gained control of the House.

What is more, the House has at long last begun to institute real reform of its procedures, which in the years to come could revolutionize its power structure. Already both the Democrats and the Republicans require a vote, by secret ballot, to confirm every committee chairmanship, although, so far, there have been no upsets; all the chairmen who were confirmed in office when Congress reassembled in January 1973 were precisely those who would have been eligible for the job anyway under the seniority system. Respect for elder statesmen is still the strongest qualification for office, but at least the rule of the chairmen is now subject to review. It is interesting, also, that when the new rules were applied, none of the committee votes was unanimous. The dam of seniority had at last been breached. Length of service is no longer the automatic guarantee of leadership.

Early in 1973, the Democratic caucus also whittled away some of the power of the committee chairmen to send their bills to the floor of the House under the "closed rule," which bars amendments, while other reforms have for the first time given the party leadership a direct voice in Democratic members' committee appointments. Some House hearings have been opened up to public scrutiny. The lower chamber has adopted a new million-dollar electronic voting system, which records each member's vote on an overhead scorecard and provides the result on a computer printout. The vote of the whole House, which used to take an average of half an hour, has been reduced to a few minutes, symbolic perhaps of the more substantive changes that are now in prospect.

All these reforms were instituted quietly, without much fanfare, but their impact on the future role of the House of Representatives is likely to be profound. The days of the feudal baronies, indeed, might already be over, in the process of being replaced by King Caucus. Such formerly dominant grandees as Wilbur Mills of Arkansas, chairman of the crucial Ways and Means Committee, have in 1973 seen their prerogatives eroded almost overnight, sometimes with their own connivance, and transferred to the party caucus, which is dominated by liberals. After thirty years on the committee, and as chairman since 1958, Mills's detailed mastery of the country's tax laws is said to be unsurpassed anywhere in government and is probably still sufficient to give him effective control, at least for a while, over an awesome range of items: federal taxation, foreign tariffs and trade quotas, Social Security, and federal welfare benefits. Like all other committee chairmen, Mills got his job through seniority, but he is also one of the chairmen who would have attained his post anyway through sheer ability. A wily politician, he has embraced with apparent ardor the reforms which have recently weakened his power, but for motives that may not be as pure as they appear. It is sometimes suggested he would like to see the caucus run wild for a time—adding protectionist clauses to his trade bill, for example, or legislating massive and impractical tax cuts—simply in order to prove the new system unworkable, to teach the House a lesson, as one of his colleagues put it. But maybe it simply reflects the one clear principle that has always guided his political conduct: He likes to finish up on the winning side. In its profile of the enigmatic Arkansan, the Nader organization declared, "Mills maintains his invincible image by remaining non-committal until a consensus has developed, and then going its way; sometimes being so strategically positioned, he creates the consensus." Holding the key to such crucial issues as tax reform, the creation of national health insurance, and America's tariff relations with the rest of the world, Mills is still a power to be reckoned with, although he has hinted that because of ill health, his present term in Congress may be his last.

As President Nixon entered his second term in office at the beginning of 1973, there were the makings of a classic constitutional struggle for power between the two main branches of government, a struggle that in the light of history might well prove to be the dominant theme of the Nixon Presidency. The two main issues at stake were the same as those that had haunted Congress for a full decade: how to bring back under control the President's power to wage an undeclared war, and how to reassert congressional control over the federal purse strings. The issues were compounded by the President's apparent contempt for the Congress and his determination to extend the presidential prerogative into areas that had hitherto, by tradition and constitutional specification, belonged to Congress.

Although Nixon had himself spent four years in the House of Representa-

tives and two in the Senate, and as Vice President had ex officio presided over
the Senate for a further eight years, he had never felt himself at home in the
legislative branch. He had not stayed in either house long enough to accumulate the seniority that would have allowed him to enter the establishment, the
inner club. Besides, he was even then too much of a loner, too ruthlessly
ambitious, too concerned with building his own career on the investigation of
domestic communism, to enter fully into the day-by-day minutiae of legislation. There are those who believe he did not fully understand the workings
of Congress when he came to the White House, where he promptly isolated
himself—as had no other President before him—from the leaders across town
on Capitol Hill. He simply had no stomach for those face-to-face confrontations that are occasionally necessary if the President is to win the confidence
of his Congress. The fact that he had been the only President in this century
who throughout his term in office faced a Congress controlled by the opposition party, only served to reinforce a natural inferiority complex.

Nixon's personal problems with Congress were further compounded by his
White House staff, who took upon themselves the role of palace guard to
insulate the President yet further from any meaningful contact with the
political leaders in Congress. His principal domestic advisors, H. R. Haldeman, John Ehrlichman, and Peter Flanigan, were wholly innocent of the inner
workings of Congress when they arrived at the White House at the beginning
of 1969 fresh from careers in advertising and big business. All three of them,
in the words of the columnists Rowland Evans and Robert Novak, looked upon
Capitol Hill "as an awkward and obnoxious obstacle, a hostile foreign power."
They sought for the President not compromise, but domination. Congress, in
their tightlipped authoritarian view, was to do as it was told; if it refused to
do as it was told, a strong President could anyhow ignore its will. At one White
House staff meeting just before the vital Senate vote on the antiballistic
missile, Haldeman turned to one of Nixon's aides who was responsible for
liaison with the Hill and said, "You shouldn't be sitting here, you ought to
be up in the Senate telling Hugh Scott how to vote." The idea that a senior
senator, then the Republican Party whip, could be so ordered around by the
White House is almost breathtaking in its arrogance. Yet it was to remain only
too characteristic of the attitude of the White House staff during the President's first term. Such pressures, repeated again and again during those first
four years, imperceptibly led to the mood of hostility towards the President
that has festered and lingered to this day.

By the time Nixon embarked on his second term in office, the rapport
between the White House and the leaders in Congress, a rapport which is
essential to the smooth working of government in America, had never in this
century stood so low. By seeking to appropriate to himself total control over
the processes of government, by unleashing the B-52s over Hanoi without so
much as a word of explanation to Congress, by sending his Attorney General
up to the Hill to assert the astonishing doctrine that the President had the

power to forbid all 2.5 million federal employees from testifying before Congress, Nixon had seemed to many to be seeking nothing less than the surrender of his political adversaries. "I am not certain whether there is a legislative route to end this bloody travesty," Mike Mansfield, the Senate majority leader, had confessed of the Hanoi raids. But, he added, "the time is long since past when we can take shelter in a claim of legislative impotence." In the House, Speaker Carl Albert, struck much the same note when he declared that he would work "harder than I have ever worked in my life" to win back Congress's place as an equal partner in government.

Neither Mansfield nor Albert are in any sense leaders bent on acquiring power for its own sake. On the contrary, both are men of mild and gentle disposition, with little taste for the politics of confrontation. Years of exercising influence in the more subtle corridors of Congress have left them with a decided preference for conciliation. Both men, too, share a respect bordering on awe for the office of the presidency. Yet when the Ninety-third Congress convened at the start of 1973, it did so in a mood of crisis and confrontation. Three actions by the President had finally served to shock Congress into a reaffirmation of its own strength, its own prerogatives. The first of Nixon's actions had been his escalation of the war in Vietnam without the slightest attempt at consultation with either the Foreign Relations Committee or with anyone else in the Senate, which has the power under the Constitution both to declare war and to raise and support armies. The second was his initial refusal to allow White House aides to testify before the Senate on their role in the Watergate affair. The third was his refusal to spend money that Congress had specifically authorized, and to do so in a manner disdainful and contemptuous of the authority of Congress.

Congress saw in all of this an almost deliberate attempt at provocation, an effort by an authoritarian President to gather all significant governmental authority into the White House. Consequently, their mood as Nixon entered upon his second term after one of the biggest electoral landslides in history was not at all submissive, but angry—an angrier mood than many Congress-watchers had seen in a lifetime. As the New York *Times* put it on the day the new Congress convened:

> A Chief Executive determined to conduct war and foreign affairs without constraint or even consultation, determined to shield the Administration's effective policymakers from Congressional cross-examination by the vastly enlarged use of the doctrine of executive privilege, and determined to arrogate to himself total control over Federal spending decisions is a President seeking nothing less than the surrender of his adversaries. Congress cannot escape responding to these direct challenges to its authority.

To its credit, the Congress—a body some of its critics had not long before written off as a constitutional relic—did not attempt to escape the challenge.

The opening of the Ninety-third Congress in 1973 may be seen in retrospect as the moment when the constitutional pendulum began at long last to swing once more away from the White House toward the legislators on Capitol Hill. Its first important victory came on the question of executive privilege over the Watergate affair, when Senator Sam Ervin of North Carolina, a courtly but tough constitutionalist, threatened that if the President would not allow his aides to testify publicly and under oath before his committee, he would have them arrested. "Divine right went out with the American revolution and doesn't belong to White House aides," Ervin had declared. "What meat do they eat that makes them grow so great? I am not willing to elevate them to a position above the great mass of the American people. I don't think we have any such thing as royalty or nobility that exempts them. I'm not going to let anyone come down at night like Nicodemus and whisper something in my ear that no one else can hear.* That is not Executive privilege. It is Executive poppycock." Ervin, who has been called "the last of the founding fathers," won an important battle over the Watergate hearings that has already done much to stop the erosion of congressional power, demonstrating that when it has the will and a determined champion to lead it, Congress still has an awesome authority which can reach into the inner recesses of the White House itself. "I don't like the surgeon's knife," Ervin had said of his role, "but sometimes a cancer comes—a cancer on the body politic that has to be eradicated in some way."

The struggle over federal spending will not be over quite so quickly, although here again the newly aroused Congress has embarked upon a genuine effort to regain its full constitutional authority, as laid down by the Founding Fathers, "to lay and collect taxes, duties, imposts and excises, to pay debts and to provide for the common defense and general welfare of the United States." The issue that had initially led to crisis was a complicated one which revolved around the President's request for a federal spending ceiling to be placed on federal expenditure for 1973. After long debate, both Houses of Congress declined to hand this carte blanche to the President. It was their right and their responsibility to set the level of federal expenditure. But the President ignored this expression of the congressional will and imposed a spending ceiling anyway. There was a further squabble over funds the Congress had voted for a water-purity bill. The President, declaring the bill recklessly expensive, exercised his undoubted constitutional right and vetoed it. Whereupon Congress passed the measure again over the President's veto, exercising *its* undoubted constitutional right to override a veto by a two-thirds vote. But again, the President ignored the will of Congress and simply refused to spend the money, impounding the funds he said were excessive. He was to use the

---

*The President had offered to allow his aides to testify in secret to Ervin. Nicodemus was a Pharisee who came to Jesus secretly at night to ask about his teachings.

same tactic again and again to block spending programs authorized by Congress on the grounds that if he did not impound the appropriated funds the Congress's costly programs would lead either to inflation or greatly increased taxation. For its part, Congress complained that the President was expanding illegally upon his constitutional authority: By impounding their funds he was altering the spending priorities that it is the right of the Congress to establish.

The issue was further compounded by the archaic budgetary procedures of Congress, where there is, astonishingly, no central point at which the federal budget is reviewed as a whole. When the President sends his budget up to the Hill it is considered in several pieces, with each individual committee working in an insulated compartment of its own. The question of priorities is never really considered by the whole House or Senate, nor are the various committees' decisions made with any reference to what revenues are available. In the House of Representatives, where the bills originate, the Appropriations Committee considers each spending bill one by one and sends them separately to the House for a vote. What is worse, other legislative committees like Education and Labor are sometimes able to send up spending bills that bypass Appropriations altogether—a system almost guaranteed to produce an irresponsible approach to spending and taxation. Even more slipshod is the failure of the Appropriations Committee, which determines the overall spending program, to link its work to that of the Ways and Means Committee, which rules over revenue-raising. "They might as well be on separate planets," Representative Donald Riegle has said. "Without any goal-setting at the outset, everything that follows is haphazard."

Congress has got by on this archaic system for years, but under the pressure of Nixon's aggressive onslaught on their prerogatives, both the House and the Senate have finally been shocked into the process of reform. Already, the seniority system is being undermined, power is in the process of being transferred to the party caucus, and now even the House's haphazard methods of controlling the budget are coming under scrutiny, with proposals that would produce the most basic reform of congressional procedure in half a century. A plan submitted by a joint committee on budget control would give future congresses the power both to set an annual limit on spending and to decide national spending priorities. Under the reforms, the Senate and House would each have a new budget committee, charged with taking an overall view of both revenues and spending. More important still, Congress and not the President would retain the final word on total spending and priorities.

It is hard to imagine that such reforms would have passed through Congress without the urgency of seeing their own prerogatives so widely under siege from the White House. "There is no question that five years ago almost every member of Congress would have found some reason to be against the proposal," said a member of the committee that had drafted the reforms. But times had changed more swiftly than anyone had foreseen. Indeed, it may well prove an important part of Nixon's legacy that he finally shocked the Congress into putting its own two houses in order, the better to withstand his constitutional encroachments. The battle is by no means over, and it is in any case unlikely to end in a clearcut victory for either side, but Congress under President Nixon has discovered, sometimes to its surprise, that it can still act as the most influential legislative body in the world. The question now is whether it also has the will.

CHAPTER IX

Supreme Court

Changing Pace

"The Constitution is what the judges say it is."

—CHIEF JUSTICE CHARLES EVANS HUGHES

Of the three great pillars that support the U.S. Constitution, perhaps the oddest is the Supreme Court, an élite institution set in a populist country, a closed and even secretive body at the heart of the most open society in the world. At once the guarantor of change and the guardian of American liberties, the Court is unique to the United States. There is no other body anywhere else quite like it.

It has often been said that the nine Justices who make up the Court are to a modern President what the Church was to a medieval monarch. Like the Church, they are supposed to be concerned not with what is expedient, but what is right; they deal with the spiritual health of the nation as well as the material; they have a mystique and a mythology unknown to other institutions in the New World; and they can meddle so infuriatingly in the great affairs of state that more than one modern President has been impelled to echo the cry of Henry II, "Who will free me from this turbulent priest!"

The mystique of the Court is carefully nurtured. The nine Justices, black-robed and somberfaced, convene in an overblown replica of a Greek temple opposite the U.S. Congress on Capitol Hill. When the Justices assemble for their deliberations, the Court crier calls out in a voice loud enough to strike the watching public with awe, "Oyez! Oyez! All persons having business before the Honorable, the Supreme Court of the United States, are admonished to draw near and give attention. . . . God bless the United States and the deliberations of this Honorable Court!"

Thus garbed with the approval of the Almighty, the nine justices solemnly shake hands with each other, then get down to the business of the day, cloistered from the influence of legislators or lobbyists, Presidents or the press. Their deliberations take place in private; only their carefully wrought decisions are made in public, and it is one of the Court's proudest boasts that their disputes (and there have been many) have never been aired in the press. That alone makes it an institution unique in the American experience.

There is a myth, infinitely cherished by many Americans, that theirs is a government of laws, not men, that it is the function of the Supreme Court to interpret the Constitution impartially and judicially, just as the Founding Fathers wrote it, and that the Court is accordingly somehow "above politics." Nothing could be further from the truth. The Supreme Court is in fact so far from being "above politics" that the nine members of the bench have normally all served in the field of practical politics at one time or another, and owe their positions as Justices to another politician who in all probability appointed them for political reasons. The Court, said George Washington, is the keystone of our *political* fabric, and Justice Felix Frankfurter used to say that constitutional law is "applied politics, using the word in its noblest sense." But beyond even that, the Court has also taken upon itself in the past twenty years a still wider role: the task of dealing with the political issues that the politicians themselves have found too sensitive to handle. On matters from the breakdown of racial segregation and the abolition of the death penalty to the apportionment of welfare payments, it is the Court that has taken the initiative. Indeed, since 1953 it has probably had more influence on the lives of ordinary Americans than all the legislation passed by Congress put together.

It is commonly believed (and by some, devoutly hoped) that the Court that now serves the nation is about to enter one of its habitual periods of hibernation after the controversy that has recently surrounded it. That is in fact the rhythm of history. Periods of great activism, like the one now drawing to a close, alternate with periods of quietism and consolidation. Like all other political institutions, the Court has had its periods of reaction as well as its periods of reform. As early as 1800, Thomas Jefferson was grumbling about the Supreme Court as that "subtle corps of sappers and miners constantly working underground to undermine the foundations of our confederated fabric." Half a century later, the infamous Dred Scott decision, which gave the Court's official approval to slavery, was an important factor in the breakdown of constitutional government that led ultimately to the Civil War. In our own times the Supreme Court struck down much of President Roosevelt's New Deal legislation. Angry at the rejection of his legislation, Roosevelt accused the Court of improperly setting itself up as a third house of Congress—a superlegislature. Later, he precipitated a constitutional crisis by threatening to increase the size of the Court so that he could pack the bench with his own nominees. He based his request on the flimsy grounds that he would be doing the "nine old men" a favor by reducing their work load. Of course nobody believed him, and Roosevelt was eventually forced to drop his Machiavellian plan. In exchange, the Court made a tacit agreement not to enter "the political thicket," going into a period of quietism that ended only with Eisenhower's appointment of Earl Warren as Chief Justice in 1953.

Until that time, the Court was widely regarded as the guardian of the nation's private property rights; within a year of Earl Warren's appointment it had launched a social revolution. The high point came in 1954 with its famous decision *Brown* v. *Board of Education,* which declared with bald simplicity, "Separate educational facilities are inherently unequal," a sentence which began the great wave of black emancipation that changed the fabric of American society.

At first, Warren had seemed an unlikely reformer: appointed by Eisenhower in consideration for his political support at the 1952 convention, he was a man of whom it was said, "he never suffered from an abstract thought in his life." In his earlier days, Warren had earned a well-deserved reputation as a right-wing conservative, a former Republican governor of California who took a leading part in bundling American citizens of Japanese ancestry into detention camps during World War II. ("If the Japs are released," he had said, "no one will be able to tell a saboteur from any other Jap.") Even after the war, he was, according to one Democratic opponent, "the personification of reaction." He had been Governor Dewey's runningmate in the presidential election of 1948 and no one could have seemed a safer conservative bet when he was elevated to the Bench. His metamorphosis into the most liberal Chief Justice in history is perhaps the classic example of the mysterious change that nearly always affects a man when he dons the black robes and enters what has been called a modern Temple of Karnak. The same thing has happened to other men time and again. Felix Frankfurter, another member of the Warren Court, had been regarded as "little more than a Bolshevik" when he was appointed by President Roosevelt, but he became under Warren the Court's conservative conscience, the prime defender of the doctrine of judicial restraint, and a hero of the right wing. On the other hand, Warren's senior Associate Justice, Hugo Black, became the foremost liberal advocate on the Court, even though in his youth in Alabama he had been a member of the Ku Klux Klan.

Under the Supreme Court system, of course, the Chief Justice is theoretically only *primus inter pares,* "first among equals." He presides over the sessions at which the Court's decisions are announced, he assigns the opinions when he is in the majority, but otherwise he is no different from any of the other eight Justices. The accomplishments of the Warren Court were therefore far more than the achievements of a single man. They were, rather, a collective effort in which the entire Court had sensed the strong tide of events and sought to make the law respond to it. But in this effort, the role of the Chief Justice had been crucial; the Court, when he came to it, had been deeply divided, on philosophical grounds as well as on political. By exercising his leadership, Warren was able to bring them together on the more important issues, so that even the *Brown* v. *Board of Education* decision had come down from a unanimous Court (although Warren was to boast later he had written "every blessed word" of it himself). Above all, Warren was an activist and a reformer. Under earlier Courts, the great majority of cases had centered around matters of property; now cases involving the Bill of Rights and the Fourteenth Amendment took priority. Warren sought to explain his activist role by saying it was inevitable, that once such a case had come up to the Court the Justices were bound philosophically to hear it. To people who asked him if he was not going too fast on matters like civil rights, he invariably answered, "We haven't anything to say about how fast we go. We go with the cases that come to us, and when they come to us with a question of human liberties involved in them, we either hear them and decide them, or we let them go and sweep them under the rug, only to leave them for future generations."

Warren and his colleagues were never men to sweep things under the rug. By any standards, they used their legal authority more boldly than any Court has ever done before. They struck down racial segregation, made rulings about how the states should appoint their legislators, put restrictions on the observance of religion in public schools, transformed the rights of criminal defendants, and finally and most controversially, decreed that massive busing should be used to achieve an acceptable racial mix in the nation's schools.

The liberal achievements were built on the foundation of the Fourteenth Amendment to the Constitution, ratified in 1868 and intended to protect the rights of the newly freed slaves. It reads, in part:

> No state shall make or enforce any law which shall abridge the privileges or immunities of citizens of the United States; nor shall any State deprive any person of life, liberty, or property, without due process of law; nor deny to any person within its jurisdiction the equal protection of the laws.

Because of the flexibility of its "due process" clause, and the discretion it gives the Court to intervene in the internal affairs of individual states, the Fourteenth Amendment was seized upon by the Warren Court to push through virtually all its social reforms. It was first used to outlaw school segregation, then to curb some of the excesses of local police interrogation. It has been used to stop some of the gerrymandering of local election procedures and to open the doors of the voting booths to the poor black citizens of the South. Ironically enough, it was also the Fourteenth Amendment that had been used by the conservative Justices of an earlier epoch to outlaw the income tax and veto the progressive economic legislation of the later New Deal—underlining once again the truth of Chief Justice Hughes's famous aphorism, "The Constitution is what the judges say it is." Even under a written constitution, it is not the laws, but the men who interpret the laws, that are all-powerful. The Constitution does not change, but the judges do.

In criminal law, as in its interpretation of the social demands of the Constitution, the Warren Court was no less progressive in its rulings. Here, its most important—and to conservatives, its most outrageous—decision was taken in 1966 in an action called *Miranda* v. *Arizona*. The case involved a white girl who had allegedly been raped by a twenty-three-year-old Mexican-American called Ernesto Miranda. After his arrest by two Phoenix policemen, Miranda wrote out a full confession in which he admitted and described the crime and signed a statement that he had made his confession voluntarily, without threats or promises, and "with full knowledge of my legal rights, understanding any statement I make may be used against me."

The Warren Court, in a 5 to 4 vote, overturned Miranda's conviction on the grounds that he had been so scared by the interrogation that he had in effect been compelled to bear witness against himself, even though the police had never threatened him or beaten him physically. The Court nevertheless held that no statement made by an arrested suspect could be used against him in court unless he had been told of his right to remain silent and to have a lawyer present. From then on defendants in criminal cases were armed with an unprecedented legal protection. As a result, any suspect now taken into custody may indicate in any way that he does not wish to answer the police questions, and the police must immediately stop their interrogation. Although Miranda himself was later retried and convicted on other evidence, police claim the Supreme Court ruling ties their hands to the extent that criminals frequently escape scotfree. It was the Miranda ruling, as much as any other, that led candidate Richard Nixon to attack the Supreme Court for "weakening the police forces" in the United States.

Again and again during his 1968 campaign, Nixon attacked the rulings of the Warren Court. He personally led the assault on the Court's criminal-law rulings, speaking with melodramatic effect during his nomination address of "sirens in the night" and murder and rape on the streets, which he put down to the decisions of the Supreme Court that had given, as he put it, "the green light to crime." In particular, he claimed that because of the Supreme Court's rulings on *Miranda* and other cases, no more than one in eight major crimes committed led to arrest, prosecution, conviction and punishment. "From the point of view of the criminal forces," he said, "the cumulative impact of these decisions has been to set free patently guilty individuals on the basis of legal technicalities. The tragic lesson of guilty men walking free from hundreds of courtrooms across the country has not been lost on the criminal community." Nixon, however, did not point out to his audiences that Miranda had in the end been convicted, even though his confession had been ruled out as inadmissible evidence. Nor did he make clear that in the seven out of eight major crimes that went unpunished, the reason in the majority of the cases was that the criminal had not been caught by the police. Only political finessing of a remarkable order could attach the blame for that onto the Supreme Court, but Nixon left the impression with his audiences that the Court's "barbed wire of legalisms" had materially contributed to the rise in unpunished crime.

On civil rights, he left the attack to others, notably Senator Strom Thurmond of South Carolina, the spearhead of his so-called southern strategy. The South had been outraged by the Court's rulings on desegregation and busing, and Nixon's surrogates exploited this to the full. The candidate himself declared, "I don't think there is any Court in this country, including the Supreme Court of the United States, that is qualified to be a school local district and make the decision as your local school board."

The new President thus came to office determined to recast the Court in his own—conservative—image. "Presidents come and go," he said, "but the Supreme Court, through its decisions, goes on forever." In fact, the President declared, except for his contributions to the cause of world peace, "there is probably no more important legacy that a President can leave in these times than his appointments to the Supreme Court." As it turned out, during his first three years in office, fate was to give Richard Nixon four separate opportunities to leave his permanent imprint on the composition of the Court. His manner of handling them looked at one time as though it would lead to a major constitutional crisis. In a series of bitter clashes with the Senate, which has the right to advise and consent on the Court appointments, one Justice was forced to resign, two of the President's nominees were rejected, three more had to be discarded before they ever came to nomination, and another Justice was threatened with impeachment. In each case, the battleground was political, the fight intensely partisan, with Nixon apparently determined to transform the Court into an appendix of the power of the Presidency.

As a result of these battles, the once-invincible liberals on the Court have been reduced to a rump of three, while four more, including the Chief Justice, are now Nixon appointees, conservatives all. Given the normal attrition of infirmity and old age, moreover, it is likely that before Nixon leaves office there will be an outright majority of his appointees on the Court. Already the shift in the balance of power has begun to have a profound effect on the nature of the decisions handed down by the Court.

In 1973, the nine men on the Supreme Court were:

Name	Age	Appointed By
Warren E. Burger (Chief Justice)	66	Nixon
William O. Douglas	75	Roosevelt
William J. Brennan	67	Eisenhower
Potter Stewart	58	Eisenhower
Byron R. White	55	Kennedy
Thurgood Marshall	65	Johnson
Harry A. Blackmun	64	Nixon
Lewis F. Powell	66	Nixon
William Rehnquist	49	Nixon

Nixon's first opportunity to "do something" about the Court, as he had promised, came as the result of a miscalculation by his predecessor, Lyndon Johnson, who in his final months in office had attempted to rush through the elevation of his old friend Abe Fortas from Associate Justice to Chief Justice.

The opportunity had arisen through Earl Warren's decision to retire, "effective at your pleasure," as he told Johnson. The old wheeler-dealer seized with relish this chance to dish his successor and saddle him with a Court fixed in its liberal image. "I will accept your decision to retire effective at such time as a successor is qualified," he wrote Warren, in a blatant attempt to negotiate the succession. "When I nominated Fortas," Johnson said later, "I did so for the same reasons I had first appointed him to the Court: because he was the most experienced, compassionate, articulate, and intelligent lawyer I knew, and because I was certain that he would carry on in the Court's liberal tradition."

Unfortunately for Johnson, Fortas was regarded as far too liberal for the Republicans and the Southern conservatives in the Senate, all of whom, as Johnson admitted, "were horrified at the thought of a continuation of the philosophy of the Warren Court." And when Johnson made the tactical error of nominating Homer Thornberry, yet another liberal crony, to fill the vacancy that would be created by Fortas's elevation, the effect was to kill the chances of *both* nominations.

The conservatives were furious. The leader of the Senate opposition, Robert Griffin of Michigan, declared, "It is highly unusual for a President to subject himself to a charge of cronyism in connection with a nomination to the Supreme Court. And never before in history has any President been so bold as to subject himself to a charge of cronyism with respect to *two* such nominations at the same time."

Under the Constitution, the power to appoint Supreme Court Justices is shared by the President, who alone has the authority to nominate, and the Senate, which has the right to "advise and consent" on the President's choice. Previously, the Senate's powers had been used sparingly. Of all the twentieth-century nominees up to that date, only one—John J. Parker, selected by Hoover in 1930—had been rejected.

The Fortas hearings were characterized by a rancor that did justice to neither side. At stake was the future control of the entire Court. The conservatives, calculating that Nixon would become the next President, were determined not to let Johnson hurry through an appointment that, after November, would become Nixon's. They were assisted by the curiously evasive manner of the nominee when he took the stand before the Senate Judiciary Committee.

There were several discreditable rows in the hearing room about Fortas's stand on the obscenity laws, which had been notably relaxed under several recent rulings. But Fortas's chances of success were effectively killed by a dramatic revelation halfway through the hearings that he had accepted a fee of fifteen thousand dollars for conducting a summer seminar at the American University near his home in Washington.

In the eyes of the Senate opposition, the fee was exorbitant, while its source was to prove even more questionable. The five donors who had put up the money were described by Senator Strom Thurmond as representing "a complex of business and financial holdings that scarcely could be extricated from anything touching upon the Court." The revelations about Fortas's outside earnings, coupled with the charges of cronyism, effectively squashed any chances he still had for obtaining confirmation, and Fortas, recognizing the realities, asked Johnson that his name be withdrawn. Fortas's troubles, though he did not yet know it, were in fact only just beginning.

A complex and sensitive man, born of working-class Jewish parents in Memphis, Tennessee, Fortas was acknowledged to be one of the most brilliant lawyers of his generation, with an enviable reputation for humanity and liberalism. During the *Miranda* hearings he had been instrumental in swaying the decision of the High Court towards its momentous verdict. As Fortas began to argue his case, one of Miranda's lawyers had passed a note to a friend in court: "If God be Fortas, who can be against us?"

Through his friendship with Johnson he became one of the half-dozen most influential men in Washington, although he had at first been reluctant to give up his lucrative private practice to enter the cloistered world of the Supreme Court and was virtually drafted into the job by the President, who told him, "I'm sending fifty thousand boys to Vietnam and I want you to go to the Supreme Court." Yet even after he was appointed to the Bench, the back door of the White House was always open to a visit from Fortas, who once described his main contribution to Johnson's Presidency as "analytical help." He affected to be modest about his close ties with the President, but modesty did not prevent him from entering his occupation in a 1966 edition of *Who's Who* as "presidential advisor" and listing his address as "care of the White House, 1600 Pennsylvania Avenue, Washington, D.C."

His private life was both lavish and cultured. He lived in an elegant Georgetown mansion, drove a restored Rolls-Royce, and was a gifted amateur musician who included David Oistrakh and Pablo Casals among his personal friends. In his biography of Fortas, *A Question of Judgment*, Robert Shogan tells a characteristic story of the Justice's friendship with Casals, for whom he once helped to organize a musical festival in Peurto Rico. On the eve of the festival, a seam broke in Casals's cello "and nothing would do but for Fortas to take it personally to an expert in New York for repairs." He boarded the plane, strapped the cello in the neighboring seat, and ordered one martini for himself and another for the cello. Then he gulped down both drinks himself. "I was nervous," he explained. "Carrying a man's cello is like carrying his wife."

On another occasion, he said in an after-dinner speech there were two things about himself that had been vastly exaggerated. "One is the extent to which I am a presidential advisor, and the other is the extent to which I am a proficient violinist. I am a very poor violinist, but very enthusiastic, and my relationship with the President has been exaggerated out of all connection with reality." But Fortas was being modest. Johnson phoned him almost every night, seeking reassurance in Fortas's hawkishness on the war, seeking his advice on policy matters, even on economics, although once on the court Fortas was supposed to have put politics behind him and certainly was not supposed to act as advisor to the executive branch.

Below the new Justice's wry and cultured exterior there lurked a streak of ruthlessness that his colleagues found both puzzling and disturbing, while his fascination for money was thought by some to be little short of avaricious. Like many lawyers who came to Washington with the New Deal, Fortas found that in private practice he could make himself fabulously rich, partly as a result of his undoubted abilities, but partly as a result of his inside knowledge of the workings of power in the capital city. Success had become its own justification, and Fortas began to behave as though he were omnipotent, above the rules that guide the conduct of ordinary mortals. Long before he entered the Supreme Court, his law firm of Arnold and Porter was well-known in Washington for taking up good causes, but as a famous New Deal lawyer once remarked, "Their good works in the past didn't stop them from representing every stinking interest in town." As the New York *Times* put it, there was something about Fortas's attitude toward the Court that was "insufficiently holy."

Besides, there was at the center of his character a sense of self-esteem that often bordered on the arrogant. He once told an influential senator who had disagreed with him about a Presidential appointment, "No one can doubt that you are completely unsuited for any position which requires the exercise of judgment and balance. If and when . . . we need guidance as to our responsibilities to the President or to the Government, we certainly will not consult a person who is so obviously irresponsible as yourself." It was not an endearing letter, nor one that was calculated to win him the friends in the Senate he would later come to need. Even when disaster struck, he was unable to admit that it had been brought about by his own conduct. "It was," he said, "just as if an automobile hit me as I stepped off the curb."

The second Fortas crisis, the one that hit him like an automobile, came in the shape of a *Life* article published in the early months of the Nixon Administration. The article revealed that soon after joining the Supreme Court Fortas had taken a fee of twenty thousand dollars from a charitable foundation run by a financier named Louis Wolfson, who later ended up in jail for playing fast and loose with the regulations of the Securities and Exchange Commission. Much later, Fortas had paid the money back, but the damage to his already tarnished reputation proved irreparable—especially when it came to light later that the twenty thousand-dollar fee was meant to be an annual one, to last as long as he or his wife should live. There was no evidence that Fortas was in breach of any criminal code, nor that he had ever used his influence in any improper way on Wolfson's behalf. There was certainly an appearance of impropriety, however, and President Nixon and his Attorney General, John Mitchell, had no intention of letting slip this opportunity to get rid of Fortas once and for all.

For Nixon and Mitchell, the prospects were tantalizing. Here, much sooner than either of them had thought possible, was a chance to recast the Warren Court in their own image. There were hazards in this course, and the President was probably aware that if it came to light that he was trying to interfere with the workings of the judicial branch of government, their carefully made plans would come to naught. So they trod through the thicket with extreme delicacy. Nixon summoned Republican leaders from Capitol Hill to a meeting at the White House and told them, "It is most desirable not to involve this matter in partisanship." He warned that there would be "no aid and comfort to anyone doing something rash."

Meanwhile, the Justice Department, which had been working night and day on the case, took the decision not to press criminal charges against Fortas, although Mitchell hinted broadly that the department knew more about the affair than had been revealed by *Life*. Later, he made a well-publicized visit to the Supreme Court for a conference with the Chief Justice in which he showed him "certain documents"—which later turned out to be copies of Fortas's contract with the Wolfson foundation. It was a clever maneuver, through which Mitchell threw the onus of taking action onto the Supreme Court itself, and so bypassed the politically damaging course of impeachment proceedings or a criminal prosecution, which would have inevitably led to charges of partisanship on the part of the administration.

In the end, Fortas left quietly, under pressures from his chief and from the liberal press, which had supported him for so long but which deserted him now. In a sometimes rambling letter to Warren, Fortas announced he wished to resign from the Court and said he hoped that public controversy would thereupon cease so that the Court could get on with its work without the harassment of debate concerning one of its members. "There has been no wrongdoing on my part," Fortas said. "There has been no default in the performance of my judicial duties in accordance with the high standards of the office I hold."

With that, he retired to his Georgetown home for the rest of the day to play Mozart and Haydn on his violin. If he practiced hard enough, he told a reporter, someone might offer him a job as second fiddle.

With Fortas out of the way and Warren himself on the verge of retirement, Nixon was now faced with the tantalizing prospect of filling two vacancies on the Court and so ending once and for all the liberal bias he found so objectionable. The course ahead looked smooth enough when, within a week of Fortas's resignation, Nixon nominated Warren Burger as Chief Justice and saw him approved by the Senate by a vote of 74 to 3. But who would the Senate approve to fill the Fortas seat, a seat traditionally reserved for Jews? Nixon's first choice was Clement Haynsworth, a judge from South Carolina who looked distinguished enough and seemed to fill the President's requirements exactly. He was a conservative, a southerner, a "strict constructionist," and young enough at fifty-six to stand a good chance of making his conservative views prevail through many years' service on the High Court. Unfortunately, he had a reputation for being antiblack in his judgments and, what was worse for his chances of confirmation, antilabor. Once again, the Senate girded itself for a fight, orchestrated by the powerful lobbyists of the American labor movement and led on the floor by the young senator from Indiana, Birch Bayh.

Due to sloppy staff work somewhere in the Justice Department, the administration had failed to uncover damaging evidence concerning the nominee's financial affairs which, as one labor leader described with some exaggeration, "makes Fortas look like an altar boy." In fact, there was never any real evidence that Haynsworth had acted improperly, but in the overheated atmosphere that had followed the Fortas affair, the slightest ethical taint was enough to jeopardize the candidate's chances of confirmation. Nor was Haynsworth helped by the President, who insisted on making the battle a political one. "If Judge Haynsworth's philosophy leans to the conservative side," he said, "in my view that recommends him to me. I think the Court needs a man who is a conservative." Actually Haynsworth's judicial record was not nearly so conservative as either the President or the labor movement made out, and in the opinion of most experts was both competent and nondoctrinaire. But by deliberately choosing the ideological battleground, the President had doomed Haynsworth's chances. In the end, he was rejected in the Senate by a vote of 55 to 45.

Having made its point over Haynsworth, however, the Senate was now in a conciliatory mood and ready, in the words of Senator George Aiken of Vermont, to approve of "anyone who hasn't been convicted of murder—recently."

What happened next was deeply revealing of the character of Richard Nixon when he finds himself in a corner. Rather than nominate one of the many fully qualified and acceptable southern conservatives who were available, he reached instead for the most provocative nominee he could find. It was as though he was seeking revenge for the slight he had just suffered and wished to humiliate the senators who had been the instruments of that slight. When the name of G. Harrold Carswell was presented to the Senate, its members openly reacted in disbelief. Carswell was clean enough financially, but his record as a judge was so mediocre and his position on civil rights so tarnished that the New York *Times* was moved to observe that his nomination "almost suggests an intention to reduce the significance of the Court by lowering the caliber of its membership." When the Justice Department had asked Carswell for a list of his legal articles and writings, he replied that he had written none. He furnished instead a list of some twenty-five opinions that the *Times* said "read, for the most part, like plumbers' manuals."

By nominating Carswell, the President had given the impression, as one caustic observer remarked, that he was shopping around for duds and bigots as if he feared that well-qualified men could not be trusted once elevated to the Court. Even his supporters were apologetic. Senator Roman Hruska of Nebraska probably sealed the nominee's fate when he replied in a television interview to a question about Carswell's mediocrity: "There are a lot of mediocre judges and people and lawyers. They are entitled to a little representation, aren't they, and a little chance? We can't have all Brandeises, and Cardozos and Frankfurters and stuff like that here." With friends like Hruska, how would the judge from Florida fare when he faced his enemies?

Carswell, handsome and youthful, was from Tallahassee, a town in northern Florida that is still very much a part of the old Deep South. His upbringing just across the state line in Georgia had been in the strictly segregated atmosphere of that part of the country at that time. In 1948, as a rising young lawyer, he had written an article for a local weekly newspaper in which he made the following statement on racial integration:

> I am a Southerner by ancestry, birth, training, inclination, belief and practice. I believe that segregation of the races is proper and the only practical and correct way of life in our states. I have always so believed, and I shall always so act. . . . I yield to no man . . . in the firm, vigorous belief in the principle of white supremacy, and I shall always be so governed.

Twenty-two years later, Judge Carswell was to say he was "aghast" at his youthful statement which was now "obnoxious and abhorrent" to his personal philosophy. Deeper probing by the press and the Senate, however, revealed that his adherence to the practice, if not the principles, of racial segregation had lasted longer than the judge wished to admit. It was disclosed that he had been a member of an all-white golf club in Tallahassee and had been instrumental in arranging the transfer of the club from the municipality into private hands to avoid integration.

Once again, Nixon's plans for the Court had gone awry. With the hearings before the Senate only days away, Senator Robert Griffin pulled him aside at a White House meeting on the issue and told him privately, "Mr. President, the Carswell nomination is in bad shape. The support for the judge has eroded —it has eroded about as far as it could go."

The original recommendation of Carswell had again come from John Mitchell's Justice Department. So two days after his meeting with Griffin, the President called Mitchell's deputy, Richard Kleindienst, into his office and, as *Newsweek* described it, told him, "I am taking you off all your other duties.

I want you to spend the rest of your time—day and night—on this nomination. You got me into this mess: now you get me out of it."

Under Kleindienst's overall supervision, the White House mounted its biggest lobbying operation of the year with a crudity that was breathtaking. What was worse, it was openly contemptuous of the Senate's prerogatives. One White House aide phoned a Republican senator from Pennsylvania, Richard Schweiker and told him, "You will be a hero in Pennsylvania if you vote for Judge Carswell. Your vote will put the nomination across. There isn't *anything* you couldn't get for your state from the White House as a result."

To another doubtful senator, William Saxbe of Ohio, Nixon wrote a personal letter that seemed to challenge the Senate's constitutional right to vote against the White House nominee. "What is centrally at issue," Nixon wrote, "is whether [the President's] responsibility can be frustrated by those who wish to substitute their own philosophy or their own subjective judgment for that of the one person entrusted by the Constitution with the power of appointment." This highly questionable thesis angered more senators than it appeased. The Senate is jealous of its dwindling prerogatives, and many of its members strongly objected to the President's suggestion that their duty to "advise and consent" consisted merely of rubber-stamping the nomination. The President's case, said Birch Bayh, "is wrong as a matter of constitutional law, wrong as a matter of history, and wrong as public policy."

The recipient of the President's letter did in fact vote for Carswell, though none too happily. "I'll vote for him," Saxbe was quoted as saying. "He's a son-of-a-bitch, but at least he's our son-of-a-bitch." If Carswell was rejected, Saxbe added, he had a good idea who they would be saddled with next: "Some South Carolina judge—but make damn sure first that he puts his slaves in escrow."

Then there was the case of Margaret Chase Smith, the formidable senator from Maine. The White House aides had not dared to lobby *her*, or even ask how she might vote, for fear of arousing her famous wrath. But Senator Smith had told Nixon privately she intended to vote for his nominee; Nixon told Bryce Harlow, his aide on the Hill; Harlow imprudently passed the word to Senator Edward Brooke of Massachusetts in an attempt to influence *his* vote; and Senator Brooke told Margaret Smith. Senator Smith was so furious at this breach of her confidence she immediately switched her vote to No.

The White House had bungled its case so badly, the scene was now set for a famous defeat. Sure enough, for the second time in a row the Senate rejected the President's nominee to the Supreme Court, this time by a vote of 51 to 45.

There were recriminations aplenty. The Attorney General's wife, Martha Mitchell, called the Arkansas *Gazette* at two o'clock in the morning to complain about the No vote cast by Senator William Fulbright of that state. "No right, no rhyme or reason why I have to withhold my thoughts," Martha shrilled. "I'm so damn mad I can't stand it: I want you to crucify Fulbright, and that's it."

There was another famous explosion down at the White House. When news of the Senate's vote came through, the President burst out with a string of obscenities that so shocked his normally discreet staff his words were reverberating around Washington within twenty-four hours.

Here was the old Nixon back with a vengeance, the notoriously bad loser, the man who carries a grudge for every defeat. He was still furious the next day when he strode into the pressroom at the White House. His words to the press (and via them to the watching world) were full of bitterness as he accused his opponents on the Hill of hypocrisy, prejudice, vicious character assassination, and malicious maligning of both Haynsworth and Carswell. "They have been falsely charged with being racist, but when all the hypocrisy is stripped away, the real issue was their philosophy and strict construction of the Constitution . . . and the fact that they had the misfortune of being born in the South," the President declared. "As long as the Senate is constituted the way it is today, I will not nominate another southerner and let him be subjected to the kind of malicious character assassination accorded both Judges Haynsworth and Carswell."

His attack on the Senate was a characteristic attempt to set up a straw man with which to make the best of a bad job and try to swing a few votes in the South from those citizens gullible enough to believe Carswell had been defeated merely because he was a southerner. The real blame, of course, lay nearer home, and Nixon knew it. That April day in 1970 was perhaps the nadir of Nixon's first term in office, the culmination of a bad nomination and an inept operation—Nixon's Bay of Pigs, as several newspapers dubbed it. Everything that could go wrong with the operation had gone wrong, from Mitchell's failure to investigate Carswell's past record, the breach of Senator Smith's confidence, the attempt to bully the Senate into confirmation, but above all the cynical determination of both Nixon and Mitchell to win electoral advantage in the South regardless of the consequences in lowering the quality of the Supreme Court and offending the sensibilities of the Senate. It was a sorry performance all round, dictated in the first place by Nixon's obsessive attempts to degrade the one institution in American society that was still highly respected. His attacks on the Senate, as Tom Wicker pointed out in the New York *Times*, may or may not have obscured this record—but they certainly revealed the man.

What happened to the Supreme Court after that famous day should have been largely anticlimactic. Nixon nominated and the Senate quickly approved Judge Harry Blackmun of Minnesota to fill the empty seat. A well-respected lawyer, a close friend of Chief Justice Warren Burger (with whom he had gone to Sunday school), a conservative, and an obviously competent, if innocuous,

Justice, Blackmun had no difficulty in obtaining his confirmation. But the bench's buffetings by the storms of politics were by no means over yet. Conservative allies of the President tried, and failed, to get their revenge for the Carswell defeat by attempting to impeach the last of the Court's great liberals, Justice William O. Douglas, for alleged financial improprieties. His opponents had also been angered by an article Douglas had written, although it was never quite clear whether they were more enraged by Douglas's temerity in comparing the contemporary American establishment with the dynasty of George III or by the publication of these views in a girlie magazine. In any event the impeachment proceedings came to nothing.

Another flurry of controversy erupted at the end of 1971, however, when two of the Court's most honored members, John Harlan and Hugo Black, resigned because of mortal illness. These two giants of the Warren era, men of high integrity and shining intellect, had for years kept the Court aloof from the maneuvers of party politics. By the end of the year, both were dead, and their departure gave Nixon a further chance to remold the Court in his own image. Here was a historic opportunity; Patrick J. Buchanan, one of the President's aides, left no doubt that Nixon intended to seize it. The next Court, he suggested, "will be known as the Nixon Court, not as the Burger Court or the Warren Court." There could be no clearer indication that the President intended to persist in his determination to diminish the independent stature of the Supreme Court.

The worst suspicions were confirmed when the Justice Department floated the names of several people, of whom it became known they were seriously considering three: Senator Robert Byrd of West Virginia, a former member of the Ku Klux Klan who had earned his law degree at night school only in 1963 and who had never practiced at the bar at all; Herschel H. Friday, a Little Rock attorney, of whom the Arkansas *Gazette* said he had spent much of his legal labor over the past dozen years "turned to the purpose of keeping black children out of white schools"; and Judge Mildred Lillie of the California Court of Appeals, a nonentity whom the American Bar Association determined "not qualified" by the margin of 11 to 1. (It is said one liberal Justice read some of Judge Lillie's opinions that night and promptly got drunk).

Justice Harlan was reported to have been so outraged by the administration's relentless pursuit of mediocrity he seriously considered writing the President a letter of protest from his hospital bed, while even conservatives on the Court began wondering aloud whether Nixon was trying to "denigrate the Court." Senator Edward Kennedy said the President had showed himself to be "a radical in the true sense of the word, a man who seeks to undermine one of the basic and vital institutions of our nation." Members of the faculty at Harvard Law School published a statement saying the President's action "demeans the Court and risks undermining public respect for it."

There is little doubt that if he had persisted with his nominations Nixon would have precipitated a new and even graver constitutional crisis. It is due in no small degree to the strength of the American constitutional system, and especially the Senate, that Nixon was forced in the end to abandon his disastrous course and submit the names of men who were sufficiently qualified, intellectually and morally, to sit on the nation's highest court. They were Lewis Powell, Jr., a member of Virginia's largest law firm and a past president of the American Bar Association, and William Rehnquist, a relatively young and extremely bright Goldwater Republican who had worked as assistant Attorney General in the Justice Department. ("You've got the wrong man," Rehnquist had joked when reporters asked him about the rumors that he might be nominated. "I'm not a woman, I'm not a southerner, and I'm not mediocre.")

Today, the Supreme Court is in a state of hiatus—not quite yet the Nixon Court that had been forecast, but still a long way from the activism of the Warren years. Under Burger, the Court has also been preoccupied with the administrative reform of the judicial process in the United States and has been comparatively restrained in its social judgments. It refused, for instance, to delay the court-ordered desegregation of school districts in Mississippi, although on cases of criminal law, the four Nixon appointees have generally voted together in favor of the so-called law-and-order position. But on the whole, the Court's performance in the years immediately after the death of Black and Harlan has been ambivalent. It has, in one major decision, effectively abolished the death penalty; it has, in others, undermined the right of reporters to keep silent about the source of their information and effectively made the definition of obscenity a matter of local option. But it has also, in a wider sense, withdrawn from the political role assumed by the Court under Earl Warren; its ideological balance has been altered fundamentally, and the Court no longer sees itself as a major instrument for reform. In that respect, Nixon has probably achieved his ambition of converting the Court into a body of narrow legal interpretation rather than the Platonic guardian of the national purpose the Court had become under Chief Justice Warren. At any rate, there is evidence that the President was pleased with his handiwork. Just before his landslide re-election in 1972, he was asked, "Mr. President, do you consider the Supreme Court now to be in balance, or do you think it needs another dose of strict constructionism if that occasion should arise?" Nixon grinned. "I feel at the present time," he replied, "that the Court is as balanced as I have had an opportunity to make it."

PART FOUR

The World Scene

CHAPTER X

Foreign Affairs

1. Isolated America?

"It is not our power but our will that is being tested tonight."
—PRESIDENT RICHARD NIXON *on the eve of the U.S. invasion of Cambodia,*
1970

During President Nixon's first term, the United States crossed a historic watershed in its relations with the rest of the world. Simply put, the Pax Americana was coming to an end, giving way to a more sober realization that in the world of the 1970s the two superpowers were no longer dominant. For reasons that were partly economic, partly military, but also in a deeper sense spiritual, the United States no longer had the capacity to meet all of the commitments it had acquired after World War II. The American tent, which, in the words of Roy Jenkins, had once stood gloriously and uniquely on the top of the highest hill, was now being lowered, and a new era of American foreign policy was clearly about to begin. The nation was in flux and with it the assumptions upon which it had built its foreign policy for almost a generation.

There is a deep irony in the fact that the task of reconciling Americans to their diminished role in the world had fallen upon Richard Nixon, the harsh anti-Communist of an earlier epoch. Yet here he was, conducting personal diplomacy on a level unparalleled in recent history, reaching agreement in Moscow on the limitation of nuclear arms, and in Peking freeing America at last from the ideological hostilities he himself had done so much to foster. In the middle of his first term, the President was forced to end America's monetary hegemony over the rest of the western world, thus destroying other old assumptions. He had also articulated a new policy for the United States, based on the premise that the Cold War was finally fading and the old bipolar rivalry between America and the Soviet Union was to be replaced by a new balance of power. Above all, the troops were coming home from Vietnam, ending an involvement which more than any other had undermined the assumptions of confrontation and containment of Communism on which the old foreign policy had been based. The traditional policy had grown, as Churchill once said of the British Empire, "in a fit of absence of mind." The United States, it is worth recalling, became a world power reluctantly and abruptly, the result of German and Japanese aggression in World War II and the exhaustion of both its allies and its enemies after it. When the Cold War erupted in 1947, it was the United States, almost alone, that had carried the burdens and responsibilities of maintaining peace in Europe. For twenty more years, at first under the very real threat of Soviet expansion, America had remained an interventionist power, finding the role more and more to her taste as the years went by.

The interventionist role was in fact perfectly attuned to the American psyche of that era, combining as it did an innate sense of idealism and a pragmatic belief that all problems are soluble if attacked with sufficient nerve and energy. The idealism, the notion that America could save the world not only by her example but by her exertions, was perfectly expressed by that true believer in the Pax Americana, Dean Rusk, who remarked on one occasion, "We have no quarrel with the Communists. All our quarrels are on behalf of other people." The tough pragmatism that always underpinned the idealism came in an early National Security Council document to the effect that Soviet behavior could be changed "only by a demonstration of superior strength—never by negotiation." And until the tragedy of Vietnam, the policy generally worked. American influence expanded on a global scale, defense treaties were concluded with forty-two foreign nations, the United States spent over $150 billion on foreign aid and stationed over a million of her troops abroad, twice the total of all other nations in the world combined.

There is a school of revisionist historians that claims all this was done as a form of disguised imperialism, that the real, if unstated, aim of American policy was to expand the influence of her system of capitalism to the farthest corners of the globe. Now that it has passed, the threat of Soviet expansion seems to these historians more like a specter than a reality, and they believe that because Lyndon Johnson was wrong in committing American troops to Vietnam, Harry Truman was equally wrong in committing them to Europe. But in Europe the threat was real enough at the time—or at least it *seemed* real enough—and, for all its flaws, there are many nations in the world that have reason to be profoundly grateful for the American help which saw them through the perils of the immediate postwar era.

Over the years, however, the interventionist epoch underwent a subtle sea-change. U.S. policy, which had begun as a strictly limited operation to contain the nationalist expansion of the Soviet Union, developed imperceptibly into a universal crusade, ideological as much as practical, in which the aim was to confront and contain Communism wherever in the world it appeared. The epoch which had begun with the solid accomplishments of the Truman Doctrine, NATO, and the Marshall Plan, progressed through several stages, reaching its highest point in the ringing rhetoric of John Kennedy's inaugural address, a stirring call to action the very sound of which falls oddly indeed on the ears of a generation disillusioned with the idea that "we shall pay any price, bear any burden, meet any hardship, support any friend, oppose any foe to assure the survival and the success of liberty." It seems so long ago; so many shattered dreams have passed, so much has gone wrong with America's foreign policy since Kennedy issued his summons to man the barricades of the New Frontier, that his inaugural address reads today as though it were as remote as Henry V's speech on the field of Agincourt. Yet it was delivered, in his metallic New England accents, only in the last decade:

> Now the trumpet summons us again. Not as a call to bear arms, though arms we need. Not as a call to battle, though embattled we are. But a call to bear the burden of a long twilight struggle, year in and year out, "rejoicing in hope, patient in tribulation"—a struggle against the common enemies of man: tyranny, poverty, disease and war itself. . . .
>
> I do not shrink from this responsibility—I welcome it. I do not believe that any of us would exchange places with any other people or any other generation. The energy, the faith, the devotion which we bring to this endeavor will light our country and all who serve it. And the glow from that fire can truly light the world.

As the world now knows, the rhetoric foundered in the tropical climate of Vietnam; and before it did, Kennedy himself was dead. Whether American policy would have been different if Kennedy had lived, whether the disillusionment would have been so great if his successor had not made the cardinal error of committing drafted troops to fight what was in effect a colonial war, are questions that make for intriguing speculation. Yet they will remain forever unanswerable. What happened in Vietnam is irreversible. When President Nixon arrived at the White House he was left to deal with the world as it was, not as it might have been. And in the world as it was, the problem of Vietnam was central; the lessons learned there were at the root of America's changing attitudes toward herself and toward the rest of the world.

As a result of the lessons learned in Vietnam, it seems a reasonably safe assumption that the United States will never again intervene with ground troops in the affairs of another country without the most direct threat to her national self-interest. Indeed, it may be an equally safe assumption that the next major mistake in American foreign policy will come about not through any failure to have learned the lessons of Vietnam but rather from having learned them *too* well, just as the original commitment to Vietnam came about in a sense because an earlier generation had learned too well the lessons of Munich and the consequences that follow a policy of appeasement—and, pursuing the parallel back even farther, just as the appeasers showed at Munich that their generation also had learned too well the lessons to be drawn from the awful slaughter in the trenches of France and Flanders in World War I.

The consequences of the Vietnam experience in shaping the attitudes of the younger generation of Americans can hardly be overstated. It has shattered, probably forever, their belief in the old axioms that peace is indivisible, that Communism must be confronted and contained wherever it raises its head, that the United States has a moral responsibility to defend what used to be called the "Free World," that America's international influence depends principally upon its military ascendancy, that the United States is somehow a more "moral" nation than other, less fortunate lands. It has brought them the insight that nuclear might, however overwhelming, cannot ever be used in the normal processes of diplomacy, that when faced with the defiance of a small, ideologically motivated, and ruthless country, the most powerful nation the world has ever known can indeed stand by as a frustrated giant, helpless in the sense that it cannot, or will not, put to use the fullest panoply of its nuclear arsenal.

The Vietnam experience has been particularly acute for the generation of young policymakers who are just now reaching positions of power and influence in the United States. Dr. Henry Kissinger, the impresario of the new order, has correctly perceived that because Vietnam was their introduction to world politics they have no memory of the time when American-supported structural innovations like NATO and the Marshall Plan were successful or of the motivations which prompted these enterprises. As a result, Kissinger believes, the American today oscillates dangerously between being ashamed of power and expecting too much from it. "The danger of the rejection of power," he has written, "is that it may result in a nihilistic perfectionism which disdains the gradual and seeks to destroy what does not conform to its notion of Utopia. The danger of an over-concern with force is that policymakers may respond to clamor by a series of spasmodic gestures and stylistic maneuvers and then recoil before their implication."

Yet it was precisely because of the success of the earlier innovations such as NATO and the Marshall Plan that the Americans of Kissinger's generation fell into the trap of believing that they could go on applying them forever, even in situations which were not remotely comparable to those that applied in Europe after the end of World War II. It took the longest and most divisive war in their history to make that lesson plain, and even today Kissinger and Nixon express the belief that the war was worth all the agony it produced, on the argument that order and stability can only exist in the world if the United States is there to maintain it. It was the nation's mission to stand firm in Indochina, not because anyone believed any more in the domino theory, or in the myth of an expansionist China, or even in the importance of supporting a friendly regime against conquest by its Communist neighbor, but simply to demonstrate that the United States was still capable of standing firm. Not to have done so, in this argument, would have caused the Soviet Union to renew again its probing of American weaknesses, and thus destroy the new balance of power so laboriously erected during the President's first term. As Nixon had said when he ordered American troops into Cambodia, "It is not our power but our will that is being tested tonight."

Maintaining the balance of power has, under Nixon, been raised to the same holy status that once belonged to the policy of containment. The attempt has been made, quite consciously, to recreate on a global scale the nineteenth-century Concord of Europe which, by recognizing the "legitimacy" of the *anciens régimes*, maintained peace for a while after the Napoleonic wars. Nixon strives to bring into being a *world* balance of power, a balance sometimes expressed in the arcane language of the diplomatic strategists as an algebraic formula: "the $2\frac{1}{2} + y + z$ powers world," a world of five major units in which the $2\frac{1}{2}$ represents the United States, the Soviet Union, and China, and the y and the z Western Europe and Japan respectively. The President himself made the point more simply in his New Year address of 1972:

> We must remember the only time in the history of the world that we have had any extended period of peace is when there was a balance of power. It is when one nation becomes infinitely more powerful in relation to its potential competitor that the danger of war arises. So I believe in a world in which the United States is powerful. I think it will be a safer world and a better world if we have a strong, healthy United States, Europe, Soviet Union, China and Japan, each balancing the other, not playing against the other, an even balance.

Such an attempt to recreate the dynamics of the Concord of Europe of a century and a half ago rests, at best, on doubtful logic. It assumes that the five powers concerned should be roughly equal in power and influence, as they were in Europe after 1815, but this is simply not true today. Western Europe, for example, is still a long way from becoming a unified force on the world stage; Japan has no military power to speak of; China cannot compare with the United States and Japan in economic power and technology. And what of the rest of the world, in Asia, Africa, South America? It is interesting that the President hardly speaks today of the role of the United Nations in maintaining his balance of power, an institution that the United States was instrumental in founding but that it has come to regard more recently with contempt and disdain. There is little place for the smaller countries of the world in the President's new scheme of things, in which the world is to be divided into spheres of influence among the great powers—economic, military, diplomatic. Whether such a five-cornered balance of power is applicable in global terms to the vastly different world that now faces the final quarter of the twentieth century remains to be seen. Whether it is the correct objective of the United States has become the subject of intense debate among those responsible for shaping the future of American foreign policy. Whether it will last is open to considerable doubt. But that it represents an historic reversal of America's postwar concept of its role in the world is beyond all question. The new policy, whether for good or ill, abrogates the principle that the United States should be "infinitely more powerful in relation to its potential competitor," the principle on which American foreign policy had been built for the previous twenty years.

Nixon himself claims his new policies will secure for the world "a generation of peace," but there has been a high price to pay for some of his initiatives. By leaving Vietnam in a manner described as that of "a gunslinger firing away as he departs an unfriendly saloon," he had stirred a deep disquiet, both at home and abroad, that American power should be so lacking in restraint. Further distress was caused by the brash and sometimes brutal way in which John Connally, then Secretary of the Treasury, had conducted the negotiations that led to the devaluation of the dollar. Even the normalization of relations with China had been conducted in a manner needlessly provocative of some of America's oldest allies, who were offended that he had not consulted them in advance. As a result, there was a feeling in many foreign offices around the world that American policy had become erratic and unpredictable. Hamilton Fish Armstrong, the distinguished former editor of the establishment quarterly *Foreign Affairs*, expressed the feelings of many critics when he wrote in the autumn of 1972 that "radical changes in the structure of our foreign policy undertaken recently without notice to friends and allies have strengthened a feeling that American policies are conceived for American purposes only." Gratitude for the immense sums given for foreign aid since the war, and especially for the help given to Europe in the Marshall Plan, had largely evaporated. And, Armstrong wrote, "just as the [Vietnam] war sharpened all our internal conflicts, so it has accentuated foreign criticism of American civilization and intensified the resentment of foreign governments that the United States seems more and more to ignore their political interests and economic needs." Far from setting an example for other nations to copy, American civilization had, in a sense, become an example of what to avoid.

Yet with the dominance of the two superpowers now drawing to an end, such changes in the American attitude had perhaps become inevitable, and would probably have taken place anyway, even without the trauma of Vietnam to speed them along. America is no longer looked upon as a nation different from all others, setting a moral example for all the others to emulate; in a world where matters of trade, agriculture, and money have become the dominant foreign policy issues, few people really expect American policy to be conceived for other than "American purposes only." To believe otherwise is to indulge in the politics of nostalgia.

Of course many other ingredients have gone into the President's new policies—the fact that the Soviet bloc no longer acts as a monolith, the economic renaissance of Europe, the difficulty of using nuclear might for any positive diplomatic objectives, to name only three—and there are many people who see in the President's concepts a rationalizing of America's dwindling influence over her allies in Europe and Japan, but it has been above all the searing experience of Vietnam that has given the main thrust to the Nixon Doctrine and the resultant fact that America and her people are now being forced into a slow retraction rather than an extension of their influence in the world. Some critics see in this the danger of a too-complete retraction, that following David Hume's remark about the Athenians, who "finding their error in thrusting themselves into every quarrel, abandoned all attention to foreign affairs," America too is in the process of turning inward, away from the affairs of the wider world into a position that is sometimes called "the new isolationism."

This is certainly not true of the President himself, whose main interest is still in foreign affairs, but for many of his countrymen the experience of Vietnam has radically altered their perceptions about their country and its role. Henry Kissinger recognized the new mood when he remarked, "in the 1920s we were isolationists because we thought we were too good for this world. We are now in danger of withdrawing from the world because we believe we are not good enough for it." And it is probably true that in private at least, the America of the 1970s will continue to turn its attentions inward. In a series of public-opinion polls taken on behalf of Potomac Associates just before the presidential election of 1972, it was found that a remarkable 87 percent of all Americans agreed with the broad outline of the Nixon Doctrine that "the U.S. should continue to play a major role internationally but cut down on some of its responsibilities abroad." The poll also found that only slightly more than half of the American public felt the U.S. should come to the defense of its western European allies with military force if they were attacked, while almost three quarters of the public felt the nation should now think less in international terms and more about domestic problems. The authors of the report concluded that "although Americans are far from the isolationism of pre–World War II days, they are, indeed, turning measurably inward."

Public opinion on foreign affairs is not of course self-generating, but simply a reflection of the current pressures and crises that exist in the world and the relative success or failure of the government's response to them. A declining public interest in foreign affairs is not therefore the cause of the new isolationism but rather a reflection of it. And while President Nixon remains in the White House it can be safely assumed that foreign affairs will continue to exercise its fascination for him and receive perhaps more than its fair share of his attention. But in the broad sweep of history in the third quarter of the twentieth century it now seems certain that what Roy Jenkins has called America's period of benevolent dominance will finally come to an end, and the period of "benign selfishness" is about to begin.

2. The World of Henry Kissinger

"President Nixon has shown great strength, great skill. In summoning me to his side, too. I had never met him when he offered me this job. I was astonished. After all, he was acquainted with the unfriendly and unsympathetic attitude I had always assumed towards him. Yes, indeed, he showed great courage in turning to me."
—Dr. Henry Kissinger, 1972

The one man who more than any other has been responsible for carrying out President Nixon's new foreign policies is the fascinating yet elusive figure of Dr. Henry Kissinger, a Jewish refugee from Nazi Germany who has risen in his adopted country to a position of power and influence unmatched by any bureaucrat of modern times. Filling a role almost as important as that of the President himself, Kissinger was the supreme impresario of foreign policy at one of the critical turning-points in American history, and under his guidance foreign affairs may fairly be said to have become the showpiece of the Nixon Presidency.

Given to great flights of abstract Germanic philosophizing about the fundamental nature of foreign relations, shy yet cocksure, highly visible yet wholly insulated from the normal processes of accountability in a democracy, this owlish and tireless professor has been the star of an otherwise lackluster administration, sure now of his place in the history books of the future.

His beginnings were relatively inauspicious. Born in 1923 in the Bavarian village of Fürth, just outside the city of Nuremberg, Heinz Alfred Kissinger was the eldest son of a teacher at the local high school for girls, acquiring at an early age a proper Jewish respect for learning and scholarship. In 1933, when the Nazis came to power in Germany, Heinz Kissinger was only ten years old, and he spent the next, impressionable years under the growing shadow of Nazi intolerance and humiliation. Before long, he was expelled from his school and forced to go to an all-Jewish institution; at about the same time, his father was dismissed from his teaching post at the high school. Seeing the horrors that were approaching, the Kissingers, like so many other Jewish families, finally fled from their homeland in 1938, first to London, then later as immigrants to America, where they arrived just before the outbreak of Hitler's war in Europe.

Some of his biographers have insisted that the key to Kissinger's character lies in the trauma he suffered during these impressionable years when he was driven as a refugee from his homeland, his father's career destroyed, his own future clouded by the uncertainties of exile. Kissinger himself rejects this tidy theory. "That part of my childhood is *not* a key to anything," he told one interviewer. "I was not consciously unhappy. I was not acutely aware of what was going on. For children, those things are not that serious. It is fashionable now to explain everything psychoanalytically, but let me tell you, the political persecutions of my childhood are not what control my life." Perhaps not, but what *has* lingered in Kissinger's later attitudes is a tragic awareness of the anarchy and chaos that occur when civilizations collapse, as the Weimar Republic into which he was born collapsed before the Nazi take-over. Throughout his later writings, the constantly recurring theme has been a passionate horror of anarchy, a melancholy realization that stability, both international and social, can be among the most elusive of human accomplishments and, in Kissinger's view, perhaps all the more desirable because of that.

Soon after the family's arrival in New York, the young refugee boy worked parttime at a shaving-brush factory in Manhattan, where he was given the task of squeezing the acid out of the bristles. At night, he went to high school, and after graduation he was drafted, still in his teens, into the U.S. Army. There, though he was still only a private, he was picked out for special training because of his high intelligence and sent to his native Germany just at the moment the Nazis were in the throes of their final collapse. The division to which he was attached had just captured the industrial city of Krefeld, not far from the border with Holland. Through the intervention of one of his early mentors Kissinger was given the task of reorganizing the government of this city of nearly 200,000 people. In an interview with the New York *Times* in 1971, Kissinger's close friend, Dr. Fritz Kraemer, described the abilities of this precocious draftee, perhaps adding one or two embellishments in deference to the later distinction of his protegé:

> I could only marvel at the way this nineteen or twenty-year-old did the job. In just two or three days, the government was again working in splendid fashion. Henry had planned things wonderfully. This was a prodigy. He had a fabulous innate sense of finding his way out of the most difficult situations. Here this little Kissinger had set up in three days a municipal government in a large city where everything had been run by the Nazis just two days before.

A year later, still at an age when most of his contemporaries were barely undergraduates, Kissinger was administering an entire district and had risen to the rank of sergeant. He went on from there to become a teacher at the European Command Intelligence School, where he declared to his friend one night, "Kraemer, I want to go home and get a first-class education. I know only what I teach in school. Otherwise, I know nothing." Good luck intervened again, and in the autumn of 1946 Kissinger obtained a place at Harvard University, where he remained on and off for the next twenty years, first as a student, later as a teacher, building the foundations of a brilliant academic career and going on to become one of the foremost theoreticians of the nuclear age. He became famous with the publication of his book *Nuclear Weapons and Foreign Policy,* in which he argued that in certain limited circumstances the use of small tactical nuclear weapons would be justified to halt a Soviet advance and that their use could be limited to the battlefield itself, without leading on to an all-out strategic nuclear war in which the civilizations of both participants would be destroyed. "In seeking to avoid the horrors of an all-out war by outlining the alternative," he wrote, "in developing a concept of limitation that combines firmness with moderation, diplomacy can once more establish a relationship with force even in a nuclear age." Although Kissinger's book became a bestseller ("the most unread bestseller since Toynbee," he was later to remark in his self-deprecatory way), it also earned him the opprobium of his colleagues, and Kissinger himself was before long retracting large portions of his nuclear theory. The book is interesting today for the insights it provides into the development of Kissinger's thoughts as well as for the expression of the ideas, which have *not* changed, that the linchpin of American diplomacy is the creation and maintenance of a balance of power with which to contain the Soviet Union. To a surprising degree, Kissinger still believes in the aggressive ambitions of the Soviet leaders, that they are still motivated by the essential philosophy of the Cold War, although he admits that such aggression is no longer to be expected in the form of a military advance in Europe, or a sudden grab of territory, but, as he once put it, as a "combination of military, psychological, and political pressures that always stop well short of the total confrontation that Hitler produced and which puts much greater strain on the political leadership and on the cohesion of the non-Communist countries." In Kissinger's vision of the modern world there is still, deep down, a belief that the United States was compelled to stand firm in Indochina to demonstrate *to the Soviet Union* that their analyses of American weaknesses were wrong, that a demonstration of American strength would deter them from making assumptions that would lead to renewed conflicts between the two superpowers. In short, his philosophy is still that of an essentially hardline anti-Communist who believes the hostile interests of the two superpowers can be reconciled only if America acts from a position of strength. "We must show them we, too, can be brutal," he said in private of the American invasion of Cambodia in 1970.

While still at Harvard, Kissinger had studied Spengler, Toynbee, and Kant, the achievements of Castlereagh and Metternich, and written a Ph.D. thesis in which can be discerned the outlines of the same deeply conservative philosophy that guides his conduct in the White House. "Stability based on an equilibrium of forces," he wrote of the 1815 Congress of Vienna, was responsible for maintaining peace in Europe after the downfall of Napoleon, an equilibrium that has several striking parallels to that he advocates for the postnuclear world of the future. There is an irresistible temptation to compare the world he wrote about then with the world he now believes is emerging, to compare his own achievements with those of his hero, the Austrian Prince Metternich, about whom twenty years ago he wrote a flattering biography, and whom he is still fond of quoting. "As Metternich would say," he observed at one of his famous White House briefings, "that action is worse than a crime. It is a mistake." And of the Congress of Vienna he had written, in another prescient passage, "What is surprising is not how imperfect was the settlement that emerged but how sane; not how 'reactionary' according to the self-righteous doctrines of nineteenth-century historiography but how balanced. It may not have fulfilled all the hopes of an idealistic generation, but it gave this generation something perhaps more precious: a period of stability which permitted their hopes to be realized without a major war or a permanent revolution."

In Kissinger's actions in the White House as well as throughout his writings, two familiar characteristics stand out with shining clarity: a passion for order in international affairs and a Metternichlike fascination with the mechanical devices through which that order might be achieved. "The greatest need of the contemporary international system is an agreed concept of order," he wrote in one typical passage in *American Foreign Policy*, a book published in the year he first arrived at the White House. "A new concept of international order is essential; without it stability will prove elusive." As for the means of achieving that order, Kissinger believes that when it becomes clear that certain principles cannot be compromised, even for the sake of peace, then "stability based on an equilibrium of forces is at least conceivable." Again and again there emerges Kissinger's idealization of stability as almost the highest state to which human society can aspire.

In this tidy world, the world of $2\frac{1}{2} + y + z$, equilibrium is seen as a dynamic force—*the* dynamic force in international relations—as it was perhaps in nineteenth-century Europe. It does not, however, allow for a disturbance of the equilibrium by forces outside the equation, nor does it allow morality, the judgment of right from wrong, to intrude for long into foreign affairs. What matters in any given situation is the change that might occur in the overall balance of power, however peripherally it might involve the strictly national interests of the United States. Thus, when in 1971 Bangladesh broke away from Pakistan, the United States engaged in some fairly crude gunboat diplomacy in the Bay of Bengal in an attempt to deter the Indians, the reason of course being that the dismemberment of Pakistan would leave the Russians as the dominant power in the area. On that occasion, the

American attempt at intervention clearly failed, at the cost of considerable resentment in India and bitterness in Bangladesh, the justice of whose cause was completely disregarded. Right or wrong, it had interfered with the world equilibrium, and that, for Nixon and Kissinger, could not be tolerated. As we have seen, the same principle applied also to Vietnam, where the U.S. felt obliged to demonstrate its power, even at the expense of world condemnation, in order not to provoke the Russians into believing the equilibrium had been disturbed. In the harsh words of one such critic, writing of Kissinger's negotiations over Vietnam: "In the Kissinger, as in the Metternich mind, nations possess no ideology in their relations to other nations. The Vietnamese are those Hungarians of 1848, upsetting the status quo with their absurd demands; or those wretched students wanting the vote: crush them. Why don't they keep quiet? Don't they realize there is a danger of world war?"

While his study of Metternich and the European balance of power in the nineteenth century has clearly had a profound influence on his own concept of foreign policy, it does not of course mean that Kissinger has carried the philosophy of his hero unmodified into the White House. He is far too intelligent and perceptive an observer of the modern world to do that. As he himself has more than once pointed out, Metternich was chancellor and foreign minister at a time when it took three weeks to travel from Central Europe to the ends of the Continent. He was in power at a time when wars were conducted by professional soldiers and diplomacy was in the hands of the aristocracy. Such a world cannot be compared with the world of today, where there is no homogeneous group of leaders, no homogeneous internal situation, and no homogeneous cultural background. All that is perfectly true, and yet the diplomatic techniques of the two men, and above all their belief in the preservation of equilibrium, does display striking similarities, so much so that some of Kissinger's recent critics have come to assume that he *is* Metternich, trying to apply the policies of nineteenth-century Austria, the weakest of the European powers, to the United States, the strongest and most dominant power of the twentieth century.

One such critic, in an article entitled "Just Who Does He Think He Is?," which was illustrated with an etching of a bespectacled Dr. Kissinger in the full diplomatic dress of the Austrian Empire, claimed that the nineteenth-century concept of the balance of power would not work in the world today because, among other things, it did not have to concern itself with public opinion. "The mass of the people," it quoted Metternich with satisfaction, "is always inert"—which was probably true, too, or at least as true today as it was then. It is also true that as Secretary of State in everything but title, Kissinger has been protected from the mass of the people, and from public opinion, and is wholly immune from the probing questions of both Congress and the people. He has never been elected to public office; he has never once testified before Congress; he has constantly been able to surprise even senior officials in the government bureaucracy with his spectacular flights from one world capital to another. In Kissinger's world it is not only the mass of the people that is inert; it is also the entire State Department bureaucracy. Indeed, he firmly believes that it is a necessary part of his function to insulate himself from such pressures. It is one of his axioms that decisionmaking can grow so complex in a modern society that the process of producing a bureaucratic consensus can overshadow the purpose of the effort—that, as he once put it, "the committee approach to decision making is often less an organizational device than a spiritual necessity." Henry Kissinger is by nature and conviction a loner—and something of an arrogant one. In a remarkable interview he gave at the end of 1972 to the Italian journalist Oriana Fallaci, the size of his ego became almost embarrassingly apparent. Yes, he admitted, he had been successful. And why? Because, as he put it:

> The main point stems from the fact that I've always acted alone. Americans admire that enormously. Americans admire the cowboy leading the caravan alone astride his horse, the cowboy entering a village or city alone on his horse. Without even a pistol, maybe, because he doesn't go in for shooting. He acts, that's all: aiming at the right spot at the right time. A Wild West tale, if you like.

Insulated he may be, arrogant he certainly is (although, as *Time* commented, the idea of Henry Kissinger as Jimmy Stewart does have a certain ridiculous charm), but at the same time he is not a man insensitive to the climate of his times, nor one who is unaware of the disillusionment of public opinion with American foreign policy over the past decade. In a more thoughtful speech given before the National Press Club earlier in 1972, Kissinger expressed his own feelings about the causes of unhappiness with considerable eloquence:

> We are living through one of the most difficult periods of our time. Some say we are divided over Vietnam; others blame domestic discord. But I believe the cause of our anguish is deeper. Throughout our history we have believed that effort was its own reward. Partly because so much was achieved here in America, we have tended to suppose that every problem must have a solution and that good intentions should somehow guarantee good results. Utopia was seen not as a dream but as our logical destination if only we traveled the right road. Our generation is the first to find that the road is endless, that in traveling it we will find not Utopia but ourselves. The realization of our essential loneliness accounts for so much of the frustration and rage of our time.

Cynics might reply that Kissinger's eloquence is more existential than pragmatic, that his "essential loneliness" comes about because, through Vietnam, America has lost its golden aura and become hated or at least criticized throughout much of the world—and Americans love to be loved, and need to be admired and respected for their actions. When, on top of all that, they did not even win in Vietnam, the anguish became unbearable. Nevertheless, Kissinger's words are not those of a man interested solely in the cynical ploys and maneuvers of great power diplomacy, nor those of a man contemptuous of public opinion, nor of a man who believes, in the words of one of his biographers, "that Henry Kissinger's only meaningful constituency is a constituency of one," but rather those of a man who understands only too well the meaning and the melancholy of the age he has helped to create.

Henry Kissinger came to Nixon's staff, much to his own surprise, after the election of 1968. He had been the resident foreign policy advisor during the campaign to Governor Nelson Rockefeller of New York, and was bitterly disillusioned when Rockefeller failed to win the nomination at Miami, making a remark there which has since been much quoted against him: "That man Nixon is not fit to be President." Kissinger seemed to fear that Nixon's lifelong quest for public office, the lifestyle of the perennial candidate, would make him vulnerable in office to the whims and pressures of a fickle electorate. Besides, he felt Nixon as a politician was essentially weak, a trimmer with no philosophy. Yet in spite of these doubts and the harsh words he had spoken in a moment of defeat, he did not hesitate for long before climbing aboard the Nixon train. And as it turned out, the two men found they had much more in common than either of them had supposed. Kissinger perhaps helped Nixon to fulfill his own passion for order, and once in office the new President's own fascination with foreign affairs quickly came to the fore, so that with Kissinger at his right hand and a relatively weak though intensely loyal William Rogers in residence at the State Department, it soon became plain that U.S. foreign policy would in this administration be determined almost entirely from the White House. Kissinger was able to see the President more often than any of his other policy appointees, certainly more often than the Secretary of State, and his performance in both concept and execution has gone far beyond that of any previous White House aides, from Wilson's Colonel House and Kennedy's Bundy to Johnson's Walt Rostow.

Kissinger and Nixon found they shared a distaste for the machinery of the State Department. Almost their first objective, therefore, was to obtain a mastery over the cumbersome bureaucracy at Foggy Bottom, where the State Department is located, which as Kissinger perceived had tended to develop a momentum and a vested interest of its own, and one that threatened to paralyze the successful application of the President's policies. The bureaucratic staffs that were supposed to support the decisionmakers were, in Kissinger's view, an encumbrance and an obstacle to the flexibility he so ardently desired. "Creativity must make so many concessions to orthodoxy that it may exhaust itself in doctrinal adaptations," he once observed.

Part of his technique was to make the bureacrats write theses, to make them "think harder" and, like a Harvard professor, to reject their written papers if they failed to match his own standards of "rigor." This sort of government by memorandum, with Kissinger as the sole arbiter of the resulting options that went before the President, had the double effect of tying up the federal bureaucracy in a spate of questionable studies and of concentrating power more firmly than ever in the hands of the National Security Council staff, which he heads. For the able and highly trained diplomats over at Foggy Bottom, the experience was traumatic. Not since the dark days of McCarthyism had their stock fallen so low or their skills been so spurned by the White House. Nothing illustrated the secondary role to which they had been relegated better than the manner in which the President's historic mission to China was handled. In the first place, the arrangments for the trip were handled in secrecy in the basement of the White House. Senior members of the State Department only heard of the mission after Kissinger had returned from his first secret flight to the Chinese capital. That decision had been the President's. After the first exciting message came through from an intermediary hinting that the Chinese might be ready for a meeting at the summit, Nixon thought for two days about who should go to Peking to make further soundings, then reportedly told Kissinger: "I've thought about it. I will send you." State Department officials were not even informed.

The Peking summit itself turned out to be an even greater source of embarrassment for the State Department, for although Rogers went along on the trip, it was Kissinger who attended the President's only meeting with Mao Tse-tung on the first day of the visit, while next morning Rogers was again excluded as Nixon and Kissinger began their talks with Chou En-lai. Rogers, however, is one of Nixon's most loyal supporters, and if he has suffered any resentment at his diminished role, he has kept it to himself. Rogers's function throughout the Nixon Presidency has been less and less concerned with the development and conduct of foreign policy, but more, in Henry Brandon's words, with "the protection of the President from the self-assertions of the bureaucracy."

While Rogers has accepted his role with forbearance, other officials in the Department have responded with less grace and more anguish to the inevitable problem of morale brought about by the neglect and underutilization of their talents. "In my twenty-five years here, I've never seen morale so low," said one foreign service officer. "It's at rock bottom." William Turpin, a foreign service officer for over twenty years, wrote sadly after returning from an overseas post that he had found "that the never excessively nimble pace of work at Foggy Bottom is in fact even more lethargic than formerly, and that the officials one encounters are nowadays even more discouraged about their activities than one had been used to finding them." Part of the problem of course is that these able and talented men and women, shut out from the processes of policymaking, are simply left with not enough to do. Discouragement, lethargy, caution are the inevitable fruits of this unwanted idleness—and because they have become discouraged, lethargic, and cautious, they are shut out even more firmly by those who wield the real power. Whenever a problem arises that could enter the President's orbit, the hapless officials at the State Department are shouldered aside, often because of their own bureaucratic inertia. This phenomenon is perhaps inevitable under a presidential system of government and has been going on at least since the days of Roosevelt. As the Dominican desk officer is said to have remarked during the crisis in that Caribbean country in 1964, "On Friday I was Dominican desk officer; by Friday night Rusk was; and by Sunday noon Lyndon Johnson was." Under the Nixon Administration this process has accelerated even further, and it is hardly conceivable that the Nixon White House would wait until Sunday before they took over the management of the crisis as their own.

Another main source of trouble within the State Department is its lack of a natural domestic constituency of its own; of juicy defense contracts to hand out, for example, that makes the Pentagon such a powerful force up on Capitol Hill; of the body of voters depending for their very livelihood on its decisions that gives, for instance, the Department of Agriculture its political clout. Now the State Department had even lost its most treasured attribute, a direct line of communication to the President of the United States. Early in the Nixon Presidency, when the announcement was made that the President was to visit Rumania—the first visit to a Communist country ever undertaken by a President in office since the start of the Cold War—the State Department official responsible for running the particular desk that looks after relations with Rumania only heard of the visit when he read about it on the tickers of the Associated Press.

The historic moves towards China, the visit to Moscow, the personal negotiations with the North Vietnamese—all were handled with similar secrecy. The bureaucracy was simply not informed, partly for fear that there would be a premature leak of the news, partly also because Nixon and Kissinger both enjoy secret diplomacy and the sudden disclosure of their moves to a startled and admiring world. Arthur Schlesinger once wrote, "President Kennedy used to divert himself with the dream of establishing a secret office of thirty people or so to run foreign policy while maintaining the State Department as a facade in which people might contentedly carry papers from bureau to bureau." Under Kennedy's successor that dream has come very close to reality.

In conception and execution, foreign policy under Kissinger has been run from the White House as never before in American history. Kissinger has spent countless hours alone with the President, but so shrouded in secrecy have these meetings been, the world will have to wait until the participants write their memoirs to gauge the real nature of their remarkable relationship.

Kissinger also spends a large part of his normal working day supervising the memoranda from his own staff to the President, and he is of course one of the principal participants in the full meetings of the National Security Council and the exclusive Washington Special Action Group, known as WSAG, which meets in times of crisis. Again, what goes on in the Cabinet Room or the bleak White House Situation Room where many of these meetings take place, normally remains a closely guarded secret, although just occasionally the corner of the curtain has been lifted to give a fascinating glimpse of Henry Kissinger in action. The minutes of one such meeting, which took place at the height of the Indo-Pakistan war at the end of 1971, were leaked to the press, presumably by a disgruntled bureaucrat who disagreed with the administration's handling of the crisis and set out to "get Henry" through his embarrassing disclosures.

Senior advisors from the State Department, the CIA, and the Department of Defense had been summoned to the WSAG meeting, which Kissinger chairs, to discuss America's response to the crisis on the Indian subcontinent. Kissinger opened the meeting with a blunt remark:

> I am getting hell every half hour from the President that we are not being tough enough on India. He has just called me again. He does not believe that we are carrying out his wishes. He wants to tilt in favor of Pakistan. He feels everything we do comes out otherwise.

A little later, Kissinger fired out a staccato string of questions: Are the Indians seizing territory? Is it possible that the Indians attacked first? What is the role of the United Nations? "If the U.N. can't operate in this kind of situation effectively," he remarked in one barbed aside, "then its utility has come to an end and it is useless to think of U.N. guarantees in the Middle East." Instructions were given about the content of a speech to be made by George Bush, then American Ambassador to the U.N. Steps were taken to suspend military aid to India. From somewhere within his voluminous memory Kissinger recalled a briefing he received ten years earlier about a secret document; he asked for it to be located. There was endless discussion about the massive problems facing the new nation of Bangladesh. The situation was looked at in grinding detail from every possible point of view—diplomatic, military, political, strategic—an altogether fascinating, and in some respects chilling view of the balance of power in action. Throughout it all, Dr. Kissinger illustrated beyond a shadow of a doubt that it is in the White House, not in the State Department, that the key problems of foreign policy are handled. (The minutes illustrated also that in these discussions it is Richard Nixon who remains the ultimate arbiter of American policy.)

Kissinger's virtuoso performances have not been without their flaws, however. While the public has been dazzled and not a little awed by the spectacular coups in Moscow and Peking, some other policies have met with rather less success. The Indian episode was not exactly a triumph for American diplomacy, to say the least, and some of the early hardline decisions involving Indochina turned out to be both unpopular and unworkable, particularly after Kissinger realized that his early theories that the Communists could be brought to negotiate were not going to work, and the U.S. turned instead to threats and the most massive use of air power in history. There was another highly awkward moment when just before the 1972 election Kissinger announced that "peace is at hand," only to find it had, temporarily, slipped from his grasp. He only recovered his balance in early 1973, and then at considerable damage to his prestige. When he first went to the White House, Kissinger is said to have assured friends at Harvard he would have the United States out of the war in Vietnam within months; four years later the war still raged. The American achievement, at best, was to have transferred the killing and the dying away from U.S. troops and onto those of the South Vietnamese. Indeed, throughout Nixon's first four years in office, the coldblooded use of force became a permanent adjunct to Kissinger's diplomacy for ending the war. Given his assumptions that the revolutionary government in Hanoi could be compelled to act in a "reasonable" manner just like other more orthodox nations, it was inevitable that the American use of force would go on increasing. The invasion of Cambodia led inexorably to the resumption of the air war over the North, to the naval blockade of Haiphong, and then to the final carpetbombing of Hanoi. Far from being over in months, the war had dragged on for four more years. It is now claimed that this policy worked, that the threats, the bombing, the blockade finally did bring Hanoi to accept a compromise settlement, that the years of endurance brought in the end "peace with honor." But it was a peace bought at a fearful price, in terms both of American prestige around the world and of division and discord at home.

CHAPTER XI

Defense

1. The Deterrent: Is Sufficiency Enough?

"Neither power at this time could gain that superiority, even if it wanted to, which would enable it to blackmail the other one."

—PRESIDENT NIXON, 1971

Through the gates of Malmstrom Air Force Base in Montana, hard up against the far northwestern frontier with Canada, a blue service limousine noses out past a billboard proclaiming, "Peace Is Our Profession," then accelerates away down U.S. Highway 87 across the rolling grassland of the high prairie. In the back seat of the limousine two young and crewcut Air Force captains, both wearing blue fatigues and a light silken scarf at the throat, chat together with the casual air of businessmen on their way to an appointment in the city. They wear no decorations other than the two silver bars that mark their rank, and no pilot's wings, for these officers are not flyers, but technicians.

They cruise for over eighty miles, pausing briefly along the roadside to point out to their visitors a two-acre enclosure, at first sight indistinguishable from the rest of the prairie, save that it is surrounded by a seven-foot-high cyclone fence with barbed wire strung along the top. A herd of Hereford cattle graze peacefully right up to the edge of the wire, unconcerned by the low, eerie hum coming from the center of the compound, which on closer inspection is seen to surround a large flat concrete slab weighing about eighty tons and sitting flat against the prairie like a gigantic mushroom. Just beneath it, invisible to the eye, is a device known to the officers as "the ace in the hole"—an intercontinental ballistic missile capped by a nuclear warhead.

The missile site itself is deserted, and the final destination of the two captains lies a further two miles down the road in another enclosure, again fenced out of a farmer's field, in the middle of which is a bleak one-story building equipped with bunks and a dining room. Once inside, an elevator carries the officers forty feet below the surface into a concrete capsule suspended on massive steel springs to cushion it against the effects of a nuclear blast. For the next forty hours, they will live with another pair of officers, working underground and sleeping on the surface on alternate eight-hour shifts, ready to respond at a few moments' notice to an order that can be given only by the President himself. That order, if it ever came, would spell the end of modern civilization, for these two officers have arrived on the doomsday watch, poised to launch a flight of the Minuteman III intercontinental missiles that dot the empty prairies of Montana and the plains of North Dakota, each one programmed to deliver a cluster of nuclear warheads on preset targets in the Soviet Union.

Malmstrom is one of three main American missile bases, with a silo complex stretching across an area the size of Ireland. There are 1,054 Minuteman missiles scattered across the western prairies in all, ten of them controlled by the two officers now on watch. Each Minuteman at Malmstrom is the latest model, Mark III, fitted with three independently targeted nuclear warheads, or MIRVs (Multiple Independently-targeted Re-entry Vehicles), each one programmed to fly to a separate target and each ten times more powerful than the atom bomb that destroyed Hiroshima.

Since a nuclear war can only be fought with missiles that are already in place, Armageddon is only minutes away. The Air Force officers at Malmstrom, once described by an army man as "the silent silo-sitters of the seventies," are ready to go into action at a few moments' notice. They sit at opposite ends of their computerized Launch Control capsule, each one in charge of a small latchkey which they must turn simultaneously before their missiles can be fired. Each carries a .38 revolver, with orders to shoot his fellow should he go berserk and try to take over the center; they sit far enough apart so that one man, if he did gain control, could not turn both keys together.

But that is an unlikely eventuality. The two officers are dedicated professionals, the last link in a chain that has been carefully designed to rule out the risk of an accidental or unauthorized firing. On duty, they display no more emotion than the consoles of the computers that surround them in their underground bunker. They are trained to respond to stimuli, and even if they were one day ordered to turn their keys and fire an armed missile they do not expect to become emotional about it. "It's all quite clear in my mind," says one officer. "I don't think about it much, but I don't think I'd have any reservations about turning the key." "Only the President of the United States can start the daisy chain," says the other laconically.

To launch an attack, the presidential order to fire must come either through Strategic Air Command headquarters in its underground bunker in Nebraska, or from the SAC's airborne battle staff, who cruise on eight-hour shifts in a converted jetliner known as *Looking Glass*, carrying with them the latest U.S. war plans. Once received, the President's message is decoded and authenticated and passed by direct circuit to the two men who make up the Combat Missile Crew. An electronic siren wails out a "deedle-deedle-deedle" warning them to stand by for their classified orders, which must be finally confirmed by their own base commander, who is in possession of a third launch key some eighty miles away in his headquarters.

Meanwhile, an entirely automated sequence of events is simultaneously set in motion. The MIRV's "brain" is automatically fed with the latest magnetic targeting tape, containing the latest information on its Soviet target, which has been gathered by satellite. Across the prairies, a thousand steel silo-covers begin to slide back, and less than a minute later the two Air Force captains are ready to read out from a printed list of instructions the countdown to Armageddon:

> "Page three dash eighty."
> "Check."
> "Inhibit switch is off."
> "Check."
> "Transmission rotary switches on."
> "Check . . ."
> "Launch!"
> "Launch!"

At the final order, read out from the same list of printed instructions, the two men turn their keys simultaneously downward and to the right, then after a count of three, release them back to their original positions. A heavy explosive charge has meanwhile blown the concrete cap away from the top of the silo, and seconds later the Minuteman rises in a plume of smoke and fire from its hole in the prairie to begin its half-hour journey to the Soviet Union. The process is known to the officers as "smoking a bird."

The first stages of the MIRV launch are essentially the same as those used to launch an Apollo Moon mission. Two rocket stages are cast off en route to thrust the spacebus into its ballistic trajectory. Four minutes after blastoff, the spacebus is entirely on its own, traveling at over four miles a second and climbing to an altitude of about seven hundred miles above the surface of the earth as it arcs up over the North Pole and down over Siberia.

No human command can control it now, and as it approaches its first target, the Minuteman's onboard microcomputer begins automatically to read out the target coordinates. A fast-spinning gyroscope senses any change in direction, and after a complicated checking system with the computer, it calculates the necessary velocity and direction changes and fires a small "vernier" jet to maneuver the spacebus into exactly the right attitude for firing its first MIRV. Finally, the computer gives the electronic command to fire, and the first warhead parts from the mother ship to fly free to its target, a sleek bomb with a needle nose and a flared tail, nine feet long and only two feet in girth, engineered to produce the smallest possible image on the enemy's radar screens. Within a minute, the other two warheads are fired in a similar sequence, each to separate targets perhaps hundreds of miles apart. Then, having dispatched its trio of missiles, the spacebus itself explodes into dozens of tiny pieces, which fall on yet another target and so further confuse the enemy radar system.

Each MIRV descends in a red-hot glow through the atmosphere, protected from the danger of melting by a ceramic heatshield, and as it approaches the target an altitude fuse triggers a nuclear explosion in the atmosphere. Below it, an area of fifteen square miles is totally devastated in the space of a split second.

Today, somewhere in the Soviet Union, there stands a flight of even bigger missiles, the Russian SS-9s, ready to blast out of *their* silos and programmed to explode on targets in the United States. As far as is known, the operational Russian missiles do not yet have either onboard computers or MIRV warheads, although these are now being tested and the fear is always there that, one day, perhaps quite soon, the Russians will be able to guide their missiles near enough to the Minuteman silos on the prairies to knock them out of action in a preemptive strike. To prevent that from happening, the Americans started to build an antiballistic missile site around Malmstrom, programmed to shoot down the incoming Russian missiles before their nuclear warheads destroyed the Minuteman. Work on the antiballistic missile site at Malmstrom has now been stopped as a result of the 1972 strategic arms treaty, leaving the base theoretically defenseless, although work is continuing on the ABM defenses around the neighboring Minuteman sites in North Dakota. Because they might soon be vulnerable to attack, the Air Force officers at Malmstrom are therefore already on their way to becoming obsolete, although they are expected to provide the basis of the deterrent throughout the 1970s. More important, the United States has taken care not to rely solely for its strategic defense on landbased ICBMs, but on a triad of deterrents, which also include nuclear submarines and the B-52 bomber fleet.

Somewhere out at sea, the first Poseidon submarines are now on patrol, carrying an even deadlier load than the Minutemen. With ten MIRVs on each of a submarine's sixteen missiles, the Poseidon fleet, together with the older Polaris submarines, would be able to hit about two thousand separate targets. As they are almost impossible to detect and thus difficult to knock out of action, it is expected that the Poseidon submarines, on their six-week patrols beneath the sea, will eventually become the main arm of the American deterrent. Later, they too will be superseded by a more modern fleet of nuclear submarines, known as Tridents, which at a cost of $1.3 billion each, will be able to hit targets in Russia from a range of five thousand miles, compared with three thousand for the Poseidons.

To most people, the actual use of a single one of these weapons is unthinkable. In every crisis since World War II, the use of nuclear weapons has sooner or later been ruled out as unacceptable. Nuclear technology has now reached a stage where both America and Russia can absorb the most violent attack that could be launched, even under ideal conditions of surprise, and still survive to strike back with sufficient force to inflict unacceptable damage on an enemy. For the first time in human history, men have invented a weapons system too terrible to use.

The consequences of this nuclear stalemate are likely to be permanent. In a special study of the American military establishment commissioned by the Twentieth Century Fund, Adam Yarmolinsky concluded:

> Both sides are vulnerable, and each side's security depends on the other side's ultimate vulnerability. This is a development particularly shocking for the United States, because no foreign enemy has touched the continental territory of the United States since the war of 1812—and shocking for the Soviet Union, because the ancient Russian strategy of trading space for time may no longer be a serious option. Clearly, it confronts the military establishment with a permanent dilemma in the uses of nuclear power.

Why then, if the use of such weapons is so clearly unacceptable to both sides, have they piled up in the past decade an arsenal so vast they could destroy each other many times over? And why, if each can already destroy the other, is it necessary to go on developing ever newer, ever more expensive, ever more terrible weapons with no end yet in sight? How much is enough?

The answer lies in the irresistible logic of a strategy the Pentagon calls "assured reponse." In simplified form, this theory rests on the argument that even if the Russians do strike first, the U.S. must still have enough missiles left over to launch an "unacceptable" counterattack. A formula devised by the former Defense Secretary, Robert McNamara, defines "unacceptable" damage as a quarter of the population killed and half of industry destroyed. This alone, it is avowed, is enough to make sure that the deterrent will deter. It follows that the nuclear arsenal maintained by each side must always be kept strong enough to survive the maximum possible theoretical attack by the other side. The irony is that the arms race that resulted from this argument was based in the first instance on a major misconception.

The original missile program had been initiated under a brilliant management team set up by President Eisenhower, who concluded that the necessary launch systems, guidance technology, and warheads were technically feasible by the end of the 1950s. The team set to work and developed the new missiles in a remarkably short time, so that the first operational Atlas missiles were in the hands of Strategic Air Command by the end of 1959. The Navy was at the same time working on an equally successful program to develop solid-fueled underwater Polaris missiles, and the Air Force followed with the development of the Minuteman I, which became operational early in 1960.

In spite of these successes, Senator John Kennedy seized upon the "missile gap" as a major issue in the presidential election campaign of 1960, a campaign that was based on the erroneous forecast that by 1964 America would have only 130 missiles against a Soviet arsenal of over two thousand ICBMs. In vain did Eisenhower point out that "the real test is to provide security in a way that effectively deters aggression and does not itself weaken the values and institutions we seek to defend. This demands the most careful calculation and balance, as well as steadfastness of purpose, not to be disturbed by any noisy trumpeting." But Americans in that year were in the grip of an irrational fear, brought about in part by the launching of the Russian Sputniks, and throughout the campaign the trumpeting fell on receptive ears. Kennedy made speech after speech on the theme of the alleged missile gap, declaring at one rally that "the deterrent ratio during 1960–64 will in all likelihood be weighted heavily against us." Soviet missile power, he said, "will be the shield from behind which they will slowly advance. . . . The periphery of the free world will slowly be nibbled away."

That his arguments were based on myth did not deter him, once in office, from announcing a momentous decision. The American missile force was to be multiplied by a factor of five, setting the goal of 1,000 Minutemen launchers and a Polaris fleet of 41 submarines carrying a total of 656 missiles. Only much later did it come to light that Kennedy's estimates of the Russian missile strength were greatly exaggerated. The missile gap was not, and never had been, a threat to American security. In a speech in 1967, McNamara candidly admitted as much when he said the decision to build up the American deterrent had been based on hypothetical estimates of a theoretically possible Soviet buildup rather than hard intelligence about its actual growth. Later still, reports came to light that the Air Force generals had asked for as many as 3,000 missiles and that McNamara's figure of 1,000 Minutemen was itself a compromise. "It is the smallest number I can propose without getting murdered by the Congress," he is reported to have said. In his public speech, he admitted the buildup was "a conservative hedge," and he added, "In the course of hedging against what was then only a theoretically possible Soviet buildup, we took decisions which have resulted in our current superiority in numbers of warheads and deliverable megatons. But the blunt fact remains that if we had had more accurate information about planned Soviet strategic forces, we simply would not have needed to build as large a nuclear arsenal as we have today."

But by then, of course, the die was cast. America had, in a sense, started an arms race with herself. Due to the assumption that whatever is technically feasible to produce must *be* produced, the only ceiling on weapons development became the imagination of the scientists who invented them and the skills of the technologists who built them. The Russians, naturally enough, took steps to catch up, and the deadly arms race that has dominated the past decade was on in earnest. In the lethal new acronyms of the military, MIRVs led to ABMs, ABMs in turn led to ULMs, then to SCRAM, SCAD, AWACS, and finally to SALT, which has finally put at least a partial check on the constantly spiraling race to produce the ultimate weapon of doom.

At first, the Minuteman missiles had been "citybusters," not accurate enough to aim at precise military targets, but capable of getting near enough to demolish entire cities. These were the days in which American nuclear strategy rested on the theory of massive retaliation, or the "spasm response" as it became known to the nuclear theorists. Later technology, developed largely during the McNamara years, greatly improved the aim of the landbased missiles so that by the end of the 1960s it was possible to aim a nuclear warhead directly at the Russian missiles sitting in their silos. The Russians were developing similar techniques, and although they were known to be several years behind, it looked for a while as though the superpowers would each have the ability to destroy the other's deterrent before it could be fired. The one who struck first would therefore leave the enemy helpless, its options limited to destruction without the possibility of a reply—or surrender.

The controversial answer to that threat was the antiballistic missile, the ABM, in which the Russians were thought to have an early lead. In 1970, Marshal Andrei Grechko, the Soviet Defense Minister, was able to declare, "We possess weapons capable of reliably hitting enemy aircraft and missiles irrespective of height or speed of flight, at great distances from the defended targets." Or, as Nikita Khrushchev put it more graphically several years earlier, "We can hit a fly in outer space."

The ABM, which at first sight appears to be a solely defensive weapon, has the effect, if deployed to protect the ICBM sites, of greatly strengthening the offensive capabilites of the side that possesses it. The deterrent, if it is to deter, must always be able to get through, to penetrate the enemy's defenses. The power without an ABM would therefore be compelled to build up its offensive forces to the point where they could overcome or "saturate" the other side's ABM protection—thus adding further impetus to the arms race. America became so concerned about Russian ABM deployments towards the end of the 1960s that President Johnson was impelled to write a secret letter to Soviet Premier Aleksei Kosygin warning him that the Russian buildup of defensive missiles had put him under pressure to increase greatly the American capability to penetrate any defensive system which the Russians might establish. "If we should feel compelled to make such major increases in our strategic weapons capabilities," Johnson added, "I have no doubt that you would in turn feel under compulsion to do likewise."

The once-simple nuclear equation was becoming enormously complicated. By the time President Nixon took office in 1969 a great debate was raging as to whether the United States should install its own sophisticated and highly expensive ABM system known as Safeguard, and whether Safeguard should protect American cities or the defenseless silos where the missiles were kept —or perhaps both. The key was always the Pentagon doctrine of "assured response." It was argued that if the cities were defended, the Russians would aim their ICBMs instead at the silos on the prairies, and that if the silos were protected as well as the cities, the Russians would be compelled to increase their offensive weaponry to the point where they could saturate any reasonable ABM defenses. And as the Russians built up *their* protective ABM system, so would the Americans be forced to build more and more offensive ICBMs in order to retain their own secure second-strike capability. Such an arms race could go on more or less indefinitely, each side piling more and more nuclear weapons into its arsenal simply to maintain what was in effect a nuclear stalemate.

These arguments stirred immense controversy and some spurious reasoning on both sides. At one point, the then Secretary of Defense, Melvin Laird, went before a congressional committee to declare that a dozen Safeguard ABM sites were essential because the Communist Chinese were on the verge of developing intercontinental missiles, while the Russians, he asserted, were "going for a first-strike capability—there is no doubt about that." If the American deterrent had depended solely upon the landbased Minutemen, the argument might have had some validity, but by dividing its weapons among the three arms of the nuclear triad, the American arsenal was to all intents and purposes invulnerable. There was, even at that time, no known combination of attack that could simultaneously wipe out the ICBMs, the Polaris and Poseidon submarines, and the B-52 Bomber fleet. The ABM system, at best, was a bargaining chip to trade away with the Russians at the arms talks.

Then, in the early 1970s, simultaneously with the ABM controversy, came MIRV, the hydraheaded missiles of Minuteman III, and the underwater Poseidons, which have done more than anything else to upset the delicate balance of terror on which the peace of the world depends. MIRV was a major technological breakthrough for the Americans, but one which also threatened to accelerate the arms race, for it is accepted by both sides that the greatest threat to stability is the capacity to destroy the enemy's strategic forces before they can be used. The great accuracy of the MIRV warheads gave the Americans precisely this capacity. The Russians, of course, were bound to respond, and it was not long before they expanded their ABM program and at the same time began the deployment of their massive and much dreaded SS-9 missiles, whose colossal megatonnage far outdistances that of the Minuteman and so helps the Russians overcome the disadvantages of having less accurate missiles. The SS-9, 113 feet long, can hurl a payload of six and a half tons over a range of five thousand miles. Like the Minuteman it is armed with three nuclear warheads, although unlike the American missiles they are not independently targeted but fall instead in a predetermined pattern chillingly known as a "footprint."

Ever since the war, America had stood head and shoulders above the Russians in both weapons technology and the deployment of "deliverable megatonnage," its world strategy based on the concept of nuclear superiority, but now, it was clear, the age of parity had arrived. In the words of President Nixon, "neither power . . . could gain that superiority, even if it wanted to, which would enable it to blackmail the other one." Under the direction of Dr. Henry Kissinger, the President began to redefine America's overall strategic objective from one of nuclear superiority to one of "strategic sufficiency," although it was always left unclear exactly what "sufficiency" implied, other than what Nixon vaguely termed "a flexible range of strategic options." Nevertheless, his new concept had opened the way for the first SALT agreement, the Strategic Arms Limitation Talks, which have marked an important, if tentative, step towards finally limiting the arms race. Under the agreement signed in Moscow during the President's visit in 1972, each side is now allowed to deploy only two antiballistic missile complexes: one defending its capital, the other protecting a single offensive missile site. Thus, the theory now is that neither side can completely knock out the other with a preemptive attack, but nor can either armor itself sufficiently to prevent the possibility of a retaliatory strike against it. At the same time, the number of landbased offensive weapons was frozen at the current level: 1,054 for the Americans, 1,600 for the Russians. The number of missile-carrying submarines was limited to 42 for the Russians, 41 for the Americans, although no limits have been placed on the number of warheads carried by each rocket, a fact which for the moment leaves the Americans with a distinct numerical superiority in deliverable warheads.

Since it puts no limits on the development of entirely new technologies, there is still a danger that some new and yet more terrible invention may start up the arms race all over again. Because no limit whatever was placed on the development of further MIRVs, there is still an inherent instability in the overall balance of terror. With ABMs limited and MIRVs permitted, a concentrated assault on either country's single protected missile site could easily overwhelm its defenses. The Safeguard system now being built around the Grand Forks site in North Dakota relies under the SALT agreement on only one hundred ABM interceptors. The arrival of the 101st Soviet missile would thus exhaust its defensive resources. The scenario now dreaded by the Americans is that sometime later in this decade, the Russians will have developed the technology to equip their giant SS-9 missiles with accurate MIRVs. Suppose then the SS-9s are launched in a preemptive strike against the landbased ICBMs in sufficient numbers to saturate the single ABM site in North Dakota and knock out all the other undefended silos as well? True, the submarine fleet remains intact, but its missiles are not accurate enough to knock out the hardened silos which contain the next salvo of Russian missiles. What can the President do then? On the face of it he has the sole option of ordering the underwater missiles to pour down mass destruction on the Russian population —knowing full well that the Russians, in this doomsday scenario, would respond with the virtual destruction of the now undefended United States. To a layman, the dreadful prospect is improbable. For one thing, the Russians would lose their own cities, since there is still nothing they can do to negate in advance the submarine arm of the nuclear triad. Nevertheless, this seems to be a threat, improbable or not, against which the Americans are now preparing to defend themselves. In a report to Congress in 1972, Nixon declared, "No President should be left with only one strategic course of action, particularly that of ordering the mass destruction of enemy civilizations and facilities"—a doctrine of "sufficiency" which goes far beyond the old theories of "assured destruction." In other words, it is in his view important to be able to strike back against the Soviets' retaliatory force even if they have attacked first. For this reason, the administration has been developing plans for making the ICBMs "land-mobile"—that is to say, to deploy them in movable and therefore elusive launchers. But the trouble with land-mobile ICBMs is precisely the fact that they are elusive and cannot be readily identified by satellite reconnaissance. Because of the resultant uncertainties about the size of each other's missile arsenal, both sides would then almost certainly overcompensate, building up greater than necessary forces to ensure "sufficiency" and at the same time undermining the original SALT agreement under which the overall strategic forces were frozen at their current level.

Armed with these arcane and labyrinthine arguments, negotiators for the two superpowers will be wrestling for years to come with the problems of nuclear limitation. Even given the good will of the negotiators, movement will continue to be painfully slow, for the issues are both awesome and immensely complicated, with the slightest change in the status quo having profound and often unforeseen consequences on the overall balance of terror upon which the peace of the world has rested ever since the Russians acquired the atom bomb. Sufficiency sounds fine as a slogan, but in the latter half of the 1970s will even sufficiency be enough?

2. Pentagon Power

"This office will probably be the biggest cemetery for dead cats in history."
—JAMES FORRESTAL, *Secretary of Defense, 1947*

Next to the President himself, the most powerful man in every administration since Kennedy's has been the Secretary of Defense, a post currently held by James Schlesinger, who came to office in the early summer of 1973 during the Cabinet reshuffle caused by the Watergate scandals. From his nine-by-five walnut desk in the "E" Ring of the Pentagon, Secretary Schlesinger sits astride what is in manpower still the biggest bureaucracy in the world, with enormous influence over just about every aspect of American life. Secretary Schlesinger has immediate access to the President at all times and is in direct contact with the silositters of Malmstrom through their headquarters in Omaha and with each Poseidon submarine on its mission beneath the sea. His department controls about one third of the federal budget, with an annual expenditure of over eighty billion dollars, a sum approaching the entire net annual income of the United Kingdom. The Secretary has under his command over two million men in arms and a civilian staff of over one million. Nearly three million more work in industries directly dependent on defense contracts, and it has been estimated that one voter in every ten is directly or indirectly dependent on the department for his livelihood.

The influence of the Pentagon thus reaches out to touch almost every family in the land. At one time or another it has called upon one American male in every four for military service, and the bureaucrats who inhabit its seventeen miles of corridor space wield enormous power over some of the country's biggest industries, some of the most famous members of the legislature, some of the best regarded universities and, via a huge and well-oiled public-relations machine, over public opinion itself. Its influence over foreign policy is perhaps more pervasive even than the State Department's, and the staff of its military missions overseas outnumbers that of the diplomatic corps by a ratio of 8 to 5.

In the legislature, its power is almost coercive. Defense contracts can affect the prosperity of entire states, and it is no coincidence that the politicians on Capitol Hill who most favor the military reap the largest benefits in terms of defense spending in their respective districts. Economists seriously doubt that the United States could ever again return to a full peacetime economy without causing a severe economic depression: More than 6 percent of the gross national product is now consumed by the military. It has been estimated that the Air Force alone is worth more than the net assets of the fifty-five biggest industrial corporations put together, and even the money paid out to retired officers is greater than the entire budget of the war on poverty.

This great concentration of power in the hands of the bureaucrats of the Defense Department is a comparatively modern phenomenon. The Pentagon building itself was only completed in 1943, under the pressures of the war against Hitler, and the unified Department of Defense came, under the pressures of the Cold War, only in 1947. There were fears at first that this unified command might lead to the emergence of a military caste in America with powers similar to the old German General Staff, but they quickly proved to be unfounded. The Department had been set up with great care to ensure absolute civilian control and great emphasis was laid on the constitutional position of the President as Commander-in-Chief of the armed forces. The National Security Act of 1947 provided for the appointment of a civilian Secretary of Defense to direct and control the administration of the military and to act as the President's principal advisor on all defense matters, and in practice the control of both the nuclear deterrent and the armed forces has remained securely in civilian hands. Ever since President Truman's summary dismissal of General MacArthur for his failure to obey orders, there has been no doubt about where the ultimate power over the military lay.

While the early fears of militarism have proved to be without foundation, a new problem has emerged to confront successive Secretaries of Defense: that of mastering a vast and virtually uncontrollable bureaucracy. Although in absolute terms the military establishment is now shrinking, both as a percentage of the gross national product and as a percentage of the total work force, the national security establishment is often regarded today as simply too big to run with any efficiency. This establishment, created a quarter of a century ago in response to what was seen as an immediate threat to the nation's survival, has become so vast it defies democratic regulation and has eliminated the effectiveness of the institutions supposed to control it.

Concern over the power of a runaway military-industrial complex were first voiced by President Eisenhower, who invented the very phrase in his famous farewell address of 1961. Already the United States was spending annually on its military security more than the net income of all its industrial corporations, and Ike gave a somber warning:

> This conjunction of an immense military establishment and a large arms industry is new in American experience. The total influence—economic, political, even spiritual—is felt in every city, every statehouse, every office of the federal government. . . . We must not fail to comprehend its grave implications. Our toil, resources

and livelihood are all involved; so is the very structure of our society. In the councils of government, we must guard against the acquisition of unwarranted influence, whether sought or unsought, by the military-industrial complex. The potential for the rise of misplaced power exists and will persist.

During the later Eisenhower years, a feeling had arisen that the men in uniform had somehow outwitted the civilians who were supposed to control them, a feeling that the formation of American military strategy lay not in the hands of the civilian leadership but in the hands of the uniformed Chiefs of Staff. As one contemporary critic described it, "Civilians could be briefed, flattered, outwitted, and finally absorbed by generals and admirals who systematically study all leadership patterns among men from Red Square to Wall Street." Consequently, one of the priorities of the Kennedy Administration which took office in 1961 was to establish greater civilian control over the military, and the task was given to one of the most brilliant and yet, as it later proved, sadly flawed, administrators of his generation.

Robert Strange McNamara had seemed to symbolize the very essence of the rational, can-do enthusiasm of the times, when he was nominated as Secretary of Defense by President Kennedy. He was unknown to the public, having only weeks before been appointed the youngest-ever president of the Ford Motor Company, and he brought with him to Washington a zeal for the arts of management and the somehow innocent fervor of a dedicated anti-Communist. "Soviet communism," he told his Senate confirmation hearing, "seeks to wipe out the cherished traditions and institutions of the free world with the same fanaticism that once impelled winning armies to burn villages and sow the fields with salt so they would not again become productive. . . . If the free world should lose to Communism, the loss would be total, final and irrevocable. The citadel of freedom must be preserved because there is no road back, no road back to freedom for anyone if the citadel is lost."

It is tragic to reflect that by the time the McNamara years drew to a close it was American troops who were burning villages and sowing the fields of Vietnam with salt. But at first it was the technologist rather than the anti-Communist who came through the strongest. Those early McNamara years were heady times for the Pentagon as the Secretary and his team of earnest whizkids initiated reform after vaunted reform on the structure of the entire department, setting the framework for an entire generation of defense planning.

When he took over the department, McNamara immediately appointed over 120 task forces to look into the running of the Pentagon establishment, which soon became a hotbed of intellectual activity. Four major studies in military policy and strategy were ordered, and assigned not to the military, as in the past, but to the new civilian aides. McNamara himself set the tone of ruthless, Detroit-style efficiency. Oral briefings by his staff were banned; everything had to be put down in writing because, as he once put it, "I can read faster than they can talk."

In retrospect, it is seen that McNamara's much-vaunted organizational reforms have been a spectacular failure, and much of system he instituted has since been demolished. But while he held the office his reputation was unassailable; his slicked-back hair, immaculately parted down the middle, his rimless gold glasses, his mastery of detail gave him an air of shrewd business acumen and self-assertiveness that seemed to overawe the generals and admirals who worked for him. His public press conferences and his appearances on the Hill became famous throughout Washington, showpieces almost, as, briefed to the eyeballs, he rattled off a masterful and unstoppable stream of convincing and detailed statistics. His manner was always one of absolute infallibility. Giving evidence one day before a House subcommittee, he was asked why he had ordered the closing of 672 Army bases. Could he not have made a mistake in the case of one or two? "No," said McNamara emphatically. Representative Edward Hébert, chairman of the committee, asked incredulously, "Six hundred and seventy-two decisions and not a single mistake? You're better than Jesus Christ. He had only twelve decisions to make, and he blew one of them."

McNamara's relations with the Joint Chiefs of Staff, the uniformed heads of the Pentagon hierarchy, were always abrasive. The military much resented the fact that their own long experience and practical judgments were being cast aside in favour of computer calculations, operational analyses, and abstract theories of nuclear strategy. The retired Chief of Staff of the Air Force, General Thomas D. White, declared in a moment of irritation, "I am profoundly apprehensive of the pipe-smoking, trees-full-of-owls type of so-called defense intellectuals who have been brought into this nation's capital." And the retiring chairman of the Joint Chiefs of Staff, General Lyman L. Lemnitzer, declared in an oblique criticism of the new Secretary, "A battle group commander who occupies himself with the internal details of the operation of his companies may be showing how much he knows about being a company commander. But he is also showing how little he knows about commanding a battle group. He is doing an injustice to the ability and conscientiousness of his captains. He is failing to take advantage of the great asset they represent for carrying out the mission of the organization as a whole. Finally, he is displaying his own lack of confidence in his own ability to do the assigned job."

McNamara could afford to ignore these barbed darts. Soon after he came to office, the military establishment had been dealt a devastating blow in the aftermath of the Bay of Pigs disaster, the blame for which had been fixed by the administration firmly and unfairly on the Joint Chiefs of Staff who had advised it. President Kennedy privately told a group of newsmen he could have managed the military responsibilities of the affair better than his military experts. It was a blow to their prestige from which the Joint Chiefs have never effectively recovered.

For his part, McNamara took no pains to disguise his own contempt for the military way of doing things. In the middle of the 1962 Cuban missile crisis, he insisted on making the detailed decisions in the Navy's Flag Plot, or operations center, deep in the Pentagon basement. He called up ship commanders directly over the radio and tended to ignore the advice of the Chief of Naval Operations. He pointed once to a symbol of a ship at sea on the Navy's visual operations chart and demanded, "What's that ship doing there?" The admiral in charge of naval operations replied: "I don't know, but I have faith in my officers." Not long afterwards, the admiral was quietly dropped from his post and packed off as Ambassador to Portugal. (It is interesting for students of the perennial Washington battle of press leaks that two versions of this story appeared in the press at this time: one presumably leaked by supporters of McNamara to demonstrate his ability to ride herd over the military; another by the military, to demonstrate how McNamara interfered with the day-to-day details of their work.)

The incident typified McNamara's determination to achieve absolute control over the operations of his defense establishment. At first, his reforms were received with something near to adulation by the press and the outside public. Yet in the end his career turned into one of the strangest paradoxes of recent American history.

Somehow, the nuclear strategies that had seemed so rational in the early days of the Kennedy Administration later led to the most dangerous arms race in the history of mankind. The attempts to achieve a graduated response to the threat of communism that at first had looked so liberal led directly to the bottomless swamp of Vietnam. And the new management techniques of cost control and systems analysis he instituted led later to the costly disasters of the C-5A troop freighter, the F-111 fighter, and the B-70 bomber. The assured technician who laid such brilliantly thought-out plans and wrought his way with such effectiveness on the military machine, lived to become bitterly disillusioned with the policies he had been instrumental in formulating. Behind the brash exterior, lurked a character more like Hamlet than anyone knew.

From the first, his image as a cold and calculating rationalist had been something of a veneer. Beneath it, he was an essentially humane and reflective man, an elder of the Presbyterian Church, with a warmth of personality, a charm and a gaiety that impressed all who knew him. His twin obsessions with tidiness and technology led him into errors that were basically in conflict with his underlying personality, and the combination of his fierce hatred of communism and a belief in the virtues of technology was in the end to prove his downfall. It was the commitment to Vietnam more than anything else that tarnished his reputation. He gave the impression that he knew it all, that he could handle it, when as later events demonstrated, he could not. In his celebrated profile of McNamara, David Halberstam has written tellingly of the

Secretary's trips to Vietnam during the crucial years just before the American buildup. "There was something symbolic about him during those trips," Halberstam wrote. "He epitomized booming American technological success, he scurried around Vietnam, looking for what he wanted to see; and he never saw nor smelled nor felt what was really there, right in front of him. He was so much a prisoner of his own background, so unable, as indeed was the country which sponsored him, to adapt his values and his terms to Vietnamese realities. Since any real indices and truly factual estimates of the war would immediately have showed its bankruptcy, the McNamara trips became part of a vast unwitting and elaborate charade, the institutionalizing and legitimizing of a hopeless lie." McNamara had got himself caught in the Vietnam tar-baby, and was himself largely to blame. "He did not serve himself or his country well," Halberstam said. "He was, there is no kinder or gentler word for it, a fool."

Throughout the subsequent escalation of the war in Vietnam, McNamara consistently underestimated the determination of the North Vietnamese and the Vietcong, whom he could not conceive would be able to withstand the well-planned onslaught of a superior technology. And while he failed, until far too late, to gauge the human and spiritual cost of the war, he was wrong also in his estimates of its cost in money. "We put a hundred thousand men across the beaches in a hundred and twenty days and did not impose wage or price controls, or call up the reserves," he once boasted. "The Russians could not do that." Nor, in the long run, it proved, could the Americans, and the cost was paid later in the form of an inflation that almost a decade later has still not been brought under control. Even his estimates of the cash costs of the war were wrong in two years by a total of almost twenty billion dollars.

Towards the end, he realised his errors and characteristically commissioned a massive study to find out what had gone wrong and why—a study that was to become famous later as the Pentagon Papers. By the end of 1967, he had concluded that the massive bombing policy he had initiated under the title of Rolling Thunder would not work, and he had gone before a Senate subcommittee to criticize it. A year later, he was eased out by President Johnson, who remarked cruelly, "I forgot he had been president of Ford for only one week." It marked the end of a distinguished but sad and even tragic career in the service of the United States government.

When he reviewed his inheritance in 1969, President Nixon announced that one of his highest priorities would be to bring the national security complex under control. The McNamara years, according to the new administration, had brought a state of overcentralization and over-regulation to defense matters that had become scandalously wasteful, with a whole new layer of management imposed on the bureaucratic horde working in the Pentagon. One of Nixon's aims was to restore the influence of the military at the

Pentagon against the top civilians. "I intend," said the President in a major television address, "to root out the whiz-kid approach which for years has led our programs down the wrong roads."

Melvin Laird, his new Defense Secretary, echoed the President's theme in a public speech in Chicago. Much of the harsh criticism that had been leveled at the military, Laird said, was totally misplaced. Civilians, he declared, decided national security policy; civilians decided the structure of the forces; and civilians ran the Department of Defense. The men and women of the armed forces executed these policies "with courage, determination and loyalty."

Laird formulated a new policy for defense procurement, which he defined as "fly before you buy." A new Deputy Defense Secretary, David Packard, was appointed to wield a new broom with which to sweep the Augean stables clean. "Frankly, gentlemen," Packard told the Armed Forces Management Association, "in defense procurement we have a real mess on our hands. Let's face it—there has been bad management of many defense programs in the past."

Among the many mistakes to be put right were the contracts for the C-5A cargo plane, the Cheyenne helicopter, and the F-111 swingwing fighter plane, all of which had gone badly awry. Fighter aircraft were costing five or six times more than they had a decade earlier, and the two tons of electronics equipment installed in some types of defense aircraft had proved to be about twice as costly as pure gold.

Much of the trouble dated back to a procedure devised by McNamara's whizkids known as "total defense procurement," under which defense contracts set the manufacturers a basic price to cover, often for years in advance, the cost of development, testing, and production. "It was totally unrealistic," said a Nixon Administration spokesman, "because no one looking that far ahead could be that smart." In their enthusiasm for the new art of systems analysis, the whizkids had embraced the high-speed digital computer, a tool that in the hands of the bureaucrats at the Pentagon provided astonishingly elaborate amounts of detail about the cost and progress of future weapons systems, long before construction had even begun. Unfortunately, most of the detail provided by the computers was purely theoretical, their forecasts little more than what one defense contractor has called "a rain dance operation." The whizkids thought their reams of computerized data had given them the ability to master and thoroughly control any contract, but as Albert Blackburn, a Defense Department advisor of an earlier era, has pointed out, their knowledge was based largely on illusion. "There is an old adage in the armed forces," Blackburn said. " 'If the boss wants peanuts, feed him peanuts.' The boss wanted management systems, and suddenly computer readouts were piling up on Pentagon desks. Hardly anyone read the data. It was enough to riffle through the pages and note how much in-depth information was being assembled." In the event, it all too often proved to be impossible to foresee the technical snags that could (and often did) arise during the production of an entirely new weapons system, so that again and again costs escalated far above the original "total defense procurement" contract. The new Spruance class destroyers being built for the U.S. Navy by Litton Industries are now costing over $100 million each. As recently as 1969, it was estimated in the Pentagon that they would cost $60 million, while the current destroyers in service with the fleet, built in the mid-1960s, cost only $40 million each. A new battle-tank for the Army had to be canceled when the unit cost went past one million dollars.

Perhaps the classic case of runaway costs came with the C-5A cargo plane, which the Lockheed Aircraft Corporation originally estimated it could develop for $2.7 billion. Today, the cost of the C-5A program has more than doubled, threatening more than once to send Lockheed down into bankruptcy. It is a measure of the bureaucratic way of handling its contracts that the documentation distributed through the Pentagon on the C-5A problem weighed twenty tons—most of it wrong. Meanwhile, the price for each aircraft has gone up from $28 million to over $60 million, and the plane has been constantly plagued by exactly the sort of snags that could not be foreseen in even the most sophisticated computer forecast. Landing gears have collapsed; the plane had to be grounded for several weeks after an engine fell off during a take-off run; among other defects listed by the General Accounting Office were wing cracks, lost wheels, defects in the radar altimeter, and unreliable navigation equipment.

Yet the new administration's promises to put this sort of thing to rights were not matched by their deeds. When a Pentagon management expert, A. Ernest Fitzgerald, drew some of the C-5A's problems to the attention of the Senate, he was rewarded for his diligence with dismissal from his post. Pentagon officials explained that they had discovered that Fitzgerald's original civil-service status had been acquired as a result of a "computer error" and the loss of his job was therefore a mere technicality. They denied until the end that there was any connection whatever between his testimony to the Senate and the decision to drop him. Besides which, according to a story spread around Washington by a bevy of Air Force public-relations men, Fitzgerald was involved in "a conflict of interest." So he had to go. The episode was a bad beginning for an administration pledged to bring an end to the inefficiencies Mr. Fitzgerald had dutifully drawn to their attention.

The F-111 fighter, selected by McNamara against military advice as a multipurpose, all-weather fighter for use by all three services, had an even more catastrophic history. The version intended for the Navy had to be dropped altogether, the British Royal Air Force was forced to cancel its order for fifty of the aircraft, and three of the first eight fighters sent to southeast Asia for use by the U.S. Air Force crashed in a matter of weeks. The chairman of the Senate Appropriations subcommittee on defense matters asked wryly if there was a chance one of the crashed fighters might have fallen into enemy hands. "I was hoping," he said, "they would fabricate some as near to ours as they could and see if they had as much trouble as we did. It would put their Air Force out of business."

The solution of "fly before you buy" formulated during the Laird régime was a return to the old concepts of the 1950s that had prevailed before the introduction of the crash program intended to bridge the missile gap with calculated risks and deliberate, if expensive, corner-cutting. A paper on defense reorganization prepared by Gilbert W. Fitzhugh, an insurance man, recommended "more prototypes, more hardware and less reliance on paper studies." "We think it is too much to expect anybody, any defense contractor, to put in a bid today as to how much it is going to cost him to build a weapon or a plane or a tank that neither he nor anyone else has ever built before," Fitzhugh declared.

At the same time, the Defense Department recognized another problem caused in part by McNamara's total-procurement policies, a procedure known as "the bidding and lying competition." Contractors who needed defense work desperately enough were "buying in" with unrealistically low bids for the work, which they knew would be more than made up in increased production orders and payments for last-minute changes dictated by the Pentagon. Deputy Defense Secretary Packard recalled visiting a plant that had fallen a year behind its delivery schedule on a certain defense item. "I asked the manager why he offered to do the job in one year less than was possible," Mr. Packard said. "The essence of his reply was—'Yes, we knew we could not meet the terms of the contract, but there was no way to get the contract if we told the truth.' "

Today, under Nixon as much as under any of his recent predecessors the greatest single barrier to efficient management of defense-procurement contracts can be summed upin a single word: politics. The military-industrial complex has become so pervasive, so crucial to the economic well-being of so many regions of America, that any attempt to make an effective reduction in spending is met with the opposition not only of the military, which wants the hardware, but also of Congress, which is supposed to watch over the Pentagon with an eagle eye, but which in reality often needs the defense spending for its own political reasons as much as the Defense Department does for military reasons. The result, according to Senator William Proxmire, a rare legislator who has stood against inefficient defense spending, is that the military-industrial complex has become in fact the military-industrial-bureaucratic-congressional-labor complex. In other words, the pressure on most senators and congressmen is for more defense spending rather than less.

Military spending, quite simply, is now the largest single industrial activity in America. The defense budget covers not only such obvious items as $7 billion a year for military aircraft, but such less obvious items as $1.5 million for musical instruments and $6,000 a year for flowers to place on American battle monuments. Defense money flows into every state of the Union in larger or lesser amounts, and scattered throughout the country are whole towns that are completely dependent on the military for their livelihoods.

The result is that, until very recently, congressmen partly dependent for their re-election on the votes of defense workers, have not been as critical of military spending as they might have been. Senator Gaylord Nelson summed up the problem in an article written in 1969:

> In the brief period of six years that I have been in the Senate, no military budget has been subjected by the Congress—or by the public, either—to really critical evaluation. We have passed seventy-billion-dollar military budgets after ten minutes or an hour of discussion, and whenever some of us attempted to offer modest amendments, it was a foregone conclusion what the result would be. We defaulted —the Congress, and the public—in all matters of judgment on the military budget, on the theory that the military knew best and that we were dealing with purely technical military matters and not political ones. This has been our greatest mistake.

Senator Nelson believes the atmosphere has now changed—that the military has lost its status of infallibility and that Congress as a result is more inclined to look twice at new demands for more cash. The cozy relationship that still exists between the Pentagon and the powerful chairmen of the appropriations committees, however, remains a principal stumbling block towards reform. "Do you think Richard Russell ever asked to have an installation put into Georgia?" asked a Pentagon official of the former head of the Senate Armed Services Committee. "All he had to do was to get appointed chairman and the installations came in."

The loading of defense contracts on the districts of the key committee chairmen—all hawkish southern conservatives—was nowhere more blatant than in the South Carolina district of the late L. Mendel Rivers, chairman of the House Armed Services Committee. According to a report in *Time*, River's district contained an Air Force base, an Army depot, a naval shipyard, a Marine air station, the Parris Island boot camp, two Navy hospitals, a naval station, a naval supply center, a naval weapons station, a fleet ballistic-missile submarine training-center, a Polaris missile factory, an Avco Corporation plant, a Lockheed plant, a General Electric plant, and an eight-hundred-acre plot of ground that had just been purchased by the Sikorsky Aircraft Division of United Aircraft. A campaign billboard for Rivers declared boldly, "Thank you! Democratic progress brought it! The Democratic team will keep it!" The total defense payroll of Rivers's district was a reported two billion dollars a year, and Rivers openly claimed the credit for landing 90 percent of this.

This sort of logrolling is by no means confined to Congress. Richard Nixon, in his campaign for the Presidency, was equally candid to a crowd at Fort Worth, Texas, which he told, "I can assure you that we are going to remember the state of Texas on defense contracts and certainly Texas is going to get its fair share—you can be sure of that—under my administration."

Yet another danger which played its part in the formulation of Eisenhower's farewell warning against the military-industrial complex was that of the employment of retired senior officers by defense contractors. When he spoke, 768 retired senior officers with the rank of colonel or above were employed by the hundred largest defense contractors. Today, there are more than 2,900.

The heart of the military-industrial complex is made up of only twenty-five giant companies, which between them account for over half of all the money spent on defense procurement in the United States. The biggest ten of these companies, controlling one third of the defense contracts in terms of dollar awards, together with the numbers of retired officers on their payroll, are:

	Defense Awards (Thousands of Dollars)	Number of Officers
1. Lockheed Aircraft	1,705,434	210
2. McDonnell Douglas	1,700,217	141
3. General Dynamics	1,289,167	113
4. General Electric	1,258,673	80
5. Boeing	1,170,878	169
6. American Telephone & Telegraph	1,121,512	9
7. Grumman	1,119,760	31
8. United Aircraft	995,619	48
9. North American Rockwell	702,862	not available
10. Hughes Aircraft	688,132	not available

(Source: Defense Department, year ended 30 June 1972)

These companies, together with the military, maintain a vast and efficient lobby in Washington through which they sell their new weapons systems to the Congress. James Phillips, a high Nixon Administration official, is quoted by Adam Yarmolinsky in *The Military Establishment*, as saying that the Pentagon organized its congressional lobby "like a marine corps landing," with generals, admirals, and top civilians "always ready to run up to the Hill whenever a problem develops." The Pentagon openly spends over three million a year on its Capitol Hill lobby, and it is backed up by the not inconsiderable efforts of the contractors. The government lobbyists, according to Phillips, "crawl unabashedly" all over the Hill, but the defense contractors are far more discreet. "Some congressmen look askance," Phillips said, "when a company that's 95 percent owned by the government asks them to support a project because it will increase business for them." Consequently, the contractors tended to "tiptoe up to the Hill in the middle of the night in tennis shoes and always cover up their tracks."

But even so, they found the members with important defense plants in their districts seldom had to be lobbied very vigorously because they vote the way their bread is buttered. Senator Philip Hart has described the same temptation as follows:

> As procurement moved steaily upward, every member of Congress began to develop constituencies that were in some degree dependent on defense jobs and contracts. . . . It is not politically hard for me to vote against, say, a new aircraft carrier. But if the shipyard were in my state and five thousand people were waiting for the work, I would be examining very closely, and perhaps less critically, all those reasons why the carrier might be essential to national security.

The Nixon Administration now finds itself in the same bind. In spite of its promises to bring defense spending under closer control, and its undeniable successes in some relatively limited areas, when it comes down to the hard bargain the administration has seemed as little able to reduce the cost of defense spending as any of its predecessors. Besides, there is comparatively little left over today, due to the sharply increased cost of military manpower, which now consumes 56 percent of the total defense budget, compared with only 42 percent a decade ago—and with the 25 percent estimated to be spent by the Russians on military manpower. When Congress approved the new pay standards designed to attract men into the new all-volunteer army, they at once raised the defense budget by $15 billion, according to some estimates. Allowing for inflation and lower force levels, moreover, the $22.9 billion budgeted for investment in military hardware actually provides almost $5 billion less for ships, planes, and missiles than was available in President Eisenhower's last year. At the same time, the costs of individual weapons programs has swollen astronomically, which is one reason there has been no "peace dividend" in the aftermath of Vietnam. The longterm result of this double squeeze on defense costs is as disturbing to the supporters of the military as it is to the critics who wish to see military spending further reduced. Senator John Stennis, chairman of the Senate Armed Services Committee, and a firm believer in a powerful military, has warned that "we may find ourselves, the next time we have to fight, with too few weapons so complex they don't work. Both the taxpayers and the military are ill-served if weapons are so costly that we don't have enough of them. Quality is important, but it is better to have a large number of rugged, easily maintained weapons than a few fragile, theoretically perfect ones."

In short, the United States is being forced by the huge increase in the cost of weapons to place more and more of its defense eggs in one basket. The current Polaris submarines, for example, cost about $100 million apiece, including missiles; the estimated cost of each new longrange Trident now being developed will be ten times as much. At least some of the money spent on Trident will clearly have to be taken from other defense programs, precisely the danger that Stennis has warned against. In the Air Force, the cost of each of the current fleet of B-52 strategic bombers is about $8 million, yet the supposedly aging (though still efficient) B-52s are to be replaced later in this decade by a new bomber known as the B-1, at a cost still undetermined, but likely to be at least seven times as expensive as the B-52. In fiscal 1974 the administration requested a total of $473 million for continued development and construction of the B-1 prototype, which has not yet taken to the air on its maiden flight. The project has so far scrupulously followed Laird's "fly before you buy" policies, but by the time the B-1 does fly, the country will have spent nearly $3 billion on it. It will take strong minds in Congress to turn around at that stage and refuse to build it, and there are some critics who believe that "fly before you buy" locks Congress just as firmly as the old total-procurement system into a process from which it cannot easily retreat. Yet there are many military analysts who believe the entire bomber concept will be out of date in the world of the 1980s. The B-1 will go into service as an endangered species, and in any case whatever role remains for the manned bomber in the age of missiles, can perfectly well be continued by the "aging" B-52.

But defense contracts are not built wholly on logic. Both the Air Force bureaucracy that conceived it and the contractor who builds it have an obvious interest in their own self-preservation, while according to Ernest Fitzgerald, who was dismissed for his revelations about the C-5A, the B-1 bomber was conceived "to make jobs for southern California." The plane will be built by the North America Rockwell Corporation, whose workforce had declined from 97,000 to fewer than 50,000 in 1970. A contract for the B-1 will keep it in business for at least another decade, with the first aircraft not due for delivery until 1979 at the earliest. By that time, in the opinion of many defense experts, the plane will be obsolete and worthless, a sitting duck for the latest Russian SAM-3 missiles. And while it will take the B-1 bomber four hours to fly the six-thousand-mile journey to Russia, eight successive missile salvos could have been fired, four by each side. The war might well be over before the bomber arrived over its target. So, in all probability, by the time it is ready, the Air Force will not need the B-1 at all. Yet such is the builtin impetus of the system, the effort to stop it seems beyond the power of either the Pentagon, the President, Congress, or the people. It is, in its way, the clearest example so far of the almost uncontrollable, unstoppable way the military-industrial machine rolls on.

3. Rebuilding the Army

"I want you to know that when I cross the river, my last conscious thoughts will be of The Corps, The Corps, and The Corps."
—GENERAL DOUGLAS MACARTHUR, *farewell address to West Point cadets,*
1962

Lieutenant Colonel Anthony B. Herbert, who had won more medals in Korea than any other enlisted soldier, stood stiffly to attention before the desk of his commanding officer, Colonel Thomas Reid, at the U.S. Army base in Fort McPherson, Georgia. After twenty years in the Army, which had once chosen him as their symbol of the perfect fighting man, Colonel Herbert was being dressed down for his saluting style.

"Close your fingers," snapped Colonel Reid.

"I think they are closed, sir."

"Tilt your hand."

"I think it is tilted, sir."

"Tilt your fingers in so you can see them."

"Like this, sir?"

"You slurred the word *sir.* Say it sharp."

"Yes, sir."

This petty exchange between two senior officers, both grown men well into their forties, took place at the end of 1971 after Colonel Herbert had accused two senior officers of covering up war crimes in Vietnam. The saluting lesson was the Army's way of humiliating Herbert, a man it had once regarded as the cream of the officer corps, but whose career it had now systematically set out to ruin.

After the massacre at Mylai, the Army's treatment of a junior half-colonel was perhaps in itself an insignificant incident, although it also symbolized the deep moral doubts that afflicted many Army officers in the aftermath of the disastrous war in Vietnam. Herbert had been assigned to Vietnam in September 1968 with an impeccable record. In Korea, he had won a Bronze Star, three Silver Stars, four Purple Hearts, and eighteen other decorations, more than any other enlisted soldier in the Army. Later, he had been chosen to make a world tour as the Army's symbol of the perfect fighting man, and his picture was selected to illustrate a training manual for the élite Green Berets, his face ferociously smudged with camouflage greasepaint, his attitude one of lean aggression, his finger clutching the trigger of his carbine. On his way up, the crewcut, quiet-spoken young officer, six feet three inches tall, had found time to acquire two university degrees and looked every inch the fighting American soldier, with reason to believe the Army—of which he was inordinately proud —was also proud of him. Before he got to Vietnam, Herbert had been picked out as a 5 percenter, one of the top officers of his generation, who won his promotions more quickly than his colleagues. In Vietnam, he was assigned first to a staff position and then, late in the war, took command of a combat battalion in the field with the crack 173rd Airborne Brigade.

In only fifty-eight days of combat, Herbert won another Silver Star, three more Bronze Stars, two Air Medals, and the Army Commendation Medal for Valor, and had just been recommended for the Distinguished Service Cross. "This guy is absolutely incredible," one of the younger officers in his battalion told the New York *Times*. "He is the perfect warrior—a supersoldier, if ever I saw one." A general was quoted as saying he was "one of the best, if not the best combat commander in the whole goddamned Army."

Yet the combat tour that had begun so brilliantly for the lean lieutenant-colonel ended in disaster. At the end of his fifty-eight days in the field, he was abruptly relieved of his command after his superiors had filed an efficiency report so adverse it effectively ended his chances of ever leading an Army unit again. Exactly what happened is, five years later, still unclear. The known facts are that Herbert's superior officer, Colonel Joseph Ross Franklin, had a row in the field with Herbert and later submitted an efficiency report on his junior commander, one of those Army forms in which the filing officer rates his subordinates on an alphabetical list of attributes running from adaptability, ambition, and appearance to stamina, tact, and understanding. The filing officer is provided with a list of "helpful words" for preparing the narrative description of his officers, which contain around one hundred different adjectives with which to describe each attribute of the officer under his charge. In Herbert's case, Colonel Franklin had chosen the most critical possible word to describe his appearance, ambition, dependability, loyalty, moral courage, and even his "will to self-improvement." The efficiency report prepared by Colonel Franklin was countersigned by his friend and superior, General John Barnes, who said later, "I had had Herbert up to here. I have commanded twenty battalion commanders in my time, and Herbert was clearly the worst. He is also the only one I have ever relieved." The general recommended that Herbert should never be allowed to command again.

Herbert immediately appealed the Army's actions, and eighteen months later filed official charges against his two superior officers, accusing them of covering up war crimes he had reported. According to Herbert's charges, he had one day in combat come across an American lieutenant and several

Vietnamese soldiers torturing a woman prisoner. When he told them to stop, the soldiers slit the woman's throat. Herbert says he filed a complaint with Colonel Franklin, and over the next few weeks reported seven similar incidents. He said he had seen woman detainees beaten with bamboo rods, split at the end "so that they cut the flesh like a razor." In another incident, he reported seeing a woman prisoner interrogated by using electric shocks from a field telephone. In each case, he reported later, Colonel Franklin called him a liar and told him not to be so squeamish.

Herbert's formal complaint accused Barnes and Franklin of failing to investigate or report incidents of murder, torture, and mistreatment of prisoners. The charges were later dismissed by the Army for "lack of evidence," and there in ordinary times the case might have rested. The Pentagon put out a five-page summary of the affair, pointing out that Herbert had only made his accusations a year and a half after he had been relieved of his command, and then only after his appeal had been refused. The clear implication was that Herbert had lied about the atrocities because of his bad efficiency rating. Herbert, not very convincingly, claimed the Army's lawyers had prohibited him from mentioning the charges until his appeals were settled. Much later, after he had written a book about the affair, further doubts were cast on Herbert's version of the events that led to his downfall when he appeared on a CBS television program, during which it was revealed that Colonel Franklin was on leave in Honolulu at the time Herbert said he had filed his first atrocity report. Other exaggerations in the book were examined, too, and while nothing was proved conclusively, the impression was left that Herbert had set out to seek revenge for his humiliations.

Yet doubts about the Army's version of the story also remained. Why did it insist so adamantly on keeping secret its own investigations of Herbert's charges? And why was Herbert's downfall so sudden? In fifty-eight days in combat, he had won seven medals and been recommended for one of the Army's highest decorations for bravery; his record before that had, according to the Army's own records, been outstanding. General Barnes suggested that Herbert had lied about enemy casualties and had himself been a "killer," but that does not fully explain the bad marks given to him for ambition, appearance, and "the will to self-improvement"—remarks that were later expunged from Herbert's record by an Army investigation that had found him to be a fine leader "admired by most of his subordinates." Nor does the treatment afforded to Herbert after his return from Vietnam reflect much credit on his superiors, who set out deliberately to harass him out of the Army.

He had at first been assigned to a recruiting post in Atlanta, where he promptly won the award for the best record of any re-enlistment officer in the United States. At the ceremony to receive the award, however, Herbert was put in the back row. While national television cameras recorded the event, the Cup was handed to his second in command. After that petty performance, he was given a series of ever more humiliating assignments, one of them the same deadend job at Fort McPherson that had been given to Captain Ernest Medina while he awaited trial for more than one hundred murder charges arising out of the Mylai massacre. He was denied leave, and a request to appear on a television program was approved by his commanding officer only after the taping of the show had already begun in another town. When it sets its mind to it, the U.S. Army can grind an officer it disapproves of exceeding small.

"I understand it, but I just don't want to admit I'm being sytematically screwed by the Army," Colonel Herbert told one reporter who visited him at this time. "I just don't want to admit that. I chose the Army as the expression of my life. I gave to it, took from it, believed in it. Now this."

Justified or not, the public humiliation of Colonel Herbert came at an unfortunate time for the U.S. Army, whose morale and reputation had been severely damaged by the frustrations and moral dilemmas of the war in Vietnam. The case arose at just the moment when the Army could least afford it. Memories were still all too fresh of the massacre at Mylai and the subsequent allegations that officers in the field had tried to cover it up. Then followed, within the space of a single year, the courtmartial of Lieutenant William Calley, a financial scandal involving the army's senior sergeant-major, the resignation of the commandant of West Point, further financial charges against the former provost marshal general of the Army, a parade of Army veterans who threw away their Vietnam combat medals on the steps of the U.S. Capitol, bitter accusations that American lives had been wantonly sacrificed in the battle for Hamburger Hill, revelations that senior officers had been awarded medals for bravery under false pretenses, and finally, the Herbert affair.

Herbert was no reluctant draftee, nor an antiwar activist, nor a pathetic shortterm incompetent like Lieutenant Calley, but the cream of the regular officer corps, a body that had hitherto boasted an *esprit* and a pride that its chief of staff described as "the finest on earth."

Career soldiers had looked on the Army with the dedication of a religious order, but in the aftermath of Vietnam it was clear that the Army was in deep trouble, its officer corps puzzled and defensive at the wave of antimilitary feeling that swept the country following Mylai, its enlisted men plagued by crime, drug addiction, racial conflict, rebellion against officers, and boredom. The resultant crisis in morale and discipline has been as serious as any of its top commanders can remember.

General Hamilton H. Howze, the retired commander of the 82nd Airborne Division, wrote in *Army* magazine, "The military forces of the United States face a disciplinary situation which, if not already critical, is at least one of rapidly growing proportions. Should senior officers not be able to reverse the trend towards indiscipline, this country will, not long from now, lose its status as the world's first power and stand almost helpless against those who would humble or destroy it."

And General Matthew Ridgway, a former Army Chief of Staff, said in a speech to a local West Point association, "Not before in my lifetime—and I was born into the Army in the nineteenth century—has the Army's public image suffered so many grievous blows and fallen to such low esteem in such wide areas of our society."

Can an officer today speak his mind freely and honestly without jeopardizing his career? asked General Ridgway. Can he expect promotion in due time without conforming to practices of which he deeply disapproves? Can he candidly disagree with his superiors when he conscientiously believes them to be wrong?

To all these questions, a deeply disturbed General Ridgway suggested the answer would have to be No. Officers he had spoken to at the Army War College—"carefully selected, thoughtful, senior officers"—had told him that to win Army promotions today it was essential to make a record in a combat unit, a record which was judged by the "body count" of the enemy dead.

"To achieve these results," General Ridgway said, "the unit commander could not tell the truth, the whole truth and nothing but the truth. He had to repudiate the code . . . indelibly engraved in the hills of West Point—the code on which the Corps of Cadets was nurtured—don't lie, cheat or steal."

The officer corps, he concluded, is the heart of any military establishment. "If they fail, disaster follows."

The source of the disaster that has overtaken the American army today can be summed up in a single word: Vietnam. "The price of Vietnam has been a terrible one," said a senior officer who had fought there. "A truly terrible one. In terms of casualties, in terms of the loss of men and treasure, in terms of morale, it was a terrible price the Army has had to pay." Ironically, it was only after the painfully slow withdrawal from Vietnam had begun that the deeply corrosive effects of that war on the morale of the Army were fully appreciated.

After the withdrawal began, troops in many units rejected the slightest semblance of military discipline. In Vietnam, thousands of them turned to drugs—often heroin—to escape the rigors of combat and to express their opposition to a war in which a large percentage of them no longer believed. Incidents of assaulting their officers with explosives—a sport known as "fragging"—grew to alarming proportions: In 1970 alone, there were 271 officially reported cases of officers killed or wounded by "fragging." One unit in Vietnam, called out to parade before a visiting general, blew up the reviewing stand with stolen explosives; another unit cheered when its gung-ho colonel was blown to pieces by a mine.

Desertions and absences without leave also increased. In 1971, the last full year of an American fighting commitment in Vietnam, 177 out of every 1,000 soldiers were listed at one time or another as "absent without leave." Nearly half of them stayed away from their units longer than a month and were therefore officially classified as "deserters." And 4 out of every 100 of those who returned home had become addicted to heroin. As recently as 1972, the FBI reported it had picked up 21,211 military deserters and turned them over to the military authorities.

"With their longish hair, black power wristbands and peace medallions, the rumpled, love-beaded draftees now lining up at the Long Binh urinals for pre-departure heroin detection tests bear little resemblance to the tough professionals who led the way into Vietnam six years ago," wrote a Washington *Post* reporter in Vietnam. Most of them had been barely teenagers then. In the following six years antiwar sentiment had become the force that unified their generation—and they wanted to be a part of that force, not a dispirited remnant of America's southeast Asia fighting machine.

In a bitter attack on the Army's record in Vietnam, Lieutenant Colonel Edward L. King quoted his own black ward orderly on the attitude of ordinary draftees towards the war they had been called upon to fight:

> If you was anything but a grunt, it wasn't too bad. I mean all the lifers, they was getting promoted and they could get a little whiskey when they wanted and the generals and the colonels they was livin' high on the hog. But if you was a grunt —nothin' man. And we had to turn up the bodies: old General Ewell he was somethin' else about killin' gooks. The platoons, they'd better turn in a good body count or else they stayed out in the bush forever. Didn't make no difference what kind of bodies—even pigs and chickens counted—just so you reported them as bodies. . . .
>
> I ain't goin' back over there again; nobody gives a damn about the cats over there. They're just there so's the lifers can get promoted. Look at all them cats up in the wards without no legs, or arms, or balls. . . . Look at the lootenant down the hall there, no eyes left—a damn mine done nearly tore his head off. And what for, sir? You don't see ol' General Westmoreland limpin' around here with no plastic legs. Fuck no, ain't nothin' good 'bout that war, sir.

By the end, it was only too clear that the ward orderly's bitterness was shared by a disturbing number of his fellow soldiers, most of them draftees, many of them black, who had been sent to fight for their country in the most unpopular campaign in the Army's history. For the most part, the young troops hated their own army with a ferocity unmatched in the annals of modern warfare.

The Army touched bottom in those desperate days of 1968 and 1969, when there were over half a million men on active duty in Vietnam. America's commitment of ground combat troops has ended now, and with it some of the bitterness has begun to lift also. By 1975, the Army will have shrunk to about half its maximum Vietnam size, with troops recruited as volunteers instead of reluctant draftees. This transformation, now well under way, will perhaps prove the Army's salvation as it prepares itself for its post-Vietnam role. "I have a feeling that we've touched bottom now and are finally heading up," says Major General John Bennett, commander of the Fourth Mechanized Infantry Division at Fort Carson, Colorado. "But the only way to keep a fighting unit in trim is to give it plenty to do."

General Bennett and other top Army leaders admit there is still a long way to go to repair the damage done to the troops in Vietnam. At Fort Carson, the Army has been experimenting with an amnesty program for drugusers and has reduced the spit-and-polish, known to the American Army as Mickey Mouse. A psychedelically painted coffeehouse has been opened on the base, paid for out of Army funds, where the troops are encouraged to air their dissident views. Full colonels are ordered to attend the "rap sessions" in the coffeehouse in which the atmosphere is usually violently antimilitary, anti-officer, and antiestablishment. The officers who attend strive hard to make contact with their men, but for many of them it is clearly a distasteful task. "Let's face it," said one officer. "You join the Army, you've got to have dicipline. You've got to have rules, you've got to enforce them. Ain't none of that here any more."

The Army today faces two quite separate problems arising from the trauma of Vietnam. One concerns the discipline, recruiting, and attitude of its enlisted men; the other, the morale of its corps of professional officers. Of the two, the latter is perhaps the more intractable.

After the end of the war in Korea in the early 1950s, senior Army officers found themselves for the first time in history without a clearly defined role in the defense of their country, which was at that time dominated by the theory of massive retaliation. The Army, it is true, stood watch on the banks of the Elbe, bored and uncertain, against a Soviet threat that never materialized, its role should a nuclear war break out in Europe unsure but almost certainly minor. Infantrymen, the traditional backbone of the Army, were no longer considered the main arm of defense in the nuclear age. "The difference between the Army and the Navy," said one officer, "is that the Navy knows just what it has to do—keep the sea lanes open—but argues interminably about how to do it. The Army does not know what its mission is, but would know exactly what to do if it did."

But gradually, as the country moved away from its doctrine of massive retaliation to that of a measured and flexible response to a limited war, the Army planners, under the inspired but misguided leadership of General Maxwell Taylor, then Chief of Staff, began to develop a new role for themselves. They based their plans on an overall strategy of graduated response in which, it was argued, the Army should be organized to intervene quickly and decisively in limited local wars and so serve as ever-present preventative to general war.

The Army got its first chance to demonstrate its new-found role during the crisis in the Dominican Republic in 1965, when almost 23,000 American soldiers and marines were rushed into the tiny republic before most people had realized what was happening. Their stated objective was to protect the lives of some 1,400 American citizens on the island, which most military observers now concede could have been achieved with a fraction of the troops actually used. But the contingency plans and the interservice rivalry to see who could mobilize the fastest gathered a momentum it became impossible to stop; once again, the military tail was wagging the diplomatic dog.

However dubious the objective, the landings in the Dominican Republic had increased the Army's confidence that it could apply its modern mobility to other limited wars, particularly the one it had been watching closely in Vietnam.

The early days of the Vietnam War were a heady time for the Army's senior and middle-ranking career officers. Most of them, it was true, were dedicated and patriotic men, and it was, after all, civilians who first sent them to Vietnam. But it was also undeniable that from the first many of them openly welcomed this opportunity to get into real combat, to smell the smoke of battle and earn themselves valuable promotions on the way. Obviously, as Professor Hans Morgenthau has put it, "No general was going to admit that the U.S. couldn't win this lousy little war against a couple of hundred thousand peasants in pajamas."

Vietnam gave the Army a new mission, one its career officers seized with relish. The Army brass devised a system of rotation for the precious combat commands that almost imperceptibly brought the officer corps to the brink of catastrophe. The Army, quite simply, fell into a trap first perceived by Alexis de Tocqueville over 120 years ago. While of all peoples those most deeply attached to peace are the democracies, de Tocqueville observed, their armies are the ones that most ardently long for war. The European armies of his day were officered by men who regarded military rank as related to social position. In the American army, by contrast, commissions were open to all classes; the wish for promotion was eager, tenacious, and continual. For an officer, he wrote, "each promotion has immense importance in his eyes, because his standing in society almost always depends on his rank in the army. Therefore all the ambitious minds in a democratic army ardently long for war, because war makes vacancies available and allows violations of the rules of seniority, which is the one privilege natural to a democracy."

The years leading up to the disaster in Vietnam were the years that also saw the growth of the Army organization man, the rise of the technocrats whose drive to succeed within the organization began to overshadow their dedication to their civilian masters. Older Army leaders like Bradley and Ridgway had lived strictly by the hallowed army code: duty, honor, country. The lives of their men they put above all else save the survival of the nation. The new breed of Army technocrats who succeeded them were more like the departmental managers of giant private corporations than leaders of men in combat; their main ambition was to expand the role of the Army and with it, to further their own careers. The old regimental unit, which had been the core of the American Army for nearly two centuries, was broken up and replaced by the loosely formed battle-group. And out with the regiments went the old ties of loyalty, tradition, and esprit that are so important to the morale of fighting units.

Today, many dedicated career officers in the modern American Army believe, like General Ridgway, that if they are to get on they will be forced into a system they contemptuously dismiss as "ticket punching," the effect of which, according to the critics, is to produce an officer corps of yes-men and opportunists, who will go to almost any lengths to win what they call "brownie points."

"Almost three generations of ticket punchers have now been produced," says Colonel David Hackworth. "They are easy to identify since they have the most medals and badges and, because of those, resemble walking Christmas trees. They are highly articulate, well educated, with impressive graduate degrees: smooth, slick guys who have not spent much time with soldiers."

In this analysis, the ticketpunchers get to the top because of the iniquitous statistical device known as "O.E.R"—the Officer's Efficiency Report, the very device that was used to bring down Colonel Herbert. Under the O.E.R. system, senior officers rate their juniors on everything from their ability to think logically in combat to their poise while playing bridge with the commander's wife. The report cards even state, by means of tiny figures, how many out of every hundred officers shall be marked down as "outstanding," "exceptional," "superior," or merely "excellent." The effect of a bad efficiency report can be disastrous for an officer's career, with the result that many of them will go to almost any lengths to get a good rating.

Colonel Hackworth tells of one commander who reported that when his unit fired on the range, 93 percent of the men qualified while the rest would probably never learn to fire a gun. As all the other units reported no failures, the honest officer's O.E.R. card was duly marked down with an "inability to teach his men to shoot straight." Another, who refused to fire artillery into a Vietcong village because of civilians, received an adverse comment for his "lack of aggressiveness." When one considers that such a report can help to ruin an officer's career, it is hardly surprising that the bodycounts in Vietnam were loaded with so many dead buffaloes, pigs, and chickens. It is argued by some that the pressures to produce a high bodycount led directly to the slaughter of innocent civilians at Mylai and some other villlages, as well as the handout of medals for bravery to senior commanders who circled the battlefield in their helicopters, gunning down enemy soldiers as they fled. Defense Department statistics show that the Army in Vietnam awarded its men 40,000 more Bronze Stars than were presented during all of World War II, together with 1.5 million Air Medals and 78,000 Distinguished Flying Crosses. Tim O'Brien, who served as an infantryman in Vietnam, has written a graphic account of how one such medal came to be awarded:

> Bullets slashed out of the bushes. One of them hit a GI in the leg; he dropped and began to bleed. A grenade sailed like a football into a clump of squirming American soldiers. It exploded and two GIs fell. "Jesus!" they screamed in unison. "Medic!" The bushes erupted again. A young lieutenant was shot in the groin. He crumpled but did not scream. The GIs began to return fire, tentatively at first. Then the whole platoon turned their M-16s into the bushes, toward the invisible enemy, emptying all they had into a short stretch of the Vietnam jungle. But they shot blindly, putting a bullet through a buddy's chest.
>
> Overhead, circling in his command helicopter, the battalion commander watched the firefight. When it ended, he buzzed the trees for ten minutes, waiting for the platoon to establish a secure landing zone for him. Then he landed. The wounded GIs were dumped into the chopper's tiny cabin and the colonel's helicopter roared and was gone. The soldier with the chest wound, shot by his friends, died on the way to the hospital. The lieutenant lost his left testicle. The battalion commander won a Distinguished Flying Cross.

The head of the Army during this turbulent period, first as field commander in Vietnam, then as Chief of Staff at the Pentagon, was General William Childs Westmoreland, an impeccably groomed product of West Point, a general whose uniform never revealed a wrinkle or a crease even in the heat and mud of Vietnam. Throughout the war, Westmoreland was always the optimist, always seeing the light at the end of the tunnel, always demanding more troops to pursue his fruitless policy of attrition against the forces of the Vietcong. In the end, after the disastrous Tet offensive of 1968, he tried to force mobilization of the reserves on a reluctant President. Instead, he was relieved of his command and brought home to the Pentagon as Army Chief of Staff.

Criticism of Westmoreland's handling of the crisis in the Army has been brutal, even among his own junior officers, who complained he was not flexible or modern enough to revitalize the army. In July 1972 he was retired with full honors, standing erect as ever in a dazzling white dress uniform at his farewell parade to speak not of the Army's problems, but of pride. "As I look back on my life," he said, "I thank God for the opportunity that was given to me to be a soldier. If given that opportunity again, I would, with the same pride and with even greater humility, raise my hand and take once again the soldier's oath. Goodbye, and Godspeed."

Westmoreland's successor as Chief of Staff, General Creighton W. Abrams, the same man who had succeeded him in Vietnam, promises to be a very different head of the Army. "If he changes the Army even half as much as he changed the war in Vietnam, nobody will recognize it," said one military acquaintance. Abrams is considered to be one of the best strategists in the Army today. He conducted brilliantly the reduction of the American presence in Vietnam from well over half a million men to fewer than fifty thousand.

Where Westmoreland looked like an Army recruiting poster, Abrams walks with a slouch, chainsmokes cigars, and seems not to notice when the ash spills down over his crumpled uniform. He is known to his colleagues as "gruff and grizzled," adjectives which apply equally to his manner as to his appearance. He believes firmly that in the Army, commanders are responsible for the actions of their subordinates. "Whenever somebody's army performs badly anywhere in the world," he once said, "it's because of leadership. The men are all the same. If you see bad performance, it's because of bad leadership."

As it moves from the concept of a large "citizen army," made up mainly of draftees, to a much smaller force of volunteers, the new American Army that Abrams now commands is in need of firm leadership as never before. The change to an all-volunteer Army deeply worries many American critics of the military. They believe such an Army will be a poor man's Army, its rank-and-file troops made up mainly of blacks, its officers cut off from the mainstream of civilian thought. Such an Army, it is argued, will be composed entirely of career military men who are isolated, even alienated, from the people they have sworn to defend. Such an Army, its critics believe, would make it too easy and too cheap for national leaders to make the initial decision to wage war.

Joseph Califano, a former Deputy Secretary of Defense, believes there are profound dangers in society's harboring two or three million men dependent solely for their livelihood on the most powerful military machine in the history of mankind. "The very concept of a highly paid volunteer army," he writes, "reflects the continuing erosion of the will to sacrifice, particularly on the part of our affluent citizens." Califano believes that to say to the affluent "now we will lift from you any concern that your sons might have to fight a war is further to pander to the more selfish baser instincts of their human nature. . . . What is of profound concern is that so many of our leaders eagerly support any move to ease the burden of the affluent and make it easier to engage in military adventures abroad at a time when the nation desperately needs a real measure of sacrifice at home and the strictest inhibitions on further military adventures in far-off lands."

Such arguments have little historical validity in the American experience, however. Until 1948, America had never drafted its young men into the Army in peacetime, and there is no evidence that voluntary service and militarism go hand in hand. Historically, it is countries like France and Germany, with strong traditions of militarism, that have turned to the draft to fill the ranks of their standing armies; the two countries with the strongest traditions of civilian control over the military—Britain and the United States—have normally relied on volunteer armies, at least in peacetime.

It is in any case not the shortterm draftees but the regular officer corps that determines the direction of the military, and America already recruits every one of its senior officers on a voluntary basis. There is not the slightest shred of evidence that the elimination of junior draftees will in any way weaken the tradition of civilian control or alter the basic psychology of the professional officers on whom the Army already depends.

Of much more concern is the argument that in the present atmosphere of antimilitarism in America, not enough properly qualified volunteers are today willing to join a force that is openly despised by so many of their fellow youngsters. Already many universities have been forced to abandon their Reserve Officer Training Corps (ROTC) under pressure from the campus activists. Before the Vietnam war, ROTC programs accounted for over 60 percent of all new officers entering the Army, but by the end of the war less than half that number of officers came up through ROTC.

By definition, these university graduates are the young men who possess the highest qualities of leadership and education—the young men the Army needs most. If they continue to defect in such large numbers, the impact on the American Army of the future will be profound—more profound, perhaps, than the abandonment of the draft. In the end, the most lasting legacy of the war in Vietnam may well be this new reluctance of college graduates to volunteer for a military career.

The more thoughtful planners of the new volunteer Army clearly recognize that one of their most difficult tasks in the immediate future will be to attract into the Army young men of high caliber. To restore public confidence in the Army, to heal its war wounds, to regain the pride that has taken such a buffeting in the aftermath of Vietnam, will be the Army's chief mission in the last half of this decade. Melvin Laird, then Secretary of Defense, recognized the problems back in 1970, when he told a graduating class of cadets at West Point, "Never be defensive about your profession, for you have a noble mission and a high calling."

Three years later, the Army is, if anything, even more defensive about its mission. The wave of war weariness that has swept many parts of the United States today threatens to isolate the Army from the mainstream of civilian life and drive its officers inward in resentment or resignation.

As the Army's own magazine put it, of all the calamities that have befallen the United States in the early 1960s, this isolation of the professional officers from the citizenry they serve could prove to be among the most grave.

PART FIVE

Communicators

CHAPTER XII

Newspapers

1. *The Wayward Press*

"A popular government without popular information or the means of acquiring it, is but a prologue to a farce, or a tragedy, or perhaps both."
—PRESIDENT JAMES MADISON, "Father of the Constitution"

"In America the President reigns four years, but journalism rules forever and ever."
—OSCAR WILDE

"Let me control the headlines and I shall not care who controls the editorials."
—FREDERICK T. BURCHALL, New York Times

No country on earth boasts a press as theoretically free and unfettered as the United States. As Supreme Court Justice Felix Frankfurter once pointed out, freedom of expression is the wellspring of American civilization. It has been the protector of the nation's democracy, the guardian of its liberties, the chief safeguard against the abuse of political power. "The basis of the government being the opinion of the people," wrote Thomas Jefferson, "the very first object should be to keep that right: and if it were left to me to decide whether we should have a government without newspapers or newspapers without a government, I should not hesitate for a moment to choose the latter."

In a sense, the United States owes its very existence to those journalists and pamphleteers who two hundred years ago defied the colonial censorship laws in order to give expression to the growing sentiment for independence. Soon afterward, the freedoms they fought for were enshrined in the new nation's Bill of Rights, which guaranteed with direct simplicity that Congress shall make no laws abridging the freedom of speech, or of the press. Ever since, the tradition of a free press has been one of the four cornerstones of American democracy.

The inheritors of that tradition—the reporters, editors, and commentators who staff America's newspapers and television networks today—are privileged as a result to work in the most open society in the world. They grumble, like journalists everywhere, that the real centers of decisionmaking are growing more and more remote, that politicians and officials have recently become more hostile to their probings, that the people's right to know, of which they are the guardians, is being eroded by the vast machinery of modern political news-management, and that under the Nixon Administration they have been forced to engage in a fight to maintain their basic freedoms as intense as any since the Bill of Rights was first ratified. While there is some validity to all of these complaints, it is nevertheless true that the fundamental liberties of the press remain, if not unmolested, at least intact, even under a President who has evinced more hostility towards the newsgatherers than any that has occupied the White House since Herbert Hoover.

Newspapers, said a great editor of the London *Times*, live by disclosure. Judged by that touchstone, American newsmen have established an access to the inner recesses of government decisionmaking—that access which is at the heart of responsible press disclosure—on a scale that leaves their colleagues from other lands gasping with envy. What was the process through which the nation got itself involved in the quagmire of Vietnam? By deep probing, the press finds out—and publishes. The Watergate affair, the massacre at Mylai, the mental-health problems of Senator Thomas Eagleton, the extent of corruption in the New York police department, the President's hostile attitude towards India in the war with Pakistan, the racist background of Supreme Court nominee G. Harrold Carswell, the real effects of the bombing of North Vietnam—all these, and many more, are issues that would probably never have come before the American people had it not been for the probings and disclosures of the press. It is an enviable record.

In the greatest test of their freedoms in a lifetime, the court battle over their right to publish the secret Pentagon history of the American involvement in Vietnam, the newspapers won a famous victory. True, it was marred by the fact that for the first time in its history the government of the United States asked for and was granted an injunction against publication until the case was settled—a precedent of prior restraint that many American journalists believe may have grave implications for the future. But on the fundamental issue of the right to publish, the newspapers won. Neither in Britain, nor in France, nor in any of the other great democracies, could that have happened. Nowhere but in America has the press even sought to establish the right to publish its government's official secrets. And nowhere but in America would that right have been granted.

Because of its protected position under the Constitution, the American press has always seen itself in an adversary relationship to government. From the beginnings of the Republic, Presidents and lesser politicians have complained loudly and often about the treatment they have received at the hands of the newspapers. Thus George Washington, the first President, was once impelled to describe press attacks against him as "outrages on common decency," and from that day to this the relationship has always been an uncomfortable one.

Under President Nixon, the relationship is perhaps more hostile than it has ever been. Nixon's own antipathy toward the press was of course well-known long before he entered the White House, but during his administration coordinated attacks on the integrity and fairness of the press have been raised to the status of high policy. His aides have embarked on a deliberate campaign to discredit the nation's press and television that left newsmen outraged and defensive. Verbal onslaughts by Vice President Agnew have been backed up by open threats and by legal and economic reprisals calculated to intimidate the most influential newspapers and television networks.

"This war on the press goes well beyond that which always exists between any administration and the journalists who write about it," wrote the New York *Times* in a 1972 editorial. According to the *Times,* the relationship between the Nixon Administration and the press could at that time only be described as "dismal." The administration's animus and its aggressive attempts to rein in the press were visible on many different fronts, from its attempts to impose prior restraint in the Pentagon Papers case to the Justice Department's use of its subpoena power to coerce reporters to turn in their private notes. Implicit threats had been made to take legislative action against the television networks, and the President had vetoed funds for public broadcasting and virtually destroyed the White House news conference, an important forum, said the *Times,* "in which reporters used to be able to force a Chief Executive to provide at least a partial accounting to the public of his policies and the motives behind those policies."

The campaign against the news media had begun only a few months after the Nixon Administration had taken office, when Vice President Agnew made his now-famous attacks on the newsmen of the television networks. Taking as his theme "the instant analysis and querulous criticism" by the network commentators after a recent speech on Vietnam by President Nixon, Agnew focused his attention on what he called "this little group of men who not only enjoy a right of instant rebuttal to every Presidential address, but, more importantly, wield a free hand in selecting, presenting and interpreting the great issues of the nation." The American people, said Agnew, would not tolerate this concentration of power in government: "Is it not fair and relevant to question its concentration in the hands of a tiny, enclosed fraternity of privileged men elected by no one and enjoying a monopoly sanctioned and licensed by government?"

The Vice President's speech had been demagoguic and partisan, an amalgam of half truths and resentments, presented under the cover of legitimate criticism with the clear aim of intimidating the bearers of the news. It was simply not true, for example, that the television news programs are "licensed by government." The licenses are granted by the Federal Communications Commission to the owners of the thousands of individual stations. Agnew had also claimed in his speech that when Winston Churchill rallied public opinion against Hitler's Germany "he didn't have to contend with a gaggle of commentators raising doubts about whether he was reading public opinion right, or whether Britain had the stamina to see the war through." Not only was that statement untrue in respect to Britain, it also failed to grasp the more significant truth that it was Hitler rather than Churchill who did not have "a gaggle of commentators" to contend with. But there was just enough justice in Agnew's speech, taken as a whole, to inflame public opinion against the press.

A week after his attacks on the networks, the Vice President was at it again, taking as his target this time the "liberal" eastern press, notably the New York *Times* and the Washington *Post*. "The day when the network commentators and even the gentlemen of the New York *Times* enjoyed a form of diplomatic immunity from comment and criticism of what they said is over," he warned. "Yes, gentlemen, the day is past." Agnew denied that he sought to intimidate the press, but Norman Isaacs, then president of the American Society of Newspaper Editors, disagreed. "It is an attack," he said, "not merely on our mistakes of judgment—and which many of us admit—but on the basic principle of free speech."

Agnew's onslaught, however, had touched a raw nerve in the American people. What most worried the targets of his attacks were not so much the implicit threats they contained ("perhaps it is time the networks were *made* to be more responsive to the views of the nation") as the unhappy realization that many Americans, perhaps even a majority, agreed with Agnew. The Vice President's first speech, carried live on the networks, triggered an avalanche of mail, phone calls, and telegrams. The three networks counted over 150,000 responses to his broadcast; the Vice President's own office received over 75,000. The final tally stood well over 2 to 1 in favor of Agnew. A few months later, when CBS commissioned a public-opinion survey on the constitutional guarantees contained in the Bill of Rights, they found to their alarm that their guaranteed freedoms no longer found majority support among the people polled. Fifty-five percent of the sample said that even in peacetime they would deny the press the right to report any news story "if the government feels that it's harmful to our national interest." For the press, here was shocking evidence that the Vice President had succeeded in shifting the blame for the so-called credibility gap, which had hitherto plagued both the Johnson and Nixon administrations, firmly away from the White House and onto the shoulders of the journalists who reported them. The conclusion, disturbing but irrefutable, was that the American people no longer trusted their sources of news.

That they were unpopular and out of tune with large segments of public opinion had been clear to the press for some years past. There had been an earlier crisis of confidence at the Democratic National Convention in 1968, when the press became the chief target of criticism for Mayor Daley and the actual target of assault by some of his police officers. "Get the man with the camera" and "beat the press" had been the battle cry of Chicago's boys in blue as they went on their rampage through the streets. "Man, the pigs have gone wild," one fleeing demonstrator called to the newsmen covering the riot. "They're not after us; they're after you!" According to the official Walker Report on the riots, a total of forty-nine newsmen were clubbed, gassed, or arrested "apparently without reason" as they went about their job of reporting the news. "The only people who can possibly feel at ease at this convention are those who have been to a hanging," wrote Russell Baker of the New York *Times*. Yet when it was all over, Mayor Daley was blandly able to put the blame for the riot on "press bias" and "biased coverage" on television. And the people believed him. Opinion polls taken soon afterwards showed that the vast majority of people preferred to accept Mayor Daley's version of what had happened on the streets of Chicago and simply to disbelieve what they had seen with their own eyes on television and read in the morning newspapers. It was a classic example of shifting the blame for the events they had provoked from their own shoulders onto those of the journalists who reported them— of executing the messenger carrying bad tidings, as the emperors of Persia were said to have done in an earlier millennium. Or, as Walter Lippmann, perhaps the greatest of all American journalists, wrote back in 1922, "When there is panic in the air, with one crisis tripping over the heels of another, actual dangers mixed with imaginary scares, there is no chance at all for the constructive use of reason, and any order soon seems preferable to any disorder."

Like so many of the other ills that afflict American society today, it all began in Vietnam. As early as 1962, when John Kennedy was still President, a small corps of young newsmen in Saigon began reporting that developments in Vietnam were far graver than the public statements indicated. Kennedy was particularly infuriated with the reporting of David Halberstam of the New York *Times*, whom he once tried to get the *Times* to withdraw. Halberstam's pessimistic accounts of the progress of the war, appearing day after day on the front page of the prestigious *Times*, so outraged Mme. Nhu, the Vietnamese president's sister-in-law, that she announced, "Halberstam should be barbecued, and I would be glad to supply the fuel and the match." Other correspondents, notably Neil Sheehan, then of United Press, and Peter Arnett and Malcolm Browne of the Associated Press, were similarly castigated by officials both in Saigon and Washington for reporting that the South Vietnamese government was on its way to losing the war. Frederick E. Nolting, Jr., a former ambassador to Vietnam, charged that the *Times*'s reporting was partly responsible for the overthrow of the Diem regime and the American escalation and casualties that followed.

Dale Minor, himself a correspondent in Vietnam, reported on the techniques used to discredit the young correspondents who were filing such pessimistic reports from Saigon in the early days of the war:

In Vietnam, in order to discredit reporters' copy, a mass character-assassination campaign is conducted, repeated whenever it is deemed necessary, in which the standard picture looks something like this: American reporters in Saigon are young, immature, inexperienced, and irresponsible. They are infatuated with their own importance and with the importance of their personal opinions. They are lazy, cowardly and clannish. They seldom, if ever, get out of Saigon, and they spend their time in hotel bars lapping up gin-and-tonics and interviewing each other. Their criticism is carping, their judgment uninformed and unsound, their attitudes a product of fashionable cynicism and unconcerned ignorance. They are supercilious, arrogant, rude, and thoughtless. They don't bathe often enough, and they are generally biased against the forces of good. And last, but far from least, they are responsible for all the confusion in the American public about the war and about American policy in Vietnam. They misrepresent, either from incompetence, ill-will, or both, the real situation. They focus on negative trivia at the expense of "the big picture." The credibility gap is all their fault. They are two-bit, half-baked Cassandras who are, on the whole, doing a disservice of almost treasonable proportions to the great American public. In short, they are not "on the team."

The bitterness of the reaction by officials in the American military headquarters in Saigon and in the Johnson White House had to be seen to be believed. "Here come the men from the *Hanoi Times,*" exclaimed one government official in Washington as two reporters from the New York *Times* walked into a conference. Yet who today would claim the young correspondents who reported from Saigon ten years ago were wrong and the officials right? Once again, the bearers of bad tidings, however accurate, were blamed for creating a situation that they simply reflected, as was their duty. In the end, of course, public opinion did swing against sending drafted troops to fight a colonial-style war ten thousand miles away, largely because of the Tet offensive of 1968, which finally broke Johnson's back. But for four whole years before that, the reporters in Saigon ploughed a lonely furrow, fighting sometimes to get their on-the-spot assessments accepted even by their own head offices back in America.

It was not a noble day for American journalism when *Time* wrote a stinging attack on the objectivity of the Saigon press corps, which included two of its own staff members, Charles Mohr and Mert Perry, who felt obliged to resign in protest. And a number of hawkish columnists in the United States, led by Joseph Alsop and Marguerite Higgins, bitterly criticized the Saigon reporters for undermining the American war effort, charging that they were "soft on communism." Later, when Harrison Salisbury of the New York *Times* became the first American newsman to visit Hanoi and reported that, contrary to the impression given by United States communiqués, on-the-spot inspection indicated that American bombing had been inflicting considerable civilian casualties, he was castigated in several other newspapers, who questioned his basic right to report from an enemy capital. It was a difficult moral issue, which split the press just as it had split the people. But as Walter Lippmann wrote:

Mr. Salisbury's offense, we are being told, is that in reporting the war as seen from Hanoi, he has made himself a tool of enemy propaganda. We must remember that in time of war what is said on the enemy's side of the front is always propaganda, and what is said on our side of the front is truth and righteousness, the cause of humanity and a crusade for peace. Is it necessary for us at the height of our power to stoop to such self-deceiving nonsense?

If government communiqués are used to mislead the people, then who is to tell them the truth, if not the press? If their reports contradict each other, who is to decide who is right and who is wrong? To whom does the journalist owe his primary allegiance: to his newspaper, to his government, to his editor, or to the people? Most thoughtful journalists would answer that he owes it to the people. But if the people decide they would rather not know, what then? These are the blood-and-bone issues that the war in Vietnam thrust before American journalism. And though the war is now finally drawing to a close, they are issues that refuse to go away.

If memory serves, it was Will Rogers who once described America as a loose amalgam of forty-eight states, bound together by the *Saturday Evening Post.* It was a statement that says as much about the nature of American journalism as it does about the United States, for although the *Saturday Evening Post* is long since dead, the outstanding characteristic of American newspaper journalism today is still its preponderantly local nature. There is simply no such thing as a national American newspaper, and even the New York *Times* and the *Wall Street Journal* have only tiny circulations away from the main metropolitan area where they are published. As Ben Bagdikian of the Washington *Post* has observed, "We have local papers because our localities control their own schools, police, taxes, highways welfare distribution, and other functions handled in other countries by centralized government. No matter how much we admire the New York *Times*, the *Wall Street Journal*, and the *Christian Science Monitor*, and no matter how quickly they can be delivered in other cities, they cannot tell the local citizen what he needs to know to govern himself intelligently in his own town."

So while television today does provide a genuinely national news service, written journalism is still based on the one-town daily newspaper. And while television has inevitably made considerable inroads, the newspaper genre remains surprisingly healthy. Newspapers are big business, wealthier by far than television, with a total annual income that now exceeds eight billion dollars. Fifty years ago, there were just over 2,000 daily newspapers in circulation throughout the United States; today, that figure has fallen surprisingly little, with well over 1,700 dailies scattered across the country. What is new is that the vast majority of these newspapers today enjoy a local monopoly. Of the 1500 cities with daily newspapers, only 37 have two or more dailies in competition. But this trend towards local monopoly has been more than offset by the huge increase in radio and television outlets and other types of specialized print media that have burgeoned in the past generation. Professor Raymond B. Nixon of the University of Minnesota has pointed out in his study of local journalism, "There can be no doubt that more American communities now have daily access to a far larger volume of information, opinion and entertainment than ever before. The principal media not only compete vigorously with each other: they also supplement and complement each other in a manner that was impossible when newspapers alone were the chief means of mass communication."

The scattered nature of American journalism puts a large burden of responsibility on the two national news agencies, the Associated Press and United Press International, who provide the country's dailies with virtually all of their overseas coverage and the bulk of their news from out of town and the federal capital. Only the most affluent metropolitan dailies can afford to cover the world without the help of the agencies, who spend a staggering amount of money on their news coverage. United Press alone spends about a million dollars every week to cover the news for its five thousand subscribers, with hundreds of correspondents in cities across the United States and around the world filing daily copy on everything from the movements of the President in the White House to the Olympic Games in Munich, the latest word from Moscow to accounts of the street fighting in Belfast or the war in Vietnam.

The agency men are the real workhorses of journalism, and their news judgments set the standards for all but a handful of the news outlets in America, including the nationwide news broadcasts on all three television networks, whose nightly programs are based largely on the work of the agencies. What correspondents such as Roger Mudd or Dan Rather report on the air is their own work, but what Walter Cronkite reads from the studio has normally been compiled from the reports of the Associated Press and United Press International. The men who control the flow of news from the agencies are therefore, in a sense, the most powerful journalists in America, unsung and usually anonymous. However, as Richard L. Tobin has written:

> The most powerful man in the United States is not the President, the Secretary of State, a member of Congress, a Senator, a Governor, the chairman of AT&T, or the head of Harvard University. The most powerful man in the United States is the key man on the general desk of AP or UPI, by whatever name at whatever hour in the twenty-four. For most rip-and-read radio broadcasters (which is to say virtually all the small stations in this country) depend utterly on the competence and integrity of the wire services and their news tickers, and only the very best of our 1,754 daily papers have available to them anything but wire service copy from out of town. The responsibility is an awful one, though less frightening when one realizes that [these are men] of utter integrity and objectivity. . . . Truth is their religion and an informed democracy their goal, whether they would admit it or not. The nation could not function long without them.

Most American journalists would be embarrassed by that description. They like to think of themselves as worldly men, adopting a hard and often cynical approach to a vocation that is neither a profession nor a trade, nor really anything in between. The stereotype appears again and again in novels and films, and even, occasionally, in factual histories of the press. In the opening paragraph of his history of the New York *Times, The Kingdom and the Power,* Gay Talese declares, for instance, that most journalists are "restless voyeurs" who see the warts on the world, the imperfections in people and places. The sane scene that is much of life, the great portion of the planet unmarked by madness, does not lure them like riots and raids, crumbling countries and sinking ships, bankers banished to Rio and burning Buddhist nuns—gloom, he says, is their game, the spectacle their passion, normalcy their nemesis.

There is truth in that description, of course—some truth, but also much that is pure parody. Today, newspaper journalists particularly are questioning as never before the underlying assumptions on which their craft is based. In the pre-McLuhan days, before the medium was the message, the function of the reporter was a simple one: He held up a mirror to an event to reflect its surface. Who? what? when? where? was his code. When he had answered those questions to his satisfaction, he adjourned to the nearest bar and left the editorial writers and columnists to brood over the wider significance of what he had written.

The tradition was well recalled by Ernest Hemingway. "After I finished high school," he once wrote, "I went to Kansas City and worked on a paper. It was regular newspaper work: Who shot whom? Who broke into what? Where? When? How? But never Why, not really Why."

Under the impact of television, these old traditions have to some extent lost their value and lost their meaning. On the national scene, at least, it is television that is today best equipped to reflect the mere surface impression of events. And the more thoughtful newspapermen realize that, partly because of television and partly because of the growing complexity of the world they cover, their own craft is being compelled to change its basic approach to the news. *Why* has for the first time become a respectable question to pose on the front page of their newspapers, no less than in the editorials. It is no longer enough for newspapers to present a straight report that the President has announced he is opposed to school busing or that a dozen people have been killed in a race riot in Newark. Why has the President made his announcement? What are the implications, both political and social? Why did the race riot break out? What are the uderlying social condtions that led people to destroy their own city? More and more, the better American newspapers are basing their reporting on a new, analytical approach to the news, on interpretation and explanation, and above all on *understanding.*

Traditionalists believe they thereby lose their objectivity, that interpretation of the news leads reporters to inject their own personality and their own subjective opinions into their reports. This is to confuse interpretive reporting with the journalism of advocacy, which has also enjoyed a new vogue in recent years. There is all the difference in the world, for instance, between the journalist who reports on the evidence of his own eyes that the U.S. bombing of North Vietnam is both killing civilians and in his judgment proving ineffectual in its stated purpose of destroying the North Vietnamese ability to fight, and the journalist who states that the bombing is immoral as well as ineffective and that the President should be brought to trial for war crimes. One is fact, the other comment. But it is also a fact and good interpretive reporting when the correspondent points out that public announcements to the effect that the United States "has used great restraint in its bombing policy and has not deliberately bombed the North Vietnamese dikes" are based on erroneous logic, if not on downright falsehoods. For, as Anthony Lewis wrote in a dispatch to the New York *Times,* in some parts of North Vietnam the only dry ground runs along the top of the dikes. They carry the roads along which military convoys pass, and sometimes they are the sites for antiaircraft weapons. To claim, as the Pentagon did, that the United States was aiming its bombs at the roads, but not at the dikes which supported them, was to stretch the truth to the point of absurdity. News reports—and there were plenty of them—that simply reported the words of the official spokesman to the effect that "the water conservancy system is not a target in our air efforts supporting South Vietnam's defense against North Vietnam's invasion" were as false for what they left out as they were on the surface true for what they put in.

It is not a simple matter to unravel the truth from the half truths and outright propaganda in which the modern news-managers wrap their public statements, but the effort is now being made by the best American reporters. The underlying principle was well perceived by the late Elmer Davis, head of the Office of War Information during World War II, when he wrote:

> "This kind of dead-pan reporting—so-and-so said it, and if he's lying in his teeth it isn't my business to say so—may salve the conscience of the reporter (or of the editor, who has the ultimate repsonsibility) as to his loyalty to some obscure ideal of objectivity. But what about his loyalty to the reader? The reader lays down his nickel, or whatever, for the paper, in the belief that he is going to find out what is going on in the world; and it does not seem to me that a newspaper is giving him his nickel's worth if it only gives him what somebody says is going on in the world, with no hint as to whether what that somebody says is right or wrong."

That official government spokesmen, Secretaries of State and Defense, and even Presidents do on occasion lie to the press, should come as no surprise to those who have watched the techniques of news management grow under successive administrations. Sometimes they are caught out, as in the now-classic incident during the last year of the Eisenhower Administration when Francis Gary Powers was shot down over the Soviet Union while on a reconnaissance mission in his high-altitude U–2 aircraft. It was only two weeks before the scheduled summit meeting in Paris, and officials were anxious not to rock the diplomatic boat. When the U–2 failed to arrive in Norway after its flight across the Soviet Union from Turkey the story was put out that a weather-reconnaissance plane was missing. At the time, the papers were dominated by news of Princess Margaret's wedding in London, and the story of the missing plane received only secondary emphasis. Four days later, Nikita Khrushchev made a dramatic appearance before the Supreme Soviet to announce that an American "spy plane" had been shot down deep inside Russian airspace.

The State Department, apparently believing that Powers was dead, denied that he had been on a spy mission. They clung to the story that he had been on a weather-reconnaissance flight over Turkey, but suggested he might have lost consciousness due to oxygen failure near the Soviet border. It was possible, therefore, that the plane might have continued to fly automatically into the Soviet Union but, said the State Department spokesman with grave emphasis, "There was absolutely no—*no*—no deliberate attempt to violate Soviet air space." His statement, to put it bluntly, was a barefaced lie, which soon became apparent when the Russians produced not only the wreckage of the aircraft but also the pilot, alive and well after he had parachuted from the U–2 when it was struck by the Soviet missile. Khrushchev demanded an apology, Eisenhower refused, and the Paris summit collapsed. If American officials regretted the lie, it was only because they had been caught out. James Hagerty, Eisenhower's press secretary, was later quoted as saying ruefully, "If there was any mistake in the U–2 affair, it was that we moved too fast on our cover story."

Other incidents, of equal seriousness, have occurred under every President since then. Kennedy attempted to conceal the Bay of Pigs affair, Johnson his intention to escalate the Vietnam War, Nixon his support for Pakistan in the war with India. Such lies, high officials will argue, are the coin of diplomacy; regrettable though they may be, they are indispensable in the conduct of international affairs, where to present the unvarnished truth may compromise America's national security and divert them from their own true high purpose. The argument is plausible, but where does it leave the journalist whose duty it is to uncover the truth of these affairs? It is an awesome responsibility for a reporter to publish facts that the President insists will jeopardize the nation's security. Twice during the 1960s James Reston of the New York *Times* found himself in possession of such information: He had known for over a year that the United States was flying the U–2 over the Soviet Union to photograph its missile bases, and he knew in advance about the planned invasion of the Bay of Pigs. On both occasions, he chose either to not publish or to play down the explosive information he possessed. Over the Bay of Pigs affair, he persuaded the *Times* to tone down its story of the planned invasion of Cuba and to delete all references to the involvement of the Central Intelligence Agency. After the invasion had failed, even President Kennedy was to admit that if the *Times* had published all it knew, the government would have been compelled to cancel the invasion and so avoid a humiliating fiasco.

Reston himself had consulted with Kennedy over the information that the *Times's* reporters had so painstakingly gathered in Miami and Guatemala and had been persuaded that publication would prejudice the success of the invasion. So he advised his editors in New York not to publish. He is later said to have had second thoughts about his decision. According to Gay Talese, debate over whether or not to publish caused a major row among the senior editors at the *Times*, one of whom was said to have become so infuriated with Reston that he quivered with emotion and turned "dead white." Turner Catledge, then executive editor at the *Times*, was also to regret that the paper had not published everything it knew. "Our primary obligation is to our readers," he said. "I wouldn't know how to interpret our obligation to the government."

In his memoirs, Catledge said he thought Reston had allowed his news judgment to be influenced by his patriotism. With the benefit of hindsight, he says, the *Times* might have printed more and, if they had, might have caused a cancellation of the invasion. But then he goes on to ask the questions that must disturb all those who advocate responsible press disclosure: "What if Castro's Cuba had indeed been ripe for 'liberation' by the CIA and the Cuban exiles? Should we then have upset invasion plans?" Catledge suggests that that, again, is the sort of speculation and would-be statesmanship a newspaper editor should avoid. "Our job," he says, "is to print the facts, insofar as we can ascertain them. That is what we did, and I think we have nothing to regret."

While New York can still lay claim to be the communications capital of the United States, with the country's most important newspaper, all three television networks, and the two important national newsmagazines all headquartered there, the real heart of American journalism lies two hundred miles to the south in the steamy climate of Washington. William L. Rivers, author of *The Opinion Makers*, believes that if instead of building the nation's capital on the mudflats of the Potomac the founding fathers had set it down in the turbulent center of a great city, American attitudes towards politics might today be profoundly different. Washington is an inbred city that lives, breathes, and endlessly talks about little but politics. For politicians and those who write about them, no city is more exciting; for those with other passions, no city is so stultifying. "None of the incisive minds who were honored during the Kennedy years of attempting to unite poetry and power lingered longer than it took to have dinner at the White House," wrote Rivers. "The result of intellectual estrangement has been the elevation of the journalist. In other world capitals—which, significantly, are part of the structure of cosmopolitan cities—he must vie with the novelist and the critic in analyzing and interpreting public affairs. In Washington, the journalist wins by default."

The Washington press corps has all the trappings of an élite. Its members are for the most part college-educated, comfortably housed, highly paid (with a median income exceeding twenty thousand dollars a year), and exceedingly pampered. There are seven hundred of them in all, including a hundred foreign correspondents, with a White House corps made up of perhaps a hundred "regulars" who like to think of themselves as the élite of the élite. Special quarters are set aside for them inside the White House, complete with leather armchairs and an atmosphere like that of an exclusive gentlemen's club; chartered aircraft are laid on to carry them wherever the President travels; they perambulate constantly in the shadows of the great; they are the willing recipients of many a whispered secret and the even more willing purveyors of the daily statements of the President, which they receive, spoonfed, on mimeoed sheets from the White House staff. They are summoned by discreet announcements over a public loudspeaker to the President's press secretary's briefings, which take place twice a day, and to the President's own press conferences, which under Mr. Nixon take place once every two months or so, if they are lucky. But so cut off are they from the real workings of the Nixon White House that several of the regulars, after four years, have yet to shake the President's hand. It is perhaps significant that the chief revelations about the administration's involvement in the Watergate affair came not from the resident White House press corps, but from reporters on the ordinary Washington police beat.

Among the White House regulars are some of the keenest and most independent minds in Washington, although there are others who display a herd instinct so strong they will not file a story until they have checked it out with a colleague. They *loathe* being out on a limb, and because they are so closely packed their dispatches inevitably begin to take on the same coloration. A scathing review of their work by John Kenneth Galbraith in *New York* magazine declared:

> Nearly all of our political comment originates in Washington. Washington politicians, after talking things over with each other, relay misinformation to Washington journalists who, after further intramural discussion, print it where it is thoughtfully read by the same politicians. It is the only completely successful closed system for the recycling of garbage that has yet been devised.

Perhaps the most invidious reporting that emanates from Washington is that which results from the briefings by high administration officials, known in the trade as "backgrounders," or even, under Nixon, "deep backgrounders." At its most refined, the technique of the background briefing is to produce

Henry Kissinger, or whoever, before a closed meeting of the White House press corps to give a detailed account of the administration's policies that the correspondents are then free to publish as their own—provided they do not identify the source. It is a form of compulsory plagiarism that leads a score of virtually identical stories to crop up in the next day's papers containing the identical facts, which the mystified reader is left to assume were independently excavated by the correspondents under whose bylines the stories appeared.

Some correspondents argue that the background briefing is an essential part of modern news-collection and that without it they would be deprived altogether of their insights into the thinking of high administrative aides like Kissinger. That is true, as far as it goes, and that the background briefing does have its uses is of course undeniable. But too often the briefings are used not to inform, but to mislead. That happened in 1971 during the Indo-Pakistan war, when Kissinger told the press corps one thing while privately pursuing another. What he told the press was dutifully recorded, without attribution, and the public was misled, quite deliberately, about the administration's actions. It was only when the minutes of the secret meetings came to light that the press realized just how badly they, and the American people, had been lied to.

The press learned a lesson from that episode, and as a result their skepticism deepened. But still the cozy relationship continues, a little more mistrustful now than it was, but essentially unchanged. Some of the more thoughtful correspondents, however, are disturbed at the deception they are forced to practice on their readers. Bill Moyers, who in his time has been both a distinguished journalist and a former press aide to President Johnson, and who therefore knows a thing or two about planting what he calls the "official version of reality," believes the indiscriminate use of backgrounders as a source of hard news causes harm and creates an unbelieving and untrusting public. It has become too easy, he writes, for public officials to use the backgrounder as a primary instrument of policy, propaganda, and manipulation, based on the principle that "the interests of national security dictate that the lie I am about to tell you not be attributed to me."

The main problem is that reporters thus wittingly become a party to the kind of doubledealing and concealment the press so often condemns on the part of government. But Moyers believes there is little hope for change. The government will go on calling backgrounders as long as it wants to put its best face forward and, writes Moyers, "Reporters will be there to report dutifully what isn't officially said by a source that can't be held officially accountable at an event that doesn't officially happen for a public that can't officially be told because it can't officially be trusted to know." But, he concludes, "don't quote me on that."

Just how absurd the official deception can be was well illustrated during President Nixon's summit meeting in Bermuda with Edward Heath, the

British prime minister. The Downing Street press corps, known in Britain as the lobby, had gathered with a few of their American colleagues to be fed their daily account of what the two leaders had discussed by Donald Maitland, the prime minister's press secretary. The rules of the meeting were the normal ones: Nothing that was about to be disclosed was to be attributed directly or indirectly to any official, British or American, and all the facts that were provided were to appear in their newspapers as if divinely inspired on the brows of the individual correspondents. Maitland was well into his secret briefing when a local cameraman stumbled into their meeting and began taking photographs of the assembled correspondents. This went on for a while until Maitland noticed what was happening and turned towards the photographer to ask in his precise Scots accent, "Excuse me, what is that you are doing?"

"Taking pictures for the local paper," replied the enterprising but now-embarrassed photographer.

"Oh, but you *can't*," Maitland told him. "You see—this actually isn't happening. We are not here."

It was meant humorously, but who, one wonders, was deceiving whom?

2. Pentagon Papers

"The only way to assert the right to publish is to publish."
—BEN BAGDIKIAN, *Washington* Post, *1971*

The affair over the Pentagon Papers began quietly that Sunday morning in June 1971. John Mitchell, then Attorney General, went to the door of his Watergate apartment in Washington to pick up the four-hundred-odd pages of the New York *Times*, its front page that Sunday dominated by a picture of Tricia Nixon, the President's elder daughter, and her bridegroom, Edward Cox, who had been married in a ceremony at the White House the previous day, a ceremony Mitchell and his wife had attended. It is not unreasonable to suppose they first read the account of the wedding before going on to digest the copy that appeared below an unsensational three-column heading, also on the front page, that read: VIETNAM ARCHIVE: PENTAGON STUDY TRACES 3 DECADES OF GROWING U.S. INVOLVEMENT.

It was Mitchell's first inkling of a story that was destined to lead to the biggest clash in a lifetime between the press on the one hand and the government on the other, with Mitchell himself leading the administration's assault on the press's right to publish the secret Pentagon documents.

Reaction that first Sunday morning was surprisingly muted. Mitchell received a call from the Defense Secretary, Melvin Laird, who was about to appear on the CBS program *Face the Nation.* He too had read the *Times*'s story and felt certain he would be asked about its disclosures on the TV program. What was he to say? Mitchell advised him to tell them the matter had been referred to the Justice Department. Incredibly, though, Laird was spared that embarrassment. Facing a panel of two correspondents from CBS and one from the New York *Times,* Laird was not asked a single question about the Pentagon Papers during the entire half-hour program. The same apparent lack of interest was displayed in the rest of the press. The Associated Press, which services over 1,200 newspapers and 3,000 television and radio stations throughout America, carried not a word. UPI put out its first story on Sunday afternoon, although its editors had received their first copies of the *Times* the previous evening. Of the three television networks, only NBC made any reference at all to the disclosures, and the two main newsmagazines, *Time* and *Newsweek,* which appear on the newsstands on Monday mornings, decided the news was not important enough to warrant any last-minute changes in make-up.

Thus one of the greatest newspaper scoops of all time arrived in the world with all the explosive power of a damp squib. The *Times* itself was partly responsible for that. It had led off its series with a generally unsensational report, carried under a mild headline, and had prepared the reports under a shroud of secrecy that would have done credit to the CIA, so that most of its own staff members did not learn about the story until they read it in the paper. Still, the *Times* had clearly not expected its coup to fall into such an echoing void as this. Max Frankel, the Washington bureau chief, had manned his office all day that Sunday waiting for the expected "quick government response," but it never came.

Mitchell, although he had been alerted to the story by Laird, did nothing all day, and on Sunday night the *Times* published its second massive installment of the secret papers. This time, however, as bureaucratic Washington recovered from its weekend sleepiness, the story did not go unchallenged. Conferences were urgently summoned at the Justice Department, the Pentagon was asked to furnish a memorandum on the security aspects of the *Times's* publication, and at about seven o'clock that night, just two hours before the deadline for the next edition, the decision was taken to ask the *Times* to desist. In the absence of the publisher, Arthur Ochs "Punch" Sulzberger, who was in Europe, the Justice Department phoned through a cable from Mitchell to Harding Bancroft, one of Sulzberger's top aides and himself a former diplomat. Its tone was unmistakable:

> I have been advised by the Secretary of Defense that the material published in the New York *Times* on June 13, 14, 1971, captioned "Key Texts From Pentagon's Vietnam Study," contains information relating to the national defense of the United States and bears a top-secret classification. As such, publication of this information is directly prohibited by the provisions of the Espionage Law, Title 18, United States Code, Section 793. Moreover, further publication of information of this character will cause irreparable injury to the defense interests of the United States. Accordingly, I respectfully request that you publish no further information of this character and advise me that you have made arrangements for the return of these documents to the Department of Defense.

Receipt of the message apparently caused a major argument up on the executive floor of the *Times's* offices in New York. According to Sanford Ungar's well-documented account of the affair, Sydney Gruson, special assistant to the publisher, and Abe Rosenthal, the newspaper's managing editor, were said to be "screaming and yelling at each other. It was just like a movie." Gruson was arguing for suspension of the series on the ground that nothing more could be gained by further provoking the administration, a suggestion that sent Rosenthal into a frenzy. Finally, the publisher was roused from his bed at the Savoy Hotel in London and asked to make the final decision. James Goodale, head of the *Times*'s legal department, was put on the line. "We cannot afford for the future of this newspaper to stop publication now," he told Sulzberger. "It would be terrible." Sulzberger agreed and gave orders for the series to go ahead. A telegram was sent off to the Justice Department stating that "The *Times* must respectfully decline the request of the Attorney General, believing it is in the interests of the people of this country to be informed of the material contained in this series of articles." Not long afterwards, the presses began to roll with the third story in its series: "Vietnam Archive: Study Tells How Johnson Secretly Opened Way to Ground Combat." In a foretaste of the way the emphasis was already beginning to shift away from the content of the Vietnam archives onto the right of the newspapers to publish them, the *Times* report that day was overshadowed by an even larger headline carrying the news of the paper's own fight with the Justice Department: MITCHELL SEEKS TO HALT SERIES ON VIETNAM BUT TIMES REFUSES.

Thus the battle was joined. "Think what it would have meant in our history and in the history of the newspaper business," Rosenthal said later, "if the headline had been, 'Justice Department Asks End to Vietnam Series and Times Concedes.' I think it would have changed the history of the newspaper business."

In the space of three days, the *Times* had taken three decisions which were indeed to change the history of the American newspaper business : to publish the story, to publish the documents on which they were based, to refuse to accept the Attorney General's demand to cease publication. A year afterwards, when the dust was just beginning to settle, Abe Rosenthal wrote his own assessment of the impact on the *Times* of those three brave decisions that were to win the paper a Pulitzer Prize:

> The essence is this: Three times the reporters, editors, executives of the Times had placed before them, in one big bundle that simply would not go away, all those blood-and-bone issues that people spend lifetimes evading.
> In the bundle were the meaning of true patriotism and national interest; the meaning and purpose of a profession, a lifetime; the meaning, duties, obligations of a free press; fear for self, for career, for the future of a newspaper; the need to see clearly what was judgment, what was ego, what was morality. As somebody said, except for sex, there it all was.

The bundle of blood-and-bone issues that Rosenthal so eloquently wrote about had dropped into the *Times*'s lap three months earlier when Daniel Ellsberg, a former government employee who had himself helped to prepare the study, handed over to Neil Sheehan of the *Times* Washington bureau an enormous bundle of Xeroxed copies of government documents: the Pentagon Papers. Their contents are by now well-known: a documented study of the growing involvement in Vietnam, the inside story of how President after President, from Truman through to Johnson, slowly entangled himself in the war in Vietnam—first in a guerrilla war, then in a major ground war in the South, and finally in the aerial war over the North. And at each step of the way, the government's true purposes were concealed from the public.

Ellsberg himself had been an early hawk in the war, had voluntarily gone on ground combat missions there, but as the war dragged on he had become completely disillusioned with the American purpose. Perhaps the key to Ellsberg's decision to leak the Pentagon study to the press was his rejection of the widely accepted theory that the United States had stumbled unknowingly into a "quagmire" in Vietnam. On the contrary, Ellsberg believed, each successive American President was "striding with his eyes open into what he *sees* as quicksand, renewing efforts and carrying his followers deeper in, knowingly." Whatever his true motives, Ellsberg was so disillusioned by September 1969 that with a few assistants, he secretly ran off Xerox copies of thousands of pages of the Pentagon study, covering over the Top Secret markings on some of the pages before putting them through the machine. At first, he apparently intended to show them only to "authorized people" like Senator William Fulbright, chairman of the Foreign Relations Committee, and Senator George McGovern, who was already indicating his intention to run again for the Presidency. When that course failed to get the publicity he sought, Ellsberg turned instead to the New York *Times*, picking out Sheehan as his chosen receptacle for the documents apparently on the basis of an antiwar review Sheehan had recently written for the *Times* book section, in which he had concluded that "the leaders of the United States, including the incumbent President, Richard Milhous Nixon, may well be guilty of war crimes."

Ten years earlier, Sheehan had been one of the young trio of reporters whose dispatches from Saigon had so infuriated President Kennedy. A pugnacious Irish-American, he had a rather abrasive reputation at the *Times*, and his article in the book review section was thought by some to have damaged his reputation for objectivity. It was natural, therefore, that when he presented his scoop to his superiors there was concern at first about its authenticity and about the reliability of its source. But once they had examined some of the documents for themselves, the *Times* executives were won over. "Because I had been intimately involved in covering that same stuff myself," Max Frankel told Sanford Ungar, "I was able very quickly to reach the judgment that it was fair, it was not grinding too many axes, it was not just a bunch of Vietnam doves sounding off or anything like that. . . . I remember saying to Neil very early on that 'if this is the quality of most of the thing, it's a gold mine.' He thought it was."

Even though the authenticity of the documents had now been thoroughly established, the top brass at the *Times* had some of its most agonizing decisions still to resolve—those "blood-and-bone" issues that as Rosenthal rightly said simply would not go away. Should the papers be published in a consecutive series, as its editors wished, or in a huge one-day package, which the lawyers argued would at least prevent the government from issuing any request for prior restraint on publication? More important, perhaps, should the *Times* publish the actual documents or simply the news summaries it had based upon them? Several of the publisher's top aides were known to believe it would be irresponsible to publish the documents in their entirety; there was military security to consider; codes might be broken; America's allies might be compromised. Against this, the editors, led by James Reston, argued that the documents were an integral part of the study. Without them, rumors and speculations would build up. Ghosts would be created in people's minds: What great secrets were being concealed? Why was the *Times* afraid to publish them? And beyond that, they believed, they had a responsibility to their readers to give the full flavor and tone of the great internal debate within the government on the conduct of the war in Vietnam.

Then there were the more abstract moral issues to consider. How could the *Times* justify publishing "stolen" documents? What godgiven right—which some called arrogance—did the editors of the *Times* have to unilaterally declassify government secrets? Does the freedom of the press have its limits, and if so, what are they, and who decides them?

After prolonged debate, the editors arrived at the conclusion that to publish would be entirely within the law. From the beginning, they had agreed that they were prepared to support a test case in the courts, but that they would not defy the courts' decisions. They did not believe their constitutional freedoms meant they were simply free to publish what the government decided it would allow them to publish; they meant, on the contrary, that the only way to establish the right to publish was to publish. Perhaps, as they pondered their decision, the dictum of John Wilkes, the great English champion of press freedom, came to mind. Asked by a French visitor how far liberty of the press extended in England, Wilkes had replied, "I cannot tell, but I am trying to find out." That was the spirit in which, two hundred years later, the editors of the New York *Times* approached the great decisions that lay before them.

As to the charge that the documents were stolen, Rosenthal replied, "We are dealing with decisions made in government that affect the people. Can you steal a decision that was made three years ago and that has caused consequences that a country now pays for, good or bad? How can you steal a decision like that? How can you steal the mental processes of elected officials or appointed officials?" Thus the *Times* arrived at its three brave decisions: to publish the story, to publish the documents, to split them into a ten-part series that would court government intervention.

Once its decisions had been taken, the *Times* mounted one of the most massive technical operations in the history of journalism. Altogether some seventy-five employees took part in the colossal, months-long task of sifting through the papers, checking each document against the facts that had been printed at the time, analyzing the historical background against which they took place, tracing each episode as it developed, putting each into its correct perspective. It was, as Abe Rosenthal later pointed out, a great intellectual achievement, heightened by the intense time pressures under which the team was compelled to work. To ensure complete secrecy, the *Times* eventually took over nine rooms in the Hilton Hotel in New York, equipped with typewriters, filing cabinets, a library of books, and two safes in which they kept the documents. When other members of the staff asked where their missing colleagues had gone, they were told, "Don't ask." The team worked twelve to fifteen hours a day on the project, not always harmoniously, and there were said to have been several wild quarrels in the confined space in which they worked. But secrecy had been maintained, and no one got wind of what they were up to.

As the 13 June deadline approached, a make-up man was seconded to the team at the Hilton to arrange the layout of the reports, which were set in type in a special composing room, with each typesetter sworn to silence. All along, the *Times* editors had feared that one of the newspaper's rivals—the Washington *Post*, perhaps, or the Los Angeles *Times*—would learn of their project, and maybe even obtain copies of their own of the Pentagon Papers. But, as it was, the *Times* maintained its shroud of secrecy so well that its great coup reached the newsstands without so much as a whisper reaching the outside world. Even Daniel Ellsberg learned that the papers had finally been published only when he received his copy of the *Times* at his home in Cambridge, Massachusetts, that Sunday morning.

For three consecutive days, those readers of the *Times* with the stamina and the interest to read through the closely packed pages of documents were treated to rare insights into the methods, the manner, the planning processes, and the intellectual assumptions that had led their country into the most divisive war in its history. That there were serious flaws in the Pentagon study was admitted even by those who had compiled it. There was, for instance, no detailed account of the mental processes of the successive Presidents who had to make the final decisions; the Pentagon researchers had not had completely open access to the files of the Joint Chiefs of Staff; there were no minutes of the National Security Council meetings; nor did the study include transcriptions of the telephone calls on which some of the most crucial decisions had been based. Incomplete though it may have been, however, the study revealed in damning detail the processes through which the Vietnam decisions had been arrived at—and the manner in which their true purpose had been consistently concealed from the American public. As Daniel Ellsberg said, "To see the conflict and our part in it as a tragedy without a villain, war crimes without criminals, lies without liars, espouses and promulgates a view of the processes, roles and motives that is not only grossly mistaken but which underwrites deceits that have served a succession of Presidents." Now, for all the world to see, here they were: the liars, the villains, the honestly misguided men, the baffled leaders, their mistakes and miscalculations exposed by the most massive leak of government documents in American history.

But on the fourth day, it abruptly ended. The previous afternoon, the *Times* had been hauled into court by the Justice Department to answer allegations that the articles it had already published had "prejudiced the defense interests of the United States" and that those still to come would result in "irreparable injury" to the country. U.S. District Judge Murray I. Gurfein, who was serving his very first day on the bench, granted the government's request for a restraining order until a full hearing could be held later in the week. "Any temporary harm that may result from not publishing during the pendancy of the application for a preliminary injunction is far outweighed by the irreparable harm that could be done to the interests of the United States government if it should ultimately prevail," he ruled. For the first time in American history a newspaper was thus faced with a prior restraint on publication. It was, said the *Times* in an editorial the next morning, "an unprecedented example of censorship." But, as it had promised all along, it dutifully agreed to abide by the court's decision.

If the *Times* was upset at the court's ruling, Daniel Ellsberg was furious. However, as Sanford Ungar reported, his anger was not directed so much at the Justice Department as at the *Times*. "He felt strongly," said Ungar, "that for the Papers to have maximum impact a newspaper had to be willing to defy an injunction against publication, at least for a day or two, even at the risk of being found in contempt of court; Ellsberg had told two U.S. senators that they ought to be willing to go to jail to end the war, and he had no difficulty in extending that principle to cover the publisher of a newspaper." Believing that the *Times* had let him down, Ellsberg sought new outlets for his documents. He turned first to the television networks, but they were feeling especially timid in the aftermath of Agnew's attacks on their objectivity and turned Ellsberg's offer down flat. Eventually he made contact with the Washington *Post* and later with a series of other newspapers so that new extracts from the documents began cropping up in cities across he country. The Washington *Post* ran its first story on Friday, June 18, but after protracted legal wrangling in the courts, it too was proscribed from publishing further installments pending a final decision by the courts.

There was a curious incidental episode in the midst of the *Post*'s involvement with the courts when two reporters were dispatched to the home of Chief Justice Warren Burger, whom the *Post* believed might act in an emergency basis in his capacity as circuit judge for the District of Columbia, where the *Post* is published. The two reporters were given the assignment of finding out whether Justice Department emissaries had arrived at Burger's home to seek a legal stay that would prevent the *Post* from publishing its next planned installment on the papers. Failing to get an answer on the Chief Justice's telephone, the two reporters rang his front doorbell—and faced on the doorstep the astonishing sight of Burger in a bathrobe carrying a long-barreled steel gun. "The Chief Justice did not seem glad to see us," one of the reporters said later when he recounted the episode to his editor. The *Post* toyed for a while with the idea of carrying a report on the encounter, but prudence prevailed and the story was killed. Sooner or later, the *Post*'s executives felt the Pentagon Papers case was bound to be brought before the Supreme Court, and they felt no urge to complicate their case needlessly.

Back at the New York *Times*, the forays of other newspapers into the Pentagon Papers affair was viewed with mixed emotions. Journalism is a competitive business, and the Times, after all, had just brought off an historic scoop. Now here they were, prohibited from publishing it by the courts, while their rivals were beginning to catch up. It was only natural that they should feel discriminated against. Finally, however, the Justice Department spread its net to the other papers that had begun to publish extracts from the Pentagon study: the Washington *Post*, the Boston *Globe*, and the Chicago *Sun-Times*, which had also, in the words of the Attorney General, now "got into the act." By the end of the week, the *Post*, too, was proscribed from publishing further installments from the Papers. It was now up to the courts to resolve the issue.

The first test came in Judge Gurfein's court in New York, where Whitney North Seymour, for the government, argued that the issue was a very simple one: "whether when an unauthorized person comes into possession of documents which have been classified under lawful procedures, that person may unilaterally declassify these documents in his sole discretion." The *Times* had all along based its case on the argument that it did have that right; the government's case, it felt, was too simplistic, and the newspaper submitted fifteen affidavits to the court to show that classified material was used regularly by the newspapers. The most eloquent argument to this effect was presented by Max Frankel, chief of the Washington bureau of the *Times*, who told the court that regular daily articles prepared by his bureau were a combination of known facts, prised-out secrets, and deliberate disclosures of secrets. "They are recognized within the profession and among readers as the most valuable kind of journalism," he said, "and have *never* been shown to cause 'irreparable harm' to the national security."

"Without the use of 'secrets,'" Frankel contended, "there could be no adequate diplomatic, military, and political reporting of the kind our people take for granted, either abroad or in Washington, and there could be no mature system of communication between the government and the people."

The relationship between a small and specialized corps of reporters and a few hundred American officials on which this kind of reporting was based, while it often mystified even experienced professionals, was essential to the practice of responsible journalism. The government's complaint against the *Times* therefore came, in Frankel's view, "with ill grace," because government itself had regularly and consistently, over the decades, violated the conditions it now suddenly sought to impose on the press. The sudden complaint by one party to those dealings struck him as "monstrous and hypocritical"—unless, he wondered, it was essentially perfunctory, for the purpose of retaining some discipline over the federal bureaucracy.

As it developed, Frankel's affidavit gave a rare and fascinating insight into the mysterious workings of the Washington press corps and the philosophy that lay behind it. Journalists, who work all their lives with concrete facts, are not normally given to philosophizing about the abstract principles on which their profession is based. Perhaps one of the most valuable side-effects of the Pentagon Papers affair was the way in which they were now forced to articulate their fundamental tenets—tenets that most of them, as practical men, had hitherto only half-consciously pondered. Now, in court, one of its most experienced practitioners put into words the creed on which he had based his professional life.

The heart of Frankel's argument was that everything the American government does, plans, thinks, hears, and contemplates in the realms of foreign policy is stamped and treated as secret—and then unraveled by that same government, by the Congress, and by the press in one continuing round of professional and social contacts, and of cooperative and competitive exchanges of information:

> The governmental, political and personal interests of the participants are inseparable in the process. Presidents make "secret" decisions only to reveal them for the purposes of frightening an adversary nation, wooing a friendly electorate, protecting their reputations. The military services conduct "secret" research in weaponry only to reveal it for the purpose of enhancing their budgets, appearing superior or inferior to a foreign army, gaining the vote of a congressman or the favor of a contractor. The Navy uses secret information to run down the weaponry of the Air Force. The Army passes on secret information to prove its superiority to the Marine Corps. High officials of the Government reveal secrets in the search for support of their policies, or to help sabotage the plans and policies of rival departments. Middle-rank officials of government reveal secrets so as to attract the attention of their superiors or to lobby against the orders of those superiors. Though not the only vehicle for this traffic in secrets—the Congress is always eager to provide a forum—the press is probably the most important.

Frankel disclosed a few of the countless occasions on which he himself had been made privy to government secrets: when President Kennedy, at the height of the Cuban missile crisis, had provided him with a transcript of his conversations with Andrei Gromyko, the Soviet foreign minister; when President Johnson, standing waist-deep in his Texas swimming pool, had recounted his confidential discussions with Prime Minister Kosygin at Glassboro; when Dean Rusk told him that Laos was not worth the life of a single Kansas farmboy, and that the SEATO treaty, which Rusk later invoked so elaborately in defense of the intervention in Vietnam, was a useless instrument. Similar dealings, said Frankel, continue to this day. Their purpose was not to amuse or flatter a reporter, but variously to impress him with their stewardship of the country, to solicit specific publicity, to push out diplomatically useful information without official responsibility and, occasionally, even to explain and illustrate a policy that can be publicly described in only the vaguest terms. "This," he concluded, "is the coin of our business and of the officials with whom we regularly deal." Some of the best examples of the regular traffic in secrets he had so elaborately described were to be found in the Pentagon Papers. To urge, as the Attorney General had done, that the press publish "no further information of this character" was in effect to tell reporters to stop doing their job.

Rarely indeed had the general public been offered such a frank and open disclosure of the procedures through which much of the information they read in their newspapers finds its way into print.

A day later, after working on his opinion through the night, Gurfein delivered a verdict that substantially supported the position taken by the *Times*. While security agents and some foreign governments might have been given "the jitters" over publication of the Papers, Gurfein said, no cogent reasons were advanced to show why the documents vitally affected the security of the nation. At most, they had caused embarrassment. The Constitution did not merely protect the opinions of the editorial writer or the columnist; it also protected the free flow of information which informs the public about the government and its actions.

"The security of the Nation is not at the ramparts alone," Gurfein declared. "Security also lies in the value of our free institutions. A cantankerous press, an obstinate press, a ubiquitous press must be suffered by those in authority in order to preserve the even greater values of freedom of expression and the right of the people to know. . . ."

"These are troubled times," the judge went on. "There is no greater safety valve for discontent and cynicism about the affairs of government than freedom of expression in any form. This has been the genius of our institutions throughout their history. It is one of the marked traits of our national life that distinguish us from other nations under different forms of government."

For Mitchell and his lawyers at the Department of Justice, the portents were not good. Although it was overturned on appeal, so that for the moment the prohibition continued, Gurfein's ruling had clearly tipped the scales in favor of the press and the preservation of its right to publish. At the same time,

the confrontation between the newspapers and the administration had become the burning issue before the country, bigger now by far than the issues
contained in the Papers themselves, which the editors of the *Times* had fought
so hard to bring before the people.

The following week, the *Times* petitioned the Supreme Court for a review
of the affair, merging its case with that of the Washington *Post*, and demanding an immediate hearing to resolve the great constitutional issues that had
been presented. The Supreme Court was at this time in a state of hiatus:
Warren Burger had taken over the Chief Justiceship from Earl Warren but,
perhaps luckily for the newspapers, the Court still retained the liberal majority
that had made its recent rulings so obnoxious to the conservative administration. Only a year later, the Court was to have more conservative cast, but as
the Pentagon Papers case went before it, there were still four sure liberals
among its nine members, as well as three conservatives (including two appointed by President Nixon) and two, Justices Potter Stewart and Byron
White, who were thought to hold the balance. It is another of the ironies of
this famous case that had the Supreme Court hearings come only twelve
months later the balance of the Court would have shifted to the hardline
conservatives, and the outcome would in all probability have been profoundly
different—for the press, for the government, for the country, and doubtless
for the Court itself.

The Justices could not have known it at the time, but the Pentagon Papers
case was the very last to be heard by a Court that still retained a bare liberal
majority. Before its next term began, both Justices Black and Harlan were to
resign under the shadow of terminal illness, to be replaced by two out-and-out
conservatives nominated by Nixon. As it was, the Court was already the
subject of unprecedented controversy, caused by the failure of the President
to secure the nomination of Judges Clement Haynsworth and G. Harrold
Carswell to the High Court, while Burger, the new Chief Justice, had himself
become a controversial political figure.

Burger, as his encounter with the two reporters from the Washington *Post*
had perhaps indicated, had no love for the press. Only a month before the
hearings on the Pentagon Papers he had suggested in a Washington speech
that the news media were largely to blame for what he called "the end of
rational thought process" in America. When the hearings on the Papers
began, his hostility toward the press was manifest. During the oral arguments,
he searchingly questioned the lawyers for the newspapers on what he saw as
an attempt by the press to set up a double standard of conduct—one set of
principles for themselves, another for the government. There was on one
hand, he said, a firm claim made by newspapers that the Constitution forbade
them to reveal their own sources, even by a grand jury investigating criminal
matters, because otherwise those sources would dry up, while on the other
hand they denied that same right to the government: "You say the newspaper
has a right to protect its sources, while the government does not."

It was an argument that disturbed many newspapermen. But the parallel was not exact. When Daniel Ellsberg was revealed as the source of the *Times*'s revelations, its lawyers did not seek to suppress that news, and in the case now before the Supreme Court, the newspapers did not seek to *compel* the government to release its secret documents, but rather to assert their right to publish facts which its own investigative reporting had uncovered. Burger's argument was in fact an extremely simplistic one; the shoe he sought to thrust onto the foot of the newspapers just did not fit.

Burger also protested against the "unseemly haste" in which the case had been conducted. In his dissenting opinion, published later, the Chief Justice castigated the *Times* for what he called "the frenetic haste" in which it had proceeded, and spoke sarcastically of its claim to assert sole trusteeship of the public's right to know on the virtue of a journalistic scoop: "The consequences of all this melancholy series of events is that we literally do not know what we are acting on." Would it have been unreasonable, he asked, for the *Times* to have given the government the opportunity to review the entire collection of documents and determine whether agreement could be reached on publication?

In the atmosphere that had surrounded the *Times*'s acquisition of the papers, that again was scarcely a realistic suggestion. Was the *Times* to go hat-in-hand to the White House each time it uncovered a fact which might be displeasing to the government? Such a course, in the opinion of most journalists, would be tantamount to giving the government the right of prior restraint that went against all the traditions of free journalism. But the Chief Justice had more to say: "To me it is hardly believable that a newspaper long regarded as a great institution in American life would fail to perform one of the basic and simple duties of every citizen with respect to the discovery or possession of stolen property or secret government documents. That duty, I had thought—perhaps naively—was to report forthwith to responsible public officers. This duty rests on taxi drivers, Justices and the New York *Times.*"

It was the old argument of authoritarianism versus liberty, of the *Times*'s urgent desire to lift an unprecedented ban on publication versus the Chief Justice's wishes for "orderly litigation." But Burger possessed only one vote out of nine, and, proving once again the truth of Chief Justice Hughes's famous aphorism that "the Constitution is what the lawyers say it is," the Court as it was then constituted returned a decision in favour of the press by a count of 6 to 3. The press had won a famous victory.

It was a measure of the widely differing views on the principles involved that the nine Justices produced nine separate opinions on the case. Among those in the majority, Justice Black stood most firmly for a strict interpretation of the Constitution. "I believe that every moment's continuance of the injunctions against these newspapers amounts to a flagrant, indefensible, and continuing violation of the First Amendment," he declared. "For the first time in the 182 years since the founding of the Republic, the federal courts are asked to hold that the First Amendment does not mean what it says, but rather means that the government can halt the publication of current news of vital importance to the people of this country."

Under the protection given by the Founding Fathers, said Justice Black, "the press was to serve the governed, not the governors. . . . The press was protected so that it could bare the secrets of government and inform the people. Only a free and unrestrained press can effectively expose deception in government. And paramount among the responsibilities of a free press is the duty to prevent any part of the government from deceiving the people and sending them off to distant lands to die of foreign fevers and foreign shot and shell. In my view, far from deserving condemnation for their courageous reporting, the New York *Times*, the Washington *Post* and other newspapers should be commended for serving the purpose that the Founding Fathers saw so clearly. In revealing the workings of government that led to the Vietnam war, the newspapers nobly did precisely that which the Founders hoped and trusted they would do."

There was rejoicing at the *Times* and at the *Post* and at newspapers across the country when news of their victory was flashed down the news agency wires on the afternoon of 30 June, just seventeen days after the first install-ment of the documents had appeared in the columns of the *Times*, and only a bare two weeks after the first prohibition on publication had been ordered. At the *Times*, a jubilant wireroom assistant ripped the first flash from the news ticker and ran into the newsroom shouting, "We won!" Sulzberger and Rosen-thal hugged one another. "We won it!" Rosenthal exclaimed. "We've won it all. We've won the right to print." Next morning, the *Times* carried a huge triple-decker headline of the size the normally sober newspaper reserves for only the most momentous occasions:

SUPREME COURT, 6–3, UPHOLDS NEWSPAPERS
ON PUBLICATION OF THE PENTAGON REPORT;
TIMES RESUMES ITS SERIES, HALTED 15 DAYS

When the euphoria wore off, however, and newspapermen began to analyze the effects of the battle they had won, they were to make a more sober assessment of the impact of their victory. Prior restraint—death to a free press —now had a precedent; for while the Justice Department had lost the overall argument, it had emphatically proved it *could* obtain a prohibition on publica-tion while a case was being reviewed in the courts. And in the rapidly shifting mood of the Supreme Court, there was no guarantee that the press would win a second victory there. There could also be no doubt that the controversy had damaged the always-delicate relationship between the press and the govern-ment; with the Nixon Administration in power, the breach was in some areas now total.

For the government, too, the case presented some grave dilemmas. As *Time* declared in the week the Court delivered its opinion:

> The fact that for the first time, the difference had to be resolved by the Supreme Court indicates a breach that threatens the orderly processes of a democratic society. Regardless of the legal issues, the newspapers saw a higher morality in exposing the secret history of decisions that had led to a dangerously unpopular public policy. Appeal to a higher morality by an individual or an organization is often necessary —and always dangerous. No government of law can passively permit it—or simply repress it. Therein lies the administration's dilemma. There may be too many Daniel Ellsbergs in the U.S. now for a President to ignore their will.

The hostility shown towards the press by some members of the Supreme Court also carried ominous portents for the future. In 1971, the press won; but could it win again in 1972—or 1975? There were many who doubted it. Within a year of the Pentagon Papers case, Burger had been joined on the bench by two other Justices with an authoritarian cast of mind: Justices Lewis Powell and William Rehnquist. Black and Harlan were dead, and there were serious doubts about the health of Justices Douglas and Marshall, both of whom voted against the government in the Pentagon Papers hearing. Before President Nixon's second term is over, it seems probable that he will have obtained a conservative majority on the bench, which has been his aim ever since he entered the White House. Norman Isaacs, past President of the American Society of Newspaper Editors, voiced the fears of many newsmen when he wrote, "Given a six- or seven-justice majority, a Nixon Court can apply a straitjacket that can inhibit, if not immobilize, news coverage for a generation, if not longer."

The way the tide was running became clear almost exactly a year to the day after it passed down its historic ruling, when the Supreme Court was called upon to make a further judgment on reporters' privileges guaranteed in the First Amendment. The issue on this occasion was the right of a newsman to withhold information obtained in confidence from his sources—the heart of his ability to put before the people what is going on.

A black New York *Times* reporter called Earl Caldwell had won the confidence of Black Panther leaders on the West Coast and, based on the confidential information they gave him, had written a series of articles on the movement. On the evidence of his published reports, he was summoned to appear before a grand jury and ordered to bring his notes and tape recordings of interviews he had made with the Black Panther leaders. The presumption was that Caldwell would be asked by the grand jury to reveal the sources of his information. Caldwell, however, refused to appear to answer the grand jury's questions and, together with two others, the case eventually reached the Supreme Court. There, to the dismay of the newsmen, the Justices ruled against him by a vote of 5 to 4. The majority of the bench held that the constitutional protection claimed by the newsman was outweighed by the general obligation of a citizen to appear before a grand jury or at a trial "to give what information he possesses."

The ruling was a direct challenge to the right claimed by reporters in all free countries to protect their sources of information. Without it, many stories would never be written, many exposures of political deals and corruption would never be made, the activities of organized crime would be shrouded even more heavily in a veil of secrecy, and the hopes and plans of dissident groups would only rarely come up into the fresh air of public discussion. What worried journalists the most was the belief they held, rightly or wrongly, that since his failure in the Pentagon Papers case the Attorney General, John Mitchell, had gone after the press in a quite deliberate attempt to intimidate them. The Caldwell case was not isolated; there had been a positive drumbeat of writs demanding that reporters deliver up information they had gathered in confidence in the execution of their duties. The Supreme Court ruling seemed to offer evidence that their hardwon victory in the Pentagon Papers affair was in fact a hollow one—that having lost the battle, the authoritarians in government were now engaged in a campaign to win a wider war. As Justice William O. Douglas put it in his dissenting opinion in the Caldwell case:

> Today's decision is more than a clog upon news-gathering. It is a signal to publishers and editors that they should exercise caution in how they use whatever information they can obtain. . . . Entrenched officers have been quick to crash their powers down on unfriendly commentators.
>
> The intrusion of government into this domain is symptomatic of the disease of this society. As the years pass the power of government becomes more and more pervasive. It is a power to suffocate both people and causes. Those in power, whatever their politics, want only to perpetuate it. Now that the fences of the law and the tradition that has protected the press are broken down, the people are the victims. The First Amendment, as I read it, was designed precisely to prevent that tragedy.

Thus, only a year after its apparent great victory, the press was once more forced onto the defensive against the conservative, authoritarian tide that swept through many American institutions since the arrival of President Nixon in the White House. Under the second Nixon Administration, the constitutional rights of a free press may indeed be heading for an even greater confrontation with all those forces in the country that, in the name of order and stability, seek to repress those rights. Thanks to the Watergate affair, that now seems rather less likely, and the persistent, aggressive investigative reporting of the Washington *Post* and other newspapers which brought that affair to light has done much to restore both the prestige and the self-confidence of an embattled institution.

CHAPTER XIII

Television

1. The Networks

"Try it, you'll like it!"
—Catchphrase popularized by Alka-Seltzer commercials, 1971–1972

The casual viewer of American television might be forgiven if on his first exposure to the medium he concluded he had arrived in a country populated solely by neurotics, hypochondriacs, and the constipated. For between eight and sixteen minutes out of every hour on network television, his eyes and ears are assailed by a cacophony of commercials seeking cynically and quite openly to exploit every vulnerability of the flesh and of the psyche. The inadequacies of middle age thus yield with miraculous ease to regular dosages of iron tonic or antacid pills. Use of the right confidence-boosting hairspray or deodorant is guaranteed to overcome the sexual insecurities of the young. Even the rigors of old age, they suggest, can be alleviated by a gentle admixture of the youth-giving laxative recommended by the ebullient actress on the box (although in the genteel wording of the ads people hardly ever suffer from "constipation" but from a subtler affliction known on television as "occasional irregularity"). Watch for only one hour and you will find a cure for everybody's hangup. The lonely housewife, it insinuates, can somehow overcome her domestic frustrations by spending hundreds of dollars on a new kitchen appliance from which—wonder of modern wonders!—she can extract the cubes of ice without actually having to open the refrigerator door. Her husband meanwhile is encouraged to compensate for his general insignificance in the world by the purchase of a shining new automobile, which in the phraseology of the seventies comes equipped not just with four wheels and an engine but with some indefinable quality known as "pizazz"—guaranteed to set him apart from his neighbors as a man to be reckoned with. Insomnia, heartburn, acne —all are catered for on American television, the universal problemsolver. Inferiority complexes, the dread of social ostracism, all the inadequacies of modern man each miraculously dissolves, as on and on it goes, from eight to sixteen minutes in every hour, from before breakfast until well after supper, Sundays and holidays especially included.

Complaining about the commercialism of American television, someone once said, is like criticizing the lions for eating Christians. You have to make allowances for the nature of the beast. And by its nature television in America dedicates itself wholly and solely to the principles of commercialism. To understand that is the first step toward understanding television as it is presently constituted in the United States. Alexander Kendrick of CBS once observed that "there are those in the industry who believe broadcasting can move men, and even some who believe it could move mountains, but they are outnumbered by those who believe all it has to do is to move goods."

The influence of commercialism is felt not only in the average twelve minutes of advertising, but more insidiously in the forty-eight minutes of programming that makes up the rest of the broadcasting hour. It is a common belief, widespread but erroneous, that the networks use television to sell goods to their audiences; in fact, they use the medium to sell audiences to their sponsors. Thus, even the old cliché used constantly by the networks to apologize for the quality of their fare, "we give the people what they want," is strictly inaccurate. The true purpose of the networks is to produce for the advertisers the audiences *they* want. If the demographic make-up of the audience is unsuitable the program is dropped, however popular it may have been with the viewers. The CBS network, for instance, used to run a national program of rural comedy and music called *Hee Haw*, unsophisticated and lowbrow, but immensely popular with its audiences and with a rating that brought it consistently into the top ten of the week. For the advertisers, however, *Hee Haw* produced the *wrong* audiences. They were country folk, who are not as beguiled by the commercials as citydwellers; they were older people, when the advertisers were in search of the young; they were poor, and the advertisers needed the affluent. So, at the height of its success, *Hee Haw* was abruptly dropped.

The melancholy influence of the advertisers can be detected even in the make-up of the programs themselves. With the honorable exception of the news broadcasts, the fare is universally bland, unexciting, and excessively timid. Controversy is generally shunned, issues avoided, self-censorship commonplace. Anything that might challenge, anything that might stimulate, anything that might cause its audience to think, is expressly, and by fiat, forbidden. Every night, the programmers reason, 75 million Americans are going to watch television anyway, irrespective of the fare, so whatever else you do, don't offend them. The formula is not so much to give the viewers what you think they want as to avoid giving them what you know they don't want. The result, inevitably, is a diet of Pablum that can be digested without effort, a soporific against which the steady drip, drip, drip of the commercials can almost unconsciously be absorbed and assimilated. Little wonder a recent survey found more than half the audience said they preferred watching the ads to watching the programs.

The constant appeal to the lowest common denominator in their audiences can impose a tyranny on broadcasting standards as rigid as any decreed by those governments who control the content of their television programs in the interests of the state. Under both systems the audiences perhaps come to like only what they know. But, as the Pilkington Committee report on British television pointed out over ten years ago, "Had they been offered a wider range from which to choose, they might have chosen otherwise, and with greater enjoyment." Arguing that a television service that caters only to majorities can never satisfy all, or even most of the needs of any individual, the commiteee put a damning finger on that widely used excuse for mediocre broadcasting: "Give the public what it wants." The phrase is misleading, the Committee said: "It appears to be an appeal to democratic principle but is in fact patronising and arrogant, in that it claims to know what the public is, but defines it as no more than the mass audience, and limits its choice to the average of experience."

Under the commercial pressures that prevail, it is therefore hardly surprising that the programs on the three main networks—ABC, CBS, NBC—look so similar. In their ceaseless quest for ratings, they have arrived at precisely the same formula for delivering the maximum possible audience. "It shines with the clarity of a mathematical law," says *The New Yorker* magazine. "All have achieved complete homogenization of comedy, drama, variety, news, sports, public affairs that will produce exactly the same mild tangy taste. No foreign ingredients—undue sponteniety, excessive dullness—have been allowed to intrude. Now that the identical formula has been found, the companies can dismiss their chemists and replace them with accountants, to keep track of the identical profits."

Occasionally, just occasionally, the practitioners of this black art themselves rebel against the system they have created. In 1970, Les Brown, an editor of the entertainment trade magazine, *Variety*, made a study of the industry called *Televi$ion: The Business Behind the Box*, in which his main characters are two of the men from the networks who helped select the nation's favorite television programs, one from CBS and one from NBC. By the end of the book, both had resigned. "Each," said Brown, "professed to have reached a point in his life when he desired to make a meaningful contribution to society. The reader may make what he will of the fact that two men with great influence over the program matter of one of the most pervasive and powerful communications forces in all history were giving up the office to do something *important.*"

It is an atmosphere which drives producers and writers of integrity to despair. They have written into their programs characters who are black and seen the networks turn them into whites; they had had entire episodes killed by the networks for fear of giving "offense." They have been ordered to avoid the issues of war, of urban life, of Vietnam. In a documentary play about the Nuremberg war crimes tribunal some years ago, all mention of the gassing of the Jews was deleted from the script at the request of the sponsor—who

happened to be a supplier of domestic cooking gas. The objections carry to
the edge of absurdity, and sometimes beyond. Once, the writer of *My Favorite
Martian* was required to change a line in his script on the grounds that "a
Martian would never talk like that." That story was revealed by David Rintels,
himself a television writer, in evidence before the Senate Subcommittee on
Constitutional Rights. From his own experience, Rintels told the subcommittee of a script he had helped prepare that dealt with an eighteen-year-old
draftee going into his first combat in Vietnam. The boy was accompanied by
a magazine photographer, and the script explored the nature of bravery, with
photographs from the first mission showing the boy looking afraid, although
he behaved bravely. On the second mission, anxiously turning to see whether
the photographer was still following him, the boy is killed. It was a plausible
enough story in a realistic enough setting, and it might have told viewers
something about the character of combat in Vietnam. But the viewers never
saw it. When he took his script to the networks, Rintels was given the usual
timid line:

> The producer liked the story well enough—a character study that would allow
> us to say something about truth and bravery, he kindly called it—to forward it
> to the network for its required approval. The network liked the story, too. They
> wanted only one change. Vietnam is controversial, you know.
>
> My collaborator, wise in the ways of television, felt his heart sink. If they
> wanted the story moved to Korea, or Germany during World War II, the usual
> gambits, we were prepared to make a fight of it.
>
> No, not at all. Keep the story fresh and contemporary by all means. Keep it
> in the present. Just change the locale to Spain, make it a bullfight instead of a
> war, and make the soldier into a matador. That way, when the bull charges, the
> matador can look to see whether the photographer is taking more pictures
> and . . .

In the 1970s, however, attitudes have begun to change somewhat in the
executive suites of the networks, where the final decisions are taken. TV has
lately been showing movies about homosexuals (where once the very word was
forbidden on the public airwaves), and there have been one or two notable
medical programs about such controversial subjects as abortion and venereal
disease, while a number of comedy programs (many of them borrowed from
the BBC) have taken a midly refreshing attitude towards racial prejudice and
sex, notable among them *All in the Family, Maude,* and *Sanford and Son.* But
in too many cases the old attitudes die hard. Early in 1973, at the time the
prisoners were coming home from North Vietnam, CBS prepared a bitter
antiwar drama about a blinded Vietnam veteran called *Sticks and Bones.*
Under pressure from its affiliate stations, CBS dropped the play, declaring it
"unnecessarily abrasive" at a time when the emotions of Americans were
dominated by the returning POWs. One station manager in Detroit flatly

declared the program was "inappropriate for TV in Detroit where our working-class audience would be offended." The American Civil Liberties Union protested the network's "corporate cowardice," and the play's producer, Joseph Papp, charged that CBS had become "the creature of its affiliates and the servant of petty censors." The episode serves to show that when American TV flirts with serious material, it does so at its peril. The play had been strongly and sometimes bitterly opposed both by an overwhelming majority of local station managers and by the commercial sponsors, whose support is of course essential if this sort of production is to be presented regularly on American TV. Even before it decided to drop the program, CBS had run into trouble with its sponsors and had sold only two of the twelve commercial minutes allocated to *Sticks and Bones*. When it was replaced by an old movie called *The Cincinnati Kid*, the sponsors immediately moved in to buy all but one of the unsold commercial minutes. For the managers of TV stations, steeped as they are in the commercial ethos that their principal duty is to maximize profits, the lesson of *Sticks and Bones* was probably all too plain: Controversy on TV does not pay.

Occasionally, a lonely voice is raised in protest against these practices. Newton Minow, a former chairman of the Federal Communications Commission, obtained attention when he described television as a "vast wasteland," and Nicholas Johnson, another commissioner, has written that virtually every intelligent and independent observer has concluded that American television is "a national scandal of criminal proportions." Their cries, however, fall largely on deaf ears and are easily dismissed by an industry that nets some three billion dollars every year from its advertisers. Who, after all, is paying the piper? From their own standpoint, the commercial one, their efforts are rewarded by an astonishing degree of success. It is estimated that by eight thirty on a typical winter's evening around eighty million Americans—one in every four—has his feet up in front of the TV set. In the average home, the television set is turned on some five and three-quarters hours every day, while from the time he enters nursery school to the day of his retirement the average male viewer will have watched television for nine full years of his life. That means he has been exposed to well over one million separate commercial messages via the medium of television.

It is the colossal size of this nightly audience that advertisers find so irresistably attractive. For the top shows such as *Flip Wilson* or *Marcus Welby, M.D.*, the networks can sell the breaks for well over eighty thousand dollars a minute, a rate that works out at something over four dollars for every thousand homes "delivered" to the advertisers. The control of the three billion dollars that is spent on television advertising each year, however, is concentrated in relatively few hands; it has been estimated that almost half of it comes from only twenty to twenty-five major companies who use television as their prime sales tool.

At the present time, television in America is dominated by the three main networks: the American Broadcasting Companies, the Columbia Broadcasting System, and the National Broadcasting Company. Their corporate headquarters in New York are three buildings know in the trade as Black Rock (CBS, from the color of its handsome black skyscraper on Sixth Avenue), Thirty Rock (NBC, from its address at 30 Rockefeller Plaza), and Little Rock (ABC, because ABC has always trailed its two big brothers), and it is upon these three rocks that the foundations of network television have been built. Each company is allowed by law to own only five stations; the rest of the network is made up of hundreds of privately owned "affiliates" who plug into the main network programs but who also compete with them for the advertising dollar. The three nightly network news programs, for example, are each carried by some two hundred affiliate stations. The revenue from the national programs finds its way back to corporate headquarters in New York, in exchange for which the networks pay the affiliates a fee for carrying their programs and in addition turn over some of the commercial time (known euphemistically as "station breaks") for the affiliates to fill with local advertising. They also deliver up their huge audiences to the affiliates when the time arrives for local programming, which the FCC now requires each of its licensed stations to produce for a certain time each day.

If broadcasting standards on the networks are low, those on the local stations are even worse. "The men who own local stations have the mentality of movie exhibitors," says Walter Cronkite, the anchorman on *CBS Evening News*. Rivalry between the affiliates and their parent networks, both commercially and ideologically, is also intense. The networks claim the affiliates find the networks patronizing, New York–oriented, and more liberal than they normally like. Indeed, part of Vice President Agnew's attacks on the news programs of the television networks was calculated to drive a wedge between the affiliates and the networks—and he may well have succeeded. The day after his attack, the networks all issued statements deploring his attempts to intimidate television's coverage of the news; but from the affiliates, with very few exceptions, there was silence. Most of them, in fact, agreed with Agnew, and not long afterwards a hand-vote was taken at a meeting of NBC affiliate stations on the question of bias in the news. Approximately 60 percent of the station-owners voted that the news they carried every night from their own network headquarters *was* biased, specifically in its coverage of the war in Vietnam. Some affiliates, it was reported, put up a slide on their screens whenever a well-known news analyst appeared on the air carrying the caption, "This does not represent the view of this station."

The relationship between the networks and their affiliates, always delicate, could be in for some profound changes in the later 1970s, and some observers believe the balance may have already tilted in favor of the affiliates. The reason is mainly commercial. At present, they argue, commercials are national, but markets are local. Consumers in Florida, for example, cannot be expected to display much enthusiasm for ads trying to sell antifreeze, nor are Chicagoans the most likely market for suntan lotions, but national advertising, necessarily indiscriminate, ensnares them both in a process both wasteful and costly. The advertisers currently buy time on national television simply because it is easier, but with the introduction of computers into the already arcane art of time buying they may in the very near future find it more efficient to purchase a hundred local spots rather than a single national one. If these forecasts are true, the effect on television could well be the most profound since the discovery of the medium itself, shifting the balance of power away from the programmers in New York and onto the shoulders of the local affiliates. The fragmentation of the national audience, which has so often been predicted will follow the invention of multichannel cable television or cassette TV, seems much more likely to come about as a result of this apparently trivial shift in the commercial balance of power in favor of the local stations. Sadly, however, one must conclude that any accompanying change in the quality of the programs is likely to be only for the worse, since the local stations have neither the professional expertise nor the temperament to improve on the offerings of the networks.

A foretaste of things to come was provided by two recent government rulings, both calculated to enrich the airwaves with more diverse and innovative programs, but which have had precisely the opposite effect of driving down standards even farther. The first such ruling came from the Federal Communications Commission, the body that regulates television in America, which late in 1971 ordered the networks to turn over half an hour of prime time each night to local stations in the top fifty markets. The FCC's aim was the laudable one of encouraging the affiliates to produce local programs of a quality that would appeal to peak-hour audiences. The ruling was supposed to open the door to a host of independent producers, lead to a diversity of new programs, improve the overall standard of viewing in cities across the country. But the FCC failed to reckon with the shortcomings of local television stations, who simply saw in the new rules a chance to turn a fast dollar. The lowest common denominator, it turned out, could go lower yet as audiences between the hours of 7:30 and 8:00 P.M.—the half hour all three networks eventually chose to present to their affiliates—were faced with reruns of programs made five or even ten years earlier or local revivals of such bewhiskered favorites from the 1950s as *What's My Line?* and *Truth or Consequences.* In short, said *Newsweek* in a comment on the new ruling, "one half-hour of prime TV time each night has been given over to a dismally dull collection of network reruns, retreads and rejects." "The FCC has turned the business upside down," declared one network producer. "And while they're making a shambles of it, they keep telling us how rotten television is."

A year later, the networks received what could in the end prove to be an even more stunning blow, when the Justice Department filed antitrust suits intended to force them to give up their financial interests in all entertainment programs. The suits complained that the networks had hitherto used their control of prime time to block what it called "free and open competition in the broadcasting of entertainment programs." Although the networks at present produce only about 10 percent of the entertainment programs they broadcast, buying the rest from independent producers in Hollywood and elsewhere, the suits alleged they had virtual control over the so-called independents also, using their economic muscle to coerce them into turning over a part of their profits on the threat of shutting out their programs from national television altogether. The suit was a complicated one, but would in effect bar the networks from either producing their own entertainment programs or from participating financially in their production by others. The intention, said a Justice Department spokesman, was twofold: "We want the networks to quit producing their own programs; their own programs obviously have a better chance of getting on the air than somebody else's programs, and that's not fair. And we want them to quit bankrolling or buying syndication rights, or whatever, for outside productions. Obviously those productions have a better chance of getting on the networks too."

The suit will probably take years to wind its complicated way through the courts, but the implications for broadcasting could be catastrophic. The networks themselves saw it as a recipe for certain disaster, and many independent observers would agree with them. The most likely result would be to hand over control of network programming to the advertisers, who under the new system would probably become the main buyers of entertainment programs. Thus, instead of relieving the problem of commercialism, the Justice Department's suit would merely compound it. Fred Friendly, a former president of CBS News who now works in the field of public television, declared that to evict the networks "would only turn TV over to a bunch of equally shoddy characters, the advertising agencies and the movie companies," and the outcome would be to depress standards even farther. The networks were even more outspoken in their condemnations. "Absolutely ridiculous," was the comment of one network spokesman when he heard the news. An FCC official observed that, if successful, the ruling would convert the networks into "mere conduits" for programs produced by outsiders. Behind it all was the suspicion that the Nixon Administration had filed its suit for political motives, perhaps to take its revenge on the "small and unelected élite" Vice President Agnew had so bitterly criticized, perhaps to take the heat off its own antitrust difficulties (the allegations were still fresh that the Justice Department had dropped an antitrust suit against ITT in exchange for financial favors at the forthcoming Republican Party Convention). Whatever the reason, and whoever wins the battle in the courts, the ultimate loser is likely to be the long-suffering viewer.

2. Public TV: Promise and Perils

"Public Television possesses a great advantage over commercial television: it can enjoy the luxury of being venturesome."
—*Carnegie Report on noncommercial TV, 1967*

"If you imitate the commercial structure, all we have is a network paid for by the government, and it just invites political scrutiny of the content."
—*DR. CLAY WHITEHEAD, director, White House Office of Telecommunications Policy, 1972*

In the autumn of 1970, viewers of American television were offered an unusual experience: *Civilisation* had reached the United States. The thirteen-part serial of that name, narrated by Sir Kenneth Clark, had been prepared for the British Broadcasting Corporation and put on the air in America under the sponsorship of the Public Broadcasting Service, a fledgling network financed by public money and private grants, which it is fair to assume most viewers had barely heard of until *Civilisation* appeared on their screens. The series proved to be a turning point in the fortunes of the new network, which had been formed only three years earlier under a bill drawn up by President Johnson in an attempt to provide the viewing public with something more than the escapist pulp they were offered on commercial television. Clark's urbane and witty commentary, together with some hauntingly beautiful photography, turned *Civilisation* into an instant success with its American audiences—a demonstration that television can be esthetically satisfying without being dull, educational without tasting like medicine, stimulating without being strident or controversial. It proved, above all, that culture (or at least middlebrow culture) could be popular. In commercial terms, of course, its audience was tiny when put alongside the tens of millions who watched the commercial television programs, but it came to American television like a breath of fresh air and was warmly welcomed by the critics. One described it as "surely the most remarkable program series in American television" and found it "more pertinent to contemporary life by far than anything CBS, ABC and NBC proffered as 'relevant.' " The series had in fact already been turned down by the three major networks and came to PBS as a result of a donation from the Xerox Corporation. Next season, PBS followed it up with a series called *Masterpiece Theater,* a weekly series of drama again purchased from the BBC that featured such historical reconstructions as *Elizabeth R* and a television adaptation of Dostoyevsky's *The Possessed.* Again, the audiences were captivated, the critics delighted, and the series became so popular in some cities where it was shown that episodes of *Elizabeth R* actually drew larger ratings than programs on some of the commercial stations. Here, belatedly, was evidence that entertainment programs on television could be both appealing and satisfying without devoting themselves entirely to an élite audience of college professors and other highbrows.

It was no accident that these two series, which finally established the reputation of American public noncommercial television, had originated with the BBC, a publicly financed corporation that had developed over a span of some fifty years the critical mass of money and talent needed to produce this type of program. *Civilisation* alone had taken the BBC more than three years to produce, with the funding committed in advance; PBS in America was by comparison an impecunious infant. The BBC has an annual revenue that works out at well over three dollars a citizen; the American PBS, which has to service over two hundred stations, receives only seventy-four cents a citizen. At its present rate of progress it is anticipated that public television in America will be forced to subsist on foreign fare for many years to come, a condition which has led one critic to observe wistfully that the United States will probably celebrate its two hundredth anniversary as a nation by watching a series on the American Revolution produced by British television.

Public broadcasting in America was a bold concept, born as the result of a report submitted to President Johnson in 1967 by the Commission on Educational Television, which had been financed by the Carnegie Corporation. Until then, noncommercial television had been a fragmentary scattering of so-called educational stations, starved of funds, and whose very name was calculated to put off the average viewer. The Commission coined the name "public television" as a substitute and filed a highminded report, written by E. B. White, full of somewhat overblown rhetoric:

> I think public television should be the visual counterpart of the literary essay, should arouse our dreams, satisfy our hunger for beauty, take us on journeys, enable us to participate in events, present great drama and music, explore the sea, the sky and the woods and the hills. It should be our Lyceum, our Chautauqua, our Minsky's, and our Camelot. It should restate and clarify the social dilemma and the political pickle.

The idealism of the commissioners was impeccable; their concrete proposals as to how the new network should be structured and financed, however, were sadly lacking in realism. In its research among the hundred or more educational stations then in existence, the commission had heard a constant and beguiling refrain: "From station to station the lament rises: so much that might be done, so much that needs doing, so receptive the small audience now reached, so little resources with which to operate." Obviously impressed, even moved, by the plight of the scattered individual stations, the commission took a fatal step. It recommended that they, the local stations rather than a new national network, should become what it termed the "bedrock" of public television—a principle precisely the opposite of that on which the BBC, a national body, had been built and from which it derives its strength. The commission took the view that localism was essential if the new service was to avoid the pitfalls into which it perceived the commercial networks had fallen. "If we were to sum up our proposal with all the brevity at our command," their report said, "we would say that what we recommend is freedom. We seek freedom from the constraints, however necessary in their context, of commercial television. We seek for educational television freedom from the pressures of inadequate funds. We seek for the artist, the technician, the journalist, the scholar, the public servant freedom to create, freedom to innovate, freedom to be heard in this most far-reaching medium. We seek for the citizen freedom to view, to see programs that the present system, by its incompleteness, denies him."

Central to this freedom it extolled in such flowery prose was the principle of localism. Networking appeared to the commissioners to be incompatible with the purposes of public television because it presupposed a single audience, where public television sought to serve differentiated audiences. It was, however, a naïve belief, and soon proved to be a vain hope, that such local fragmentation would lead to an improvement in the quality and diversity of television. The painful truth is that high-quality television, by its nature, requires large *lumps* of money, concentrated money, if it is to produce successful programs. To scatter funds, however generously, among upwards of two hundred separate stations is a sure recipe for mediocrity. An hour of quality drama costs at the very least $150,000 to produce, and no single station could afford an outlay of that magnitude on anything like a regular basis, although in combination they clearly might. Money, technical resources, talent must all be gathered in a critical mass, and applied in a mass, if television is to fulfill its expensive promise. The Carnegie Commission, whether through ignorance or a misguided faith in the abilities of the local stations, rejected that basic truth, and the television service they created has suffered from the effects of their folly ever since.

The second key to the establishment of a healthy noncommercial television service was, of course, financial security. Here the commission rejected the idea of an annual license fee to be collected on all television sets (the method by which the BBC in Britain is financed) on the grounds that it would be too unpopular and too difficult to collect. Instead, they recommended the creation of a permanent trust fund based on a tax on the sales of new television sets, a sensible proposal which would have relieved the broadcasters of the political pressures that would surely arise if they were forced to apply to Congress, hat in hand, for an annual appropriation. To subject themselves to regular buffetings at the hands of the politicians was the certain path to political interference and even political control of their destiny.

Sadly, that is precisely what has happened in the five years since the Public Television Act was passed. Congress rejected the sound advice of the commission and ruled that the federal funds essential to the new service's existence must come in the form of direct grants from the government, thereby ensuring that whenever it applied for new funds the Public Broadcasting Service would be placed in the political arena to answer for its programs. Indeed, public television has been paying the price for this congressional timidity ever since, doubly handicapped now by its own insistence on the "bedrock of localism" and by a system of funding that threatens to undermine its continued independence.

Under the Johnson bill that created public television, the system was also put under the control of a complex jumble of bureaucratic bodies that has further hindered its development. In the beginning there was the Corporation for Public Broadcasting (CPB), federally chartered and forbidden by law to operate a network. In an attempt to surmount that dilemma, a second organization was formed in 1969 known as the Public Broadcasting Service (PBS), a membership corporation with individual stations as members, deriving its income entirely from grants by the CPB. The efforts of these two organizations overlapped and sometimes conflicted with those of the two public television bodies already in existence, the Ford Foundation whose generous grant had created National Educational Television (NET), which had in turn spent several millions of dollars to establish a current affairs operation known as the Public Broadcasting Laboratory (PBL). To those wise in the ways of bureaucracies, the system appeared unworkable, with tier upon tier of committees, boards of directors, chairmen, presidents, general managers, and ordinary program-producers all maneuvering for their own advantages. This was diversity all right, but hardly in the sense Congress had intended. Interservice rivalries quickly became apparent, and NET found to its surprise that instead of becoming the main production arm of the new network, as it had hoped, it was relegated to a secondary role, one producer among many, although it did retain control of the biggest single outlet in the country, the public broadcasting station in New York City, which with its passion for acronyms it renamed WNET, a station that soon established for itself a reputation for extreme liberalism. NET's public-affairs offerings were meanwhile superseded by those of yet another organization, which called itself the National Center of Television (NPACT), headquartered under the watchful eye of the parent organizations in Washington.

With a forest of new initials calculated to confuse even those élitists who were alleged to watch public television, it is hardly surprising that the new network at first failed to establish a clear identity. Ironically enough, the first really successful program to be aired by the tangled network, the brilliant children's program *Sesame Street,* was produced by an organization outside the reach of the bureaucrats, an independent nonprofit company based in New York called the Children's Television Workshop. While the network itself now began to produce a few programs that were genuinely innovative (*The Advocates,* in which both sides of important public issues were discussed in depth, and William Buckley's *Firing Line,* one of the most intelligent and stimulating talk shows on television, chaired by an extreme conservative to boot), many others fell well below the accepted standards of professionalism. "We've learned that there isn't that much talent," said John W. Macy, the civil servant who was chosen as the first president of CPB, in a rather dismal excuse for the amateurish approach to programming found on many of the public broadcasting stations. One well-known reviewer began his article on a program that had been sponsored by Ford, "I would not watch this program unless you paid me to. You did. I did." And a reporter on the local public broadcasting station in Washington, WETA, was quoted as saying after his program had been scrapped, "We'd have done better on the corner with a bullhorn." But these were early days, and much was forgiven (although there was also much to forgive).

From the start, the network's own productions were also the subject of occasionally intense and partisan controversy, both internal and external. Several PBS documentaries were turned down by the local stations, including one entitled *Banks and the Poor,* in which the banking industry was severely taken to task for avoiding its social responsibilities, particularly in slum neighborhoods. Then J. Edgar Hoover succeeded in intimidating the network into blocking a segment of *The Great American Dream Machine,* a program that had had the temerity to criticise the FBI. Even *Sesame Street* was initially found unacceptable by a few stations in the South because of its racially integrated cast.

In many ways PBS was its own worst enemy, seemingly intent on provoking the wrath of those from whom it obtained its funds. *Banks and the Poor,* for instance, had closed with the stirring music of *The Battle Hymn of the Republic* played over a rolling list of the names of ninety-eight senators and congressmen who were shareholders or directors of banks, with the clear and provocative implication that they were to blame for the state of affairs portrayed in the program. That they were also the same senators and congressmen who voted the funds that made the program possible could hardly have been calculated to increase their generosity when the new appropriations were considered.

Concern over the service's use of its finances was also widespread, particularly over the money spent on an expensive new building in Washington in which the network planned to house its burgeoning bureaucracy and over the salaries paid to two current-affairs commentators, Sander Vanocur, who came from NBC at a reputed salary of $85,000 a year, and Robert McNeil, a Canadian formerly with the BBC, who was paid $65,000 a year. The Nixon Administration was particularly upset at Vanocur's appointment, considering him to be one of the most discernibly anti-Nixon commentators on television. The size of his salary was an incidental issue, but it served as a whip with which to chastise public broadcasting generally, which the Nixon Administration had come to believe was displaying a consistently hostile bias, a "welfare of the airwaves for America's liberal and left-wing élite," as one of them termed it. It was pointed out that PBS was paying Vanocur a salary precisely twice that of Senator John O. Pastore, chairman of the subcommittee that authorizes public television funds. To the critics again, the network seemed to have embarked on a needlessly extravagant course. In their defense, NPACT declared it had taken on Vanocur in order to win a national audience for itself. "You have just got to have a name," said Gerald Slater, the PBS general manager. "A name brings you an audience, gets out guests, brings visibility."

And with NPACT, the *Civilisation* series, and *Masterpiece Theatre*, the network began to obtain the visibility it sought. For the first time, audiences began to take notice of public television, which had by now extended its network to some 223 stations across the country with approximately thirty million Americans turning to its programs for some part of their weekly television-viewing. Its annual appropriation had meanwhile risen from $5 million in 1969 to $35 million in 1971 and was eventually intended to reach over $100 million which together with the private grants would bring in close to $200 million a year, a figure at last large enough to guarantee a flow of quality programs. There were even promises from President Nixon that legislation would soon be offered for "improved financing" for public broadcasting, with the hope that here at last CPB would obtain the longterm financial security and freedom from political pressure it had so ardently sought. But that was not to be. In reaching out for a national audience, PBS found it had set itself on a collision course with the Nixon Administration. Indeed, far from encouraging the service as it emerged as a fourth genuinely national network with programs that could fill in the large gaps left by commercial television, the administration instead took it to task for its boldness. Dr. Clay T. Whitehead, a brilliant and conservative young man of thirty-three whom Nixon had appointed director of the Office of Telecommunications Policy within the White House, disagreed profoundly with the network's new course and soon set about the task of correcting it.

Whitehead told a convention of public broadcasters in Miami at the end of 1971 that by trying to compete with the commercial networks, public broadcasting was jeopardizing its permanent financing. The threat was explicit: "If you imitate the commercial structure," Whitehead declared, "all we have is a network paid for by the government, and it just invites political scrutiny of the content." If PBS chose to establish a centralized network, he warned, "then permanent financing will be some way off in the future." It was Whitehead's view, backed by the President, that the bulk of public money provided by the government should bypass CPB altogether and go direct to the local stations. Here was a clearly politically motivated move that could undermine all PBS had worked for, a declaration of open warfare on public broadcasting with even direr implications than Vice President Agnew's attacks on the news programs of the commercial networks. The technique, indeed, was chillingly similar: an attempt to drive a wedge between the more conservative local station managers and the élitist "easterners" who were alleged to control the network.

Later, Whitehead aired his objections to PBS before the Senate Subcommittee on Constitutional Rights:

> No citizen who feels strongly about one or another side of a matter of current public controversy enjoys watching the other side presented. But he enjoys it a good deal less when it is presented at his expense. His outrage—quite properly—is expressed to, and then through, his elected representatives who have voted his money for that purpose.

The administration's antagonism towards PBS, it was now clear, was based more on political objections to the content of its recent programs than on a philosophical difference about the nature of the network. While Whitehead expressed his outrage at the allegedly leftwing bias of the programs, the President's press secretary, Ron Ziegler, found it reprehensible that "91 percent of prime time TV programs were produced by 7 stations out of 220," most of them "in the Northeast." Direct political interference with its programming was now at hand.

Nixon followed up his young aide's threats in the summer of 1972 when he unexpectedly vetoed a measure which had passed both houses of Congress providing increased funds for public television, a move that threatened to undermine the continued independence of the new service. The President's veto did not seek to cut off funds entirely, but to freeze them at the present levels and to force CPB to hand over a larger share of what remained to the local stations.

The President's veto had come because of his displeasure at public broadcasting's attempts to centralize its service, in contravention of the rule that it must rest on a "bedrock of localism." He argued that the major purpose of the service at its inception in 1967 was to encourage "innovative and diverse" programming from local stations around the country, but that this purpose had since become corrupted by its increasing disregard for "localism." In vetoing the bill, which would have authorized the expenditure of $155 million on public television over the following two years, the President expressed his concern "that an organization, originally intended to serve only local stations, is becoming instead the center of power and the focal point of control for the entire public broadcasting system."

The President's veto began a profound if sometimes shrill debate about the whole future of public television in America. The sponsor of the original bill, Representative Torbert H. Macdonald, Democrat of Massachusetts, called it "an incredible sacrifice of the public interest on the altar of partisan politics." Douglass Cater, who had worked with President Johnson on the original Public Broadcasting Act, said it put the fate of public television in "deep peril." Supporters of the President replied that "the corporation cannot continue to enjoy taxpayer subsidy while it permits its production staff to produce news and public-affairs programs biased in favour of a single liberal-to-leftist viewpoint."

By 1973, it was becoming clear that what the administration really objected to was any sort of independently produced public affairs programming on public television, a freedom which is, or ought to be, the bedrock of any responsible television service in a modern democracy. "Public affairs is at the very heart of public television," writes Jim Lehrer, an NPACT correspondent. "Without it, PTV is reduced to a safe, comfortable medium for little children and people who like Russian ballet, English drama and French cooking, but does nothing to add to the public's knowledge and understanding of important American events and issues." Yet it was just this safe and comfortable medium that the Nixon Administration was determined public television should become. Henry Loomis, a former official of the United States Information Agency, who was put in charge of CPB by Nixon, has since altered in fundamental ways the relationship between the network and its parent body, leading to suspicions that what he sought to create was a domestic USIA, a propaganda network for use as a conduit by the administration. Loomis left no doubt that what he objected to the most were the independent public affairs and discussion programs that make up almost one third of the network's output. He has since set out, with some success, to prune them drastically. In a sharp struggle for power with CPB's chairman, Thomas B. Curtis, in the spring of 1973, Curtis was forced to resign, accusing the Nixon White House of "tampering" with the work of the supposedly independent board.

Indeed, the continuing hostility and interference from the White House has put formidable handicaps before public television as it is presently constituted. In the face of this presidential antagonism to centralized programming, just what is the future of public television to be? Its lack of independence and money, compounded by its own failures of imagination and balance, seem to have put its future in dire peril. To suggest, as some critics did, that the network should now go elsewhere for its funds is simply unrealistic: The $200 million needed to produce effective programs can never be raised entirely from private sources. Yet the Whitehead formula seems to offer an equally blighted future; to spread the government's largesse among 230 or so local stations merely ensures docility and mediocrity. Douglass Cater has said that one can make a case that the Nixon White House, whether by design or not, has so polarized the arena that survival may not be worth the effort. Public television in America may not yet be altogether washed up, as some of its adherents believe, but its future is in direr jeopardy today than at any time since the service first began.

3. The Nightly News

"The American people would rightly not tolerate this concentration of power in government. Is it not fair and relevant to question its concentration in the hands of a tiny, enclosed fraternity of privileged men elected by no one and enjoying a monopoly sanctioned and licensed by government?"
—VICE PRESIDENT SPIRO AGNEW, 1969

The chief pride and glory of commercial television in America is its coverage of the news. In a country lacking national newspapers, the suppertime newscasts of the three major networks have in the single decade since they adopted the half-hour format become the social cement that binds together audiences in urban Manhattan and rural Alabama, the aerospace workers at Cape Kennedy and the hillbillies of the Tennessee mountains, the gregarious sophisticates who live in Beverly Hills and the isolated farmers who till the Great Plains, all drawn together for the first time into a genuinely national audience. Statistics show that the majority of these Americans now rely mainly on the television newscasts for their impressions of what is happening in the world. In that sense, the regular news programs of the three main networks have become the most important source of news in America. Just how well do they perform?

Technically, their productions are a lavish mixture of journalism and show business, costing at a conservative estimate around $120 million a year. The producers of the CBS evening news alone spend up to $30,000, excluding overheads, to cover the news of a single day, barely pausing to consider the costs as they open up communications satellites to bring in a three-minute report from Vietnam or a summary of the day's developments in the Middle East. With the advent of the communications satellite, the news directors of American television have made McLuhan's "global village" into a daily reality, with events almost anywhere in the world within the instantaneous reach of their cameras.

Journalistically, however, in spite of all the expenditure, national television news is little more than an illustrated headline service. The dictates of time and the pressures of other events compel it to cover the news in snippets: three sentences from a speech by presidential candidate George McGovern followed by a glimpse—and it is rarely more than a glimpse—of the South Vietnamese assault on Quangtri, then the first commercial break; thirty seconds of silent film of Henry Kissinger climbing into and out of a car in Paris, over which the commentator bravely tries to say something of significance about the progress of the peace talks, then another commercial; a building falling down in St. Louis, a new transit system opening in San Francisco, two more minutes of analysis and roundup, a further commercial—and the news is over.

Richard Salant, president of CBS News, once set up in type the complete spoken text of his nightly program and found it would fit into less than half a page of the New York *Times*. With normally five commercial breaks, each of one minute, even the news programs' "half hour" is reduced to a bare twenty-five minutes. "When I read statistics that show 60 percent of Americans get all or most of their news from television," says Av Westin, a former producer of the ABC evening news, "I shudder. I know what we have to leave out."

Of course it can be argued that the average viewer actually prefers to receive his daily Iliad in a nutshell. The TV news programs are comprehensive and impartial, even if they are not complete; the regular viewer of the CBS or NBC nightly news is at least kept aware of all the significant public developments in the United States (although their coverage of foreign affairs is woefully deficient), and he still has access to his daily newspaper for fuller coverage of events in which he is interested. The television newsmen are themselves perfectly aware that their service is at best complementary to the service provided by the newspapers, "For further details consult your local newspaper," as the old radio newscasts used to say. Even Mr. Salant's experiment of setting up his program in type is misleading. His broadcasts claim the audience's attention for a full twenty-five minutes every night; there are not many readers who spend longer than that over the hard news coverage in their daily newspapers—most indeed probably spend very much less time than that on the real news before they move on to the editorials, the columnists, the crossword puzzle, and the ads. The difference between television and newspaper coverage of events is that the reader of the New York *Times* can choose for himself between the items he wishes to read in depth and those he wishes merely to skim. On television, the news director makes that choice for him. Perhaps as a result he actually receives a broader perspective from television than he does from the newspapers.

For all its shortcomings, the impact of television's coverage of affairs is profound. There is scarcely a public institution in the country dependent for its effectiveness on the power of communication, whether it be politics, the presidency, or the press, that has not felt the impact of television and itself been transformed by its presence. That is because television involves people in the news in a way the press could never do. It was largely television coverage of the protests of southern blacks led by Dr. Martin Luther King that convinced many northerners that the problem also concerned *them*, although most of them had probably never even visited the Deep South. It was television's coverage of the Tet offensive of 1968 that finally turned public opinion against the continuing involvement of American troops in Vietnam. It was television, not the press, that took millions of people from around the world on the first voyages to the moon. It was television that created the law-and-order issue in the United States, bringing the evidence of crime and violence into every living room. Most people led lives that were as secure and crimefree as they had ever been; it was television that convinced them they were threatened.

Two events that occurred in 1972 illustrated this phenomenon perfectly. The first was the shooting of Governor George Wallace of Alabama, the second the kidnapping and murder of the Israeli athletes at the Olympic Games in Munich. One night in May viewers of the CBS evening news watched in horror as Arthur Bremer thrust his .38 revolver through the crowd to shoot down Wallace in full view of the CBS cameraman. For millions of people, it was almost as if Wallace had shed his blood in their own living rooms. The impact on the emotions was enormous, ordinary people were outraged by the attempted assassination in a way they could never have been by a newspaper account of the tragedy. The violence, via the medium of television, reached out and touched them all. Two months later there was a similar outpouring of grief and frustrated rage at the Olympic Games tragedy, which again was brought straight into the living room, much of the drama coming in live as it happened via the ABC network's Olympic satellite. And again, the viewer, helpless and captive before the electronic tube, felt the assault as a direct threat to his own security.

In what is perhaps the biggest political story they have had to cover in a lifetime, the networks again illustrated the complementary nature of television's reporting of the news. At first, the Watergate affair had been very much a newspaper story, dependent for its impact on the mass of detailed and lengthy revelations uncovered by investigative reporters working in one of the oldest traditions of American journalism. Television in those early weeks could do little more than headline the main developments and flesh out the personalities who were involved. The running, that is to say, was made by the printed press, and it was upon the printed word that the informed citizen had to depend for his basic understanding of the events. Once the affair had moved into public session, however, television came into its own, capturing live as it happened the drama and conflict of the Ervin Committee hearings in the Senate in a way the following day's newspaper accounts could never do.

In its coverage of these visible happenings, especially those that the networks have been able to cover live, television has been a superb medium of communication. It falls short of its potential when it attempts to cover events that are not visible, especially those that take place in the mind. How do you film a President in the process of taking a decision? How can you explore on television the financial crisis that led to the devaluation of the dollar? Even in its reporting from Vietnam, which has rightly been called television's first war, its efforts have been only partially successful. Since television lives on pictures, and the battlefield for the hearts and minds of the Vietnamese is not pictorial, there has been virtually no coverage of an aspect of the war that was perhaps the most vital of them all.

Towards the end of the American ground commitment in Vietnam, John Laurence, the CBS correspondent there, filed a series of moving and balanced reports on the activities of one infantry company as it went on patrol: Charlie Company, a part of the First Air Cavalry Division. The series began with the departure of Charlie Company's well-liked commander, a captain, and went on to record the arrival of a new commander, who was intensely disliked. Members of the company talked freely to Laurence about their hopes and their fears; the film showed them receiving home mail, going into action, looking after their wounded, and in the end threatening to mutiny because of an order to attack they regarded as stupid. It was superb television, moving and shocking, and it displayed as no other medium could have done the nature and feel of combat in Vietnam from the point of view of the ordinary G.I. But like virtually all the film reporting from Vietnam it showed the war from the bottom up. There was not—and by the nature of the medium there could not have been—an explanation of why the Army had sent this particular platoon on patrol, what the overall strategy of the senior commanders had been, or what this action looked like from above. It captured brilliantly the nature of the war as viewed from platoon level, but it barely touched on the loftier issues that are beyond the reach of television. There have been many films on television to put alongside the series on Charlie Company; there have been none that have recorded in similar detail the daily activities of, say, General Creighton Abrams, the Vietnam commander. That the series on Charlie Company represented the truth is undeniable: Laurence and his crew deservedly won an award for their coverage. But their series fell far short of representing the whole truth, and that is the main handicap of television: It simplifies, it distorts, it makes the world more dramatic than it really is, more interesting, more controversial.

The appeal of television is to the emotions rather than the intellect. In the words of Robin Day, a prominent British TV commentator, "For television journalism this means a dangerous and increasing concentration on action (usually violent and bloody) rather than on thought, on happenings rather than issues, on shock rather than explanation, on personalities rather than ideas." There are even those who argue that the distorting effect of television has undermined the fundamental security of modern society. Thus Vice President Agnew, in the less strident part of his attack upon the networks, expressed the concern of many when he asked if their ongoing exploration for more action, more excitement, more drama, did not somehow threaten the national search for peace and stability. And Byron Shafer, a political scientist at the University of California, has blamed television news for the polarization of American society:

> If TV news is a major factor in unraveling the American social fabric, and if it has a heavy effect on the way we (fail to?) adjust to the new pluralism, it is also an influential teacher when it comes to the type of political decisions that could meet the problem. What it teaches is not the "old politics" of hard work and compromise, but the "new politics" of theatricality. The key characteristic of the world presented through TV is that life is apocalyptic. The news can deliver only the major events of the day—the outstanding deviations from civil norms.

That, however, is the nature of the medium. It cannot avoid giving an apocalyptic view of the world, however hard it tries to give a balanced account of public events. Television lives on pictures, and it is in the end the most dramatic pictures that people will remember. The image of George Wallace falling before the bullets of his would-be assassin is frozen for ever in the mind of every viewer who saw it, while the worthy attempts to cover less dramatic and perhaps more significant happenings fade insensibly into oblivion. Short of censorship, there is nothing that the most highminded critic of television news coverage can do to alter that basic truth.

In America, news and documentary programs on television have an additional impact, the consequences of which may be even more profound than the effect of these repeated acts of violence. American television no less than the American people reflects an ethic that is fundamentally activist. If a problem presents itself, the problem must be solved. If injustice exists, it must be eradicated. If abuses occur, they must be eliminated. The American impulse is to act, to *do* something. As in society as a whole, so in the enclosed world of television: Since the days of the late Ed Murrow, the best American communicators have never believed that the medium is the message. To them, society is the message; the function of television's coverage of the real world is to spur action.

In his days at CBS, Murrow had a quotation from Thoreau hanging on his office wall: "It takes two to speak the truth—one to speak and another to hear." Implicit in that code is the suggestion that simply by making people aware, television is already moving them to act. Or, as Michael Novak has written:

> The cultural religion of television is not Buddhist. Its aim is not nirvana. Its aim is not quiet. Its aim is not serenity in the contemplation of inevitable tragedy. . . . The television documentary is a morality play whose purpose is to move us to action.

Over the years, the producers of the best news and documentary programs on the major networks have absorbed that ethic to the point where it has become a part of their bloodstreams. Murrow himself fathered the genre in his famous series of the 1950's entitled *See it Now,* the series which was instrumental in bringing down Senator Joseph McCarthy back in 1954. Murrow was not alone in criticizing the junior senator from Wisconsin for his unprincipled and vicious attacks on alleged former Communists, but he was the first to bring the searchlight of television to bear on McCarthy's techniques. For an hour that spring night the viewer was shown a series of typical attacks by the senator on a number of individuals. After each fact came Murrow's refutation as he pointed out the errors in McCarthy's facts, the holes in his logic, his attempts to destroy through the technique of the smear. And at the end of his broadcast Murrow made his now famous attack on McCarthyism and all it stood for:

This is no time for men who oppose Senator McCarthy's methods to keep silent, or for those who approve. We can deny our heritage and our history, but we cannot escape responsibility for the result. There is no way for a citizen of a republic to abdicate his responsibilities. As a nation we have come into our full inheritance at a tender age. We proclaim ourselves—as indeed we are—the defenders of freedom, what's left of it, but we cannot defend freedom abroad by deserting it at home. The actions of the junior senator from Wisconsin have caused alarm and dismay amongst our allies abroad and given considerable comfort to our enemies, and whose fault is that? Not really his. He didn't create this situation of fear; he merely exploited it, and rather successfully. Cassius was right: "The fault, dear Brutus, is not in our stars but in ourselves."

Good night, and good luck.

It was perhaps the finest broadcast in the history of American television, certainly the bravest, and the first direct blow it ever struck in the cause of righteousness. "This is what TV is for," one viewer wrote to Murrow afterwards. The program was not the last to deal with the evils of McCarthyism —Murrow followed it up with several more—nor was it the only occasion on which he spoke out in a cause he believed to be just, but it is with that single paragraph spoken at the conclusion of a broadcast nearly twenty years ago that the tradition was established that television no less than the press could be used to right wrongs, to remedy injustice, to speak out against cruelties, to move people to act. And it is perhaps back to that same single paragraph that television's present difficulties with the authoritarians in government can be traced.

Murrow and *See It Now* are both long since dead, but the tradition Murrow established lives on in the evening news programs, all three of which employ a resident columnist to interpret and analyze the news. Eric Sevareid of CBS, David Brinkley of NBC, and Howard K. Smith and Harry Reasoner, who alternate in the job at ABC, are all responsible and fairminded men who two or three times a week undertake the difficult task of adding perspective and depth to television's coverage of the news. CBS, for one, prefers to call Sevareid a "news analyst" rather than a commentator, but the distinction is a fine one, and his analysis has more than once led to accusations from a conservative administration that his elegantly phrased essays have a natural bias towards liberalism. Sevareid himself would probably not deny it: An honest search for truth, particularly on such a broad-brush medium as television, must start from certain basic premises, and the intimate nature of television is such that it could hardly fail over a period of years to project personality and the underlying rock of belief on which that personality is based. The main point, however, is that Sevareid and his colleagues—like Murrow before them—are motivated not by the propagandist's desire to project his own point of view, but by the professional journalist's desire to inform the public. While the rest of their programs answers the how, what, when, where questions—which some still call "the facts"—the analysts attempt to answer the more difficult questions of why. It is a role (unique to American television) that has led them into a bitter conflict with an administration that believes television has no business to ask the question *why*, particularly not after an address by the President.

Vice President Agnew is no McCarthy, but at the core of all his criticism of the media is his sense of outrage that television can be permitted a point of view. "The purpose of my remarks tonight," he said in his attack on the networks, "is to focus your attention on this little group of men who not only enjoy a right of instant rebuttal to every Presidential address, but, more importantly, wield a free hand in selecting, presenting and interpreting the great issues of our nation."

For millions of Americans, Agnew declared, the network reporter who covers a continuing issue—like the ABM or civil rights—becomes, in effect, the presiding judge in a national trial by jury. Of the men who produced and directed the network news, he said, most Americans know practically nothing —"other than that they reflect an urbane and assured presence seemingly well-informed on every important matter." The Vice-President concluded his attack by questioning the networks' basic right to cover the news of the day as they saw fit. "Now, my friends," he declared, "we'd never trust a power such as I've described over public opinion in the hands of an elected government. It's time we questioned it in the hands of a small and unelected élite. The great networks have dominated America's airwaves for decades; the people are entitled to a full accounting of their stewardship."

The Vice President's attack on the networks had come as a direct result of their practice of following public addresses by the President with what he called "instant analysis and querulous criticism." The administration had been particiularly incensed by the reaction of some commentators to a recent address on Vietnam, in which the commentators, having "inherited" the President's vast audience, came on the air, according to Agnew, to express hostility to what they saw.

The Vice President was bitterly critical of one commentator who twice contradicted the President on his exchange of letters with Ho Chi Minh. The President had claimed the letters from Ho were intransigent, but Marvin Kalb of CBS had pointed out that in his opinion the letters contained "some of the softest, most accommodating language" yet. A commentator on another network had reached the conclusion about the President's address that "there was nothing new in it politically." But the Vice President reserved his sharpest criticism for the third network, ABC, who had obtained a considerable journalistic coup in persuading Averell Harriman, a former head of the American negotiating team in Paris, to come into the studio for an interview on the President's address. Harriman, whom Agnew compared to Coleridge's Ancient Mariner, was, in the words of the Vice President, "under compulsion to justify his failures."

The heart of Agnew's argument was this statement:

> . . . the President of the United States has a right to communicate directly with the people who elected him, and the people of this country have the right to make up their own minds and form their own opinions about a presidential address without having a President's words and thoughts characterized through the prejudices of hostile critics before they can even be digested.

The main significance of Agnew's speech was this indication that the Nixon Administration believed the President had the right to commandeer the airwaves to act as a sort of presidential conduit direct to the people, unchallengeable and inviolate. Those who ran the networks disagreed strongly with this interpretation of the role of television. They found Agnew's speech deeply disturbing, at once an appeal to prejudice and an attempt to deny to television the freedom of the press. Evidently, said Julian Goodman of NBC, the Vice President would prefer a different kind of reporting on television—"one that would be subservient to whatever political group was in authority at the time."

"Those who might feel momentary agreement with his remarks," Goodman observed, "should think carefully whether that is the kind of television they want." Agnew's arguments seemed to question the basic purpose of journalism on television. To many of them it seemed that analysis of political remarks by the President, or any other politician, provided it was conducted dispassionately and fairly, was an essential function if the people were to be kept fully informed. What other way was there of putting a presidential address into perspective? Part of the argument was the old one, noted in the previous chapter on the press, of objectivity versus interpretation, and which approach came closer to the truth. Partly, too, it was due to the common tendency of politicians (not confined to America) to reject as biased any report which does not support their own point of view. David Brinkley of NBC put it well when he declared, "If I went on the air tomorrow night and said Spiro Agnew was the greatest American statesman since Washington, Jefferson, Madison, Adams, and Hamilton, the audience might think I was biased. But he wouldn't." What happens, Brinkley found, was that people projected their own bias on television: "If we report a story in a way that supports the views they already hold, then we're honest, fair, and objective. If we report it in such a way as to differ with the views they already hold, then we are biased, slanted, and unfair. This is a fact of life and we have to live with it. Anyone who can't live with it shouldn't go into journalism."

It is an equal fact of life that ever since television became the chief instrument of national communication, its relationship with the White House has been abrasive. There is a story that on one occasion President John Kennedy phoned the chairman of the FCC, Newton Minow, to ask, "Did you see that goddam thing on Huntley-Brinkley?" When Minow replied that he had, Kennedy told him, according to David Wise's article "The President and the Press," in *Atlantic Monthly*, "I want you to do something about that. You do something about that." To some, Kennedy's call was seen as a demand that the FCC take Huntley-Brinkley off the air, or at least censor its product, but Minow wisely gave the President time for calmer second thoughts. Next morning, he phoned one of the President's aides instead, and said to him, "Just tell the President he's very lucky he has an FCC chairman who doesn't do what the President tells him."

Johnson, too, was demanding and often abusive of television. It was during his Presidency that the networks were required to install a permanent TV hookup to the White House, and at one time Johnson asked for the networks to provide "hot" cameras, manned throughout the day, ready for the President to commandeer the airwaves at a moment's notice. It is said that the President once went on the air so fast the duty technicians did not even have time to put up the Presidential seal to warn viewers what was coming. "Son," Johnson told the technician, "I'm the leader of the free world, and I'll go on the air when I want to." Johnson was also not above phoning correspondents personally to complain about stories they had reported, grumbling on one occasion direct to a startled copy editor on the UPI news desk about a typo in a report the agency had just circulated.

Under earlier Presidents, journalists have recounted these stories with some amusement, never taking them entirely seriously as threats to the way they were allowed to do their job. Under Nixon, however, the threats have been seriously intended and seriously received. Agnew's speeches have been only a part of a concerted drive to bring the networks to heel. Individual network reporters have been investigated by the FBI after they had filed stories unpleasing to the administration. A group of Nixon supporters in Florida attempted to block the license renewal of a local station that had revealed Judge G. Harrold Carswell's segregationist past. And attempts have been made to control the networks by threats to their local affiliates. Toward the end of 1972, Clay Whitehead unveiled a plan that many in television saw as a direct attempt at intimidation. Whitehead offered to introduce legislation extending the local stations' franchises from three years to five and at the same time make it considerably more difficult for outside groups to bid for the same licenses. As a *quid pro quo* Whitehead insisted that the local station managers should be held responsible for the content of network news programs. "There is no area where management responsibility is more important than news," he said. "The station owners and managers cannot abdicate responsibility for news judgments. When a reporter or disc jockey slips in or passes over information in order to line his pocket, that's plugola, and management would take quick corrective action. But men also stress or suppress information in accordance with their beliefs. Will station licensees or network executives also take action against this ideological plugola?" Whitehead held that, at the peril of losing their franchises, the station licensees should have the final responsibility for news balance—whether the information came from their own newsrooms or from a distant network—and to make quite sure the station managers realized about whom he was talking, he added a comment about "so-called professionals who confuse sensationalism with sense and who dispense élitist gossip in the guise of news analysis." The threat of government reprisal was quite explicit: "Station managers," he said, "who fail to act to correct imbalance or consistent bias in the network—or who acquiesce by silence—can only be considered willing participants, to be held fully accountable at license renewal time."

Whitehead's proposal, like many others that have come from his office, was wholly impracticable. For one thing, there is simply no way in which station managers, however willing, can monitor network news programs before they come down the line. The managers see the programs at the same time the viewers do; there is no mechanism that can be devised to allow a couple of hundred station managers scattered across the country to exercise prior control over the content of a daily news broadcast. Nor is it proper that they should do so; in any responsible form of journalism the final control over what is broadcast or what is printed must rest with the editor in control of the program and not with half-informed outsiders worried about a commercial threat to their livelihood. In any case, who, if not the government, is supposed to measure the amount of bias in any given news program? On any analysis, Whitehead's suggestions come closer to outright censorship than any that have come out of the White House in its entire history.

There is, however, a safeguard: A bill containing such requirements would be almost bound to fail in the Congress, which has the final responsibility over the FCC and, indirectly, over the television networks. But legislation was perhaps not Whitehead's main intention. The publication of his warnings was probably by itself enough to influence the content of future news programs, simply by putting the producers on the defensive, by making them nervous about broadcasting news the government does not like, by creating a climate of opinion in which coverage of controversial subjects became unacceptable to the more timid local station managers.

Taken by itself, Whitehead's proposals could probably have been fairly lightly dismissed by a profession not unused to criticism from politicians. But taken as a whole, the concerted attacks on both television and the press that came out of the Nixon White House during its first four and one-half years in office has provided, on any objective assessment, the greatest threat to the freedom of broadcasting and of the press that has ever been mounted in America. Thanks to the Watergate scandal, and also to the natural resilience and toughness of many of those who practice the art of journalism, that threat has probably now receded somewhat. The threat, however, was real enough while it lasted, and its lessons have still to be fully digested by a profession not normally given to introspection.

CHAPTER XIV

Lobbyists

1. Boodlers

"The way to a Senator's Aye is through his stomach."
—SAM WARD, legendary "king of the Washington lobbyists"

For every member of the U.S. Congress at work in Washington, it is estimated there are between eight and ten professional lobbyists seeking by fair means, and sometimes by foul, to influence his vote. On matters that range from gun-control legislation to health care, postal rates, and airline mergers, the members of this mysterious and little-understood profession act as the essential lubricant that oils the relationship between the men and women who sit in Congress and the special-interest groups the lobbyists have been hired to represent.

It is not for nothing that the lobbyists are often referred to as a fourth branch of government. Some two thousand separate and sometimes competing organizations maintain offices in the capital, with lobbyists representing everything from the two hundred members of the National Peanut Council to the gigantic labor organizations, from the fifteen thousand members of the National Apple Institute to the nearly one million members of the National Rifle Association—all with the single purpose of influencing legislation in Congress or the decisions of the executive branch in the interests of their members. Every trunk airline maintains at least two lobbyists in Washington. After suffering relentless attacks in Congress, the pharmaceutical industry has increased its Washington bureau from ten to more than seventy, with a budget that has grown in the past decade from less than $150,000 to $3.6 million. The oil lobby maintains a large staff that works hard to maintain the industry's depletion allowances. There is a highway lobby; a railroad lobby; a sugar lobby; a medical lobby, which has successfully blocked attempts to introduce a national health service for almost a generation; and—a recent phenomenon —several public-interest lobbies, notably that led by the consumers' crusader, Ralph Nader, who has been particularly effective in the field of road safety and pollution controls.

The lobbyists' function, protected by law, is that of persuasion. They maintain close contact with senators and congressmen of both parties and their staffs. They whip up public opinion whenever their interests seem threatened.

They troop up to Capitol Hill to give expert testimony before congressional committees. They spend much time with the various regulatory agencies, such as the Federal Communications Commission, the Civil Aeronautics Board, and the Federal Trade Commission. Half of the measures introduced in Congress are said to have been originally drafted in the offices of the lobbyists, who between them spend well over a billion dollars a year on their activities.

There is no means of telling just how many lobbyists are at work in Washington today or precisely how much they spend on their work. So full of loopholes is the Federal Lobbying Act that many lobbying organizations don't bother to register at all and prefer to call themselves "information-gatherers" or "public-relations officers" rather than lobbyists. Lobbying is also an activity that can be purchased on an ad hoc basis: There are about three hundred law firms in Washington that will provide lawyer-lobbyists, for a fee, for their commercial clients, while many of the best lobbyists are themselves former congressmen, including the AFL-CIO's Andrew Biemiller, a former congressman from Wisconsin, and Frank Ikard, a former congressman from Texas, who runs the oil lobby, one of the biggest and most influential of them all.

Back in the nineteenth century, the lobbyists were known as "boodlers," a disreputable group of men who won themselves a lurid reputation for gaining their ends through a more or less indiscriminate mixture of "broads, booze, and bribes." In the years after the Civil War, the section of Pennsylvania Avenue that proceeds through the heart of Washington from the Capitol to the White House was lined with gambling dens and bawdyhouses where willing senators were regularly provided with free refreshments and other pleasures of the flesh. Places with names like the Wolf's Den and the Band Box became "the recognized clearing houses for purchasable votes." Under a succession of mediocre Presidents, corruption rose to alarming heights, while Congress was reduced in many matters to a role picturesquely described by one senator as that of cattle to whom the lobbyists were merely required to say Haw and Gee in order to win their legislative support.

The aura of corruption has lingered over the reputation of the Washington lobbyists to this day. From time to time a fresh scandal comes to light to give further impetus to the unsavoury legend. As recently as the fall of 1972, a former senator was convicted of accepting an unlawful $14,500 gratuity from a Washington lobbyist who had hoped thereby to influence his vote on postal-rate legislation. In the same year there were suspicions, openly voiced but never proved, that the ITT Corporation had tried to buy its way out of an antitrust suit by offering to underwrite much of the cost of the Republican Party Convention that was to have taken place in San Diego. Further suspicions were aroused when a $300,000 donation from the dairy industry found its way into the coffers of President Nixon's re-election campaign fund soon after the government had announced it would raise the price-support levels for milk.

Because of these shady transactions, it is widely believed in Washington that a lobbyist who wants legislation or a favor from the executive branch buys it with cold cash, usually in the form of a donation to the politician's next election campaign. "You don't tell him what you want," one veteran lobbyist has said. "He knows. You tell him you understand he has a tough campaign coming up—or he had a tough campaign—and you'd like to help cover the costs. Then you leave an envelope with cash in it. The real reason you are giving the money is never mentioned."

Most lobbying activities are much more circumspect these days, however, and open bribery is the exception rather than the rule. For one thing, the legislature is on the whole a far more honest body than it was in the past. For another, most members of Congress are more addicted to power than they are to money—and power in Congress means votes. A shrewd lobbyist knows that help in winning a congressman another term at the polls is a far more persuasive technique than offering him an open bribe. The powerful labor lobby, for example, maintains an electronically stored bank of information on union members around the country, which it uses on Election Day to get out the crucial union vote to help elect those congressmen who have been friendly, or to help defeat those it opposes. The effect of this support on the congressman's subsequent voting record is said to be salutary.

Another variation of the technique is to whip up public opinion in the congressman's district on matters that engage the lobbyist's interests. The National Rifle Association—which, incidentally, claims it is not a lobbying organization at all—boasts that it can deluge Congress with a million letters and telegrams at twenty-four hours' notice whenever a measure is proposed to control the ownership or sale of guns. "I'd rather be a deer in the hunting season than a politician who has run afoul of the N.R.A. crowd," one western senator remarked not many years ago.

Not that blondes or booze have disappeared altogether from the lobbyist's repertory. Congress was recently startled when a bevy of exceptionally pretty airline stewardesses swarmed through the corridors of the Capitol, sweetly trying to charm as many Senators and congressmen as they could find into voting against a proposed merger between two big airlines. Another well-known lobbyist maintains a country estate west of Washington, complete with a well-stocked fishing stream and a large and comfortable lodge in which to entertain the friends in the capital he wishes to influence.

Lavish parties are regarded as one of the essential tools of the lobbyist's trade. "Don't leave out the parties," one veteran staff member of a Senate subcommittee told James Deakin, a Washington reporter. "They're damned important, especially with the new Congressman. The new man arrives in town with his wife. They're both a little awed. And what happens? All of a sudden, they are invited to a little dinner party given by the Washington vice president for a billion dollar corporation. They're impressed, but there's more to it than that. Let's say the Congressman is a liberal. He's suspicious of big business. What does he find? The big shot is a darned nice guy. He doesn't have horns and a tail. He charms the wife and he's deferential to the Congressman. They go away feeling a little differently. Maybe it doesn't affect the way he votes, at least not right away. But it's a softening up process." (Although not all the lobbyists' attempts to win influence through entertainment are successful. One lobbyist not long ago sent four cases of French champagne to a senator from whose party he had been excluded, with the note, "Senator, hope you and your guests enjoy this at your party Thursday." The cases were returned unopened by the senator's chauffeur without acknowledgment—and without the desired invitation.)

The image of the lobbyist as a man who wakes up in midmorning and lunches with influential Senate committee chairmen at a private table in the Rib Room at the Mayflower, casually picking up information vital to his interests and dropping equally casual hints about his client's attitude on, say, the latest nomination to the Supreme Court, provides an enduring and entertaining Washington legend. The picture, however, is incomplete. Andrew Biemiller, director of the labor movement's legislative department, has said of the craft of which he is one of the acknowledged masters, "We haven't perfected lobbying by magic. We've gotten people to understand this is a fulltime operation, a careful operation, and one in which you don't try for the spectacular."

Over the past decade, the broad-based labor lobby has been the prime mover in winning congressional support for such progressive legislation as Medicare, the war on poverty, important civil-rights bills, and approval for a loan to the Lockheed Corporation, whose collapse would have threatened many union jobs. It was also largely responsible for the defeat of two successive Supreme Court nominations, although it has also had its own share of setbacks, notably over its repeated attempts to repeal the section of the Taft-Hartley Law which prohibits the closed shop in American industry.

The labor movement's lobbying activities are part of a well-coordinated strategy worked out at weekly meetings in Biemiller's office. The six staff lobbyists gather together with other lobbyists from individual unions to report on the status of legislation in which the unions have an interest. Each man then receives his assignment for the week and is sent off to Capitol Hill to work on winning the support of the congressman or senator he knows best. The unions mounted one of their biggest lobbying operations of this decade to block the Supreme Court nomination of G. Harrold Carswell, who they believed was inimical to labor's interests.

One wavering senator was skillfully won over by Ken Young, a top AFL-CIO lobbyist who, seeing the senator's political difficulties back home, set about a subtle and successful lobbying operation to win him over. The senator had hinted that he might be persuaded to vote against Carswell if he could be assured of the support of influential voters in his home state. Young immediately set about making contacts with the senator's old law school and politically active people in local law firms who were upset at Carswell's lack of qualifications.

"I waited a couple of weeks," Young said, "and then I went back to the senator. He started grinning and said, 'I'm sure it would just amaze you to know that I got a lot of letters from the law school professors and lawyers.' "

"What do you think?" Young asked.

"I'm not going to announce my position for another week," the senator replied. "And I think it would be extremely helpful if I got more letters."

Once again the lobbyists got to work, more letters poured in from the senator's home state, and finally of course he was persuaded to vote against the Carswell nomination, a vote that without energetic lobbying might easily have gone the other way.

Public arm-twisting of this sort is one of the most common forms of the lobbyist's art. When the television industry took alarm in 1973 at the prospect of having their license renewal applications actually scrutinized, instead of being automatically approved as they had generally been in the past, the National Association of Broadcasters launched a massive campaign to introduce a bill into Congress which would have the effect of making their licenses automatically renewable—a bill which would have the effect of shutting out prospective competitors in perpetuity, as though the broadcasters now licensed actually owned the public airwaves. "A broadcaster should not have to spend a major portion of his time battling challenges for his licences," the NAB said, "—ofttimes by irresponsible people who have only to make promises and threats." The NAB accordingly formed a Washington task force to whip up public support for their protective bill. One task-force memorandum sent to broadcasters throughout the country urged each station to call together its employees and get them into the battle. "They and their families have many contacts," it said, in an apparent threat to the broadcast employees. "It should be explained that their *jobs are only as good as their licenses.*" They were also urged to persuade state legislators, mayors, police chiefs, fire chiefs, "or anyone else in your community with whom you closely work" to deluge Congress with pleas for the passage of the bill.

Such efforts, it must be admitted, are usually highly successful, although the activities of the lobbyists do on occasion backfire. The American Medical Association, for instance, has begun to alienate many of the legislators on Capitol Hill through its adamant opposition to anything that smacks of "socialized medicine" (see pp. 477ff); more and more congressmen have become suspicious of the activities of the military lobbyists; and more of them today are also having to take into account the work of the counterlobbyists, such as Ralph Nader and John Gardner, the chairman of Common Cause, a citizens' lobby that has among other things campaigned against financial secrecy in lobbying operations.

Then there is the story of the White House lobbyist who a few years back was instructed by President Johnson to inform a Texas congressman of the good news that the Pentagon had decided to close one of its bases and transfer its personnel to another base in the congressman's district. The call was received by Democratic Congressman Joe Kilgore, who listened patiently while the lobbyist explained how important the new base would be to his district, how much money it would bring in to his voters, how Kilgore was such a great friend of the President's, and how Johnson was taking good care of him —with the unspoken implication that he would one day want the favor returned.

When the lobbyist got to the end of his announcement, Kilgore told him: "You've got the wrong congressman. It's my district that's losing the base. Clark Fisher's district is getting the base."

The lobbyist quietly hung up—doubtless hoping to live to lobby another day.

While the activities of the lobbyists are normally discreet and rarely come to the attention of the wider public, just occasionally the corner of the curtain is lifted far enough to give a fascinating, if disturbing, glimpse of the cozy relationship they have developed over the years with both the legislative and executive branches of government. One such glimpse of what the Washington *Post* has called the dismal swamp of American politics—"a world inhabited by lobbyists and fixers and by politicians with short memories"—came to light in February 1972 with the now-notorious ITT affair, the first major scandal to afflict an administration that has become more immersed in the dismal swamp than any since the days of Warren Harding.

The allegation could be stated simply: In exchange for a gift of up to $400,000 to finance the Republican Party's forthcoming convention in San Diego, Nixon's Justice Department would drop antitrust suits against ITT. The circumstances that led up to this allegation opened up the world of the Washington lobbyists to unprecedented scrutiny.

The previous summer, the Justice Department had been pressing with considerable vigor an antitrust suit designed to strip ITT of the brightest jewel in its conglomerate crown, the immensely profitable and newly acquired Hartford Fire Insurance Company. The Justice Department's antitrust chief, Richard McLaren, had shown he was determined to push the Hartford case right up to the Supreme Court in an attempt to clarify the government's powers to limit the growth of conglomerates, about which he was known to be deeply concerned. Then, at a private dinner meeting on May 12, ITT's president, Harold Geneen, told a Republican congressman that ITT would pledge up to $400,000, if needed, to finance Nixon's renomination convention, at that time planned for San Diego. On July 23, the Republicans announced the convention would, indeed, take place at San Diego, at the specific request of the

President, who regarded that southern Californian city as his "lucky town." One week later, the Justice Department stated it was dropping its suits against ITT and had reached an out-of-court settlement under which the conglomerate would be stripped of several smaller affiliates, but allowed to keep the Hartford.

Later, when news of the donation to the Republicans came out, the Justice Department hotly denied there was any link between these two events. ITT's contributions, they declared, were quite unconnected with the dropping of the antitrust suits. While that may have been true, and was never conclusively proved one way or another, many people found it strange, to say the least, that the Republican Party could accept such a large financial contribution from a giant corporation whose future was at that same moment in the hands of the Justice Department of a Republican administration. The most likely answer, of course, was that no one was supposed to know; that this sort of thing happens all the time; that as Senator Roman Hruska later put it, "Conventions all over America are bought all the time by the business community." Still, to less partisan observers, it was disturbing that the two cases were so closely linked. "The worst thing about it is that they don't even realise that what they've done is wrong," said Representative Paul McCloskey, a Republican opponent of Nixon. "It's indecent for the former chief law-enforcement officer [John Mitchell, then the President's campaign manager] to be the chief politican bagman, and it's indecent for the Secretary of Commerce [Maurice Stans] to be your chief political fund raiser. And they don't even see that it's indecent."

Mitchell's involvement in the affair came to light early in 1972 when someone at the White House phoned ITT to ask whether its contribution was to go direct into the President's campaign chest or to the Republican National Convention. The inquiry so alarmed ITT's Washington lobbyist, Dita Beard, that she at once penned a sarcastic—and supposedly confidential—memorandum to her immediate boss, Bill Merriam, an ITT vice president.

"I'm so sorry we got that call from the White House," she wrote. "I thought you and I had agreed very thoroughly that under no circumstances would anyone in this office discuss with anyone our participation in the convention, including me." Other than Mitchell, H. R. Haldeman, two California politicians, and Nixon himself, no one had known, she said, from whom the $400,000 had come. She was convinced, moreover, that what she called "our noble commitment" had gone a long way towards helping negotiations on the mergers, and she concluded her memo with a revealing and most damaging final paragraph:

I hope, dear Bill, that all of this can be reconciled . . . if all of us in this office remain totally ignorant of any commitment ITT has made to anyone. If it gets too much publicity, you can believe our negotiations with Justice will get shot down. Mitchell is definitely hleping us, but can't let it be known.

Please destroy this, huh?

Unfortunately for Mrs. Beard, her confidential memo was leaked by someone at ITT and subsequently fell into the hands of Jack Anderson, Washington's muckraking journalist, who of course promptly published it. What followed might have been taken from the pages of a thirdrate thriller, with ITT's lobbyist as the unwilling but undoubtedly colorful star.

A hard-drinking, tough-talking, twice-married mother of five children, Dita Beard was clearly no shrinking violet. "I started raising hell when I was born," she said as the drama unfolded, "and I ain't quit yet." The daughter of an itinerant Army colonel, she had once been engaged to three men at the same time and had served during World War II with the Red Cross in Casablanca and Corsica, where she claimed she used to fly on P-47 missions sitting on the pilot's lap. She had drifted into ITT after the war and found her job there got better and better as the years went by. "It had been beautiful until those sons of bitches pulled this one on me," she said. When Brit Hume, Anderson's young legman, first went to see her at the ITT offices on L Street in Washington, he found her "an astonishing sight," wearing a short-sleeved sweatshirt and a pair of faded yellow cotton slacks, her horned-rimmed glasses held together by a paper clip. She reminded him of Tugboat Annie.

But when Hume faced her with his copy of the memo, tough Dita Beard spilled it all. Mitchell had told her, she said, that Nixon had given the order to "lay off ITT"—although Hume says she immediately changed the phraseology to "make a reasonable settlement, please." It was difficult to tell exactly what role Dita Beard had played in the settlement, for, as *Newsweek* put it, "like roosters and press agents, lobbyists are pleased to think that their crowing makes the sun come up," and it was not impossible that Mrs. Beard was exaggerating her role in the ITT settlement. Nevertheless, her memorandum had raised serious concern all around town. Mitchell immediately issued a statement terming her allegations "totally false." He added, for good measure, "The President has never, repeat never, made any request to me directly or indirectly concerning the settlement of the ITT case, and I took no part in the settlement."

By this time, the affair had reached the Senate Judiciary Committee, where Jack Anderson appeared to make a dramatic accusation. "The public record on this episode is blotted with falsehood," he declared. "The aura of scandal hangs over the whole matter. If Mitchell says under oath what he said in the statement he issued it will be one of the most arrogant displays of perjury this committee has ever heard."

There was, of course, one person whose presence before the committee might have cleared this up, once and for all. But Dita Beard, who had not long before been regarded as one of the half-dozen most powerful lobbyists in Washington, was by now in disgrace, disowned by the company as a crackpot and a drunk, her allegations of misconduct, according to Acting Attorney General Richard Kleindienst, simply the result of "a memorandum written by a poor soul—it's just a sad situation." The discredited lobbyist herself had some time before dropped out of sight, spirited away by E. Howard Hunt, later of Watergate fame. She later turned up in the intensive-care unit of a Denver sanatorium suffering from what her doctors described as angina pectoris. So instead of Dita Beard, the committee heard from witnesses called specifically to discredit her. One of them was Dr. Victor Liszka, a Hungarian-born surgeon who had known Mrs. Beard for nine years and who told the Committee that Mrs. Beard had been an excessive drinker who also suffered from a heart disease. When she wrote the memo, he hypothesized, she might have suffered an attack which could have caused her heart to fail to pump sufficient blood to provide oxygen for the brain. In such a case, her thoughts would not flow in a logical order. "She would become so disoriented that she would be incapable of a legal act, such as signing a will or a contract." It was unlikely that even as tough a lobbyist as Dita Beard could have dictated any sort of memorandum during a heart attack, but Dr. Liszka was by now in full flow. "Having lost the facility of judgment," he went on, "putting things together in an uncontrolled fashion—she could have written an inaccurate memo." She was, he concluded triumphantly, both "mad and disturbed" at the time she wrote it.

Unfortunately for Dr. Liszka, it turned out he had once been on the payroll of ITT to whom he had reported about Dita Beard's health for years without mentioning her emotional problems. He also acknowledged after he testified that he had at one time been investigated for possible Medicare frauds (he was later cleared, but his wife was indicted) and had moreover conferred with the Justice Department before giving his testimony. Skepticism about his credibility was therefore in order.

Further skepticism was aroused when it was disclosed that all of Mrs. Beard's papers had been hastily thrust through the ITT office shredder. Although it was claimed these contained nothing more damaging than tourist brochures, newspaper clippings, speeches, and drafts of legislation, destroyed by company policy intended to combat "man's squirrel-like instinct to keep everything," it was clear that things were not running too smoothly for either the beleaguered company or its allies in the Justice Department and the Republican Party. Realizing their attack on Mrs. Beard had backfired, they next tried another ploy. It was not long before the memorandum itself was under attack. Expert witnesses were produced before the committee to swear that as the result of "microscopic, ultra-violet fluorescence and highly sophisticated microchemical analyses" it could be said that the memo in Anderson's possession had been typed six months *after* everyone thought it had. It was, therefore, a scientifically proved forgery. What is more, Mrs. Beard, still in her Denver hospital bed, now denied she had ever written the memorandum at all. So there was nothing for it but for a special subcommittee to fly out to the Rocky Mountains and interview the invalid lobbyist at her bedside.

There, reclining on a pile of pillows, with a plastic tube inserted up her nostrils, Dita Beard testified that No, she had never written the memorandum in question, although she did admit having penned another one containing "similar language." She had not repudiated her memo earlier, she said, because ITT officials refused to believe her. Questioning continued for some two and a half hours, then, as if on cue, Mrs. Beard suddenly clutched her chest and fell backward, moaning in pain, her arms outstretched to her attendant doctors. The senators scuttled away, as one writer described it, "like abortionists at the first sign of a mortal fiasco." As they left, her doctors solemnly told them, "she will probably never be able to testify again as long as she lives."

So Mrs. Beard never did get to tell the full story of her famous memorandum. The affair fizzled out to an inconclusive end. Richard Kleindienst, who had been heavily implicated in the allegations of collusion, went on to succeed John Mitchell as Attorney General, Mitchell moved on to become the central figure in an even bigger scandal, and Richard Nixon went to Miami for his convention instead of San Diego. ITT kept the Hartford, and according to most accounts, even got its $400,000 back. It, too, was involved in a later and larger scandal, in which it was charged that the company had offered a fund of a million dollars to stir up economic and political disorder in the Republic of Chile in order to keep the Marxist Salvador Allende from coming to office. But that, as they say, is another story.

When the San Diego convention was abandoned and moved abruptly to Miami, the charges in the earlier case were quietly dropped and have never been conclusively put to the test, one way or another. Still, while it lasted, the Washington merry-go-round has never enjoyed a more public ride. As for the world of the capital lobbyists, it is clearly quite as colorful and quite as disreputable as it ever was in the days of the Wolf's Den and the Band Box.

2. Public Citizen, Inc.

"I am trying to tell people that if they can just organize to make the establishment obey its own rules, they will have created a peaceful revolution of tremendous proportions."

—RALPH NADER, 1972

He works from a shabby, almost tumbledown office in an unfashionable part of Washington, draws a salary of no more than five thousand dollars a year, owns no car, gives no parties, scrubs his teeth with baking soda, which he considers more efficient than toothpaste, and has set himself the audacious goal of a "qualitative reform of the industrial revolution," no less. To his admirers he is an American Mahatma Gandhi, simple to the point of saintliness, singleminded to the point of fanaticism, yet at the same time as shrewd —and often shrewder—than the worldly men of business and law who are the targets of his reforms. To his enemies he is also a fanatic, the national scold, a man intent—like Samson—on bringing the pillars of American capitalism crashing down. In short, Ralph Nader is an original American eccentric and one of the most significant figures to emerge in the United States in the past ten years.

He is the people's lobbyist, the citizen crusader, who in the bare seven years since the General Motors apology first thrust him into national prominence has become one of the most powerful forces in Washington. His lean six-foot-four frame has become a familiar sight at congressional hearings as wholly incorruptible, always in earnest, marshaling his facts with all the subtlety of an artillery barrage, he has brought to public attention for the first time the threat of mercury poisoning from fish, the unhygienic methods of handling meat and poultry, the overcozy relationships between the federal bureaucracy and the corporations they are supposed to regulate, the deadly dangers to miners and textile workers from occupational lung diseases. At least seven laws for the protection of the consumer have been passed almost entirely through his efforts, and his lonely crusade to compel Detroit to design safer cars has saved thousands of lives on the highways. His ideals of public service have inspired a whole host of imitators and spawned a new school of law firms dedicated to looking after the interests of the ordinary citizen. He himself believes the people can be encouraged to look upon citizenship as "a profession, an expertise"—and a fulltime profession at that.

His dedication to his own ideals is awe-inspiring. "Ralph's great strength is his spiritual quality," one congressional aide has said. "He moves around town like some fifteenth-century Franciscan, compelling men to act for the good." He lives in an eighty-dollar-a-month roominghouse, has virtually no possessions, works twenty hours a day, and displays utter contempt for leisure and the normal comforts that most Americans take for granted. "Someday we'll have a legal system that will criminally indict the president of General Motors for [his] outrageous crimes," he once told a college audience in his characteristic, bludgeonlike prose. "But not as long as this country is populated by people who fritter away their citizenship by watching TV, playing bridge, and mah-jongg, and just generally being slobs."

Members of his staff, indeed *all* responsible citizens, are expected to display the same degree of dedication, which over the years has become almost monklike in its intensity. If members of his staff take a night off to go to the cinema, they are said to be regarded next day as virtual dropouts. And there is a story that when Nader's chief aide, Ted Jacobs, took his family for a weekend at the beach, Nader asked him whatever they did when they got there. "Oh, we lie on the beach, we read the papers, we go for walks, we have lunch on the porch," Jacobs replied. Nader was genuinely incredulous: "That takes *all weekend?*"

He takes the message from his own campaigns with a deadly seriousness that amounts almost to crankishness, with a touch of self-dramatization thrown in. He refuses ever to ride in a Volkswagen, a vehicle he has described as "a portable funeral parlor," and on a recent visit to Japan he ate nothing at an elaborate banquet featuring the local delicacy, raw fish. "Ever since a guy described amoebic dysentery to me when I was nineteen," he explained, "there is no way I'll eat strange stuff." He is liable to harangue air hostesses about the poor quality of airline food, and after accepting a ride in a Firebird he at once rolled down the window, explaining to his startled host, "This is one of the models that leaks combustion gas."

In his public speeches, too, he makes his points with the same ferocity, using outrageous comparisons as one of his chief bludgeons. Americans, he likes to point out, spend nine times more on control of bad breath than they do on air pollution. "Do you know," he says to his college audiences, "you can be arrested for urinating in the street, but industry is free to pollute the nation's rivers and lakes?"

"Why don't we talk about the really big forms of violence?" he asks. "I don't know of any hippies or yippies who have managed to smog New York City or contaminate the Gulf of Mexico. But I know companies that have done that." Do they realize the government spends more money to protect migratory birds than it does on auto safety? Are they aware that General

Motors spent $250 million to change its signs to read, "GM: Mark of Excellence" but spent only one tenth of that figure in the past twenty years to develop alternative propulsion systems that will not pollute the air? Out it pours, outrage after outrage, naïve in its way, but perhaps all the more effective for that. For there is guile as well as idealism in Nader's speeches, which are always backed up by action—action to prod the federal bureaucracy into movement, law suits against General Motors, a citizens' handbook on Congress that qualitatively assesses the effectiveness of each member of the Senate and House of Representatives, testimony before Senate committees demanding action—always immediate action.

Every time he branches out into a new field, takes on some new corporate giant, his enemies happily predict that Nader has a last overreached himself. "We are witnessing the balkanization of Nader," one hostile lobbyist remarked recently. "It may be the end of him; I hope so." But Nader of course survives, a permanent and important part of the Washington landscape. "Ralph hasn't changed," says an old associate. "He's still a basically sound fanatic."

The private Nader is a decidedly softer figure than the ferocious public image; he is shy in his personal relationships, with a surprisingly quiet and gentle voice. He was born in 1934 in the small Connecticut village of Winsted, the younger son of Lebanese immigrants who ran a local restaurant called the Highland Arms. His father, Nathra Nader, who had arrived in America with twenty dollars in his pocket, instilled in his son an early respect for the democratic traditions of their adopted country. "When I went past the Statue of Liberty," Nathra Nader has said, "I took it seriously." The Highland Arms gained a local reputation as a disputatious place; it was said in Winsted that you always got a dollar's worth of conversation with every ten-cent cup of coffee. A local doctor, one day ordering a drink in the restaurant, told Nathra Nader he scaled his fees according to the patient's income. "I like that idea!" the older Nader replied. "For you the martini is five dollars. For a poor man, it's ten cents."

As foreigners, the family were outside the Connecticut mainstream. Ralph was brought up to speak Arabic as well as English and the Arab influence has lingered to this day, not least in the use to which he puts the English language. Some of his biographers have suggested he does not really understand English, in the sense that he does not hear the poetic echoes, the emotive nuances of English words. "If to a poet words are tuning forks, then to Nader they are hammers and chisels," Charles McCarry has written, suggesting that in the Near East, where people are largely illiterate and mostly devout, language is designed to appeal to the ear and the heart rather than the eye and the mind. This tradition has perhaps also played its part in shaping the hyperbole of Ralph Nader.

As a schoolboy, Nader was a passionate collector of baseball statistics and at fourteen was already reading his way through the turgid pages of the *Congressional Record.* Later he went to Princeton, the most aristocratic of the eastern universities, where he majored in Russian and Chinese. His father, proud enough to be able to afford to pay for his children's education himself, forbade him to apply for a scholarship, while it is said Nader characteristically chose Princeton above other colleges because the air was cleaner there. He had a distinguished academic career, taking time out to campaign unsuccessfully against the use of DDT on the college campus on the ground that it was killing birds and might be doing harm to the students. He also became a famous hitchhiker, later boasting that all the time he was at college he never once traveled on public transportation. After Princeton, he went on to Harvard Law School, almost like a true son of the eastern establishment. He was disappointed, however, in the education Harvard had to offer, feeling that it concentrated far too much on turning out smooth establishment lawyers for the benefit of large corporations. "Harvard was simply unbelievable," he remarked, "a high-priced tool factory."

By this time, he was already concerned with auto safety, a subject he came to after the death of a college friend in a crash. He had already amassed an awesome file of statistics when he was drafted into the U.S. Army in 1959. He spent the next six months working as a chef, preparing huge quantities of food for the soldiers at Fort Dix, once helping to make banana cake for forty thousand men. When he was discharged from the Army, his papers declared with a sublime unawareness of the future: "Equivalent civilian status—executive chef."

Nader spent the next six years in obscurity, accumulating the data for his book on the GM Corvair, *Unsafe at Any Speed,* and was generally regarded in these years as something of a crackpot. In 1964, he got a job with Daniel Moynihan in the Labor Department as a consultant on highway safety, working mainly at night when the department was deserted. "Ralph was a very suspicious man," Moynihan later told Charles McCarry. "He used to warn me that the phone at the Labor Department might be tapped. I'd say, 'Fine ! They'll learn that the unemployment rate for March is 5.3 per cent, that's what they'll learn!' But he kept on warning me."

This feeling of paranoia, the idea that people are shadowing him, tapping his phones, prying into his private affairs, at first only added to Nader's crackpot status. Then came the GM affair, which proved that Nader's suspicions had been only too well founded (see Chapter Five, Section Two). It is now clear that the humble apology he forced out of the chairman of General Motors that March day in 1966 marked a turning point in America's industrial civilization: David had felled Goliath. Nader, characteristically enough, was not in the hearingroom when Roche made his celebrated apology. He was stranded on the sidewalk outside his roominghouse, frantically trying to summon one of Washington's notoriously fickle taxis to carry him to Capitol Hill. When he arrived, breathless and apologetic before the Senate hearing, Roche's testimony was over. "As I waited and waited and waited to get a cab," he told the committee, "and as my frustration mounted, I almost felt like going out and buying a Chevrolet."

The key part of Nader's own testimony that day was the statement, "I am responsible for my actions, but who is responsible for those of General Motors? An individual's capital is basically his integrity. He can lose only once. A corporation can lose many times and not be affected."

This time, however, General Motors had lost once too often. The hearings thrust Nader into national prominence overnight. They gave him a constituency that today brings in over ninety thousand letters a year. They were to prove the foundation of a national consumer movement more powerful than any since Upton Sinclair had campaigned against the packers of diseased and filthy meat in his book *The Jungle* back in 1906. They have provided the basis, financial and moral, of all that Nader has achieved since.

Today, the consumer movement he personifies is still primarily a concern of the affluent. The poor, the underprivileged, the racial minorities, are more concerned with basic movements to establish their civil rights and with escaping from their own poverty than they are with the flaws in the doorlocks of a new Rolls-Royce or the rape of national forests by logging companies, although Nader himself vehemently denies that his movement does not appeal to the underprivileged. "Who do they think gets cheated, diseased, crippled, and generally screwed if not the minorities and the poor?" he asks. As far as it goes, that is perfectly true. Nevertheless, his movement has been notably unsuccessful in recruiting blacks, for instance, and his Raiders, almost all of them, are products of expensive private schools and the most élite eastern universities, young men and women who can afford the idealism to rise above the subtle system of corruption that causes ordinary workers to accept shoddy workmanship and inferior produce. Most people, after all, spend their lives as producers as well as consumers, and it takes an altogether out-of-the-ordinary spirit to complain about the practices that bring him his own weekly paycheck. As Sylvia Kronstedt of New York City's Department of Consumer Affairs has perceptively observed:

> Our guilt is shared. The executives at the top of the machine may profit more from consumer fraud, but that is merely a structural reality, and not the foundation of the fraud, nor the driving force behind its perpetuation. In order for deceit to flourish, compromise and complicity must permeate the economic system. And at every level the motivation is the same; each of us wants more for himself, and to get it we are willing to cheat, facilitate cheating, ignore cheating, or rationalize cheating. The fact that those at the top are getting more does not alter the fact that we're all grabbing. . . .

Our general failure to view the madness of the marketplace as a complex and full-blown human problem, instead of a somewhat romanticized confrontation between good and evil, has thrust the consumer advocate into the role of heroically protective white knight, a role that, besides being unrealistic, has the potential for working to the consumer's detriment.

In the 1970s, Ralph Nader, the original White Knight, sits at the hub of what has become a virtual conglomerate of consumerism. There is the Center for the Study of Responsive Law, the Center for Auto Safety, the Fishermen's Clear Water Action Project, Public Citizen, Inc., and many others, spending altogether almost a million dollars a year on their various activities. Nader raises the money through royalties on the organizations' publications, his lecture fees (at three thousand dollars an appearance), public donations, and grants from private foundations, some of them running into hundreds of thousands of dollars. Nader is no longer the single-issue evangelist, the Lone Ranger of consumerism; he has become a brand name. "He's franchising himself like a chain of fried chicken restaurants," complains the president of the First National City Bank, the target of one of Nader's critical reports.

That is the main criticism against the Nader movement today: that Nader is spreading himself too thin, that the quality of his work has begun to suffer because he no longer has the time to supervise all his projects effectively. Nader is no stranger to criticism, of course. From his earliest days he has been the subject of invective from corporate interests, who sometimes portray him as a direct threat to the survival of American capitalism. "Nader behaves like a dictator," the American Automobile Association declared in a dispute about the effectiveness of airbags. It went on to accuse him of "creating public paranoia with the whistle-blowing Gestapo technique." Even the owners of Corvair cars, which Nader had exposed as "deathtraps on wheels," have rallied against him, forming the Corvair Club of America to defend the car against Nader's campaigns, doubtless feeling that their own judgment was under attack for having bought the vehicle in the first place. Other lobbyists have called him an egomaniac who makes more speeches in a year than a presidential candidate. His technique of issuing complaints to the press before they have been seen by the organizations under attack has been likened to McCarthyism.

In the past, Nader has always shrugged off such attacks with ease. When it gets down to motives, he has invariably been able to demonstrate that he is on the side of the angels, while his critics have in some way been tainted by money, politics, or corporate interests. He is justly proud of some of his earlier reports, like that on the Federal Trade Commission, which was later backed up almost word for word in an investigation undertaken by the Nixon Administration and which led to the most sweeping reorganization in that moribund agency's existence. But lately, other studies have come in for severe and sometimes justified criticism even from those parts of the press that sailed off on a prolonged honeymoon with the Nader movement at the end of the 1960s. "The press let him get away with unforgiveable sloppiness without the slightest criticism," says Joseph Rigo, a New York banker. "It is easier to write off a stateful of professional colleagues as hacks and cowards than believe that Nader's victims might have a point when they say that his investigators don't know what they are talking about."

Rigo was upset at Nader's attack on the First National City Bank in a report which many bankers found sloppy and ill-informed. He was particularly unhappy at the constitution of Nader's investigatory team, most of whom were law students, "young, socially oriented, and totally uncorrupted by knowledge of their subject." There were further accusations that Nader had overreached his own resources when he released a 1,200-page report on the use of land and power in California that had been prepared by a team of twenty-five young Raiders. "His investigators have come up with a report that is flawed by minor inaccuracies and burdened with its own bias," wrote the *Wall Street Journal.* "Worse, it is largely irrelevant." The main charge against the team of young Raiders was that they had made blanket accusations of corruption and conflict of interest against California legislators which they had failed to back up with a single specific instance of wrongdoing. "They moved in and moved out, pillaging and raping as they went," complained A. Alan Post, a California legislative analyst. "We can't afford to do that sort of thing on a day-to-day basis here."

The nagging concern that Nader, equipped with insufficient data, has begun to shoot from the hip, has also been growing stronger lately. The press, once so uncritical, now pounces on every inaccuracy. The Associated Press, for example, reported that Nader had slipped up in a speech at the University of Utah, when he charged that makers of orange juice were making $150 million by watering their product, and in his characteristic style, comparing this sum to the $8 million bank robbers take in each year. The $150 million figure, however, was immediately challenged. "Nader says now he was talking about a ten-year period," says the AP. "But he didn't say so in his speech." There was a further example of shooting from the hip when Nader charged darkly that General Motors had advance knowledge of the Nixon Administration's wage-and-price freeze. When Cabinet officials challenged him to prove it, however, he was forced to back down, saying that the evidence was "circumstantial."

There is no doubt that by institutionalizing himself Nader has become prone to the problems of bigness and quality control that he criticizes in others. His Raiders are now producing massive and detailed reports at a rate which sometimes exceeds two a month; it is obviously impossible for Nader to watch over them all with the same care he devoted to his own reports on the Corvair and the FTC. He has chosen instead to delegate the work, to rely on others, and some of them are simply not as good at it as he is.

Nader himself believes the complaints about inaccuracy are exaggerated.

"We neither have government authority, nor do we have corporate wealth and power," he said in a recent newspaper interview. "So the extent of our acceptance is pretty much in proportion to the acceptance of values and facts by the community. Where else does our power come from? We can't prosecute anybody, tax anybody, regulate anybody, can't get campaign funds, we can't generate three million votes or anything. It's the classic model of accountability. Every day some columnist says, 'Ah, they've gone too far' and this and that. We can't make many mistakes."

Further, he believes that criticisms that he is spreading himself too thin miss the more fundamental point that he is trying to achieve his objectives by example, to instill in the entire United States a new concept of citizenship—full time, active, and participatory. He has even written a manual for students, spelling out to them how they can organize their own Public Interest Research Groups, and he later hopes to move on to form similar groups among retired people, who have the spare time, the skills, and the experience to become a powerful new force in the consumer movement. He has written in his handbook:

> Building a new way of life around citizenship action must be the program of the immediate future. The ethos that looks upon citizenship as an avocation or opportunity must be replaced with the commitment to citizenship as an obligation, a continual receiver of our time, energy and skill. And that commitment must be transformed into a strategy of action that develops instruments of change while it focuses on what needs to be done.
>
> This is a critical point. Too often, people who are properly outraged over injustice concentrate so much on decrying the abuses and demanding the described reforms that they never build the instruments to accomplish their objectives in a lasting manner.

In the long run, Ralph Nader's greatest contribution to society may not be the legislation he has personally forced Congress to adopt, or the new accountability he has thrust onto the big corporations, or the protection he has individually won for the consumer, but rather the formation of this entirely new concept of participatory citizenship, which by example he has spread in seven short years to law schools and universities across the entire nation. Like all great leaders, his first concern has been to take care of the succession: Through his example, it now seems certain that the consumer movement will become an important and permanent part of American society.

3. The AMA: Health and Politics

"If we want to keep politics out of medicine, we must get into politics."
—Dr. Gunnar Gundersen, *former president, American Medical Association*

Jim Rieger and his wife, both textile workers in the industrial city of Cleveland, were expecting their second child when disaster struck. They had been married a couple of years and had already learned from their first experience how expensive it was to have a baby in America. But Mr. Rieger had hospital insurance through his employer, a clothing manufacturer, and although he had been temporarily laid off work because of a local trucking strike, there seemed to be no reason why they could not afford a second child.

The baby, however, was two months premature, and while giving birth Mrs. Rieger suffered a cardiac arrest. Her heart stopped beating during labor and to save her life she had to be given an emergency tracheotomy to help her to breathe and electroshock treatments to restart her heart. Then she caught pneumonia, and her lungs collapsed. She was put at once into the intensive-care unit at Cleveland Metropolitan Hospital, where she was kept for two months. The baby, a girl, lived for six months, five of which were spent in the infant intensive-care unit at the same hospital. The cost of this personal tragedy for the Rieger family was $20,000 in hospital bills. Mr. Rieger's insurance company paid only $350 of that, and although he was back at work by the time the bills arrived, he was earning only $120 a week, with an unpaid debt hanging over his head that he could not possibly meet.

Not long afterwards, someone from the credit department at the hospital called up on the telephone and said, "Mr. Rieger, you owe us some money. When are you going to come up with it?"

"I told them I couldn't get twenty thousand dollars," Mr. Rieger replied. "And the lady on the phone said, 'Why don't you go to a finance company and borrow twenty thousand dollars?' I asked her which loan company would give me that much money. . . . I told them that if they would come down to a reasonable amount that I could possibly handle, I would be more than glad to handle it. Because, like I said, they saved my wife's life."

In the end, the Riegers were forced into bankruptcy. Their stove, refrigerator, and television set, all of which had been brought on credit, were repossessed. "They came right away and took them," Mr. Rieger told the Senate Subcommittee on Health, which was holding hearings on the cost of hospital care in America. "I tried calling the bank that I had [financed] the stove and refrigerator and TV through; I explained to them that I would like to revive it, but they wouldn't talk to me. What can I do? . . . As it is, the only way I can buy anything I want or need, no matter how bad a necessity it might be, is by paying cash for it."

The shocking thing about the tragedy that struck the Rieger family is that it could happen to anyone. Similar stories were told again and again to the Senate Subcommittee in its hearings during 1971: A boy who was paralyzed playing football had plunged his family into financial destitution; a bank president in Denver injured in a road accident was faced with costs at a rehabilitation center of $3,000 a month, which was not covered by his normal medical insurance; a university professor died from cancer of the brain, leaving his widow with staggering hospital bills.

The stark fact is that the United States remains the only industrial nation in the world without some form of compulsory health-insurance program to cover all its citizens. As a result, almost all Americans are forced to take a colossal gamble on their health, never certain whether their private insurance policies will cover the costs if they are struck by catastrophic illness or accident. Although old-age pensioners, poor people on welfare, and sufferers from certain chronic illnesses do now receive free treatment under Medicare and Medicaid legislation, these programs reach fewer than eight million Americans, while families still at work, those normally regarded as the secure backbone of the affluent society, remain the most vulnerable of all.

After Mr. Rieger had finished his testimony at the Senate Subcommittee's hearings, Senator Edward Kennedy observed:

> Mr. Rieger, this could happen to anyone, this kind of problem. The complications of childbirth that were involved produced this extraordinary medical bill, $20,000 in four or five months. This could happen to anyone in this country. And, of course, the question I think we as Americans have to ask ourselves is, "Why do we have to have a system which adds such a financial burden to the pain and trauma and sense of loss that you felt in terms of your infant, and the extraordinary kinds of hardships that your wife has been confronted with?"
>
> I think you should be asking us, "Why in this nation of ours don't we have a health system that is more compassionate, more concerned, and more sensitive to these kinds of needs?" That question is long, long overdue.

In 1971, every man, woman, and child in America spent an average of $358 on health care, by far the highest per capita figure in the world. And yet, by the standards of other western countries, the United States is not a healthy nation. In the measurement of male life expectancy, actuarial tables prepared by the World Health Organization put America eighteenth among the nations of the world, with an average male life expectancy of 66.8 years against well over 71 years for the men of Scandinavia and surpassed even by such comparatively poor countries as Greece and Italy. It is sometimes suggested that American males die earlier because of the stresses of modern business, but that theory is demolished by the actuarial tables that show that the poor die sooner than the rich and that black men in America die sooner than whites—and black men, of course, are not conspicuous in the higher echelons of management where stress is said to bring on heart disease.

In the figures for infant mortality, the picture is equally bleak. Each year some eighty thousand American babies die before they reach their first birthday—an infant-mortality rate that is worse than East Germany's and fourteenth among the countries of the world—first in wealth, fourteenth in infant mortality. In slum areas, of course, the rate is far worse than that, with forty-five deaths for every thousand live deliveries by black women in the ghettoes of Chicago, roughly the same as the infant-mortality rate in Ecuador. It has been calculated that if, with adequate medical care, the infant-mortality rate in America could be reduced to the level of Sweden's, over fifty thousand lives would be saved every year.

Clearly, the problems of infant mortality are partly brought on by poverty. In testimony given to the Senate, Dr. Martin Cherkasky, director of the Montefiore Hospital and Medical Center in the Bronx declared:

> In the southern Bronx with 650,000 people, mostly Negro and Puerto Ricans— mostly at the poverty level—the infant mortality rate per thousand live births is 37.3, while in the northern Bronx, primarily middle-class white, it is 18.8. A gap of twenty-five blocks and a social and economic gap of astronomical proportions dooms twice as many babies to death in the greatest city in the greatest country in the world.

While this state of affairs might be put down to the poverty that blights America's ghettoes, the lack of adequate medical care has in the past decade also become one of the major problems facing middle-class Americans, as the testimony before Senator Kennedy's subcommittee clearly displayed. Partly as a result of the blight of inflation that has recently afflicted American health care, health-insurance premiums have risen 165 percent in the space of a single decade, doctors' fees by 60 percent, and hospital charges by 170 percent, so that in large cities like New York it now costs at least a hundred dollars for a single day in the hospital. As a group, the country's quarter of a million practicing physicians have become the highest-paid workers in the world, with a median income that exceeds $50,000. And yet, for all the expenditure, medicine remains, in the words of Senator Kennedy, "the fastest growing failing business in the nation," and one out of every seven Americans now has no health insurance at all, either because he cannot afford it or because he has a health problem that insurance companies will not insure.

The root of the problem of health care can be summed up in a single word: commercialism. Medicine in America is run on the principles of business. Deliberately and by choice, the medical profession has built its edifice upon the philosophy of unregulated capitalism. Good health is a commodity to be purchased; a service is offered, fees are set at a rate the market will bear, government interference is abhorred as "socialistic," and any attempt at reform is reviled as a blow to he traditions of liberty. As a result, those who can afford it are offered the best, the most expensive, and the most lavish treatment offered by medical practitioners anywhere in the world. The American Medical Association demands high standards from the physicians who make up its membership and claims that the care they provide is unsurpassed. As far as it goes, that is perfectly true—for those who can afford it. The principle collapses, however, because of the simple fact that medical treatment is a service that is at some time or another required by every member of society, by the poor as well as the rich, by those who cannot afford expensive treatment as well as by those who can afford it, by the indigent and the unlucky members of society as well as by those who are hardworking and thrifty.

When good health is a commodity to be purchased, those without money must go without the commodity. The principle of much American medicine is as simple and brutal as that. In the Deep South, where black poverty is endemic, health standards among the remaining black field workers are abysmal. After a tour of Bolivar County in the delta region of Mississippi, Carl M. Cobb of the Boston *Globe* wrote:

> Asked what they do when a patient is dying and has no money, one doctor said bluntly, "If there is a nigger in my waiting room who doesn't have three dollars in cash [a day's wage for a black man], he can sit there and die. I don't treat niggers without money."

The doctor's attitude was not an isolated one, Cobb found. "No money, no medicine, it is as simple as that," another (black) doctor told him. "Why, if I was giving away my service, I'd have 'em lined up clear to the Mississippi River."

The problem, however, is not simply one of poverty. Medicine that is run as a business also ignores the fact that the average consumer of medical services, however wealthy, approaches his purchase in ignorance. As Elton Rayack has pointed out in his study of the professional power of American medicine, the physician is in a position to create a demand for his own product, decide whether or not drugs are required, whether or not hospitalization is desirable, and whether or not surgery is necessary. In all these matters, the consumer must rely upon his faith in the integrity and competence of the physician. If it is a business, it is one that in financial terms is heavily loaded in favor of the medical entrepreneur and against the unfortunate and unwilling consumer.

Because they are businesses, run on sound commercial principles, it is common for hospitals to make certain that payment is assured before they will accept a patient. An elderly and relatively rich English widow on holiday in San Francisco recently suffered a slipped disc that required her temporary hospitalization, but because she carried a form of insurance that was locally unfamiliar, the ambulance men who arrived to carry her on a stretcher from her hotel to the hospital demanded payment for their services—in cash— before they would accept her. And just before Christmas in 1969, a ten-year-old Chicago boy suffered a seizure at home and was rushed by his father to the nearest hospital. The boy was dying, but before the hospital would admit him the father was subjected to an interview by the accounts department on his financial status: Did he own his own home? For whom did he work? What type of medical insurance did he carry? When the father protested, he was informed, "If you don't like the service here, take him elsewhere." In desperation the father drove his son, who was by this time passing into a coma, along the expressway into another hospital where he—and his financial status—was already known. The son died soon after arrival there, but that did not prevent the first hospital (which had in effect rejected him) from sending a bill for their services: $12.50 for use of the emergency room and $7.00 for the doctor's fee.

In all these cases, the evidence that American health care is at once an open scandal and a national disgrace would seem to be overwhelming. The case for the creation of a comprehensive, all-embracing national health service would seem to be equally overwhelming. It is now more than ninety years since Bismarck set up in Germany the first compulsory system of health insurance and over sixty years since David Lloyd George laid the foundations of a similar system in Britain; in America, pressures for such a service have been building up for well over a generation, yet until now they have been successfully resisted by the medical profession itself.

In the past fifty years, the American Medical Association has spent well over ninety million dollars in its relentless battle to retain the practice and control of medicine in private hands. "The dread of outside interference has led the AMA to oppose even the mildest and most constructive official and semi-official intrusions, including compulsory inoculation against diphtheria and compulsory vaccination against smallpox, the mandatory reporting of tuberculosis cases to public-health agencies, the establishment of public venereal disease clinics and of Red Cross blood banks, federal grants for medical school construction and medical student loans, Blue Cross and other private health insurance programs, government subsidies to reduce maternal and infant deaths, and free centers for cancer diagnosis," writes Richard Harris in his book *A Sacred Trust.* He might also have added to this melancholy list the AMA's opposition to publicly financed polio immunization, equal opportunity in medical education, and health benefits for veterans of World War I. In each case, the AMA's opposition has been based on the argument that they constituted "bureaucratic interference with the sacred rights of the American home," and even that some of them would tend "to promote Communism."

The AMA has long been regarded as one of the most powerful lobbies in Washington, with an annual operating budget that approaches thirty-million dollars, drawn mostly from membership dues drawn from the 156,000 doctors who belong to the association and from advertising revenues from its many publications. The association registers only eight full time lobbyists in Washington, four who deal with its relations with Congress and four who deal with the various offices of the executive branch, such as the Department of Health, Education, and Welfare, the White House, and the Veterans' Administration. In 1971, they reported, as required by law, an expenditure on lobbying of only $114,800, but this represents merely the tip of the iceberg. The fact is that almost everyone who belongs to the association, from the nine hundred members of the headquarters staff in Chicago, the fifty members of the legislative office in Washington, the officials of the state and county medical societies, down to many individual members, are engaged in political activities of one form or another. Because of its status as a tax-exempt institution, the association is actually forbidden to make direct financial contributions to political candidates or to engage directly in their campaigns, but these loose requirements have been neatly circumvented by the formation of a supposedly "independent" operation known as the American Medical Political Action Committee (AMPAC), whose board of directors is appointed by the AMA's own board of trustees and which receives direct financial contributions from the AMA for "educational purposes." AMPAC is thus able to participate directly in the electoral process, providing campaign literature, advice on precinct organization, instruction on voter-registration drives, and help in getting out the vote on Election Day. It has been estimated that the association spends over eight million dollars a year on its various political activities, a total many times greater than the figure officially reported for its lobbying operation.

From their offices in Washington, the lobbyists of the AMA can flood the office of an influential senator or congressman with a avalanche of mail from its supporters around the country. It has been able to put enough pressure on President Nixon to persuade him to drop an appointee as HEW's top health officer of whom the Association disapproved. It provides favored legislators with detailed research and spokesmen to help his electoral campaign. It has brought a small army of doctors' wives into the battle against medical health insurance. In its fight to keep medicine in private hands, it has marshaled all the modern techniques for the manipulation of public opinion. It has even managed to obtain the right to examine the scripts of popular television shows such as *Dr. Kildare* and *Marcus Welby, M.D.*, in order to check not only their medical accuracy but their ideological content as well. And some years ago one of its affiliate organizations offered cash prizes of three thousand dollars apiece to newspapers which published the best editorial cartoons attacking the national health-insurance concept.

On Capitol Hill, where its influence is perhaps the greatest, it has learned to exert its pressures subtly and indirectly. "We make friends by doing little favors," one of the AMA's Washington lobbyists was once quoted as saying. "I may help a congressman write a speech. Another may want to know how to get his son into medical school. I tell him how. Still another needs advice on getting his sick wife into hospital, and I help." An experienced lobbyist knows not to make an approach to a congressman who opposes him, but concentrates on known friends or those who may be sympathetic to the crusade. Winning friends in order to influence people is the basis of his creed. "Psychological pressures are far sounder than financial or political pressures," one highly successful lobbyist told Richard Harris. He went on to describe his technique in a highly revealing glimpse of the lobbyist's art:

> I spend far the largest part of my time on personal attention. Say, for example, that I'm talking to a Senator who is a member of a key committee and I notice that he's coming down with a cold. Well, after I leave I stop off at the nearest drugstore and send a messenger with a bottle of cold tablets to him. Who could accuse me of trying to buy anyone with a dollar's worth of cold tablets? But it's remembered. It's thoughtful. Or say one of his staffers is leaving to take another job back home. I hear about it, and the next time I see the Senator I mention what a good egg this fellow is and I'd like to give him a nice sendoff. How about if I bring a pile of steaks and a case of Scotch to the Senator's house and we all have a cookout? After all, the man is leaving, so how could it be considered pressure? But it's another thoughtful act. . . .
>
> Slowly, slowly, we become friends, and before long I can come and go at will. If I'm careful, he'll never even realize what's happened. One time, I was standing out in the corridor with a Senator I'd become friendly with when a lobbyist for another outfit went by. The Senator didn't like him, and when the man was out of earshot he turned to me and said, "Another lousy lobbyist!" He'd forgotten that I was one, too.

When crucial bills are pending, the activities of the lobbyists become intense. During its campaign against President Johnson's Medicare legislation, the AMA moved into high gear and spent almost a million dollars in a period of only three months. "The pressure was the most intense I've ever experienced," one senator remarked soon afterwards. "I had made it absolutely clear that I was going to vote for the bill, but the AMA wouldn't listen. They

Lobbyists

sent a delegation from home to visit me—my doctor, my wife's doctor, three other doctors I was friendly with back home, and four state party officials who had a lot to say about campaign funds. They were here for a week, and they pounded away at me every chance they got. It was intolerable. I learned later that the local medical society picked up the tab for their trip, which came to over five thousand dollars."

A little later, the AMA mounted a massive publicity campaign, sending every member of Congress seventy-one magazine-style pages of literature opposing Medicare. Senators were flooded with letters from their constituents, much of it of the variety known in Washington as "canned mail." Joseph Tydings, a freshman senator from Maryland, conscientiously and a little naïvely set about writing replies to the letters that poured into his office. Of the first 350 replies sent from his office, 72 came back marked "no such street," "addressee unknown," or "deceased." In its efforts to protect the privileged status of its members, the AMA does not hesitate to whip up an entirely spurious public reaction to prove that it is on the side of the people.

In its opposition to government interference in matters of health care, the AMA, writes Ed Cray in *In Failing Health*, has drifted with the nation "first into prosperity, then into conservatism and finally into complacency."

The AMA has been conducting its fight against what it unfailingly refers to as "socialized medicine" ever since Harry Truman unexpectedly won re-election in 1948 and returned to the White House determined to enact compulsory health-insurance legislation. The inauguration was scarcely over when the association began to build up a $3.5 million "war chest," for which each AMA member was assessed $25. Realizing that "you can't beat something with nothing," they based their campaign on support for voluntary health insurance while violently attacking any form of compulsory scheme. Perhaps the best-remembered slogan of that campaign was a poster that appeared in the waiting rooms of some ninety thousand doctors across the country showing a touching nineteenth-century scene with a country doctor sitting head in hand by a small sick girl while the father stands by helplessly and the mother weeps. The caption read:

KEEP POLITICS OUT OF THIS PICTURE!
When the life or health of a loved one is at stake, hope lies in the devoted service of your Doctor. Would you change this picture?
Compulsory health insurance is political medicine. It would bring a third party—a politician—between you and your Doctor. It would bind up your family's health in red tape. It would result in heavy payroll taxes—and inferior medical care for you and your family. Don't let that happen here!

In the face of this onslaught, the Truman bill was quietly buried in committee up on Capitol Hill; the AMA had persuaded the "do nothing" Congress that public opinion was opposed to the formation of a national health service in America and had succeeded in drowning out the results of a Gallup poll that showed that a majority of Americans were even then in favor of national health insurance.

Eisenhower's election in 1952 ensured that medicine would be left securely in private hands for eight more years, although Ike did create a new Cabinet-level department to coordinate health, education, and welfare activities. But America still had no form of federally financed health care, even for the indigent poor and the sixteen million old people, two thirds of whom were living on incomes of less than a thousand dollars a year.

Federal aid for health care for the aged was therefore one of the principal domestic issues in the presidential election of 1960, when John Kennedy accused the Republican Party candidate, Richard Nixon, of taking the position that the country could not afford medical care for the aged. Nixon's position, following the AMA theme, was that the issue was between voluntary and compulsory insurance. The tide seemed to be running in Kennedy's direction, and the votes of people over sixty-five undoubtedly helped him into office, leading a worker at the Democratic National Committee headquarters to observe, "From where I sat, I'd say it was those fellows at the AMA who put Kennedy in the White House."

Soon after his inauguration, therefore, Kennedy declared that Medicare for the aged would be the first order of business for his administration. Yet when his bill was introduced in Congress (providing for ninety days of free hospital care, outpatient services, nursing-home care, home visits for pensioners, and certain other benefits), the AMA described it as "the most deadly challenge" that the medical profession had ever faced and called upon its 180,000 members to wage an all-out effort to defeat it. The AMA fought its battle all through Kennedy's Thousand Days. At one point its women's auxiliary launched a countrywide drive they called Operation Coffee Cup, during which doctors' wives invited their friends to sip coffee and listen to a tape recording by Ronald Reagan, who was just then beginning to dip his toes in the political waters of California. "One of the traditional methods of imposing statism or socialism on a people has been by way of medicine," Reagan said, urging his listeners and their friends to write letters to Congress. "If you don't do this," he went on, "one of these days you and I are going to spend our sunset years telling our children and our children's children what it was once like in America when men were free." The hostess then passed out pens, writing paper, and preaddressed envelopes and stamps.

Some time later, Kennedy appeared before a rally of senior citizens at Madison Square Garden to give an important policy address on Medicare. There, to everyone's surprise, he delivered what is regarded as one of the worst speeches of his career. The AMA at first demanded equal free time on the television networks to reply to him, but when this was denied they bought an hour of prime time and also rented Madison Square Garden, at a cost of some

$100,000, to make a pitch to the audiences watching at home. The TV presentation began with a shot of the littered arena left behind by Kennedy's audience, then switched to a shot of Dr. Edward Annis, head of the Association's speakers' bureau, who declared to the empty auditorium, "I'm not a cheerleader, I'm a physician." It was the cue for a vehement and effective assault on Kennedy's rally:

> These people know how to rally votes, rally support, rally crowds and mass meetings. That's quite a bit of machinery to put behind something, isn't it? Who can match it? Certainly not your doctors. . . . Men and women of America, I appeal to your sense of fairness! Nobody—certainly not your doctors—nobody can compete in this unfamiliar art of public persuasion against such massive publicity, such enormous professional machinery, such unexplained money, and such skillful manipulation!

Dr. Annis was credited with a great propaganda victory. As one labor official put it, "his distortions were simply more credible than Kennedy's truths." Partly as a result of this contest, the President's Medicare proposals went down to defeat in the Senate. In his biography of Kennedy, Theodore Sorensen said the President "never got over the disappointment of this defeat."

In the end, it was President Johnson who finally persuaded Congress to pass the Medicare bill in the heady days after his landslide victory in the elections of 1964. Johnson's consummate ability as a politician, his long experience as the Senate Majority Leader, had made him wise in the ways of converting dreams into programs. It led him now to the conclusion that the bill stood no chance of passage without the active support of Congressman Wilbur Mills, chairman of the crucial Ways and Means Committee, which had hitherto been the graveyard of all previous Medicare legislation. Mills has been described as the most cautious man in the House, where his committee is sometimes known as the In No Way and By No Means Committee, and he was worried about the actuarial soundness of the Medicare plans. Mills moved slowly, "but he was also a man who knew how to count votes," as Johnson said of him later. "He never liked to be overrun or defeated or outdistanced, and he rarely was." After Johnson's landslide victory, Mills finally became convinced that Medicare's hour had come, and he was persuaded by Johnson to help sponsor it. "On a great controversial issue like this one," wrote a New York *Daily News* columnist, "Mills wasn't a conservative or a liberal or a moderate. He was a politician. And he has always been a consummately adroit one. If he couldn't stop the bill, he was naturally going to turn it to his own purposes, even if it meant that he ended up sponsoring it."

Although his indecisiveness is proverbial throughout Washington (someone once said Shakespeare wrote a play about him), on this occasion Mills changed his mind literally overnight. Taking the three main proposals before his committee, he had them drafted into a single bill between suppertime and breakfast the next day. "Mills did it so fast," one of Johnson's aides remarked, "the Republicans were struck dumb." Next morning, Mills presented his proposals to the President. Johnson asked him how much it would cost. "About five hundred million dollars a year," Mills replied. Then, according to Johnson, he put the essential question: "What do you want to do about it, Mr. President?" The answer came in the form of one of those Texas tales with which Johnson loved to regale his friends, especially those who also came from the South:

> "I told him about the test that had been given to a man in Texas who wanted to be a railroad switchman," Johnson said. "One of the questions he was asked was: 'What would you do if a train from the east was coming at sixty miles an hour, and a train from the west was coming at sixty miles an hour on the same track, and they were just a mile apart, headed for each other?'
>
> "The prospective switchman replied: 'I'd run get my brother.'
>
> " 'Now why,' he was asked, 'would you run get your brother?'
>
> " 'Because,' the fellow answered, 'my brother has never seen a train wreck.'
>
> "I told Wilbur I thought I would run and get *my* brother if the Ways and Means Committee reported out this extended Medicare Bill he had described to me," Johnson went on. "I approved the proposal at once . . ."

And so two southern politicians exchanging folksy Texas stories in the White House formed an alliance that finally outmaneuvered the lobbyists of the AMA. A few months later the Medicare bill was passed into law. "In the opinion of many knowledgeable people." wrote *Medical World News*, "the AMA's own strategy of uncompromising resistance contributed to the dimensions of its defeat." And a union lobbyist remarked at the time, "If you want to get something defeated in Congress, just say the AMA backs it."

Outmaneuvered, outgunned, out of touch with public opinion and a growing part of its own profession, even now the AMA continued its fight against Medicare. There were threats—though they never materialized—that doctors would boycott the new health-care program, and Dr. Annis declared that the bill had been passed by what he called "every mockery of the democratic process," and that the nation's physicians had been betrayed by "appeasers," "collaborators with the enemy," "labor bosses" and "power hungry political leaders."

Some members of the medical profession were now beginning to revolt against the rigid, unyielding line laid down by the central hierarchy. But at the AMA headquarters the residue of bitterness at their defeat remained, and when in 1968 Johnson nominated as his new Secretary of Health, Education, and Welfare Wilbur Cohen, the man who had helped Mills draft the legislation, the White House was flooded with over a thousand telegrams, all carrying the same message: "Please do not appoint Wilbur J. Cohen Secretary of HEW. It is my opinion that he is an enemy of American medicine."

Johnson named him to the Cabinet notwithstanding. "That last campaign against him," the President wrote in his memoirs, "is the kind of unpleasant thing a dedicated man has to expect if he devotes part of his life to public service."

Cohen, however, was a lame-duck Secretary of Health, Education, and Welfare, since Johnson had already announced his intention not to seek re-election. When President Nixon entered the White House early in 1969 he chose as the new Secretary his close friend Robert Finch, a man who was probably the most liberal of all Nixon's close associates. Finch was hardly installed in the sprawling HEW complex when he became involved in a bitter six-month clash with the increasingly conservative leadership of the AMA. Finch wished to name Dr. John Knowles, general director of the Massachusetts General Hospital, as his Assistant Secretary for Health and Scientific Affairs, the administration's top health officer. Knowles was a well-known Republican who had helped organize a political committee known as Doctors for Nixon in the 1968 elections. Medically, however, Knowles was a radical: He was known above all for his support of the idea of a comprehensive prepaid health-insurance program for all Americans. Not long before his appointment was first mooted, he had gone before a Senate subcommittee to declare his support for such a scheme. "The program," he said then, "must cover the indigent as well as the average middle-income family, who don't qualify for Medicaid or Medicare and who suffer considerable financial stress during catastrophic illness."

Sensing that Knowles would turn out to be an enemy within the camp, the AMA set out to block his appointment, selecting as their instrument the late Senator Everett Dirksen, the Senate Minority Leader, to whose last campaign the association was said to have donated some $150,000. Finch, however, stuck by his nominee. In June 1969 he called Knowles in Boston to tell him the President had approved the appointment and a few days later told a reporter from the Los Angeles *Times* that if Nixon did not back the nomination "he'd have to find another Secretary."

Unknown to Finch, the AMA was at this time mounting a last-ditch stand against the nominee inside the White House itself. Not much is publicly known about the pressures they were able to exert there, but they must have been considerable, since within a week Nixon had capitulated. Finch emerged from a five-hour meeting with the President and his two top aides to tell a press conference:

> I have reluctantly and regretfully decided and today advised Dr. John Knowles that the protracted and distorted discussion regarding his appointment as Assistant Secretary for Health and Scientific Affairs has resulted in a situation in which he would not be able to function effectively in this critical position.

So Knowles was thrown to the wolves, directly as a result of the pressures exerted by the AMA. Finch himself did not long survive the débâcle and was later to resign from the turbulent department under great physical and mental stress. But he did succeed in having the last word in the matter of Knowles's replacement, choosing another known supporter of Medicare and a critic of the AMA, Dr. Roger Egeberg, dean of the University of Southern California Medical School. This time, the AMA was not consulted about the appointment before Nixon sent it up to Capitol Hill for confirmation. It seemed that the AMA may have won a battle but lost the war. "I admire Dr. Knowles's forward look," Egeberg told a press conference, "and I hope to have the same forward look."

Attention was now switched from the usual Washington fascination over the political infighting to a crisis that had blown up over the costs of the Medicare scheme, which had far exceeded all the estimates. The Medicaid part of the program, that which provides health care for patients on welfare and certain others, had reached the point of financial collapse and was moreover reaching only 7.5 of the 45 million people Congress had intended it to cover. The scheme was described by the Nixon Administration as "badly conceived and badly organized." About this time, horror stories began appearing in the press describing doctors who were making fortunes out of the federally funded plan. By 1972, one Washington physician was found to have earned $250,000 in the previous year, $120,060 of which came in the form of Medicaid payments for treating the poor. A number of other Washington doctors were also being investigated for similarly inflated earnings. Today, the annual cost of the entire Medicare program has risen to over $7 billion, nearly three times the estimates when the bill was first passed. The Senate Finance Committee reached the conclusion that the rising costs were getting so far out of hand that the future of the scheme was being threatened. Doctors' fees, however, were only a comparatively small part of the problem, accounting for less than 20 percent of the total expenditure. The rest was going on huge increases in the costs of hospital and nursing-home care.

By now, a number of bills are pending before Congress to create a fullscale national health service in America, notably one sponsored by Senator Edward Kennedy and another, milder proposal that has the backing of the Nixon Administration. But the AMA remains adamant in its opposition to anything that smacks of what it likes to call "welfarism." "A piece of the roof came off with Medicare," said Dr. Annis in 1971. "Now the whole structure is threatened as we knew it would be sooner or later." In a later telephone interview with the New York *Times*, Dr. Annis declared, "Some people think that people are entitled to health care as a matter of right, whether they work or not. This is just as absurd as saying that food, clothing and shelter are a matter of right—one step further than that is a revolutionary system bordering on Communism."

Dr. Annis's extreme position, however, no longer receives the support of a majority of American doctors, and partly due to its intransigent opposition to reform in the past, the AMA itself has begun to lose some of its influence in medical circles. By 1971, fewer than half the nation's practicing doctors were dues-paying members of the association, whose retiring president that year made an appeal for internal reform because of the growing feeling by many doctors that the AMA does not represent them. Membership is now estimated at some 156,000 dues-paying doctors—less than half the nation's total of 334,000 physicians. There was a loss of some 12,000 members in 1970 alone, partly because dues had been raised from $70 to $110 to finance an advertising campaign to raise the image of American doctors, and partly because several state medical societies (notably that in New York) had ruled that its members need no longer belong to the AMA. It is believed many others would probably drop out, too, if they were not dependent upon the association for such things as patient referrals, hospital privileges, malpractice insurance, and other fringe benefits offered by membership.

There is widespread disaffection among the eight thousand young doctors who enter the profession each year, and occasionally the simmering revolt breaks into the open. At a 1971 meeting of the Medical Committee for Human Rights, which is largely made up of young and progressive doctors who regard the AMA as a "menace to health care," one delegate was seen wearing a button with the inscription "Caution: AMA May Be Hazardous to Your Health." And at a recent convention of the AMA itself, there were chaotic scenes as blacks, spokesmen for the poor, and dissident doctors tried to seize the platform to state their demands. There were shouts of "fascism" from the floor as they did so. The AMA threatened to adjourn the meeting, but Dr. George Tolbert, a black doctor serving the poor in Mississippi, declared, "I don't like this shouting of fascist and pig. I've come a long way to be here, and I want to be heard." Together with thirty-five other dissidents he was heard, taking the floor to accuse the AMA of neglecting the health problems of the poor and emphasizing curative rather than preventive medicine.

All this may be a sign that the AMA is becoming more responsive to the wishes of its rank-and-file members and even those members of the profession who are now outside the association. At the 1972 meeting of the AMA's ruling body, the House of Delegates, the Alaska representatives submitted a resolution asking the AMA to make its governing board "more accessible to the membership and the actions of the board more open to view, and that more opportunity be given to express different views." This and other reform resolutions, however, were voted down by a considerable majority. Any shift in the association's stance will be a painfully slow one, and the association remains today one of the most conservative bodies in American politics. In a poll released in 1972, the AMA claimed its stance was backed by a majority of doctors; two thirds of whom were said to be still in favor of the traditional fee-for-service private practice of medicine over any national health insurance plan. According to the poll, some 62,000 doctors favored the maintenance of the current practice, although it is perhaps worth noting that only 94,000 members had responded to the poll. And 62,000 doctors out of a nationwide total of 334,000 hardly represents a majority, even by the AMA's standards of measurement.

In the country as a whole the tide in favor of a full health-insurance system is inexorably growing, and Dr. Sidney M. Wolfe of Ralph Nader's Health Research Group believes "there is definitely a shift in the balance of power in terms of impact on Washington." Once again, the key to success may be the cautious figure of Congressman Wilbur Mills, who has recently openly come out in support of the comprehensive nature of the health-care bill proposed by Senator Kennedy. And a number of senators and congressmen have in recent years begun to hire doctors and other health workers to positions on their staffs to help counteract the propaganda input of the AMA's lobbyists. The AMA will doubtless put up a stiff fight against compulsory health-insurance to the bitter end; but it is a fight they seem destined sooner or later to lose.

CHAPTER XV

Advertising

Ulcer Gulch, U.S.A.

"Nobody ever went broke underestimating the taste of the American public."
—H. L. MENCKEN, *1880–1956*

"The consumer isn't a moron; she is your wife."
—DAVID OGILVY, *Madison Avenue executive, 1963*

It is sometimes said that the tone of American civilization is set by the advertising executives who work on New York's Madison Avenue. Here, at the heart of the American advertising industry, where nearly half the advertising expenditure in the entire country is controlled, they like to claim that their craft is the "sparkplug" of the American economy, a necessary part of the business machine that brings comfort, luxury, and ease to millions. And they often quote approvingly the words of Winston Churchill to the International Advertising Conference of 1924. "Advertising," he said then, "nourishes the consuming power of men. It creates wants for a better standard of living. It sets up before man the goal of a better home, better clothing, better food for himself and his family. It spurs individual exertion and greater production."

The decade in which Churchill spoke was one of the golden ages of American advertising, the start of the first great consumer-led boom of the twentieth century, a time in which American advertisers increased their expenditures by over 50 percent. Madison Avenue looks back to one day in that decade which many believe was the greatest in the history of their industry: the day in December 1927 when old Henry Ford finally paid attention to their blandishments. Under the pressure of growing competition from General Motors, he stopped producing his all-black, one-version Model T and turned to Madison Avenue to build up sales for the newer, prettier, more consumer-oriented Model A. Ford bought full-page ads in two thousand newspapers for five consecutive days to sing the praises of the Model A, at an unprecedented cost of nearly $1.5 million. The campaign, as Madison Avenue still fondly remembers, was stunningly successful. Mounted police were called in to keep order outside the Ford showrooms in Cleveland, over a hundred thousand people jammed the showroom in Detroit, and in New York Ford claimed a million people turned out to view the company's first new automobile since before the start of World War I. It was just two years before the Great Crash, and the purchase of a new car was being heralded as "the most potent statistic of the Coolidge prosperity." It was a potency to which Madison Avenue had contributed to no small degree.

Back in those innocent materialistic days of Babbitt and Main Street, business and advertising were venerated as never before—or since. "The man who builds a factory," President Coolidge had said, "builds a temple; and the man who works there worships there." Advertising in that era was regarded, often quite literally, as the priesthood of this new religion of consumerism. Bruce Barton, the founder of one of the biggest Madison Avenue empires, wrote at that time that if Jesus Christ were living then he would almost certainly be "a national advertiser." And an insurance company pamphlet characterized Moses as "one of the greatest salesmen and real estate promoters that ever lived."

While times have now certainly changed, and that old exuberant innocence has been lost, perhaps forever, Madison Avenue today still retains most of the trappings of those golden years—including egos unmatched for size anywhere north of Wall Street. "When you hire a Napoleon," one copywriter replied when asked why he was resigning, "you don't put him on iron rations." Beneath this brash and glittering self-confidence, however, all is not well in the world of advertising in the 1970s. The glossy days are gone, and nobody knows when they will return. Unemployment on the Avenue is reputed to be the worst since World War II, and the agencies that operate there are caught today in one of the biggest upheavals in their history—ensnared both by a profits squeeze that could last for years and by a fundamental change in the attitudes of big business to their functions. There are many who believe the entire nature of Madison Avenue could be transformed by the end of the present decade.

Appearances in the world of advertising, however, are everything. On the surface at least, the agencies strive hard to make themselves appear as glossy as they have ever been, with dazzling rewards for those who are successful. The bulk of national advertising—around 75 percent of it—is conducted by no more than fifty of the large agencies, the majority of them clustered along Madison Avenue. The five largest agencies of all, those with the highest worldwide billings, are, according to *Advertising Age:*

	Billings (1971) *(in millions of dollars)*
1. J. Walter Thompson	774
2. McCann-Erickson	593.9
3. Young and Rubicam	503.5
4. Ted Bates & Company	424.8
5. Leo Burnett Company	422.7

J. Walter Thompson, the largest, oldest, and probably the stuffiest advertising agency in the world, became a symbol of the Nixon establishment during the President's first term in office, having provided him with H. R. Haldeman, his chief of staff; Ron Ziegler, his press secretary (who used to handle the Disneyland account); and Dwight Chapin, his appointments secretary. Several of the JWT men fell from grace, however, during the Watergate affair, an episode that has not helped the world of advertising, where industrial espionage is more commonly practiced and more readily accepted than it is in the world of government. JWT has also been having its own share of problems in the 1970s, having lost in an eighteen-month period such famous clients as Ford, Pan Am, Singer, and Firestone Tires, and seen its profits plunge to the bare break-even point.

It is a surprisingly small world, this state known as Madison Avenue. The part that houses the advertising industry runs for only about a mile, concentrated between the 200 and 800 blocks of the handsome Avenue, an area known to the cynics as "Ulcer Gulch." In all, perhaps 25,000 people work here, about half of them women. There are creative writers who turn up at the office, invariably late, wearing trendy clothes and showy psyches (one twenty-nine-year-old, hired at a salary of $65,000 a year, reported to work on his first day carrying a golden typewriter). There are account executives, those who actually meet the clients, who tend to be more sober and conservatively dressed. There are space buyers, artists and TV producers, media specialists and PR men, whose talents, even in the 1970s, can command salaries of $80,000 a year and more.

The highest rewards commonly go today to those who work in the power-houses of the agencies, the so-called creative departments, which are staffed by an odd and often bizarre breed of conforming nonconformists—a part of the economic establishment that gives the appearance of not wishing to admit it. One has the feeling that most of them secretly, or even openly, despise the jobs that pay them so handsomely. But the idiosyncrasies of the creative staffs are benignly tolerated at most advertising agencies. They are the ones, after all, who bring in the bread and butter, and it is recognized on Madison Avenue that the creative juices are not stimulated by regular office hours or conservative clothes. "It is with the advertising man as with the cow," they say on the Avenue. "No browsing, no milk." At one agency a leading copywriter is known to curl up under his desk when he is thinking particularly hard. "My God," complained an executive at another agency, "we hired a new copywriter the other day—a very good copywriter, too—and he came to work in bare feet." "You could set off a bomb in the creative department at nine thirty in the morning and at nine forty-five still have a full creative staff," says the treasurer at Ogilvy and Mather. And David Ogilvy himself, one of the most successful creative advertisers of all, has written of his craft:

> I hear a great deal of music. I am on friendly terms with John Barleycorn. I take long hot baths. I garden. I go into retreat among the Amish. I watch birds. I go for long walks in the country. And I take frequent vacations, so that my brain can lie fallow—no golf, no cocktail parties, no tennis, no bridge, no concentration; only a bicycle.
>
> While thus employed in doing nothing, I receive a constant stream of telegrams from my unconscious, and these become the raw material for my advertisements. But more is required: hard work, an open mind, and ungovernable curiosity.

The rewards for such activity are high: Ogilvy has made himself a multimillionaire and lives for much of the year in a twelfth-century French chateau he bought from the proceeds of the telegrams he received from his unconscious.

But there is another side to the coin, and that is fear. It is not for nothing that Madison Avenue's best-known luncheon club is called The Golden Ulcers, with the cynical motto, "What good is happiness if it doesn't bring you money?" This is the original home of the twentieth-century rat race, and the insecurities of the advertising world are inseparable from the rewards that come to its successful practitioners. "The advertising industry is a great business of compromise," says one Madison Avenue man. "But you compromise the wrong things—your peace of mind, health, sanity." No other industry in the nation has the same horrendously high turnover rate, estimated by *Advertising Age* at around 25 percent of all the personnel on Madison Avenue every year. It is accepted as a basic truth here that unless you own the business, you are going to get fired some day. And on Madison Avenue it may be today. You are never quite sure; in advertising, personal uncertainty and a faintly desperate insecurity are the twin names of the game. Samm Sinclair Baker, who worked for thirty years on the Avenue, writes in *The Permissible Lie:*

> One thing most agencymen have in common is *fear*—based on the uncertainty of keeping an account, holding a job. . . . You can smell this fear when you enter a conference room. You can see it in the stony or falsely smiling faces, the staring or shifting eyes. You can hear it in the braggart voice and the uncertain stutter of the unsure. Often this fear is based on the individual's lack of ability, which frequently masquerades as over-confidence.

Baker also tells an old story of two account executives meeting one day on Madison Avenue:

"You knew Harry Bloops, the account supervisor and veep at Norman, Craig and Kummel, formerly at Ketchum-MacLeod and Grove, right?" asks one.

"Sure," says the other. "Great guy. The greatest pal. What about him?"

"He dropped dead this morning."

"That's awful. Terrible. What did he have?"

"I think it was a heart——"

"No, no—I mean—what accounts did he have?"

Behind all the insecurity, there is also a lingering suspicion that many admen are faintly ashamed of their profession. Back in the 1960s, the Gallup-Robinson "Mirror of America" surveyed the opinions of admen about their profession and, more revealingly, what they believed other people thought of their craft. A hundred housewives were asked how respectable, honest, hardworking, neurotic, and heavy-drinking they thought admen were, and a hundred admen were asked how they thought the housewives would rate them on each subject. It turned out that the housewives held a far higher opinion of the admen than the admen thought they would. Thus, forty-three housewives called the admen "respectable," while only nine admen thought they would; twenty housewives described the admen as "honest," while only four admen thought they would; three housewives believed admen were neurotic, while twenty-eight admen thought they would.

In those days, it was fashionable to portray admen as clever manipulators of the public mind. In *The Hidden Persuaders*, one of the biggest bestsellers of the 1950s, Vance Packard credited the advertisers with molding the mind of the unsuspecting public by the use of the black arts of psychiatry and the social sciences, by making appeals that were beneath the level of awareness, by acting as truly "hidden" persuaders. "The stuff with which we work is the fabric of men's minds," the president of the Public Relations Society of America had admitted, and Packard's thesis was based on the antihumanism of this approach:

> Typically, they see us as bundles of daydreams, misty hidden yearnings, guilt complexes, irrational emotional blockages. We are image lovers given to impulsive and compulsive acts. We annoy them with our seemingly senseless quirks, but we please them with our growing docility in responding to their manipulation of symbols that stir us to action. They have found the supporting evidence for this view persuasive enough to encourage them to turn to depth channels on a large scale in their efforts to influence our behavior.

According to Packard's thesis, these salesmen of the subconsious built images for their products that would arise before an unaware public's "inner eye" at the mere mention of the product's name, once they had been properly conditioned. The advertisers had found that most consumers were totally unable to make any objective distinction between different brands of cigarettes or beer or whisky, and when blindfolded were quite incapable of distinguishing their favorite brands. The admen therefore concluded that people could be encouraged to discriminate between products *unreasonably* through the device of imagebuilding. "Basically," said Pierre Martineau, a leading adman of the day, "what you are trying to do is create an illogical situation. You want the customer to fall in love with your product and have a profound brand loyalty when actually content may be very similar to hundreds of competing brands." To create this illogical loyalty, he said, the first task "is one of creating some differentiation in the mind—some individualization for the product which has a long list of competitors very close to it in content."

One of the main complaints of this and similar critiques of the world of Madison Avenue was that advertising had discovered it was more profitable to appeal to the more discreditable human emotions: fear, greed, jealousy, ambition, and snobbery. While these are still the main ingredients of the Madison Avenue mix, fifteen years after he wrote the *Hidden Persuaders*, Packard's thesis is no longer in vogue.

One reason is that a more sophisticated public has today tumbled to the tricks that Madison Avenue tries to play on the pysche. Thanks to the modern consumer movement, for example, most intelligent viewers are now aware that some of the products shown on television are not what they are made to appear. The tricks employed are in many cases too obvious, and each time a story appears in the press or a public complaint is filed with the Federal Trade Commission exposing the fake photography employed by the admakers, the public's skepticism for *all* advertising is insensibly deepened. One case of deception that received wide publicity when it went to the Supreme Court showed Colgate-Palmolive's Rapid Shave Cream apparently shaving sandpaper, while a voice explained, "To prove Rapid Shave's super-moisturizing power, we put it right from the can onto this rough, dry sandpaper. It was apply, soak—and off in a stroke." What the advertisement did not make clear was that the "sandpaper" shown on television was not sandpaper at all: It was a sheet of transparent plastic coated with sand. It was demonstrated that actual sandpaper would have to be soaked for eighty minutes in order to achieve the effect shown on the commercial.

Another case of outright deception came to light when the FTC complained that a TV commercial showing the lack of distortion in the windows of a car had been filmed with the windows rolled down. As to those frequent commercials where the housewife is shown cleaning a filthy floor with some magic wax and one swipe of her duster, it has been revealed that in order to achieve the apparently miraculous effect the floor is first covered with powdered graphite. Those commercials where the car filled with Shell gasoline is shown to win a mileage test, every time, are equally phony: The other car, the one that loses, has been filled with a type of gasoline not commonly available to ordinary motorists. All of Shell's major competitors put exactly the same "special ingredient" into their gasolines that Shell boasts will make its car run an "extra" mile. Campbell's Soup was exposed when the FTC found it had placed glass marbles in the bottoms of the bowls of soup it advertised in order to force the chunky ingredients up to the surface. Colgate-Palmolive once carried a commercial which purported to show how gentle its dishwashing liquid was by having a manicurist soak someone's hand in the product. What the commercial did not make clear was that the liquid used in the ad was *cold*. Its cleaning action on dishes does not begin until it is mixed with hot water.

So the list of deceptions grows; and public confidence in advertising declines. Perhaps as a result, the public today is not so easily gulled as it once was. People are more cynical about the claims of the advertisers, more easily bored by the constant stream of commercials, particularly on television; simply exhausted by the unending flow of superlatives that come flowing from the television screen; and above all, stunned to the point of insensibility by the endless assaults on their minds.

Advertisers themselves recognize this dangerous threat to their future. Stephen A. Greyser, vice president of the American Academy of Advertising, declared in testimony to the FTC in 1972: "A substantial body of consumer behavior research tells us that the consumer is hardly a helpless pawn manipulated by the will of the advertiser. We know, for example, that almost all consumers are very selective in what advertising they pay attention to, perceive, evaluate, and remember—let alone act upon." Maybe so, but advertisers still understand that a basic truth of their trade is that products sell in the marketplace for quite irrational reasons. They know, for instance, that in selling a cake mix it is important to let the housewife add milk or an egg to the package—she likes to believe she has done some of the work, too. And sometimes ads are directed plainly and bluntly at the public's desire to *spend* —spend on anything, it hardly matters what. In 1973, a national advertiser offered a cutout coupon for a gadget called an "English fog fine mist sprayer." The headline over the ad read, in its entirety: UTTERLY USELESS AND ONLY $2.98. The advertiser offered a complete moneyback guarantee if the purchasers were not delighted with his product.

Back in the golden years of advertising in the 1950s, when television was a new and comparatively less important medium of advertising than it is today, the bulk of commercial messages appeared on the printed page, either in the daily press or in the glossy magazines, where it was a simple matter to flip over and skip the uninteresting pages. The ads the consumers chose to read were those that directly concerned them, or amused them, or otherwise caught their attention. The point was, they did not have to read them unless they actually *chose* to do so. And they chose to read only a tiny proportion: It has been estimated that the average woman is exposed to more than 1,500 printed advertisements every day, but actually reads only 4 of them.

In the modern world of television, however, the consumers are captive.

They must sit through the commercials whether they like it or not. Thus the unconstipated suffer with the sourpuss through the advertisements for laxatives, men are indiscriminately bombarded with advertisements for women's skin cream, the women are caught with the men in commercials that sing the praises of the latest razorblade. As a result, they become monumentally bored and irritated by advertisements they are compelled to sit through even though they have no possible application to themselves. In a sense, they have thereby become inoculated against the effects of *all* advertising. Not long ago *Fortune* came to the conclusion that the consumer is on to the game. "The language of advertising, it said, "is no longer manipulating him. It's not deceiving him. It's not even making him mad. It's just boring the hell out of him."

There is a real danger for advertisers in the 1970s, on television at least, that their commercials have become counterproductive, that they serve to irritate and annoy more consumers than they attract. Alfred Hitchcock, the famous maker of suspense films, once remarked, "Seeing a murder on television can be good therapy. It can help work off one's antagonisms. If you haven't any antagonisms, the commercials will give you some." Even David Ogilvy has said he is "angered to the point of violence" by the commercial interruption of programs. At the very end of his otherwise defensive book, *Confessions of an Advertising Man,* Ogilvy admits to some heretical thoughts:

> As a practitioner I know that television is the most potent advertising medium ever devised, and I make my living from it. But, as a private person, I would gladly pay for the privilege of watching it without commercial interruptions. Morally, I find myself between the rock and the hard place.
>
> It is television advertising which has made Madison Avenue the arch-symbol of tasteless materialism. If governments do not soon set up machinery for the regulation of television, I fear the majority of thoughtful men will come to agree with Toynbee that "the destiny of our Western civilization turns on the issue of our struggle with all that Madison Avenue stands for." I have a vested interest in the survival of Madison Avenue, and I doubt whether it can survive without drastic reform.

In the 1970s, some of the reforms that Ogilvy advocated have begun to be introduced to the world of advertising from the unlikely source of the Federal Trade Commission, a hitherto moribund agency that Ralph Nader once likened to "a self-parody of bureaucracy, fat with cronyism, torpid through inbreeding unusual even for Washington, manipulated by the agents of commercial predators, impervious to governmental and citizen monitoring."

Nader made those remarks as recently as 1969, but since then several startling changes have occurred. Under the supervision of Miles W. Kilpatrick, a Republican lawyer from Philadelphia with a strong reputation for conservatism, the FTC made an unprecedented effort to set the house of advertising in order. One of its early successes was almost revolutionary in its impact on Madison Avenue: a commercial that at first sight looked like any other when it appeared on American television screens early in 1972. The scene was familiar enough, a mother and her two children preparing a meal in their pleasant suburban garden, a large loaf of Profile Bread prominent in the foreground. The spoken text, however, was startlingly unfamiliar:

"Does Profile have fewer calories than other breads?"
"No, Profile has about the same per ounce as other breads."
"To be exact, Profile has seven fewer calories per slice."
"That's because it's sliced thinner."
"But eating Profile will not cause you to lose weight. A reduction of seven calories is insignificant."

Never before had there come out of Madison Avenue such an heretical flight of fancy: an ad that pointed out the shortcomings of its sponsor's product showing that it *wasn't* unique. When they saw the Profile spot, old hands on the street nearly died of shame. "This kind of economic masochism is not only ludicrous," said one, "it's untenable." "The whole business has been put into a vast confusion," another complained.

The Profile commercial had not been broadcast by free choice. The agency that prepared it, Ted Bates and Company, the fourth largest advertising agency in the nation, had been *ordered* to prepare the advertisement by the Federal Trade Commission; the "countercommercial" was run to correct the impression left by earlier Profile ads that the FTC had ruled were "deceptive." In the earlier commercials, following the time-honored Madison Avenue tradition, the agency had touted Profile as a diet loaf, with the clear implication it would help consumers to lose weight. It was not exactly dishonest to claim that Profile had fewer calories per slice than other breads, but in failing to point out that this was because the slices had been cut thinner than usual, it was certainly misleading, and even deceptive.

Madison Avenue of course has been getting away with practices like this for years (copywriters call it "legitimate puffery"). But never before had they been faced with the wrath of an official government agency for their deceptions. And never before had they been forced to repent for their sins in public. Robert Pitofsky, then head of the FTC's Bureau of Consumer Protection, led the new drive against unfair and deceptive advertising. He declared bluntly that it was his intention "to explore the limits of the FTC's power in dealing with mass advertising techniques," about which, he said, the Commission was feeling "great concern." In thus choosing to fight fire with fire, Pitofsky brought the action against the bakers of the Profile loaf, the Continental Baking Company (a subsidiary of ITT), and its agency on the grounds that their wares had been deceptively advertised. Continental said it disagreed with the FTC's view "that consumers inferred from our Profile Diet Plan advertising that Profile Bread would by itself cause weight loss," but it also said it did not wish to enter into litigation over what it called a "small volume" product and would therefore agree to enter into a settlement of the action. Whereupon the FTC promptly ordered Continental to devote one quarter of Profile's advertising budget for the following year to countercommercials disclaiming its properties as a weight-controller.

The ruling caused consternation on Madison Avenue. The concept of what constitutes "unfair and deceptive" advertising is obviously subject to broad interpretation, said *Fortune,* one of the glossy trade magazines widely read by businessmen and their advertising executives. "The manner in which the FTC has chosen to interpret it lately has been giving both agencies and advertisers fits." Its article was ominously headlined: "Those Throbbing Headaches on Madison Avenue."

Sure enough, the FTC's action against Continental did not prove to be an isolated case. The commission moved swiftly with other suits against similar advertisements, including those of the Sugar Association, and one against another product of the Continental Baking Company called Wonder Bread. The Wonder Bread ads were aimed at small children and suggested, in the words of one commercial, that "Wonder helps build strong bodies twelve ways." "Each delicious slice," said the ad in the all-too-familiar hyperbole, "supplies proteins for muscle, minerals for strong bones and teeth, carbohydrates for energy, vitamins for nerves. . . . Help your child grow bigger and stronger. Serve Wonder Bread. It helps build strong bodies twelve ways."

It was all true, every word. The Wonder Breads ads, however, did not point out the nutrients they praised so extravagantly were required to be put into such breads by law and were therefore to be found in *all* enriched loaves, including those produced by Wonder Bread's competitors. The FTC claimed Continental was representing Wonder Bread as unique, an outstanding source of nutrients, distinct from other breads. The Commission found, moreover, that the commercials exploited both the emotional concern of parents for their offspring and "the aspirations of children for rapid and healthy growth." It asked the courts to bar Wonder Bread from making their claims without at the same time making clear that its product is just like any other enriched bread.

Continental has said it will fight the case right up to the Supreme Court. "The issue," said the firm's president, "is whether or not advertisers have the right to publicize certain qualities which their products share with others." It has been suggested that if the FTC succeeds in this and other pending cases, the effect will be to undermine the whole purpose of advertising. Some manufacturers have threatened that unless the FTC quenches its enthusiasm for the consumer they will abandon television advertising altogether rather than expose their products to attack. The suits could therefore revolutionize the practice of advertising, a practice that has hitherto been one of the cornerstones of American capitalism and the affluent society.

The cries of alarm that have arisen at this prospect have been shrill. "What's the New Consumerism doing to us?" asked one salesman. "Why, it's just grinding us out of business, that's what." "I think the ultimate target is free enterprise itself," complained another. And *Fortune* in 1972 clearly disapproved of the Commission's new-found solicitude for the consumer:

> Inoculated with the New Consumerism, the fifty-seven-year-old Commission is prancing around like an adolescent. It was set up to prevent unfair competition, but found its mandate confusing and frustrating, since the process of preventing unfair competition, unless conducted with great sagacity, itself results in stifling competition. . . . Too much regulation of advertising and selling, over the long run, can only be self-defeating and do the consumer more harm than good.

The FTC, however, has so far proved to be deaf to the complaints of business. Under its aggressive former chairman, Miles W. Kilpatrick, who was appointed by President Nixon in 1970, the commission issued well over four hundred complaints involving consumer issues in a two-year period. It accused the four largest makers of breakfast cereals of falsely advertising that their products act as bodybuilders and proposed that they be broken up into smaller companies, partly on the grounds that they spend so much on advertising that they have been able to monopolize the market and keep prices artificially high. It has criticized General Motors for claiming that its Chevrolet Chevelle has "ten advantages" that keep a car from "becoming old before its time." It has ordered filling stations to post the octane ratings for their various grades of gasoline. It has launched a program that would make national advertisers produce documentary evidence to back up their claims; after analysis of some three hundred claims from thirty-two companies making goods ranging from electric shavers to cough remedies, the Commission found that 30 percent were inadequately documented, another 30 percent were supported by data too technical for consumers to understand, and thirteen assertions were backed by no evidence at all. And it has helped sponsor a series of further countercommercials against the leading brands of analgesics, in which the actor Burt Lancaster appears before a row of six big-selling pain tablets to declare bluntly, "The American Medical Association has found remedies like these to be either irrational, not recommended or unsound."

Although many of the cases are still pending before the courts, the effect of the assault on the advertising industry has been profound. "We're worried stiff," said one leading executive on Madison Avenue. "The danger to advertising has reached a point critical to its continued existence," said another. While such cries of pain may be as exaggerated as some of the recent advertising claims, it is clear that if the FTC's actions are backed by the courts, they could revolutionize the practice of advertising in America.

In the 1970s, Madison Avenue is no longer quite the glittering symbol of American capitalism that it used to be. The tough attitude of the FTC is one part of the problem; another, which may perhaps in the long run prove to be even more intractable, is a slow but fundamental change in the attitude of big business towards the full-service advertising agencies. Advertising expenditure still accounts for some twenty billion dollars each year (of which around nine billion, or 45 percent, is handled on Madison Avenue), but the rate of expansion in the 1970s has slowed down quite dramatically and is now actually less than the rate of growth of either the gross national product or of personal consumption expenditures. Significantly, a survey of businessmen undertaken by the *Harvard Business Review* in 1971 revealed that most managers now feel that they spend too much on advertising, and their attitude towards the fundamental purpose of the advertising agencies is also becoming markedly more critical. Furthermore, there has been a drift away from the Madison Avenue agencies in recent years, so that of the top one hundred advertisers in America, at least twenty now have their own official house agencies, which handle at least a part of their own advertising needs.

During the golden years of the 1950s and early 1960s, the years of the *Hidden Persuaders,* when the influence of Madison Avenue was at its height, American advertising agencies were held in awe by the world of business. There was a mystique and a prestige in the so-called full-service agencies, which insisted on providing their clients not only with glossy and expensive advertisements, but with a whole range of other marketing services that Madison Avenue held was inseparable from the basic service: market research, media contact, space buying, public relations, and a whole shopping list of other equally arcane services. The convention was for clients to pay the agencies a commission of 15 percent on all its advertising. Thus the greater the budget the agency could squeeze out of the client, the larger its own profits. It was one of the most blatant con games in the history of big business, but for over thirty years the American Association of Advertising Agencies decreed that this outmoded method of compensation was an inviolable condition of membership. The rule was eventually outlawed by the FTC, but the tradition remained, and, in the words of David Ogilvy, "any advertising agent who rejected the conventional commission arrangements was a cad."

Today, there are signs that the tradition is at last on its way out. Many clients have caught on to the game and concluded they no longer need the unnecessary, unwanted, and often frivolous window-dressing offered by the full-service agencies. There has been a growing trend to demand services on what Madison Avenue calls an "à la carte" basis. Many of the larger agencies are still holding out for the full-service concept, but dozens of enterprising smaller agencies have sprung up in the past decade or so and are now offering their clients a "creative only" service, for which they charge a flat fee—irrespective of the amount of money they can persuade their clients to spend on placing the advertisements in the press or on TV. To meet the new demand, it has been estimated that more new agencies were formed in the years between 1965 and 1971 than in any other period in the history of advertising. The bigger agencies contemptuously dismiss these newcomers as "boutiques," but they have nevertheless established a beachhead on Madison Avenue that may well transform the fundamental nature of advertising in America. What more and more clients want today is a smaller package of services, supplied by a smaller number of people, at a smaller price. The trend is expected to grow even faster in the years ahead and could undermine the whole organizational structure of the more traditional agencies. Already the pressures have caused some of the biggest names on the Avenue to cut back on their overextended services. At Young and Rubicam, for example, the research department was recently cut back from a staff of 178 to one of only nine. Edward Buxton, publisher of *Ad Daily,* has chronicled what happened when The Interpublic Group of Companies wielded its broom:

> They wiped out eight companies and some four hundred executives, including a crowd of such unorthodox experts as interior decorators, food scientists, social workers, State Department specialists, international banking experts, five Army generals, and a dozen $40,000 generalists who never knew why they were hired in the first place. And more. They dumped several planes, including the luxurious flying living room assigned to Marion Harper (called "Harper's Ferry"), a ranch and riding academy, a Swiss financial firm whose nature and functions were vague, two of its Centers for New Product Research, including an expensive eye camera to measure pupil dilation of eyeballs when exposed to ads. They also dumped their chairman, Marion Harper, who must certainly have earned the long-distance record for expanding agency services. At its zenith, his conglomerate was indisputably the fullest of the full-service agencies.

The glossy world is clearly not what it once was, and *Fortune* recently quoted the president of one of the top ten agencies speaking nostalgically of "those wonderful years when money was coming in so fast you could hardly count it." Alas, he added, "they're all going to be tough years from now on."

PART SIX

Society

CHAPTER XVI

Beliefs

America's Religions

"Have all the Christianity you wish, cherish it as much as you can, enthrone it in your church, but keep it from the public schools. Let us be Protestants or Catholics, agnostics or Jews in our churches or homes; in our public institutions, however, let us be American."
—RABBI JOSEPH KRAUSKOPF, *president, Central Conference of American Rabbis, 1904*

Even in the godless seventies, it is possible to describe the United States as a religious country, on the surface perhaps more religious today than for the major part of the nation's history. At the time of the Civil War, only 16 percent of Americans adhered to an organized religion. Today, two Americans out of every three officially belong to one of the four main religious groups—Protestants, Catholics, Jews, and the Eastern Orthodox—and affiliation to church or synagogue remains a central characteristic of American life.

The social fabric of the nation today is to a remarkable degree the product of religion. From its seventeenth-century roots in New England, Protestantism has reached out to affect the entire tone of American morality, and its lingering effects can still be felt in many areas, from the imposition of local "blue" laws to the curiously moral fervor with which older Americans still speak of "the work ethic." Catholic immigrants have had a profound influence on the shape of both city governments and the American labor movement. Jews have been an important element in molding the school system and the professions. The Baptists—both black and white—helped to shape the attitudes of the Deep South. The upper Midwest is still permeated by the traditions of Lutheranism, the desert regions of Utah and Idaho by the cultural impact of the Mormons. Even in the 1970s, many Americans vote the way they do because of their religions, and the influence of their beliefs on the national and international scene has on occasion led to major political consequences. The work of the fundamentalist Protestant groups led directly to the enfranchisement of women and the experiment of Prohibition; the support given by American Jews was probably decisive in the formation of the state of Israel; the drive for racial equality in the South has derived an important part of its leadership from the black Baptist Church.

It is well known that almost 5 million Americans are members of the various Jewish congregations; it is not so well known that there are almost as many members of the various branches of the Eastern Orthodox churches, mostly of Greek, Russian, and Armenian origin. According to the National Council of Churches, there are today over 87 national churches or religious groups with a total membership of 133 million persons—two thirds of the whole population—with an astonishing diversity of allegiances, ranging from the 57,674 members of the Soul Saving Assembly of the U.S.A. to the 48 million members of the Roman Catholic Church, from the 86,000 members of the Bulgarian branch of the Eastern Orthodox Church to the 13 million Methodists. There is a fundamentalist sect in the hills of Tennessee that uses snakes and the drinking of poison as a part of its ceremonies, and it is estimated there may be as many as half a million American members of the various eastern religious groups: Hindus, Buddhists, and Moslems.

In 1972, membership of the main American religious groups was listed as follows:

Methodists	13,425,000	
Southern Baptists	11,628,000	
Other Baptists	14,029,000	
Lutheran	8,806,000	
Presbyterian	4,137,000	
Episcopal	3,285,000	
Mormons	2,073,000	
Other Protestant	17,582,000	
	Total Protestant Churches:	74,965,000
	Roman Catholic Church	48,555,000
	Jewish Congregations	5,870,000
	Eastern Orthodox Churches	4,038,000
	Total religious-group membership:	133,418,000

(65.66 percent of the total U.S. population)

Source: National Council of Churches, *Yearbook of American Churches,* 1972 edition

In the seventies, changes in church membership have been erratic and uneven. The Catholics in the past decade have about held their own in membership (although attendance at church has declined). The moderate, ecumenical Protestant groups have shown a comparatively large decline in both membership and attendance; the more conservative Protestant groups—and some of them are very conservative indeed—have flourished as never before.

Numbers, of course, tell only a part of the story of America's religion, and perhaps only a small part at that. For all their vast membership, there are few people today who would deny that the progressive denominations of the religious mainstream are in spiritual trouble, in America as elsewhere in the western world. Christianity, say some, may be losing its power to grip the imagination. In a nationwide survey taken in 1971, it was revealed that 75 percent of the general public felt religion as a whole was losing its influence on American life. Even more disturbing for the religions, the poll found this view was shared by 59 percent of the Protestant ministers, 61 percent of the Roman Catholic priests, and 63 per cent of the Jewish rabbis. If the shepherds are losing their faith, who remains to lead their flock? The poll also showed that nearly four in every ten young Protestant and Roman Catholic clergymen, and six in ten young rabbis, had seriously considered leaving the religious life. "It used to be that as a Bishop you knew what your role was," Episcopal Bishop C. Kilmer Myers told *Time*, "but in just five years all that has changed. People today want someone to direct them, but not authority figures. They are looking for holy priests—for gurus." So while belief is not yet dead in America, it is beginning to take on more and more noninstitutional, nonsecular forms. The so-called Jesus movement, for example, has burgeoned since the 1970s began, and religious themes often crop up in popular entertainment, with such hits as *Jesus Christ Superstar* and *Godspell* attracting overflow crowds at churchs, theaters, and outdoor rallies. In June 1972, more than 75,000 young people poured into Texas for Expo 72, a religious festival chaired by the evangelist Billy Graham, with the young people chanting with apparent fervor; "Two bits, four bits, six bits, a dollar. Everyone for Jesus stand up and holler."

In terms of church membership, the biggest decline in this decade has been suffered by the Methodists, once the largest single Protestant group of all, whose circuit-riders were responsible for bringing religion to the old frontier. Once described as God's light cavalry, organized to pursue and overtake the fugitives that had fled into the wilderness from His presence, the circuit-riders were in the authentic tradition of American puritanism. Peter Cartwright, the most famous of the itinerant preachers, said that when the circuit-rider felt God had called him to preach, he had less need to hunt up a college or a Bible institute than he had a hardy pony or a horse. With his Bible and his hymn book in his saddlebag his Methodism could set the whole West on fire. The people of the frontier, he said, did not want "manuscript sermons," they wanted instead a preacher who could "mount a stump or a block or an old log, or . . . stand in the bed of a wagon, and without note or manuscript, quote, expound, and apply the Word of God to the hearts and consciences of the people." In this century, President Theodore Roosevelt spoke of Methodism's "fiery and restless energy of spirit" and the wide play it gave to individual initiative—qualities that, he said, "tended to make it peculiarly congenial to a hardy and virile folk, democratic to the core, prizing individual independence above all earthly possessions and engaged in the rough and stern work of conquering a continent."

With the continent now conquered and the qualities Roosevelt praised so highly gone somewhat out of fashion in an increasingly urban world, American Methodism has fallen upon hard times, having lost over half a million members in the past five years, the largest drop in membership of any church in American history. At the 1972 Methodist General Conference in Atlanta, Bishop F. Gerald Ensley blamed the drop in Methodist membership on "the decline in Christian belief" and declared that "probably not for centuries has the witness of Christian people on ultimate questions been so hesitant and uncertain."

What was true for Methodism, however, did not apply equally to all religions. On the outer fringes of Protestantism, for example, church membership has been growing steadily in the past decade: Christian Scientists, Mormons, Jehovah's Witnesses, and other fundamentalist Protestant sects have more than held their own in recent years. In a study of the sociology of religion, Dean M. Kelley, himself a Methodist minister, found that "amid the current neglect and hostility towards organized religion in general, the conservative churches, holding to seemingly outmoded theology and making strict demands on their members, have equaled or surpassed in growth the yearly percentage increases of the nation's population." Here, surely, is one of the oddest paradoxes of the modern age: Success, at least in terms of membership, comes to those churches that maintain a body of unshakable (if outmoded) beliefs, strict internal discipline, zeal, exclusiveness, and a distinct code of ethics, while the more liberal virtues of tolerance, ecumenism, and relevance to modern problems provide a formula for religious failure. As Kelley argues, once a church lapses into such an approach, as the Methodists have, decline in numbers is sure to follow. The inescapable conclusion must be that in religion, as in another sense in politics, a growing number of Americans are turning in this skeptical world to those bodies that explain the mysteries of human existence in ultimate terms.

The United States has been described as a pluralist society built on Protestant foundations with important Catholic and Jewish embellishments. Americans sometimes like to claim that the original colonies were founded for the sake of religious liberty, but as Ernest Bates has pointed out in *American Faith*, that was a myth that came into existence around the time of the War of Independence when men had forgotten the facts, a myth that has been thoroughly discredited by modern historians. In only one colony, Rhode Island, did the myth completely fit the facts, and, says Bates, "the founders of 'Little Rhody' fled thither not to escape from religious tyranny in England but to escape from persecution by their fellow-colonists in Massachusetts."

Religion there was aplenty, of course, and it was to play an important part in shaping American society. The first settlers, it has been said, brought their religion with them as naturally as their provisions of food and clothing; the early religious organizations were brought to the New World from Europe, where they had all originated—from the faith of the Pilgrim Fathers to that of the Irish Catholics who flocked to America in the years after the great potato famine in the 1840s; from the Anglicanism of the early Virginia settlers to the Judaism of the nineteenth-century immigrants from Czarist Russia.

In the colonial era, religion in America was a largely local phenomenon, determined by the church adherence of the original settlers. Thus, in broad terms, Anglicanism was the predominant religion in Virginia, Congregationalism in New England, Presbyterianism in the middle colonies, and Quakerism in parts of Pennsylvania.

At first all these churches were, of course, Protestant churches. At the time of the War of Independence there were only 20,000 Roman Catholics and some 6,000 Jews in the thirteen colonies, which at that time had a total population of about 3.5 million. America was regarded, like most of the countries of Europe, as a Christian nation, and also an overwhelmingly Protestant one. Indeed, it was common until comparatively modern times for Protestant historians to claim that the settlement of America had been delayed until after the Reformation (presumably by God) in order to save the new nation from the superstitions of the old Catholic Church. "If the discovery of America had been achieved four centuries or even a century earlier," wrote Leonard Woosley Bacon, a Protestant historian of the late nineteenth century, "the Christianity to be transplanted to the western world would have been that of the Church of Europe at its lowest stages of decline." It was a breathtaking claim (which incidentally ignored completely the experience of those parts of the continent colonized by the Spanish, French, and Portuguese), but, more to the point, nobody could possibly make such an exclusive claim for his religion in the pluralist America of today.

The transformation of the practice of religion in America goes back to the War of Independence when the established Anglican Church was overthrown entirely and many of its members, who accepted loyalty to the British Crown as an integral part of their religion, fled to Canada, the Bahamas, or the West Indies. The patriotic churches of New England, which had been very largely instrumental in fermenting the spirit of revolution, were at first reluctant to give up their new-found predominance. It took what Jefferson called "the hardest struggle of my life" to achieve what is today the outstanding characteristic of American religion: its total separation from the state, at the time a wholly unprecedented experiment. As it was, the Congregationalist state of New Hampshire yielded to the principle of disestablishment only in 1817, Connecticut in 1818, and Massachusetts in 1833.

The practical effects of the new doctrine of pluralism manifested themselves during the later part of the nineteenth century, and then in two peculiarly American fields: the arrival of large numbers of Catholic and Jewish immigrants, who filled up the large cities, and the Americanization of Protestantism, especially among those sects that carried their gospel to the expanding frontier. As the boundaries of American civilization moved slowly westward, the Protestant churches began to fragment, the rightwing or more conservative groups nearly always breaking away from the main bodies. In each case, the new groups drew further and further away from the original European religions the early settlers had brought with them. At this time, too, the Church of Jesus Christ of Latter Day Saints, better known as the Mormons, became the first truly American religion, its founders all born on American soil, its body of doctrine exclusively American in origin.

The principles of the new pluralism, however, were more readily planted than its practice, and even in America the adherents of various religions frequently became involved in sectarian violence. The Puritans hanged Quakers in Boston, Catholics fought bloody battles with Protestants in Maryland, the Mormons settled on their desert home in Utah only after they had been driven by murder and physical violence from earlier settlements in Illinois and Missouri, and the years immediately before the Civil War saw the rise of a violently anti-Catholic fundamentalist party called the Know-Nothings. Hundreds of thousands of fundamentalist Protestants in both North and South joined the Know-Nothings in the late forties and early fifties, winning the governorship of Massachusetts in 1854. They were given a good chance of carrying the Presidency in the national elections of 1856, when their nominee was ex-President Millard Fillmore, but like the Whigs before them they split over the issue of slavery at their nominating convention, when some fifty northern members walked out. Fillmore consequently received only 8 of the 149 electoral votes, and from then on the Know-Nothings disappeared as though they had never been. Yet their spirit of intolerance lived on well into the present century, notably in the rise of the infamous Ku Klux Klan, another fundamentalist and racist group, which became powerful in the 1920s with the declared aim of restoring America to its mythical state as a white Protestant country.

The end of the Protestant era in American history was the product of the great flood-tide of immigration in the period 1880–1910. Large numbers of Roman Catholics from central and southern Europe began to join their fellow religionists who had arrived some decades before from Ireland and Germany. At the same time, major Jewish communities grew up in several of the larger cities, and it was at this time too that members of the Eastern Orthodox Churches first arrived in the United States in significant numbers. After World War I, when the cities were in the process of becoming for the first time the real centers of power in America, the newer Roman Catholic and Jewish arrivals began to exercise an influence on society out of all proportion to their actual numbers. Under their impact, America's Protestant religions began to lose their power to shape the character of whatever it is we call Americanism. That faith which had in an earlier epoch molded American culture now began to lose its identity. Henceforward, it was the strength of

American culture that molded faith, so that by 1933 Alfred North Whitehead was to say of American Protestantism, "Its dogmas no longer dominate; its divisions no longer interest; its institutions no longer direct the patterns of life."

Since the end of the Protestant era, America has held on to its uniquely pluralist tenets with remarkable success. While being a WASP—a White Anglo-Saxon Protestant—is even today regarded in some circles as a great social, economic, and cultural advantage, neither Catholicism nor, to a lesser extent, Judaism is considered a bar to the highest offices in the land. Indeed, since the election of President John Kennedy in 1960, it is considered equally respectable to belong to any one of the three principal faiths. As Murray Stedman has noted, "The religion of America has become not Protestantism or Catholicism or Judaism or some mixture of the three, but Americanism."

Nearly one quarter of all Americans today are members of the Roman Catholic Church, making up by far the largest single religious minority in the nation, three times the size of any other religious body. Its 48 million adherents make it one of the largest Catholic churches in the world, and certainly the richest, with combined assets that run into tens of billions of dollars and an annual income that runs into billions.

Until comparatively recently, to be Catholic in America was to be discriminated against, to be regarded as something less than a first-class citizen. Most Catholics came to America under the spur of poverty and were often regarded by the older Americans as superstitious and uneducated, poor and indolent. It was to America's undoubted advantage, however, that it did let them in and permit them in time to become full-fledged citizens. The nation benefited enormously from its new immigrants, especially in the era of industrialization, although prejudices against the Catholics continued and in some cases still continue to the present day.

After the defeat of Al Smith in the presidential election of 1928, it was widely assumed that no Catholic could successfully aspire to occupy the White House. For years afterward those who made that assumption refused to be convinced by the overwhelming evidence that no Democratic candidate could have carried the White House that year, Catholic *or* Protestant. In any event, it was not until 1960 and the election of John F. Kennedy that Roman Catholicism finally became an acceptable religion for an American head of state. Only a few years before Kennedy's election, there had been an outburst of anti-Catholic prejudice when Justice William J. Brennan was nominated to the Supreme Court by President Eisenhower, and Brennan was only confirmed by the Senate after a minor constitutional crisis in which he was made to swear before a congressional committee that his Catholicism did not conflict with his Americanism.

As Kennedy moved towards his candidacy in the late 1950s, he realized that his faith would be one of the main obstacles he would have to overcome. He was helped in his approach by his understanding of American history, Protestant as well as Catholic, so that Lawrence H. Fuchs was able to write of him, in his book *John F. Kennedy and American Catholicism:*

> He did not regard every voter who doubted the desirability of a Catholic in the White House as a bigot. As he told Unitarian Ted Sorensen, he would have to answer all reasonable as well as unreasonable questions. He could not afford to be defensive or silent to questions which seemed unfair or insulting. This approach was far different from that of Al Smith, who could not understand anti-Catholic attacks as having any reasonable basis at all. Kennedy understood their historical roots.

In the presidential campaign of 1960, Kennedy shrewdly chose to meet the issue of his Catholicism head-on, notably in the primary election in the predominantly Protestant state of West Virginia and, after his nomination, at a televised meeting with the Protestant ministers of Houston, a Texas city that was then still very much a part of the old southern Bible Belt. As Kennedy had expected, the ministers were suspicious of his religion, expressing fears that he would help win financial support for Catholic parochial schools and that in forming his foreign policy he would fall under the influence of the Vatican. Kennedy answered the hostile questions calmly and effectively, demonstrating particularly that he stood firmly beside the religious clauses of the First Amendment to the Constitution, which demands from the government a position of strict neutrality on all matters of religion. In his most widely remembered quote in the Houston debate, Kennedy told the ministers that what mattered in a candidate was "not what kind of church I believe in, for that should be important only to me, but what kind of America I believe in."

Kennedy's performance in Houston brought him tremendous dividends in terms of public acceptance. Theodore White concluded that "when he had finished, he had not only closed Round One of the election campaign—he had for the first time more fully and explicitly than any other thinker of his faith defined the personal doctrine of a modern Catholic in a democratic society." Television films of the debate were shown to the electorate in both North and South. It was claimed this had the double effect of placating the fears of Protestants about the candidate's Catholicism and of arousing the simultaneous indignation of northern Catholic groups at the hostility shown by the ministers. It is now generally agreed that Kennedy managed to defuse the religious issue just enough to win him a paper-thin victory—a 119,000-vote plurality—and it is significant that Kennedy trailed the rest of the Democratic ticket in areas that were predominantly Protestant. But however narrow the margin, the victory was won: Catholicism was finally accepted as part of the mainstream of American culture, and it is today widely conceded that the religious issue could never again bar a candidate from seeking the highest office in the nation. Indeed, Kennedy was barely installed in the White House before people began to wonder what all the fuss had been about.

Today, nearly a decade and a half after that famous victory, Catholics have made enormous strides towards winning both full equality of opportunity and acceptance from other groups. When Kennedy was elected President, only one fourth of the nation's college students were Catholics; today, one third of them are, and recent studies have shown that Catholics under forty are just as likely to be college graduates and to be economically successful as comparable American Protestants.

Those figures represent a remarkable transformation, achieved in the span of a bare dozen years. Yet for all their material achievements, the Roman Catholic Church in America is today as beset by doubts and as torn by internal dissent as Catholic churches in many other parts of the industrialized world. Largely because of the turmoil that has followed Pope John's historic Vatican Council II, the Catholic Church in America has become almost as split and as diversified as the Protestants. It was a Catholic Archbishop who announced in the 1960s that the war in Vietnam should be blessed as a struggle for civilization, and there is no evidence that most members of his flock did not agree with him. Today, however, a Catholic priest or nun is just as likely to be in the vanguard of dissent, and several of them have shown themselves prepared to go to jail for their antiwar beliefs.

It has been a remarkable—and remarkably swift—transformation, and for many American Catholics the experience has been unnerving. John Deedy, managing editor of the Catholic magazine *Commonweal*, expressed the ambivalent feelings of most Catholics toward the reforms that have swept their religion in the past decade in an article he wrote in 1972, just ten years after Pope John's Vatican Council II set in motion the forces which have, in effect, produced a new Catholicism:

> Pope John's council gave the church a deeper understanding of its nature; it gave it a purer liturgy, episcopal collegiality, and a keener appreciation of the role of the laity; it put the church at last on line on religious freedom; it repudiated old libels about the Jews; and it conceded the operativeness of the divine in churches other than the Catholic church solely. Considerable advances these. But the church of "most splendid light" that John saw evolving from a council which would produce all this is instead a shadowy, fractious church of no little crisis, one in which there is diminishing conformity and an astonishing degree of doctrinal freelancing, not only on the part of ill-informed laity, but also among the church's professional theologians. And how does one explain that?

How indeed? Yet although a large part of the unhappiness of many American Catholics with their Church is spiritual, there are other more domestic reasons for dissatisfaction. The Catholic hierarchy, for example, is still monopolized by the Irish, with the majority of American cardinals of Irish descent, even though the Irish today make up only 17 percent of the total Catholic population in America. While one Catholic in every four is of Latin-American descent and one in every six is Italian, there is not a single Spanish-speaking or Italian-American archbishop presiding over any of the Catholic sees within the United States.

The Catholic school system has also faced a crisis in the seventies. American Catholicism was once described as a school system with churches attached, and Catholics have often been accused of using their parochial school system to escape the chaos of the public schools, particularly in the big cities. "Most black people join the Catholic Church so that their kids can attend parochial schools," the head of an all-black Catholic school in Detroit told *Newsweek* in an unusually frank interview. In Philadelphia, the Catholic Church educates one child out of every three who live in the city. Yet in the 1970s, the church is having to close down many of its schools for reasons that are chiefly financial. So although there are still over eleven thousand Catholic schools in the United States, most of them providing a higher standard of education and far stricter discipline than the public schools, they are being closed down at the average rate of one school every day, largely because of a crisis of costs that remains unresolved.

The Catholic parochial schools are the victims of two forces: a shortage of the nuns and priests who had for years provided them with teachers at very little cost; and more important, the American tradition of total separation between church and state. The first amendment to the Constitution quite specifically bans Congress from making laws about the establishment of religion, and this has always been interpreted to mean that no public money could go for the support of church schools. In recent years, however, several states had got around this constitutional provision by a variety of formulas, generally known as parochiaid. Pennsylvania, for example, provided "payment of services" to parochial schools for children educated there, while Rhode Island devised a scheme under which teachers in the parochial schools were paid a proportion of their salaries by the state. But in 1971, the Supreme Court found these plans unconstitutional, both under the First Amendment prohibition on the establishment of religion and under the Fourteenth Amendment, which provides equal protection under the laws. In an 8 to 1 verdict, the Court ruled that the government supervision that would be needed to make sure government money was not being diverted to religious purposes would amount to "excessive entanglement between government and religion." Other indirect forms of subsidy, such as providing state-run schoolbuses, were allowed to continue, on the grounds that the state was providing for the welfare of the individual child, but any sort of direct financial assistance was prohibited. The ruling has caused much unhappinesss among the Catholic community, which believes large amounts of state money are necessary if the school system is to continue in its present form. President Nixon seemed to agree with them, and had at one point promised his help, but so far this has come to nothing.

These are material problems, however, and the malaise that afflicts the Catholic Church today is more spiritual than material, a malaise that is thought by many Catholics to be both lasting and profound. A large part of the unhappiness arises from the same causes as the unhappiness felt by Catholics in industrialized societies elsewhere: the Church's unyielding positions on birth control, divorce, and dissent. Many liberal Catholics have also been concerned with what they regard as the profound chauvinism of the American Church, which one radical Catholic said, "has blessed our excursion into southeast Asia more blindly and obediently than any other religious group in the nation." And a Catholic sociologist, Father Andrew Greeley, has declared, "I believe the present leadership of the church to be morally, intellectually, and religiously bankrupt."

In 1971, the Gallup organization polled American Catholics and came up with some startling findings. More than a third of them, they discovered, no longer regularly attend Sunday Mass, two out of every three had not been to confession in the previous two months, and three out of every five families believed it was possible for good Catholics to ignore the Pope's condemnation of artificial birth control (findings borne out by the official National Fertility Study, which also concluded that, despite the strictures of the Church, Catholic women were increasingly using unapproved methods of contraception—by 1970, Roman Catholic couples had sharply reduced the number of children they were having and intended to have). Even more surprising for Catholics was the answer they gave to the question, If your child decided to leave the Church, do you think he could still be saved? Although membership in the Roman Catholic Church has traditionally been regarded as the only means of salvation, almost eight Catholics out of every ten answered Yes to the Gallup question.

The problems faced today by many individual Catholic laymen were eloquently expressed by John Robben in an article he wrote for the New York *Times* in 1972. Robben was born and raised in a devout Catholic household; he ate fish on Fridays, attended Mass regularly, went to confession and communion. Then, like so many Catholics, he split with the Church over the issue of birth control:

> If you remove one brick from a structure of belief, other bricks begin to fall. After our fifth child we began practicing birth control. This, for a Catholic, is a sin, and the priest, when I went to confession, wouldn't absolve me because I wouldn't stop practicing it. I left the confessional still laden with mortal sin, and condemned to hell if I should die, and yet in a way feeling suddenly free. I'd never go into a

confessional again. That was the second brick. The third was communion, the fourth mass itself, and the structure was down.

In the collapse of his adherence to his religion, Robben concluded that the biggest thing he was free of was authoritarianism. Formerly, he had relied on the Church's "experts" to explain to him the rules for salvation, but, he says, the "experts" of the Catholic Church were at this time themselves beginning to pull a few bricks: "Meat on Friday, for example—which had once been a sure route to hell—was now suddenly O.K." Sooner or later, Robben believed, the Church would itself change other rules, like birth control. "I was simply going to beat her to it," he said.

Like the majority of other Americans, Robben still believes in God; what he rejects is the authority of his church. Here, perhaps, is the quandary faced by all bodies of organized religion in America today—by the Methodists no less than the Catholics, by the Jewish congregations no less than the Episcopalians—that to adhere too rigidly to a body of dogma and theology many of its liberal members regard as outmoded, is to drive them away from organized religion altogether, yet to change with the times, to revise its tenets according to the modern principles of ecumenism is, as Robben discovered, to pull away the bricks from the religion's fundamental structure of belief, a course that ends in driving away the traditionalists, those on the opposite wing of the church who seek from their religion not doubt but certainty, an explanation of the human mystery in ultimate terms.

It is a dilemma which the more fundamentalist religions find easier to cope with than those that seek to modernize both their function and their faith. Before Vatican II the Catholic Church in America belonged in the first category of religions; today, it sits unhappily and uncomfortably in the latter. There it is likely to remain at least for the rest of this decade.

CHAPTER XVII

Minorities

1. Students: Beyond the Revolution

"The youth of America is their oldest tradition. It has been going on now for three hundred years. "

—OSCAR WILDE, 1893

As the United States emerged from the cataclysmic year of 1968, a large segment of its better-educated youth was in a state bordering on rebellion. Across the country, campus after campus was disrupted by rioting, strikes, and violent protest, which were directed ostensibly against the war in Vietnam, but which many observers believed had much more profound, even metaphysical, causes. It seemed as though a whole generation was rising up to cast off the hypocrisies and social assumptions of their elders. To some, this new generation of Americans was at the vanguard of a social transformation as sweeping in its implications as those that occurred during the Renaissance, the Reformation, and the rise of Christianity in ancient Rome. To others, the excesses of the new youth culture, and especially its rejection of the old conventions, represented "an aberration from the moral order of American society," as President Nixon's Commission on Campus Unrest ruefully put it.

At any rate, the alarm of the older generation was widespread. In the spring of 1969 a group of twenty-two congressmen returned from a tour of American colleges to report that the problem of student unrest was "far deeper and far more urgent" than most realized, going way beyond the efforts of organized revolutionaries that some had been inclined to blame for all the trouble. A year later, Walter Hickel, then Secretary of the Interior, wrote in his famous letter to the President that "our young people, or at least a vast segment of them, believe they have no opportunity to communicate with Government . . . other than through violent confrontation." And it was the opinion of the President's commission (headed by William W. Scranton, former governor of Pennsylvania) that the unrest was rooted in the rise of a new youth culture, which had found its identity in the rejection of the work ethic, the materialism, and the conventional norms and pieties of the older America. "Indeed," said the commission's report, "it rejected all institutional disciplines externally imposed upon the individual, and this set it at odds with much in American society." Sometimes, the leaders of the rebellion themselves were quite explicit in their admission that this was, indeed, a struggle between two generations, holding two quite disparate sets of values. "The struggle is no longer between the wage-earner and boss, but between capitalists and their sons who do not want to tend the store," said Tom Hayden, one of the founders of the revolutionary student movement. "The so-called generation gap is a new kind of class struggle. The struggle is not a vague Marxist equation: It's a very personal family feud."

Generational conflicts have of course been one of the universal themes of mankind: it was Aristotle who first commented on the strong and sometimes intemperate passions of youth "who cannot bear to feel slighted and are indignant if they imagine themselves unfairly treated." It is also true that throughout history one of the clearest signs of social decay has been the *lack* of conflict beteeen one generation and the next, a condition that occurs only in static or decadent civilizations.

Nevertheless, it is by now obvious to everyone that the change in fundamental lifestyles that has taken place in America in the space of the last decade has been marked by more than the ordinary stress that occurs when one generation succeeds another. The reasons are obscure and sometimes mystifying and are only connected in the most peripheral sense with the overt cause of so much of the college turmoil of the last decade. For while the war in Vietnam was certainly the *object* of much of the protest, it was by no means the only cause of the malaise that afflicted the young. The turmoil was just as widespread and often even more violent in other societies like France and Japan where the war was hardly an issue at all, or at least not in any practical sense. And even in America, the youth rebellion was already well under way before the trauma of Vietnam added so greatly to its impetus in the last four years of the decade. This rebellion has led to lasting changes in the attitudes of young people toward the old shibboleths of sex, family, church, and what they often call "the system"—changes that one suspects would have taken place anyway, without the issue of Vietnam. One must therefore look elsewhere for the forces which led to its birth.

An obvious starting point is the sheer size of the younger generation. Just about half the total population is now under 25 years old, the result of the biggest and most prolonged baby boom in American history. For decades before the end of World War II the American birth rate had been fairly static, rarely varying by more than 100,000 from year to year. Then, in 1947, as the troops returned home from the war, there was a sudden and startling increase. Total births jumped 800,000 in a single year—up by nearly a third over 1946. Each year after that the numbers went up, until by 1960, when the boom reached its peak, there were 4.3 million births, the most ever, compared with only 2.7 million in 1946 and 2.4 million a generation earlier in 1934 at the height of the Depression. As a result, by 1974 there will be twice as many Americans aged fourteen as aged forty. Even in ordinary times this demographic shift in the balance of power between the generations would have had far-reaching implications. But times were far from ordinary in the late sixties when the first wave of the bulge came of college age, and numbers alone cannot account for the transformation that has taken place in the attitudes of young people towards the society in which they find themselves. This is particularly true of the sons and daughters of the middle classes, those who go on to college, the true inheritors of the affluent society. "This is not just a new generation," said *Time* in 1970, "but a new kind of generation."

Not everyone would share that view, even today, and there are some who believe that differences in class are just as important in shaping basic attitudes as differences in age. The election results of 1972, for example, demonstrated that the young generation—or at least those of them who bothered to vote —divided on much the same party lines as their parents. And Richard Scammon, the social analyst, had a valid point when he wrote: "The working class kid from the Italian-American half of Cambridge whose father is a fry cook in the White Tower Restaurant, and the Harvard undergraduate son of a Scarsdale physician have less in common with each other than either does with his own parents." If the "working class kid" has followed his father to become a fry cook, too, that is probably perfectly true. But the chances are better than fifty-fifty that he has not; and if he has also gone on to college—as the majority of young Americans now do—the generation gap is likely to be even more profound.

In the well-educated middle class at any rate, the postwar baby boom *has* produced a new kind of generation. They have been shaped, collectively, by entirely new forces, both social and technological. They have no memories of the Depression and World War II, the two great upheavals that molded the attitude of their parents. They are the first "permissive" generation, reared under the benevolent guidance of Dr. Spock. They are the first generation to have grown up with television, which has exposed them since infancy to outside and even worldwide influences. They are, as a generation, far better educated than their parents and far more affluent than their parents were at the same age. By the end of the 1960s, more than twice as many young people were living alone, away from the influence of their families, than lived alone at the beginning of the decade. And five times as many of them go away to college as in the 1930s. As a result of all these factors, family influences have become relatively less dominant; outside influences, particularly from their own peer groups, much more so.

All these have been common experiences. Yet other influences, which even at the start of this decade seemed dominant, have now disappeared from the equation altogether, and there are many pitfalls for the sociologist who lumps them all together in casual generalizations about students. Such is the speed of change with which one college generation succeeds another that by the fall of 1973, those who were starting their last year at college came to political awareness at a time when America was racked by war, riots, and political assassinations, with the draft and antiwar demonstrations a part of their personal experiences. Those who were just entering college had been shaped by very different forces; they were only thirteen, for example, during the Chicago riots of 1968 that did so much to shape the political attitudes of the seniors. Meanwhile, the draft has ended, the American combat role in Vietnam is over, eighteen-year-olds have won the vote, and for three successive years, the campuses had been uncommonly cool. The revolution that so fired their elders has run its course, even turned sour, since this decade began. "For five years," David Broder has remarked, "they tried canvassing, marching, demonstrating, striking and protesting. Nothing has seemed to work. In short, they have been turned off by politics."

Nevertheless, the upsurge of the late sixties has left a permanent imprint on the collective attitudes of the young. Values have changed in basic ways. "The shagginess and chosen poverty of student communities have nuances that may be tremendously important for the future," Paul Goodman has commented. "We must remember that these are the young of the affluent society, used to a high standard of living and confident that if and when they want, they can fit in and make good money. Having suffered little pressure of insecurity, they have little need to climb, just as, coming from respectable homes, they feel no disgrace about sitting a few nights in jail. By confidence they are aristocrats—*en masse.*"

This new kind of student is the product of a new kind of university. The old ideals of a university dedicated to providing a "liberal education" for an élite band of undergraduates rather than mere vocational training for the masses, the ideal classically expressed by Cardinal Newman more than a century ago that the university was to be an "alma mater, knowing her children one by one, not a foundry or a mint or a treadmill," has been largely replaced in postwar America by the idea that education is the means to national growth. Universities have become, in one famous phrase, "the knowledge industry." Clark Kerr, former president of the University of California, America's biggest, and an early prophet of the new order, says that "the basic reality, for the university, is the widespread recognition that new knowledge is the most important factor in economic and social growth." What railroads did for the second half of the last century, he argues, what the automobile did for the first half of this century, education may do for the remainder of the twentieth century. The results of his prophecy, however, have so far not been entirely happy.

The American universities had actually been moving toward this goal for almost a hundred years, putting greater stress on graduate research and study, rather on the German model, than they did on the simple teaching of undergraduates. Academic freedom in the United States had come more and more to mean *Lehrfreiheit,* the freedom to teach, rather than *Lernfreiheit,* the freedom to learn. But the more recent trend toward "using" universities to fulfil national goals really began with World War II and has continued at an accelerating pace ever since. As Edwin Diamond has pointed out, the end of the university's political innocence came perhaps in July 1939, when Enrico Fermi and the other physicists working on the idea of a nuclear chain-reaction found they needed $6,000 worth of graphite to complete their experiments. No individual university physics department could possibly come up with such a sum, and it took nothing less than the famous letter from Einstein to President Roosevelt to get the project going. Three years later, the academics were at war, developing radar, proximity fuses, navigational devices, and the atom bomb itself. Scientific knowledge had become the essential ingredient for national survival.

This trend, already apparent in the 1940s, received a terrific new impetus at the end of the 1950s when Russia began the space age with the first of the orbiting Sputniks. The trauma suffered by all Americans at having been beaten into space by the Russians can hardly be imagined today, but it was perhaps the decisive event of the decade, not only for scientists but for the entire concept of American education. It was "to get America going again" that John Kennedy was elected to the White House just a few short years after the first Sputniks had shattered the easy going confidence of the Eisenhower years, and it was not long before Kennedy had embraced the philosophy that education is the path to national power. He declared in one message to Congress:

> This nation is committed to greater advancement in economic growth; and recent research has shown that one of the most beneficial of all such investments is education, accounting for some *forty per cent* of the nation's growth and productivity in recent years. In the new age of science and space, improved education is essential to give meaning to our national purpose and power. It requires skilled manpower and brainpower to match the power of totalitarian discipline. It requires scientific effort which demonstrates the superiority of freedom [italics added].

Nothing could be further from the old ideals of the universities as repositories of intellectual integrity, centers of thought, than the role which Kennedy was now casting for them. It was as though he was deliberately seeking to turn them into the foundries and treadmills Cardinal Newman had so abhorred. For many, it was a profoundly disturbing development.

On one level, however, that of numbers, the new policy brought some remarkable achievements. In the 1930s, barely one high school graduate in ten went on to college. Twenty years later the proportion had almost exactly doubled, and in the 1970s over half the young people who finished high school will receive some advanced education. In the last ten years alone, the actual number of college undergraduates in America has leapt from less than three

million to almost eight million, and it has been estimated that more masters'
and doctors' degrees will have been awarded between 1965 and 1975 than in
the previous half-century.

While the effects of this academic revolution can still only be dimly perceived, it has meant that America more than any other society the world has
ever known has during the past decade come close to achieving the dream of
universal education. The comparison with the rest of the world is startling.
Recent studies have calculated the percentage of twenty-to-twenty-four-year-
olds enrolled in higher education in various advanced countries as follows:

TABLE

Country	Per cent Enrolled In Higher Education
U.S.A.	23.9*
France	14.1
U.S.S.R.	11.8
Canada	8.6
Great Britain	8.5
Italy	7.7

Source: Organization for Economic Cooperation and Development, Paris, 1969

*The figure of 23.9 percent used by the OECD differs from the 50 percent mentioned earlier
because of the different age groups used as a base.

On the face of it, therefore, Americans are now far and away the best-
educated people in the world. According to the Census bureau, almost a third
of the undergraduates now at college are the sons and daughters of parents
who never even completed high school—so that the son of the fry cook in
Cambridge today has, in fact, an excellent chance of getting a college education. Indeed, even the average American black now has as good a chance of
receiving a university education as the average Englishman or Canadian. The
consequences can hardly fail to be profound—both for America, and for the
rest of the world.

There is, however, another side to the picture, and it is here perhaps that
the key to the student unrest of the previous decade is to be found. American
universities are on their way to becoming an integral part of the capitalist
system of production, as Kennedy obviously intended they should, a foundation stone of the power structure, inescapably linked to government, big
business, and the defense establishment.

Kennedy's Presidency saw a remarkable transformation in the status of
American intellectuals. His were the years in which large numbers of professors (particularly, it seemed, if they came from Harvard) descended from their
ivory towers to claim positions of considerable power and prestige in Washing-

ton. They were, in David Halberstam's phrase, "the best and the brightest" of their generation, and just as big business had been regarded as the national savior of the 1920s, so education became the cure-all of the 1960s. Men from a profession with a traditionally liberal outlook suddenly became a part of the conservative establishment, with a vested interest in maintaining the status quo. Education, in a sense, had lost its independence.

The interchange worked in both directions. Academics flocked into government and federal money poured into the universities, so that between 1940 and 1964 federal expenditures for research and development increased over two hundred times. By 1968, the federal government was spending $17 billion a year for research and development—more than the entire gross national product of Denmark—while something like one-half the funds for such universities as MIT, Caltech, Stanford, and Berkeley were coming from the government in the form of research contracts.

As a result, the professor, the graduate student, and the college administrator have increasingly become a part of corporate America, linked more to their disciplines and those who pay for their research than to their own universities. "When a man's reputation is national," Professor Neil Smelser of Berkeley has remarked, "he does the things that enhance his reputation—and teaching isn't one of them." As long ago as 1964, a report of the Carnegie Foundation for the Advancement of Teaching was already referring to a "crisis of values" in American education. The cause of this crisis, the report maintained, was "a limitless supply of research funds, consulting opportunities, easy promotions, dazzling offers." It said the heavily bid-for young men produced by this system were likely to have no sense of institutional loyalty whatever, while students were just impediments "to the headlong search for better grants, fatter fees, higher salaries, higher rank." There is of course a certain appeal in the idea of a university without walls that results from such a system, with the intellectuals tied to their subjects rather than to their students or their colleges, but it is an idea that sits unhappily with the ancient theory of the university as an alma mater. The cozy establishment niche discovered by large numbers of faculty members and graduate students has altered in basic ways the relationship between the university and the society it serves.

Another major cause of the unhappiness that erupted during the 1960s has been the depersonalization of the student, due largely to the sheer size of the "multiversity" in which he has received his education. The giant American universities today, with 40,000 or 50,000 students on a single campus, have become conglomerates of knowledge and, some would argue, precisely that treadmill warned against by Cardinal Newman. While the multiversity, with all its faults, is perhaps the inevitable fruit of the belief in higher education for all, it can have disturbing effects on its students. So big has the University of California become, it now files the names of its 100,000 students on IBM cards, stored in a computer; at the University of Illinois, rows of TV monitors have been suspended from the ceiling of the bigger lecture halls in order to give the students at least a glimpse of their teachers; and across the country, term grades are now commonly sent out not by name but by code number. By the mid-1960s, indeed, the machine was becoming perilously close to replacing the teacher, at least as a means of communicating information, and it was possible for students to emerge from the university production-line almost like the fruits of a modern factory, "untouched by human hand." If that seems an exaggeration, it was one that was often fostered by the multiversities themselves, fascinated like so many Americans with the sheer technology of the new teaching devices, and encouraged in their headlong rush toward computerization by the salesmanship of the companies that made the hardware. "IT CAN BE JUST ONE BIG CAMPUS, LINKED BY THE BELL SYSTEM NETWORK," said the headline on one advertisement published by the AT&T over a large map of the United States. Through the Bell System, the advertisement promised, taped and live television lectures could be transmitted simultaneously to classrooms across the country, so that professors "and other resources" could be shared by all. Bell's Tele-Lecture system, moreover, "allows widely separated audiences to hear a lecture, then participate in question-and-answer sessions with the speaker." If that sounds more like science fiction than education, well, it *is* science fiction, almost a parody of the training techniques used to produce the Alphas in Aldous Huxley's *Brave New World*. And the depersonalization of the student implicit in the use of these new techniques was in large part responsible for the malaise that erupted in violence and protest during the 1960s.

It was perhaps no accident that the student uprising began at Berkeley, the most advanced university in the most technologically minded state in the Union. It is significant, too, that the enemy against which the students rebelled was increasingly identified as the impersonal university, the machine, the administration. "I am a UC student," ran the most common slogan, "please do not bend, fold, spindle, or mutilate me." Others echoed the same, almost despairing theme: "Nobody Knows My Name," and "Are You a Student or an IBM Card?" The university, like the nation, said Jerry Avorn, a student at Columbia, seemed to be like a great complex vending machine that had become rusted with age: "The only way to make it work right is to kick it hard."

Several of the leaders of the first Berkeley revolt had begun by identifying themselves with the civil-rights movement and had taken part in the Freedom Rides in Mississippi and Alabama in the early years of the decade, but when the revolt erupted on the Berkeley campus in the fall term of 1964, the civil-rights objectives quickly slid into the background, to be replaced by a confused and not always articulate attack on the university bureaucracy. The First Battle of Berkeley, as Professor Lewis Feuer has rightly said, was a battle of generations.

The Berkeley revolt has gone down in history as the first significant white-collar rebellion in our time. The leaders of the movement thought quite seriously that they were living through the first heady moments of a new revolutionary dawn. And in a way, of course, they were right. By 1968 violent student revolution had become worldwide, with university demonstrations reported by a United Nations study group taking place in fifty countries that year. To some, it seemed that the whole of western society had reached a point when, like Rome, it was about to collapse, because, as one French politician put it, "belief is dead."

In America, the spearhead of the student revolutionaries was a small but immensely influential group of militants who called their organization Students for a Democratic Society (SDS). For SDS, the American university had at last found its role: It was to be an instrument of revolution. Their object was frank destruction of the American system. Their precise aims, however, were often confused and wildly romantic, so that when asked what his revolutionary program was, Tom Hayden, one of the founders of SDS, was able to reply, "We haven't any. First we will make the revolution, and *then* we will find out what it is for." If today's six demands are met, tomorrow there will be six more. The politics of absurdity could hardly go any farther, and yet it seemed for a while that SDS was on the way to destroying the American system of higher education. One of the SDS leaders at Columbia University is reported to have exclaimed at the height of the disturbances there, "As much as we would like to, we are not strong enough as yet to destroy the United States. But we are strong enough to destroy Columbia!" Fanaticism was in the saddle. When faced with the deliberate confrontations of violence that had been precipitated by the militants, often on the most spurious of pretexts, some members of the academic community yielded to their blackmail. They capitulated, both morally and intellectually, to the calls for "students' rights" and "relevance" that had become the slogans of the revolutionaries.

The humane, liberal, and eminently *reasonable* men who ran the universities showed that there was an intellectual softness, a moral mushiness at the core of their liberal philosophy; when threatened with violence or the issuance of revolutionary demands, it simply collapsed. It is true, they faced a terrible dilemma: At heart, they sympathized with the majority of the students in their unhappiness with the system, with the war, with the government in Washington, with their demands for black rights, for "relevance" and the rest. As a result, they tried to compromise. And compromise, after all, is the essence of the liberal philosophy—abuse can be righted by prompt and enlightened reform—but compromise with the forces of destruction becomes an impossible objective, as the universities found when they tried to reason with the militants. But the militants were not interested in compromise, in reason; their goal was revolution.

Sometimes the university administration capitulated in despair and called in the police to bring order to their disrupted campus—action that the militants had probably wanted all along and that usually had the effect of turning the moderate students into militants, too. Sometimes the administration simply gave in to the radicals' demands, however absurd. Professors of biochemistry began to include in their examinations such "relevant" questions as the definition of civil disobedience. In some universities, written examinations and formal grades were abolished altogether, and students, including freshmen, invited to write their own courses. At Harvard, where the role of the Reserve Officers' Training Corps had become an issue, the SDS demanded the removal of ROTC from the campus altogether. After several incidents of violence, the university agreed, whereupon the SDS escalated their demands and "Abolish ROTC" became the new slogan. The goal may have been a valid one, but for the revolutionaries, the aim of these actions was never to achieve the ostensible reforms demanded, but to undermine and ultimately to destroy the institution of the university. The slogan was only a tactic. Professor Nathan Glazer of Harvard astutely observes that "the terrible effect of such an approach is to introduce corruption into the heart of the movement, and into the hearts of those who work for it, because the 'insiders' know that the *ostensible* slogans are only tactical, that one can demand anything, no matter how nonsensical, self-contradictory and destructive, because the aim is not the fulfillment of demands, but the creation of new radicals who result from the process of putting forward such demands: violence by the revolutionaries, counterviolence by the authorities, radicalization therefore of the bystanders, and the further 'building of the movement.' What justifies this process, of course, is the irredeemable corruption of the society and all its institutions, and therefore the legitimacy of any means to bring it down."

At Columbia University, in the heart of New York City, revolutionary students effectively shut down the university for a whole month with a strike that had begun over the issue of where to build a new college gymnasium. But this was simply a pretext, as one of the leaders later admitted. "The point of the game was power," he said. "It was revolution. . . . Everywhere, the purpose was to destroy institutions of the American Establishment." Finally, a thousand policemen were called in to evict the occupying students. Seven hundred were arrested, over one hundred injured. "Somehow the whole night seemed unbelievable," wrote the New York *Times* the next day, "a mixture of moods that seemed to have no relationship to each other: violence and compassion, talk of hatred and death and talk of gentle philosophers, ugliness of action and speech, and moments of tenderness, a place of learning become a place of destruction."

When San Francisco State blew up, the issue again was the relevance of the education provided by the university. Demands were made by the rebel leaders, some reasonable, some not, but all *non-negotiable*, as the new phrase had it. "The Bible says there's a time for everything," declared Nathan Hare, leader of the San Francisco militants. "I think this is a time for hate." Bombs were found on the campus, roving bands of vandals began breaking into classes, and again police were called in to quell the disturbances. For two weeks there were daily confrontations between the six hundred policemen and some three thousand or so militant students, with examples of brutality on both sides. Leo Litwak, an associate professor of English at the university, wrote later of the two-week trauma:

> One of my colleagues, protesting a brutal arrest, was thrown down, handcuffed, led away with a riot stick pressed to his throat. An officer squirted Mace in his eyes. Another came from behind—"How do you like this, you fancy-pants professor?"— and cut his head open with a blow from a riot stick that knocked him cold. The professor was charged with resisting and interfering with an arrest.

In campus after campus, similar scenes were repeated. There are many who believe American higher education came close to total collapse in that six-month period that led up to the biggest confrontation of all, on the streets of Chicago during the Democratic Party's national convention. "This is the apocalypse, it really is," said Mary Lovett of the University of Pennsylvania. Her feelings were echoed by thousands of students all across America.

At Berkeley, where the movement had begun, the rebellious student leaders seized upon the issue of black studies to force that troubled campus into the worst confrontation yet. A group of militants calling themselves the Third World Liberation Front issued a series of demands, which were rejected, and then called a student strike, which was on the whole unsuccessful. They resorted instead to violence. Groups of fifty to a hundred demonstrators took to snakedancing through the campus, smashing office windows with clubs, throwing rocks into libraries and classrooms, breaking up lectures, and making the normal life of the university intolerable.

Governor Reagan, a hardline conservative, dramatically proclaimed a state of extreme emergency that brought the university to a standstill and had the effect of turning over control of the campus to the sheriff of Alameda County, whose men, promptly nicknamed the "Blue Meanies," soon made it clear they were not inclined to treat the students with much finesse. But order of a sort was at first restored. Then, in the spring of 1969, came the worst and most violent clash of all. The issue was "People's Park"—not Vietnam, not the relevance of university studies, but a quarrel over the proper use of a small and derelict piece of university-owned land led to the gravest student disorders of the decade. The students decided to take the park, which suddenly acquired a symbolic importance far transcending the rights and wrongs of what was on the face of it a trivial issue. But by this time, the Alameda sheriff's men had decided "to teach Berkeley a lesson." The National Guard was called in to ring the campus with bayonets; the police, armed with shotguns, opened fire on one demonstration, killing one onlooker and blinding another; a few days later, an Army helicopter appeared over the rooftops of Sproul Plaza near the center of the campus and indiscriminately sprayed tear gas over the entire area. Students, trapped on the campus by the rings of armed guards, had no means of escape, and children in nearby elementary schools ran gasping and coughing from their classrooms. Berkeley had the appearance more of a battlefield than of an institute dedicated to the ideals of thought and learning.

The 1960s ended with Richard Nixon in the White House and a fragile quiet on the nation's campuses. But the college turmoil had not yet quite run its course. The new decade was in fact barely four months old when Nixon ordered American troops into Cambodia, and thereby triggered a new spasm of student rage, which ended in the tragedy at Kent State, where four bystanders were killed when National Guardsmen opened fire on a crowd of demonstrators.

That weekend at Kent State turned to tragedy after a rally on the ten-acre commons in the center of the campus had fallen under the complete control of the militants. About eight hundred students went on a rampage through the grounds, smashing windows and setting fire to the university's ROTC building; when firemen arrived, the students threw rocks at them, cut their hoses, and had to be dispersed with tear gas. Ohio's Governor, James Rhodes, ordered in the National Guard and arrived at Kent in person the next morning to denounce the troublemakers as "worse than the Brown Shirts and Communists and vigilantes—they're the worst type of people that we harbor in America." He declared a state of emergency and banned all further demonstrations, bringing in some nine hundred National Guardsmen to make sure his orders were enforced.

By Monday, when about a thousand students gathered on the grass to test the governor's ban, the tension at Kent State was palpable. "We just couldn't believe they could tell us to leave," one student said afterwards. "This is *our* campus." They stood their ground as National Guard officers warned them through bullhorns, "Evacuate the commons area. You have no right to assemble." The students replied with shouts of "Pigs off the campus! We don't want your war!" Tear gas was fired to disperse the students, who began to flee, occasionally tossing canisters of expended tear gas back at the troops. What happened next has never been clearly established, but whether on orders from their officers or through simple panic, a group of the Guardsmen quietly dropped to their knees and discharged a ten-second burst of rifle fire towards the crowd. Four students, none of them radicals, or even demonstrators, were killed, another ten wounded. Inside those ten seconds, Kent State had become the site of an authentic American tragedy.

A week later, 75,000 young people crowded into Washington to protest both the invasion of Cambodia and the killings at Kent State. By this time, there had been riots in more than twenty universities and more than two hundred colleges had been closed down for at least one day, eight of them for the rest of the term. In California, all twenty-eight campuses of the state's vast university were shut for four days on the orders of Governor Reagan. The National Guard had to be called out to keep order in Maryland, Illinois, Wisconsin, Kentucky, and New Mexico. More than 5,000 federal troops were hastily moved into Washington in expectation of massive disruptions, but in the end the day passed in comparative peace.

No one knew it then, but the Cambodia moratorium turned out to be the last great student uprising of the era. Almost immediately afterwards, an inexplicable calm settled on most universities. Although there have been sporadic and isolated outbursts since then, including another massive and peaceful demonstration in Washington in the spring of 1971, it was clear that the student revolt had run out of steam. Its leadership became increasingly quarrelsome and fragmented; "energy levels," it is said, were low; and even the renewal of the bombing over North Vietnam in the election year of 1972 raised scarcely a murmur of organized protest. Anger had been replaced by a sence of futility. There was a widespread feeling that the antiwar movement had failed in its basic objectives, and the movement itself seemed to be afflicted with an overwhelming sense of weariness. A "National Emergency" rally called at the U.S. Capitol that election year drew only a handful of protestors, and they were welcomed in words that spoke for the despair of them all. "Well," Julius Hobson had said, "for the one-thousandth god-damned time, welcome to Washington to stop these idiots." There could be no starker admission that the passions of the late sixties were spent.

In the 1970s, older Americans take comfort in the fact that the overt causes of the youth rebellion have now been removed. The draft and the war have both apparently passed into history, youth has been given the vote, and with the removal of these immediate reasons for unrest the universities can resume their old placid ways. Or so they fervently hope. Meanwhile, they remind themselves that even at the fever pitch of 1968 and 1969, the student rebellion commanded the loyalty of only a small proportion of the young and had far less direct impact on their government than the classic student revolts of the past—those at the beginning of this century in Czarist Russia, for example, those of the German students of 1848, or even the Bosnian student movement that disrupted the Balkans sixty years ago and lit the fuse that led directly to a world war. There is truth in all these arguments, of course, although closer scrutiny of the recent American student movement does not support the sanguine view that with the end of the war in Vietnam all is now well in the kingdom of the young.

Even at the time, a survey by the National Student Association in analyzing the disturbances during the first six months of 1968, found that of the 221 college demonstrations that occurred during that most turbulent period of all, only 45—fewer than one fourth—were directly related to the war in Vietnam or other military factors. Of the rest, 97 were related to the aims of the black power movement and 50 the reform of their own universities. Nor were the proportions taking part in the demonstrations all that tiny. At the end of the decade, a Gallup poll reported that nearly one out of every three college men and one in every four college women had participated in a demonstration of some kind. Clearly, much deeper forces than those of simple political protest were at work.

And even though a new quiet had settled on the colleges and universities by the start of President Nixon's second term, the attitudes and lifestyles of the young suggest that a transformation of historic proportions has taken place in America in the space of the past decade, with the main impact on the fundamental role of America in the world yet to be fully felt. The great upsurge in higher education that continued throughout the 1960s might, in fact, now have reached its peak. Today, with room to spare in many universities, there is a new skepticism abroad about the basic value of a college degree.

On a purely material level, the possession of even an advanced degree is no longer quite the certain passport to a high salary that it was even five years ago. The boom in higher education that tripled the annual harvest of Ph.D's between 1959 and 1970 has begun to slow down since the Nixon recession in the opening years of this decade, and many Ph.D. graduates, caught by a simultaneous decline in spending by both the universities and the federal government, have found it harder to land the plum jobs they had expected. In 1973, New York State even went so far as to declare a freeze on all doctoral programs throughout its university system, the result of what it called "deep concern" over the expansion of such programs in the past and the evidence that present and future needs are being met. There are even some who believe America has now become saturated with advanced graduates and that the time has come for a reduction in the numbers of its educated élite.

On a more fundamental level, there are signs today that more and more students are turning away from the purely material goals of their parents and from the technological training needed to achieve those goals. Six out of every ten students now say they want a life "different" from that of their parents. In Frederick Dutton's phrase, they are turning away in significant numbers from a "working and saving" outlook to one in favor of "doing and using." When the American Council on Education polled the freshmen in some five hundred colleges and universities across the country in the fall of 1972, it found the new students were measurably less inclined to start careers in the physical sciences, education, and engineering and more inclined towards becoming doctors, lawyers, and social scientists. Of those who were leaving college, the council found more than two thirds of them agreed that "much of what is taught in college is irrelevant to what is going on in the outside world." Now that the war in Vietnam is over, and with it the draft, the poll also found the political preoccupations of the young were changing, too. The overwhelming concerns of the freshmen, they found, were the pollution of the environment (mentioned by 89.6 percent of the almost 200,000 students interviewed) and the support of consumer protection (mentioned by 76.3 percent).

The changes in the career attitudes of college women have been perhaps even more radical. In a poll conducted by *Fortune* in the spring of 1973 at Stanford University, only 3 percent of the women wanted to go into "women's jobs" such as housewife, secretary, or nurse, down 12 percent from the class of 1965. And four times as many women in the class of 1973 said they intended to go into medicine, law, and other professions compared with that earlier class.

There are some who call the modern students the New Barbarians, armed in William Shannon's phrase, "with college degrees and glib phrases, but ignorant." Yet, if the recent polls are any guide, there is more hope than despair to be found on the college campuses in the 1970s. And it may still turn out that the enduring hero of American youth in this era is not Herbert Marcuse or Che Guevera or the other heroes of the "old" New Left, but the very American, very positive figure of Ralph Nader.

2. Race: Still the American Dilemma

"Racial injustice is as American as apple pie. But so is the struggle against it."
—KENNETH CLARK, *black educator, 1973*

Just as the passions of the youth revolt appeared to spend themselves in frustration during Nixon's first term in office, so too did the simultaneous uprising of the nation's blacks. The blind rage that led to the riots of the sixties —in Watts, Detroit, Newark, and a score of other cities—has for some reason subsided now. The mood of helpless violence that swept through the black ghettoes after the assassination of Dr. Martin Luther King in 1968 has evaporated and been replaced by more constructive political action: in the 1970s, even the revolutionary Black Panthers have turned away from confrontation with the police to seek power through the ballot box. White Americans sometimes assume that the reason for all of this is that the blacks have achieved their immediate objectives, that the calm of the 1970s is an indication that the underlying causes of the black revolt have at last been removed. Black Americans are now free to vote, in the South as well as in the North; school desegregation has been pressed by the courts to its limits, while the worst excesses of poverty are being rapidly removed. Such a belief, however, harbors a dangerous delusion. For all its surface calm, for all the undoubted progress that was made in the decade of the 1960s, black Americans are aware that the majority of their goals have not been met, not by a long way.

On all sides, there is evidence that what they came to call the Second Reconstruction is drawing to an end. The Civil Rights movement that led to the major reforms of the sixties is at a standstill, while Johnson's Great Society program has today been largely discredited, and much of its apparatus dismantled by a President who has openly abandoned integration as a goal of national policy. The United States today is in just as much danger as it was in 1968 of falling into the condition warned against by the President's commission on race relations, of a society split irretrievably into two, black and white, separate and unequal. As a result, to be black in America is still for a large part of the time to be angry.

The anger of black Americans is a phenomenon that has only peripheral connections with their economic status or with their professional standing in society. It is the result of having been treated for generations as second-class citizens, a condition two black psychiatrists, Drs. William Grier and Price Cobbs, have termed cultural paranoia. In this analysis, the black American has come to regard every white man as a potential enemy unless proved otherwise and every social system set up against him unless he personally finds out differently. Grier and Cobbs submit that it is *necessary* for a black man in America to develop a profound distrust of his white fellow citizens and of the nation. "He must be on guard to protect himself against physical hurt," they write. "He must cushion himself against cheating, slander, humiliation, and outright mistreatment by the official representatives of society. If he does not so protect himself, he will live a life of such pain and shock as to find life itself unbearable." Many factors, of course, have contributed to the discrepancies between black and white in America, but the major factor remains racial discrimination. Hostility toward black people is still a central characteristic of American life, a hostility which Gunnar Myrdal, in his classic study of race relations of thirty years ago, termed "the American Dilemma."

Segregation of the races *by law* has vanished in America in the thirty years that have passed since Myrdal first postulated his thesis. Lunch counters, cinemas, schools, public transportation, and all the rest have been opened up to the black community, in both North and South, and the minority groups share in theory the full and equal rights enjoyed by their fellow citizens. However, the old system of *de jure* segregation, enforced by law, is in the process of being replaced by a system of *de facto* segregation, brought about in large part by the white exodus to the suburbs. (James Baldwin has said that *de facto* segregation means that blacks are still segregated but nobody did it.) The odious apparatus employed in the Deep South to shore up its system of apartheid may have been dismantled, segregation may have largely disappeared in public places, but it remains as strong as ever it was in housing patterns, and housing patterns play an increasingly important part in enforcing, willy-nilly, segregation in other spheres of life—in schools, for instance, and even in employment, where the inability of minority groups to follow the movement of industry to the outer rings of the metropolitan areas has contributed significantly to the black unemployment rate. Most whites still seem to fear and shun social contact with blacks and do not want a black person living next door.

That is not to deny that the lot of black Americans has improved measurably over the past twenty years. Of the 23 million black Americans, one third of them are now, in an economic sense, members of the middle class: white-collar workers, teachers, professionals. One out of every four working blacks, moreover, now earns more than $10,000 a year, and the number employed in skilled trades and crafts has increased by 69 percent over the past decade.

Even among middle-class blacks, however, the gains of the recent past have been uneven. While the more affluent among them are now beginning to move into the suburbs, they are doing so in only tiny numbers—820,000 of them during the decade of the 1960s—and suburbia today remains overwhelmingly white. When the blacks do move into suburban areas, they find that all too often their new white neighbors begin to move out, and the area very quickly becomes a sort of overflow ghetto. The stark fact is that in spite of all the progress that took place in the decade of the 1960s, the nation was more segregated at the end of it than it was at the beginning. Nor are the newly affluent blacks evenly distributed between the professions: a disproportionate number of them are either teachers or government workers, while their share of managers and proprietors of businesses remains minute. It was once estimated during the 1960s that in proportion to their numbers, Chinese-Americans derive forty-five times as much income from Chinese-owned businesses as blacks do from black-owned businesses, and even in the heart of the black ghettoes it is uncommon for blacks to own the small grocery stores they patronize. Of the 300,000 physicians in the United States, only about 8,000 are black, less than 3 percent of the total (and still only just over twice as many as there were in 1910, when most blacks lived in the rural South). In industry, General Motors has appointed its first black board member in the 1970s, yet only about a dozen of the 1,300 GM dealerships are owned by blacks. Of the nation's 100,000 millionaires, it has been estimated that only 35 are black. And while many insurance companies are run by blacks, very few banks are, with the result that the raising of capital is still one of the major obstacles barring the way for the black businessman.

To be black in America is not necessarily to be poor, but even though one third of them are now members of the middle class and a third work in more or less secure jobs in industry or on farms, another third of them—7.7 million people—live below the official poverty level, compared with only 10 percent of the white population. Unemployment in the 1970s has also averaged around 10 percent for blacks, or slightly less than double the white rate, with as many as 31.7 percent of the black teenagers without jobs in 1971. To be black in America is not necessarily to be poor or unemployed—but poverty and unemployment are much more likely conditions for blacks than they are for whites.

While many other groups in America have also known what it is to be poor, the poverty of many blacks is of a special and spiritual kind, not to be defined in statistical terms. Michael Harrington has written that "if a group has internal vitality, a will—if it has aspirations—it may live in dilapidated housing, it may eat an inadequate diet, and it may suffer poverty, *but it is not impoverished.*" For too many black families, even today, to have aspirations is to dream an impossible dream. Yet many white Americans assume that if blacks are poor it is somehow their own fault, that if they only tried harder they would be able to break out of their impoverished society. According to this argument, deeply believed by many white Americans, every other ethnic group in American history started off poor and exploited—the Irish, the

Italians, the Poles, the Jews, the Chinese—and if these once downtrodden and backward immigrants have been able to fight their way up into the affluent society, how is it that the blacks have not?

The answer is easy: the whites have prevented them from doing so. The fact is that the black American of today faces a problem of aculturalization that is not only different in scale, it is different in *kind* from that faced by the older ethnic groups who came here as immigrants. For the black, the problem goes back to its historical roots and the fact that he was brought to the American continent in slavery, a process which by deliberate calculation wiped out all pride in his ancestry and all knowledge of his ethnic origins. Other groups that have come to America have been able to retain the social institutions of their homeland, some link with their past. The Irish and the Italians had the support of the Roman Catholic Church. The Chinese, however badly they were exploited economically, were at least able to maintain their strong ties of family. Even the American Indian retains some legacy from his ancestors. Only the blacks have been cut off without the hope of redress from their past, stripped of their language, their culture, their ancestry, their names, and in the days of slavery not even allowed legally to marry. The result has been a catastrophe for the black family and the black community as a whole, the effects of which have lingered to this day.

Alexis de Tocqueville was perhaps the first to point out that the slavery that was introduced into America was different in its consequences from the institution of slavery imposed by the ancients. Slavery itself led to almost the same immediate ills in the ancient world as in the modern, but the consequences of these ills were different. In antiquity, the slave was the same race as his master and was often his superior in education and enlightenment. Aesop and Terence were among the slaves of antiquity, after all, and many civilized men captured in war were later subjected to servitude. In the ancient world, only freedom kept the master and his slave apart, and freedom once granted, they mingled easily. Therefore the ancients had a very simple means of delivering themselves from slavery and its consequences: namely, to free the slaves. The freedman and the man born free were so completely alike it was soon impossible to distinguish between them. But in America, as de Tocqueville observed, the consequences of freeing the slaves were different, because, as he put it, "the insubstantial and ephemeral fact of servitude is most fatally combined with the physical and permanent fact of difference in race. Memories of slavery disgrace the race, and race perpetuates memories of slavery. . . . I see that slavery is in retreat, but the prejudice from which it arose is immovable."

There was another consequence of the American form of slavery not much dwelt upon by de Tocqueville, and that lay in the fact that its very introduction was an inherent contradiction to the ideals of a people who believed that society was based on a contract freely entered into by free men. The "peculiar institution" could therefore only be justified by denying the black slaves their status as human beings, by regarding them as biologically, morally, and irredeemably inferior to the white man, and by denying them the right to enter into a contract of any sort, even marriage. The practice of separating men from their womenfolk, children from their mothers, was thus both legal and common, as can be seen from advertisements for the sale of slaves, like this one published in a New Orleans newspaper around 1830:

> NEGROES FOR SALE—A negro woman, 24 years of age, and her two children, one eight and the other three years old. Said negroes will be sold SEPARATELY or together, as desired. The woman is a good seamstress. She will be sold low for cash, or EXCHANGED FOR GROCERIES. For terms, apply to Mathew Bliss & Co.

More than one hundred years have passed since the American slaves were freed, but two consequences of the institution have been felt down to the present day. The first is a problem in the heart of the whites, the American Dilemma again, the persistent belief that the blacks are an inferior race and the consequent unwillingness of many white Americans to accept them as fellow human beings. The principle desire of the blacks is to be treated like men. Yet, as James Baldwin has put it, "people who have mastered Kant, Hegel, Shakespeare, Marx, Freud and the Bible find this statement utterly impenetrable."

The second part of the problem passed down by the singular nature of American slavery is a problem for the blacks, and one with which they have been struggling ever since emancipation: the fragmentation of the black family. In the words of the abolitionist Wendell Phillips, the Emancipation Proclamation freed the slave but ignored the Negro. "Never was a people less prepared for freedom," Charles Silberman has written in his history of the racial crisis, *Crisis in Black and White,* and he went on:

> Slavery had emasculated the Negro males, had made them shiftless and irresponsible and promiscuous by preventing them from ever assuming responsibility, negating their role as husband and father, and making them totally dependent on the will of another. There was no stable family structure to offer support to men or women or children in this strange new world. With no history of stable family ties, no knowledge even of what stability might mean, huge numbers of Negro men took to the roads as soon as freedom was proclaimed; the right to move about was seen as a crucial test of freedom. Thus there developed a pattern of drifting from place to place and job to job and woman to woman that has persisted (in a lesser degree, of course) to the present day.

There are many people today who believe the crumbling of the family structure is the root cause of a great many of the problems of black people.

In some slum areas in the northern cities, one third of the black families are now headed by women. In Daniel P. Moynihan's report on the black family in America, he concluded that the causes were to be found in the attack on manhood brought about by discrimination, by the over-rapid urbanization to which the black family had found difficulty in adjusting, in the endemic poverty to be found in the black slums. Black critics, however, have repudiated Dr. Moynihan's argument with some heat. Drs. Grier and Cobbs, for instance, point out that other men have borne discrimination and remained men. Families have adjusted to urbanization since the beginning of time. Other Americans have lived in poverty, but few of them have been trapped there for so long as the black American.

No! No! No! they cry. The problem of the black family is not these challenges. The problem is a latter-day version of the problem faced by the slave family. How does one build a family, make it strong, and breed from it strong men and women when the institutional structures of the nation make it impossible for the family to serve its primary purpose—the protection of its members? The black family is weak and relatively ineffective because the United States sets its hand against black people and by the strength of wealth, size, and numbers *prevents* black families from protecting their members.

They believe, moreover, that a basic cause of black frustration is this inability of so many black families to protect their members—not all of them, of course, but a significant number, particularly in the big city ghettoes, where crime, poverty, and harassment by the authorities are everyday hazards on a scale unknown to white families. To be black and poor in America is to suffer almost every day from verbal and physical abuse, to endure the exploitation of landlords, shopkeepers, and employers, to receive brutal and humiliating treatment from the police, to put up with frequent unemployment, inadequate jobs, poor schools, and squalid housing. Much more than segregation itself, these are the main sources of discontent among the poorer blacks today. These are the forces before which they feel so helpless and enraged. These are the forces that lead to anger. These are the forces that prevent black families from protecting their members. And these are the forces that provide the tinder in American society.

The state of the black community today can be compared to the state of the big-city ghettoes in which so many of its members live: The violence of the 1960s has passed, but the scars remain. In Detroit, Newark, Los Angeles, and especially in Washington, D.C., it is possible still to walk along streets that bear the marks of the rioting of half a decade ago. Along Fourteenth Street in Washington, the scene of one of the worst riots of 1968, almost nothing has changed—except, perhaps, for the worse. Shops that were looted remain derelict and shuttered up, the blocks that were burned down are overgrown with weeds now, making instant playgrounds for the ghetto children. Business has all but fled from this area. There is an overall atmosphere of decay and neglect. A white visitor here meets an inescapable feeling of hatred and resentment, usually in the form of verbal abuse or jostling on the sidewalk. One has the feeling that the distance between this place and the "other America," the world outside, has grown wider in the years that have passed since the rioting.

In the 1960s, the blacks were at the center of attention, due not just to the violence, but also to the progress that was made in the years after Martin Luther King came to Washington to proclaim on the steps of the Lincoln Memorial, "I have a dream." In the five years that followed, blacks made more real progress toward equality than they had in any comparable period since emancipation: the programs of the Great Society, the growth of a new black middle class, the end of segregation of the public schools by law, the three major civil-rights acts, and help and sympathy with their struggle from many whites.

In the 1970s, the mood has changed. It is no longer the blacks who are at the center of attention—it is the so-called Silent Majority, the counter-reformation of mostly working-class whites, resentful at compulsory busing, hurting from inflation, and frightened by the black militancy that seemed to many of them a threat to their own security. These are the people President Nixon wooed so successfully away from the Democratic Party in the national election of 1972, first in the South, then increasingly in the working-class areas of the urban North. As a result, programs to help the poorer blacks have been muted and cut back, some of them abandoned altogether. As Peter Goldman said in an article in *Newsweek,* while the Second Reconstruction is not yet dead, it is today sorely diminished.

The liberal coalition that brought so many of the gains of the previous decade has been dissipated. The whites among them have moved on to other issues, other causes. The media has switched its attention elsewhere. The black leadership itself has lost its momentum, among both moderates and revolutionaries. Martin Luther King is dead, and under his lackluster successor, the Reverend Ralph Abernathy, his movement has been passing through a severe financial crisis. Of the other leaders of the sixties, Malcolm X and Whitney Young are also dead. Eldridge Cleaver, one of the first to articulate the rage of the blacks, is in exile, and so, for a long period, was Stokely Carmichael. Rap Brown has been sentenced to jail for a New York stickup. Bobby Seale and Huey Newton have left the national scene to run for local office in Oakland. In any case, the inflammatory rhetoric of the revolutionaries has lost much of its attraction in the Nixon era. It has been said the blacks today don't have, and perhaps don't want, a single leader who could be killed with one bullet.

It is often claimed that politics is the civil-rights movement of the 1970s, and here the black community has made considerable progress, especially in the old South, where every election sees the return of more and more black office holders. The younger black leaders today are working their way within the system—men like Julian Bond, the attractive politician from Georgia, and Jesse Jackson of Chicago, who played a prominent role in the unseating of Mayor Daley at the Democratic National Convention of 1972. A black caucus has also emerged in Congress, and its power in the years to come is thought by many to be one of the more hopeful signs that blacks in America will eventually be able to win their fair share of political control, on the national scene as well as in their own communities. But even in the field of politics, apathy is widespread. In the elections of 1972, black participation was the lowest since 1960. According to the Joint Center for Political Studies, only 58 percent of the black registered voters in the cities went to the polls that year. Four years before, the portion was 87 percent. In Washington, D.C., the city with the largest concentration of blacks in America, the participation of all voters in the 1972 election was only 27 percent. Electoral apathy on this scale is a sure sign that the blacks have lost the expectations they once had that they could make the national government more responsive to their needs.

While the so-called Second Reconstruction may today be sorely diminished, some gains have survived, chief among them black pride. "There's a new brother about," one of their leaders has said. Blacks as a result are prouder of their color today than they have ever been. "Black is Beautiful" is more than just a slogan: it is a new sign of ethnic pride, an indication that blackness is a badge of honor, not a source of shame.

Ever since the Supreme Court decision of 1954, it has been an article of faith among progressive Americans that one of the main roads to racial equality was prominently and clearly signposted "education." The Court's historic statement in *Brown* vs. *Board of Education* had been explicit in its belief that to separate children solely because of their race "generates a feeling of inferiority as to their status in the community that may affect their hearts and minds in a way unlikely ever to be undone." That decision has proved to be one of the important turning points—perhaps *the* important turning point —in the history of American race relations in the past three generations. (From it has flowed the national policy of integration which has since broken down *de jure* segregation in every aspect of American life, leading to the equal voting laws, the Civil Rights Act of 1964, much of Johnson's Great Society program, and the federal busing orders of the 1970s.)

The idea of using public education as the principal means of lifting from the blacks the burdens of inequality was based on one of America's oldest and most cherished traditions, the belief that the public school was the linchpin of the American Dream. In making education available to all, the United States made democracy available to all. For generations, the mission of the schools had been to provide a free outlet for ability, to guarantee the equality of opportunity upon which the American way of life had been built. In Horace Mann's famous phrase, the schools were to be "the great equalizer of the condition of men—the balance wheel of the social machinery." The ideal had worked for white Americans; now it was time to apply it also to blacks. "Having a white child sit next to my Negro child is no guarantee that mine will learn," a black leader in Harlem had said, "but it is a guarantee that he will be taught."

Yet the ideal of integrated education is now in retreat, under attack from white parents, who are opposed to busing their children; from political and social scientists, who have concluded that the policy does not work, that 'schools make no difference'; and even from some black activist groups who have espoused the cause of separation. The reason is that most schools are no longer segregated by law; they are segregated because society is segregated.

Until the 1970s, it was widely assumed that school segregation was a problem of the South. The early Supreme Court decisions had all been directed against school systems where segregation had been maintained by law, and these were all, without exception, to be found below the Mason-Dixon Line. However, since this decade began, the fact has slowly dawned that the most segregated schools today are generally to be found in the North and the West, the result of segregated patterns of housing, the familiar story of whites fleeing to the suburbs. The school systems of Washington, Newark, Detroit, Chicago, even New York, are all more segregated in fact than the school system in Birmingham, Alabama. Indeed, of the fifteen largest cities with nonwhite majorities in their schools, only five are in the South, while seven are in the North and Northeast and three in the West and Midwest. These cities, with the percentages of nonwhite children in their school systems, are:

City	Percentage of Non- white Students
Washington, D.C.	96
Newark, N.J.	88
San Antonio, Tex.	79
New Orleans, La.	73
Oakland, Calif.	73
Atlanta, Ga.	72
Baltimore, Md.	68
St. Louis, Mo.	68
Detroit, Mich.	67
Chicago, Ill.	65
Philadelphia, Pa.	64
New York, N.Y.	62
Cleveland, Ohio.	60
El Paso, Tex.	60
Birmingham, Ala.	57

In many of these cities, there is no hope of achieving any semblance of racial integration, simply because there are not enough white children in the system to dilute the great concentration of blacks. No amount of busing, of black children or of white, can alter that basic fact. But in other cities, where the balance between the races is not yet hopelessly distorted, the federal courts have intervened in an attempt to restore some degree of integration in the public schools. In many cases, the tool they have employed has been that of busing, a decision which has led to some of the most agonizing political controversies of the decade. The ubiquitous yellow school bus has in the 1970s become a symbol of conflict. To many white parents, the buses represent a threat to their suburban security, based on the twin fears that they will either import the problems of the ghetto into their pristine neighborhoods, or, what is to them even worse, carry off their own children into the violence and squalor of the ghettoes.

Because of these emotional overtones, the problem of busing is often vastly exaggerated. Most opponents of busing tell lurid stories of little children being carried thirty, even forty miles away from their homes, and spending more time in the schoolbus than they do in their classrooms. Yet long-distance busing of this nature has been ordered in only a tiny proportion of the cases, and there—in cities like Los Angeles, for example—the children in most instances already travel quite long distances by bus to get to school. In the vast majority of cases, the distance to be traveled is rarely more than four or five miles, and sometimes much less than that. American children, moreover, have been traveling to school by bus for generations now: almost twenty million of them already go to school by bus for reasons quite unconnected with segregation. In the fall of 1972, Elliot Richardson, then Secretary of Health, Education, and Welfare, announced that only about 3 percent of the children who traveled to school by bus at public expense did so because of desegregation orders.

For all that, the issue remains one of the most explosive in American society. Feelings on both sides run strong and deep. In the House of Representatives, Edith Green, a white Republican congresswoman from Oregon, declared, "If the federal government is going to reach its long arm into my house and say, 'We are sorry but your children are going to be bused thirty miles,' I say the government has gone too far." To which Shirley Chisholm, the black congresswoman from Brooklyn, replied, with scorn, "Your only concern is that whites are affected. Where were you when black children were being bused right past the white schools?" There are few objective observers who would deny the validity of both points: No mother, black or white, can be expected to take kindly to the idea of having her children taken by court order to schools outside their own neighborhood. Yet, when housing patterns are so segregated, how else is integration of the races to be achieved? The dilemma is not easily resolved. At the same time, it is hard to avoid the conclusion that what many white parents oppose is not what President Nixon has called "busing for the sake of busing" but integration itself. In many areas where busing has been ordered, the amount of white rage that has been generated has far exceeded the dimensions of the actual problem—and, indeed, after initial noisy protests, most integration schemes, in both North and South, have gone ahead far more smoothly than anyone expected.

The first big test of the new busing orders came at the start of the school year in the fall of 1971 in Pontiac, Michigan, a bleak General Motors factory town about thirty miles north of Detroit with a population of some 85,000 and a school enrollment that was about one-third black. Over the years, the bulk of the Pontiac school system had been divided into two camps, black and white, partly as a result of segregated housing-patterns, partly as a result of gerrymandering by the city leaders, who had again and again redrawn the boundaries of the various school districts in the city in order to keep black children out of the white schools. As long ago as 1969, the local branch of the National Association for the Advancement of Colored People had filed suit on behalf of a black mother, Mrs. Sadie Davis, charging that the Pontiac schools were keeping her son Donald in an all-black school in violation of the Supreme Court decision of 1954.

Eventually, Federal Judge Damon Keith, himself a black, rejected the city's argument that segregation in the Pontiac schools was the result of housing patterns, observing that school boundaries had been redrawn whenever blacks had moved in to a previously all-white neighborhood. That constituted illegal segregation, and he ordered each of the 36 previously all-white schools in Pontiac to admit blacks in a ratio that varied from 20 to 36 percent. The tool to be used was busing. Some 9,000 of the city's 24,000 children were to be carried an average of two and one-half miles, a trip that takes at most fifteen to twenty minutes. The longest distance any child had to travel under the Keith plan was six miles, and many of the children still had less than a five-minute bus-ride to school. In their first six years at school, moreover, children were to be bused for only three of them. In the next three years, they would be bused to school for two of them, and for their final four years, the high school years, they would not be compulsorily bused at all, since the two high schools in Pontiac were already integrated. Thus, for most children the Keith plan meant they would be bused to school for purposes of racial integration for only five of their thirteen years in school.

The scheme hardly represented the threat of "massive busing" that many people had feared; yet the Keith decision, which was later upheld by an appeals court, caused outrage in Pontiac. An organization of militant white parents calling themselves NAG, the National Action Group, marched on Washington to demand an end to the desegregation plans and also began to organize a boycott to keep their children out of school. An antibusing rally was held in a Pontiac stadium under the slogan "Bus judges, not children." A few weeks before the schools were due to open, six alleged members of the local branch of the Ku Klux Klan cut a hole in the chain-link fence around the schools' transport yard and dynamited ten of the buses that were to carry out the court order. On the day the schools opened, the tension in Pontiac was palpable, reminiscent in a way of those occasions of fifteen years earlier when the schools in Little Rock and Birmingham had first been desegregated. In Pontiac, the scene seemed all too familiar. Five women chained themselves to the gate of the transport yard to stop the buses from leaving on their first collection round. As the black children and black teachers arrived at their new schools, they were met by pickets of angry white adults yelling, "Nigger! Nigger!" Rocks were thrown at some buses, and children had to be protected on their way to school by cordons of sheriff's deputies and state police. There were few who saw it who could doubt that the anger of the whites was the result not so much of "civil rights," as they claimed, but of racism. How else could one explain those haunting shouts of "Nigger!" as the black children filed into their classrooms?

Many white children had stayed away from school that first day, and some 1,500 white children were registered at so-called freedom schools, hastily organized by some of the militant white parents. But in spite of all the heat it generated during those first few days, the school system in Pontiac has since returned to a state approximating normality. It is estimated that only 200 white children stayed away from the system permanently, although the backlash continued during the following year's election campaigns, when George Wallace won one of his most important primary victories in Michigan, largely as a result of the controversy over busing. The fact remains that although the Pontiac schools would not be integrated without a busing program, and although the Keith plan has been implemented with relatively little strife in the schools, most parents in the city are still bitterly opposed to the busing scheme, including, it must be admitted, many blacks.

A nationwide poll taken on behalf of Potomac Associates during 1972 strongly supported the belief that most American parents, both black and white, were against enforced busing of their children to achieve integration in the public schools. The poll found that only 7 percent of the white parents in America favored enforced busing, and even among black parents this solution received only minority support: 24 percent of the black parents polled said they were in favor of enforced busing, compared with 41 percent who said they favored instead quality education "in place." The results seemed to indicate beyond any doubt that the majority of Americans of both races rejected the policy through which standards of integration are currently applied. The consequences of this belief are yet to be fully felt. The Supreme Court decision of 1954 had in the end broken down school segregation which was required by law; the rationale for breaking down *de facto* segregation came much later, articulated in recommendations published in 1967 by President Johnson's Commission on Civil Rights. Its main conclusion was:

Negro children suffer serious harm when their education takes place in public schools which are racially segregated, whatever the source of such segregation may be. Negro children who attend predominantly Negro schools do not achieve as well as other children, Negro and white. Their aspirations are more restricted than those of other children and they do not have as much confidence that they can influence their own futures. When they become adults, they are less likely to participate in the mainstream of American society, and more likely to fear, dislike and avoid white Americans. The conclusions drawn by the U.S. Supreme Court about the impact upon children of segregation compelled by law—that it "affects their hearts and minds in ways unlikely ever to be undone"—applies to segregation not compelled by law.

The ideal here expressed, that integrated education is the means through which blacks are to be brought into the American mainstream, is today under widespread attack, not only from white parents who object to the busing of their children that follows from the application of such ideals, but also from many sociologists who contend that induced integration does not bring about the intended effect: It does not enhance black achievement, it does not lead to greater self-esteem, it does not in itself improve race relations, it does not increase black opportunities for higher education. In a phrase, "schools make no difference."

The most important such conclusion came in a survey commissioned by Congress during the 1960s and undertaken by James Coleman, a sociologist at Johns Hopkins University. The Coleman Report, as it came to be known, challenged just about every assumption that had previously been made about the effects of integration on black children. After sifting through studies commissioned at some 4,000 schools and including some 600,000 children and 60,000 teachers, Coleman discovered that while black children were already behind whites when they first arrived at school, they were even further behind at the end of school. The biggest variations in achievement between black children and white, moreover, took place not between schools but within the same school. The implications of this discovery for the future of integrated education seemed devastating. The inescapable conclusion was that massive busing would not work, did not improve student achievement, and had little effect on racial harmony. Coleman's conclusion, in a nutshell, was that schooling made no difference. It was family background that made the difference.

Such findings come as heresy to those who still believe in the ideal of the public school as "the balance wheel in the social machinery," and they have led to acrimonious debate among the social and political scientists whose work in the past has been enormously influential in shaping public policy. In the words of one of them, Professor David Armor of Harvard, "without the legitimacy provided by the hundreds of sociological and psychological studies it would be hard to imagine how the changes we are witnessing could have happened so quickly. At every step . . . social science research findings have been inextricably interwoven with policy decisions." So this was no mere "scuffle in the Groves of Academe"; it was a deadly serious threat to the whole idea of integration, "a spear," as one writer put it, "pointed at the heart of the cherished American belief that equality of educational opportunity will increase the equality of educational achievement."

The argument that as a result of these findings in the Coleman report—and some others—the policy of enforced busing should be abandoned, has led to a heated and sometimes bitter debate among educators, parents, and black leaders alike. To some, the new attitude towards integration seemed very like laying the blame for racial problems on its victims. It has also led to a withdrawal from the commitment to education as a means of bringing its black minority into the American mainstream—or at least given such a withdrawal a certain respectability. President Nixon has asked for large cuts in federal spending programs, much of which would have gone on providing what is known as "compensatory education" for minority groups, while his former domestic-affairs advisor, Dr. Daniel P. Moynihan, made a famous remark, under the influence of Coleman's findings, which has since been much quoted against him. It was, he said, perhaps now time for a period of "benign neglect" in America's treatment of its racial problems. The report also seemed to give aid and comfort to outright segregationists, those who had believed all along that mixed schooling would not work (while ignoring the fact that the Supreme Court rulings had made it clear that segregation should be overthrown not just for practical sociological reasons, but, in the last analysis, because it was wrong—morally wrong). But the findings are plain. In urban schools throughout the country, reading achievements have been dropping steadily for at least a decade as enrollments have brought in more and more children from minority families. In New York City, the largest school district in the country, it was found in 1973 that 66.3 percent of the elementary pupils and 71.3 percent of the junior high school and intermediate pupils were reading a year or more behind the level for their grade.

The fact is that black children from the ghettoes do badly in school because they do not learn to read properly in their first two years in class. This inability to read and write increases in importance as they progress through the school system, so that black children fall further and further behind the older they get. The progression can be compared to two trains traveling on parallel tracks but at different speeds: They start off side by side, but the farther they travel, the farther they pull apart. The gap accelerates, the process is geometric: Because a ghetto child cannot learn to read, he begins not to care, he withdraws from the system, regards his teachers with hostility and eventually develops an angry and aggressive attitude towards an alien outside world. Sooner or later, he becomes a dropout, full of self-hate and useless to society. The whole process is a vicious circle, and because American education is geared so strongly to middle-class values, the deprived child of the ghetto is more likely than ever to reject its values.

This is a problem that is being recognized more and more by black educators, that, in a sense, the battle of the ghetto child is won or lost between the ages of three and six. These are the years in which children actually learn the most. To fall behind in this crucial preschool period becomes a handicap few children are able to overcome. They are not able to learn to read at school because they have not acquired what educationalists call "reading readiness" in the period before school. The reason, in most cases, is that they come from nonverbal households where such skills are simply not there to be learned. The home environment is often overcrowded and blighted by poverty. The child has few toys and probably no books. Often there is not a pen or a pencil in the household. Adults speak to the child in monosyllables. As a result the child never acquires the stimulation to his memory, inquisitiveness, and judgment that the middle-class child acquires unconciously, without even knowing it. When the ghetto child arrives at the age of six at a school which, as often as not, assumes that he has already acquired these basic skills, he is therefore almost bound to fail.

Charles Silberman has graphically chronicled the process which follows in his *Crisis in Black and White.* Coming from a nonverbal household, Silberman says, the ghetto child has never been obliged to listen to several sentences spoken consecutively. The speech he does hear tends to to be grammatically and syntactically simple, with the result that "the child is unable to follow the middle class teacher who rambles on for several sentences at a time. . . . From the standpoint of syntax and vocabulary, the teacher might as well be talking in another language." Teachers, says Silberman, take for granted that children know *what* things are, and assume that their job is to answer *why* they are. But these children do not know what things are, and nothing in their environment has taught them to ask why. Inevitably, therefore, they do not learn to read adequately; and their failure in school confirms and enhances their own sense of lack of worth.

The clear conclusion from all this would seem to be that it is kindergarten education that is now needed to free the ghetto child from the effects of his culturally starved environment—that it is nursery schools which are just as much, if not more, the balance wheels of the society of the future. The radical reorganization of nursery-school education that would appear to be necessary to correct this situation, however, seems to be as far away today as ever it was. In America, the dropout problem, and with it, much of the urban race problem also, still begins in the cradle.

3. Uppity Women

"After all, women are a sex to themselves, so to speak."
—Sir Max Beerbohm, *The Pervasion of Rouge*

Not long ago, the role of women in American society was based on certain universal and seemingly immutable assumptions. Mother, wife, homemaker— these were the roles to which every normal American woman was assumed to aspire and expected to conform. The feminine ideal, in those halcyon days of the 1950's, was one of blameless domesticity. American women were marrying earlier than ever before, having more babies than ever before, isolated in their new homes in suburbia as never before. The housewife was wooed by by the advertisers, idealized by her magazines, pampered by more household gadgets than any other women in the world. It was widely assumed that the character- istic American recourse to technology had liberated her forever from the toil and drudgery of woman's work. The new supermarkets relieved her of the burdens of daily shopping, prepackaged foods reduced by a half the time she needed to spend on the family cooking, while her up-to-date kitchen, equipped with its deep-freeze, dishwasher, eyelevel ovens, and dazzling array of labor- saving electrical appliances, was said to be the envy of all other women everywhere, leaving her more time than ever to devote to the rearing of her children and the care of her men. It had all seemed a part of the American Dream.

Then, sometime during the troubled decade of the 1960s, the dream soured. Betty Friedan wrote a book called *The Feminine Mystique,* in which she argued that women were losing their human identities in this suburban world of house, home, and children. This book had an enormous influence on the attitudes of women across the nation, and there followed, perhaps inevitably, a reaction to the mindless stereotypes of the later 1950s. The whole status of women as individuals began increasingly to be called into question. By the time the decade ended, many women had found that they were not as content as they had supposed with the role in which they had been cast.

At first the disenchantment of the women had been masked by the more violent and more conspicuous uprisings of America's blacks and America's youth. However, when in the early years of the 1970s both of those two

movements had temporarily run their course, the Women's Movement remained. Some called it the New Feminism, others Women's Liberation.
While only a tiny minority of women have paraded through the streets
carrying slogans denouncing the sexist attitudes of male chauvinist pigs, or
publicly thrown their bras into trashcans in protest, almost all of them have
been affected by a new awareness of their changing position and their changing aspirations.

Since this decade began, there have been important improvements in the
status of women in American society. The more public changes have taken
place in the role of women at work: legal changes, promising them more
equality with men, and fairer opportunities in the professions. But perhaps
even more profound are the invisible changes, the signs of a fundamental and
probably permanent transformation in the average American woman's attitude toward marriage, sex, and the family, changes that most men and many
women find difficult to articulate and perplexing to understand.

Thus, in 1972 a writer in that bastion of male journalism, the *Wall Street
Journal,* was able to quote with approval the strictures of John Stuart Mill of
a century ago, that the principle that regulates the existing relations between
the two sexes is wrong and ought to be replaced by "a principle of perfect
equality, admitting no power or privilege on the one side, nor disability on the
other." As a plea in behalf of equal pay for equal work, the principle was easy
to grasp and easy to grant. But when he came to examine the Women's
Liberation movement of his own day, the writer found himself confused. The
movement, as he saw it, was fuzzy. The women he had listened to were clearly
possessed by deeper dissatisfactions and were groping for something more than
equal opportunity or equal pay. But it was not clear what. He therefore
concluded, "They don't know what Women's Lib is because they don't really
know what they want out of life." Or, as Lord Byron put it in *Don Juan:*

> There is a tide in the affairs of women,
> Which, taken at the flood, leads
>   —God knows where.

It is true, the search for a clear definition of the Women's Liberation
movement is not always helped by the attitudes of the more militant women
themselves. Feeling deprived and sex-typed, their most public arguments have
concentrated for much of the time on what often appear to be trivial symbolic
issues: whether to call themselves Mrs., Miss, or Ms.; whether the presiding
officer at their meetings should be called a chairman, chairwoman, or chairper-
son; protests against what they regard as sexist advertising—those for per-
fumes, for instance, that carry the headline "One More Pleasure You Can
Give Him," or those for National Airlines that entice businessmen to "Fly
Cheryl" in a not-very-subtle appeal to sexual adventure. There have been
well-publicized invasions of all-male bars and, on the extreme wing of the

movement, the claim that "feminism is lesbianism." All of which has tended to confuse the onlooker and detract attention from the vaguer but more substantial discontent of the American woman, particularly in her role as wife and mother.

It is sometimes claimed that the institution of marriage itself is the chief instrument through which the oppression of the modern American woman is perpetuated. Marlene Dixon writes, for instance, that "in all classes and groups, the institution of marriage functions to a greater or lesser degree to oppress women; the unity of women of different classes hinges upon our understanding of that common oppression." Later in the same article she goes on to claim that the most original and creative politics of the women's movement has come from a direct confrontation with the issue of marriage and sexuality: "The cultural revolution—experimentation with life-styles, communal living, group child-rearing—have all come from the rebellion against dehumanized sexual relationships, against the notion of women as sexual commodities, against the constriction and spiritual strangulation inherent in the role of wife." Naturally enough, most men—and, it must be admitted, many women, too—have felt themselves threatened by this attack on one of the most hallowed institutions in American society, an institution which, for all the attacks, is entered into by more women today than ever before. As recently as 1940, 17 percent of American women in their thirties had never been married; today, the proportion is down to only 7 percent. In other words, more than nine American women out of every ten—including most members of the Movement—are married. Ms. Dixon's angry rhetoric notwithstanding, it is unlikely that the institution is about to be swept away in a new cultural revolution. And yet there is, without any doubt, a restlessness among American women with their traditional role in marriage, perhaps even among a majority of them. Some of the causes of this conflict are common to women everywhere in the modern technological world; others are peculiar to the women of America—and nowhere else, it might be noted, has the New Feminism grown so fast or taken root so deeply as in the United States.

In most respects, this is still a largely middle-class phenomenon, due in part to the suburban housing patterns and the suburban lifestye into which most young middle-class wives are thrust. Yet it is a life to which the college-trained American woman, better-read and more ambitious than ever before, is almost wholly unsuited. Consequently, she is often ill-prepared to cope with two enormous traumas that normally come to her in the course of her marriage. The first usually comes early, with the arrival of children. Until then, she has more often than not been a working wife with interests and an occupation in the wider world. Then, quite abruptly, she is plunged into a vastly different world of isolated domesticity, typically as the homemaker of a nuclear family in a dormitory suburb, her role restricted to caring for her home and rearing her babies. As one young college-educated mother has put it:

The plunge from the strictly intellectual college life to the 24-hour-a-day domestic one is a terrible shock, and it is no wonder that we stagger through the first few years of child-rearing wondering what our values are and struggling to find some compromise between our intellectual ambitions and the reality of everyday living.

In most other societies, the change in lifestyle involved in becoming a mother and housewife is nothing like so severe as it is in American suburbia. The young wife, in this setting, is all too likely to become unhappy, finding an outlet in frustration with her role, in overprotection of her children—or, increasingly, in militant feminism. In a crosscultural study prepared during the 1960s, a group of social scientists compared families in various parts of the world with those in a New England suburb, which they named Orchard Town. The American women, they reported, were far more worried about the "correctness" of their own behavior and that of their children than were the women in Mexico, the Philippines, India, Okinawa, and Kenya. In part, this was because the American women were so isolated and had as their principal task the rearing of their children. The two authors of the report, Leigh Minturn and William W. Lambert, concluded that "the mothers of Orchard Town are unusual in that they are relatively isolated and spend much of their time alone with their children and in exclusive charge of them. Their belief that they must guide their children's development along proper channels, their anxiety about conforming to ideal norms that are culturally unclear, and their conviction that no one else can adequately substitute for a mother makes them reject alternative caretakers even when they are available. The relatively high emotional instability of these mothers appears to be due, in part, to the large amounts of time they spend in charge of children."

Throughout history, of course, women have always borne the main burden of bringing up the children. In the past, however, they have also had a greater or lesser share in other related and supplementary activities that have traditionally been a part of the woman's role—making clothing, for instance, taking in laundry, producing and marketing garden produce and eggs, supplementing the family income in a variety of ways—activities that not only gave her a degree of culturally accepted economic worth unknown to the modern suburban housewife, but that also brought her into wider contact with the outside world. Like her men in that somewhat idealized agrarian world, she too had a life outside the family. But in the middle-class America of today, these traditional activities have wholly vanished. In her book *Man's World, Woman's Place*, Elizabeth Janeway makes the point that these women's skills, once so vitally important to feeding and clothing mankind, have deteriorated today into hobbies. They have become adult play—leisure-time activities which imitate the realities of work. "For children," she says, "such play is a necessary part of learning to live. In maturity, it is a substitute for living." The woman in such a world is thrown back upon herself alone, her traditional roles atrophied to the specialized task of bringing up children. The arrival of cheap consumer goods has removed for ever the middle-class need to make and grow things at home. "Families don't make things any more," says Ms. Janeway, "they buy them."

It follows, therefore, that the woman who wishes to find some fulfillment beyond her children, or who, for economic reasons, needs to do so, must look for such fulfillment in work outside the home. And this is an outlet towards which more and more married American women have turned. After World War II, when the troops returned home from Europe and Asia and the postwar baby boom began in earnest, the proportion of women in the U.S. work force had dropped off sharply, and only began to pick up again in the later 1960s. By 1970, however, more than four married women out of every ten had outside jobs, twelve million of them with children at home under the age of eighteen.

But this, it seems, is considered a dual role that produces even greater conflicts of values in many women. Brought up in the American belief that the care of her young children is her prime responsibility in life, the working mother begins to suffer, in many cases, from feelings of guilt—torn, in a sense, between her twin roles.

The ideological pressures placed upon such working mothers from neighbors or relatives can be intense, as Alice Rossi, a professional sociologist and herself a working mother, has recounted in an interview by the magazine *Psychology Today*. Ms. Rossi lived with her family in Chicago, about a mile and a half from the lake shore. During the summer holidays other women in the neighborhood would take their children down for a swim and a lakeside picnic. "You know," she said, "summer is the hardest time for a working mother. So when these homemaker neighbors would take off for the lake they would say things to our children like 'Isn't it too bad that your mother isn't at home so she could take you to the beach, too?' As you can imagine, that made our kids feel just great. The point is learning to cope with that kind of invidious social pressure. But that's hard because the pressure strikes right where a woman's residual guilt is likely to be, and women haven't communicated the right coping skills to each other yet." Ms. Rossi coped with her own problem by taking her children for twilight picnics instead.

Other feminists have urged a myriad of ad hoc solutions to this problem of permitting the working mother to get out of the home, a problem many of them recognize as one of the biggest obstacles towards the full recognition of Women's Liberation: the creation on a massive scale of adequate day-care centers for their children, an upgrading in the status of day-care jobs, and such concepts as group-families, community living, and the development of surrogate mothers. So far, however, they admit to little progress. The dilemma they are in lies in the nature of the American family. At the very moment that more and more middle-class mothers aspire to professional or other careers, they have lost the services of nannies and housemaids, and because of the nuclear nature of their households, they have lost the help of their older relatives also. The grandmother or unmarried aunt who lives as a part of the family is an all-but-vanished concept in middle-class America. Nor is there much sign that Grandma is about to be rediscovered by the liberated American mother, who is forced by the nature of society into a solo performance, either as a fulltime household drudge or compelled to carry the heavy burden of two often-conflicting roles.

Still, in spite of these handicaps, more and more American women are finding it possible to combine work and home. For one thing, they tend to marry later than ever before. The median age of women at marriage increased by a whole year during the 1960s, and while most of them do still get married eventually, it means they have spent longer as single working women and are therefore more likely to have both the ambition and the necessary skills and experience to resume their jobs after the birth of their children. Their families, in the 1970s, tend also to be smaller than they have been in the past, thanks in part to a revolution in the use of contraceptives—and, increasingly, the liberalized abortion laws in many states, due most recently to a 1973 Supreme Court decision. Because of the smaller size of their families and the fact that women are living longer than ever, most of them are spending a relatively smaller proportion of their lives as active fulltime mothers. For a woman who has two children close together in age, the time she needs to spend away from her career, even if she devotes herself fulltime to the children in their nursery years, is often not much more than six or seven years.

While for most women the first trauma of married life comes with the change of lifestyle brought by the arrival of the first baby, a second and sometimes greater trauma comes when the children begin to leave the domestic nest. The shock, particularly for women who have not previously had a career outside the home, can be profound. As one such mother has put it:

> The woman who, in her early thirties, sees her last child enter school and then faces blankly the next forty years left to her by the actuaries with no notion of how to realize herself as an individual, is likely to blame the marriage for her plight.

These, then, are some of the reasons so many American women have begun to take an active interest in the New Feminism. These, too, are the reasons why more of them are joining the U.S. work force. Back in 1940, just over one quarter of all women over the age of sixteen had a job; today, that proportion has almost doubled. Twenty-three million American women now have fulltime jobs with another eight million working partime.

In contrast with other western countries, this growth in the female work force is a very recent phenomenon. In both France and Britain, for instance, the employment rate among women has remained fairly constant since 1900, at a rate of some 50 percent in France and 40 percent in Britain. Women have approached that rate in America only since the 1960s (leaving aside the wartime years when many more women did enter the work force, but had to leave it again immediately afterwards).

In spite of the recent growth, the world of work in America is still very much a man's world, and here the Women's Liberationists have easily understandable grounds for their protests. In the first place, women are usually paid less than men for the work they do. According to one federal survey, the average woman employed in a fulltime job in 1972 was earning only three dollars for each five dollars paid to a man with a similar job. Primarily because of the recent arrival of so many women at the bottom end of the pay scale, the gap between the average woman's pay and the average man's has actually declined since 1955. Job discrimination on the ground of sex is also still prevalent in many fields. Thus, the proportion of working women who are managers and proprietors is today less than one in every twenty, compared with three in every twenty working men who fall into these categories. What is more, the women's share of managerial jobs is also slightly less than it was fifteen years ago. In some professions, the proportion of women who are employed at all remains small. Only 7.6 percent of the nation's 300,000 physicians are women, only one per cent of the surgeons. Even gynecologists tend to be male by a ratio of more than nine to one. In a survey of America's biggest 1,300 business corporations conducted by *Fortune* in 1973, it was found tht of the 6,500 officers and directors of these companies who earned more than thirty thousand dollars a year, only eleven were women. On the other hand, not surprisingly, more than 90 percent of the nation's secretaries, typists, and telephone operators are women, although in some jobs there has been an interesting change of sex in the past twenty years or so. Bank clerks, for example, used to be overwhelmingly male in the United States; today, they are just as likely to be women. And some sales work is still cast by sex for no logical reason whatever. For what subliminal sexual motives, for instance, do American men buy their underwear from women, while women buy their shoes from men? Tradition and established patterns of employment still seem to play an important part in the selection of employees for certain jobs.

In a nation devoted to the principles of equality, it is surprising how very few women make it to the highest reaches of their society. There is today not a single woman member of the Senate, there has never been a woman member of the Supreme Court, only two women have ever sat as full members of the Cabinet, and the idea of a woman as President of the United States seems as remote today as it was in 1920, when women first won the national right to vote. *Fortune* concluded after its survey of women in business that working women had all too often to be "twice as good" as men to reach the same level. "The unexceptional woman, unlike the unexceptional man, never seems to make it," the magazine said, and it summed up women's aspirations in business in the words of a New York lawyer: "Women want their share of mediocre managers at the top."

It will doubtless be many years, if ever, before that transformation comes to pass. Nevertheless, there are few who would deny that change has now begun to improve the overall status of women in America, who are at last beginning to escape from their destiny in the Doll's House to which social attitudes had for so long confined them. The changes that are coming were symbolized in a historic vote in the Senate in March 1972, when that now all-male body (but which then had one woman member, since defeated for re-election) voted overwhelmingly to approve the Twenty-Seventh Amendment to the U.S. Constitution—otherwise known as ERA, the Equal Rights Amendment—which specifies that women are to receive absolute equality with men before the law. If ratified within seven years by three quarters of the state legislatures, the amendment will have the effect of putting men and women, for the first time, on an absolutely equal constitutional footing. ERA was by no means guaranteed an easy passage through the various state assemblies and several of them have already rejected the amendment, partly on the grounds that it tends to give women "too much" equality. If enacted, it will make them subject, like men, to the military draft (if the draft, now ended, should be restored). It will remove special women's labor laws (or make their provisions equally applicable to men). For these reasons, much of the opposition to ERA has come from women themselves, especially in the states of the rural South and West. It is still not clear whether ERA will be ratified by sufficient states or not, but it is thought likely to find its way into the Constitution before the measure expires in 1979, one more landmark in the emancipation of the American woman. Or, as Aileen Hernandez, former president of NOW, the National Organization for Women, has summed it up, "Today, the glacier, tomorrow the avalanche."

Nevertheless, many Americans, both male and female, seem still to be unaware of what revolutionary changes would be introduced when and if ERA does pass into law. Not only would women be equally subject with men to the draft, they would, according to most interpretations, also be subject to combat duty. An article in favor of ERA which appeared in the *Yale Law Journal* suggested, for instance, that "the effectiveness of the modern soldier is due more to equipment and training than to individual strength. Women are physically as able as men to perform many jobs classified as combat duty, such as piloting an airplane or engaging in naval operations. . . . Women in other countries, including Israel and North Vietnam have served effectively in their armed forces. There is no reason to assume that in a dangerous situation women will not be as serious and well-disciplined as men."

At work, ERA would bring equally revolutionary concepts to bear. Women would no longer be exempted from hazardous jobs such as mining, while all the labor laws relating to the type of work a woman could do would either have to go, or be applied equally to men. Those in favor of ERA suggest that while such laws were provided to put right the undoubted abuses and exploitations of the past, times have now changed and many of the protective work laws now discriminate against women and are used to deny them extra pay.

But perhaps the biggest changes of all would come in the domestic status of women in America. Under ERA, a woman would no longer be obliged to change her name on marriage, while husbands would no longer be obliged automatically to provide financial support to their wives. Instead, that duty would fall upon the partner most able to provide it. Alimony would become equally available to both husbands and wives in divorce cases and special laws protecting women from certain sexual offenses—though not from rape— would have to be abolished. Married women would have an equal say with their menfolk in choosing where they wish to live and a wife's refusal to follow her husband to a new home would no longer amount to desertion or abandonment.

If ERA ever came about, it would represent an avalanche indeed.

CHAPTER XVIII

Crime

1. The Mob

"A nationwide crime syndicate does exist in the United States of America, despite the protestations of a strangely assorted company of criminals, self-serving politicians, plain blind fools, and others who may be honestly misguided that there is no such combine."

—SENATOR ESTES KEFAUVER, 1951

"Nobody will listen. Nobody will believe. You know what I mean? This Cosa Nostra, it's like a second government. It's too big."

—JOE VALACHI, 1962.

When the smash-hit film of *The Godfather* played at cinemas in New York, invariably to full houses, it was common for the audiences to stand up and cheer at each scene of gruesome gangland murder. Appearing first as a bestselling novel, then as the most commercially successful movie of the decade, Mario Puzo's romanticized story about a New York Mafia "family" of a generation ago clearly stirred deep public feelings of fascination, and even admiration, for the world of organized crime and violence.

New Yorkers have always shown a talent for glorifying the activities of the gangsters who live in their midst, regarding them largely as colorful characters from a Damon Runyon novel, semifictitious men with romantic names like "Pete the Greek" and "Crazy Joe," men whose deeds of evil take place in an unreal underworld, remote from the workaday city outside the cinema or the newspaper headlines. The idea that even in this complicated modern age things can be "fixed" by a simple deed of violence, appears to be deeply satisfying to many law-abiding Americans, for whom the Mafia has always held a sinister attraction.

This attitude sometimes makes it hard for them to unravel fact from fiction. Even as they cheered the mayhem inside the cinema, killings that could have been lifted straight from the story of *The Godfather* were taking place in real life, outside in their own streets, almost every week. By the middle of 1972, it was obvious to everyone that a major war had broken out among the Mafia families of New York—a war that was taking the lives of one gangster every ten days. Yet the myth persisted that the quarrel of the mobs was a private feud that had little or no effect on the lives of the ordinary citizens who were getting such a thrill from the scenes of violence on the screen.

The New York *Daily News* expressed the commonly held view in an editorial written at the height of the gangland killings in April 1972: "We cannot help feeling that these killings are ridding society of some characters who won't be missed sorely, if at all, and are saving police, prosecutors and courts a lot of work and taxpayers a lot of money."

Organized crime in New York and other large cities across the nation, however, is not quite so easy to dismiss. The truth is that the kingdom of crime, with Cosa Nostra at its heart, reaches out to taint the quality of life of every large city in America. Its effect is felt in statehouses and city halls, on the streets of the urban ghettoes, in labor unions and transportation, and even in the halls of the U.S. Congress itself. In short, organized criminals prey not only on each other but on the economic and political life of every community in which they have been able to set up a base.

In a study pepared for President Johnson's Task Force on Crime, Donald Cressey found that organized syndicates controlled all but a tiny part of the illegal gambling in the United States. They were the principal loansharks. They were the principal importers and wholesalers of narcotics. They have infiltrated certain labor unions, where they extort money from employers and, at the same time, cheat the members of the union. They have a virtual monopoly on some legitimate enterprises, such as cigarette vending machines and jukeboxes. They own a wide variety of retail firms, restaurants and bars, hotels, trucking companies, food companies, linen-supply houses, garbage-collection routes, and factories—and, probably the fastest-growing racket of recent years, the distribution and production of pornography. Until recently, the owned a large proportion of Las Vegas. They own several state legislators and federal congressmen and other officials in the legislative, executive, and judicial branches of government at the local, state, and federal levels. Some government officials (including judges) are considered, and consider themselves, members.

In New York alone, it is estimated the people pay hundreds of millions of dollars a year in artificially high prices for services and commodities controlled by crime. At one time or another, such unlikely service industries as laundries, commercial window-washing, long-distance haulage, air freight, and florists have fallen completely under the domination of the crime syndicate. "You can fill every letter from A to Z and find them," says one former New York detective, "or from birth to death—some own diaper services and some own funeral homes." Even the petty burglaries and muggings of the drug addict that plague the streets of the big cities can be traced to the multiplier effect of the organized gangs that control both the wholesale supply of narcotics and the skills necessary to get rid of the stolen goods. "Almost every bit of the crime we study has some link to organized crime," says Milton Rector, director of the National Council on Crime and Delinquency.

Perhaps the most extraordinary thing about organized crime is the fact that America has tolerated it for so long. At the beginning of the 1960s, J. Edgar Hoover, head of the FBI, denied that there was such a thing as the Mafia, and even today no important Mafia figure has ever made his way onto the FBI's list of the "Ten Most Wanted Men." When another Mafia figure is rubbed out in a seedy section of Brooklyn or lower Manhattan, the public is titillated for a few days, but rarely are the people outraged enough to demand an end to the activities of the underworld. It is a chilling fact that of the hundreds of gangland killings that have taken place in New York in the past thirty years, only one has ever been brought to a successful prosecution. In Chicago, the ratio is even worse.

Yet as the President's Commission on Law Enforcement and Administration put it:

> Organized crime is not merely a few preying on a few. In a very real sense, it is dedicated to subverting not only the American institutions, but the very decency and integrity that are the most cherished attributes of a free society. As the leaders of the Cosa Nostra and their racketeering allies pursue their conspiracy unmolested, in open and continuous defiance of law, they preach a sermon that all too many Americans heed: the Government is for sale; lawlessness is the road to wealth; honesty is a pitfall and morality a trap for suckers.

The underworld has grown to what it is today because of a basic contradiction first observed by Walter Lippmann over forty years ago. By their moral convictions, Lippmann noted, Americans first prohibited all sin, then by their liberal convictions kept their prohibitions from being enforced. Laws made to control morals act like a protective tariff and encourage the business of the underworld by turning over to crime the services from which it profits, such as gambling, prostitution, narcotics and, in that day, the consumption of alcohol. Unlike the wholly predatory criminal, the members of the organized underworld have a real social function to perform: they provide services for respectable members of society. "The fact," wrote Lippmann, "that it employs methods such as bribery, terrorism and murder, which we all deeply deplore, should not divert our attention from the main point, which is that the underworld performs a function based ultimately on a public demand." Crime was strong in America, he concluded, "largely because Americans are too moral to tolerate human weakness, and because they are too great lovers of liberty to tolerate the tyranny which might make it possible to abolish what they prohibit." As a result, they are left to defy the devil with a wooden sword.

There is no doubt that the real success of the Mafia and its allies today, and the degree to which their activities are publicly tolerated, depend on the quality of these traditional, routine services provided to meet a demonstrable public demand. To this extent, crime will remain a social problem in America, rather than a simple matter of law enforcement. In spite of the great social upheaval that has taken place since Lippmann's day, the Americans remain a deeply moralistic nation, and it is inconceivable, even in the 1970s, that they will consider in the forseeable future the legalization of such activities as prostitution, drug supply, or the more pervasive forms of gambling. As a result, organized crime will continue to find a fertile field in which to cultivate its nefarious deeds.

In money terms, organized crime in America is sometimes claimed to be the largest business in the world. Federal agencies estimate its revenues at well over thirty billion dollars a year, more than the annual cost of the war in Vietnam when the American involvement there was at its peak. Illegal gambling operations alone generate a sum believed to be three times the amount spent on U.S. aid in foreign countries, while Meyer Lansky, the crime world's top financial expert, once boasted to a reporter, "We're bigger than U.S. Steel."

In spite of Lansky's grandiose comparisons, the structure of crime in America is in fact less like a unified and centralized business corporation than it is a loosely knit association of groups with common interests, an affiliation on the lines of the AFL-CIO rather than a single organization like U.S. Steel. At the heart of this affiliation is a body variously known as the Mafia, Cosa Nostra, or the Mob, itself a loose confederation of "families" bound together like feudal baronies by understandings, agreements, and formal "treaties."

The growth of this organization is, in its way, a traditional American success story. The American Mafia began back in the 1880s during the great wave of European immigration into the United States, when the first rural bandits came across to prey on their fellow Italian and Sicilian immigrants. The rudimentary organization that grew up in the urban slums of America was popularly known in those days as "the Black Hand," and specialized in crude extortion threats directed exclusively against their fellow Italians.

Most of the Italian immigrants who arrived in America during this period were unskilled laborers of peasant stock from one of the most solidly rural backgrounds in Europe. "The Italian comes in at the bottom, and he stays there," wrote Jacob Riis at this time. Speaking poor or little English, they found jobs in the cities as shoemakers, barbers, and garment workers—the bottom of the pile, with other ethnic groups like the Irish, who had arrived forty years earlier, in control of the political machinery. For some of the more aggressive children of the second and third generation, still trapped in their urban slums, the background provided a natural breeding ground for crime.

The first Mafia leader of note to operate in America was a sadistic immigrant known as Lupo, "the Wolf," who flourished in New York until World War I. Lupo and his fellow gangsters, who spoke virtually no English, were later to be contemptuously dismissed by their American-born successors as "Mustache Petes," because of their rural mannerisms and the Garibaldi-type whiskers most of them affected.

In those days, the Mafia was only one of many criminal gangs that were spawned in the turbulent new urban areas of burgeoning America. The ethnic, economic, and political turmoil that characterized many big cities in this period saw the rise and fall of criminal gangs of widely differing national backgrounds. In New York, Jewish gangsters were dominant; in Boston, they were Irish; in San Francisco the dominant gang was known as the "Sydney Ducks," expatriates from Australia, as well as rival groups of Chinese Tongs.

It was in a sense therefore an ethnic accident that the Sicilian Mafia had achieved a predominant position in the world of crime at the very moment that crime, through Prohibition, suddenly became profitable beyond the dreams of the most ambitious gangsters. It was the arrival of Prohibition more than any other single cause that set the Mafia on its modern course. By banning the public sale of alcohol, the U.S. Congress and the state legislatures in effect turned over the liquor industry to crime. The Mafia grew on the enormous profits of bootlegging into a monster whose hold on the underworld it has never relinquished. The late 1920s were golden days for the American underworld, and the gang bosses that came into prominence then, figures like Al Capone, "Lucky" Luciano, and Frank Costello, have taken their place in the American pantheon of crime alongside the legendary outlaws of the old frontier (most of whom, incidentally, carried Anglo-Saxon names—the first in the ethnic succession of American crime). At the height of Prohibition, it is estimated that the gang of Al Capone alone was making as much as sixty million dollars a year from its bootlegging operations.

While Prohibition was enormously profitable to the Mafia in terms of power and money, it was to prove expensive in terms of blood. War frequently broke out between the rival bootlegging gangs, culminating in the infamous St. Valentine's Day Massacre of 1929, when seven of "Bugs" Moran's men were machine-gunned to death in a Chicago garage by a bunch of Capone's hoodlums disguised as police officers. Like virtually all Chicago gangland killings, the St. Valentine's Day Massacre was never solved, but it led, together with the repeal of Prohibition a couple of years later, to the calling of the first gangland ceasefire. From 1934, when the crime syndicate was first formed, until the early 1960s, when gang warfare broke out again in New York, there was virtually no internecine criminal warfare other than that sanctioned, ordered, and approved by the rulers of the syndicate itself.

The wealth that was generated during Prohibition enabled the gangsters of the Mafia to establish a kind of hegemony over American crime that has lasted until the present day. Over the years, they have made their alliances with members of other ethnic groups, many of whom are now in a sense honorary members of the Mafia, to whom they are informally tied through the overall syndicate of crime. As the bulk of Italian immigrants have long ago moved on to respectability, affluence, and power, so the natural constituency of the Mafia, the urban Italian slums, has dwindled also. Crime will remain, but the peculiarly Italian pattern that so much of organized crime has followed in the past three generations, is already beginning to change. The present leaders of the Mafia are thought by some to be the last of the line—men whose rich sons and grandsons will, in the time-honored American tradition, find social acceptance in the world of "respectable" money in the pattern of all American success stories.

For years, the FBI refused to acknowledge that the Mafia existed, but thanks to widespread (and often illegal) wiretaps undertaken by assorted law-enforcement agencies in the past decade, its composition is now widely known, even down to the names of the hundreds of "buttons" or soldiers who make up the rank-and-file membership of that hitherto-mysterious organization. The American Mafia today is believed to consist of at least twenty-four families, gangs of between seventy-five and a thousand men, sworn to loyalty by an oath of blood, often though not necessarily related, and always of Italian or Sicilian extraction. The organization is ruled by a "commission", a sort of Supreme Court of crime, made up of the heads of the most powerful individual families and regarded as the ultimate authority on organizational disputes, with jurisdiction over the entire United States, the Bahamas, and parts of Canada. Its power is nebulous but absolute, and it can in extreme cases order the execution of a family boss who falls out of line. All other Mafia executions are ordered by the individual bosses, occasionally on instructions from the commission.

The existence of the commission was only proved in 1957, and it came about almost by accident. A New York state police sergeant stumbled one night across an assembly of some seventy-five Mafia chieftains and their lieutenants gathered for a summit meeting on the estate of Joseph Barbara in the remote upstate township of Apalachin. Three weeks before the Apalachin summit, the Mafia chieftain Albert Anastasia had been shot dead in a barber's chair in the Park Sheraton Hotel in Manhattan, and it is assumed the surviving leaders had gathered in committee to discuss the redistribution of their affairs following his death (which some observers believe may have been ordered by the commission itself). As the local police closed in on the meeting, many of the gangsters fled. Some escaped, but among those rounded up and arrested were Vito Genovese, Joseph Profaci, "Joe Bananas" Bonnano, and John Scalish, the Mafia boss in Cleveland.

Here was clearcut evidence that the activities of the Mafia were organized on a nationwide basis. Yet if it had not been for the chance discovery of an alert local police sergeant, suspicious of the flashy cars he saw driving down a rural lane, it is possible that no one would have ever had the slightest suspicion that the Mafia's high commission had ever met, or even that it existed.

It is believed now that the commission was formed as long ago as 1934, when the country was divided up into Mafia territories following the particularly bloody internal strife that took place in the aftermath of the bootlegging days. Subassignments are thought to have been made according to racket, so that in the East Coast syndicate one chieftain was given control of the garment industry, another of narcotics and prostitution, a third the numbers game, and so on.

In their book on the Syndicate, *Murder Inc.*, Burton Turkas and Sid Feider, the investigators, explained how the commission came into being:

> It was quickly realized, of course, that no one of them would ever stand for one single boss—or czar over all. Each regarded himself as a big shot and was fanatically jealous of his position. But it was explained how there could be central control based on cooperation, without sacrifice of individuality. . . .
>
> A board . . . of all the bosses could arbitrate intermob disputes by meeting and talking and deciding who was right and wrong. That was the key that finally decided them. Each boss remained czar in his own territory, his rackets unmolested, his local authority uncontested. In murder, no one—local or imported—could be killed in his territory without his approval. . . . In fact, no lawlessness on an organized scale could take place in his domain without his sanction and entire consent unless he was overruled by the board of governors. And even then, he would have a say in the discussion. It was state's rights in crime . . .

Soon, the criminal bands across the country saw the strength of the union. The Capone crowd came in from Chicago, and mobs from as far away as Boston, Miami, and Detroit joined in the confederacy of crime, until it was nationwide.

Over the years, the commission has varied in size from nine to twelve members, and since the outbreak of war between several of the New York families, it has in recent years been in a state of unusual flux. The present members of the Commission are thought to be:

1. Carlo Gambino, New York City
2. Joseph Colombo, New York City (incapacitated)
3. Paul Sciacca, New York City (in semiretirement)
4. Carmine Tramunti, New York City
5. Stefano Magaddino, Buffalo, NY
6. Angelo Bruno, Philadelphia
7. Joseph Zerilli, Detroit
8. Paul deLucia, Chicago

The ninth seat remains vacant while a successor to the late Vito Genovese emerges. Genovese, who died in jail in 1969, was once widely regarded as the most powerful of all the Mafia bosses, revered and feared by the rest like an Old Testament Patriarch. According to those who remember him, he had the appearance of a courteous old gentleman: majestic, but humble. At the height of his power, Genovese lived in a modest suburban home in New Jersey, where he kept an array of cheap plaster statues of saints on his bedroom dresser— for the Mafia leaders are, as often as not, devout and regular churchgoers. He personally cooked the spaghetti when his eight grandchildren visited him; he drove a two-year-old Ford and owned not more than ten cheap suits. He was worth, at that time, around $25 million to $30 million, to all outward appearances a gentle and respectable businessman, the treasurer of the County Line Steel Corporation of Amityville, New York, which was his "front" business. Few would have guessed he was one of the most notorious criminals of his age, an extortionist, a usurer, and a ruthless killer.

Today, following Genovese's death (from natural causes), together with the attempted assassination of Joseph Colombo and the flight from America of the old Chicago boss, Salvatore Giancana, it is assumed that the commission's strength is not what it once was. In New York, the outbreak of the bloodiest interfamily warfare since the early thirties is perhaps a sign that the old confederacy is beginning to break up. But from its Sicilian origins until the present day, the Mafia has shown great powers of cohesion and endurance. It may well be that the current bloodletting will lead in the end to yet another truce as a new generation of bosses takes over the syndicate.

While the leadership of Cosa Nostra is exclusively Italian or Sicilian, the Syndicate has over the years absorbed criminals from other groups. "We got Jews, we got Polacks, we got Greeks," Jackie Creone, a Chicago member once observed. All outsiders, however, serve in a subordinate or affiliated capacity, with one notable exception—a Jewish financial wizard, Meyer Lansky, whose special expertise in the field of casino gambling enabled his Italian partners to make more money than they could without him.

Gambling is far and away the Mob's most lucrative business, with a revenue estimated by federal officials at up to twenty billion dollars a year, of which about one third represents pure profit for the mob. During the last decade, the most profitable gambling operations were based on the one state in America where casino gambling is legal: the state of Nevada. Under Lansky's guidance they developed a technique known as "skimming" that was—almost—foolproof. The Mafia simply gained control of the casinos, then skimmed off part of the cash profits before the figures reached the ledger books.

Lansky has been described as the financial genius of the underworld whose skills have amassed for him a personal fortune of perhaps $100 million. For years, Lansky lived modestly in an oceanfront apartment near the Fontainebleau Hotel on Miami Beach, where he was known to his neighbors as "a perfect gentleman." While he was there, he was watched almost constantly by the FBI, on whom he came to rely for his protection from rivals in the underworld. On one occasion, it is said, he slowed down his car to allow his FBI tail to catch up, either as an act of conscious irony or in the belief that the G-men would provide him with a more efficient bodyguard than any that could be hired from within the family.

But the law has now caught up with Meyer Lansky in a way he hadn't bargained for. In 1971, he was indicted by a federal grand jury in Nevada for conspiring to defraud the U.S. Government of income tax on some $36 million in profits from the syndicate's gambling operations. He skipped to Israel to avoid the federal subpoena, but had to leave again when he was refused permanent asylum there and was finally arrested on an airliner at Miami International Airport. He had flown from Tel Aviv to Zurich, then to South America, where he reportedly offered a million dollars to any country that would take him in. However, he was turned away from Rio, Buenos Aires, Asuncion, La Paz, Lima, and Panama City, to arrive, haggard and defeated, back where he had started out a year and a half before. He was later indicted and convicted of a criminal contempt. Without him, it can be fairly assumed the Mob's gambling operations in Las Vegas have fallen on leaner times.

With a few rare exceptions like Lansky, the basic unit of Mafia operations remains the famous family, in which total allegiance is paid to one man, the Boss, or *il padrone* as he is normally known to the members. The function of these powerful dons, all of them millionaires, is like that of the chairmen of large corporations: to maintain order and maximize profits. They demand, and usually get, total obedience from subordinate members of the family; it is rare indeed for violence to break out within the ranks of a single family.

The dons rule their world of organized crime by fear. Collectively, their organization is so powerful no outsider has yet been able seriously to threaten it. They have enough muscle and enough money to put any competitor out of business by sheer violence. Their criminal activities today are normally sevenfold: gambling, narcotics supply, usury, labor racketeering, the infiltration of legitimate businesses, extortion, and the political fix.

Usury is an activity that nets the Mafia billions of dollars a year through a technique that is both simple and effective. The Mafia, a rich organization, lends its money to people who cannot raise loans through orthodox channels: gamblers down on their luck, small business operators who find themselves on the verge of bankruptcy, narcotics peddlers who borrow money to purchase heroin, or anyone else who needs to raise cash in a hurry. The Mafia's interest rates, however, run at the rate of 20 percent a week; or, as the gangsters put it, "six for five"—borrow five dollars on Monday, pay back six by Saturday noon, when the debts fall due. As collateral for the loan, the borrowers put up their bodies. If they fail to meet the repayment deadline, they receive not a dunning letter from the credit corporation but a visit from the Mafia goon squad. Stories of beatings, limb-breakings, debtors left hanging from hotel windows by their legs, are commonplace. Murder, however, is frowned upon by the loansharks; dead bodies can make no repayments.

Shylocking of this nature is also the classic method by which the Mafia gains control of legitimate business operations. As Robert Morgenthau, a former U.S. Attorney in New York, put it, "A hoodlum will lend a businessman money at high rates. If the businessman is unable to pay up, he soon finds himself with a new partner. The hoodlum will take over a part, or most, of the business and retain the respectable businessman as a front."

In other cases, well-known public officials have been trapped in the same manner. James Marcus, formerly water commissioner for New York City and one of Mayor Lindsay's close advisors, went to the Lucchese family for a loan when his investment firm got into difficulties. He got forty thousand dollars at an annual rate of interest that worked out at 104 per cent. When he was unable to pay it back, the family got what it probably wanted all along: influence in high places. Marcus was eventually sent to jail for arranging financial kickback to the family on a contract to clean a Bronx reservoir.

In labor racketeering, the Mob's tactic is normally one of simple extortion. Small nonunion employers are the commonest victims, and in the classic cases the employer will one day receive a visit from the Mob to inform him that his business is thenceforward "unionized." The employees, naturally, are never told, and never receive any of the benefits of union membership, although the employer is nevertheless forced to pay fees to the mythical union "organizers" as well as the workers' initiation fees and monthly dues. In another variation, the Mob, for a fee, guarantees the employer that he will have fewer strikes and lower wages to pay than his competitors. The resulting profits are split fifty-fifty, although in each case the real loser is the exploited worker, who as often as not does not even realize he has been "unionized."

Perhaps the most evil of the Mafia's current activities is the wholesale trade of narcotics, chiefly heroin, which is said to bring in profits of around thirty million dollars a year. Statistics on the heroin trade are notoriously unreliable, but depending whose figures you believe, it is estimated there are now between 300,000 and 560,000 heroin addicts in the United States, perhaps 200,000 of them in New York City alone. The social toll of this epidemic of heroin abuse in terms of young lives ruined and the petty, though often violent, crimes committed on the streets by desperate young addicts in search of the cash with which to raise their next fix has become a national scandal. For those between the ages of fifteen and thirty-five, drug overdoses have become the most common cause of death. The city's former police commissioner, Patrick V. Murphy, estimated that at least a quarter of all crime was committed by addicts. The story is the same across the country, particularly in the northern cities with large ghetto populations of poor and often desperate blacks. In Detroit, drug abuse has reached critical proportions; authorities there attribute as much as 70 percent of that city's armed robberies to drug addicts. "It's a monster," one Detroit policeman told *Time*. "And it's getting worse."

Across the country as a whole, the American Bar Association informally puts down 33 to 50 percent of the holdups, burglaries, muggings, and thefts committed in the nation's thirty-four major urban centers to heroin addiction. Another nationwide study estimates that drug addicts need to steal a colossal $2.4 billion a year to support their habit. Young women on heroin often turn to prostitution to bring in the cash, and earnings from this source alone are put at $457 million.

A huge share of this money, of course, ends up in the hands of the dealers. At the street level, where the money first changes hands, the dealers are never members of Cosa Nostra, who reserve for themselves the far less dangerous role of importers and wholesalers. The McClellan Committee estimates that the drug wholesalers expect a return of about 6 percent on the gross income obtained from heroin sales.

Unlike gambling and loansharking, which are almost exclusively preserves of the Mafia, there is no monopoly in the heroin trade. The Mob faces competition, particularly in California and Detroit, where aggressive young blacks have seized a major share of the market. As a result, gang warfare on a major scale has broken out in the latter city, which for once does not seem to involve the gangsters of Cosa Nostra. The black dealers, who call themselves "Jones Men," appear to have learned a thing or two, however, from their white competitors and have begun to go after one another in the time-honored Mafia way. "You can get a guy killed here for two hundred bucks," said one ghetto liquor-store owner, and it is estimated that as many as one hundred such killings took place in the drug underworld in Detroit in 1971. When a dealer is assassinated his competitors turn up for the funeral like gangsters out of *The Godfather*, lining the streets for blocks around with their flashy white Cadillac El Dorados.

The nucleus of the international heroin trade, however, is still firmly in the hands of the members of the Mafia, both in the United States and in Europe, where much of the heroin is refined. Donald Cressey has compared the heroin trade to an hourglass, with ten to fifteen Cosa Nostra members occupying the thin waist of the glass. The top section consists of the hundreds of Turkish or Asian farmers who grow the crop, receiving around $35 a kilogram for pure opium; the bottom of the glass by the retail dealers, the "piece men," and the "quarter kilo men," who get the heroin onto the streets. Somewhere down the line, the price increases from the $35 a kilo paid to the growers to about $225,000 paid for a kilo of refined heroin by the addicts of New York. A large percentage of that represents profit for the Mafia middleman.

A key functionary in each of the twenty-four main Mafia families across the country is the *consigliere*, or counselor, who has the same rank as the family's underboss but controls no hierarchy of "buttons" of his own. His position is normally one of long tenure, a senior advisor to the boss and other members of his family, and one of his important roles is often that of the official family corrupter. It usually falls to the *consigliere* to supervise the bribery and intimidation of police, judges, internal-revenue agents, and other public officials whose help is needed to protect members of the family from arrest and prosecution. They set about their job so efficiently that when the New York State Joint Legislative Committee on Crime made a study of over 1,700 cases in state courts during the decade of the 1960s, they found that in New York City 44.7 percent of the indictments against known members of organized crime were dismissed by Supreme Court judges, four times as many as the average. Ralph Salerno, perhaps the most knowledgeable outside expert on the workings of the Mafia, estimates that the votes of about 25 members of the U.S. Congress can be delivered, when needed, by the Mob. In New Jersey, perhaps the most corrupt state of all, the Justice Department disclosed in 1969 that "a great portion of the Internal Revenue Service was controlled by organized gambling syndicates." Since then no fewer than 131 elected and appointed officials have been indicted on various charges of corruption, in which the hand of the Mafia has always been apparent, particularly in the area around the port of Newark.

Newark is perhaps the most depressing city in the United States, a place that represents an urban catastrophe rather than a living community. It stands, only ten miles west of Wall Street, behind the polluted, hideously ugly water-front of the Hackensack River, surrounded by stinking fat-rendering plants, oil refineries, and dilapidated old factories. It is reputed to have the worst air pollution, the poorest ghettoes, and the worst urban crime rate in the nation. It is here that the Mafia obtained the firmest stranglehold on any city in America.

The story of Newark's corruption by the Mafia goes back to the days of Prohibition in the 1920s, when its port became the bootleg capital of the Eastern Seaboard. The Mob got a hold on the state then that it has only just relinquished, buying a mayor here, a judge there, a police chief or a political leader somewhere else. Its grip was reinforced when many of the leading gangsters moved across the Hudson River from New York in the early 1940s to escape the rigors of Thomas E. Dewey's drive against racketeers.

By the late 1960s, organized crime was estimated to gross up to a billion dollars a year in the state. The two main activities were gambling, which was controlled out of Newark by Ruggiero Boiardo, a gangster known as "Richie the Boot," and corruption at the Newark docks, controlled by Gerardo Catena, the acting boss of the Genovese family. It was reported that the syndicate was stealing tens of millions of dollars worth of goods each year from the docks, and the Mafia had gained control of at least two dozen New Jersey unions, ranging from the Teamsters to restaurant workers.

"Scandal after scandal whimpered to a silent and forgotten end," writes Fred J. Cook, who has made a study of crime in Newark during this period. "More than twenty indictments have been returned against public officials over the years; officials have been criticized and censured; business firms and contractors doing business with the city have been indicted. But seldom has anyone had the misfortune to be convicted."

During its investigations into the activities of the New Jersey Mafia, the FBI obtained several wiretaps at the headquarters of a local captain called Angelo (Gyp) De Carlo that throw fascinating, if chilling, light on the methods and manners of the modern underworld. The tapes, obtained over a period of nearly four years during the 1960s, show how the gang leaders train each other to "get" a judge or an income-tax inspector. They chitchat endlessly about their nefarious exploits, exaggerating greatly their own importance and toughness as they go.

Richie the Boot, who died in jail in 1973, had built himself a citadel in suburban New Jersey that could have come straight from the film of *The Godfather*, complete with a lifesize statue in the grounds of the Mafia leader himself, sitting on a white horse and surrounded by nine busts, mounted on stone pedestals, of members of his family. Behind the garden greenhouse, according to the FBI tapes, there was an incinerator for disposing of human bodies. Here, the tapes reveal, Richie the Boot used to dispose of the bodies not only of the victims of his own business activities, but also of those passed on by Thomas Lucchese, then the boss of one of New York's five families. Other families used to dispose of their surplus bodies by using an ingenious doubledecker coffin, provided by a Mafia mortician, so that only those mourners in the know ever noticed the double weight carried by the muscular Mafia pallbearers. But Boiardo had devised a system of getting rid of unwanted bodies in his incinerator without the fuss of using the double coffin.

One conversation between De Carlo and a petty gangster called Anthony (Little Pussy) Russo, went, according to the FBI, like this:

RUSSO: I seen too many. You know how many guys we hit up there?
DE CARLO: What about the big furnace he's got back there?
RUSSO: That's what I'm trying to tell you! Before you go up there . . .
DE CARLO: The big iron grate.
RUSSO: He used to put them on there and burn them.

Later in their macabre conversation, Russo told De Carlo, "He'd give them to me, and we'd take them up."

The tapes are not solely concerned with murder and mayhem. They also record the pettier tribulations and frustrations involved in running a modern Mafia gang. On one occasion, the FBI logged a conversation in which a group of gamblers complained they had wandered around Brooklyn for hours trying to find the hide-out where a dice game was supposed to be in progress. In trying to help their henchmen find the game, the leaders in New Jersey were unable to put their hands on a telephone book later than the 1958 edition.

Then there were complaints from the Mafiosi that their New York gambling operations were being raided only a few days after they had paid big bribes to local law-enforcement officers. "It'd be all right if they'd let you go thirty days," De Carlo complained. "But we're paying twelve thousand a month. . . . Two nights after we opened we were pinched! Three thousand for a shake! We ain't working for the law! Somebody from the narcotics squad wanted a shake! Two nights later, the chief of some theft squad wanted . . ."

Later De Carlo told his subordinates, "You guys have gotta do something! You gotta concentrate and try and make connections. You made them all with the law down in Newark. Everybody can be made."

The disastrous race riots that swept Newark in 1967 finally opened the eyes of the rest of the nation to the extent of the malaise there. The commission appointed to investigate the riots found that an important underlying cause was "a pervasive feeling of corruption." They reported they had been told time and time again by knowledgeable officials: "There is a price on everything at City Hall." There was one report that a man walked into the State House at Trenton one day asking to be made a judge, an appointment for which he produced from a leather bag the going rate of fifteen thousand dollars—in cash.

Frederick B. Lacey, later the federal prosecutor in many of the New Jersey corruption cases, said in a public speech just before the trials began, "Unless you . . . arouse an apathetic public to stem the tide of crime in this nation, our society as we know it is doomed." He went on later, "Organized crime is, in the vernacular, taking us over. . . . It cannot operate without corrupting law enforcement personnel. I flatly state that it will not even go into a municipality unless and until it has bought its protection against raids and arrests."

The tale that unfolded as the trials began revealed as never before how the money and the muscle provided by the Mafia had subverted the entire city of Newark—and much of the rest of New Jersey with it—to the extent that organized crime could clearly get away with anything it wished. Up to the present time, those indicted include ten mayors, nineteen councilmen or commissioners, four political leaders, three present or former state legislators, two Secretaries of State, two county detectives, and one U.S. congressman. The charges against them ranged from extortion and fraud in the handling of bank funds to accepting bribes to protect the gambling operations of Joseph Zicarelli, a reputed Mafia figure. In addition, Monmouth County's chief of detectives committed suicide, and the Newark Police Director was indicted for "willfully" failing to enforce the state's gambling laws.

Soon after President Nixon came to office, unbeholden to any local politicians in predominantly Democratic New Jersey, his Justice Department began the crackdown that has since shaken the Newark underworld to its foundations and put several of the known Mafia leaders behind bars.

In the aftermath of the scandals that then came to light, a Republican administration was swept into office in the elections of 1969, pledged to put an end to the crime and corruption that had plagued the state for so long. There were people who then believed the worst of New Jersey's nightmare of crime was over and that the state had finally turned over a new leaf, ready to purge the last germs of organized crime from its public life.

Less than three years later, however, there were ominous signs that not much had changed in New Jersey after all when the new Republican Secretary of State, Paul J. Sherwin, the second most powerful man in the new administration, was indicted on charges of extortion and bribery. "In a state that has witnessed scores of indictments and convictions involving alleged corruption," wrote the New York *Times*, "today's indictments are regarded . . . as the most startling of them all." Sherwin has denied the charges, but late in 1972 he was found guilty of conspiring to influence the award of a state highway contract in return for a ten thousand dollars contribution to the state Republican finance committee. It was never alleged that Sherwin had lined his own pockets, but he was sentenced from one to two years in jail and fined two thousand dollars, pending his appeal.

By the time the 1970s arrived, the Mob was feeling itself beleaguered by the forces of the law more keenly than ever before. Partly for that reason, Joseph Colombo, head of one of New York's five families, made the extraordinary decision, early in 1970, to take the cause of the Mafia to the public. He organized a protest movement called the Italian-American Civil Rights League, which engaged in a series of public antics that is said to have deeply shocked the secretive dons of an older generation. Claiming that Americans of Italian descent were being harassed and victimized by the Justice Department, Colombo began to take upon himself the role of public spokesman for an abused minority. He appeared on late-night television shows, where he claimed he had formed his Civil Rights League because Italian-Americans were being discriminated against. He himself, he declared piously, was just an honest businessman, engaged in real estate with a part share in a florist's shop and a funeral home, yet wherever he went, he and his associates were being followed and harassed by federal agents. It was, he declared, unfair and un-American and ought to be stopped.

In April 1970, Colombo astonished the FBI by throwing up a picket line outside their New York headquarters to protest the arrest of his son. The League set up quarters in many areas of Brooklyn, where police discovered they were no longer free to walk in and frisk a suspect as they had done in the past. "We have to be very careful about the civil rights aspect of things," a baffled policeman told the New York *Times*.

At first, Colombo's League was a brilliant success, claiming a membership of 150,000, most of them honest Italian-Americans who had nothing to do with crime but who liked to flock to Colombo's rallies to express their pride in their ethnic origins. The large Italian-American community in New York seems to have been suffering from a feeling of neglect, almost a persecution complex, because of the attention given to other ethnic groups like the Puerto Ricans and the blacks. Colombo's new organization gave them an outlet for their pentup frustrations. The League's biggest coup came when Colombo persuaded both the FBI and the producers of *The Godfather* to drop the terms *Mafia* and *Cosa Nostra* from their vocabulary.

All this came to an abrupt end at Colombo's second annual *celebrazione* in 1971, an open-air rally at Columbus Circle in the heart of Manhattan, which had been called by the League to proclaim pride in its Italian descent. The circle was festooned with red, white, and green streamers—the Italian colors—pennants went on sale proclaiming "Italian Power," and circulating through the festival crowd was Joseph Colombo, beaming broadly and shaking hands with everyone in sight. Suddenly, almost inaudibly, shots were fired, and Colombo fell to the ground with two bullets in his brain. Almost immediately, another volley of shots felled his assailant, a young black who had been posing as a photographer. To this day, no one knows who killed the assailant; it is presumed the shots were fired by one of Colombo's bodyguards who escaped in the turmoil as professionally as he had shot the would-be assassin.

Colombo survived five hours of brain surgery, but has remained permanently incapacitated, unable to play any further part in the affairs of his family. Even as he lay in Roosevelt Hospital, his bed was guarded night and day by private detectives and members of his staff in a style familiar to all Mafia aficionados. No one was allowed to enter his room without the approval of his bodyguard and, fearing a second attack, his staff set up a ring of button men around the hospital corridors. "You watch this stairway," a *Time* reporter overheard one *caporegime* instruct a younger man. "If someone goes into the hallway, you follow him. If he gets into the elevator, you get in with him. And if he gets off on the floor, you tell him he can't go no further."

Under Colombo's rule, the old Profaci family had grown into one of the most powerful in New York, involved in rackets that were generalized rather than narrowly specialist. The family had become a sort of conglomerate of crime, with interests in gambling, loansharking, hijacking, and the take-over of legitimate businesses, especially bars, nightclubs, and Manhattan garment firms whose owners had fallen in too deeply with the loansharks.

Colombo was the youngest of the five Mafia chieftains in New York, having been given command of the Profaci family in 1962 at the age of forty. He had been involved in internecine warfare before, during the celebrated "Bananas" war of the early 1960s, when he negotiated the truce between the feuding families. It was reported that he originally obtained his power as a result of a cunning doublecross, having been picked out by two of the Mafia bosses of that decade, Joe Bonanno and Joe Magliocco, and given the job of exterminating their three main rivals: Thomas Lucchese, Carlo Gambino, and Stefano Magaddino. Colombo went instead to the other three bosses and tipped them off, an event that is believed to have unleashed the so-called "Bananas" war that eventually led to the overthrow and disappearance of Joe Bonanno.

The shots that brought down Colombo started a classic struggle for power among the Mafia families of New York that, according to various estimates, has so far taken the lives of between fifteen and twenty-seven gangsters in one of the bloodiest outbreaks of Mafia violence since the truce of 1934.

His shooting was also the first attempt to assassinate a Mafia leader since Albert Anastasia was shot in his barber's chair at the Park Sheraton Hotel in 1957. The contract for Anastasia's murder is believed to have passed through the late Joseph Profaci to the Gallo brothers, Albert and "Crazy Joe," who felt that such signal service had earned them a more important role within the family than Profaci, the "olive oil king," was prepared to grant them. The Gallo brothers—touched, said one writer, "with the kind of madness that drives sharks berserk in a blood-stained sea"—challenged the authority of the boss himself and were widely believed in the underworld to have been behind the shooting of Joe Colombo, who took over the family on Profaci's death in 1962.

"Our information is that practically everyone in the Colombo family exclusively blames Joe Gallo for the shooting," said one New York detective. It was therefore only a matter of time before the vengeance of the Colombo family found its victim. And as Crazy Joe Gallo celebrated his forty-third birthday at a predawn champagne party in Umberto's Clam House in Little Italy, a group of four gunmen walked in from the street and shot him dead.

Gallo's funeral at the Greenwood Cemetery in Brooklyn was theatrically familiar. As the mourners filed past the grave, each dropped a single red rose on the burnished bronze coffin and cried, "Take him, Big Boy! You've got him now, Big Boy!" Gallo's sister Carmella was heard to vow, "The streets are going to run red with blood, Joey!"

Sure enough, within the next six days five other bodies were found in and around New York, murdered in the classic Mafia way. That same week, the rival factions of the Colombo gang officially declared war and "went to the mattresses" in their fortified hide-outs. Six months later, the war was still running at full pitch, having taken the lives, according to some law-enforcement officers, of perhaps twenty-seven Mafiosi, including Thomas Eboli, the powerful underboss who had been left in temporary charge of the Vito Genovese family, as well as two innocent bystanders, who were gunned down as they stood at a bar in the Neapolitan Noodle Restaurant on the Upper East Side. The innocent men were meat wholesalers, out for dinner with two business associates and their wives, apparently assassinated in a case of mistaken identity. The police believe the killer was an out-of-town gunman hired by a rival family to murder two members of the Colombo gang who had been standing at the bar only minutes before. Mayor Lindsay, angered at the killings, declared the murder of innocent citizens by the gangland executioners was "an outrage which demands that the romanticization of the Mob must be stopped and gangsters run out of town." But federal investigators were skeptical. "Forget it," said one. "They'll just go into hiding." And so they did.

By this time, it was evident that the Profaci family feud had triggered off a major shift of power among the five families of New York. The most common theory was that the Eboli killing had been ordered by Carlo Gambino; in any event, it was a move that left the formerly dominant Genovese family almost leaderless, with its other acting boss, Jerry Catena, already in jail for refusing to answer questions for New Jersey authorities. The removal of Eboli was thought by some Mafia watchers to be a move that could pave the way for Carlo Gambino to take over the remnants of that once-powerful family. At the same time, it was known that Gambino had just completed negotiations to absorb some fifty seasoned members of the rebellious Gallo faction from the Colombo family. Together, the addition of those forces would give Gambino the power to move for complete control of all the Mafia families in New York. "Carlo wants to swallow up everybody," one Mafia boss was overheard saying.

It is thought Gambino believes that the Mafia is under greater pressure from law-enforcement agencies than it has ever been, and that the only way to ensure its survival is to dissolve some of the weaker families altogether and merge their activities first into two groups, then into one sole family. Gambino reportedly has been importing Mafiosi from Sicily in order to revive the old discipline and traditions, and he is said to favor the reopening of the Mafia's membership books, which have been closed since 1957, to allow the initiation of new and tougher blood.

With the situation more confused perhaps than it had ever been, the status of the five families stood as follows:

1. Gambino Family
    Boss: Carlo Gambino
    Underboss: Aniello Dellacroce
    Consigliere: Joseph Riccobono
    Membership: 1,000
    Activities: Gambling, Brooklyn waterfront, citywide garbage carting
2. Genovese Family
    Boss: Frank Tieri (acting, following death of Vito Genovese)
    Underboss: Jerry Catena (in jail)
    Thomas Eboli, underboss, assassinated, 1972
    Consigliere: Michele Miranda
    Membership: 600
    Activities: Gambling, loansharking, docks
3. Bonanno Family

Boss:	Natale Evola (died, 1973)
Underboss:	Frank Mari
Consigliere:	Michael Adamo
Membership:	400
Activities:	Trucking and narcotics

4. Profaci Family

Boss:	Joseph Colombo (incapacitated)
Acting Boss:	Joseph Yacovelli
Consigliere:	Benedetto D'Alessandro
Membership:	200
Activities:	Gambling, hijacking, usury, infiltration of legitimate businesses

5. Lucchese Family

Boss:	Carmine Tramunti (acting—under indictment)
Underboss:	Steve LaSalla
Consigliere:	Vincent Rao
Membership:	150
Activities:	Narcotics, gambling, garment industry

The war that broke out in 1972 could eventually drag in all five families. "What we have now," says Ralph Salerno, "is evidently and patently a fight that's going on between the various groups. Basically, what it spells out is that crime is not as well organized as it used to be." Salerno, like other Mafia-watchers, does not know how the current war will end, but he believes the total effect will be to weaken the structure of the Mafia. At the same time, many of the older members of the syndicate are now going to jail after the crackdown of the strike forces set up at the Justice Department and of local law-enforcement agencies. As a result, says Salerno, "more top people have gone to jail in the past five years than in the previous fifty. And that's also beginning to take its toll. I think the quality of the leadership has begun to deteriorate quite a bit."

As if to prove him right, the New York Mafia, in the middle of its private wars, received its heaviest blow in years towards the end of 1972 when a special force of 1,200 policemen swept through the city in a predawn raid, serving grand-jury subpoenas on over 600 alleged Mafiosi. The Brooklyn District Attorney Eugene Gold called it "the most massive investigation of organized crime in the history of this country." He proudly took two busloads of reporters to view the source of the police department's information: a broken-down housetrailer in a Brooklyn junkyard which had been used as a Mafia headquarters for over six months. Police had successfully planted a bug there and set up an observation and listening post on the top floor of a high school across the street. There they recorded over 300 miles of tape as Paul Vario, a *capo* in the Tramunti family, met with his cronies to plan their alleged crimes.

"The view from the summit has not been pretty," said the Brooklyn district attorney. He reeled off a list of deals said to have been struck in the trailer that gave a staggering insight into the sheer scope of the modern Mafia's activities: the sale of narcotics, extortion, loansharking, bookmaking, assault, robbery, burglaries, counterfeiting, hijacking, receiving stolen property, forgery, possession and sale of weapons, labor racketeering, stolen automobiles, untaxed cigarettes, insurance frauds, arson of businesses, the cutting-up of autos and boats, prostitution, and violation of Alcohol Beverage Control Laws. He also revealed that one hundred police officers had visited the trailer at various times, presumably to receive their payoffs for cooperating with the gang.

The cases will take years to wend their way through the courts, and forecasts that two hundred *Mafiosi* could end up in jail may yet prove too optimistic. But for the two thousand or so surviving members of the city's five families, it may be a sign that the good days are at last coming to an end.

2. FBI Story: The Hoover Legacy

"Law enforcement is only as effective as the citizens demand."
—*J. Edgar Hoover, director, FBI, 1951*

Visitors to the offices of the Federal Bureau of Investigation on Pennsylvania Avenue in Washington, after being encouraged to leave their fingerprints behind in the bureau's files, are often taken to see a macabre exhibit in the anteroom of the Director: the white plaster death mask of John Dillinger, the notorious bankrobber of the 1930s, whose ghostly features have been staring out from under its glass case for the past forty years. Lovingly preserved around the deathmask are other memorabilia of that famous night when Dillinger was shot down by the FBI as he strolled from the Biograph Cinema in Chicago. The outlaw's silver-rimmed glasses are there, scarred by one of the FBI bullets that felled him, there is the straw hat he was wearing, and a corona cigar, still wrapped in cellophane, that was found in the dead bankrobber's shirt pocket that summer night so long ago.

The legend it has built up around Dillinger says more for the FBI's genius for publicity and its curious predilection for glorifying secondrate bankrobbers than it does for the size of the menace represented by the lonely outlaw and his ilk. Although the FBI had tagged him "Public Enemy Number One," Dillinger was in fact no great shakes as a bankrobber, even by the standards of forty years ago, and his deeds actually pale into insignificance when put alongside those of his more sinister contemporaries such as Al Capone, whose reputed 127 murders never once attracted the attention of the FBI.

The truth is that the FBI gained much of its reputation for infallibility in a blaze of gunfire and heroics against a band of largely petty criminals, from Dillinger himself to "Pretty Boy" Floyd, "Baby Face" Nelson, "Ma" Barker, and "Old Creepy" Karpis, loners all, and little more than what one writer has called "the human tumbleweeds of crime"—car thieves, minor bankrobbers, freightcar burglars, waterfront pilferers. Yet while the bureau was busy winning glory against these often pathetic outlaws, it ignored altogether the much more dangerous threat of organized crime, whose very existence it persistently denied for more than a quarter of a century.

The failure of the FBI to move against the organized crime syndicate in the years when it was gaining its stranglehold in city after city is one of the more puzzling aspects of American law enforcement in the past half-century. Many theories have been advanced for the FBI's downright refusal to acknowledge the existence of the Mafia, most of which rest on the personality of the legendary J. Edgar Hoover, who directed the bureau from 1924 until his death in 1972. Some argue that Hoover's bureaucratic vanity led him to avoid organized crime because its time-consuming investigations could never yield the same impressive statistics as attacks on simple crimes like bankrobbery; others argue that Hoover wished to protect his incorruptible agents from the temptations that would inevitably come their way if they tangled with the Syndicate; still others say Hoover was so jealous of the FBI's reputation he would never allow his investigative agents to take second place in a national crimefighting unit. Whatever the reasons, the fact remains that it was only the arrival of Robert Kennedy at the Justice Department in 1961 that forced Hoover, belatedly and much against his will, to enroll the FBI in the fight against the nationwide crime syndicate. And even then, according to Jack Anderson, the FBI assigned precisely four investigative agents to the Justice Department's seventeen-city drive against the Mafia. As a result, until very recently the FBI was organized to fight the crime pattern of the twenties and thirties, and not set up to do battle with the organized syndicate that drains the United States of billions of dollars a year.

"The FBI has so coveted personal credit that it will sacrifice even effective crime control before it will share the glory of its exploits," writes Ramsey Clark, Hoover's nominal boss as Attorney General under the Johnson Administration, in his book *Crime in America*. "This has been a petty and costly characteristic caused by the excessive domination of a single person . . . and his self-centered concern for his reputation and that of the FBI."

Here is perhaps the key that explains why for thirty years Hoover constantly belittled the activities of organized crime, and when he finally did come to acknowledge its existence insist that it was purely a matter to be dealt with by local police forces. He was perhaps quite simply afraid that if he tackled the Mafia, he might fail in the task—and failure was something J. Edgar Hoover could not countenance. Back in the 1950s, when Senator Estes Kefauver was holding his compellingly convincing hearings on organized crime in cities across the nation, he concluded that "much of the responsibility for what is going on rests squarely upon federal enforcement agencies." To remedy the situation, he proposed the creation of a National Crime Commission, to be staffed partly by the FBI, which would act as an information bank on the activities of the crime syndicate. Hoover, however, would have none of it. Such a commission, he declared, might lead to the establishment of a national police force, and in his view "nothing could be more dangerous to our democratic ideals." In fact, as Kefauver pointed out, there was no connection between his suggestions for a federal crime commission and a national police force, but Hoover's power was such that his conservative supporters in Congress were persuaded to kill the proposal in committee. America has been paying the price ever since.

Hoover's contention that the crime syndicate did not exist was finally exploded in 1957 when the New York state police stumbled across the Mafia summit at Apalachin. Their discovery was followed by an immediate, though shortlived, public outcry. Under the pressures that resulted, William Rogers, then Attorney General, launched the first "special group" in the Justice Department to investigate the syndicate. Under Milton R. Wessel, a former Assistant U.S. Attorney, the group prepared the first detailed recommendations for dealing with organized crime on a nationwide basis, including a streamlining of federal criminal prosecution procedures to equip it to deal effectively with the modern syndicate.

During its investigations, the special group found that some of the most important syndicate leaders were men of outstanding public reputation with no criminal records, so that they were able, by the use of modern public-relations techniques, to create the appearance of legitimacy and to deceive the public into thinking they were the distinguished representatives of ordinary big business. And just as with big business, management of the syndicate operated on a wholly different level, often miles away from the crime that was committed. This separation had two important consequences to law enforcement, the group said: "First, each level operates as insulation to the higher level, since criminal law enforcement loses effect the further it strays from the specific, physical criminal act. Second, the leaders can remove themselves from the subpoena power of any particular local prosecutor. Even the most vigorous district attorney finds it virtually impossible to investigate where the real culprits are outside his subpoena jurisdiction." The primary cause of law enforcement breakdown, its report concluded, was the splintered structure of American enforcement agencies. It went on to criticize, albeit indirectly, Hoover's reluctance to bring the FBI into the fight:

> It is a startling fact that nowhere in Government does there exist a permanent force capable of unifying action of the thousands of federal, state, local and special law enforcement units all over the country. Nowhere is there even a clearing house to which police or prosecutors can turn for advice on where criminal intelligence can be found.

The remedy to all of this, the group found, was to create an office on syndicated crime with the mission of serving as a nerve center, maintaining communication between the law-enforcement units, and drawing together a truly unified prosecutive effort against syndicated crime. To members of Wessel's group, the case seemed overwhelming. Yet once again Hoover was instrumental in turning it down, and in less than two years the special group was disbanded. "According to the stories, our unit was dissolved because we had aroused the jealousy of older agencies that resented our authority over crimes in their jurisdiction," Wessel told the *Saturday Evening Post.* His aides were even more outspoken in their criticism of the FBI director. "Hoover was very cool to the whole idea of the Attorney General's special group," said Richard Ogilvie, who was in charge of the group's midwestern office. "He ordered that the FBI files, containing the very information we needed on organized crime, were to be closed to us. Furthermore, he forbade any agents even to talk to members of the special group."

Once again, Hoover's entrenched system of bureaucracy had prevented effective action being taken against the Mafia. The group had served its purpose—public opinion had been appeased for a while—but now it could be safely dismembered, leaving the FBI's public reputation and its jurisdiction intact. Even at this late date, Hoover was simply not prepared to launch an all-out assault on the citadels of organized crime. As William W. Turner, an FBI agent himself for ten years, put it in his book *Hoover's FBI,* "The essential problem was just the opposite from the one the Bureau had been used to in bank robberies and other crimes it had investigated; there, the challenge was to identify the subject and garner sufficient evidence to convict him. The organized crime figures were already known for the most part, and the problem was to detect them in a criminal act. This could only be done by a prolonged intelligence effort, not a crash program. The FBI, of course, had not made such an effort in the past. At headquarters there was no division devoted purely to organized crime—not even a section. In the field, there were no Mafia specialists, no Mafia file."

This state of affairs continued until Robert Kennedy took over the Justice Department under his brother's administration in 1961 and immediately insisted that the FBI join fully in the drive against organized crime. Hoover again resisted, but for once found himself outgunned by the young Attorney General, whose fraternal ties with the White House were too strong to be ignored. JFK himself was reported to be appalled at Hoover's obsession with communism at this time and was, according to the Washington *Post,* "unable to carry on a coherent conversation with him." For a while, it appeared that Hoover was in danger of being fired by the Kennedys as a result of their frustrations with the lack of relevance to the problems of the 1960s, but in the end Hoover yielded to their pressures. For the first time since he took over the bureau twenty-seven years earlier, a division was finally set up to deal with the major figures in the Syndicate. The drive was always provided by Kennedy, but Hoover was powerless to object. Within two years the new section had compiled the first full intelligence file on the activities and composition of the crime syndicate and had begun to obtain impressive results against some of the most vicious mobsters.

Kennedy's fight against the Mafia and its affiliates made a spectacular breakthrough in the summer of 1962 when Joseph Valachi, a hitherto insignificant Mafia button man, became the first member to break the Mafia's oath of silence, *omerta*, for which the family's penalty was death. Valachi, a member of the Vito Genovese family, had been sent to the Atlanta penitentiary for selling heroin on a conviction obtained by the Federal Narcotics Bureau. There were rumors inside the prison that he had been marked for death for "spilling his guts" to the narcotics agents who had prosecuted him. One day in June 1962, Valachi seized a two-foot piece of pipe and clubbed to death a fellow prisoner he mistakenly believed to be his assigned executioner. Facing a death sentence for his murder and with nothing more to lose, Valachi "sang" as no member of the Mafia had ever sung before.

Kennedy later arranged for Valachi to tell his story in the Senate, where he revealed for the first time how the Mafia was organized, how its "commission" functioned, and how it allocated its territories. Faced with this cast-iron evidence, Hoover was finally persuaded that the Mafia did in fact exist, even though only a few months earlier he had written, "No single individual or coalition of racketeers dominates organized crime across the nation." But now, at last, he changed his tune and characteristically moved in to claim for his FBI most of the credit for the discovery. Valachi's testimony, he said later, simply "corroborated and embellished the facts developed by the FBI as early as 1961 which disclosed the makeup of the gangland horde," while he smugly maintained that all the Valachi information "was known to the Bureau or had been obtained from informants of the Bureau."

It was an astonishing, though characteristic, reversal of the line he had steadfastly maintained in the teeth of all the evidence for years past, but with his genius for seizing the credit that rightly belonged to others he now began parading his new discovery to the press and public. He even invented a new name for the Mafia, calling it "La Cosa Nostra," in order to enhance the impression that this was an entirely new form of organized crime which had suddenly been discovered by the fearless G-men of the FBI. He got the name from an FBI wiretap in New York in which two Mafia gangsters were heard to refer to "cosa nostra," which simply means in Italian "our thing." Hoover seized on the new name, putting it into capital letters as "La Cosa Nostra," a piece of grammatical nonsense meaning "The Our Thing." But curiously enough, the name has stuck, and is commonly used today to describe the Mafia, even apparently by its own members, standing as one more tribute to Hoover's talent for public relations.

Had John Kennedy lived to serve a second term and his brother Robert stayed on at the Justice Department, it is likely that Hoover would have been quietly retired when he reached his seventieth birthday on New Year's Day, 1965. But that of course was not to be. There was a cruel irony in the fact that Robert Kennedy was in the middle of a conference on organized crime when Hoover came through on the telephone to break the news of the events

in Dallas. According to the account of the assassination by William Manches-
ter, Hoover announced in an expressionless voice, "I have news for you. The
President's been shot." He said he thought it was serious and promised to call
back with more details as soon as he had them.

Eighteen minutes later, the call came. "The President's dead," Hoover
announced, then hung up. Although Robert Kennedy stayed on at the Justice
Department for a few more months under President Johnson, the two men
are reported never to have spoken to each other again. Hoover immediately
reverted to his old ways, channeling all his information direct to the Johnson
White House. By now, of course, it was becoming more difficult than ever to
dislodge the syndicate of organized crime. As President Nixon put it when six
years later he announced his administration's own crime drive, "Not a single
one of the twenty-four Cosa Nostra familes has been destroyed; they are more
firmly entrenched than ever."

History has since put much of the blame for that state of affairs on the
shoulders of J. Edgar Hoover, the one man who had the power and the prestige
to crush the syndicate in its formative years, but who chose instead to look
the other way.

When Hoover died in 1972, President Nixon ordered that his body should
lie in state in the rotunda of the U.S. Capitol, an honor normally reserved for
Presidents, war heroes, and the giants of Congress. In the following two days,
over 25,000 people filed past his coffin, draped in the red, white, and blue
colors of the American flag, in a remarkable tribute to the world's most
powerful policeman, a man whose public career had spanned a quarter of
America's history as a nation. In his funeral eulogy, the President fulsomely
declared that the United States was a better country "because this good man
lived his long life among us." Hoover, said Nixon, "was one of the giants, a
man who helped keep steel in America's backbone and the flame of freedom
in America's soul."

Newspaper obituaries were less kind to the seventy-seven-year-old director.
The general consensus was that Hoover was a legend who had outlived his own
time. "It was fitting that the director died in his sleep," one bitter FBI agent
was quoted as saying. "That is the way the bureau was run lately."

In his last years, Hoover had grown out of touch with the changing mood
of America. He was an authoritarian in an increasingly permissive society, a
rigid moralist among a people grown more tolerant, a doctrinaire anti-Communist in a country where the threat of domestic subversion had long since passed
—if indeed it had ever existed at all. His views and his values seemed more
and more to represent those of a vanished America, and the question of his
retirement had time and again been considered by the White House, only to
be rejected by the President himself—partly, it now appears, over difficulties
Hoover was creating over a series of wiretaps conducted in the aftermath of
the Pentagon Papers affair. There were fears in the White House that Hoover

might "use" his FBI wiretap files in some manner against the President. But there was a widespread and growing feeling that, if he had lived, Hoover would sooner or later have to be dropped. "Hoover wasn't of sound mind," one of his chief aides, William H. Sullivan, said later in an interview with the *Los Angeles Times*. He was thought in the bureau to be no longer rational, and in his last years the bureau had suffered a whole series of public embarrassments. Morale in its upper echelons was said to be the lowest it had ever been, and in the months before Hoover's death several of the FBI's ablest assistant directors had left or been forced out because of policy disputes with the increasingly irascible director. But the old man's staying power rested on fear as well as on respect for his past services.

It was widely believed around the capital that Hoover's dossiers "had" something on everyone, and until the end he was treated with the greatest deference by those in Congress who had the task of approving his budgets. "That fellow was a master blackmailer," Sullivan said after Hoover had died. "And he did it with considerable finesse, despite the deterioration of his mind. He always did that sort of thing: The moment he would get something on a senator, he'd send one of the errand boys up and advise the senator that we're in the course of an investigation and we by chance happened to come up with this data on your daughter. But we wanted you to know this—we realize you'd want to know it. But don't have any concern, no one will ever learn about it. Well, Jesus, what does that tell the senator? From that time on, the senator's right in his pocket." Hoover was not always so circumspect: The celibate director had widely circulated around Washington spicy details concerning the private lives of more than one well-known American, and his dossiers on the famous were said to have been President Johnson's favorite bedtime reading.

But by the end, Hoover was visibly aging; his face had grown pale and his jaws slack, his once-curly hair was now straight and thin, he was given to moods of withdrawal and daydreaming, and under his direction the FBI had in his last years entered a stage of near-paralysis. The bureau's legendary efficiency began to suffer, too. Hoover was badly embarrassed when activists raided the FBI's secret files in Media, Pennsylvania, and circulated ream after ream of papers showing how the bureau kept a detailed watch on meetings of domestic protest groups to which he was ideologically opposed—even an Earth Day rally attended by Senator Edmund Muskie had been monitored. Then Hoover himself prematurely leaked word of an alleged leftwing plot to kidnap Dr. Henry Kissinger before anyone had been indicted and had publicly called Dr. Martin Luther King a liar and his old boss, Ramsey Clark, a jellyfish. Toward the end, the word *senility* was widely whispered around Washington, and Hoover became the butt of some bitter jokes, both private and public. One satirical snippet, circulated only a few months before his death, had Hoover engaged in conversation with President Nixon:

NIXON: I wanted to see you to discuss with you the matter of retirement.
HOOVER: Why, that's ridiculous. Why, you're still a young man.
NIXON: I'm not talking about my retirement, Mr. Hoover. I'm talking frankly
         about your retirement.
HOOVER: Why, Mr. Roosevelt, I can't believe you're saying that.

In the end, Nixon was spared the embarrassment of throwing his old friend
to the wolves. In May 1972, after a full day's work in the office, Hoover died
suddenly during the night in his neo-Georgian house in the Washington
suburbs. For the United States as well as for the bureau, an era had ended.

The Hoover era had begun forty-eight years earlier under the administration
of Calvin Coolidge, when the ambitious young lawyer was chosen at the
astonishing age of twenty-nine to retrieve the bureau from the corruption and
incompetence it had fallen into in the dark years under President Harding.
Hoover, who had already been at the Justice Department for five years, clearly
stood out from his contemporaries as a totally incorruptible young man with
a penchant for long hours, hard work, and outstanding ability. "He dressed
better than most, a bit on the dandyish side," wrote Jack Alexander in his 1937
profile of the director. "He had an exceptional capacity for detail work, and
he handled small chores with enthusiasm and thoroughness. He constantly
sought new responsibilities to shoulder and welcomed chances to work over-
time. When he was in conference with an official of his department, his
manner was that of a young man who confidently expected to rise."
      When Harlan Fiske Stone was appointed Attorney General under the new
Coolidge Administration, determined to rebuild the then Bureau of Investigation after the image of Scotland Yard, Hoover was recommended to him as
"a lawyer of uncommon ability and character." Just how uncommon a
strength of character he possessed was revealed in his interview with the new
Attorney General, as described by Don Whitehead in his officially sanctioned
FBI Story:

> Hoover took a seat. Stone peered over his glasses and the two men looked at each
> other over the desk. Then Stone said abruptly, "Young man, I want you to be acting
> Director of the Bureau of Investigation . . ."
>   Finally Hoover said: "I'll take the job, Mr. Stone, on certain conditions."
>   "What are they?"
>   "The Bureau must be divorced from politics and not be a catch-all for political
> hacks. Appointments must be based on merit. Second, promotions will be made on
> proved ability and the Bureau will be responsible only to the Attorney General."
>   The Attorney General scowled and said, "I wouldn't give it to you under any other
> conditions. That's all. Good day."

From the start, Hoover's confidence and cunning had thus given him a
personal grip on the bureaucratic workings of the bureau he was not to

relinquish until his death. Freed from the inhibitions of outside politics and the rest of the civil service, he was able to shape the bureau in his own stern image, demanding that his agents have either a law or accountancy degree and quickly turning the bureau into one of the most efficient crimefighting units in the world, with an enviable reputation for probity. Today, the bureau he created employs some twenty thousand people, including nearly nine thousand special agents, and not one of them has ever been convicted of a crime (at least up to the time of Watergate).

During the first decade of his tenure, Hoover overhauled and modernized the entire structure of federal law enforcement in America. The Identification Division, modeled on Scotland Yard's, was created in 1925, and now possesses over 200 million sets of fingerprints. The Crime Laboratory followed in 1932, bringing science for the first time to the aid of police work in the United States. Three years later, Hoover founded the National Police Academy to train through the resources of the FBI the leadership élite of police forces throughout the country. Later still, the National Crime Information Center was formed, which today enables over four thousand law-enforcement agencies to enter records on thirty-five separate computer systems, controlled from the headquarters of the FBI.

From the earliest days as director, Hoover expected the same rigid standards from his agents to which he subjected himself. Personal affairs at the bureau were strictly regulated. No one was allowed a coffee break. Agents were expected to dress in a white shirt, dark suit, felt hat, and a white handkerchief in the breast pocket. Staff were reprimanded for being overweight or for reading *Playboy* magazine. A clerk was once dismissed for playing with a yoyo in the halls; another for keeping his girlfriend in his apartment overnight.

Within the bureau, Hoover's word was rarely questioned, leading sometimes to absurd results. The director was in the habit of writing comments in the margins of his staff's memoranda in bright blue ink. On one occasion, the story goes, Hoover received a memorandum that filled the page so full there was no room left for Hoover's blue ink, and the note was returned with the comment, "Watch the borders." His puzzled but obedient aides are said to have dispatched agents to patrol the Canadian and Mexican borders for a week. On another occasion, after inspecting a new batch of recruits, he passed the word to get rid of "the one that looks like a truckdriver." One of the recruits was duly dismissed, but when Hoover attended the class's graduation party he complained, "That truckdriver—I thought I told you to get rid of him."

The groundwork for Hoover's reforms were laid during the 1920s, but the FBI only caught the public imagination during the rash of bankrobberies and kidnappings during the thirties. The hero worship of Hoover and his men began in earnest in the vintage year of 1934, when FBI agents killed Dillinger, Nelson, "Ma" Barker, and her son Fred. Hoover made his own first arrest when he personally brought in Alvin ("Old Creepy") Karpis. Hoover, with his penchant for simplifying the war on crime into a straightforward battle between the good guys and the bad guys, had melodramatically dubbed Karpis "Public Rat Number One," and had been nettled at having to admit before the Senate Appropriations Committee that he had never personally arrested anyone. He is said to have left the hearing room "boiling mad." Determined to put right this slur on his heroic image, he flew at once to New Orleans, where his agents had just located Karpis. According to Karpis's autobiography, published in 1971, Hoover stayed safely under cover until his men had Karpis cornered, then rushed forward to bind his hands with an agent's necktie. It seems that in the excitement he had neglected to bring along any handcuffs. But Hoover had made his arrest and obtained the glory he now openly sought. The legend was burgeoning.

"At the outset," writes Fred J. Cook in his biography of Hoover, "the effect may have been beneficial, helping to nourish a healthy public regard for law and contempt for criminals, but there is always danger when such excessive praise, lacking the counterweight of effective criticism, is lavished on any man or any agency over a period of decades. When a man becomes the convert to his own heroic image, when he embraces the idea of his own infallibility, he rapidly becomes to himself an issue and a cause more important than any other. In Hoover's case, the evidence of the years plainly says that, however reluctant Hoover may have been in the beginning, he came to revel in his role and to become one of the first and greatest victims of his own publicity."

Perhaps Hoover's greatest public-relations coup was the coining of the word *G-men* to describe his fearless agents. At his arrest in 1933, "Machine Gun" Kelly had supposedly pleaded as he surrendered, "Don't shoot, G-men! Don't shoot!" It was presumed that Kelly meant "government-men," and Hoover immediately seized upon his phrase to increase the public hero worship of his force. It enabled him to preserve the picture, always cherished by Americans with their heritage of frontier violence, of good versus bad, and Hoover was a master at coining ever-more-lurid descriptions of the criminals he sought. As Hank Messick wrote in his biography, *John Edgar Hoover:*

> When the Director spoke of "scum," of "rats," of "craven beasts," of "vermin" and "vultures," the public could understand and applaud. No mumbo jumbo about environment, social conditions, broken homes, no talk about job opportunities and rehabilitation—the only good punk was a dead one. It was a return to the code of the old West with the FBI serving as a national posse and, occasionally, a lynching party. If a bank robber was shot down without cause, so what? The G-men had saved the government the expense of a trial.

Hoover's genius was not solely dependent on public relations, however. He was also perhaps the most efficient bureaucrat the country has ever seen, always on top of the subtle undercurrents of power in Washington, and his crime-fighting statistics were lovingly garnered not only with an eye to publicity but also for the practical purpose of pushing his budgets through Congress. Only once were his figures questioned—when the late Senator Kenneth McKellar, a Democrat from Tennessee, tried to cut some $225,000 from the FBI's annual appropriation. He was criticized for his temerity by Senator Arthur Vandenberg "as a miser whose parsimony would cause the threat of kidnapping to hang once more over every cradle in America." Whereupon Hoover's full budget request was passed by a resoundng voice vote. In the House, which has the responsibility for reviewing the bureau's spending, Representative John J. Rooney, chairman of the Appropriations subcommittee, declared, "I have never cut the FBI's budget and I never expect to." In his last year in office, Hoover asked for, and of course was granted, an appropriation well over $200 million, not one penny of which was queried by the Congress. At the same time, he was supervising the construction of a vast new FBI headquarters, which will be completed in 1974, on Pennsylvania Avenue. Not only will the new headquarters be the third largest building in Washington (coming only after the Pentagon and the House's Rayburn Building), it will give the FBI physical autonomy from its political masters across the road in the Justice Department. Typically, Hoover had vetoed a suggestion by the Washington Fine Arts Commission that, in order to blend the massive new building in with the rest of Pennsylvania Avenue's architecture, it should be fronted by freestanding Corinthian pillars. Absolutely not, said Hoover; columns make ideal cover for assassins.

Hoover's campaign against the bankrobbers, kidnappers, and murderers went on throughout the 1930s. During the war, the FBI switched its main efforts to searching out Nazi spies and sympathizers, seizing thirty-three German agents over one weekend in 1941. After the war, it was the pursuit of Communists that Hoover took as his main objective, including the arrest of Julius and Ethel Rosenberg, the atom-bomb spies, who were later executed.

But however successful the FBI was in its chosen fields of endeavor, there were still those curious blind spots over organized crime, the protection of civil-rights workers in the South, and the extreme sensitivity that would brook no criticism. As late as 1969, Hoover tried to demand that TWA fire one of its pilots who had dared to criticize the FBI's attempts to foil a hijacking attempt. A runaway marine, Raphael Minichiello, who later became a folk hero in his own right in his native Italy, had commandeered a TWA jet in Los Angeles and demanded to be flown to Rome. In New York, where the plane stopped for refueling, a swarm of FBI men in flak jackets surrounded the plane, ignoring the pleas of Captain Donald J. Cook to stand back. "We want everyone away from this plane. This boy is going to shoot us," Cook had pleaded from the cockpit window. Sure enough, as the agents closed in, Minichiello fired a shot into the cockpit ceiling. Only then were the FBI agents persuaded to back off and leave the plane to fly peacefully to Rome. When he arrived there, Cook held a press conference in which he strongly criticized the FBI's tactics. "The Rome police put the FBI to shame," he said. "The FBI just thought they were playing at Wyatt Earp and wanted to engage in a shootout with a supposed criminal and bring him to justice. They would have wound up unnecessarily killing this boy and, probably, completely destroying a seven-million-dollar aircraft and wounding or endangering the lives of four crew members." As captain of the aircraft, he felt it was his responsibility to decide how to deal with the hijacking, a decision, he said, "that cost less in gunpowder and more in gasoline."

Hoover was furious at the captain's outspoken comments. The bureau authorized a statement calling Cook's comments "irresponsible" and claimed that he had made them in order to portray himself as "the sole hero of the escapade." TWA, it was suggested, ought to fire the captain for his impertinence. Fortunately, it never did, but the episode clearly illustrated Hoover's intolerance of criticism, from without or within.

In his later years at the bureau, his strict one-man régime going back nearly half a century had led inevitably to a certain amount of sycophancy. "Let's say you're an agent," one insider told the New York *Times*. "Go in there and tell him he looks better than ever, that you are inspired by his leadership, that he's saving America and you hope he lives for ever. As soon as you leave there will be a memo from the director saying, 'This man has executive ability.' A lot of agents have caught on." It was common for agents to solicit autographed photographs of the director, whom they privately called The Man. The executive in charge of the bureau's Miami office once had one of his agents fly up to Washington carrying a birthday cake for Hoover on his lap. On another occasion, when the director was out of town, an agent spilled coffee over the rug in Hoover's office. Unable to remove the stain, the staff had an exact duplicate of the rug made up over the weekend and installed before Hoover returned.

Hoover, in short, was unique. The man and the machine he had created were so intertwined that as long as he lived, the fundamental questions about the role of the FBI in modern society, the problems about its political control and its jurisdiction, were never effectively discussed. While he remained in office, modernization of the bureau or any searching review of its role in the very different society to the one in which he had grown to maturity was inevitably postponed.

The director's own view of the bureau's role was clear. "The FBI," he wrote, "is strictly a fact-finding agency, responsible in turn to the Attorney General, the President, the Congress, and in the last analysis, the American people." That was doubtless true, although in nearly half a century under his personal control, the agency had become powerful enough to use its own discretion about which of its investigations to press, which to softpedal. In theory, the bureau was charged with investigating some 180 different federal violations, ranging from kidnapping, bankrobbery, and extortion to sabotage, espionage, treason, and civil-rights violations. Under Hoover, the bureau had been spectacularly successful in the cases it chose to press; less successful in other fields, such as organized crime and civil rights, which the Director chose largely to ignore; and downright perverse in its vendetta against domestic communism, which it pursued long after any supposed danger had passed.

Hoover's death therefore precipitated a lively debate about the future and the basic functions of the bureau. How should it be controlled? Should its jurisdiction over acts of subversion be separated from its investigations of crime? Were new checks and balances needed to control its awesome power?

There was widespread agreement that the new director's term should be limited by law in order to prevent a new Hoover from establishing a life tenure on the office. A Congressional act of 1968 already stipulated that the new permanent director must, like Justices of the Supreme Court, be confirmed by the Senate. But naturally enough in an election year, there were widely differing views on how the more fundamental problems should be solved. Courtney Evans, a member of the Democratic Party's policy council, suggested that "a way must be found to maintain the integrity of the FBI, at the same time providing policy guidance and direction in security and intelligence investigations, particularly in areas where there is likely to be a legitimate difference between freedom for individual citizens and security for the government itself." The more conservative Nixon Administration tended on the other hand towards a harder line and had for several years been pressing for even wider use of such techniques as wiretaps and electronic eavesdropping devices in cases involving campus unrest, racial disorders, and the leftwing protest movement.

Here, however, was a political hot potato the President chose not to handle until after his re-election. In order to avoid turning the succession into an election issue, he named only an acting director, L. Patrick Gray III, a fifty-five-year-old former Navy captain who had been an Assistant Attorney General, and who was utterly loyal to Richard Nixon. Just how misguidedly loyal he had been only came to light six months later, when Gray was swept out of office, along with so many other of Nixon's appointees, in the turmoil of the Watergate scandal. As it later turned out, Nixon's appointment of this former submarine commander, who was used to obeying orders and who seemed to be awed and spellbound in the presence of the mighty, had been a direct attempt by the White House to seize political control of the FBI— to use it, according to some, as a party political police force. For all his faults, that is something J. Edgar Hoover would never for a moment have tolerated.

During the election campaign itself, Gray had demonstrated he was little more than a creature of the Republican White House, traveling around the country in a government aircraft at a reported expense to the taxpayers of nearly half a million dollars in order to make speeches on behalf of a political candidate. Gray further provided FBI information, some of it confidential, for use in the President's campaign, once sending out a telex message to twenty-one FBI field offices ordering agents there to gather information on criminal justice that might have political implications. The information was required, he said, "to give the President maximum support during campaign trips over the next several weeks." A number of agents quite properly refused to comply, and when he was tackled by the Senate about his cable, Gray reportedly replied, "Wouldn't you do that for the President?"

This alone was enough to arouse the deepest reservations among the Democratic members of the Senate Judiciary Committee when his nomination as permanent director was sent up for confirmation after the election was safely over. But worse was to come. It became apparent during the hearings that Gray had displayed an obedience to his political superiors that amounted, on the most charitable assessment, to appalling naiveté. He disclosed he had sent many of the FBI's confidential files on Watergate to people in the White House who were themselves implicated in the affair. He had allowed John Dean, then the President's counsel, to sit in on FBI questioning of fourteen White House officials, seemingly unaware that this might inhibit their testimony. When three of the aides later asked to see FBI agents alone, Gray turned over transcripts of their interview to Dean, who he admitted to the Senate had on one occasion probably lied to him. By this time appalled at his candor, the White House began privately calling him "Tattletale Gray," indicating he no longer had their full support. Gray's chances of confirmation by the Senate were, in any case, now remote. It was not long afterwards that the acting Director bowed to the inevitable and withdrew his name from further consideration.

Later, even more damaging evidence came to light, showing that Gray had been totally subservient to the White House. Allegations were made that he had personally destroyed two folders containing incriminating documents handed to him by White House aides John Dean and John Ehrlichman, who had "ordered" him to dispose of them. The documents included cables forged by the Watergate conspirators in an attempt to show that President John Kennedy was implicated in the assassination of Ngo Dinh Diem, the president of South Vietnam, in 1963. Gray also destroyed a dossier prepared by the conspirators on Senator Edward Kennedy's accident at Chappaquiddick in 1969, although he said he had never examined the papers, which he kept for months before disposing of them in the furnace of his Connecticut home. Friends of Gray's told the Washington *Post* the acting Director felt he had been "set up" by the White House. "He is just sick about all this," the friend said, "and thought Mr. Dean and Mr. Ehrlichman were his superiors and that he had to follow orders and could not believe anyone in the White House would act dishonestly." So the obedient Mr. Gray had done as he was told.

When the story came out in the Washington *Post*, Gray abruptly resigned, stating he felt that personal acts of judgment were now being publicly called into question and that his own continued presence at the helm had become an embarrassment to the bureau. His departure, he said, was required "to preserve in both image and fact the reputation, the integrity and the effectiveness of the FBI." (Clarence M. Kelly, a former FBI man who was chief of police in Kansas City, was subsequently named Director.)

Gray had been openly despised by many senior members of the bureau's staff, who blamed him for a precipitous drop in morale since his arrival, brought about in part by his politicization of the bureau's activities. Now that he was gone, there was a widespread feeling of simple relief. "He did more to hurt us in one year," a field agent said, "than J. Edgar Hoover did in forty-eight." That is not a pretty epitaph, but in the eyes of most observers it had been well earned by the all-too-loyal L. Patrick Gray III. As for the bureau itself, the Watergate boil may just have been lanced in time for everyone concerned—particularly those in the Senate who must confirm the Director's appointment, and those in the House who supervise the bureau's budget—to prevent the FBI from ever again falling so dangerously into the political thicket. At the very least, there is now an awareness that the FBI could be—and under Richard Nixon very nearly had been—turned over into an instrument of political will. Nothing could represent a more dangerous threat to the liberty of individual Americans.

Bibliography

The books and articles here listed have been invaluable in providing both background and mood and also for specific quotations, which I have generally indicated in the text. In addition, I would like to acknowledge my debt to the mass of information culled from the daily editions of the New York *Times* and the Washington *Post*, surely the two finest newspapers in the country, and also to *Time, Newsweek, Fortune, New Republic, Atlantic Monthly, Harper's Magazine,* and *Washington Monthly,* all of which I have read avidly and with profit.

General

Alsop, Stewart, *The Center.* New York: Harper & Row, 1968.

Barone, Michael, *et al.,* *The Almanac of American Politics.* Boston, Mass.: Gambit, 1972.

Britannica Book of the Year. Chicago: Encyclopedia Britannica, 1972

Brogan, D.W., *The American Character.* New York: Alfred A. Knopf, 1956.

Gunther, John, *Inside U.S.A.* New York: Harper and Brothers, 1947.

Halberstam, David, *The Best and the Brightest.* New York: Random House, 1972.

Heren, Louis, *The New American Commonwealth.* New York: Harper & Row, 1968.

Johnson, Lyndon B., *The Vantage Point.* New York: Holt, Rinehart & Winston, 1971.

Peirce, Neal R., *The Megastates of America.* New York: W.W. Norton, 1972

Schlesinger, Arthur M., *The Crisis of Confidence.* Boston: Houghton Mifflin, 1969

Statistical Abstract of the United States. Washington, D.C.: U.S. Dept. of commerce, 1970

Tocqueville, Alexis de, *Democracy in America.* New York: Doubleday, 1969.

Watts, William, and Free, Lloyd M., *State of the Nation.* Washington, D.C.: Potomac Associates, 1973

White, Theodore H., *The Making of the President, 1960.* New York: Atheneum, 1961

White, Theodore H., *The Making of the President, 1964.* New York: Atheneum, 1965

White, Theodore H., *The Making of the President,* 1968. New York: Atheneum, 1969

Chapter One: Cities

Abrams, Charles, *The City is the Frontier.* New York: Harper & Row, 1965
Bradbury, Ray, "Los Angeles is the Best Place in America." *Esquire,* October 1972.
Buckley, William F., *The Unmaking of a Mayor.* New York: Viking Press, 1966.
"California: A State of Excitement." *Time,* 11 November 1969.
Cameron, James, *The USA: A Visitor's Handbook.* New York: Time-Life Inc., 1973.
"Chicago's Daley: How to Run a City." *Newsweek,* 5 April 1971.
Coleman, Terry, *Going to America.* New York: Pantheon, 1972.
Green, Constance McLaughlin, *The Rise of Urban America.* New York: Harper & Row, 1965.
Hale, Dennis, and Eisen, Jonathan, *The Californian Dream.* New York: Collier Books, 1968.
Harris, Fred R. & Lindsay, John V., *The State of the Cities: Report of the Commission on the Cities in the '70s.* New York: Praeger Publishers, 1972.
Jacobs, Jane, *The Economy of Cities.* New York: Random House, 1969.
James, Henry, *The American Scene.* New York: Horizon Press, 1967.
Lindsay, John, *The City.* New York: W.W. Norton, 1969.
McWilliams, Carey, *Southern California Country.* Los Angeles: Duell, Sloan & Pearce, 1946.
Mumford, Lewis, *The Urban Prospect.* New York: Harcourt, Brace & World, 1968.
Rand, Christopher, *Los Angeles, the Ultimate City.* New York: Oxford University Press, 1967.
Riis, Jacob, *The Battle with the Slum.* Macmillan, New York:, 1902.
Royko, Mike, *Boss.* New York: Dutton, 1971.
Sternlieb, George, "The City as Sandbox." *Public Interest,* Fall, 1971.
"The Cities: Waging a Battle for Survival." *Time,* 17 March, 1969.
The Cities: Waging a Battle for Survival. Newsweek. 17 March, 1969.
Walker, Robert A., *Chicago.* London: Allen & Unwin, 1954.
Wagenknecht, Edward, *Chicago.* Norman: Univ. of Oklahoma Press, 1964.
Weisman, Steven, "Why Lindsay Failed as Mayor." *Washington Monthly,* April 1972.
Wells, Annette, *The Los Angeles Guide Book.* L.A.: Sherbourne Press, 1972.
"What Makes a City Great?" *Time,* 14 November 1969.
Whalen, Richard, *A City Destroying Itself.* New York: William Morrow, 1965.
White, Morton, White, Lucia, *The Intellectual versus the City.* Cambridge, Mass.: Harvard University Press, 1964.
Wolfe, Tom, *New York, New York.* New York: Dial Press, 1964.

Chapter Two: The Land

Cordtz, Dan. "A Tough Row to Hoe." *Fortune*, August 1972.

Dunne, John Gregory, *Delano: Story of the California Grape Strike*. New York: Farrar, Straus & Giroux, 1967.

Duscha, Julius, "Butz Makes Hay Down on the Farm." New York: New York *Times Magazine*, 16 April 1972.

Gentry, Curt, *The Last Days of the Late, Great State of California*. New York: Putnam's, 1968.

King, Seth S., "The Family Farm is Not Dead." *Saturday Review*, 29 July 1972.

"Little Strike that Grew to La Causa, The." *Time*, 4 July 1969.

Partsch, Francis L., "Corn Belt Blues." *Wall Street Journal*, 23 November 1971.

"Time to Plant a New Farm Policy." *Time*, 26 February, 1973.

Chapter Three: The South

Brenner, Joseph, M.D., *Children in Mississippi*. Statement to U.S. Senate Subcommittee on Manpower and Employment, 1967.

Coles, Robert, *Farewell to the South*. Boston: Little, Brown, 1972.

Hunger USA Revisited: Citizens' Board of Inquiry into Hunger and Malnutrition in the U.S.A. Atlanta, Ga.: Southern Regional Council, 1972.

McGill, Ralph, *The South and the Southerner*. Boston: Little, Brown, 1963.

Morris, Willie, *Yazoo*. Harper's Magazine, June 1970.

"New Day A'Coming in the South." *Time*, 31 May 1971.

Poverty: Hunger and Federal Food Program. Washington: U.S. Government Printing Office, 1967.

Randall, James G., *The Civil War and Reconstruction*. Boston: Heath, 1937.

Sherrill, Robert, *Gothic Politics in the Deep South*. New York: Grossman Publishers, 1968.

Simkins, Francis Butler, *A History of the South*. New York: Alfred A. Knopf, 1963.

Sinder, Allen P., *Change in the Contemporary South*. Durham, N.C.: Duke Univ. Press, 1963.

Woodward, C. Vann, *Origins of the New South*. Baton Rouge, La.: Louisiana State University Press, 1951.

Chapter Four: Money

Baruch, Hurd, *Wall Street, Security Risk*. Washington, D.C.: Acropolis Books, 1971.

Bloom, Murray Teigh, *Rogues to Riches*. New York: Putnam's, 1971.

"Change and Turmoil on Wall Street." *Time*, 24 August, 1970.

Elias, Christopher, *Fleecing the Lambs*. Chicago: Henry Regnery, 1971.

Gerber, A.B., *The Bashful Billionaire*. New York: Lyle Stuart, 1967.

Keats, John, *Howard Hughes*. New York: Random House, 1966.

Kwitny, Jonathan, "The Richest of the Rich." *Fortune*, May 1968.

Lamott, Kenneth, *The Moneymakers*. Boston: Little, Brown, 1969.

Lapham, Lewis H., *The Coming Wounds of Wall Street. Harper's Magazine,* May 1971.

Leffler, George L., *The Stock Market.* New York: Ronald Press, 1963.

Lundberg, Ferdinand, *America's Sixty Families.* New York: Halcyon House, 1939.

Lundberg, Ferdinand, *The Rich and the Super Rich.* New York: Lyle Stuart, 1968.

Mayer, Martin, *Wall Street, Men and Money.* New York: Harper Brothers, 1969.

Ney, Richard, *The Wall Street Jungle.* New York: Grove Press, 1970.

Nielsen, Waldemar A., *The Big Foundations.* New York: Columbia University Press, 1972.

"Polaroid's Big Gamble." *Time,* 26 June, 1972.

Rolo, Charles J., and Lebon, George J., *The Anatomy of Wall Street.* Philadelphia, Pa.: J. B. Lippincott, 1968.

Sobell, Robert, *The Big Board.* New York: Free Press, 1965.

"Tossing Snake Eyes." *Wall Street Journal,* 1 August, 1972.

Trebble, John, *The Inheritors.* New York: Putnam's, 1962.

"Wall Street on the Ropes." *Fortune,* December, 1970.

"Winds of Scandal on Wall Street." *Newsweek,* 12 October, 1970.

Chapter Five: Industry

Bainbridge, John, *The Super Americans.* New York: Doubleday, 1961.

Beman, Lewis, "The Great Merger Frenzy." *Fortune,* April 1973.

Engler, Robert, *The Politics of Oil.* New York: Macmillan, 1961.

Galbraith, John K., *The Affluent Society.* New York: Houghton-Mifflin, 1969.

    The New Industrial State. New York: Houghton-Mifflin, 1971.

    Investigation of Conglomerate Corporations: Antitrust Subcommittee, House of Representatives, US. Govt. Printing Office, 1971.

Keats, John, *The Insolent Chariots.* New York: Lippincott, 1958.

Lapham, Lewis H., "Alaska and the Conservationists." *Harper's Magazine,* May 1970.

Louis, Arthur M., *Alaskan Oil. Fortune,* July 1972.

Mills, C. Wright, *The Power Elite.* New York: Oxford University Press, 1956.

Mintz, Morton, and Cohen, Jerry S., *America, Inc.* New York: Dial Press, 1971.

O'Connor, Richard, *The Oil Barons.* Boston: Little, Brown, 1971.

"Pan Am's Route into the Red." *Fortune,* January 1972.

Sloan, Alfred P., Jr., *My Years With General Motors.* New York: Doubleday, 1963.

"Seattle Under Siege." *Time,* 4 January 1971.

Serrin, William, "Profile of John Roche." *Detroit Free Press,* 1971.

Stern, Philip M. *The Great Treasury Raid.* New York: Random House, 1962.

Tugendhat, Christopher, *Oil: The Biggest Business.* New York: Putnam's, 1962.

Vanderwicken, Peter, "G.M.: The Price of Being Responsible." *Fortune,* January 1972.

White, William H., *The Organization Man.* New York: Simon & Schuster, 1956.

Chapter Six: Labor

Blue Collar Workers: A Symposium on Middle America. New York: McGraw-Hill, 1972.

Bok, Derek C. and Dunlop, John T., *Labor and the American Community.* New York: Simon and Schuster, 1970.

Boyd, James, "From Crusade to Collusion." *Washington Monthly,* March 1972.

Cornier, Frank and Eaton, William, *Reuther.* Englewood Cliffs, N.J.: Prentice-Hall, 1970.

Hume, Brit, *Death and the Mines.* New York: Grossman Publishers, 1971.

Johnson, Haynes and Kotz, Nick, "The Unions." Washington *Post,* April 1972.

Marx, Herbert L. Jr. *American Labor Today.* New York: H.W. Wilson, 1965.

Mills, C. Wright, *New Men of Power.* New York: Harcourt Brace, 1948.

Rayback, Joseph G., *A History of American Labor.* New York: Macmillan, 1965.

Rothschild, Emma, "GM in More Trouble." *New York Review of Books,* 23 March 1972.

Serrin, William, *The Company and the Union.* New York: Alfred A. Knopf, 1973.

Chapter Seven: The Presidency

Broder, David, *The Party's Over.* New York: Harper & Row, 1972.

de Toledano, Ralph, *One Man Alone.* New York: Funk & Wagnalls, 1969.

Dutton, Frederick G., *Changing Sources of Power.* New York: McGraw-Hill, 1971.

Evans, Rowland, Jr. and Novak, Robert D., *Nixon in the White House.* New York: Random House, 1971.

Hickel, Walter, *Who Owns America?* Englewood Cliffs, N.J.: Prentice-Hall, 1971.

"Interview with the President, An." *Time,* 3 January 1972.

Lubell, Samuel, *The Hidden Crisis in American Politics.* New York: W.W. Norton, 1971.

Mazo, Earl, *Richard Nixon.* New York: Harper Bros., 1959.

Nixon, Richard M., *Six Crises.* New York: Doubleday, 1962.

Reedy, George E., *Twilight of the Presidency.* New York: Mentor Books, 1970.

Whalen, Richard J., *Catch the Falling Flag.* Boston: Houghton Mifflin, 1972.

Wills, Garry, *Nixon Agonistes.* Boston: Houghton Mifflin, 1970.

Chapter Eight: Congress

Clark, Senator Joseph S., *Congress: The Sapless Branch.* New York: Harper & Row, 1964.

Freidin, Seymour K., *A Sense of the Senate.* New York: Dodd, Mead, 1972.

Grazia de, Alfred, *Congress: The First Branch of Government.* New York: Anchor Books, 1967.

Hinckley, Barbara, *The Seniority System in Congress.* Bloomington: Indiana University Press, 1971.

Making Congress More Effective. New York: Committee for Economic Development, 1970.

Riegle, Donald, *O Congress.* New York: Doubleday, 1972.

Truman, David B., *The Congress and America's Future.* Englewood Cliffs, N.J.: Prentice-Hall, 1965.

Weaver, Warren, Jr., *Both Your Houses.* New York: Praeger Publishers, 1972.

Who Runs Congress? Ralph Nader Congress Project. New York: Bantam–Grossman, 1972.

Wilcox, Francis O., *Congress, The Executive & Foreign Policy.* New York: Harper & Row, 1971.

Chapter Nine: Supreme Court

Kilpatrick, James J., "The High Court: Where Now?" *National Review*, November 1971.

McCloskey, Robert G., *The Modern Supreme Court.* Cambridge, Mass.: Harvard University Press, 1972.

"Nixon's Court." *Time*, 1 November 1971.

Shogan, Robert, *A Question of Judgment.* Indianapolis: Bobbs-Merrill, 1972.

Simon, James F., *In His Own Image.* New York: David McKay, 1973.

Warren, Earl, *A Republic, If You Can Keep It.* New York: Quadrangle Books, 1972.

Chapter Ten: Foreign Affairs

Armstrong, Hamilton Fish, "Isolated America." *Foreign Affairs*, October 1972.

Brandon, Henry. *The Retreat of American Power.* New York: Doubleday, 1973.

Dutton, Frederick G., *Changing Sources of Power.* New York: McGraw-Hill, 1971.

Jenkins, Joy, *Afternoon on the Potomac.* New Haven, Conn.: Yale University Press, 1972.

Kennan, George F., "After the Cold War." *Foreign Affairs*, October 1972.

Kissinger, Henry A., *American Foreign Policy.* New York: W.W. Norton, 1969.

Kolko, Joyce, and Kolko, Gabriel, *The Limits of Power.* New York: Harper & Row, 1972.

Landau, David, *Kissinger: The Uses of Power.* Boston: Houghton Mifflin, 1972.

Morgan, John, "Kissinger and Metternich." *New Statesman*, June 1972.

Tucker, Robert W., *A New Isolationism: Threat or Promise?* Washington, D.C.: Universe, Potomac Associates, 1972.

Chapter Eleven: Defense

Ambrose, Stephen E., and Barber, James A., Jr., *The Military and American Society.* New York: The Free Press, 1972.

Califano, Joseph A., Jr., "The Case Against an All-Volunteer Army." *Washington Post*, February 1972.

Donovan, James A., *Militarism USA.* New York: Scribner's, 1970.

Jay, Peter A., and Osnos, Peter, "Army in Anguish." Washington *Post,* September, 1971.

Lapp, Ralph E., "Can Salt Stop MIRV?" New York *Times,* 1 February 1970.

Mollenhoff, Clark R., *The Pentagon.* New York: Pinnacle Books, 1972.

O'Brien, Tim, *Medal Mania.* Washington *Post,* 1973.

"Particular Tragedy of Robert McNamara." *Time,* 5 July 1971.

Raymond, Jack, *The Military and American Society.* NY: Free Press, 1972.

Report by the President's Commission on an All-Volunteer Armed Force. New York: Collier, 1970.

Rodberg, Leonard S. and Shearer, Derek, *The Pentagon Watchers.* New York: Anchor Books, 1970.

Yarmolinsky, Adam, *The Military Establishment,* New York: Harper & Row, 1971.

Chapter Twelve: Newspapers

Black, Alfred, and Boyland, James, *Our Troubled Press.* Boston: Little, Brown, 1971.

Catledge, Turner, *My Life and the Times.* New York: Harper & Row, 1971.

Krieghbaum, Hillier, *Pressures on the Press.* New York: Thomas Y. Crowell, 1972.

Lippmann, Walter, *Public Opinion.* New York: Macmillan, 1961.

Marbut, F.B. *News from the Capital.* Carbondale, Ill.: Southern Illinois University Press, 1971.

Minor, Dale, *The Information War.* New York: Hawthorn Books, 1970.

Moyers, Bill, "Read This Please." New York *Times,* 6 January 1972.

Reston, James, *The Artillery of the Press.* New York: Alfred A. Knopf, 1967.

Rivers, William L., *The Opinion Makers.* Boston: Beacon Press, 1965.

Rosenthal, A.M., "What a Free Press Is All About." New York *Times,* 11 June 1972.

Talese, Gay, *The Kingdom and the Power.* Cleveland and New York: The World Publishing Co., 1969.

Ungar, Sanford J., *The Papers and the Papers.* New York: E.P. Dutton, 1972.

Witcover, Jules, "Two Weeks That Shook the Press." *Columbia Journalism Review,* Sept.–Oct. 1971.

Wicker, Tom, "The Greening of the Press." *Columbia Journalism Review,* May–June 1971.

Chapter Thirteen: Television

Brown, Les, *Television: The Business Behind the Box.* New York: Harcourt, Brace, Jovanovich, 1971.

Friendly, Fred W., "Politicizing TV." *Columbia Journalism Review,* March–April 1973.

Groombridge, Brian, *Television and the People.* Harmondsworth, England: Penguin Books, 1972.

Kendrick, Alexander, *Prime Time.* New York: Little, Brown, 1969.

Mayer, Martin, *About Television.* New York: Harper & Row, 1972.

Schramm, Wilbur, and Nelson, Lyle, "Financing Public TV." *Columbia Journalism Review*, January–February 1973.
Survey of Broadcast Journalism, 1969/70; 1970/71; 1971/72; 1972/73
Whale, John, *The Half-Shut Eye*. New York: St. Martin's Press, 1969.
Wise, David, "The President and the Press." *Atlantic Monthly*, April 1973.

Chapter Fourteen: Lobbyists

Boyd, James, "How to Succeed in Business Without Really Trying." *Washington Monthly*, April 1972.
Buckhorn, Robert F., *Nader: The People's Lawyer*. Englewood Cliffs, N.J.: Prentice-Hall, 1972.
Cray, Edward, *In Failing Health*. Indianapolis and New York: Bobbs, Merrill, 1970.
Deakin, James, *The Lobbyists*. Washington, D.C.: Public Affairs Press, 1966.
Harris, Richard, *A Sacred Trust*. Baltimore: Penguin Books, 1969.
Health Care In America. Washington, D.C.: U.S. Government Printing Office, 1969.
"Interview with Ralph Nader." Washington *Post*, 5 December 1971.
Kennedy, Edward M., *In Critical Condition*. New York: Simon and Schuster, 1972.
McCarry, Charles, *Citizen Nader*. New York: Saturday Review Press, 1972.
Nader, Ralph, & Ross, Donald, *Action for a Change*. New York: Grossman Publishers, 1971.
"Nader's Shoddy Product." *Wall Street Journal*, 2 November 1972.
Rayack, Elton, *Professional Power and American Medicine*. Cleveland and New York: The World Publishing Co., 1967.
"Spread Too Thin." *Newsweek*, 14 April 1972.

Chapter Fifteen: Advertising

Baker, Samm Sinclair, *The Permissible Lie*. Boston: Beacon Press, 1968.
Buxton, Edward, *Promise Them Anything*. New York: Stein & Day, 1972.
Harvard Business Review, March–April 1972.
Loomis, Carol J., *Advertising Age*.
Mayer, Martin, *Madison Avenue, U.S.A.* New York: Harper Bros., 1958.
McGinnis, Joe, *The Selling of the President, 1968*. New York: Trident Press, 1969.
Ogilvy, David, *Confessions of an Advertising Man*. New York: Atheneum, 1966.
Packard, Vance, *The Hidden Persuaders*. New York: David McKay, 1957.
Seldin, Joseph J., *The Golden Fleece*. New York: Macmillan, 1963.
"Those Throbbing Headaches on Madison Avenue." *Fortune*, Feb. 1972.

Chapter Sixteen: Beliefs

Bates, Ernest Sutherland, *American Faith*. New York: W.W. Norton, 1940.

Brauer, Jerald C., *Protestantism in America*. Philadelphia: Westminster Press, 1965.

Deedy, John, "Troubled Vatican." *Commonweal*, Summer 1972.

Ellis, John Tracy, *American Catholicism*. Chicago: University of Chicago Press, 1969.

Frazier, E. Franklin, *The Negro Church in America*. New York: Schocken Books, 1963.

Fuchs, Lawrence H., *John F. Kennedy and American Catholicism*. New York: Meredith, 1967.

Giannella, Donald A., *Religion and the Public Order*. Chicago: University of Chicago Press, 1964.

Glazer, Nathan, *American Judaism*. Chicago: University of Chicago Press, 1957.

Hudson, Winthropp S., *American Protestantism*. Chicago: University of Chicago Press, 1961.

Kelley, Dean, *Why Conservative Churches Are Growing*. New York: Harper & Row, 1972.

"Methodist Malaise." *Time*, 8 May 1972.

Robben, John, "Roaming Catholics." New York *Times*, 24 February 1972.

Spence, Hargzell, *The Story of America's Religions*. New York: Holt Rinehart & Winston, 1960.

Stedman, Murray S., Jr., *Religion and Politics in America*. New York: Harcourt, Brace and World, 1964.

Chapter Seventeen: Minorities

"American Woman." *Time* (Special Edition), 20 March 1972.

Armor, David J., *The Evidence of Busing*. The Public Interest, 1971.

Bander, Edward J., *Turmoil on the Campus*, New York: H.W. Wilson, 1970.

"Black America Now," *Newsweek*, 1 February 1973.

Brown, Michael, *The Politics and Anti-Politics of the Young*, Beverly Hills, Calif.: Glencoe Press, 1969.

Diamond, Edwin, "The Violent Years." *Newsweek*, 23 June 1969.

Dutton, Frederick G., *Changing Sources of Power*. New York: McGraw-Hill, 1971.

Faltermayer, Edmund, "Youth after the Revolution." *Fortune*, March 1973.

Frederick, Mostellers, and Moynihan, Daniel, *On Equality of Educational Opportunity*. New York: Vintage Books, 1972.

Garskof, Michelle Hoffnung, *Roles Women Play*. Belmont, Calif.: Cole, Brooks, 1971.

Glazer, Nathan, "The Campus Crucible." *Atlantic Monthly*, July 1969.

Grier, William H., and Cobbs, Price M., M.D., *Black Rage*. New York: Bantam Books, 1969.

Hodgson, Godfrey, "Do Schools Make a Difference?" *Atlantic Monthly*, March 1973.

Janeway, Elizabeth, *Man's World, Woman's Place*. New York: Dell, 1971.

Litwak, Leo, "Battle for a College." *Look*, 27 May 1969.

Mead, Margaret and Kaplan, Frances, *American Women*. New York: Scribner's, 1965.

Myrdal, Gunnar, *An American Dilemma*. New York: Harper Bros., 1944.

Silberman, Charles E., *Crisis in Black and White.* New York: Vintage Books, 1964.
"Sisterhood is Beautiful: A Conversation with Alice S. Rossi." *Psychology Today,*
　　　August 1972.

Chapter Eighteen: Crime

Clark, Ramsey, *Crime in America.* New York: Pocket Books, 1971.
"Conglomerate of Crime." *Time* 22 August 1969.
Cook, Fred J., *The FBI Nobody Knows.* New York: Macmillan, 1964.
Cook, Fred J., "The People v. the Mob." New York *Times,* 1 February, 1970.
Cressey, Donald R., *Theft of the Nation.* New York: Harper & Row, 1969.
Kefauver, Estes, *Crime in America.* New York: Doubleday, 1951.
Messick, Hank, *John Edgar Hoover.* New York: David McKay, 1972.
Mollenhoff, Clark R., *Strike Force.* Englewood Cliffs, N.J.: Prentice-Hall, 1972.
Turkus, Burton B. and Feder, Sid, *Murder Inc.* New York: Permabooks, 1951.
Turner, William W., *Hoover's FBI.* Los Angeles: Sherbourne Press, 1970.
Tyler, Gus, *Organized Crime in America.* Ann Arbor: University of Michigan Press,
　　　1962.

Index